OUR NAME MAY SAY IT ALL BUT OUR FURNITURE SPEAKS FOR ITSELF

BRITISH ANTIQUE REPLICAS LTD
SCHOOL CLOSE, QUEEN ELIZABETH AVENUE
BURGESS HILL (NEAR BRIGHTON) WEST SUSSEX
RH15 9RX, ENGLAND
Fax (0444) 232014
Telephone BURGESS HILL (0444) 245577

MILLER'S
Antiques
PRICE GUIDE

THERE ARE MANY ANTIQUE
SHIPPERS IN BRITAIN BUT...

...few, if any, who are as quality conscious as Norman Lefton, Chairman and Managing Director of British Antique Exporters Ltd. of Burgess Hill, Nr. Brighton, Sussex.

Thirty years experience of shipping goods to all parts of the globe have confirmed his original belief that the way to build clients' confidence in his services is to supply them only with goods which are in first class saleable condition. To this end, he employs a cottage industry staff of over 50, from highly skilled antique restorers, polishers and packers to representative buyers and executives.

Through their knowledgeable hands passes each piece of furniture before it leaves the B.A.E. warehouses, ensuring that the overseas buyer will only receive the best and most saleable merchandise for their particular market. This attention to detail is obvious on a visit to the Burgess Hill showrooms where potential customers can view Photographic records of what must be the most varied assortment of Georgian, Victorian, Edwardian and 1930s furniture in the UK. One cannot fail to be impressed by, not only the varied range of merchandise, but also the fact that each piece is in showroom condition.

As one would expect, packing is considered somewhat of an art at B.A.E. and the manager in charge of the works ensures that each piece will reach its final destination in the condition a customer would wish. B.A.E. set a very high standard and, as a further means of improving each container load, their customer/container liaison dept., invites each customer to return detailed information on the saleability of each piece in the container, thereby ensuring successful future shipments.

This feedback of information is the all important factor which guarantees the profitability of future containers. "By this method" Mr. Lefton explains, "we have established that an average £12,500 container will immediately it is unpacked at its final destination realise in the region of £20,000 to £25,000 for our clients selling

the goods on a quick wholesale turnover basis."

In an average 20-foot container B.A.E. put approximately 75-100 pieces carefully selected to suit the particular destination. There are always at least 10 outstanding or unusual items in each shipment, but every piece included looks as though it has something special about it.

Burgess Hill is 15 minutes away from Gatwick Airport, 7 miles from Brighton and 39 miles from London on a direct rail link (only 40 minutes journey), the company is ideally situated to ship containers to all parts of the world. The showrooms, restoration and packing departments are open to overseas buyers and no visit to purchase antiques for re-sale in other countries is complete without a visit to their Burgess Hill premises where a welcome is always found.

BRITISH ANTIQUE EXPORTERS LTD,
SCHOOL CLOSE, QUEEN ELIZABETH AVENUE,
BURGESS HILL, WEST SUSSEX RH15 9RX, ENGLAND.
Telephone BURGESS HILL (04 44) 245577.
Fax (04 44) 232014.
Tel from USA 011 44 444 245577

MEMBER
LAPADA
MEMBER

MEMBER

MILLER'S
Antiques
PRICE GUIDE

Consultants
Judith and Martin Miller

General Editor
Josephine Davis

1995
Volume XVI

BCA

LONDON   NEW YORK   SYDNEY   TORONTO

MILLER'S ANTIQUES PRICE GUIDE 1995

Created and designed by
Millers
The Cellars, High Street,
Tenterden, Kent, TN30 6BN
Tel: 0580 766411

This edition published 1994
by BCA
by arrangement with Miller's

CN 4854

Consultants: Judith & Martin Miller

General Editor: Josephine Davis
Editorial and Production Co-ordinator: Sue Boyd
Editorial Assistants: Sue Montgomery, Marion Rickman, Jo Wood
Production Assistants: Gillian Charles, Lorna Day
Advertising Executive: Elizabeth Smith
Advertising Assistants: Sally Marshall, Liz Warwick
Index compiled by: DD Editorial Services, Beccles
Design: Stephen Parry, Jody Taylor, Darren Manser
Additional photography: Ian Booth, Robin Saker

Bromide output by Perfect Image, Hurst Green, E. Sussex.
Illustrations by G.H. Graphics, St. Leonards-on-Sea
Colour origination by Scantrans, Singapore
Printed and bound in England by William Clowes Ltd,
Beccles and London

Front cover illustrations:
Top l. *A Meissen group of The Spanish Lovers, modelled by J.J. Kändler,
c1741, some damage, 7in (17.5cm) high. S*
Top r. *A George III silver coffee pot, London 1775, 10½in (27cm). S*
Below. *A Chippendale mahogany desk, Goddard-Townsend School, Newport,
Rhode Island, c1765, 39½in (100cm) wide. S(NY)*

£250 FREE

TOWARDS ANY PIECE OF FURNITURE FOR EVERY
£1000 SPENT FROM OUR TRADE PRICE LIST;
£500 FREE FOR EVERY £2,000 SPENT –
THE LIST IS ENDLESS . . .

FINE HAND-MADE REPLICA FURNITURE TO A
STANDARD UNSURPASSED THIS CENTURY.
MADE BY MASTER CRAFTSMEN IN BURR
WALNUT, YEW AND MAHOGANY INCLUDING
DINING TABLES, SIDEBOARDS, CHAIRS, COCKTAIL
CABINETS, DESKS, FILING CABINETS, DESK
CHAIRS, BOOKCASES AND HAND-MADE
BUTTONED LEATHER UPHOLSTERED CHAIRS AND
CHESTERFIELDS.

**TOGETHER WITH A FINE MACHINE MADE
ECONOMY RANGE OF EXCELLENT VALUE
FAITHFUL REPRODUCTIONS**

SEND FOR BROCHURE OR VISIT
15,000 SQ FT OF SHOWROOMS

OVER 1,000 ITEMS ON DISPLAY

BRITISH ANTIQUE REPLICAS

SCHOOL CLOSE, QUEEN ELIZABETH AVENUE
BURGESS HILL (near Brighton)
WEST SUSSEX RH15 9RX

TEL: (0444) 245577

KEY TO ILLUSTRATIONS

Each illustration and descriptive caption is accompanied by a letter code. By reference to the following list of Auctioneers (denoted by *) and Dealers (•) the source of any item may be immediately determined. In no way does this constitute or imply a contract or binding offer on the part of any of our contributors to supply or sell the goods illustrated, or similar articles, at the prices stated. Advertisers in this year's directory are denoted by †.

AAV	*	Academy Auctioneers & Valuers, Northcote House, Northcote Avenue, Ealing, London W5. Tel: 0181 579 7466.
ABB	*	Abbotts Auction Rooms, Campsea Ashe, Woodbridge, Suffolk. Tel: 01728 746323.
AG	*	Anderson & Garland (Auctioneers), Marlborough House, Marlborough Crescent, Newcastle-upon-Tyne. Tel: 0191 232 6278.
AH	* †	Andrew Hartley, Victoria Hall, Little Lane, Ilkley, W. Yorks. Tel: 01943 816363.
AHL	•	Adrian Hornsey Ltd., Three Bridge Mill, Twyford, Bucks. Tel: 01296 738373.
AJ	•	A. J. Partners, Stand J28, Gray's-in-the-Mews, 1-7 Davies Mews, London W1. Tel: 0171 629 1649.
AL	• †	Ann Lingard, Ropewalk Antiques, Ropewalk, Rye, Sussex. Tel: 01797 223486.
ALL	*	Bristol Auction Rooms, St John's Place, Apsley Road, Clifton, Bristol, Avon. Tel: 0117 973 7201.
ALS	• †	Allan Smith Antiques, Amity Cottage, 162 Beechcroft Road, Upper Stratton, Swindon, Wilts. Tel: 01793 822977.
APO	• †	Apollo Antiques Ltd., The Saltisford, Birmingham Road, Warwick. Tel: 01926 494746.
ARE	• †	Arenski, 185 Westbourne Grove, London W11. Tel: 0171-727 8599.
ASA	• †	AS Antiques & Decorative Arts, 26 Broad Street, Pendleton, Salford 6, Lancs. Tel: 0161 737 5938.
ASB	• †	Andrew Spencer Bottomley, The Coach House, Thongsbridge, Holmfirth, Huddersfield. Tel: 01484 685234.
B	*	Boardman, Station Road Corner, Haverhill, Suffolk. Tel: 01440 730414.
BBA	*	Bloomsbury Book Auctions, 3/4 Hardwick Street, Off Rosebery Avenue, London EC1. Tel: 0171-833 2636.
Bea	*	Bearnes, Rainbow, Avenue Road, Torquay, Devon. Tel: 01803 296277.
BIR	• †	Birchall's, Cotebrook, Tarporley, Cheshire. Tel: 01829 760754.
BKK	• †	Bona Arts Decorative Ltd., 19 Princesmead, Farnborough, Hants. Tel: 01252 372188.
Bon	* †	Bonhams, Montpelier Galleries, Montpelier Street, London SW7. Tel: 0171-584 9161.
Bri	*	Bristol Auction Rooms, St John's Place, Apsley Road, Clifton, Bristol. Tel: 0117 973 7201.
BWe	*	Biddle and Webb, Ladywood Middleway, Birmingham. Tel: 0121 455 8042.
C	*	Christie, Manson & Woods Ltd., 8 King Street, St James's, London SW1. Tel: 0171-839 9060.
C(S)	*	Christie's Scotland Ltd., 164-166 Bath Street, Glasgow. Tel: 0141 332 8134.
CAG	* †	Canterbury Auction Galleries, 40 Station Road West, Canterbury, Kent. Tel: 01227 763337.
CAI	•	Cains Antiques, Littleton House, Littleton, Nr Somerton, Somerset. Tel: 01458 272341.
Cai	•	Caithness Glass Ltd., Inveralmond, Perth, Scotland. Tel: 01738 37373.
CB	•	Christine Bridge Antiques, Tel: 0181 741 5501.
CHA	•	Chapel House Antiques, 32 Pentood Industrial Estate, Pendre, Cardigan, Dyfed. Tel: 01239 614868 & 613268.

ChC	•	Christopher Clarke, The Fosse Way, Stow-on-the-Wold, Glos. Tel: 01451 830476.
CNY	*	Christie, Manson & Woods International Inc., 502 Park Avenue, New York, NY 10022, USA. Tel: (212) 546 1000. (including Christie's East).
CoH	* †	Cooper Hirst Auctions, The Granary Saleroom, Victoria Road, Chelmsford, Essex. Tel: 01245 260535.
CRA	•	Cranks Antiques, Powerscourt Townhouse Centre, Dublin 2.
CSK	*	Christie's South Kensington Ltd., 85 Old Brompton Road, London SW7. Tel: 0171 581 7611.
DA	* †	Dee Atkinson & Harrison, The Exchange Saleroom, Driffield, East Yorks. Tel: 01377 253151.
DaD	*	David Dockree, 224 Moss Lane, Bramhall, Stockport, Cheshire. Tel: 0161 485 1258.
DAV	•	Davies Antiques, 44a Kensington Church Street, London W8. Tel: 0171 937 9216.
DeA	•	Delphi Antiques, Powerscourt Townhouse Centre, Dublin 2. Tel: 00 353 1 679 0331.
DFA	• †	Delvin Farm Antiques, Gormonston, Co. Meath, Southern Ireland. Tel: 00 353 1 841 2285.
DMC	*	Diamond, Mills & Co, 117 Hamilton Road, Felixstowe, Suffolk. Tel: 01394 282281.
DMe	• †	Daniel Meaney, Alpine House, Carlow Road, Abbeyleix, Co. Laois, Ireland. Tel: 00 353 502 31348.
DMT	•	David Martin-Taylor Antiques, 558 Kings Road, London SW6. Tel: 0171 731 4135.
DN	*	Dreweatt Neate, Donnington Priory, Donnington, Newbury, Berks. Tel: 01635 31234.
DRA	• †	Derek Roberts Antiques, 25 Shipbourne Road, Tonbridge, Kent. Tel: 01732 358986.
DRU	•	Drummonds of Bramley, Birtley Farm, Horsham Road, Bramley, Guildford, Surrey. Tel: 01483 898766.
DUN	•	Richard Dunton, 920, Christchurch Road, Boscombe, Bournemouth, Dorset. Tel: 01202 425963.
DW	* †	Dominic Winter Book Auctions, The Old School, Maxwell Street, Swindon, Wilts. Tel: 01793 611340.
E	*	Ewbank, Welbeck House, High Street, Guildford, Surrey. Tel: 01483 232134.
EL	*	Eldred's, Robert C. Eldred Co. Inc., 1475 Route 6A, East Dennis, Massachusetts, 02641-0796, USA. Tel: 0101 (508) 385 3116
ELR	*	Eadon Lockwood & Riddle, 411 Petre Street, Sheffield. Tel: 0114 618000.
F	*	Francis Fine Art Auctioneers, The Tristar Business Centre, Star Industrial Estate, Partridge Green, Horsham, Sussex. Tel: 01403 710567.
FB	• †	Fenwick Billiards, The Antiques Pavilion, 175 Bermondsey Street, London SE1. Tel: 01823 660770.
FLE	*	Fleury's, The Square, Cahir, Co. Tipperary, Ireland. Tel: 00 052 41226.
FP	•	For Pine, 340 Berkhampstead Road, Chesham, Bucks. Tel: 01494 776119.
G&CC	• †	Goss & Crested China Ltd., 62 Murray Road, Horndean, Hants. Tel: 01705 597440.

GAK * †G. A. Key, 8 Market Place, Aylsham,
Norwich, Norfolk. Tel: 01263 733195.

GeC • †Gerard Campbell, Maple House,
Market Place, Lechlade-on-Thames, Glos.
Tel: 01367 252267.

GH * Giles Haywood, The Auction House, St.
John's Road, Stourbridge, W. Midlands.
Tel: 01384 370891.

GHA • †Garden House Antiques, 116-118 High St,
Tenterden, Kent. Tel: 01580 763664.

GRF • Grange Farm Ltd., Grange Farm,
Tongham, Surrey. Tel: 01252 782993.

GRG • †Gordon Reece Gallery, Finkle Street,
Knaresborough, N. Yorks.
Tel: 01423 866219.

HAL • †John & Simon Haley, 89 Northgate,
Halifax, W. Yorks. Tel: 01422 822148.

HAW • †Haworth Antiques, 26 Cold Bath Road,
Harrogate, N. Yorks. Tel: 01423 521401.

HCH * Hobbs & Chambers, Market Place,
Cirencester, Glos. Tel: 01285 654736.

HER • Heritage Antiques, Unit 14, Georgian
Village, Camden Passage, London N1.
Tel: 0171 226 9822.

HEW • †Muir Hewitt, Halifax Antiques Centre,
Queens Road Mills, Queen's Road/ Gibbet
Street, Halifax, W. Yorks.
Tel: 01422 347377/366657.

HOLL* †Holloways, 49 Parsons Street, Banbury,
Oxon. Tel: 01295 253197.

HON • †Honan's Antiques, Crowe Street, Gort,
Co. Galway. Tel: 00 091 31407.

HSS * †Henry Spencer and Sons, 20 The Square,
Retford, Notts. Tel: 01777 708633.

JH * Jacobs & Hunt, Lavant Street,
Petersfield, Hants. Tel: 01730 62744.

JHo • †Jonathan Horne (Antiques) Ltd.,
66B & C, Kensington Church Street,
London, W8. Tel: 0171 221 5658.

JNic * †John Nicholson, The Auction Rooms,
Longfield, Midhurst Road, Fernhurst,
Haslemere, Surrey. Tel: 01428 653727.

JO • †Jacqueline Oosthuizen, The Georgian
Village & 23 Cale Street, Chelsea, London
SW3. Tel: 0171 352 6071.

JP • †Janice Paull, Beehive House, 125
Warwick Road, Kenilworth, Warwicks.
Tel: 01926 55253.

KEY • †Key Antiques, 11 Horse Fair, Chipping
Norton, Oxon. Tel: 01608 643777.

L * Lawrence Fine Art Auctioneers,
South Street, Crewkerne, Somerset.
Tel: 01460 73041.

L&E * †Locke & England, Black Horse Agencies,
18 Guy Street, Leamington Spa,
Warwicks. Tel: 01926 889100.

LANG* Langlois, Westaway Chambers, Don St.,
St Helier, Jersey. Tel: 01534 22441.

LF * †Lambert & Foster, 77 Commercial Road,
Paddock Wood, Kent. Tel: 01892 832325.

LIO • †Lions Den, 11, St Mary's Crescent,
Leamington Spa, Warwicks.
Tel: 01926 339498.

LRG * Lots Road Chelsea Auction Galleries,
71 Lots Road, London SW10.
Tel: 0171-351 7771.

LT * †Louis Taylor Auctioneers & Valuers,
Britannia House, 10 Town Road, Hanley,
Stoke-on-Trent. Tel: 01782 214111.

M * Morphets of Harrogate, 4-6 Albert Street,
Harrogate, North Yorks.
Tel: 01423 530030.

MA • Manor Antiques, 2a High Street,
Westerham, Kent. Tel: 01959 64810.

MAT * Christopher Matthews, 23 Mount Street,
Harrogate, Yorks. Tel: 01423 871756.

MCA * Mervyn Carey, Twysden Cottage,
Benenden, Cranbrook, Kent.
Tel: 01580 240283.

McC * †McCartneys, Portcullis Salerooms,
Ludlow, Shropshire. Tel: 01584 872636.

MEA * Mealy's, Chatsworth Street, Castle
Comer, Co. Kilkenny, S. Ireland.
Tel: 00 353 564 1229.

Mit * Mitchells, Fairfield House, Station Road, Cockermouth, Cumbria. Tel: 01900 827800.

MJB * †Michael J. Bowman, 6 Haccombe House, Netherton, Newton Abbot, Devon. Tel: 01626 872890.

MJW • Mark J. West, Cobb Antiques Ltd., 39a High Street, Wimbledon Village, London SW19. Tel: 0181 946 2811.

MofC • Millers of Chelsea Antiques Ltd., Netherbrook House, 86 Christchurch Rd, Ringwood, Hants. Tel: 01425 472062.

MSh • Manfred Schotten, The Crypt Antiques, 109 High Street, Burford, Oxon. Tel: 01993 822302.

MSW * †Marilyn Swain, Westgate Hall, Westgate, Grantham. Tel: 01476 68861.

OCP • †Old Court Pine (Alain Chawner), Old Court, Collon, Co. Louth, S. Ireland. Tel: 00 353 41 26270.

OCS • The Old Curiosity Shop, 30 Henley Street, Stratford-upon-Avon. Tel: 01789 292485/269679.

ORI • Oriental Gallery, 1 Digbeth St, Stow-on-the-Wold, Glos. Tel: 01451 830944.

OS • †Oswald Simpson, Hall Street, Long Melford, Suffolk. Tel: 01787 377523.

P * †Phillips, Blenstock House, 101 New Bond Street, London W1. Tel: 0171 629 6602.

P(Ch) * Phillips North West, New House, 150 Christleton Road, Chester, Cheshire. Tel: 01244 313936.

P(L) * Phillips Leeds, Hepper House, 17a East Parade, Leeds. Tel: 01532 448011.

P(O) * Phillips, 39 Park End Street, Oxford. Tel: 01865 723524.

P(S) * Phillips, 49 London Road, Sevenoaks, Kent. Tel: 01732 740310.

PAO • †P A Oxley, The Old Rectory, Cherthill, Nr Calne, Wiltshire. Tel: 01249 816227.

PC Private Collection.

PCh * †Peter Cheney, Western Road Auction Rooms, Western Road, Littlehampton, Sussex. Tel: 01903 722264/713418.

PEx • †Piano-Export, Bridge Road, Kingswood, Bristol. Tel: 0117 568300.

PHay • †Peggy Hayden, Yeovil. Tel: 0935 21336.

PT • †Pieces of Time, Grays Mews, 1-7 Davies Street, London W1. Tel: 0171 629 2422.

RA • †Roberts Antiques. Tel: 01253 827794.

RBB * †Russell, Baldwin & Bright, Fine Art Salerooms, Ryelands Road, Leominster, Hereford. Tel: 01568 611166.

RdeR • †Rogers de Rin, 76 Royal Hospital Road, London SW3. Tel: 0171-352 9007.

REL • Relic Antiques at Brillscote Farm, Lea, Malmesbury, Wilts. Tel: 01666 822332.

RID * †Riddetts of Bournemouth, 26 Richmond Hill, Bournemouth, Dorset. Tel: 01202 555686.

RP • Robert Pugh. Tel: 01225 314713.

RUM • †Rumours Decorative Arts, 10 The Mall, Upper Street, Camden Passage, Islington, London N1. Tel: 01582 873561.

RWB • †Roy W. Bunn Antiques, 34-36 Church St., Barnoldswick, Colne, Lancs. Tel: 01282 813703.

S * Sotheby's, 34-35 New Bond Street, London W1. Tel: 0171 493 8080.

S&S * Stride & Son, Southdown House, St John's Street, Chichester. Tel: 01243 780207.

S(G) * Sotheby's, 13 Quai du Mont Blanc, CH-1201 Geneva. Tel: 41(22) 732 8585.

S(NY) * Sotheby's, 1334 York Avenue, New York NY 10021, USA. Tel: 212 606 7000.

S(S) * Sotheby's Sussex, Summers Place, Billingshurst, Sussex. Tel: 01403 783933.

SA • Somerville Antiques & Country Furniture Ltd, Killanley, Ballina, Co Mayo, Ireland. Tel: 00 353 96 36275.

SAD • Old Saddlers Antiques, Church Road, Goudhurst, Kent. Tel: 01580211458.

SAF * Saffron Walden Auctions, 1 Market Street, Saffron Walden, Essex. Tel: 01799 513281.

Sim * †Simmons & Sons, 32 Bell Street, Henley-on-Thames, Oxon. Tel: 01491 571111.

Som • †Somervale Antiques, 6 Radstock Road, Midsomer Norton, Bath, Avon. Tel: 01761 412686.

SK(B) * Skinner Inc, 357 Main Street, Bolton, MA 01740, USA. Tel: 0101 508 779 6421.

SLN * C.G. Sloan & Co. Inc., 4920 Wyaconda Road, North Bethesda, MD 20852, USA. Tel: 0101 301 468 4911.

SPI * Spink, 5, 6 & 7 King Street, St. James's, London SW1. Tel: 0171930 7888.

STA • †Michelina & George Stacpoole, Main St, Adare, Co Limerick, Ireland. Tel: 00 353 61 396409.

SUL • Sullivan Antiques (Chantal O'Sullivan), 43-44 Francis Street, Dublin 8. Tel: 541143/539659.

SWB • †Sweetbriar Gallery, Robin Hood Lane, Helsby, Cheshire. Tel: 01928 723851.

SWO * †Sworders, G. E. Sworder & Sons, 15 Northgate End, Bishops Stortford, Herts. Tel: 0117 965 1388.

TM * Thos. Mawer & Son, The Lincoln Saleroom, 63 Monks Road, Lincoln. Tel: 01522 524984.

TOL * Turn On Ltd, Antique Lighting Specialists, 116/118 Islington High St, Camden Passage, London N1. Tel: 0171 359 7616.

TPC • †The Pine Cellars, 39 Jewry Street, Winchester, Hants. Tel: 01962 867014.

UP • Utopia Pine & Country Furniture, Lake Road, Bowness on Windermere, Cumbria. Tel: 015394 88464.

VH • Valerie Howard, 131e Kensington Church St, London W8. Tel: 0171 792 9702.

VS * †T. Vennett-Smith, 11 Nottingham Road, Gotham, Nottingham. Tel: 01602 830541.

W * †Walter's, No. 1 Mint Lane, Lincoln. Tel: 01522 525454.

W&W • †Walker & Walker, Halfway Manor, Halfway, Nr Newbury, Berkshire. Tel: 01488 58693 or 01831 147480.

WAB • Warboys Antiques, Old Church School, High Street, Warboys, Cambridge. Tel: 01487 823686

WAG • †The Weald Antiques Gallery, 106 High Street, Tenterden, Kent. Tel: 01580 762939

Wai • Wain Antiques, Peter Wain, 7 Nantwich Road, Woore, Shropshire. Tel: 01630 647118.

WAL * Wallis & Wallis, West Street Auction Galleries, Lewes, E. Sussex. Tel: 01273 480208.

WBB • †Sir William Bentley Billiards, Standen Manor Farm, Hungerford, Berkshire. Tel: 0181 940 1152/01488 681711.

WELD • J W Weldon, 55 Clarendon St, Dublin 2. Tel: 00 353 1 771638.

WIG • †James Wigington. Tel: 01789 261418.

WIL * Peter Wilson, Victoria Gallery, Market Street, Nantwich, Cheshire. Tel: 01270 623878.

WL * Wintertons Ltd., Lichfield Auction Centre, Wood End Lane, Fradley, Lichfield, Staffs. Tel: 01543 263256.

WTA • †Witney and Airault, Prinny's Gallery, 3 Meeting House Lane, The Lanes, Brighton, Sussex. Tel: 01273 204554.

WW * Woolley & Wallis, The Castle Auction Mart, Castle Street, Salisbury. Tel: 01722 321711.

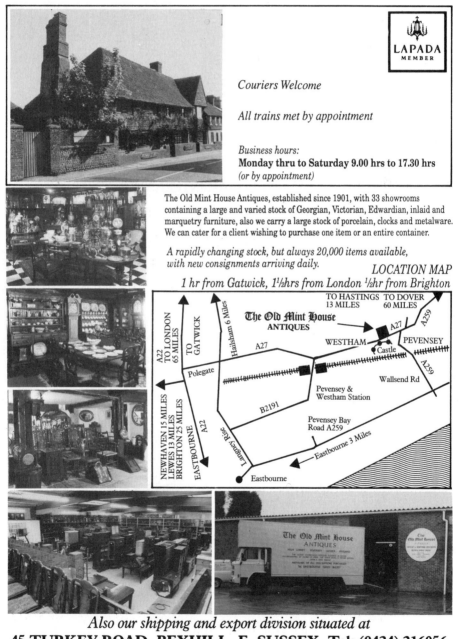

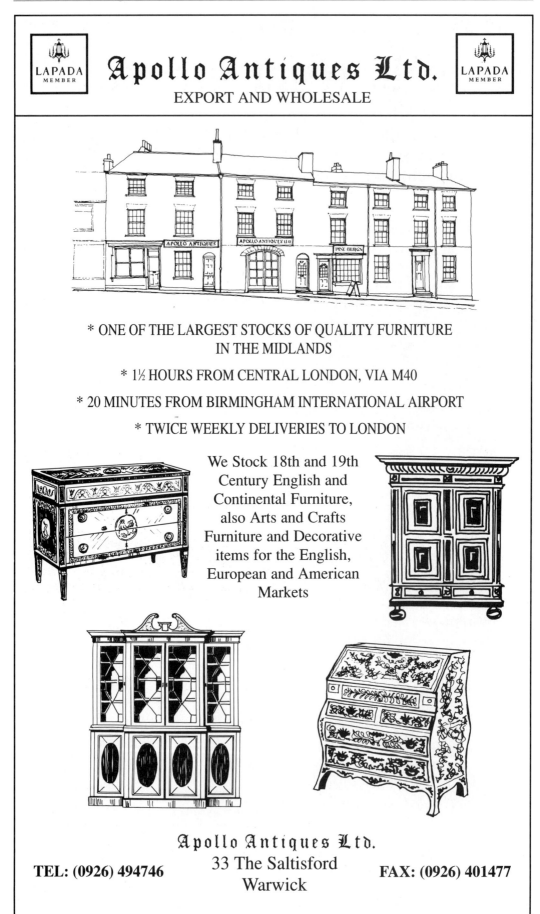

LAKESIDE
A CASE FOR FINE QUALITY

Whether you are looking for an individual piece or high volume, at Lakeside both quality and attention to detail are foremost. Lakeside furniture can also be adapted to suit the needs of the individual by varying the dimensions or materials used. An established firm with customers worldwide, our reputation precedes us.

For more information see our colour advertisement at the back of this guide

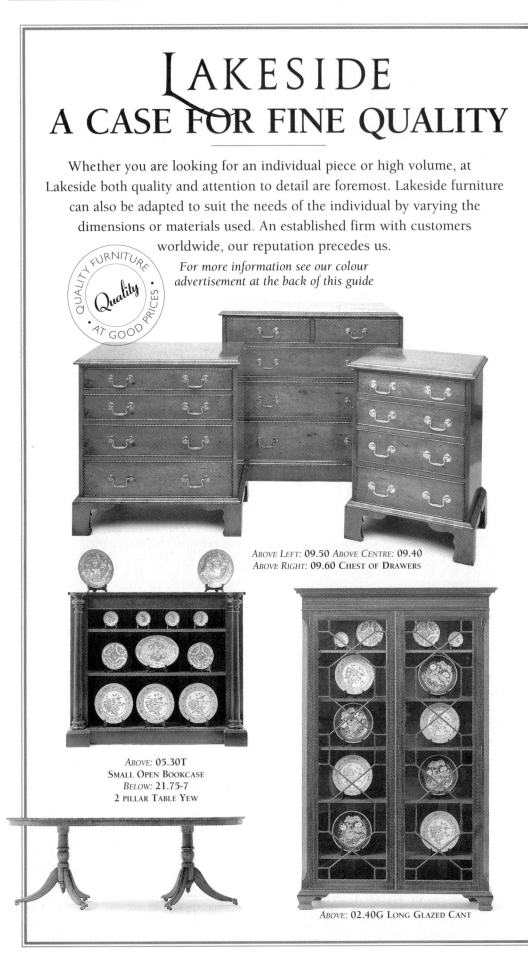

ABOVE LEFT: **09.50** *ABOVE CENTRE:* **09.40**
ABOVE RIGHT: **09.60** CHEST OF DRAWERS

ABOVE: **05.30T**
SMALL OPEN BOOKCASE
BELOW: **21.75-7**
2 PILLAR TABLE YEW

ABOVE: **02.40G** LONG GLAZED CANT

21.MC
MAHOGANY TWO DOOR CANT

05.25H
TALL OPEN BREAKFRONT

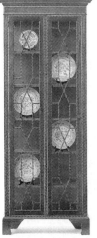

ABOVE: **94.91**
GLAZED SIDED CABINET
ABOVE RIGHT: **05.10H**
SMALL OPEN BOOKCASE

LAKESIDE
l i m i t e d

Old Cement Works, South Heighton
Newhaven, East Sussex BN9 0HS
Tel 0273 513326 Fax 0273 515528

20

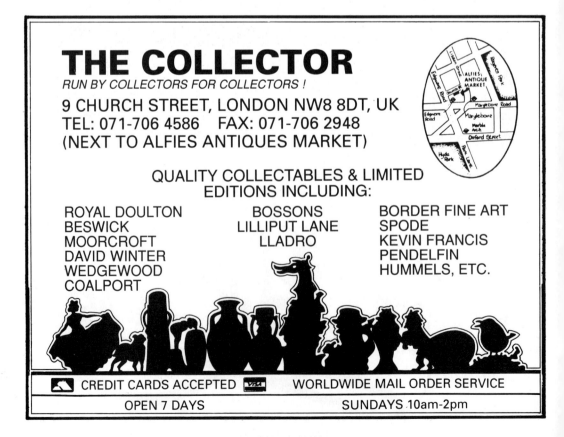

ACKNOWLEDGEMENTS

The publishers would like to acknowledge the great assistance given
by our consultants:

FURNITURE: **Richard Davidson,** Romsey House, 51 Maltravers Street, Arundel, Sussex.

TWENTIETH CENTURY
CHINESE CERAMICS: **Peter Wain,** 7 Nantwich Road, Woore, Shropshire.

CLOCKS: **Derek Roberts,** 25 Shipbourne Road, Tonbridge, Kent.

TEXTILES: **Joy Jarrett,** Witney Antiques, 96-100 Corn Street, Witney, Oxfordshire.

PAPERWEIGHTS: **Lady Langham,** J30/31 Gray's Mews, Davies Mews, London W1.

TOYS: **John Haley,** 89 Northgate, Halifax, W. Yorkshire.

BOOKS: **Catherine Porter,** Sotheby's, 34-35 New Bond Street, London W1.

MECHANICAL MUSIC &
MEDICAL INSTRUMENTS: **John Baddeley,** Sotheby's, 34-35 New Bond Street, London W1.

MASON'S IRONSTONE: **Valerie Howard,** 131e Kensington Church Street, London W8.

FOCUS ON AMERICA: **Lita Solis-Cohen,** 1031 Meetinghouse Road, Rydal, Pennsylvania 19046-2423, USA.

CONTENTS

INTRODUCTION

In the introduction to last year's edition of the *Miller's Antiques Price Guide* we reported a mood of 'cautious optimism' in the antiques market and although most areas of the trade have enjoyed a more prosperous year, the market is still a difficult one to predict.

There are signs of recovery, particularly in the furniture market – at the start of the year, Robert Copley, Director of the Furniture Department, Christie's reported he was 'extremely encouraged' by the results of their first English and Continental Furniture sale adding, 'Lots which had previously failed to attract interest sold in excess of their top estimates.' A handsome Regency oak and gilt writing table doubled its pre-sale expectations, selling for £27,600 against a pre-sale estimate of £7,000 to £10,000. Lower to medium range furniture which over the last few years has contributed to unsold lots at auction is now selling.

One encouraging sign is the re-emergence of the private buyer at auction who is making the most of the keen prices, recognising that as the recession comes to an end, and the market improves, prices will increase. Perhaps too they have discovered that antiques are a good alternative to other financial investments, which are at present not reaping the rewards they once did. However, Michael Collins of Collins Antiques in Wheathampstead, commented to Miller's that he felt until the property market showed improvement the antiques market would remain fairly quiet.

The nature of the trade has been changed by the recession; with many antique shops forced to close due to crippling overheads, fairs have boomed as dealers have made this their main outlet. Fairs at Olympia, Grosvenor House, the NEC, Birmingham and Harrogate to name just a few are all flourishing and the quality of the antiques on display is improving.

'Celebrity Sales' have been very much in the news. Barbra Streisand's collection of 20th Century Decorative and Fine Arts (see page 745) was auctioned at Christie's in New York. The sale totalled £4.2 million, with the 'Streisand factor' pushing some items way over estimates.

In London the Phillips Bayswater sale of the kitchenware that belonged to the much-loved cookery writer Elizabeth David also received extensive press coverage. The sale fetched three times as much as was expected at £49,000, for a collection that ranged from Tupperware boxes to a heavy pine table. The buyer who paid £300 for five wooden spoons captured the mood of the sale by saying 'I'm hoping some of the magic will rub off.' The event awakened interest in kitchenalia (see page 743) and as the country-style kitchen seems here to stay, this is an area that will become increasingly popular.

Both Streisand and David have a huge following and the provenance of their collections should ensure they remain valuable for years to come. However, it is unwise to be too star-struck when buying at auction as in many cases objects associated with public figures can become almost worthless as the popularity of the personality involved wanes. Buy pieces that you like for their own sake and you are unlikely to go too far wrong.

One of the 'fun' sales of the year was an auction of golf memorabilia at Phillips in Chester, where a 180 year old Spode porcelain bowl, held together with car body filler, its inscription barely legible, sold for a record £16,100. The bowl has now been professionally restored to its former glory and recognised as the first known golf trophy.

This year, Miller's have provided more detailed introductions on three areas – furniture, textiles and toys and increased the coverage on books, book illustrations and medical instruments, an increasingly popular collecting area. There is also a new feature on posy holders. Lita Solis-Cohen, our American consultant, introduces our new 'Focus on America' section. As well as providing an overview of the market place, Miller's consultants also give advice on restoration, fakes and forgeries, individual manufacturers and possible areas of investment – see Richard Davidson's introduction to the Furniture section on the wisdom of buying Edwardian, for example, page 27.

It is our aim to make the Guide easy to use. In order to find a particular item, consult the contents on page 23 to find the main heading, for example Porcelain. Having located your area of interest, you will find the larger sections have been sub-divided. If you are looking for a particular factory, designer or craftsman, consult the index which starts on page 801.

Please also remember Miller's pricing policy: we provide you with a price GUIDE not a price LIST. Our price ranges are worked out by a team of trade and auction house experts, and are based on actual prices realised. They reflect variables such as condition, location, desirability and so on. Don't forget that if you are selling it is possible that you will be offered less than the price range.

Lastly, we are always keen to improve the Guide. If you feel that we have left something important out, or have any other comments about the book, please write and let us know; we value feedback from the people who use this Guide to tell us how to make it even better.

FURNITURE

Good news for owners of antique furniture - prices are beginning to rise after years of dismal trading!

Signs that stability has been creeping back into the market are evident by the huge success of antiques fairs around the country, the slow-down of antique showroom staff lay-offs and the odd smile seen on dealers' faces, all indicating the worst may have passed. Further signs of an improving market, albeit a slow one, are shown by the increased level of trade in lower to medium range furniture. In previous years these items contributed to the large number of lots which remained unsold in salerooms and which dealers found difficult to move at any price.

Those who were in the fortunate position to buy during this difficult period were able to pick up many bargains. However, those days are now gone, decisions have to be made quickly as dealers are becoming more confident and decisive. Looking to the future, as European and American economies continue to improve, prices will continue to rise as trading confidence returns.

However, this long awaited upturn in the market has not put dealers off finding something to complain about. When asked how business is going, most claim they are doing well but that it is difficult to find new stock and prices for anything of good quality are sky high.

NEW COLLECTING AREAS

With traditional antique furniture becoming both scarce and prohibitively expensive, particularly 17thC and 18thC furniture, young buyers are now looking at collecting areas neglected by their parents. I shall always remember a dealer who worked for a well known firm in London just after WWII, telling me how Regency furniture was really only thought of as secondhand and not worthy to be put alongside the Queen Anne and other 18thC pieces such as Chippendale and Hepplewhite. Today the Regency period is one of the most highly prized collecting areas.

Similarly, Victorian furniture was only bought by dealers who broke it up and made use of the timber for restoration. Much of it was burnt, being considered ugly and old fashioned by those who were attracted to the new emerging designs of the 1950s. Victorian furniture has, during the last ten to twenty years, regained popularity to the point where very good examples are hard to find.

Edwardian furniture is becoming very well established and the products of this era, although often reflecting the styles of the late 18thC, (Adam and Sheraton in particular are exciting and extremely well made), satinwood with neo-classical marquetry or painted decoration are favoured techniques.

An Edwardian satinwood and giltwood demi-lune table, the top veneered with segments and painted with a rustic scene and ribbon and flower border, with fluted frieze and circular tapering legs, with shaped stretchers,42in (106.5cm). **£4,000-5,000** *S*

The pale woods of the Art Deco period are emerging as favourites amongst younger buyers, its popularity enhanced by the likes of Elton John and other celebrities whose houses feature in interior design magazines. Although some pieces from this period have become highly priced - these being either signed pieces or known to be by a particular craftsman - there are many items that can still be picked up cheaply in salerooms or antique shops. Armchairs and sofas, as well as dining and bedroom furniture, can be restored or re-upholstered in a suitable fabric, and transformed into something very stylish.

A Victorian ebonised and gilt metal mounted credenza.
£1,300-1,500 *AH*

For those with more traditional tastes, but having to keep within a tight budget, it is well worth considering reproductions from the Victorian period to the 1930s. Sets of dining tables and chairs from the 1920s and 30s can be picked up for hundreds rather than thousands of pounds and, if looked after and maintained properly, should rise in value steadily if not spectacularly. There are now a number of dealers and auction rooms which specialise in items from the 1950s and 60s, creating a keen interest in this modern field of collecting.

Examples such as the 19thC Anglesey Desk, which sold at Christies for £1.5 million, could give the impression that all antique furniture is very expensive, and certainly it is true that rare examples of high quality furniture are only for the very wealthy. However, with some imagination there is no doubt that a house can be furnished without the outlay of great sums of money and that a lot of fun can be had along the way.

RESTORATION

Always bear in mind that a good piece of antique furniture can be ruined and its value destroyed by a bad restorer, and once the damage is done it may be impossible to rectify. The problem is how do you tell if the restorer is good or bad? Probably the best way is through personal recommendation, either from a friend or a member of the trade.

Many professional restorers today received their training at West Dean College in Sussex, sponsored by The British Antique Dealers' Association, and are now members of BAPRA, The British Antique Furniture Restorers' Association, who publish a list of members.

Furthermore, the serious restorer will probably keep a detailed record of past work which should indicate their capabilities. Also it is advisable to take a look around the workshop and assess the general standard of pieces that are being restored. If you find pieces of cheap secondhand furniture strewn around the place it is probably a good idea to take your cherished piece of Queen Anne walnut elsewhere!

Discuss with the restorer what is needed to achieve the best results and always get an indication of what it is going to cost. What may seem an easy and straightforward process may, in fact, be very time consuming and lead to a nasty shock when the time comes to pay the bill. Our advice would be to always get an estimate in writing, and to ask him to contact you if unforseen problems arise before continuing with the work.

For the professional buyer experience will enable a decision to be made as to how well a piece will respond to restoration. For the inexperienced buyer this is obviously harder to assess and there can be faults that are very difficult and costly to remedy. For example, tears and splits in table tops accompanied by warping can be very complicated to restore successfully. If you are unsure, seek professional advice before proceeding to purchase pieces that require major restoration.

There is undoubtedly much furniture at the lower end of the price scale to be found in antique shops and salerooms which is not in perfect condition. This can be bought quite cheaply and with the attention of a restorer or polisher can quite easily be reinstated to its former glory without too much difficulty or expense.

The Regency mahogany tilt-top breakfast table illustrated below, with an over-faded and water marked top, looks dreadful as it is but is typical of a piece that will respond well to restoration and in this case is basically a polishing job. The natural colour of the mahogany can be seen to be a rich reddish-brown colour. The polish has probably perished due to over-exposure to sunlight, and the ring marks indicate water damage and general neglect. The actual physical structure of the table is surprisingly good, perhaps due to the fact that it was well made in the first place and that good seasoned timber was used.

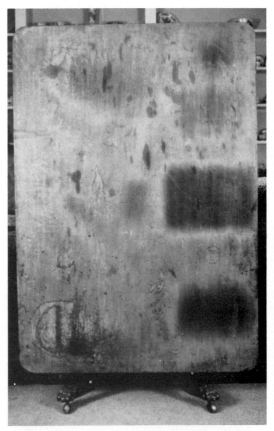

A Regency mahogany tilt-top breakfast table, with a faded, water marked top, but otherwise in good condition

To transform this table it will be a process of gently stripping off the old polish and repolishing by hand in the traditional way, then gradually building up the amount of polish applied, cutting back in between, until a smooth and soft finish is achieved, finally finishing off with wax.

WARNING: It may seem a good idea to attempt this job yourself using a proprietary stripper and varnish. However, polishing is an art learnt by years of experience and for the uninitiated this would probably lead to ruining both the piece and its value.

The illustrations here show an early Georgian wing armchair before and after restoration and re-upholstery. It is important as far as value is concerned for such chairs to have their original framework, and an inspection of a chair in this 'before' state will in all probability show some evidence of woodworm. This is not a problem provided it is not active or has been treated. The spattering of old tacks and holes where the chair has been previously re-upholstered through the years may be taken as a good sign of authenticity.

If the chair has already been re-upholstered it is worth asking about the frame and the experienced dealer will, as a matter of course, have photographed the frame beforehand.

An 18thC wing armchair during the course of restoration, and, right, re-upholstered in silk damask.

CARE OF ANTIQUE FURNITURE

Antique furniture needs to be respected, and a piece that is well cared for will appreciate in value more than a neglected item.

Here are a few simple ways to avoid unnecessary damage:
• Never place a piece of wooden furniture against or near a radiator, or in a very dry or damp atmosphere, as this will cause warping and splitting. The atmosphere can be regulated with a humidifier.
• Never use aerosol sprays on wood.

• Never let people lean on the backs of chairs.
• Never let an amateur restorer repair a piece of furniture.

There are also a few easy ways to prevent deterioration:
• Polish at regular intervals with a wax polish.
• Check regularly, and have any necessary work done before further deterioration occurs.
• Take care to avoid exposure to continued strong sunlight.

BUYING GUIDELINES

From Shops and Fairs:

Buy from shops where pieces are clearly labelled with at least a brief description and an indication of the age.

Always obtain a receipt giving the description and, more importantly, the date.

It is undoubtedly a good idea to purchase from dealers who are members of a recognised trade organisation such as the BADA or LAPADA.

From Auction Rooms:

Your receipt will not always give a description but merely the lot number, hammer price and any buyer's premium.

Remember to keep the catalogue as it is this description which will be used in the event of a problem.

ANTIQUES AS AN INVESTMENT

Owning beautiful pieces of antique furniture can bring great pleasure and this should always be the prime reason for buying. However, the investment factor is also a good excuse for indulging oneself!

Investment in antique furniture should be seen as long term. Do not expect to buy one year and to sell it the next for a profit; it can happen but it is not the general rule. It has also been proved that the better the piece the more likely it is to increase in value.

Today, very good pieces of antique furniture are becoming extremely difficult to find, even for dealers. Major auction houses in London now have only three or four sales of important furniture a year, which normally contain less than two hundred lots each, boosted by regular auctions of lesser quality items. Despite this, there is still insufficient antique furniture to satisfy demand in what is now a world market.

To someone entering the fascinating world of antiques for the first time, and even the more experienced purchaser, the best advice anyone could give is to buy the best of what you like - this will result in owning an antique that will give you great pleasure with the added bonus that it should prove to be a good investment in the long term.

Richard Davidson

OAK & COUNTRY FURNITURE

Beds

A Charles II style carved oak daybed, with cane back and seat, needlework back and seat cushions, late 19thC, 72in (182.5cm). **£550–800** *S(S)*

Bureaux

An oak bureau cabinet, the upper section with moulded cornice and a pair of panelled doors enclosing adjustable shelves, the sloping fall enclosing a fitted interior, on shaped bracket feet, c1800, 37½in (95cm). **£1,500–2,500** *CSK*

A Georgian oak and mahogany crossbanded bureau, with fall front, mahogany banded drawers with cockbeading to the drawer fronts, brass drop handles with oval back plates, standing on shaped bracket feet, 45in (114cm). **£1,000–1,400** *Mit*

An ebony inlaid walnut, oak and marquetry tester bed, with moulded cornice, panelled frieze inlaid with stylised scrolling foliage, above a geometrically panelled roof supported by bulbous turned baluster columns to the floor, with a deeply panelled three-tier headboard between scrolled foliate brackets, the footboard with urn cappings, including box spring and mattress, adapted, lacking cross struts, parts 17thC, 65in (165cm). **£7,200–8,500** *CSK*

An oak child's cradle, the panelled sides with foliate strapwork decoration, joined by chamfered uprights with finials, the ogee arched hood later carved '1781 T.M.', with rocking bars, now stabilised, repaired, early 18thC, 43in (110cm). **£1,600–2,000** *CSK*

An oak cradle, English, c1700. **£500–700** *KEY*

An oak bureau, the crossbanded fall enclosing fitted interior, on bracket feet, restored, parts early 18thC, 39in (99cm). **£1,000–1,400** *CSK*

A Georgian oak bureau, with fitted interior cupboard, pigeonholes and drawers above a well, with 3 long graduated drawers beneath a dummy drawer, on bracket feet, 38in (96cm). **£1,200–1,700** *Bri*

An oak double-dome bureau bookcase, with moulded cornice and later finials, the sloping fall enclosing a fitted interior, on later bun feet, replacements and repairs, mid-18thC, 38½in (98cm). **£4,000–6,000** *CSK*

A Queen Anne oak bureau, on bracket feet, damaged, early 18thC, 33in (84cm).
£1,500–2,000 S(S)

Chairs

An oak box seat armchair, with fielded panelled back, stamped 'E.R.' 4 times, later base, repaired, early 17thC.
£1,400–1,700 CSK

A Derbyshire oak lambing chair, the shaped back with panel, flanked by winged sides, shaped arms and enclosed seat and a panelled base with drawer to side, 18th/19thC, 45in (114cm) high.
£650–800 B

Cabinets

An oak spice cabinet-on-stand, fitted with 10 drawers enclosed by a panel door, on baluster supports joined by stretchers, part 17thC, 23in (58cm).
£450–600 P

An oak side chair, with initials carved in the cresting rail, English, c1670.
£500–600 KEY

A set of 6 ash ladder back chairs, with rush seats, Wigan, c1830.
£1,800–2,200 KEY

An oak cabinet, the upper section with 2 frieze drawers above 2 cupboards carved in high relief with The Presentation and The Epiphany, the lower section fitted with twin doors also carved in relief, with Flemish style mouldings, barley-twist columns to middle and either end, 66in (167cm).
£1,000–1,500 WL

A carved oak dwarf side cabinet, with marble top, the 3 frieze drawers above a central glazed door flanked by pair of panelled cupboard doors, shaped aprons and foliate carved scroll feet, 67in (170cm).
£950–1,200 CSK

An oak open armchair, the later top rail with central rosette, above a panelled back carved with rosettes and scratch-carved lozenge, later padded seat and turned legs joined by stretchers, stamped 'M.I.' and 'T.I.' twice, repaired and restored, late 17thC.
£500–700 CSK

An elm and ash Windsor chair,
late 18thC.
£300–400 *WIL*

A set of 8 beech and elm dining
chairs, including a pair of
armchairs, the arms of one chair
possibly replaced, slight
differences in height, early 19thC.
£1,500–2,000 *CSK*

Two oak and ash ladder back low
elbow chairs, with undulating top
rails and splats, with rush seats,
on tapered legs with pad feet
joined by turned front stretchers,
early 19thC.
£260–300 *P*

A George IV elm and ash Windsor
armchair, the splayed legs with
H-shaped stretcher, c1825.
£300–450 *S(S)*

A pair of alder and ash spindle
back chairs, with rush seats, on
tapering legs with pad feet, joined
by turned front stretchers,
together with an alder spindle
back low armchair with rush
seat, 19thC.
£250–300 *P*

A West Country oak open
armchair, the panelled back
carved with foliage, rosettes and
central Tudor Rose, turned legs
joined by stretchers, a small
section of seat moulding missing,
late 17thC and later.
£800–1,000 *CSK*

A Regency elm and fruitwood
open armchair, the deeply curved
back with vase-shaped splat,
rectangular supports and saddle
seat, on sabre legs joined by
X-shaped turned stretchers.
£650–800 *C*

*This provincial form of 'Grecian'
chair derives from the Parisian
chaise en gondle of the 1790s
which first appeared in England
in the* London Cabinet-Makers'
and Carvers' Book of Pieces *of the
early 1800s.*

An early Victorian yew and elm
Windsor armchair, with arched
back and pierced vase splat, solid
seat, on baluster turned legs
joined by crinolene stretcher.
£500–800 *CSK*

A yew wood and elm low back
Windsor armchair, c1830.
£700–900 *KEY*

Settles

A Queen Anne oak settle, with hinged seat, on stile feet, later additions, 43in (110cm). **£1,300–1,700** *S(S)*

An elm and ash comb back Windsor elbow chair, with shaped crest rail and pierced splat, on turned legs with stetchers, Thames Valley region. **£300–400** *DN*

An elm ladder back country rocking chair with rush seat, on turned front supports and cross stretcher. **£250–300** *HCH*

Settles

In medieval times the most common forms of seating were crude stools, benches and chests. The interior of a medieval home was extremely sparse, with little comfort available. Chests and benches were usually placed against walls, with benches often fixed to the panelling of smarter establishments.

A settle, therefore, is a bench or chest fitted with a section of wall panelling and fixed arms. These useful pieces of furniture sometimes had a cupboard under the seat or a hinged seat, and were often used for storing food.

In the 19thC, a large number of provincial settles were made in pine with the smaller examples now commanding a premium.

A Welsh oak settle, with box seat, early 18thC, 41in (103cm). **£500–550** *BIR*

Miller's is a price GUIDE not a price LIST.

A Lancashire oak settle, the back with 4 fielded panels and foliate, shell-carved cresting between uprights with finials, above solid seat and turned and block legs joined by conforming stretchers, seatboards replaced, repaired, late 17thC, 72in (183cm). **£3,000–3,500** *CSK*

An oak settle, with an applied top rail above the panelled back, with downswept scrolling arms supported by turned columns, with squab cushion supported on ropes and turned legs with stretchers, 17thC, 72in (182.5cm). **£500–600** *Mit*

A George III oak settle, with fielded panel back over loose squab cushion, flanked by downswept arms and raised on cabriole supports, 72in (183cm). **£400–500** *BIR*

An oak hall bench, with bobbin turned legs and similar hand rails, 72in (183cm). **£400–600** *CSK*

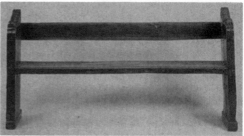

A pair of Continental baroque oak church pews, on trestle ends with block feet, 70in (178cm). **£400–500** *CNY*

Chests

A Jacobean chest, 45in (114cm).
£680-750 *WIL*

A Charles II oak and inlaid 2 part chest, inlaid in bog oak and holly, with later inlay and bun feet, damaged, 44in (112cm).
£1,000–1,500 *S(S)*

A Charles II oak 2 part chest, with geometric and turned mouldings, on later turned feet, late 17thC, 38in (96cm).
£1,000–1,400 *S(S)*

A Charles II oak 2 part chest, the drawers with mitred fielded panel fronts, on stile feet, late 17thC, 43in (110cm).
£1,000–1,500 *S(S)*

A William and Mary oak and yew 2 part chest, the drawers with mitred mouldings, on turned feet, late 17thC, 38in (96cm).
£3,200–4,000 *S(S)*

An oak chest, on stile feet, late 17thC, 39½in (100cm).
£1,000–1,500 *CSK*

An oak chest of drawers, decorated with geometric mouldings and split balusters, on stile feet, late 17thC, 38in (96.5cm).
£2,000–2,500 *OS*

A Queen Anne oak and walnut chest, the drawers with fruitwood crossbanding and sycamore stringing, on later bracket feet, early 18thC, 37in (93cm).
£1,000–1,500 *S(S)*

A Flemish oak 2 part chest, the hinged top enclosing a well, the geometrically panelled front with 3 drawers, on later stile feet, mid-17thC, 40in (101.5cm).
£1,500–2,000 *S(S)*

A French oak chest, with plank top, profusely carved with berried trailing vines, rosettes, flowers and grotesque creatures, centred with a heart and a pair of winged angels above, dated 'Ano 1794', with carrying handles to the sides, on stile feet, top repaired, 51in (130cm).
£1,500–2,000 *CSK*

A Georgian oak and mahogany crossbanded tallboy, on shaped bracket feet, 41in (104cm).
£1,500–2,000 *Mit*

An oak panelled chest, with lunette carved frieze and later panelled front, fluted stiles, late 17thC, 49in (124cm).
£800–1,000 *CSK*

An early Georgian oak mule chest, with triple crossbanded panel front above 2 drawers, on stile feet, 50in (127cm).
£600–700 *ALL*

A William and Mary walnut and oak chest, the later veneered top above 2 short and 3 long drawers, on later bracket feet, 38in (96cm).
£1,000–1,400 *S(S)*

Mule Chests

A mule chest has one or two drawers in the lower part, beneath a hinged lid.

They were made from the mid-17thC, usually from oak, and evolved into the chest of drawers in the 18thC.

An oak mule chest, with a hinged lid enclosing a lidded compartment and 3 later drawers, the panel front with initials 'AR' and 2 drawers below, on block feet, 18thC, 50in (127cm).
£500–600 *P*

An oak chest, early 19thC, 41in (105cm).
£250–300 *WIL*

A Lancashire oak mule chest, the hinged top with a fretwork gallery above an arrangement of 5 dummy and 4 real drawers flanked by quadrant pilasters, on ogee bracket feet, lacking part of one bracket foot, late 18thC, 63in (160cm).
£900–1,200 *S(S)*

A George III oak tallboy, 45in (114cm).
£700–900 *S(S)*

A pair of oak and iron bound oak chests-on-stands, each with hinged fall enclosing fitted interior with pigeonholes, on square chamfered legs, one of the stands in yew, one with label 'Pair of Countrymade Charter Chests of Oak which have always been at Dawyck'.
£1,500–1,700 *CSK*

An oak tallboy, standing on later feet, early 18thC, 44in (111.5cm).
£1,000–1,400 *Mit*

A Commonwealth oak boarded coffer, the moulded hinged top above a lunette border centred by an iron lock plate, on trestle shaped supports, mid-17thC, 45½in (116cm).
£800–900 *S(S)*

An oak coffer, the top with moulded edge above a carved frieze and central stylised foliate panel, flanked by 2 diamond panels, 18thC.
£600–700 *BWe*

Coffers

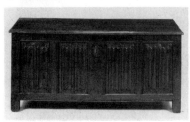

A baroque oak coffer, the hinged top opening to a well, the front and sides with linenfold panels, on plank feet, some alterations, 68½in (174cm).
£1,500–2,000 *CNY*

A George I carved oak coffer, the moulded hinged top above a strapwork frieze, the panelled front with scroll borders and lozenge carving centred by the date '1715', 49in (124.5cm).
£500–800 *S(S)*

A Queen Anne oak boarded coffer, the front carved with floral vases, initials and dated '1701', 30in (77cm).
£1,200–1,500 *S(S)*

A Gothic oak coffer, altered, early 16thC, 47in (119cm).
£1,000–1,200 *B*

> ## Coffers
>
> A coffer, by strict definition, is a travelling trunk which is banded with metalwork and covered with leather or other material.
>
> However, the word tends to be used quite freely now to describe chests of various kinds.

A Jacobean coffer, initialled and dated '1686', 51in (130cm).
£400–500 *WIL*

A Charles II carved oak coffer, with chip-carved roundel and scroll decoration, the panelled hinged top above a 4 panel front, on stile feet, 58in (147cm).
£500–700 *S(S)*

A Charles II carved oak coffer, the panelled hinged top above a strapwork frieze and a triple panel front, with lozenges bearing the date '1667' flanking a stylised arch with the initials 'MW', later lock and hinges, late 17thC, 60in (152cm).
£850–1,000 *S(S)*

Cupboards

A Flemish oak buffet, 18thC,
57in (144.5cm).
£1,500–1,700 *B*

Buffet

Buffet is the name loosely
applied to various structures
of more than one tier, with or
without enclosed sections.

A James I Westmoreland oak
court cupboard, 62in (157cm).
£3,000–3,500 *B*

A food cupboard-on-
stand, the upper part
enclosed by a panelled
door with an aperture
with ring-turned
spindles, the stand
with baluster turned
legs, 25in (64cm).
£800–900 *P*

A French Provincial oak and
chestnut buffet, the top section
with moulded cornice above
2 pierced metal-panelled doors,
each dated '1841', above 2 open
shelves, the lower section fitted
with a fielded panelled door
on block feet, mid-19thC,
32½in (82.5cm).
£800–1,200 *CSK*

An oak housekeeper's cupboard,
the top with mahogany frieze,
2 twin panelled and banded doors
over 4 shelves, the base with
6 banded pine lined drawers, brass
plate handles, standing on a plinth
and reeded pilasters, early 19thC,
72in (183cm).
£2,200–2,700 *WIL*

A Georgian standing corner
cupboard, with fitted shaped
shelves enclosed by 2 pairs
of doors with fielded panels,
45in (114cm).
£2,500–3,000 *RBB*

A Charles I oak livery cupboard,
the cleated top above a foliate
scroll carved frieze and triple
lozenge panelled front,
incorporating a central door, on
cup-and-cover turned supports
joined by stretchers, top and
stretchers replaced, some parts
later, 26in (66cm).
£2,300–3,000 *S(S)*

A Flemish oak cupboard, the moulded rectangular top above a pair of doors, each with 4 linenfold panels and iron strapwork, on stile feet, with label inside inscribed 'Bruxelles', some repairs and alterations, c1600, 63in (160cm).
£5,000–7,000 *CSK*

An oak press cupboard, on bracket feet, early 18thC, 52in (132cm).
£1,700–2,200 *B*

An oak court cupboard, 17thC, 55in (139.5cm).
£1,000–1,500 *Mit*

A Charles I carved oak press cupboard, the shallow cornice above recessed lozenge panels incorporating a pair of doors, flanked by bulbous turned pillars, the lower part with a pair of frieze drawers and corresponding cupboard doors, on stile feet, mid-17thC, 62in (157cm).
£2,000–3,000 *S(S)*

Press Cupboard

A press cupboard is an enclosed cupboard, usually in 2 parts. The upper part has either a recessed flat or canted front and the lower part is entirely enclosed by doors.

A Charles I carved oak press cupboard, 71in (180cm).
£1,500–1,700 *WIL*

A Charles II oak press cupboard, the lunette carved frieze centred by a panel bearing the date '1667' and initials 'TDC', on stile feet, later back boards, 73in (185cm).
£1,800–2,200 *S(S)*

A George II oak linen press, the moulded cornice above a pair of fielded panelled doors enclosing hanging space, the base with 3 dummy drawers above 3 real drawers, on bracket feet, mid-18thC, 50in (127cm).
£2,000–2,300 *S(S)*

A Normandy oak armoire, with central cartouche of doves above stylised quivers, 2 long doors with carved foliate and raised decoration of roses and flowers, with reeded sides and raised upon stylised carved cabriole legs, with separate cornice, 18thC.
£2,500–3,000 *B*

This armoire was a present from General Charles de Gaulle of France to General Spiers, who was the officer entrusted with his safe arrival in England during WWII.

A Welsh oak deuddarn, the projecting frieze with twin pendants above a pair of recessed ogee arched doors, 2 frieze drawers below and a pair of multi-panelled doors, on stile feet, late 18thC, 40in (102cm).
£2,500–3,000 *S(S)*

Deuddarn

A deuddarn is a Welsh variety of press cupboard with two tiers. The full name being cwpwrdd deuddarn.

A George III oak and mahogany crossbanded housekeeper's cupboard, with moulded cornice over 4 panelled doors, the lower section with 2 panelled doors flanked to either side by 3 short drawers.
£2,000–2,400 *BIR*

A George II oak linen press, the later cornice above a pair of fielded panelled doors enclosing hanging space, the base with an arrangement of 2 dummy and 2 real drawers, on stile feet, mid-18thC, 53in (134.5cm).
£1,000–1,400 *S(S)*

A George III oak cupboard, with moulded cornice above 3 drawers and a pair of fielded panelled doors, flanking central arched panel, on later bracket feet, 59in (150cm).
£1,800–2,200 *CSK*

A Charles II oak cupboard, with later moulded cornice above a guilloche carved frieze, panelled front with a pair of doors enclosing later shelves, late 17thC, 69in (175cm).
£950–1,200 *S(S)*

A George I panelled oak cupboard, the later moulded cornice above a pair of cupboard doors, now on bracket feet, originally the upper section of a larger cupboard, 61in (155cm).
£1,200–1,700 *S(S)*

Dressers

An oak dresser base, with 3 drawers, 17thC, 82in (208cm).
£2,400–2,700 *WIL*

A north Wales oak dresser, with superstructure containing 6 small drawers, possibly associated, on stile feet, repaired, mid-18thC, 86in (219cm).
£2,000–3,000 *CSK*

An oak dresser, with moulded top, on baluster turned legs, joined by stretchers, formerly with super-structure, 17thC and later, 70in (177cm).
£1,800–2,200 *CSK*

An oak dresser base, with oval plates and drop handles, on block feet, early 18thC, 64in (162.5cm).
£2,500–3,000 *L&E*

A George III oak dresser base, with raised shelved super-structure containing 3 drawers, later back rail, above 3 frieze drawers, shaped aprons and cabriole legs with pad feet, some restoration, 77½in (197cm).
£3,000–3,500 *CSK*

An oak dresser with associated rack, on ring turned legs and turned feet joined by an undertier, early 18thC, 77½in (197cm).
£1,500–2,500 *CSK*

An oak dresser base, early 18thC, 72in (182.5cm). **£7,000–8,000** *B*

A George II oak dresser, the canopied raised back with a cavetto cornice above recessed open shelves, on stile feet, drawers relined, mid-18thC, 55in (139.5cm).
£3,200–4,000 *S(S)*

An oak low dresser, with moulded top and 4 frieze drawers, on turned and block supports, repaired, 18thC, 97in (247cm).
£3,000–4,000 *CSK*

A George III style oak dresser, crossbanded throughout in burr elm, 94½in (240cm).
£1,100–1,600 *S(S)*

An oak dresser, the low rack, with 2 shelves and 5 spice drawers, 3 cockbeaded drawers and cabriole legs, 18thC, 72in (182cm).
£3,000–3,500 *WIL*

An oak, mahogany crossbanded and herringbone inlaid dresser, with contemporary delft rack, on scroll decorated cabriole legs with pad feet, 18thC, 75in (190.5cm).
£1,700–2,500 *AH*

A George III oak dresser base, with original brass fitments, on cabriole front supports, 79in (200cm).
£1,300–1,800 *WL*

An oak dresser, the shelved superstructure with a moulded cornice, the base fitted with 5 drawers in the double arched frieze, with a central flattened baluster support and undertier, on block feet, early 18thC, 58in (147cm).
£3,000–3,500 *P*

A country oak dresser, with 5 small spice drawers, mid-18thC, 57in (144.5cm).
£3,000–3,500 *HOLL*

A George II oak dresser, mid-18thC, 70in (178cm).
£5,500–6,500 *S(S)*

A Georgian oak dresser, the 2 shelf back with moulded cornice, the base with 3 frieze drawers above potboard, 62in (156cm).
£1,500–2,000 *Bri*

A George III oak dresser, with upper delft rack, inlaid decoration and crossbanding, on cabriole legs with pad feet, restored, 78in (198cm), the brass faced clock in upper section with silvered raised chapter ring, engraved 'Thomas Shinn, Mathen No. 124'.
£1,200–1,700 *L&E*

A George III oak dresser, the associated top and shelves above 3 drawers and cupboards, enclosed by a pair of panel doors, 66in (167.5cm).
£1,500–2,000 *RID*

A George II oak dresser base, the moulded top above 3 walnut crossbanded frieze drawers and a shaped apron, on cabriole legs with pad feet, 73½in (187cm).
£2,500–3,000 *S(S)*

An elm dresser, with shaped frieze over shelves, the base, fitted with 3 drawers, on square chamfered legs, 90in (229cm).
£1,300–1,700 *RBB*

A George III oak dresser, with brass knob handles, panelled sides and bracket feet, 60½in (152cm).
£4,500–5,000 *AH*

A George III oak dresser.
£2,800–3,200 *P(S)*

A George III Welsh oak dresser, on bracket feet, 72in (182cm).
£3,200–3,700 *WL*

An oak enclosed dresser base, the drawers with lipped fronts, the base moulding standing on 3 bun feet, later brass knobs, early 18thC, 85in (216cm).
£1,800–2,000 *WIL*

Stools

An oak joint stool, with later seat, the foliate scroll frieze on columnar legs with block feet joined by stretchers, 17thC.
£480–530 *P*

An oak stool, c1860.
£50–55 *SAD*

An enclosed oak dresser base, late 18thC, 76in (193cm).
£1,100–1,500 *WIL*

A north Wales oak dresser, on bracket feet, early 19thC, 66½in (168cm).
£3,500–4,500 *CSK*

A Charles II oak box seat stool, with a shaped escutcheon, on square and ring turned legs, late 17thC, 15in (38cm).
£1,400–1,800 *S(S)*

A William and Mary oak closed stool, with moulded hinged top, turned and square supports joined by spiral twist stretchers, late 17thC, 20in (50cm).
£1,300–1,700 *S(S)*

An oak dresser, with 2 frieze drawers and ogee shaped apron, on turned legs with pad feet, one repaired, later back supports, mid-18thC, 60in (152cm).
£2,000–2,500 *CSK*

A Welsh oak dresser, with brass drop handles, on baluster and block turned front legs, 18thC, 77in (194cm).
£1,200–1,700 *WL*

An oak dresser base, with 3 frieze drawers, bulbous turned supports with corner spandrels, joined by an undertier, on block feet, formerly with a plate rack, mid-18thC, 67½in (171cm).
£3,000–3,500 *CSK*

An oak stool, 30in (76cm) high.
£55–60 *AL*

Tables

An oak gateleg dining table, with single drawer, on baluster turned supports with bun feet, 18thC, 66in (168cm).
£2,500–3,000 *Bri*

A Charles II oak gateleg table, drawers missing, the square and turned legs joined by stretchers, late 17thC, 56in (142cm) extended.
£1,100–1,500 *S(S)*

An oak centre table, the moulded friezes with scrolling spandrels, on spiral twist supports joined by stretchers, repaired, late 17thC, 30½in (77cm).
£1,000–1,500 *CSK*

A William and Mary oak gateleg table, on ball turned legs and stretchers, 64in (163cm).
£1,600–1,800 *AH*

An oak drop-flap table, on triform base with uprights joined by stretchers, late 17thC, 33in (84cm).
£1,200–1,500 *CSK*

An oak refectory table, with planked top, on 4 heavy chamfered and bulbous shaped legs, united by block floor stretchers, early 17thC, 82in (208cm) long.
£2,000–2,400 *WL*

A Jacobean oak draw-leaf table, on gadrooned cup-and-cover turned legs joined by stretchers, and bun feet, 95in (241cm).
£8,000–10,000 *CNY*

A Charles II oak gateleg table, the top with a frieze drawer, the bobbin turned and square legs joined by stretchers, restored, late 17thC, 68in (172cm) extended.
£1,300–1,700 *S(S)*

An oak side table, with frieze drawer, on reel-and-bobbin turned legs joined by stretchers, on bun feet, late 17thC, 34in (86cm).
£600–800 *P*

An elm and oak refectory table, with twin plank top, on trestle supports joined by stretchers, the top early 18thC, the base early 18thC and later, 100in (254cm) long.
£3,200–4,000 *CSK*

MONARCH CHRONOLOGY		
Date	**Monarch**	**Period**
1558 - 1603	Elizabeth I	Elizabethan
1603 - 1625	James I	Jacobean
1625 - 1649	Charles I	Carolean
1649 - 1660	Commonwealth	Cromwellian
1660 - 1685	Charles II	Restoration
1685 - 1689	James II	Restoration
1689 - 1694	William & Mary	William & Mary
1694 - 1702	William III	William III
1702 - 1714	Anne	Queen Anne
1714 - 1727	George I	Early Georgian
1727 - 1760	George II	Georgian
1760 - 1812	George III	Late Georgian
1812 - 1820	George III	Regency
1820 - 1830	George IV	Late Regency
1830 - 1837	William IV	William IV
1837 - 1860	Victoria	Early Victorian
1860 - 1901	Victoria	Late Victorian
1901 - 1910	Edward VII	Edwardian

A post-Restauration design oak gateleg dining table, with twin oval drop leaves on barley sugar twist legs and square framing, 67in (170cm).
£3,000-5,000 *M*

The table was purchased in 1947 from the Grantley Hall auction of the Estate of Sir William Aykroyd for the sum of £62.10s.

A German oak and walnut refectory table, the walnut top inlaid with a chequer banded circle and central star motif raised upon six-sided oak base with 6 columnar turned legs and united by an all-round stretcher, 17thC, 72in (182.5cm) diam.
£13,000-17,000 *B*

An oak gateleg table, with 2 drawers, on bobbin turned supports, early 18thC, 61in (154cm).
£2,000-2,500 *BIR*

A Queen Anne oak low table, with moulded top above 4 turned tapering and square legs joined by peripheral stretchers, early 18thC, 21½in (55cm).
£1,400-1,700 *S(S)*

A sycamore cricket table, with a shelf and stretchers, c1800.
£1,100-1,300 *KEY*

An oak gateleg dining table, restored, late 17thC, 65in (165cm) extended.
£2,500-3,500 *CSK*

An oak side table, with bobbin twist legs, joined by stretchers, lock and drawer sides replaced, late 17thC, 34in (86cm).
£1,200-1,700 *CSK*

An oak gateleg dining table, with fitted drawer, on reel turned supports and square stretchers, 68in (173cm) extended.
£4,000-4,400 *RBB*

A Charles I oak credence table, the canted top above an arcaded frieze with applied ebonised turned and geometric mouldings, the columnar turned and square legs joined by stretchers, originally with a fold-over top and rear gateleg support, 36in (90cm).
£1,000-1,200 *S(S)*

A Flemish style oak draw-leaf table, with cleated top on 4 bulbous turned and square legs, joined by stretchers, 17thC, 38in (96.5cm).
£1,400-1,700 *S(S)*

An oak gateleg table, on columnar supports, joined by stretchers, some alterations, 17thC, 56in (142cm).
£850-1,200 *P*

A George II oak side table, on circular tapering legs and pad feet, mid-18thC, 28in (76cm).
£1,400-1,600 *S(S)*

A Queen Anne oak refectory table, requires some restoration, early 18thC, 84in (213cm) long.
£3,500-4,000 *S(S)*

An oak refectory table, the 4 plank cleated top above a carved frieze, on 4 inverted baluster turned legs united by stretchers, 17thC, 84in (213cm) long. **£4,000–4,700** *Mit*

A Charles II oak side table, with frieze drawer, 36in (91.5cm). **£4,000–4,500** *OS*

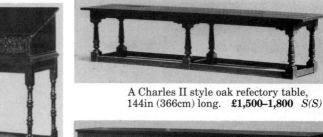

A Gloucestershire oak refectory table, the plank top with cleated ends above a rosette and guilloche carved facing frieze, on turned supports headed with entwined foliage and corner scroll spandrels, joined by associated stretchers, profusely carved with schoolboy names and initials, mostly dating from the early 19thC, the base 17thC with later stretchers, the top late 18th/early 19thC, 170in (432cm) long. **£10,000–15,000** *CSK*

Miscellaneous

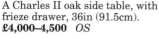

A Charles II carved oak desk box-on-stand, the sloping hinged top above a strapwork carved frieze centred by an iron escutcheon, the turned and square legs joined by stretchers, late 17thC, 34in (86cm). **£800–1,100** *S(S)*

A Charles II style oak refectory table, 144in (366cm) long. **£1,500–1,800** *S(S)*

A Charles II oak serving table, on bun feet, 207in (525cm) long. **£3,000–3,700** *S(S)*

A George IV oak hat stand, the hexagonal tapering column with a leaf carved finial and Gothic panels, on 3 splayed legs with brass terminals, 64½in (164cm) high. **£750–900** *DN*

A miniature oak commode, the concave front fitted with 3 long drawers, on bun feet, late 19thC, 24in (61cm). **£600–800** *DN*

An oak peat bucket, with brass bands, 16in (41cm) high. **£800–950** *SUL*

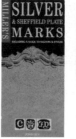

FURNITURE
Beds

An Empire style silvered iron day bed, the front rail cast with a rosette enclosed within spirals, cast with acanthus leaves and a laurel spray continuing to vitruvian scrolls cast with berries, acanthus leaves and beading, on toupie legs, 88½in (224cm) long.
£4,750–5,750 *S(NY)*

A Louis XVI style tester bed, painted green, with padded head and foot ends covered in ivory and blue chintz, gadrooned serpentine top rails, ribbon-twist edge panels flanked by pierced fluting columns with leaf finials, the rails carved with entwined scrolls and ribbon-twists, centred by a panel of ribbon-tied laurel, on turned tapering fluted legs, box spring missing, 90in (229cm) long.
£3,500–4,000 *CSK*

Bonheur du Jour

A satinwood and rosewood bonheur du jour, with hinged velvet lined surface, the whole with gilt ormolu mounts, on cabriole legs. **£3,500–4,500** *BWe*

Bonheur du Jour
A bonheur du jour is a small French writing table of delicate proportions with a raised back comprising a cabinet or shelves.

A double bed, with raised ends, lozenge parquetry panels and turned toupie feet, 61in (155cm).
£1,200–1,700 *CSK*

A French gilt metal mounted kingwood, rosewood and marquetry bed, late 19thC, 78in (198cm) long.
£2,000–2,500 *CSK*

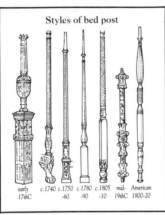

Styles of bed post

early 17thC | c.1740 -60 | c.1750 -90 | c.1780 -10 | c.1805 | mid-19thC | American 1800-20

A French Transitional kingwood bonheur du jour, by G. Cordié, with gilt metal mounts, the fold-over top enclosing 3 palissandre and tulipwood crossbanded sliding compartment covers, the apron with 2 small drawers, on cabriole legs, c1770, 26in (66cm).
£20,000–25,000 *S(S)*

Guillaume Cordié was received Maître in 1766, and died 1786.

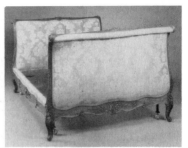

A Louis XV bed, with upholstered head and footboards, scrolled top rails joined by serpentine side rails, on cabriole legs, the whole carved with flowerheads flanked by scrolling foliate sprays, restored, mid-18thC, 82in (208cm) long.
£6,000–7,000 *S(NY)*

A pair of Louis XV style walnut beds, on carved cabriole legs with scrolled feet, late 19thC.
£550–650 *FLE*

An Empire style day bed, the cream and gilt painted frame with floral decoration, outscrolled sides and squab cushion, on turned legs, 82in (208cm).
£750–1,000 *CSK*

A late Victorian mahogany and inlaid bonheur du jour, with raised mirror back, distressed leather inset top, 36in (92cm).
£500–700 *S(S)*

Breakfront Bookcases

A late Victorian oak breakfront bookcase, with moulded fluted cornice above 4 glazed doors flanked by fluted uprights, 4 arched panelled doors below, 74in (188cm).
£2,000–2,500 *CSK*

An Austrian mahogany breakfront bookcase, on plinth base and turned feet, the locks stamped 'P. Werthei & Co. Wien 92007', late 19thC, 73in (185cm).
£2,500–3,500 *CSK*

A mahogany breakfront library bookcase, the 4 glazed Gothic tracery doors with moulded astragals enclosing adjustable shelves, the base with blind Gothic tracery doors enclosing a fitted interior, on a plinth base, early 19thC.
£10,000–12,000 *WW*

A George III style mahogany breakfront bookcase, with dentil moulded and drop-pendant cornice, on plinth base, 86in (219cm).
£1,800–2,400 *CSK*

A mid-Victorian walnut breakfront bookcase, with moulded cornice above 4 glazed doors and 4 arched panelled doors, on plinth base, 88in (224cm).
£4,000–4,500 *CSK*

A mahogany breakfront library bookcase, with moulded cornice above 4 doors, 19thC with old alteration, 87in (221cm).
£4,500–5,000 *WW*

A satinwood breakfront library bookcase, reduced, 19thC, 84in (213cm).
£4,500–5,500 *P*

An inlaid mahogany breakfront secrétaire bookcase, with dentil moulded cornice above astragal glazed doors, 6 drawers and 2 panelled cupboard doors, on plinth base with label 'Georgian Furniture, by Frederick Tibbenham Ltd., Ipswich, England', 63in (160cm).
£2,000–2,500 *CSK*

A pair of George III style mahogany breakfront bookcases, 96in (244cm).
£5,000–6,000 *CSK*

An early Victorian mahogany bookcase, 66in (168cm).
£2,500–3,000 *CSK*

Bureau Bookcases

A mahogany cylinder top bureau bookcase, on square chamfered legs, 18thC, 39in (99cm).
£5,000–5,500 *CAG*

Bureau Bookcases

All the major styles of bureaux were also made in bureau bookcase form from c1690, to match other furniture of the period. Bureau bookcases were invariably made in 2 pieces, the upper resting within the moulding on the top of the lower section, which is left unfinished and held in place by screws.

Some 18thC and 19thC bureau bookcases are so large that they are not practicable for today's smaller rooms and, therefore, not as collectable.

A George III style mahogany bureau bookcase, with moulded cornice, a pair of geometrically astragal glazed doors above sloping fall, enclosing a fitted interior of drawers and pigeonholes around a central cupboard, with 3 long drawers below, on shaped bracket feet, locks and keys stamped 'Bartholomew & Fletcher', 36in (92cm).
£1,000–1,500 *CSK*

This bureau bookcase was sold with the correspondence relating to its ordering and making.

A mahogany bureau bookcase, with dentil cornice and satinwood inlay to the break arch surmount, fitted interior, crossbanding and satinwood stringing to the fall, on bracket feet, late 18thC, 46in (117cm).
£2,500–3,500 *RBB*

A mahogany bureau bookcase, bureau late 18thC, restorations, the bookcase later, 45in (114cm).
£1,700–2,000 *CSK*

A George III mahogany bureau bookcase, the crenelated and blind fret-carved cornice above a pair of astragal doors enclosing adjustable shelves, the fall revealing stationery compartments, c1770, 45in (114cm).
£4,500–5,500 *S(S)*

A mahogany bureau bookcase, on bracket feet, parts late 18thC, restorations, 40in (102cm).
£3,000–3,500 *CSK*

A George II mahogany bureau bookcase, with brass handles, supported on bracket feet, requires restoration, 40in (102cm).
£1,700–2,200 *L&E*

A mahogany bureau bookcase, parts late 18thC, associated, with paper depository labels, 45in (114cm).
£1,700–2,200 *CSK*

A mahogany bureau bookcase, the bureau late 18thC, restorations, the bookcase later, 28½in (72cm).
£1,500–2,000 *CSK*

Dwarf Bookcases

A pair of mahogany dwarf bookcases, each with associated top above 3 pointed arched astragal glazed doors enclosing shelves, flanked by column uprights with stiff-leaf heading, on bun feet, probably German, mid-19thC, 70½in (179cm).
£1,700–2,500 *CSK*

A pair of mahogany and line inlaid dwarf bookcases, on turned tapering legs, 23in (59cm).
£1,400–2,000 *CSK*

A walnut bureau bookcase, on bracket feet, 31in (79cm).
£1,400–1,800 *CSK*

A mahogany dwarf bookcase, with breakfront top above 2 graduated tiers flanked by reeded uprights, on reeded turned tapering legs, early 19thC, adapted, 36½in (93cm).
£950–1,200 *CSK*

A George III mahogany bureau bookcase, on bracket feet, with later brass handles, 41in (104cm).
£3,800–4,500 *DN*

A George II mahogany bureau bookcase, on bracket feet, restored, c1740, 39in (99cm).
£2,000–3,000 *S(S)*

An early 18thC style scarlet lacquered and chinoiserie decorated bureau bookcase, on bracket feet, repairs, lacquer chipped, 41in (104cm).
£1,700–2,200 *CSK*

Library Bookcases

An early Victorian mahogany library bookcase, on plinth base, 81in (206cm).
£1,200–1,800 *CSK*

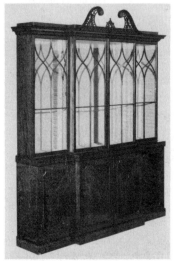

A George III mahogany breakfront library bookcase, the base with carved blind-fret key border, incorporating a spring loaded drawer, above shelves and 5 drawers with chased gilt handles, enclosed by 4 panelled doors, on plinth base, pediment of a later date, incorporating 4 electric lights, 84½in (215cm).
£8,500–12,000 *DN*

A mahogany secrétaire bookcase, the drawer enclosing fitted interior above 2 arched panelled doors, on plinth base, parts early 19thC, 61in (155cm).
£1,500–2,000 *CSK*

Secrétaire Bookcases

A George III style secrétaire bookcase, with dentil moulded cornice above 4 astragal glazed doors, the central fitted drawer flanked by 2 drawers and 4 panelled cupboard doors, on plinth base, 68in (173cm).
£1,000–1,500 *CSK*

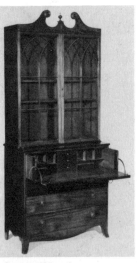

A George IV mahogany secrétaire bookcase, the base with a fitted ebony strung drawer above 4 long drawers, with brass ring handles, on splayed bracket feet, 41in (104cm).
£4,200–5,000 *DN*

A Georgian mahogany secrétaire bookcase, 41in (104cm).
£3,600–4,000 *Mit*

A George III mahogany secrétaire bookcase, on bracket feet, the whole inlaid with neo classic pendant urns, ram's mask, swags of husks, oak leaves and acorns, in coloured woods and boxwood stringing, 44in (112cm).
£6,300–7,300 *HSS*

A George III mahogany secrétaire bookcase, with later line inlay on outswept bracket feet, 39½in (100cm).
£1,500–2,000 *CSK*

> ## Secrétaire Bookcases
>
> The secrétaire bookcase was first seen c1750 and fulfills the same function as the bureau bookcase. In place of the slant front of the bureau it has a chest base. The deep top drawer pulls out to reveal a fitted interior and the drawer front lowers to form the writing surface.

A mahogany secrétaire bookcase, with moulded cornice above a pair of panelled doors, fall front enclosing fitted interior above 4 long drawers, on bracket feet, 30½in (77cm).
£1,500–1,800 *CSK*

A Regency mahogany and line inlaid secrétaire bookcase, the fall front drawer enclosing fitted interior of drawers and pigeonholes, above 3 long drawers, on bracket feet, associated, some mouldings missing, 41½in (106cm).
£1,500–2,000 *CSK*

A late George III mahogany secrétaire bookcase, on ogee bracket feet, damaged and restored, 49½in (126cm).
£3,000–3,700 *CSK*

A Regency mahogany and ebonised line-inlaid secrétaire bookcase, with bracket feet, possibly associated, restored, 45in (114cm).
£2,500–3,500 *CSK*

A mahogany and line inlaid secrétaire bookcase, on turned feet, associated, restored, 19thC, 51in (130cm).
£1,800–2,500 *CSK*

A Regency mahogany secrétaire bookcase, on turned and reeded feet, damaged, c1810, 47in (119cm).
£2,500–3,000 *S(S)*

A late Georgian mahogany secrétaire bookcase, in 2 sections, the secrétaire drawer with boxwood and ebony ovals and falling to reveal a fitted interior, on short bracket feet, 56in (142cm).
£1,700–2,200 *Mit*

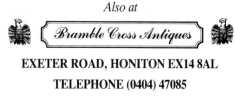

Miscellaneous Bookcases

A revolving bookcase, with mahogany veneered satinwood banded and fan marquetry top, 19in (48cm) square.
£800–1,100 *DN*

A mahogany bookcase-on-stand, on cabriole legs with hoof feet, 41½in (106cm).
£1,000–1,300 *CSK*

A George IV rosewood open bookcase, with 3 shelves above a pair of drawers, on bun feet.
£1,800–2,100 *P*

A mahogany bookcase-on-chest, with dentil moulded cornice above blind fret frieze, with central sliding astragal glazed door flanked by a pair of similar doors, above drawers, on bracket feet, re-constructed, parts late 18thC, 51in (130cm).
£900–1,200 *CSK*

An Edwardian inlaid mahogany bookcase, the broken swan's neck pediment with central urn finial, on fluted tapering legs, 37in (94cm).
£800–1,200 *CSK*

A Georgian mahogany bookcase-on-chest, in 2 sections, the top half with a swan's neck pediment, cockbeading to the drawer fronts, standing on bracket feet, 38in (97cm).
£1,600–2,000 *Mit*

A satinwood and inlaid bookcase, detailed throughout with black stringing, on a moulded plinth, 19thC, 44in (111cm).
£3,000–3,500 *S(S)*

A satin veneered and inlaid two-tier revolving bookcase, the moulded top with central fan motif, above slatted dividers and plinth base, 19in (48cm) square.
£500–800 *CSK*

A mahogany bookcase, on bracket feet, adapted and associated, 18thC, 57in (145cm).
£1,700–2,200 *CSK*

Buckets

A pair of mahogany brass banded peat buckets, 14in (36cm) diam.
£2,000–2,250 *SUL*

A George III mahogany plate bucket, with brass rim and swing handle, vertical pierced sides, 11¾in (30cm).
£1,000–1,200 *L*

A pair of early George III period mahogany and brass bound spiral reeded peat buckets, with swing handles and later brass protection liners, 14in (36cm) diam.
£12,000–14,000 *MEA*

Bureaux

A feather banded walnut and mahogany bureau, with sloping fall enclosing fitted interior, on bracket feet, restored, early 18thC, 37in (94cm).
£2,000–3,000 *CSK*

A pair of Georgian period Irish mahogany ribbed and brass bound peat buckets, with brass swing handles and T-shaped hinge mounts, 15½in (40cm) diam.
£9,000–10,000 *MEA*

A walnut bureau, early 18thC, 38in (97cm) high.
£3,300–3,800 *Mit*

A mid-George III mahogany bureau, the sloping fall enclosing a fitted interior, on later bracket feet, 48in (122cm).
£2,000–3,000 *CSK*

A walnut and feather banded bureau, with sloping fall enclosing a fitted interior, on bun feet, extensively restored, parts early 18thC, 36in (92cm).
£2,000–2,500 *CSK*

A George III period mahogany bureau, on bracket feet, 39½in (100cm).
£1,000–1,300 *MEA*

A George III mahogany bureau, the sloping fall enclosing fitted interior above 2 short and 3 long graduated drawers, on bracket feet, restored, 34in (86cm).
£1,400–1,700 *CSK*

A late George III mahogany and grained pine bureau, the crossbanded sloping fall enclosing a fitted interior, repaired, 36in (92cm).
£900–1,200 *CSK*

A George I style walnut split bureau, with banded and feathered fall, brass side handles, on shaped bracket feet, 38½in (98cm).
£4,200–4,700 *WL*

A George III mahogany bureau, on bracket feet, one now detached, alterations, 42in (107cm).
£1,000–1,500 *CSK*

A George III mahogany bureau, with hinged fall enclosing fitted interior above 4 graduated drawers, on bracket feet, 32in (81cm).
£1,700–2,000 *CSK*

A George III mahogany bureau, on ogee bracket feet, drawers possibly relined, c1760, 38in (97cm).
£1,000–1,500 *S(S)*

A Dutch walnut bombé bureau, with hinged fall enclosing fitted interior, on claw-and-ball feet, restored, 38in (97cm).
£1,700–2,500 *CSK*

A George III mahogany bureau, the fall revealing a fitted interior, c1770, 44in (112cm).
£1,500–2,000 *S(S)*

A walnut and feather banded bureau, the sloping fall enclosing a fitted interior, on bracket feet, restored, early 18thC, 36in (92cm).
£3,500–4,500 *CSK*

A George III mahogany bureau, the fall enclosing a fitted interior, now on fluted bun feet, c1770, 40in (102cm).
£1,000–1,500 *S(S)*

An early George III mahogany bureau, with interior fittings including a concealed recess, with original brass handles, on bracket feet, 36in (92cm).
£1,500–2,000 *DN*

A late George III mahogany bureau, with sloping fall enclosing a fitted interior of drawers and pigeonholes around central cupboard, veneer lifted, 36in (92cm).
£1,500–2,000 *CSK*

A line inlaid mahogany bureau, on outswept bracket feet, 47in (119cm).
£1,500–2,000 *CSK*

A mahogany bureau, part 18thC, 35in (89cm).
£1,000–1,500 *S(S)*

A mahogany bureau, the sloping fall enclosing fitted interior, on later shallow bracket feet, c1800, 48in (122cm).
£1,500–2,000 *CSK*

A mahogany bureau, with shaped interior, 4 long drawers with brass plate handles, on ogee feet, late 18thC, 36in (92cm).
£1,500–2,000 *WIL*

A walnut dwarf bureau, with crossbanded hinged fall, mainly early 18thC, 31in (79cm).
£1,300–1,700 *CSK*

A George III mahogany bureau, with interior fittings enclosed by the crossbanded fall above 2 short and 3 long drawers, with original brass handles, on ogee bracket feet, 46in (117cm).
£2,000–2,700 *DN*

A late Victorian carved oak bureau, on carved shaped bracket feet, 27in (69cm).
£500–600 *MJB*

An early Georgian walnut and feather banded bureau, on bracket feet, later parts and restorations, 36in (92cm).
£2,500–3,500 *CSK*

A figured walnut veneered bureau, in 2 sections, the fall flap crossbanded with stringing and feather banding, the oak lined drawers with engraved brass bat's-wing plate escutcheons and handles with moulded stiles, with girdle mouldings, on bracket feet, 39in (99cm).
£2,200–2,800 *WW*

An Edwardian mahogany bureau, inlaid with swags, on bracket feet, 33in (84cm).
£1,400–1,800 *S(S)*

A French inlaid kingwood bureau de dame, with marquetry hinged slope enclosing fitted interior, on cabriole legs, late 19thC, 27in (69cm).
£900–1,200 *CSK*

A George III mahogany table top bureau, the sloping front enclosing a stepped interior with drawers and pigeonholes, brass carrying handle, 16in (41cm).
£800–1,000 *MEA*

A late George III mahogany crossbanded and line inlaid cylinder top bureau, with a fitted interior of drawers and pigeonholes and baize lined pull-out writing surface, 2 short and 2 long drawers below, on later ogee bracket feet, veneer chipped, 35in (89cm).
£1,500–2,000 *CSK*

A French gilt metal mounted rosewood and marquetry bureau de dame, with three-quarter brass gallery, the floral inlaid fall enclosing fitted interior, on cabriole legs with gilt clasps and gilt sabots, 26in (66cm).
£800–1,200 *CSK*

An Edwardian mahogany and satinwood banded writing bureau, the fall front with shell motif, opening to a fitted interior above 3 long drawers, on bracket feet.
£600–1,000 *FLE*

Cabinets-on-Chests

A gilt metal mounted mahogany cylinder bureau, with associated bookcase top, the three-quarter gallery above a pair of glazed doors, the tambour slope enclosing fitted interior, brushing slide and 2 long drawers, on square tapering legs with spade feet, parts early 19thC, 25½in (67cm).
£1,200–1,700 *CSK*

A black japanned and chinoiserie decorated cabinet-on-chest, decorated overall with flowers, birds and pagoda scenes, containing 11 drawers, on later bun feet, early 18thC, later decorated, 41in (104cm).
£1,500–2,000 *CSK*

A Continental marquetry cabinet-on-chest, with elaborate foliate marquetry, 18thC.
£3,000–3,500 *BWe*

Display Cabinets

An Edwardian mahogany display cabinet, 48in (122cm).
£450–650 *WIL*

A Sheraton style inlaid mahogany display case in 2 sections, the top with a moulded dentil cornice above a mahogany collar and a pair of glazed doors, the lower half with an inlaid collar above a pair of scroll and bell flower inlaid doors, with canted corners, standing on shaped bracket feet, 36in (92cm).
£1,500–2,000 *Mit*

A late Victorian bamboo black and red japanned display cabinet, with overall floral and bird decoration, the upper section with central bevelled mirror flanked by shelves and cupboards, surmounted by pagoda-type cresting, the lower section with an arrangement of open shelves, cupboard and drawer, on outswept feet, 40in (102cm).
£1,000–1,200 *CSK*

An Edwardian mahogany and satinwood banded display cabinet, on square tapering legs joined by an undertier, with spade feet, 49in (125cm).
£1,200–1,700 *CSK*

An Edwardian mahogany and marquetry display cabinet, on splayed legs, 45in (114cm).
£1,000–1,700 *CSK*

An Edwardian mahogany and satinwood banded serpentine breakfront display cabinet, on square tapering legs with spade feet, 55in (140cm).
£1,400–1,800 *CSK*

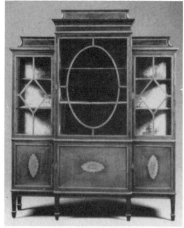

An Edwardian mahogany, line inlaid and satinwood banded breakfront display cabinet, on square tapering legs with spade feet, one loose, 60in (153cm).
£1,200–1,700 *CSK*

A rosewood display cabinet, in the manner of Charles Boulle, the frieze decorated with inlaid brass, on ormolu mounted turned feet, 19thC, 40in (101cm).
£2,500–3,000 *FLE*

A Louis XV style kingwood, marquetry and ormolu mounted double door vitrine.
£1,000–1,500 *FLE*

A Queen Anne style walnut double dome display cabinet, on bulbous turned legs joined by flattened stretchers, on bun feet, 39in (99cm).
£1,000–1,500 *CSK*

An Edwardian satinwood, mahogany and marquetry bowfront display cabinet, on spade feet, 55in (140cm).
£1,200–1,700 *CSK*

A Victorian walnut and gilt metal mounted display cabinet, inlaid throughout with tulipwood bandings and floral marquetry, the serpentine top above a glazed door enclosing velvet lined shelves, on a plinth base, 32in (82cm).
£1,000–1,500 *S(S)*

An Edwardian rosewood and marquetry bowfronted display cabinet, on square tapering legs, 60in (152cm).
£2,200–2,700 *CSK*

A French kingwood and gilt metal mounted vitrine, the stepped pediment above an ogee shaped and glazed door, on cabriole legs, 36in (92cm).
£2,000–2,500 *S(S)*

A rosewood, bone inlaid and tortoiseshell cabinet, with associated turned fruitwood finials, on bun feet, probably Spanish, the back re-strengthened, c1800, 29in (74cm).
£2,000–3,000 *CSK*

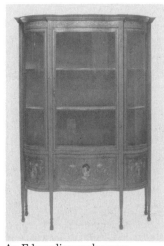

An Edwardian mahogany serpentine front display cabinet, with satinwood banding, on square tapering legs and spade feet, 51in (129cm).
£1,900–2,600 *WL*

A Chinese Chippendale style mahogany pagoda-top vitrine, the rising fluted canopy with pierced foliate finial above glazed doors, flanked by glazed sides, on square chamfered legs joined by pierced brackets, 26½in (67cm).
£1,200–1,700 *CSK*

A French ormolu mounted kingwood Vernis Martin vitrine, the velvet lined interior with later electric light and 2 glass shelves, the bombé base painted with 18thC style landscape panels, on 6 curved feet to gilt sabots, one glazed side panel replaced, signed 'H. Lebrum', late 19thC, 44in (111.5cm).
£4,000–4,500 *MJB*

A north Italian ebony and bone inlaid display cabinet, possibly Milanese, damaged, late 19thC, 47in (119cm).
£2,000–2,500 *CSK*

An Edwardian mahogany Vernis Martin style vitrine, with a hand painted panel door and sides, on cabriole legs.
£1,000–1,500 *FLE*

Vernis Martin

Vernis Martin is the generic term used to describe lacquers and varnishes used for decoration on French clocks and furniture during the 18thC.

It takes its name from the Martin brothers who were permitted to copy Japanese lacquer. It is found in many colours, but especially green.

A French gilt metal mounted kingwood vitrine, with moulded cornice above a pair of bowed glazed doors, with 2 Vernis Martin panels, on cabriole legs with sabots, late 19thC, 47in (119cm).
£2,000–2,500 *CSK*

Music Cabinets

A mahogany, gilt metal mounted and marquetry music cabinet, the marble top with pierced three-quarter gallery, the panelled door below inlaid with musical trophies, flanked by fluted uprights, on gilt metal paw feet, 25in (64cm).
£1,500–2,000 *CSK*

A mid-Victorian burr walnut and marquetry music cabinet, with three-quarter gallery above a pair of cupboard doors, enclosing fitted interior with leather lined writing slope, glazed door below, on bracket feet, 24½in (62cm).
£1,500–2,000 *CSK*

A Victorian walnut and inlaid music cabinet, the top inlaid with kingwood supported by 2 turned columns and mirror back, above a pair of panelled doors, 25½in (65cm).
£1,500–2,000 *S(S)*

Side Cabinets

A George III style line inlaid mahogany demi-lune side cabinet, with crossbanded top, central frieze drawer and a pair of oval panelled doors with a pair of panelled doors to each side, on square tapering legs with spade feet, 54in (137cm).
£600–900 *CSK*

A Regency chinoiserie black japanned and gilt cabinet, c1810, 31in (78cm).
£2,000–3,000 *S(S)*

A George IV mahogany chiffonier, fitted at the back with an open shelf with turned column supports, above a shaped front with reeded borders, one long frieze drawer with ebony stringing, and a central concave door flanked by 2 convex doors, with crossbanded ebony strung panels, on turned feet, 38½in (98.5cm).
£2,500–3,000 *DN*

A Victorian figured walnut credenza, 65⅓in (166cm).
£2,400–3,000 *WIL*

A William IV rosewood chiffonier, with raised open shelf and mirror back, the later green marble top above a drawer with cut brass inlay, raised back possibly altered, c1835, 42in (107cm).
£1,200–1,700 *S(S)*

A Victorian burr walnut and inlaid credenza.
£2,400–3,000 *P(S)*

A bowfronted burr walnut veneered side cabinet, with gilt bronze mounts and inlaid frieze, the centre inlaid door flanked by a pair of glazed doors enclosing plush covered shelves, on a plinth base, 19thC, 66in (167.5cm).
£2,500–3,000 *WW*

A mid-Victorian gilt metal mounted and inlaid walnut side cabinet, of broken D-shaped outline with foliate scroll inlaid frieze, the panelled door flanked by bowed glazed compartments, on plinth base, 59in (149cm).
£1,800–2,200 *CSK*

A late Regency mahogany dwarf side cabinet, with yellow silk pleated doors between acanthus carved volute uprights, on lion's paw feet, 37in (94cm).
£1,300–1,700 *CSK*

A Regency mahogany chiffonier, with raised superstructure on scroll uprights, on reeded bun feet, restored, 34in (86cm).
£1,500–2,000 *CSK*

An early Victorian mahogany side cabinet, the top with a gilt bronze gallery and egg-and-dart moulded edge, above shelves enclosed by a pair of glazed central doors, flanked by figured mahogany panelled doors, on a plinth base, stamped 'H. Mawer & Stephenson, London, and Gillow & Co.' No. 7957', 90in (228.5cm).
£2,400–2,700 *WW*

A Victorian walnut credenza, the boxwood strung flat top with applied gilt metal beading and ebonised moulding, on short turned feet, 67in (170cm).
£2,000–2,500 *Mit*

A mid-Victorian walnut, sycamore, purple heart and marquetry gilt metal mounted credenza, with foliate inlaid frieze above a central door with oval panel of classical urns, flanked by fluted uprights and glazed compartments, on a plinth base, 72½in (184cm).
£3,500–4,000 *CSK*

A Victorian inlaid walnut bowfronted credenza, c1860, 48in (122cm).
£2,000–2,700 *Mit*

A 'Chinese Chippendale' mahogany chiffonier, with a shelf section to the rear, supported on Gothic pierced fretwork brackets, ornate fretted top, exposed and carved floral work, central pagoda, the lower section fitted with shelves, enclosed by 2 glazed panel doors with raised moulded lancet panels, bracket feet, 19thC, 39in (99cm).
£600–800 *L&E*

A late Victorian gilt metal mounted ebonised and amboyna banded side cabinet, with classical Wedgwood plaques within scratch carved frames, flanked by fluted Ionic columns, on platform base and turned feet, 70in (178cm).
£900–1,200 *CSK*

A Victorian ebonised and burr walnut veneered cabinet, on turned feet, c1860, 58in (147cm).
£1,200–1,700 *S(S)*

An Italian walnut side cabinet, on bracket feet, with additions and restored, c1800, 49in (124cm).
£900–1,200 *CSK*

A Victorian ebonised breakfront credenza, the central door inset with a Sèvres style porcelain plaque, the whole applied with gilt metal mounts and boxwood stringing, on short turned feet, 70in (178cm).
£800–1,000 *WL*

A Victorian ebonised and gilt metal mounted cabinet, with Sèvres style porcelain mounts, the shelved interior lined in velvet, c1860, 70in (178cm).
£2,000–3,000 *S(S)*

A French rosewood side cabinet, with rococo gilt metal mounts, on short cabriole legs with gilt metal sabots, 19thC, 58in (147cm).
£2,000–2,400 *P(S)*

A Continental chestnut low cabinet, with serpentine front and sides, fitted with a frieze drawer above 2 doors with oval pleated silk panels, gilt leaf scroll mounts, 19thC, 42in (107cm).
£300–500 *DN*

A figured and burr walnut canted open tier side cabinet, 44in (111.5cm).
£660–900 *DaD*

A rosewood breakfront dwarf side cabinet, with green mottled marble top, on plinth base, reconstructed, parts early 19thC, 66in (168cm).
£1,200–1,800 *CSK*

Cabinets-on-Stands

A William & Mary walnut and marquetry cabinet-on-stand, with overall marquetry decoration of flowers in coloured woods and green stained bone, with later additions, 44in (112cm).
£4,500–5,500 *HSS*

A walnut cabinet-on-stand, with moulded cornice and a pair of astragal glazed doors, the stand with 2 drawers above arcaded apron and octagonal tapered legs, one pane cracked, the base with later parts, restored, early 18thC, 46in (117cm).
£5,000–5,500 *CSK*

A George III style cabinet-on-stand, with dentil moulded cornice above a pair of astragal glazed doors enclosing shelves, labelled 'Law, Foulsham & Cole, Cabinet Makers and Upholsterers, South Molton St. London, W.', 52in (132cm).
£1,200–1,700 *CSK*

A Victorian marquetry side cabinet, in the manner of Stephen Webb, of classical architectural form, the cupboard door flanked by shelves above a deep drawer, on square tapering legs, joined by a platform stretcher, the whole inlaid with engraved ivory Renaissance style figures and foliage with a rosewood ground, the drawer stamped 'Collinson & Lock, London, 3661', with a brass Cope & Collinson lock, with key, c1880, 42in (107cm).
£2,700–4,000 *S*

Stephen Webb was employed by Collinson & Lock after 1884 to decorate furniture with ivory and brass inlay, much of it designed by the founding partner J. S. Lock. Webb stayed with the firm after the Gillow's takeover of 1897, but eventually left to become Professor of Sculpture at the Royal College of Art.

A Dutch design ebonised cabinet, in the style of Domenico Benotti, late 17thC, 58in (147cm).
£20,000–25,000 *WIL*

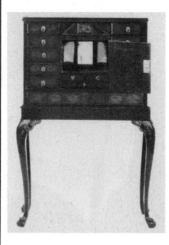

An early Georgian brass mounted black japanned cabinet-on-later-stand, with overall gilt chinoiserie decoration, on cabriole legs with pointed pad feet, restored, possibly re-decorated, 39½in (100cm).
£2,000–3,000 *CSK*

> **In the Furniture section when there is only one measurement it refers to the width of the piece unless otherwise stated.**

A Flemish ebonised, oyster veneered and tortoiseshell cabinet-on-later-stand, with later moulded top, cabriole legs and paw feet, cabinet 18thC, 33in (84cm).
£2,000–2,700 *CSK*

A japanned chinoiserie cabinet, early 18thC, 40in (102cm).
£2,200–2,600 *WIL*

A rosewood and bone inlaid cabinet-on-stand, Italian or Spanish, 19thC, 32in (81cm).
£1,700–2,200 *CSK*

A European black lacquered cabinet-on-stand, late 19thC, 30in (77cm).
£5,700–7,000 *WIL*

A South German walnut and marquetry inlaid cabinet-on-later-stand, with paper label in ink 'M. 130-16 Vargueno LLS 1200', cabinet 19thC, 24½in (62cm).
£3,000–3,500 *CSK*

Canterburies

An early Victorian mahogany three-division canterbury, with bowed slatted dividers and a drawer below, on turned tapering legs, some damage, 20in (51cm).
£1,000–1,200 *CSK*

A mid-Victorian pierced walnut canterbury, on brass casters, 26in (66cm).
£1,200–1,500 *AH*

A William IV rosewood canterbury, the serpentine topped divisions with leaf and scroll carved borders above a drawer, on turned and nulled feet with casters, damaged, 26½in (67cm).
£1,200–1,700 *DN*

A late Georgian mahogany three-division canterbury, with turned uprights, simple reeded divisions, single drawer with pressed brass knobs, on turned baluster legs with brass casters, 22in (56cm).
£1,100–1,400 *L&E*

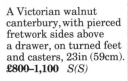

A Victorian walnut canterbury, with pierced fretwork sides above a drawer, on turned feet and casters, 23in (59cm).
£800–1,100 *S(S)*

A George IV mahogany four-division canterbury, with ring turned corners and a drawer, on turned feet and casters, c1825, 19in (49cm).
£800–1,000 *S(S)*

An early Victorian carved rosewood canterbury, with a drawer, on turned feet and casters, 20½in (52cm).
£700–1,000 *S(S)*

An Elizabeth I oak and inlaid coffer, the geometric frieze above triple arched panels with figural pilasters, mid-16thC. **£4,000–5,000** *S(S)*

An oak bedstead, the fielded panelled headboard, incorporating 2 sliding compartments with carved scroll brackets, restored, German, 18thC, 63in (160cm) long. **£7,500–9,500** *CSK*

An oak tester bed, the panelled headboard inlaid with bog oak and fruitwood and heavily carved, the turned tester on column supports, possibly Lancashire, mid-17thC and later, 64in (163cm) long. **£9,000–£11,000** *CSK*

A set of 6 ash ladder back chairs, including an armchair, early 19thC. **£700–1,000** *S(S)*

A matched set of 9 ash and elm ladder back chairs, early 19thC. **£2,800–3,300** *S(S)*

A child's oak and hide chair, on turned supports, Spanish, c1700. **£700–1,000** *S*

A set of 6 ash and alder spindle back chairs, restored, early 19thC. **£2,000–2,500** *S(S)*

A Charles I carved oak press cupboard, mid-17thC, including later components, 59in (150cm). **£1,300–1,800** *S(S)*

A George IV child's yew wood and elm Windsor armchair, c1825. **£1,300–1,500** *S*

A yew, ash and elm Windsor armchair, c1800. **£900–1,200** *S(S)*

A set of six carved mahogany Windsor armchairs, one damaged, c1890. **£3,000–4,000** *S*

An oak, walnut, carved and painted tester bed, with mattresses, labels inscribed 'Wm. Knight Hester', replacements, restored, late 16thC and later, 66in (168cm) long. **£26,500–30,500** *CSK*

A George III ash and elm Windsor armchair, c1800.
£500–800 *S(S)*

A carved oak armchair, possibly Salisbury, with carved initials 'EP', late 17thC.
£2,000–2,500 *S(S)*

An oak, elm, grained and painted tester bed, the tester with entrelac frieze, the central scroll decorated panel with lions' mask angles, the headboard with a pair of flower painted panels, alterations, 17thC and later, 90in (229cm) long.
£7,000–10,000 *CSK*

A primitive staved chair, with detachable board seat, 18thC/19thC.
£800–1,200 *S(S)*

Two ash, yew and elm Windsor armchairs, probably Nottingham, late 19thC.
£1,300–1,500 *S(S)*

A yew, elm and beechwood Windsor armchair, Thames Valley, early 19thC.
£450–550 *S(S)*

A matched set of 5 fruitwood, yew, ash and elm Windsor armchairs, probably Buckinghamshire, early 19thC.
£2,250–2,500 *S(S)*

An oak tester bed, the carved panelled canopy with a moulded cornice, headboard with stop-fluting and applied carved masks above 3 inlaid panels, 17thC and later, 87in (221cm) long. **£2,500–3,000** *S(S)*

A carved oak armchair, the cresting with arrowhead finials, one arm with the letter 'S', restored, late 17thC.
£1,500–1,800 *S(S)*

An oak chest-on-chest, with moulded cornice, on ogee bracket feet, c1760, some damage, 39½in (100cm) wide.
£3,000–3,250 *S*

An oak coffer, with twin panel front, lozenge and rosette motifs and scrolled angle brackets, c1680, 39in (99cm) wide.
£950–1,250 *S*

A boarded oak coffer, the front carved with twin lozenge panels above scroll angle brackets, c1680, 47in (120cm) wide.
£700–800 *S*

An oak chest-on-stand, the drawers crossbanded in walnut, with shaped carved apron, on cabriole legs, 41in (104cm) wide.
£4,500–5,000 *S*

Paul Hopwell Antiques

Early English Oak
Sets of chairs always in stock

Top: A set of eight (four showing) Georgian ash wavyline ladderback dining chairs. Excellent colour, condition and patination. English c1800.

Centre: A William and Mary oak side table with crossed stretcher, good colour and patination. English c1695.

Bottom: A late 17th century oak dresser base, with three geometrically moulded drawers. English c1700.

Furniture restoration service available
30 High Street, West Haddon, Northamptonshire NN6 7AP
Tel: (0788) 510636

A Queen Anne oak dresser, with moulded top above 3 fielded frieze drawers, on baluster turned and square legs, with later additions, 89½in (227cm). **£1,800–2,800** *S(S)*

A George III oak and mahogany crossbanded low dresser, with moulded edged top, panelled cupboard doors, moulded base and bracket feet, 68in (172.5cm). **£3,000–3,500** *AH*

An early George III oak low dresser, with rectangular cabriole legs and pointed pad feet, restored, 94in (239cm). **£4,000–4,500** *CSK*

An oak dresser base, with 3 frieze drawers and an arcaded apron, on cabriole legs, mid-18thC, 74in (188cm). **£3,500–4,000** *S(S)*

An oak and mahogany crossbanded dresser, 18thC, 72in (183cm). **£4,500–5,000** *S(S)*

A pair of Regency oak hall benches, with scrolled ends, on sabre legs, damaged, 47½in (121cm). **£6,500–7,000** *C*

A George III oak and mahogany crossbanded low dresser, with moulded cornice, 3 centre drawers with brass handles, fluted pilasters, panelled sides and stile supports, 73in (185cm). **£3,250–3,750** *AH*

A Charles II oak close stool, with boarded hinged cover, the panel sides with square and bobbin turning, c1680, 17in (44cm) wide. **£1,800–2,200** *S*

A Charles II oak joint stool, the square and turned legs joined by peripheral stretchers, c1680, 18½in (47cm). **£2,800–3,200** *S*

An oak dresser, the moulded top above 3 frieze drawers with geometric mitred mouldings, on turned and square legs, late 17thC, 77in (195cm). **£3,800–4,200** *S(S)*

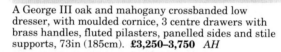

r. A George III oak dresser, with associated shelf back, above drawers and panel doors, c1800, 70in (178cm). **£2,800–3,500** *S(S)*

l. A George II oak dresser, with 3 frieze and 3 central drawers flanked by a pair of cupboard doors, mid-18thC, 66in (168cm). **£5,800–6,200** *S(S)*

An oak refectory table, with associated cleated top, on bulbous turned square legs, one stretcher replaced, early 17thC, 81½in (208cm). **£3,000–5,000** *S(S)*

An oak gateleg table, with a frieze drawer, baluster turned and square legs, altered, c1700, 61in (155cm) extended. **£2,000–3,000** *S(S)*

A Queen Anne walnut and oak gateleg table, 37in (93cm) wide. **£1,500–2,000** *S(S)*

A yew folding tea table, with arcaded apron, restored, late 17thC, 31½in (80cm). **£2,000–3,000** *S(S)*

An oak centre table, with moulded frieze, c1680, 33½in (85cm). **£2,000–3,000** *S*

An oak gateleg table, leaves restored, c1690, 39in (100cm). **£2,500–3,000** *S*

An oak gateleg table, with barley twist legs, early 18thC, 66½in (168cm). **£3,250–3,750** *AH*

An oak refectory table, with a frieze carved with S-scrolls, restored, Lake District, 18thC, 100in (254cm). **£5,750–7,000** *C*

An oak side table, with boarded top and a drawer, square and baluster turned legs, c1690, 30½in (78cm). **£3,000–4,000** *S*

An oak gateleg table, with square and baluster turned legs, c1690, 25½in (65cm). **£2,000–3,000** *S*

An oak gateleg table, with a frieze drawer, on turned legs, restored, c1680, 64½in (164cm) open. **£4,000–5,000** *S*

A Charles II oak side table, with spiral twist turned and square legs, late 17thC, 30½in (78cm). **£2,000–2,500** *S(S)*

An elm bacon settle, probably West Country, c1800, 62in (157cm) wide. **£2,750–3,000** *S(S)*

A walnut gateleg table, with a drawer, the square and spiral twist legs joined by stretchers, restored, c1690, 61½in (156cm). **£7,250–8,000** *S*

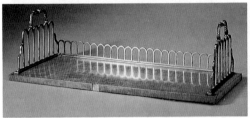

A pair of Regency rosewood and brass book carriers, with three-quarter hipped brass gallery and leaf cast handles, c1820, 19½in (50cm). **£3,000–3,500** *S*

A George IV satinwood and gilt metal book carrier, with gilt brass hipped gallery and leaf cast handles, c1825, 21½in (54cm). **£1,500–2,000** *S*

A Transitional grey painted and parcel gilt bed, with oak leaf carved apron, acanthus carved tapering legs, and original set of French silk hangings, re-gilt, 85in (216cm) long. **£20,000–25,000** *C*

A French or Italian fruitwood cradle, raised on 2 tracery carved supports joined by a shaped stretcher centred by an urn, c1825, 49½in (125cm) long. **£3,000–3,500** *S*

l. A George III mahogany secrétaire bookcase, with pierced swan's neck cresting and lancet cornice, a pair of glazed doors enclosing adjustable shelves, the fitted secrétaire drawer veneered with ovals and with 3 drawers below, on bracket feet, c1775, 100in (254cm) high. **£6,000–6,500** *S*

A George III mahogany tester bed, with stop-fluted turned spreading posts, altered, 87in (221cm) long. **£7,250–8,000** *C*

A brass inlaid rosewood and grained rosewood bonheur du jour, with hinged writing surface, c1815, 33in (84cm) wide. **£6,000–6,500** *S*

A rosewood table book tray, with spindled H-shaped gallery and a pair of leaf cast handles, c1820, 16½in (42cm). **£2,250–2,750** *S*

A French Transitional kingwood bonheur du jour, by G. Cordié, with cabriole legs, c1770, 25½in (65cm). **£8,500–9,000** *S(S)*

A satinwood and marquetry bonheur du jour, crossbanded in tulipwood, 29in (74cm) wide. **£4,500–5,000** *CSK*

A satinwood and mahogany bonheur du jour, with a shelf, the pair of doors each enclosing a drawer, with baize lined writing surface, one finial missing, c1780, 26in (66cm). **£9,000–10,000** *S*

A George III style painted satinwood bonheur du jour, with central doors flanked by cupboards. **£2,250–3,000** *CSK*

A pair of Regency inlaid rosewood book cabinets, with marble tops above crossbanded shelves flanked by inlaid pilasters, on turned tapered reeded feet, c1800, 40in (102cm).
£14,000–16,000 *S*

A George IV mahogany bookcase, in the manner of Richard Brown, with shaped cornice and glazed trellised doors, on free-standing columns, c1810, 29in (74cm).
£8,500–9,500 *S*

A Regency ormolu-mounted mahogany, ebonised and parcel gilt bookcase, the glazed doors enclosing later shelves, restored, 55in (140cm). **£38,000–40,000** *C*

A Victorian mahogany breakfront bookcase, restored, 60½in (154cm).
£6,000–7,000 *C*

A George III mahogany and inlaid secrétaire bookcase, the fall-front enclosing a fitted interior, 48in (122cm).
£4,000–5,000 *AH*

A late George III mahogany secrétaire breakfront bookcase, the moulded cornice above 2 pairs of glazed doors, each enclosing 2 shelves and 2 drawers, above a central fitted secrétaire drawer, on splayed bracket feet, 120in (305cm). **£15,000–17,000** *C*

A George III mahogany bookcase, the open body with 4 moulded shelves divided by moulded uprights between panelled pilaster strips, repaired, 132½in (336cm). **£10,000–12,000** *C*

A Regency brass inlaid ebony and ebonised open bookcase, with 5 shelves, restored, 54in (137cm). **£11,000–15,000** *C*

A George III mahogany bureau bookcase, the fall front enclosing fitted interior, 45½in (115cm).
£4,500–5,500 *Bri*

r. A Victorian walnut veneered library bookcase, with 8 pairs of glazed doors, c1845, 207in (526cm).
£10,000–11,000 *S*

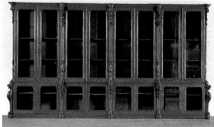

A pair of Irish mahogany brass bound turf buckets, the ringed bodies of slightly tapered form, with brass bands and brass loop handles, c1780, 17in (43cm) high.
£9,500–10,000 *S*

A pair of mahogany buckets, each with pierced brass bound body, 19thC, 12in (30cm) wide.
£4,500–5,000 *S*

A Queen Anne figured walnut bureau, in 2 parts, with later bun feet, restored, 41in (103.5cm).
£7,000–10,000 *C*

A George III mahogany bureau, with inlaid fall-front and 4 drawers, on bracket feet, 38in (97cm).
£1,500–2,000 *MSW*

An Edwardian inlaid mahogany lady's bureau, with spindle turned gallery, display shelves, the fall front with a shell motif enclosing a fitted interior, above a frieze drawer, 30½in (78cm) wide.
£480–520 *ELR*

A George I figured walnut double domed bureau cabinet, with moulded cornice, a pair of arched mirror-glazed doors, the interior with pigeonholes and 17 drawers, finials missing, restored, 43½in (110cm) wide. **£100,000–120,000** *C*

A Dutch walnut bureau cabinet, with fitted interior, marked 'VO34', c1740, 44½in (113cm).
£7,500–8,500 *S*

A German or Swiss fruitwood and burr maplewood parquetry bureau, the cylinder front enclosing a fitted interior, c1785, 43in (109cm). **£7,750–9,000** *S*

A south German baroque parcel gilt, ebonised and burr walnut bureau cabinet, inlaid with geometric strapwork, mid-18thC, 47in (119cm).
£9,000–10,000 *CNY*

A Dutch cherrywood bucket, with brass swing handle and liner, ribbed sides, baluster stem, moulded base and bun feet, mid-19thC, 16in (41cm) high. **£700–800** *AH*

A Victorian satinwood side cabinet, by Pratt of Bradford, with inlaid cupboards, c1880, 66in (167cm). **£3,500–4,500** *S*

A William and Mary black and gilt japanned corner cabinet, with red painted fitted interior, restored. **£5,000–6,000** *C*

A Dutch oyster veneered walnut cabinet, inlaid with stars and roundels, c1680, 68in (173cm). **£6,500–9,000** *S*

A Victorian painted mahogany writing cabinet, with fitted interior, c1890, 38in (97cm). **£7,000–8,000** *S*

A French gilt bronze mounted display cabinet, with marble top and 3 shelves, c1900, 57in (145cm). **£4,000-5,000** *S*

An Edwardian mahogany corner cabinet. **£5,000-6,000** *CSK*

A French jasper mounted display cabinet, with marble top, c1900, 44½in (112cm). **£4,000–4,500** *S*

A French side or display cabinet, the brocatelle marble top with a three-quarter gallery, 4 glazed doors surrounded by gilt bronze mounted mahogany, c1850, 38½in (98cm). **£5,500–6,500** *S*

A Dutch mid-18thC style floral marquetry display cabinet, the bombé lower part with 3 drawers, 61in (155cm). **£6,000–7,000** *S*

A Victorian satinwood and gilt metal mounted mirror back cabinet, c1850, 45in (114cm). **£6,000-7,000** *S(S)*

l. A Dutch floral marquetry display cabinet, the serpentine lower part with 2 short and 2 long drawers, mid-18thC and later, 65in (165cm). **£13,000–14,000** *S*

A George IV rosewood breakfront side cabinet, in the manner of George Bullock, with a Mona marble top, 4 doors inset with brass trellis, the canted corners inlaid with trailing brass leaves, c1820, 76½in (194cm). **£10,000–11,000** *S*

A Regency simulated rosewood and parcel gilt side cabinet, with later simulated porphyry top. **£2,500–3,500** *C*

A George III style mahogany and inlaid pier cabinet, labelled 'Maple & Co.,' c1910, 44½in (113cm). **£5,000–5,500** *S(S)*

A pair of French gilt metal mounted, ebonised and brass inlaid side cabinets, 47in (119cm). **£4,500–5,500** *CSK*

A George IV maplewood side cabinet, the panelled beaded front with 3 drawers and 4 doors, on carved scroll feet, c1820, 54in (137cm). **£3,500–4,000** *S*

l. A Regency parcel gilt rosewood side cabinet, with modern verde antico marble top, the doors with pleated silk panels flanked by Egyptian pilasters, c1810, 49½in (125cm). **£4,000–4,500** *S*

An Augsburg 16thC style marquetry cabinet, with hinged fall front, 37in (94cm). **£30,000–35,000** *C*

A walnut and marquetry side cabinet, the door inlaid with a vase of flowers, flanked by glazed serpentine doors, c1855, 75in (191cm). **£4,500–5,500** *S*

A Victorian boulle and ebonised cabinet, the panelled door flanked by a pair of bowed glazed doors, damaged, c1860, 72in (182.5cm). **£2,500–3,000** *S(S)*

A Franco-German rosewood side cabinet, with fruitwood carved panel, c1890. **£6,000–7,000** *S*

A mid-Victorian gilt metal mounted inlaid walnut side cabinet, with moulded top above scroll-inlaid frieze and central arched glazed doors. **£4,000–5,000** *CSK*

l. A mid-Victorian burr walnut side cabinet, with gilt metal and porcelain mounts. **£7,000–8,000** *CSK*

28th September - 2nd October 1994

The Business Design Centre
Islington Green, London

OVER ONE HUNDRED LEADING DEALERS DISPLAYING AN
OUTSTANDING RANGE OF HIGH QUALITY ANTIQUES &
FINE ART IN THE SUPERB SETTING OF LONDONS MOST
EXCITING EXHIBITION CENTRE.

Including 'Antiques for Interiors' a designed presentation by
selected exhibitors of period antiques within magnificent
room sets.

All exhibits Vetted & Datelined

For more information please contact
Sarah Marris on 071-359 3535

A pair of George III ebonised open armchairs, upholstered in buttoned red leather, repaired. **£9,000–10,000** *C*

A Chippendale period mahogany elbow chair, designed and carved in the Chinese style. **£2,000–2,500** *SAF*

A pair of George III mahogany open armchairs, the arms carved and decorated, restored. **£14,500–15,500** *C*

A pair of late George III giltwood armchairs, one stamped 'B. Harmer', the other 'HM'. **£3,000–5,000** *C*

A mahogany armchair, with interlaced splat, out-curved arms, drop-in seat and cabriole legs, mid-18thC. **£800–1,200** *S*

A pair of early George III mahogany library open armchairs, the outscrolled arms with flowerhead terminals and chamfered square legs carved with Greek key pattern, restored. **£32,000–35,000** *C*

A George II mahogany library armchair, c1755. **£3,500–4,000** *S*

A walnut library open armchair, on claw-and-ball feet, repairs to one leg. **£3,500–4,000** *C*

A George III mahogany open armchair, with umbrella shaped carved back, carved arm rests and cabriole legs, restored. **£5,000–6,000** *C*

A matched set of 4 late Victorian painted satinwood chairs, including 2 open armchairs, each with shield-shaped backs. **£3,500–4,500** *CSK*

A walnut open armchair, covered in floral petit point needlework, with channelled stylised X-frame, on hoof feet, repaired. **£6,000–8,000** *C*

A pair of Louis XV grained beech and pine fauteuils, each with foliage carved cabriole legs. **£9,500–10,500** *C*

A Louis XVI painted armchair, stamped 'L. Pluvinet', c1780.
£3,000–3,500 *S*

A Louis XV walnut armchair, stamped 'P H Poiré JME', c1770.
£3,000–3,500 *S*

An Empire painted and parcel gilt armchair, c1810.
£1,500–2,000 *S*

A set of 12 Regency style brass inlaid mahogany armchairs, caning damaged, 20thC.
£16,500–17,500 *C*

r. A Regency mahogany open armchair, the arms on panther mask monopodia supports, damaged.
£3,500–5,000 *C*

l. A Victorian carved mahogany framed open armchair.
£300–500 *F*

r. A mahogany open elbow desk chair, with rope back, on sabre legs, early 19thC.
£350–400 *PCh*

A pair of Russian birch-wood armchairs, with baluster front legs, c1835.
£2,000–3,000 *S*

A George III mahogany wing armchair, c1765, repaired.
£2,400–2,800 *S*

A pair of Directoire giltwood bergère chairs, c1790.
£9,000–10,000 *S*

A pair of George III mahogany armchairs, restored.
£2,000–3,000 *C*

A George I walnut open armchair, covered in associated wool and silk needlework, restored.
£28,000–29,000 *C*

A pair of Consulat painted armchairs, with stuffed backs and seats, c1800. **£2,500–3,000** *S*

A George II mahogany bergère chairs, on cabriole legs.
£4,500–5,000 *C*

A pair of Tuscan walnut armchairs, mid-17thC.
£5,000–6,000 *S*

A pair of George III painted armchairs, c1785.
£2,600–3,000 *S*

A pair of Louis XV giltwood fauteuils, minor restorations.
£7,500–8,000 *C*

A pair of George III mahogany open armchairs, restored and repaired.
£5,500–6,500 *C*

A pair of William IV rosewood bergère chairs, c1830. **£10,000–11,000** *S*

l. A George IV caned rosewood bergère chair, c1825.
£4,500–5,000 *S*

A Regency mahogany bergère chair.
£2,600–3,600 *C*

A pair of William IV mahogany library bergère chairs, c1835, restored.
£5,000–6,000 *S(S)*

A William IV mahogany
bergère chair, with
profusely carved toprail.
£1,500–2,000 *C*

A Louis XVI painted
bergère chair, c1775.
£2,500–3,000 *S*

A Queen Anne walnut
wing armchair, c1710.
£5,000–6,000 *S*

A George II walnut wing
armchair, on cabriole
legs and pad feet.
£4,000–5,000 *C*

A William IV rosewood
bergère chair, on turned
tapering legs.
£3,000–3,500 *C*

A pair of William IV
mahogany bergère
chairs, c1835.
£2,500–3,000 *S*

A Queen Anne walnut wing armchair,
on scroll knee and turned front
supports with hoof feet.
£8,000–9,000 *Bri*

A pair of Louis XV giltwood
bergère chairs, each toprail
centred by a foliate trail, later
gilt, restored. **£5,500–6,000** *C*

A Restauration mahogany
bergère chair, with swans'
head arm supports and sabre
legs, c1825. **£2,000–2,500** *S*

A carved mahogany
wing armchair, the seat
rail carved with shells
and leaves, possibly
Irish, mid-18thC.
£5,500–6,000 *S*

A George I walnut wing armchair,
with outscrolled arms, on cabriole
legs and shaped feet, repaired.
£3,500–4,000 *C*

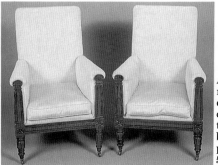

A pair of William IV
mahogany bergère
chairs, with lappet
carved turned
tapering legs headed
by flowerhead
paterae, c1835.
£7,500–8,500 *S*

A set of 5 early
George III mahogany
chairs, c1770.
£2,200–2,500 *S*

A set of 8 George III
mahogany dining
chairs, c1785.
£8,500–9,500 *S*

A set of 8 Regency dining
chairs, restored.
£10,000–11,000 *C*

A set of 6 George III
mahogany dining chairs.
£3,000–3,500 *C*

A set of 6 late Victorian balloon back dining
chairs, with embossed upholstered sprung seats.
£1,000–1,500 *JH*

A set of 6 mahogany
dining chairs, minor
restorations.
£2,200–2,800 *C*

A set of 8 mahogany dining
chairs, with leather drop-in
seats, repaired.
£3,500–4,500 *C*

A set of 12 Regency mahogany dining chairs,
including a pair of armchairs, each with a curved
and reeded panel top rail with brass inlay and
curule crossbars. **£35,000–40,000** *MEA*

A set of 12
mahogany dining
chairs, including
a pair of open
armchairs.
£6,500–7,000 *C*

A set of 8 George III
mahogany dining chairs,
some repaired.
£7,000–8,000 *C*

A set of 8 mahogany dining chairs, including a pair of
open armchairs, and another pair of chairs, 19thC.
£6,000–7,000 *C*

l. A set of 6 George III
mahogany shield back
chairs, each with
pierced husk carved
splat, serpentine drop-
in seat and square
tapering moulded front
legs, c1775.
£4,000–4,500 *S*

A set of 10 William IV rococo revival parcel gilt ebonised chairs, c1830. **£3,500–4,500** *S*

A set of 6 George II provincial red walnut chairs, c1750. **£8,500–9,500** *S*

A George I green and gilt japanned side chair, restored. **£6,500–7,000** *C*

A set of 6 Swedish painted chairs, with Egyptian supports, early 19thC. **£2,500–3,500** *S*

A set of 4 Regency bronzed and parcel gilt side chairs, with caned seats, on naturalistic legs and paw feet, restored. **£4,800-5,400** *C*

A Dutch or Portuguese Colonial walnut chair, early 18thC. **£1,400–1,600** *S*

A set of 11 George II red japanned chairs, attributed to Giles Grendey, each with shell carved toprail and solid vase splat, and another very similar with painted shell and plainer splat and supports, all with gilt chinoiserie and cane seats, c1735. **£50,000–70,000** *S*

A set of 4 Russian parcel gilt mahogany chairs, early 19thC. **£4,500–6,500** *S*

A set of 8 George III provincial mahogany spindle back chairs, c1775. **£6,500–7,500** *S*

A set of 6 Iberian walnut chairs, the backs and seats covered in nailed leather tooled with scrollwork and figures, and an armchair, c1680. **£3,000–3,500** *S*

l. A set of 6 George III mahogany hall chairs, the shield backs with eagles' heads, c1815. **£7,000–9,000** *S*

A late George III mahogany reading chair, with pear-shaped seat, restored. **£2,000–2,500** *C*

A Regency mahogany metamorphic library open armchair and steps, restored. **£4,500–6,500** *C*

A Regency rosewood dressing stool, with fringed needlework seat. **£300–400** *JH*

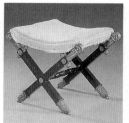

A French or Baltic mahogany and parcel gilt stool, early 19thC, 24in (61cm). **£7,500–8,500** *S*

A pair of Queen Anne walnut stools, each with padded seat, cabriole legs and pad feet, c1710, 21in (53cm). **£6,000–8,000** *S*

A pair of Louis XIV giltwood tabourets, with upholstered seats, on moulded scrolled legs joined by stretchers, late 17thC, 29½in (75cm). **£15,500–17,500** *S(NY)*

A Regency Gothic revival rosewood veneered stool, c1830, stamped '15516', 21in (54cm). **£2,000–3,000** *S*

A George I walnut stool, with floral silk needlework, restored, 21½in (54cm). **£6,000–7,000** *C*

A George III Etruscan style ebonised window seat, c1775, 41in (104cm). **£3,000–4,000** *S*

A mahogany satinwood banded stool, c1910. **£1,500–2,000** *S(S)*

A pair of George II style stools, on cabriole legs carved with eagles' masks, shells and scrolls, 28in (71cm). **£3,200–4,200** *CSK*

A pair of George III Irish mahogany hall benches, each panelled back centred by an oval panel decorated with the Coote arms, and inscribed 'Coote Qui Coote', restored, 33½in (85cm). **£41,000–45,000** *C*

l. A matched pair of Regency painted and parcel gilt stools, one top depicting a sphinx, the other a dog, repaired. **£13,000–15,000** *C*

r. A Regency decorated piano stool, with hinged cupboard, c1800. **£8,000–10,000** *S*

A Dutch walnut chest, inlaid with chequered stringing, mid-18thC, 31½in (80cm). **£2,500–3,500** *S*

A William and Mary burr walnut chest, on later moulded plinth and stand with bracket feet, 38in (96.5cm). **£2,500–3,500** *C*

A walnut chest, restored and sides re-veneered, late 18thC, 30in (77cm). **£3,000–5,000** *C*

A William and Mary oyster veneered chest of drawers, inlaid with boxwood, 37in (94cm). **£4,000–6,000** *C*

A Queen Anne japanned chest of drawers, with gilt chinoiserie decoration, 40in (103cm). **£4,500–5,500** *S*

A George I walnut chest, the quarter-veneered crossbanded top with moulded edge above a brushing slide, 4 graduated drawers below, on bracket feet, c1720, 30in (76cm). **£30,000– 35,000** *S*

A George II mahogany chest of drawers, with brushing slide, c1755, 33in (84cm). **£3,000–5,000** *S*

A George II mahogany chest, on bracket feet, c1750, 27½in (70cm). **£2,500–3,500** *S*

A George III mahogany chest-on-chest, with concave cornice and canted corners, on ogee bracket feet, 73in (185.5cm). **£2,000–2,500** *ALL*

A William and Mary oyster veneered walnut chest-on-stand, the crossbanded top with moulded edge, restored, 36in (91.5cm). **£9,000–11,000** *C*

A William and Mary oyster laburnum and marquetry chest, c1690, on associated oak stand, 40in (102cm). **£7,500–9,500** *S(S)*

A Queen Anne burr walnut chest, with spring loaded secret drawers, stamped 'SG', c1700, 37½in (94cm). **£12,500–15,000** *S*

A Victorian walnut secrétaire Wellington chest, on plinth base, 50in (126.5cm) high. **£1,750–2,250** *ALL*

A George I walnut bachelor's chest, restored, top re-veneered, 29in (74cm). **£5,500–6,500** *C*

A Dutch walnut chest, with claw-and-pad feet, c1740, 38½in (98cm). **£3,500–4,500** *S*

A George I figured walnut bachelor's chest, inlaid with feather banding, on bracket feet, restored, 30in (76cm). **£14,000–16,000** *C*

A William and Mary oyster veneered cedar chest, crossbanded overall, on later bun feet, restored, 38in (96.5cm). **£5,500–7,500** *C*

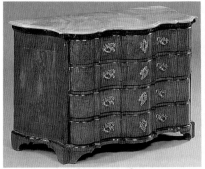

A German walnut parquetry chest, with grey marble top, c1750, 50in (127cm). **£18,000–22,000** *S*

l. A George III kingwood banded mahogany serpentine chest, with moulded banded top, leather lined writing slide, on splayed bracket feet, c1780, 34in (87cm). **£10,000–12,000** *S*

A George III plum pudding mahogany serpentine chest, 41in (104cm). **£6,500–8,500** *C*

l. A Dutch walnut chest, c1740, 35in (89cm). **£4,000–6,000** *S*

A Louis XIV ormolu mounted, ebony and floral marquetry commode, the top re-used from an earlier piece and cut down, 48½in (123cm). **£96,000–110,000** *C*

An Italian rococo painted and parcel gilt commode, mid-18thC, 51½in (130cm). **£46,000–52,000** *S(NY)*

A carved giltwood commode, possibly Portuguese, mid-18thC, 50in (128cm). **£12,500-13,500** *S*

An Italian walnut marquetry commode, late 18thC. **£19,000–25,000** *CSK*

A Venetian or Austrian walnut inlaid bowfronted commode, c1785, 49in (124.5cm). **£13,000–15,000** *S*

A George III mahogany commode, with 19thC parquetry panels, 44in (112cm). **£6,000–8,000** *C*

l. A Régence kingwood bombé commode, top restored, c1720. **£29,000–39,000** *S(S)*

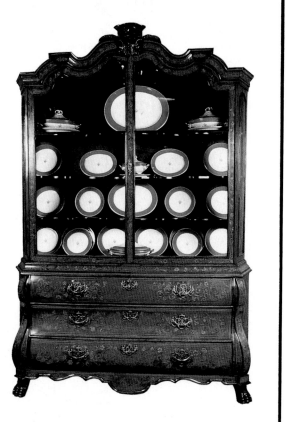

A George I walnut veneered chest-on-chest, with cross-banded moulded drawers, c1725, 39½in (100cm).
£13,000–15,000 *S*

A French Provincial or Piedmontese burr chestnut wood commode, c1710, 49in (126cm).
£12,000–15,000 *S*

An Italian marquetry commode and mirror, engraved with ivory, c1870, 58in (147cm).
£10,500–13,500 *S*

A George III mahogany chest-on-chest, c1770, 46in (116.5cm).
£3,000–4,000 *S(S)*

A Maltese walnut parquetry commode, mid-18thC, 45in (114cm).
£5,000–7,000 *S*

A George III style carved mahogany serpentine fronted commode, c1900, 41in (104cm).
£3,000–4,000 *S(S)*

A Dutch marquetry commode, c1740 and later, 35in (89cm).
£5,000–7,000 *S*

A Queen Anne walnut chest-on-stand, restored, 40½in (102cm).
£7,000–9,000 *C*

A pair of Italian marquetry commodes, inlaid with hunting scenes in engraved wood on a walnut ground, c1870, 33in (84cm).
£7,000–9,000 *S*

A Sicilican olivewood parquetry commode, top re-veneered, c1770.
£3,000–4,000 *S*

An Italian or Sicilian walnut parquetry commode, c1760.
£3,000–5,000 *S*

A George II walnut secrétaire tallboy, restored, 42in (106.5cm).
£5,000–6,000 *S*

A Régence ormolu mounted, oyster veneered kingwood commode, by François Lieutaud, replacements, extensively restored, 51in (129cm). **£22,000–25,000** *C*

l. A George III ormolu mounted kingwood and mahogany serpentine commode, in the style of Pierre Langlois, restored, 50in (127cm). **£13,000–15,000** *C*

A Victorian walnut davenport, with piano front and incised writing slide, 23in (59cm). **£2,200–2,800** *MAT*

A George III mahogany linen press, c1790, 14in (36cm). **£7,000–8,000** *S(S)*

A Victorian burr walnut harlequin davenport, c1855. **£3,000–4,000** *S(S)*

A Victorian walnut harlequin davenport, with rising stationery compartment, 21½in (54cm). **£2,500–3,000** *AH*

A George III mahogany breakfront wardrobe, 79½in (202cm). **£5,000–6,000** *C*

A George III mahogany linen press, c1780, 50½in (127cm). **£5,500–6,000** *S(S)*

A rosewood sliding top davenport, stamped 'Johnson Jupe & Co.,' 19thC, 21in (53cm). **£2,500–3,500** *AH*

A pair of George IV bowfront mahogany bedside cupboards, c1820. **£5,000–5,500** *S*

A Dutch walnut cupboard, with moulded cornice above 2 panelled doors, on bracket feet, c1730, 65in (165cm). **£9,000–11,000** *S*

A German walnut parquetry armoire, with scallop shell handles, early 18thC, 88in (223.5cm). **£30,000–35,000** *S*

An Edwardian satinwood, marquetry and later line inlaid breakfront wardrobe. **£6,500–8,500** *CSK*

r. A Napoleon III marquetry side cupboard, c1855. **£2,500–3,000** *S*

A George I walnut veneered kneehole desk, c1715, 30in (76cm) wide.
£8,000–9,000 *S*

A Chippendale style mahogany desk, by Edwards & Roberts, with leather top, 54in (137cm). **£850–950** *E*

A George III style mahogany partners' desk, the top with flowerhead carved border, 72in (183cm). **£17,000–18,000** *CSK*

A painted satinwood Carlton House desk, with galleried top, drawers, pigeonholes, cupboards and hinged compartments, 42in (107cm). **£4,500–5,500** *CSK*

A Victorian walnut pedestal desk, with green leather lined top, 9 drawers and dummy drawers at the back, c1860. **£4,500–5,500** *S*

A mid-Victorian brass mounted burr walnut desk, restored.
£12,000–15,000 *C*

A George III mahogany partners' desk, with leather lined top, 6 frieze drawers and 3 more to each pedestal, damaged, 66in (168cm). **£5,000–6,000** *CSK*

A George III mahogany desk, in the manner of Gillows, the moulded leather lined top with hinged flap above 3 frieze drawers, c1790, 53½in (136cm).
£17,000–20,000 *S*

A French rosewood veneered desk, with marble top, c1890, 35in (89cm).
£6,500–7,500 *S*

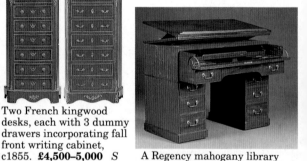

An early Victorian mahogany desk, with hinged reading slope, stamped 'Gillows Lancaster'.
£5,000–6,000 *C*

Two French kingwood desks, each with 3 dummy drawers incorporating fall front writing cabinet, c1855. **£4,500–5,000** *S*

A Regency mahogany library desk, by Gillows, each pedestal with 3 drawers and simulated drawers to reverse, restored, 49½in (126cm). **£5,500–6,500** *C*

r. A satinwood desk, inlaid with tulipwood banding, with leather lined writing surface, c1900, 54½in (138cm).
£3,000–3,500 *S*

r. An Italian walnut parquetry desk, with inlaid star motif to top, later dummy drawers fitted to back, c1770.
£4,000–5,000 *S*

Open Armchairs

A pair of Regency painted beech elbow chairs, decorated in black and gilt, the canvas seats with squabs, on turned legs headed by panels of flowers.
£2,000–2,500 *DN*

A George III style inlaid mahogany open armchair, the fluted oval back with ribbon tied Prince of Wales feathers above serpentine seat, fan inlaid headed stop-fluted tapering legs.
£1,000–1,500 *CSK*

A pair of Queen Anne style mahogany open armchairs, each with arched padded backs and shepherd's crook arms, on cabriole legs with pad feet.
£850–1,000 *CSK*

A pair of George III beech open armchairs, with seats covered in trellis pattern cotton, previously decorated.
£3,000–4,000 *C*

A matched pair of George III beechwood open armchairs, covered in close nailed yellow silk floral damask, on channelled cabriole legs, restored, probably previously painted, one chair 2in (3.5cm) higher than the other.
£3,000–4,000 *C*

A George III gilt armchair, upholstered in blue velvet, underframe with cradle marks, c1780.
£3,000–3,500 *S(S)*

A William IV mahogany open armchair, with carved top rail, above foliate carved downswept arms and foliate headed ring and reeded turned legs, seat missing.
£450–650 *CSK*

A pair of George III red painted simulated bamboo cockpen armchairs, each with arched back and splayed arms filled with pierced Chinese paling, with dished drop-in caned seat and turned legs joined by stretchers, re-decorated and one repaired.
£3,000–4,500 *C*

The design of these chairs is close to that of the set of 10 'neat bamboo chairs' supplied by John Linnell to William Drake of Shardeloes, Buckinghamshire in 1767. The dished seat on the present chairs is clearly an improvement on the original design. Such chairs were in high fashion in the late 1760s.

A pair of Georgian style, mahogany elbow chairs, with pierced interlaced Gothic splats and C-scroll carved top rails, the drop-in seats on chamfered legs, 19thC.
£600–800 *P*

A set of 3 elbow chairs, with beech simulated bamboo frames, rounded backs and rush seats, re-decorated, early 19thC.
£500–600 *DN*

A gilded mahogany and needlework upholstered library open armchair, on cabriole legs with scroll feet, seat cushion missing, late 19thC.
£850–950 *CSK*

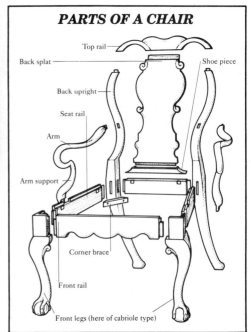

PARTS OF A CHAIR

Top rail
Back splat
Shoe piece
Back upright
Seat rail
Arm
Arm support
Corner brace
Front rail
Front legs (here of cabriole type)

A pair of Sheraton style satinwood elbow chairs, with Angelica Kauffman style panels of classical maidens, painted floral swags, urns and husks, cane panelled back and seats, on turned tapering front supports, button upholstered squab cushions, late 19thC.
£1,200–1,700 *RBB*

A George III style mahogany Gainsborough armchair, on foliate scroll carved cabriole legs with claw-and-ball feet.
£1,200–1,800 *CSK*

A George III open armchair, with serpentine crest rail, the arms with blind fret swept supports, stuffed seat, on straight blind fret legs with pierced corner brackets and pierced stretchers, legs reduced.
£1,000–1,500 *DN*

A Louis XV walnut fauteuil, the moulded frame carved with leaves and flowerheads, the arched cartouche shaped padded back with outscrolled arms and padded serpentine seat, on cabriole legs.
£800–1,200 *P*

A Victorian walnut open armchair, the show frame banded in burr walnut with boxwood and ebony stringing, with a carved crest, scroll arms and turned legs, upholstered in rose dralon.
£500–700 *DN*

A Victorian carved walnut suite, comprising an armchair, an occasional chair and a pair of side chairs, with pierced splats, incised carving, covered in green striped fabric, c1860.
£800–1,200 *S(S)*

A Victorian walnut easy chair, with open scrollwork back, padded arms, spring seat, curved apron on floral carved French cabriole supports.
£1,000–1,200 WL

A pair of Regency painted chairs, 34in (86cm) high.
£1,400–1,750 SUL

A Victorian carved walnut and upholstered spoon back armchair, covered in striped gold fabric, with padded arms and cabriole legs, on ceramic casters, upholstery worn.
£1,000–1,400 S(S)

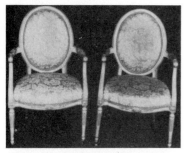

A pair of painted amchairs, each with moulded frame and padded panel, above scrolled arms and bowed seat, on half fluted legs.
£1,200–1,700 MEA

A Victorian walnut open armchair, with upholstered back, padded arms and serpentine seat, on foliate cabriole legs.
£600–800 P

A Victorian carved mahogany and button upholstered armchair, the open arms with scroll terminals, on reeded legs with ceramic casters.
£500–800 S(S)

An Edwardian satinwood armchair, with tapered legs and painted lines.
£600–800 WIL

A walnut open high back armchair, with an embroidered silk panel, late 19thC.
£1,200–1,700 CSK

Two Louis XV gilt and upholstered fauteuils, covered in blue silk, one indistincly stamped 'Cluveine', frames chipped and flaking, c1750.
£5,000–6,000 S(S)

A matched set of 5 stained beech and walnut high back chairs, including 2 armchairs, each with profuse foliate scroll carving, caned back flanked by spiral twist uprights and pierced cresting with crown flanked by putti, above caned seat and scroll legs, joined by stretchers, the armchairs with twist and block legs, minor differences in the carving, repairs, all but one variously stamped 'R.W.', 'W.R.', and 'I.P.'.
£3,500–5,500 CSK

A pair of Chippendale period mahogany elbow chairs.
£14,000–17,000 *SWO*

These chairs have been restored, presumably prior to their purchase in the 1920s, at which time the arms were altered.

A French or Flemish walnut open armchair, with pale damask upholstery, restored, late 17thC.
£1,000–1,400 *CSK*

A Louis XV style giltwood three-piece salon suite, comprising a canapé and a pair of fauteuils, on cabriole legs with scroll feet, later gilded, the canapé 77in (195.5cm).
£1,700–2,200 *CSK*

A pair of Louis XVI gilt and upholstered fauteuils, covered in claret velvet, with oval backs and stop fluted square tapering legs, c1780.
£4,000–5,000 *S(S)*

A set of 8 Louis XVI style beechwood open armchairs, repaired, some arms loose.
£1,700–2,000 *CSK*

A Dutch marquetry and walnut armchair, with vase-shaped splat and slip-in seat, c1750.
£1,000–1,700 *S(S)*

A set of 3 Dutch floral marquetry chairs, including an armchair, each decorated overall with trailing leafy branches and birds, above serpentine drop-in seat, on cabriole legs with claw-and-ball feet.
£1,500–2,000 *CSK*

A set of 4 north Italian black walnut armchairs, with stuff-over seats, mid-18thC.
£34,000–40,000 *B*

Upholstered Armchairs

A Restauration mahogany fauteuil, the moulded frame with an overscrolled padded back, bowed padded seat and scrolled arms, on scroll topped legs.
£600–800 *P*

A Regency mahogany tub bergère chair, with trellis patterned material-covered squab cushion, on reeded tapering legs and brass caps, the casters stamped 'COPE PATENT'.
£1,200–1,500 *C*

An Italian Renaissance Savonarola armchair, with scroll arms and X-shaped curule frame, upholstered in scarlet cut velvet.
£5,000–6,000 *CNY*

A Victorian armchair, with cabriole legs and casters.
£380–420 *WIL*

A Victorian carved walnut armchair, with upholstered padded back, padded scroll arm supports, and stuff-over serpentine seat, on cabriole legs.
£600–800 *P*

A three-piece bergère suite, the mahogany frames decorated in Chinese lacquer, 19thC.
£800–1,000 *FLE*

A William IV mahogany and cane armchair, with scroll arms, on lotus clad turned legs with casters, c1830.
£1,200–1,700 *S(S)*

A William IV mahogany library armchair, on reeded tapered legs.
£1,000–1,500 *CSK*

An early Victorian mahogany bergère armchair, with squab cushion, on turned front legs with brass casters.
£900–1,000 *CAG*

A George I style mahogany wing armchair.
£600–700 *CSK*

A George III mahogany wing armchair, with arched padded back, outscrolled arms and on square tapering legs.
£2,200–2,700 *C*

A Louis XVI style giltwood duchesse, the raised ends with stiff-leaf decoration above down scrolled arms, on patarae headed stop fluted tapering legs, 76in (193cm).
£1,400–1,700 *CSK*

A George IV satin birch caned library armchair, the removable padded headrest, armrests and squab cushion covered in buttoned green leather, the reeded frame with turned and reeded arm supports, on turned tapering reeded legs with brass caps, with printed paper label of Jones & Higgins Ltd/ Depositories/Dulwich, restored.
£2,000–3,000 *C*

A pair of late Victorian mahogany armchairs, each with padded back, arms and each seat, on square tapering legs, stamped 'Howard & Sons Ltd., Berners Street 175929572 and 26878633', the casters stamped 'Howard & Sons Ltd., London'.
£2,000–2,500 *CSK*

A William IV mahogany and caned library armchair, with waisted outswept back, caned back and seat with loose leather cushion, on faceted tapering legs.
£3,000–4,000 *CSK*

A pair of Victorian carved rosewood and upholstered armchairs, with spoon shaped backs, overscroll arms and bowed seats, on cabriole legs and casters, needs minor restoration, c1845.
£3,0000–3,500 *S(S)*

A carved mahogany and cane bergère three-piece suite, with green dralon seats and cushions, with eagle's head arms and claw-and-ball feet, damaged.
£2,700–3,200 *S(S)*

A George IV mahogany and caned library armchair, the outswept back carved with paterae above scroll arms, the caned seat with loose leather cushion, on reeded tapering legs.
£2,700–3,200 *CSK*

A mid-Victorian matched walnut suite, comprising a pair of armchairs, a sofa, and a pair of footstools, each moulded frame with foliate cresting above padded arms and scroll terminals, serpentine seat and floral carved cabriole legs.
£2,000–2,500 *CSK*

A Victorian showframe gentleman's armchair.
£380–420 *DaD*

An Italian walnut tub-shaped armchair, with padded back and seat, stop fluted seat rail, on fluted tapering and beaded legs headed by rosettes, early 19thC.
£600–800 *DN*

An Edwardian satin birch and polychrome painted bergère, with caned panelled back and arms within a finialled frame, the top rail centred by an oval portrait medallion, the bowed seat on turned tapered legs, each with a stiff-leaf collar.
£300–500 *CSK*

A giltwood wing armchair, upholstered in Flemish verdure tapestry, with arched back, outscrolled arms, squab seat and foliate carved cabriole legs with scroll feet, 17thC.
£2,000-2,500 *CSK*

A Victorian button back upholstered armchair, on turned legs.
£200-250 *P*

A stained mahogany and tapestry upholstered wing armchair, with downswept padded sides, squab seat, on shell carved cabriole legs with claw-and-ball feet.
£300-400 *CSK*

A Victorian button back armchair, on turned legs.
£250-300 *P*

A pair of George I style upholstered walnut wing armchairs, individually covered in peach and sage green velvet, with projecting scroll wings and seat cushions, on cabriole legs, c1930.
£3,000-4,000 *S(S)*

An Edwardian mahogany bergère chair, with caned back and padded caned arms, on square tapering legs.
£500-800 *CSK*

Dining Chairs

A set of 4 walnut dining chairs, each with shaped rail and spindle splat backs over solid seats and raised on elaborate turned supports, 17thC.
£1,700-2,200 *BIR*

A set of 8 George III style mahogany dining chairs, each with arched back and serpentine seat with close studded upholstery, on square chamfered legs with pierced spandrels, joined by stretchers.
£3,500-5,000 *CSK*

A set of 7 George III style mahogany dining chairs, including a pair of armchairs, each with drop-in seat and foliate scroll carved cabriole legs and claw-and-ball feet.
£1,500-2,000 *CSK*

A set of 10 George III style mahogany ladder back dining chairs, including a pair of armchairs, each with drop-in seat and square moulded legs joined by stretchers.
£3,000–3,500 *CSK*

A set of 8 George I style walnut dining chairs, including a pair of armchairs, with solid splats, drop-in seats and carved cabriole legs.
£2,200–3,000 *S(S)*

A set of 6 George III mahogany dining chairs, the padded seats covered in green velvet, on square tapering legs and spade feet.
£4,500–5,500 *C*

A set of 6 George III style stained hardwood dining chairs. **£1,500–2,000** *CSK*

Thomas Chippendale (1718-79)

Thomas Chippendale, born in Otley, Yorkshire, the son of a Worcestershire carver, set up as a cabinet maker in London in 1749.

He was an exponent of the rococo style, and his superb and delicate carving set new standards for furniture making. Besides elaborate and costly work, his firm made very large quantities of relatively cheap, simple furniture of very high quality.

His business, in St Martins Lane, was carried on after his death by Thomas Chippendale the Younger, c1749-1822.

A set of 8 George III style mahogany dining chairs, including a pair of armchairs.
£1,500–1,800 *CSK*

A set of 5 late George III mahogany dining chairs, together with one of a later date, each with shield-shaped back, pierced vase-shaped splat, some rails, stretchers and one leg replaced, restored.
£1,500–2,000 *CSK*

A set of 8 Gothic revival dining chairs, possibly to designs by William Porden, each curved toprail with Gothic tracery, the reeded frames with drop-in seats, sabre legs, one chair now with arms, c1815.
£2,000–2,700 *S*

By repute from Eaton Hall, Cheshire, which was built for Robert, 2nd Earl Grosvenor, by the architect William Porden (died 1822), also employed by the Prince Regent to design the Indian stables at Brighton Pavilion in 1803. Gillows of Lancaster supplied much of the furniture for the house, along with the Manchester upholsterer John Kaye (died 1840), Porden's son-in-law.

A set of 6 early George III mahogany dining chairs, with a pair of later armchairs, replacements and restorations.
£3,000–4,000 *CSK*

Reputed to be from Dublin Castle.

A set of 7 George III style mahogany dining chairs, including 2 open armchairs.
£1,700–2,200 *CSK*

A set of 7 George III style mahogany dining chairs, including one armchair, each with wavy top rail and pierced interlaced vase splat, padded seat and cabriole legs with pad feet.
£1,200–1,700 *CSK*

A set of 10 George III style mahogany dining chairs, including a pair of armchairs, each with reeded wavy top rail, pierced shell and floral carved vase splat, drop-in seats and cabriole legs with claw-and-ball feet.
£3,200–3,700 *CSK*

A set of 5 George III Chippendale style dining chairs, with drop-in seats, on moulded square supports joined by stretchers.
£1,500–2,000 *Bri*

A set of 6 George III style mahogany dining chairs.
£1,300–1,800 *CSK*

A set of 8 George III style mahogany dining chairs, including a pair of armchairs, each with shield-shaped back, and pierced vase-shaped splat with central urn and drapery, drop-in seat and moulded square legs joined by stretchers.
£1,200–1,800 *CSK*

A set of 8 George II style carved mahogany dining chairs, including a pair of armchairs, each with pierced splats and drop-in seats, on cabriole legs, 20thC.
£3,700–4,200 *S(S)*

A set of 6 George III mahogany dining chairs, each with serpentine crest rails, pierced and interlaced splats carved with urns, leaves and rosettes, drop-in seats and square tapering legs with stretchers, 2 chairs with later added arms.
£2,700–3,200 *DN*

A set of 17 George III style mahogany dining chairs, including 3 open armchairs, each with pierced foliate carved uprights, above a padded seat, on square channelled legs joined by stretchers, one damaged.
£3,000–4,000 *CSK*

A set of 5 Regency fruitwood elbow dining chairs, each with curved bar back above a single rail, scrolled arms and drop-in seat, on tapered legs.
£1,500–2,000 *BWe*

A set of 6 George IV mahogany
dining chairs, the crest rails with
ebony stringing and reeded
borders, rope twist centre rails,
the supports with roundels,
stuffed seats, on turned legs.
£3,000–3,500 *DN*

A pair of George III mahogany
dining chairs, each with stop
fluted stiles, the padded seats
covered in brown leather, one
restored and one repaired,
later blocks.
£500–800 *C*

A set of 6 George IV rosewood
dining chairs, the rail backs
carved with rosettes and scrolls,
the caned seats with squabs, on
turned and reeded legs headed
by roundels.
£1,800–2,200 *DN*

Did you know?

The earlier a set of chairs and
the more pieces in it the
greater the value; especially if
the set includes a carver or,
better still, two. The carvers
seats should be at least 2in
(5cm) wider than the others in
the set.

Use the following ratios to
assess the value of sets of
average quality compared
with a single chair price.
  A pair: 3 times
  Set of 4: 6/7 times
  Set of 6: 10/12 times
  Set of 8: 15 times plus.

A set of 6 Regency rosewood
dining chairs, with drop-in seats,
the aprons with turned
mouldings, on sabre front
legs, c1900.
£2,000–2,700 *P(S)*

A set of 4 Regency goncalo alvez
dining chairs, by Gillows, each
with waisted balloon back with
central floral patera between
channelled anthemia above a
beaded tablet, with caned seat
and yellow and ivory floral
patterned silk squab cushion, the
panelled seat rail with anthemion
rounded angles, on turned
tapering reeded legs and turned
tapering feet, one stamped
'Gillows, Lancaster', 3 with pencil
inscription 'Dixon', one with
inscription 'J. Lanson'.
£1,500–2,000 *C*
*Goncalo Alvez is one of the rarest
and most exotic tropical
hardwoods that were used by
English furniture makers in the
early 19thC.*

A set of 6 Regency brass inlaid
mahogany dining chairs, each
with outswept back with reeded
uprights and tablet horizontal
bar, above padded seat on ring
turned legs.
£2,000–2,500 *CSK*

A set of 4 Regency simulated
rosewood dining chairs.
£1,200–1,700 *P(S)*

A set of 12 Regency mahogany
dining chairs, the backs with
curved scrolled top rails and
ball decorated horizontal splats,
having drop-in seats, on
moulded sabre legs, including
a pair of armchairs.
£6,000–8,000 *P*

A set of 6 William IV mahogany
dining chairs, each with deep bar
top rail and foliate carved
horizontal splat, above drop-in
seat on baluster turned legs.
£900–1,500 *CSK*

A set of 4 Regency inlaid
simulated rosewood dining chairs,
including a pair of open armchairs,
each with bar top rail above
foliate roundel horizontal splat,
drop-in seat on reeded legs.
£700–900 *CSK*

A set of 6 Victorian mahogany balloon back dining chairs, including one carver, each with drop-in seats, supported on carved shaped cabriole legs.
£1,200–1,700 *Mit*

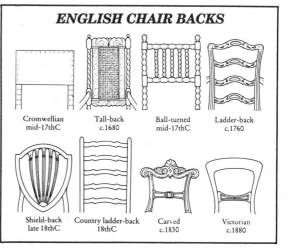

ENGLISH CHAIR BACKS

Cromwellian mid-17thC

Tall-back c.1680

Ball-turned mid-17thC

Ladder-back c.1760

Shield-back late 18thC

Country ladder-back 18thC

Carved c.1830

Victorian c.1880

A set of 4 Victorian carved oak high backed dining chairs, with upholstered stuff-over seats, above turned front and rear twist legs united by barley twist stretchers.
£450–600 *FLE*

A set of 8 Victorian walnut balloon back chairs, with carved back rails, stuff-over serpentine seats, on cabriole legs.
£3,500–4,500 *BWe*

A matched set of 12 Victorian mahogany dining chairs, upholstered in blue velvet, labelled 'From Jas. Shoolbred & Co., Tottenham Court Road, London'.
£3,000–4,000 *CSK*

A set of 6 early Victorian mahogany dining chairs, one signed on the seat rail 'Mr. Marsh, Market Place, Devizes' and one similar bearing a label inscribed in ink, one chair lacking carved brackets.
£1,000–1,400 *DN*

A set of 3 Dutch marquetry chequer strung dining chairs, each with foliate inlaid top rail, above a padded seat, on square tapering legs, some old damage, 19thC.
£500–700 *CSK*

A set of 8 Victorian decorated satinwood dining chairs, including a pair of armchairs, each circular back centred by carved leaves joined by husks, the shaped arms decorated with leaves and berries, with curved supports, the padded seats on square tapering legs decorated with husks.
£20,000–25,000 *S*

Although these chairs do not appear to follow any published design, similar hall chairs were supplied by Thomas Chippendale for Nostell and Harewood in the mid-1770s. The elegant furniture of the neo-classical period had become fashionable once again by the early 1860s, and 18thC examples were being purchased and copied by such firms as Wright and Mansfield, who exhibited a Wedgwood mounted satinwood cabinet in the Adams style at the Paris Exhibition of 1867.

A set of 6 late Victorian walnut dining chairs, by Gillow, each with padded back and fluted uprights, padded seat, collared fluted tapering legs, each stamped 'Gillow 4037'.
£800–1,200 *CSK*

A set of 8 mid-Victorian mahogany balloon back dining chairs, each labelled 'G.M. & H.J. Story, Cabinet Makers, 33 London Wall, EC'.
£1,700–2,200 *CSK*

A set of 8 mahogany dining chairs, including 2 armchairs, each with a pierced splat, over drop-in seat, on square legs, 19thC.
£2,000–2,500 *MEA*

A set of 12 Edwardian parcel gilt dining chairs, in George II style, each with a dipped and scalloped back support and generous sprung seats, on leaf-cast cabriole legs with claw-and-ball feet, 2 chairs distressed.
£7,000–8,500 *S*

These chairs were copied from a set at Stourhead in Wiltshire, which are attributed to the cabinet maker Giles Grendey and were supplied for the house c1750.

Wicker Chairs

A wicker shell-shaped lady's armchair, by Pollodian, c1910.
£200–300 *DMT*

An English wicker armchair, by Dryad of Leicester.
£300–500 *DMT*

A lady's wicker high back bedroom chair, by Heywood Brothers, c1880.
£300–400 *DMT*

An English wicker Arran chair, by Caxtons, early 20thC.
£200–250 *DMT*

An English sea grass folding armchair by Citidal, c1885.
£280–350 *DMT*

An English wicker armchair, by Dryad, c1915.
£150–220 *DMT*

A wicker high back armchair, stamped C.R. Maquire of Sydney, c1890.
£280–300 *DMT*

Miscellaneous Chairs

An English wicker corner armchair, by Aster & Co., c1900.
£200–300 *DMT*

A pair of Victorian walnut chairs, c1870.
£2,000–2,400 *Mit*

A lady's wicker chair, by Heywood Brothers, late 19thC.
£250–350 *DMT*

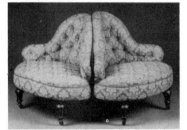

A late Victorian ebonised parcel gilt conversation sofa, comprising 4 sections, each with button down back and bowed padded seat, on fluted tapering legs, each section detachable.
£2,000–2,500 *CSK*

A mahogany child's chair, with bar top rail above caned seat, on ring turned splayed legs joined by stretchers and foot board, 19thC.
£150–200 *CSK*

A pair of French beech side chairs, each oval deep buttoned padded back in a carved wreath frame, over a circular deep buttoned seat, on carved cabriole legs with scroll feet.
£1,200–1,500 *MEA*

A Victorian child's mahogany high chair, with white hide padded back and upholstered seat flanked by down scrolled armrests, on turned tapering supports, the rounded rectangular stand on ring turned supports, stamped 3608, 48½in (123cm) high.
£600–700 *C(S)*

A Victorian walnut lady's chair, on cabriole legs.
£350–450 *M*

A Victorian rosewood lady's chair, with upholstered dralon seat and back, on cabriole legs with scrolled feet.
£300–400 *M*

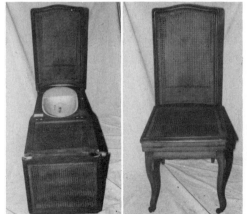

A travelling bidet chair.
£150–180 *REL*

A mid-Georgian carved mahogany corner chair, restored, some later carving.
£2,000–2,500 *CSK*

A set of 6 mahogany side chairs, repaired, mid-18thC.
£2,700–3,200 *WW*

A mid-Victorian walnut framed sociable, upholstered in blue velour, on carved cabriole legs with knurl feet and casters.
£2,000–2,500 *Bea*

A set of 6 mahogany side chairs, with Chippendale style pierced splat backs, red plush covered drop-in seats, on square chamfered bracketed front legs, with H-stretchers, early 19thC.
£2,500–3,000 *WW*

A walnut music chair, with bowed toprail, stick splats, adjustable leather upholstered circular seat, on square cabriole legs joined by a flat X-stretcher, early 19thC.
£300–500 *Bea*

A pair of Regency brass mounted mahogany side chairs in the Gothic style, the serpentine padded seats covered in nailed green horsehair, on fluted square tapering legs joined by H-shaped stretchers, with spade feet, later blocks.
£750–1,000 *C*

A set of 4 Edwardian rosewood and inlaid salon chairs.
£600–700 *WL*

A cello chair, 39½in (100cm) high.
£75–125 *WAB*

A set of 6 Victorian walnut parlour chairs, the shell and acanthus carved frames with stuffed serpentine seats, all button upholstered in salmon velvet, gadrooned fluted tapering legs on casters, the seat rails labelled 'Constantine & Co., Leeds'.
£2,500–3,500 *S*

The firm of William Constantine & Co., was established in Leeds by the mid-1830s and just over a decade later it employed about a hundred workers, including 15 carvers.

An Italian ebony and ivory inlaid side chair, with arched top rail and padded back, padded seat on block and turned legs and scroll feet joined by stretchers, late 19thC.
£1,200–1,700 *CSK*

A set of 4 early Victorian walnut framed side chairs, upholstered with woolwork, the padded backs carved with scrolling foliage within fluted uprights and on similarly carved fluted legs.
£600–800 *Bea*

A Gainsborough style mahogany upholstered chair, 22½in (57cm).
£200–240 *SUL*

A set of 5 George II walnut chairs, with pierced vase-shaped splats and slip-in claret velvet seats, on cabriole legs and pad feet, one chair damaged. **£2,000–3,500** *S(S)*

A Victorian walnut chair, with yoke-shaped top rail, shaped central splat, drop-in seat, on cabriole legs on pointed pad feet.
£300–400 *SUL*

A set of 12 mahogany chairs, some bearing a retailer's label Holdsworth & Sons, New Wells, Wakefield, the seats now with dralon covers.
£2,700–3,700 *DN*

A Regency lacquer and gilt chair, with cane seat.
£200–250 *STA*

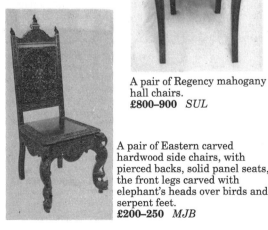

A pair of Regency mahogany hall chairs.
£800–900 *SUL*

A pair of Eastern carved hardwood side chairs, with pierced backs, solid panel seats, the front legs carved with elephant's heads over birds and serpent feet.
£200–250 *MJB*

A set of 8 Victorian rosewood chairs, each with moulded back, serpentine top rail, carved centre rail, serpentine front stuff-over seats covered in floral tapestry, cabriole legs with scroll feet.
£1,500–2,000 *WIL*

A set of 3 Swiss walnut and chestnut side chairs, 18thC, together with a similar chair, branded 'D. Meyer' above a pin wheel.
£2,000–2,750 *CNY*

A set of 4 Victorian mahogany and button upholstered chairs, with cartouche shaped backs on bowed seats covered in coral velvet, on cabriole legs.
£600–900 *S(S)*

Chests of Drawers

A William and Mary style burr walnut marquetry chest, with crossbanded top centred with inlaid foliate panel, above 2 short drawers and 2 long drawers, on turned bun feet, 37in (94cm).
£1,600–2,000 *CSK*

A William and Mary style inlaid burr elm chest, the crossbanded top with feather banding and central foliate marquetry panel with similar side panels, on bun feet, 39in (99cm).
£1,000–1,500 *CSK*

A mahogany and burr walnut chest, the associated moulded top above 2 short and 2 long crossbanded drawers, on bracket feet, early 18thC and later, 37½in (95cm).
£1,500–2,000 *CSK*

In the Furniture section when there is only one measurement it refers to the width of the piece unless otherwise stated.

A Georgian mahogany chest, 31in (79cm).
£2,500–3,000 *MEA*

An early Georgian walnut and featherbanded chest, with quarter-veneered and crossbanded top, 4 long drawers and bracket feet, alterations and re-veneering, 31in (79cm).
£1,500–2,000 *CSK*

A walnut chest, with moulded crossbanded top above 2 short and 3 long drawers, on later bracket feet, restored, early 18thC, 37½in (95cm).
£2,200–2,700 *P*

A walnut chest of drawers, inlaid overall with bog oak and fruitwood scrolling foliage, feet missing, repaired and damaged, later inlay, late 17thC.
£1,700–2,200 *CSK*

A George I walnut chest, the top with featherbanding and crossbanded edge, above a slide, 2 short and 3 long featherbanded drawers, 30in (76cm).
£6,000–7,000 *B*

A Regency mahogany bowfronted chest, crossbanded overall in satinwood and inlaid with boxwood and ebonised lines, some restorations, 39in (99cm).
£2,500–3,000 *C*

A George II mahogany bachelor's chest, with brushing slide, on bracket feet, 29½in (75cm).
£4,700–5,500 *CSK*

A late George II mahogany chest, the top with a moulded edge, fitted with 4 long drawers, on later bracket feet, 28in (76cm).
£1,500–2,000 *P*

A George III mahogany chest, on shaped bracket feet, restored, the top possibly re-veneered, 35½in (90cm).
£3,200–3,700 *C*

A George III mahogany chest, with graduated part beech and blue paper lined long drawers, on shaped bracket feet, 37in (94cm).
£1,800–2,000 *C*

A Regency mahogany bowfronted chest, with crossbanded top, on bracket feet, 42in (107cm).
£600–800 *CSK*

A Georgian mahogany serpentine chest, with 3 long drawers and canted corners, on swept apron and bracket feet, 43½in (110cm).
£1,200–1,500 *WL*

A George III mahogany
serpentine chest, inlaid
throughout with purple heart
bandings and boxwood stringing,
the 4 long graduated drawers
flanked by tulipwood banded
chamfered corners, shaped apron
with bracket feet, 39in (99cm).
£2,700–4,000 *S(S)*

A mahogany bowfronted chest,
with crossbanded top, 4 long
drawers flanked by panelled
pilasters, brass handles and
turned feet, early 19thC,
40½in (103cm).
£2,000–2,500 *DN*

A George III mahogany chest,
with 4 long graduated drawers,
brass swan neck handles, bracket
feet, requires slight restoration,
33in (84cm).
£1,500–2,000 *L&E*

A George III mahogany chest, the
top crossbanded and inlaid with a
boxwood line, above a slide and
4 graduated long drawers, on
shaped bracket feet, minor
restorations, 36in (91.5cm).
£2,200–2,400 *C*

A Georgian mahogany chest of
drawers, 40in (101.5cm).
£1,200–1,700 *Mit*

A George III mahogany and
satinwood banded bowfronted
chest, with slide above 3 drawers,
on splayed feet, 40in (102cm).
£1,200–1,700 *S(S)*

A mahogany chest, the marquetry
top with central inlaid musical
trophy, the top possibly associated,
and later inlaid, late 18thC,
36in (91.5cm).
£1,800–2,200 *CSK*

A George III mahogany chest,
with 3 short and 3 long drawers
on bracket feet, 44½in (112cm).
£1,000–1,500 *CSK*

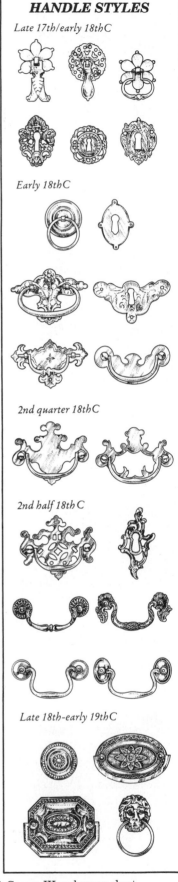

HANDLE STYLES

Late 17th/early 18thC

Early 18thC

2nd quarter 18thC

2nd half 18thC

Late 18th–early 19thC

A Regency mahogany bowfronted chest of drawers, 37in (95cm).
£750–850 *Bri*

A George III cedar veneered chest, the 4 long drawers with brass octagonal handles, on ogee bracket feet, the top drawer previously fitted with compartments and a slide, 44in (112cm).
£1,000–1,200 *DN*

A George III mahogany chest, restored, 39in (99cm).
£550–850 *CSK*

A George III mahogany chest of drawers, with plain top above 2 short and 3 graduated drawers, with brass drop handles and cockbeading to the drawer fronts, flanked on either side by reeded quarter column corners, standing on ogee bracket feet, 36in (91.5cm).
£2,000–2,500 *Mit*

A Regency bowfronted chest, with 2 short and 3 long graduated drawers, between foliate headed reeded column uprights, on ring turned legs.
£1,200–1,700 *CSK*

With a paper label 'Timothy Walford & Sons, Upholsterers, Cabinet Makers, and Appraisers, 19 Head Street, Colchester, Paper Hangings, Funerals completely furnished, old goods taken in exchange'.

A Baltic gilt metal mounted mahogany chest, with canted top above 2 drawers, between fluted angles, on paterae headed collared square tapering legs with block feet, early 19thC, 32in (81cm).
£2,700–3,200 *CSK*

A Dutch marquetry and walnut chest, the top inlaid with birds, cartouches of flowers and classical figures, profusely decorated including sides, over 4 long drawers with a double concave breakfront, raised on ball feet, 18thC, 31in (79cm).
£5,000–6,000 *B*

A mahogany chest, in 2 parts, the crossbanded top with an oval shell inlay, above a slide and 4 long drawers, on bracket feet, 37in (94cm).
£700–900 *P*

A mahogany chest, with reeded top above 4 long graduated drawers with waved aprons, inlaid with boxwood lines, on splayed bracket feet, converted from a bedside commode, 24in (60cm).
£500–600 *P*

A north European softwood chest, with three-quarter gallery above 6 long drawers, flanked by ebonised Corinthian columns, on block feet, 18thC, 35½in (90cm).
£700–900 *CSK*

A miniature mahogany chest of drawers, c1870, 13½in (34cm).
£240–280 *DUN*

Secrétaire Chests

A George I walnut secrétaire chest, inlaid overall with fruitwood and ebonised lines, the quarter-veneered top above a fitted secrétaire drawer with suede lined writing surface, 2 short and 2 long drawers, on later shaped bracket feet, the top formerly hinged, probably previously a dressing chest, 31in (79cm).
£3,500–4,500 *C*

A padouk wood brass bound military secrétaire chest, in 2 sections, with single drawer fall-front enclosing a bird's eye maple veneered fitted interior and leather lined writing surface, flanked by another small drawer, above 3 long drawers, on turned feet, with label, 'Army & Navy C.S.L. makers', mid-19thC, 39in (99cm).
£1,200–1,700 *CSK*

A Regency mahogany secrétaire chest, with a deep secrétaire drawer enclosing a fitted interior, on bracket feet, 34in (86cm).
£1,600–2,000 *CSK*

A Victorian mahogany and brass bound military chest, in 2 parts, on turned feet, 40in (102cm).
£800–1,000 *P*

A mahogany brass bound secrétaire military chest, the rectangular top above central fall enclosing fitted interior, early 19thC, 39in (99cm).
£1,200–1,700 *CSK*

A Victorian teak and brass bound military secrétaire chest, in 2 parts, the tooled leather lined fall enclosing a fitted interior, lacking feet, 39in (99cm).
£900–1,200 *P*

An early Victorian oak and brass bound military secrétaire chest, 39in (99cm). **£2,500–3,500** *CSK*

Wellington Chests

A Victorian mahogany Wellington chest, with 7 drawers and a locking pilaster, 22½in (57cm).
£1,200–1,700 *S(S)*

A Victorian walnut secrétaire Wellington chest, one with a fall front enclosing a fitted interior, flanked by a locking stile, on a platform base, 23in (59cm). **£2,000–2,500** *P*

Chests-on-Chests

A George III mahogany tallboy.
£1,200–1,500 *P(S)*

A George III mahogany chest-on-chest, with oak lined drawers and brass swan neck handles, raised on shaped bracket feet, 46in (117cm).
£900–1,200 *DMC*

A crossbanded walnut and oak tallboy, on bracket feet, some veneer missing, restored, mid-18thC.
£1,700–2,000 *CSK*

A George III mahogany chest-on-chest.
£1,400–1,800 *W*

An inlaid mahogany bowfronted chest-on-chest, with arched crossbanded cornice, outswept bracket feet, the cornice possibly associated, some damage and restorations, early 19thC, 45in (114cm).
£1,200–1,700 *CSK*

A walnut chest-on-chest, with brushing slide, 18thC, 40½in (103cm).
£2,500–3,000 *HOLL*

A George III mahogany tallboy, with drop pendant moulded frieze cornice, above 2 short and 6 long drawers, on bracket feet, damaged, 46in (117cm).
£800–1,200 *CSK*

> ## Tallboy
> A tallboy is a chest of drawers raised upon another chest of drawers. Also known as a chest-on-chest.

A late George III mahogany tallboy, with moulded cornice, brass handles and bracket feet, 45in (114cm).
£800–1,200 *DN*

A mid-George III mahogany tallboy, with part replaced dentil moulded cornice, on shaped bracket feet, 44in (112cm).
£1,200–1,700 *CSK*

A mahogany chest-on-chest, with dentil moulded cornice, on bracket feet, restored, late 18thC, 43in (109cm).
£1,000–1,500 *CSK*

Chests-on-Stands

A Regency mahogany line inlaid chest-on-chest, with urn finials above shaped pediment, 2 short and 6 long drawers, on outswept bracket feet, restored, 42in (107cm).
£1,500–2,000 *CSK*

A walnut and featherbanded chest-on-stand, the stand with a long drawer on bracket feet, early 18thC and later, 38in (96.5cm).
£1,500–2,500 *CSK*

Use the Index!

Because certain items might fit easily into any number of categories, the quickest and surest method of locating any entry is by reference to the index at the back of the book.

This has been fully cross-referenced for absolute simplicity.

A walnut chest-on-stand, with quarter-veneered and crossbanded top, the sides also crossbanded, drawers with inlaid border bands, the later stand with a drawer, arcaded apron and turned ball feet, 38in (97cm).
£1,500–2,000 *P(S)*

A George III mahogany tallboy, with dentil moulded cornice above 2 short and 6 long drawers, on bracket feet, the feet possibly associated, 47in (119cm).
£2,500–3,000 *CSK*

A pair of George III style mahogany chest-on-stands, each with pagoda cresting with pierced gallery and blind fret frieze, each stand with blind fret frieze on square chamfered legs and pierced damaged spandrels, 21½in (65cm).
£2,500–3,000 *CSK*

Miscellaneous Chests

An Indian mahogany, ivory, ebony and floral marquetry mule chest, lacking 3 handles, feet restored, 33½in (85cm).
£2,000–2,500 *C*

A George I fruitwood and walnut chest-on-stand, inlaid throughout with chevron bandings, on later cabriole legs with pointed pad feet, c1725, 38in (96cm).
£2,500–3,500 *S(S)*

A walnut and crossbanded chest-on-stand, with ebonised line inlay, cavetto cornice, 2 short and 3 long drawers, the base with 2 short drawers and later cabriole legs with pad feet, early 18thC, 39in (99cm).
£2,500–3,500 *CSK*

A George III mahogany mule chest, with hinged top, mahogany lined drawer, on block feet, 54in (137cm).
£1,000–1,500 *C*

A pair of carved walnut chests, with coloured marble tops, magazine compartments to either side, supported on tapered fluted legs.
£500–600 *FLE*

A Dutch Colonial hardwood and brass mounted chest, with nailed decoration, hinged cover and carrying handles, some damage, 18thC, 48in (122cm).
£1,000–1,200 *S(S)*

A black lacquer and chinoiserie decorated rug chest, with lift top, large engraved brass lock plate, on a stand with short square legs, 56in (142cm).
£2,700–3,200 *MEA*

Coffers

A mahogany serpentine dressing chest, the fitted frieze drawer with compartments and central hinged ratcheted mirror, above 2 further drawers, on splayed bracket feet, parts 18thC, 49in (125cm).
£1,500–2,000 *CSK*

A Spanish baroque embroidered velvet covered coffer, on later walnut stand carved with crouching beasts, on splayed legs joined by a scrolling wrought iron stretcher, 49in (125cm).
£7,000–8,000 *CNY*

A south German walnut coffer, with hinged lid enclosing a fitted interior, the front with arched line inlay and frieze drawer below, on later bun feet, late 18thC, 38in (96cm).
£700–900 *CSK*

A Dutch East Indies teak and studded brass coffer, with three drawers, a pierced brass hasp and carrying handles, 43in (109cm).
£500–600 *S(S)*

A Shiraz gilt metal close studded coffer, painted red, the hinged top above 3 apron drawers, 56in (142cm).
£850–1,000 *CSK*

Reputed to have belonged to Seyyid Said who transferred his capital from Muscat to Zanzibar.

Commodes

A George III mahogany
serpentine fronted commode,
with 2 short and 3 long drawers,
flanked by canted fluted corners,
c1770, 40in (102cm).
£3,500–4,500 *S(S)*

A George III mahogany night
commode with shaped tray top
and 2 doors above a pull-out slide,
with shaped apron, 24in (61cm).
£900–1,200 *DN*

A George III mahogany night
commode, with brass handles,
the pull-out pot holder with a
serpentine edge, fitted with a
brass swan neck handle, on
square legs, 22in (56cm).
£800–900 *WW*

Commodes

A commode is a chest of
drawers in the French style,
fashionable from the mid-
18thC, but never produced in
great quantity because the
elaborate shapes and
decoration were expensive
to achieve.

Prudishness caused the
Victorians to call any piece of
furniture designed to conceal
a chamber pot a commode.
The bedside type was
produced in great quantity
and has little antique value
although early examples are
now collectable.

A George III mahogany tray top
tambour commode, the drawer
now lacking a liner, 21in (53cm).
£1,000–1,200 *S(S)*

A George III mahogany bedside
commode, the galleried top above
a pair of cupboard doors and a
pull-out section enclosing a white
ceramic pot, on square legs, minor
restorations, 21in (53cm).
£3,000–3,500 *C*

A Louis XV style kingwood and
tulipwood bombé commode, with
marble top, gilt metal mounts,
the front with a cartouche, floral
sprays and 2 drawers, the splayed
legs ending in sabots, marble top
bears label to reverse 'Chenue
S.A.R.L., Layetier Emballeur,
Paris', restored, c1870, 37in (94cm).
£4,000–4,500 *S(S)*

A Louis XV style gilt metal
mounted red and brown japanned
and gilt chinoiserie decorated
bombé commode, the serpentine
brocatelle marble top above
2 frieze drawers and waved
apron, on splayed legs with gilt
clasps and sabots, late 19thC,
41½in (105cm).
£1,500–2,000 *CSK*

A Venetian serpentine green
painted commode, with applied
gilded mounts, fitted single
drawer above a 2 door cupboard
base, with deep scrolled feet,
18thC, 36in (92cm).
£2,200–2,700 *HOLL*

A Flemish mahogany bombé chest
of drawers, the serpentine top and
drawer fronts inlaid with
satinwood and rosewood banding,
fitted with ornate brass handles
and escutcheons, shaped apron
and claw feet, 40in (102cm).
£2,000–2,500 *MAT*

A Louis XV style gilt metal mounted kingwood and marquetry commode, with serpentine marble top above two drawers inlaid with foliate marquetry sans traverse, on cabriole legs with gilt sabots, marble damaged, late 19thC, 46in (117cm).
£3,600–4,200 *CSK*

A Louis XV style gilt metal mounted mahogany and rosewood bombé commode, with serpentine marble top, overall floral marquetry inlaid sans traverse, 2 drawers, on cabriole legs with sabots, 39½in (100cm).
£2,500–3,000 *CSK*

A Louis XV style kingwood and ormolu mounted bombé commode, with a coloured moulded marble top, ormolu handles and escutcheons, the shaped frieze having a central ormolu mount, the cabriole shaped supports mounted in ormolu and terminating in sabots, 19thC.
£2,000–2,500 *FLE*

Cupboards

A pair of inlaid mahogany bowfronted corner cupboards, each with moulded top and chequer strung edge, above shell inlaid frieze and panelled doors with central oval shell, on square tapering legs, each 27in (69cm).
£1,500–2,000 *CSK*

A north Italian walnut veneered commode, inlaid with marquetry panels of flowerheads, the top banded in tulipwood and rosewood inlaid, the 3 long drawers also inlaid and fitted with brass rosette plate ring handles, on square tapering legs, 48in (122cm). **£8,000–9,000** *WW*

A George III mahogany bedside cupboard, inlaid overall with lines, the waved gallery and rectangular top above a panelled door and pull-out section, on square legs, 21½in (54.5cm).
£1,500–2,000 *C*

A north Italian walnut and marquetry bedside cupboard, with crossbanded top above frieze, on associated square channelled legs with block feet, parts late 18thC, 16in (41cm).
£2,000–2,700 *CSK*

A late George III mahogany tray top bedside cupboard, with waved gallery, cupboard door below, on square legs, restorations, 14in (36cm).
£400–450 *CSK*

A Georgian mahogany standing corner cupboard, 42in (106.5cm).
£2,000–2,500 *Mit*

A Georgian mahogany bowfronted corner cupboard, with satinwood and ebony stringing and brass H-hinges.
£750–850 *RBB*

A George III inlaid mahogany hanging corner cupboard, the swan's neck pediment with central brass finial, above a boxwood and ebony strung collar, 33in (84cm).
£750–800 *Mit*

A French cream and brown painted armoire, on bun feet, re-decorated, late 19thC, 84in (213cm).
£1,000–1,500 *CSK*

A George III mahogany linen press, the moulded cornice above a pair of oval panelled doors, 2 short and 2 long drawers, on bracket feet, the cornice associated, restorations, 55in (140cm).
£1,000–1,500 *CSK*

A Regency mahogany standing corner cupboard, in 2 parts, c1810, 40in (102cm).
£2,500–3,000 *S(S)*

Clothes Presses

Typically a low chest with a cupboard above containing shelves, trays or runners and a hanging space.

Many fine Regency presses were gutted to make wardrobes; a mid-19thC invention.

Best prices are paid for presses which still retain good quality oak fittings.

A Georgian mahogany bowfronted hanging corner cupboard, with a moulded cornice above a pair of panelled doors, enclosing a series of shaped shelves and with 3 spice drawers at the foot, with moulded base, 29in (74cm).
£450–550 *Mit*

A George III mahogany linen press, with moulded and dentil cornice, 2 panelled doors over 2 short and 2 long drawers with brass drop handles, on bracket feet, 50in (127cm).
£1,700–2,000 *AH*

A George III mahogany linen press, the pair of doors with oval kingwood banding, enclosing sliding trays, 50½in (128cm).
£1,500–2,000 *S(S)*

A George III mahogany linen press, with moulded panel doors over 2 dummy drawers and 2 long drawers, on later turned feet.
£800–1,200 *BIR*

A George III style mahogany standing corner cupboard, in two parts, with kingwood banding, the glazed doors enclosing glass shelves, panel doors below, on splayed feet, c1910, 53in (134cm).
£1,500–2,000 *S(S)*

A George III mahogany clothes press, with dentil cornice above 2 oval panelled doors enclosing sliding trays, with brass handles and bracket feet, 49½in (126cm).
£1,700–2,200 *DN*

A George III mahogany and line inlaid bowfronted linen press, on outswept bracket feet, cornice damaged, 54in (137cm).
£1,000–1,500 *CSK*

A George III mahogany standing corner cupboard, reconstructed and including later components, 56in (142cm).
£1,200–1,700 *S(S)*

A George III mahogany linen press, with twin moulded panel doors enclosing fitted shelf interior, over 2 long drawers, on square bracket feet.
£700–1,000 *BIR*

A Regency mahogany linen press, the architectural pediment with ebonised finials, above a pair of panelled doors, on outswept bracket feet, 50in (127cm).
£1,500–2,000 *CSK*

A late George III mahogany linen press, with moulded cornice and a pair of doors with oval panels, enclosing pull-out shelves, above 2 short and 2 long drawers, on outswept bracket feet, 44in (112cm).
£1,500–2,000 *CSK*

A late George III mahogany linen press, repairs to feet, minor damage to drawer mouldings, 49½in (126cm).
£1,500–2,000 *CSK*

Davenports

A William IV rosewood davenport, the sliding top with sloped leather lined fall, above foliate headed fluted uprights, flanked by brushing slides, 4 true and 4 false drawers to each side, on foliate bun feet, 19in (48cm).
£1,200–1,700 *CSK*

An early Victorian rosewood davenport, with three-quarter gallery, leather lined sloping fall enclosing a fitted interior, on scroll supports, with 4 side drawers and opposing dummy drawers, on plinth base and turned feet, 21½in (54cm).
£1,000–1,200 *CSK*

A William IV rosewood veneered davenport, the flap with remains of old leather, with fitted interior and a side writing compartment, above 3 mahogany lined drawers with brass locks, panelled back and front and 3 dummy drawers the other side, front column supports, the plinth base on bun feet with casters, 22in (56cm).
£700–900 *WW*

A mid-Victorian bird's-eye maple davenport, with pierced brass gallery and hinged leather lined fall, fitted with hinged pencil drawer and 4 drawers, on turned uprights and concave platform base, 21½in (54cm).
£800–1,200 *CSK*

An early Victorian mahogany davenport, the three-quarter gallery above leather lined slope, 4 short drawers opposed by 4 dummy drawers to each side, with ring turned uprights on inverted platform base, with bun feet, 23in (59cm).
£900–1,200 *CSK*

A mid-Victorian burr walnut davenport, 21in (53cm).
£1,000–1,500 *CSK*

A walnut davenport, with satinwood inlaid back fitted with compartments and inkwells, curving carved supports, ending in porcelain casters, 22in (56cm).
£1,800–2,200 *JNic*

A George IV rosewood davenport, with pierced brass three-quarter gallery, the hinged leather lined fall with beaded edge enclosing fitted interior, above pencil drawer, slide, and 4 drawers, on bun feet, 20in (51cm).
£2,500–3,000 *CSK*

A walnut veneered and rosewood banded davenport, the super-structure with fitted interior, the leather lined slope enclosing a fitted interior, with 4 drawers to the side and opposing dummy drawers, on plinth base and turned feet, 23in (59cm).
£1,500–2,000 *CSK*

A late Victorian inlaid burr walnut davenport, on plinth base, 22½in (57cm).
£1,500–2,000 *CSK*

A Victorian walnut veneered davenport, on short bun feet.
£1,200–1,700 *Mit*

A Victorian mahogany davenport, with raised gallery back, the writing slope with fitted interior, stringing and crossbanding, leather inset, sliding top to base fitted with small drawer, 4 drawers to side, with inlaid ribbon and husk pendant decoration, on bracket feet, 27in (69cm).
£1,500–2,000 *RBB*

A late Victorian walnut and burr walnut davenport, on plinth base and turned feet, 21in (53cm).
£1,300–1,700 *CSK*

A Victorian burr walnut davenport, with small gallery back, sloped rising writing surface, opening to reveal a maplewood interior with a panel door to the side, opening to reveal 4 small drawers, with pierced fretwork brackets, on turned and carved supports, 23in (59cm).
£1,500–2,000 *JNic*

Desks

A George III and later mahogany tambour top kneehole writing desk, with satinwood banding, 42in (107cm).
£1,700–2,200 *S(S)*

A mahogany partners' desk, with eared leather lined top and foliate carved frieze with satyr's heads, above 6 frieze drawers, 3 further drawers opposed by a cupboard to each pedestal, on cabriole legs with claw-and-ball feet, 66in (168cm).
£3,000–4,000 *CSK*

A mahogany cylinder desk, 19thC.
£1,600–2,000 *W*

A French mahogany kneehole
cylinder desk, on tapering fluted
legs, 19thC, 49in (124cm).
£3,000–3,500 *MEA*

A satinwood and crossbanded
roll top desk, with fitted interior
and pull-out writing slide, united
by a concave stretcher shelf,
40½in (102cm).
£1,500–2,000 *MEA*

A George III style mahogany
kneehole desk, with rectangular
top, frieze drawer and further
central drawer with recessed
cupboard below, flanked by
3 small drawers to each side, on
bracket feet, 29½in (75cm).
£900–1,200 *CSK*

A George I walnut kneehole desk,
with featherbanded and
crossgrained top, on pedestals
with double bracket feet to each,
good original colour and
patination, 31in (79cm).
£10,000–12,000 *B*

A George I style burr walnut
kneehole desk, on bracket feet,
31in (79cm).
£800–1,000 *CSK*

A mahogany partners' pedestal
desk, with inverted breakfront
leather lined top, 6 frieze drawers
and a further 3 drawers to each
pedestal, with opposing cupboard
doors, on plinth bases, mid-19thC,
60in (152cm).
£3,500–4,500 *CSK*

A George I walnut, crossbanded
and featherstrung kneehole desk,
with later top, on bracket feet,
37in (94cm).
£1,200–1,500 *P*

A mahogany kneehole desk, with
rectangular moulded top, above a
frieze drawer, 3 drawers either
side of an apron drawer and
cupboard, on bracket feet,
probably reconstructed,
mid-18thC, 31in (79cm).
£1,200–1,700 *CSK*

A Georgian period mahogany
kneehole desk, on bracket feet,
29in (74cm).
£6,000–7,000 *MEA*

A George III mahogany kneehole
desk, on bracket feet, 33in (84cm).
£1,000–1,200 *P*

A late Victorian oak Gothic
revival partners' pedestal desk,
on bracket feet, 51in (130cm).
£1,700–2,200 *CSK*

A mahogany desk, the top with a sloping writing centre on ratchet, a concave centre with gadrooned edge over 2 recessed concave open shelves, flanked with 2 pedestals each with 4 graduating drawers, on plinth base, early 19thC, 52in (132cm).
£2,500–3,000 *MEA*

A mid-Victorian mahogany serpentine partners' desk, with eared leather lined top above 2 ripple moulded frieze drawers, each pedestal with arched cupboard door enclosing drawers, flanked by half column uprights, on foliate carved plinth base, 63½in (161cm).
£2,000–2,500 *CSK*

A mahogany serpentine shaped partners' desk, with leather inset top above 3 false and 3 frieze drawers, the centre with pierced angles on 2 fixed pedestals, each with 2 small cupboards, a drawer, 2 slides and 2 false drawers, on bracket feet, 53½in (135cm).
£3,200–4,000 *MEA*

A Victorian mahogany pedestal desk, fitted with a central recessed frieze drawer and four drawers to each pedestal, on plinth bases, 50in (127cm).
£900–1,200 *P*

A Victorian mahogany pedestal desk, the top inset with a panel of tooled leather, fitted with 3 frieze drawers, and 3 drawers to each pedestal, on plinth bases, 57in (144.5cm).
£800–1,000 *P*

An Edwardian mahogany kidney shaped pedestal desk, line inlaid and rosewood banded, with leather lined top, central frieze drawer and 4 drawers to each pedestal, on square tapering legs, 54in (137cm).
£1,800–2,200 *CSK*

A Victorian mahogany kneehole desk, the central drawer with sliding leather inset writing panel, 53½in (136cm).
£1,300–1,700 *S(S)*

A mahogany partners' desk, with leather lined breakfront top, 68in (173cm).
£2,800–3,300 *CSK*

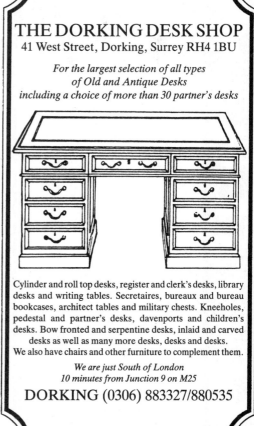

A Victorian mahogany small twin pedestal desk, the top with inkwell compartment and inset sloping surface, on pedestals each with 3 drawers.
£1,000–1,500 *BWe*

A late Victorian mahogany clerk's desk, the raised superstructure with 2 banks of 3 short drawers with locking stiles, above leather lined hinged slope, the central dummy frieze drawer flanked by 2 short frieze drawers, and 3 further drawers to each pedestal, on plinth bases, 59in (150cm).
£850–1,200 *CSK*

A mahogany lady's writing desk, with gilt bronze gallery, inlaid with stringing and satinwood, the tambour top reveals 3 satinwood drawers, inlaid marquetry flap with gilt tooled leather, stationery well and a sprung secret drawer, on square tapering legs to socket feet and shaped front undertier, the frieze drawer stamped 'Maple & Co. Ltd.', 30in (76cm).
£2,000–2,500 *WW*

A Dutch mahogany and floral marquetry pedestal desk, the moulded top with central leather lined panel, the top split, door panels cracked, mouldings loose, 58in (147cm).
£1,500–2,000 *CSK*

A late George IV period mahogany desk, with ebony stringing, the tooled leather top with a crossbanded edge over 3 frieze drawers, each alphabetically stamped, raised on pedestals each with 4 graduated drawers, on plinth bases, 64in (163cm).
£3,200–4,000 *MEA*

A late Victorian mahogany partners' pedestal desk, with leather lined top, 55in (140cm).
£1,700–2,200 *CSK*

A late Victorian mahogany pedestal desk, with tooled leather inset top, 60½in (153cm).
£800–1,200 *S(S)*

A late Victorian mahogany partners' desk, the leather lined top above 6 frieze drawers, 3 drawers to each pedestal opposed by a cupboard door, with label 'patent drawer fastening', 60in (152cm).
£1,600–1,800 *CSK*

A Victorian oak pedestal desk, with raised superstructure and sloping leather lined writing panel, 59½in (151cm).
£900–1,200 *S(S)*

A late Victorian rosewood and inlaid writing desk, with leather lined top and gilt metal pierced galleries, above 2 frieze drawers, on square tapering legs, stamped 'Edwards & Roberts', 42in (107cm).
£2,000–2,500 *CSK*

A Napoleon III plum pudding mahogany lady's writing desk, with brass mounts and stringing, 32in (81cm).
£2,000–2,500 *FLE*

Dumb Waiters

A mahogany dumb waiter, the 3 graduated circular tiers edged with C-scrolls, on stop fluted turned shaft and strapwork carved downswept legs, with pad feet, 42⅛in (108cm) high.
£1,500–2,000 *C*

An early Victorian metamorphic dumb waiter, on bun feet, 60in (152cm).
£1,000–1,700 *CSK*

A William IV mahogany two-tier dumb waiter, 24in (61cm) diam.
£1,500–2,000 *CSK*

An early Victorian mahogany telescopic three-tier dumb waiter, on circular column, with concave sided platform base and carved squat bun feet, 32in (82cm) diam.
£1,000–1,200 *CSK*

A Georgian mahogany dumb waiter, 45in (114cm) high.
£800–900 *SUL*

A William IV metamorphic three-tier dumb waiter, with rectangular top above scroll carved supports, joined by turned stretchers on stile feet, 47½in (120cm).
£1,200–1,500 *CSK*

A George III mahogany dumb waiter, the 3 graduated tiers with a central baluster turned pillar, on tripod supports, lower tier restored, c1770, 41in (104cm) high.
£1,500–2,000 *S(S)*

Jardinières

A pair of French style walnut jardinières, each upper section with gilt metal galleriy and lift-out covers, with brass and exotic wood inlay and applied with ormolu mounts and mask heads, 19thC, 40½in (103cm) high.
£2,000–2,500 *WL*

A mahogany planter, 19thC, 32in (81cm).
£1,400–1,600 *SUL*

A late Victorian walnut and marquetry jardinière, the rectangular lift-out top banded in tulipwood and decorated with an urn of flowers, the concave sides with sprays of flowers and chased brass mounts, on cabriole legs, 24in (61cm).
£1,000–1,200 *DN*

A Louis XV style crossbanded and string inlaid jardinière, with pierced rococo gilt metal mounts, the oval top with loop handles revealing liner, shaped frieze and cabriole legs with scrolled feet, 19thC, 25in (64cm).
£800–1,000 *AH*

A George III mahogany brass banded planter, 24in (61cm).
£2,200–2,700 *SUL*

A wicker jardinière, c1900, 16in (41cm) diam.
£140–150 *DMT*

Mirrors and Frames

A gilt overmantel, the frame carved with leaves, fruit and C-scrolls, pierced cresting, late 18thC, 26 by 61in (66 by 155cm).
£2,500–3,000 *MEA*

A George III mahogany jardinière, with coopered sides, 2 brass bands and loop handles, 29¼in (74cm) diam.
£1,800–2,000 *DN*

A gilt overmantel mirror, the divided plate flanked by scrolling foliage, late 18thC, adapted, 58in (147cm) wide.
£1,000–1,200 *CSK*

This mirror was sold with a copy of the original receipt.

A convex wall mirror, with acanthus finial and applied dolphin mounts, early 19thC, 43 by 31in (109 by 79cm).
£500–700 *HOLL*

A Regency giltwood and composition triple plate overmantel mirror, with dentil moulded cornice, the frieze decorated with profuse scrolling foliage and cornucopiae, above bevelled plates, flanked by half columns, 33 by 59in (99 by 150cm).
£1,200–1,700 *CSK*

A William and Mary oyster veneered, walnut and marquetry cushion mirror, the later rectangular bevelled plate within a moulded slip and outer border, inlaid with scrolling foliate arabesque panels, previously with a cresting, the marquetry later, 33 by 29in (84 by 74cm).
£1,700–2,000 *C*

A George II walnut and gilt wall mirror, with swan's neck pediment and leaf ornament, 54 by 27in (137 by 69cm).
£2,000–3,000 *CAG*

The plate is probably original but with later silvering, the gilding was probably improved in the 19thC.

A Spanish carved, gilded and painted frame, with lotus outer edge, S-scroll corners and foliate sight edge, with glass, 17thC, 17in (43cm) wide.
£2,500–3,000 *C*

A George III mirror, the giltwood frame carved with a border of C-scrolls and flowering branches, 47 by 29in (119 by 74cm).
£8,200–8,700 *DN*

A giltwood mirror, mid-19thC.
£350–450 *FLE*

A George III gilt framed wall mirror, the arched bevelled plate surmounted by triple feather plumes, c1800, 44 by 25in (112 by 64cm).
£1,500–2,000 *S(S)*

A George II carved giltwood wall mirror, with pierced foliate scrolls, the plate flanked by pilasters, and with a patarae surmount, parts missing, c1750, 51 by 28in (130 by 71cm).
£3,300–4,000 *S(S)*

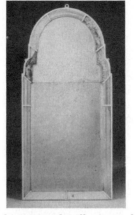

A white painted wall mirror, the arched bevelled plate flanked by divided outer plates, 18thC, later painted, 71 by 34in (180 by 86cm). **£1,200–1,500** *CSK*

A George I style carved giltwood and gesso wall mirror, the scroll pediment with a cartouche, the bevelled plate within a stipple border, the egg-and-dart surround with leaf scroll and scallop shell motifs, c1900, 66 by 34in (168 by 87cm). **£2,000–2,500** *S(S)*

A William and Mary walnut, fruitwood and inlaid cushion framed wall mirror, with arched cresting, later bevelled plate, c1700, 52½ by 31in (133 by 79cm). **£1,000–1,500** *S(S)*

A George III style giltwood mirror, the bevelled plate within pierced C-scroll and rocaille cresting surround and apron, cresting damaged, 73 by 42in (185 by 107cm). **£1,000–1,500** *CSK*

A Regency giltwood and composition girandole, the convex mirror plate in an ebonised slip and cavetto frame below a cresting of scrolling acanthus headed by an eagle, the base supporting twin scrolling branches with glass drip pans hung with drops and turned nozzles, regilded, the reverse inscribed in pencil '3/10/56' and with paper label of 'C. Thomas & Son, Carvers and Gilders, 2 New Bridge Street, Truro ...Old Frames Re-gilded', 33 by 18in (84 by 46cm). **£1,200–1,700** *C*

It is possible that C. Thomas was a descendant of John Thomas, who was a Truro cabinet maker from 1805 until c1822. He advertised a 'Fashionable Upholstery and Cabinet Warehouse' at 8 Lemon Street.

A George IV cheval mirror, with mahogany straight moulded supports, on reeded splayed legs with carved scrolls and brass terminals, 62 by 32in (157 by 81cm). **£850–950** *DN*

A Regency giltwood overmantel mirror, the bevelled plate flanked by cluster columns with overhanging feather capitals, the frieze carved with a central anthemion flanked by foliate scrolls, the inverted breakfront cornice mounted with beads, 47 by 34in (119 by 86cm). **£2,800–3,200** *C*

Cheval Mirrors

Cheval mirrors, or 'horse dressing glasses', so called because of their four-legged frame, were introduced during the last decade of the 18thC when it became possible to cast large enough mirror plates. Most examples date from 1790-1830, but they were still being made as late as 1910.

Some cheval mirrors have adjustable candleholders, usually a sign of good quality, which increase their value.

A Regency giltwood and green painted convex wall mirror, the eagle and leaf scroll cresting above a cavetto frame, applied with a border of stars, the conforming foliate apron terminating in a pendant pineapple finial, one applied star device missing, c1815, 69 by 28in (175 by 71cm).
£3,000–4,000 *S(S)*

The eagle was a popular cresting motif throughout much of the 18thC and early 19thC.

A pair of oval gilt wall mirrors, each with moulded frame and eagle cresting, 19thC, 44 by 32½in (112 by 82cm).
£1,800–2,500 *MEA*

A Regency giltwood mirror, the plate in a mirrored frame, with moulded divides and fluted border, parts of the border replaced, the back inscribed 'Front Sitting Room', 60½ by 42in (154 by 107cm).
£1,500–2,000 *C*

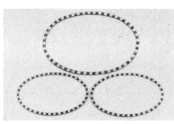

A pair of Irish oval mirrors, the frames set with royal blue glass brilliants and white glass panels with gilt dashes, early 19thC, 25in (64cm).
£6,000–8,000
A single mirror, 32½in (82cm) wide.
£7,000-8,000 *WW*

A Regency gilt convex mirror, with eagle cresting, in leaf moulded frame with ebonised and reeded band, 47 by 26in (119 by 66cm).
£1,200–1,500 *MEA*

A Hepplewhite style satinwood shield-shaped toilet mirror, the bevelled plate glass with painted acorn and oak leaf border, the stand with painted panel of horsemen in a landscape, the bowfronted base with 3 drawers, on small bracket feet, 21in (53cm).
£750–900 *RBB*

A Louis XVI carved and gilded frame, with stiff-leaf raised outer edge, a flute and husk centre, acanthus corners and rope-twist sight edge, 18in (46cm) wide.
£2,000–2,500 *C*

A Victorian mahogany cheval mirror, with arched plate and pierced supports, on a serpentine platform base, with moulded splayed feet, c1850, 64½ by 37in (164 by 94cm).
£350–400 *S(S)*

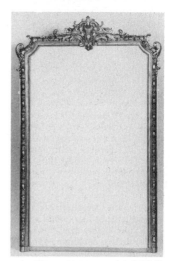

A giltwood overmantel, 19thC, 81in (205cm) high.
£1,000–1,500 *FLE*

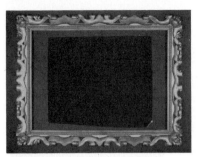

An Italian carved and gilded frame, the pierced scrolling border with putti at the corners, with cresting and cable raised inner edge, 17thC, 47½in (120cm) wide.
£4,500–5,500 *C*

A Victorian mahogany framed cheval dressing mirror, on scroll supports and casters, slight damage, 34½in (87cm) wide.
£500–700 *S(S)*

An Italian carved and gilded frame, with foliate edges and acanthus scotia, 17thC, 22in (56cm) wide.
£7,800–9,000 *C*

A Dutch carved tortoiseshell frame, with ebonised ripple inner and outer edges and oval sight edge, 17thC, 8½in (21cm) wide.
£3,000–3,500 *C*

A Basque carved frame, inlaid with bone engraved flowerheads, 17thC, 5½in (14cm) wide.
£1,500–2,000 *C*

An Italian carved, gilded and painted frame, with pierced scrolling acanthus border, 17thC, 13in (33in) wide.
£450–650 *C*

Screens

A George IV parcel gilt rosewood cheval fire screen, with painted silk panel of a medieval castle, on gilt scroll supports, sabre feet and padded footrest, c1820, 20in (51cm) wide.
£1,800-2,200 *S*

An ebonised and polychrome painted four-leaf screen, decorated in naturalistic colours with birds amongst fruiting foliage, 75in (191cm) high.
£900-1,200 *CSK*

A Continental screen, each of the 6 panels with a rococo carved giltwood border incorporating painted canvas reserves of children hunting, dancing and harvesting, the painting after the style of Johan Conrad Zekatz, probably German, c1890, 114in (290cm) high.
£6,000-7,000 *S*

A Dutch rococo painted and parcel gilt leather four-panel screen, in 12 parts, depicting figures in a landscape setting at various pursuits, in tones of red, blue, green, rose, beige and brown, 78½in (199cm) high.
£2,800-3,200 *S(NY)*

A Dutch painted leather four-leaf screen, with birds, scrolling foliage and strapwork, in gold and green within close studded borders, extensively restored, late 18thC, 86in (219cm) high.
£2,500-3,000 *CSK*

A polychrome painted and gilt embossed leather screen, the 3 panels with arched tops, each with a flower filled cartouche panel, restored, 19thC, 84in (213cm) high.
£2,000-2,500 *CSK*

A three-fold screen, with 2 papier mâché panels painted with peacocks, exotic birds, flowers, foliage and gilt heightened decoration, signed 'Robert Winn, Birmingham', the giltwood frame in Chinese Chippendale manner, mid-19thC, 96in (244cm) high.
£3,500-5,500 *P(O)*

A pair of William IV rosewood pole screens, each japanned cartouche-shaped panel depicting Scottish hunting scenes, on foliate clasped and baluster turned column, above concave sided platform base, with turned feet, 56in (142cm) high.
£800-1,000 *CSK*

A mahogany four-leaf screen, each leaf with 2 later glass panels, restored, probably previously lined, stamped '1 2 3 4' twice, 78in (198cm) high.
£2,500-3,500 *C*

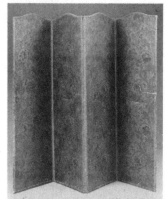

A Dutch polychrome painted and gilt four-leaf screen, each arched leaf embossed with birds of paradise amongst flowering foliage and butterflies painted in naturalistic colours, some damage, 19thC, 78½in (199cm) high.
£1,000-1,500 *CSK*

Screens

Screens were made in England from the 17thC and designed to keep out draughts as well as to decorate a room. They consist of a series of hinged boards, made in a variety of materials from lacquered or polished wood to wood frames covered in canvas, leather, paper or needlework.

Those made from delicate materials have often suffered from ill-treatment and have needed extensive restoration. The extent to which this detracts from the value will depend on the degree of damage and the calibre of restoration. Close inspection should be made of the front surface area and also of the back, which is invariably quite plain.

Some screens are very large, especially those from the 18thC, which can be as many as eight folds wide. Over the years some of these have been divided to make smaller screens. These may be missing a border at one end, the design may stop abruptly or appear to be incomplete.

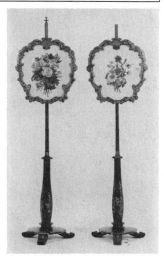

A pair of papier mâché pole screens, with botanical subjects painted on velvet, the columns decorated in gilt.
£900-1,200 *L&E*

Use the Index!

Because certain items might fit easily into any number of categories, the quickest and surest method of locating any entry is by reference to the index at the back of the book.

This has been fully cross-referenced for absolute simplicity.

Settees

A George III fruitwood hall settee of Chinese Chippendale design, with geometric trellis back, over solid seat, raised on square section supports.
£800–1,000 *BIR*

A Knole sofa, covered in worn purple velvet, the back with 18thC French floral tapestry, on concealed ceramic casters, damaged, 17thC, 85in (216cm).
£1,500–2,000 *S(S)*

A George I style mahogany double chair back settee, with padded drop-in seat, cabriole legs, carved at the knees with shells, with claw-and-ball feet, 50in (127cm).
£2,500–3,500 *JNic*

A Charles II style carved walnut and caned settle, the pierced scroll cresting surmounted by cherubs supporting a monogrammed roundel with the initials 'R.H.,' and a motto border, 'Honi Soit Qui Mal y Pense', the back and seat with scrolled open arms, on turned and S-scroll supports joined by conforming stretchers, early 20thC, 58in (146cm).
£1,000–1,500 *S(S)*

A George III style mahogany triple chair back settee, and a pair of matching armchairs, the slip-in seats covered in gold damask, the cabriole legs joined by stretchers, settee damaged, c1910, 81in (206cm).
£5,000–6,000 *S(S)*

A Regency mahogany and upholstered scroll-end settee, covered in distressed gold velvet, with 2 squab cushions, the reeded frame with a gadrooned cresting, the sabre legs with brass cappings and casters, c1810, 89in (210cm).
£2,000–3,000 *S(S)*

A Regency rosewood and brass inlaid sofa, with padded back and central tablet cresting flanked by gadrooned scrolls, overscrolled ends, on sabre legs headed with foliate cut brass tablets, terminating in brass paw cappings, 92in (234cm).
£1,200–1,700 *CSK*

A George III Sheraton serpentine back sofa, upholstered and covered in faded chintz, on square legs joined by stretchers.
£850–1,000 *L&E*

A Victorian rosewood and upholstered scroll end chaise longue, covered in green striped silk, with squab cushion, on sabre legs, c1840, 77in (198cm).
£750–1,200 *S(S)*

A George IV rosewood and upholstered scroll end settee, inlaid with cut brass, covered in gold damask, with 2 squab cushions, on turned and reeded legs ending in brass cappings and casters, damaged, c1825, 94in (209cm).
£1,200–1,700 *S(S)*

A mid-Victorian rosewood twin chair back sofa, 76in (193cm).
£850–1,000 *CSK*

A Regency simulated bamboo triple chairback settee, each back with railed top above an X-shaped splat, with curved arms, on turned tapering legs, the squab cushion covered in green and white patterned material, the seat replaced with a solid panel, with metal corner blocks, 56in (142cm).
£1,000–1,800 *C*

A William IV giltwood sofa, with
pale blue upholstery, 93in (236cm).
£4,500–5,500 *CSK*

An Edwardian mahogany and
marquetry rococo design drawing
room suite, comprising a pair of
armchairs and a 2 seater settee,
inlaid throughout with ivory
acanthus scrolls and stringing,
on cabriole legs with scroll
feet, c1910.
£2,500–3,500 *S(S)*

A Victorian carved walnut and
button upholstered settee, on
turned and fluted legs with
ceramic casters, c1860,
76in (193cm).
£2,700–3,300 *S(S)*

A Regency ormolu mounted
ebonised settee, with serpentine
padded back, out-scrolled arms
and seat covered in red velvet,
the back centred by a patera
flanked by foliage, on reeded
sabre legs and brass caps,
remounted, 87½in (222cm).
£2,500–3,000 *C*

An early Victorian rosewood sofa,
the padded back, squab cushion
and splayed sides covered in red
floral damask, the back flanked
by scroll finials, on gadrooned
turned tapering legs and later
brass caps, 85½in (217cm).
£1,700–2,200 *C*

*The palmette enriched and voluted
arm supports, and flowered tablet
above reeded columnar legs, relate
to the George IV 'antique' or
Grecian style that continued to be
popular into the early years of
Queen Victoria's reign.*

A William IV rosewood sofa, with
padded back and foliate carved
overscroll ends, on stylised foliate
clasped tapering legs, 75in (191cm).
£2,700–3,300 *CSK*

A Victorian mahogany settee,
with serpentine scrolling back
with roll-over ends, exposed
carved show frame, on short
turned legs.
£650–750 *Mit*

A Regency ebonised and parcel gilt settee, on turned tapering legs, brass caps and ceramic casters, the casters stamped 'PMS' beneath a crown, one leg broken, 80in (203cm).
£1,000–1,500 *C*

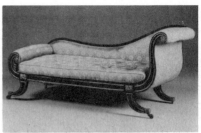

A Regency simulated rosewood and parcel gilt chaise longue, covered in patterned green silk, on sabre legs headed by flower heads, with brass caps, 77in (196cm).
£3,500–4,000 *C*

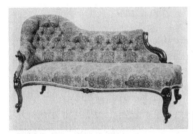

A Biedermeier walnut sofa, with padded back and outscrolled arms, padded seat, on scroll feet, early 19thC, 85in (216cm).
£800–1,200 *CSK*

A mid-Victorian walnut sofa, on foliate headed cabriole legs with scroll feet, 53in (135cm).
£1,500–2,000 *CSK*

A Victorian rosewood single high end couch, with buttoned back, serpentine front, covered in floral tapestry, with cabriole legs, carved with scrolls and leaves, 72in (182cm).
£750–850 *WIL*

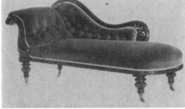

A Victorian mahogany and button upholstered chaise longue, covered in purple velvet, on gadrooned turned feet and casters, 73in (185cm) long.
£700–1,000 *S(S)*

A fruitwood daybed, with arched back, foliate carved outswept ends and padded seat on splayed legs, probably Austrian, mid-19thC, 47in (120cm).
£850–1,200 *CSK*

An Edwardian mahogany framed settee with camel back, winged arms, cabriole legs with carved shoulders, on claw-and-ball feet.
£500–700 *M*

An Edwardian matched mahogany, satinwood and ivory inlaid salon suite, comprising 2 low seat chairs, 4 side chairs, 2 armchairs and a settee, with vase shaped splats, bowed seats and gold fabric upholstery, 39in (100cm).
£1,300–1,700 *S(S)*

A mahogany sofa, with padded back, outscrolled arms, squab cushions, square fluted legs, the casters stamped 'Bartholomew & Fletcher', with floral loose covers, 80in (203cm).
£1,600–2,000 *CSK*

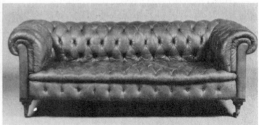

A Chesterfield sofa, the button back, outswept arms and seat in red leather upholstery, on turned tapered legs.
£3,500–4,500 *CSK*

A walnut and burr walnut triple chair back settee, on cabriole legs with claw-and-ball feet, damaged and repaired, 61in (155cm).
£1,700–2,200 *CSK*

A Biedermeier style mahogany and gilt decorated sofa, with block feet, c1900, 69in (175cm).
£1,200–1,700 *CSK*

An Empire style giltwood sofa, the padded back with reeded and scrolled top rail, above similar downswept arms on winged female bust supports, padded seat, on fluted square tapering legs, 48in (122cm).
£900–1,200 *CSK*

A Louis XV style walnut sofa, and a pair of matching tub armchairs, sofa 82in (208cm).
£1,000–1,500 *CSK*

A Louis XVI style giltwood duchesse brisée, with foliate carved arched top rail above padded arms on paterae-headed fluted tapering legs, 80in (203cm).
£1,800–2,200 *CSK*

A Victorian walnut settee, the frame carved with flower heads, with arched button back, sides and seat, on turned tapering fluted legs.
£800–1,000 *CSK*

A Louis XVI style giltwood and cream upholstered canapé, on foliate headed fluted legs, late 19thC, 52in (132cm).
£1,200–1,700 *CSK*

A giltwood canapé, upholstered in yellow damask, on foliate headed cabriole legs, probably Italian, mid-19thC, 84in (213cm).
£1,500–1,800 *CSK*

Locate the source
The source of each illustration in Miller's can be found by checking the code letters below each caption with the list of contributors.

A Louis XVI style carved giltwood occasional sofa, 19thC.
£2,000–2,500 *M*

A Syrian mother-of-pearl and bone inlaid triple chair back sofa, with overall profuse geometrical and foliate decoration, pierced arched panelled back, padded seat and square legs, 59in (150cm).
£1,000–1,500 *CSK*

A kelim upholstered sofa, with padded back and arms, on ring turned legs, 84in (213.5cm).
£1,800–2,200 *CSK*

A French style giltwood three-piece salon suite, comprising a settee and 2 wing back armchairs, with elaborate pink floral upholstery, on cabriole forelegs with carved knees.
£1,000–1,700 *BWe*

Sideboards

An inlaid walnut and parcel gilt sideboard, the crossbanded top with scrolling foliate marquetry, above 3 frieze drawers, on foliate headed faceted tapering legs joined by flattened stretchers, on bun feet, 50½in (151cm).
£1,000–1,500 *CSK*

A George III mahogany bowfronted sideboard, inlaid throughout with satinwood bandings, stringing and harewood medallions, the top now with a three-quarter gallery, the 3 frieze drawers and a door surrounding an arched apron, on tapered square legs, c1790, 72in (183cm).
£4,000–4,500 *S(S)*

A George III style mahogany serpentine fronted sideboard, with shallow raised back, tambour enclosures and drawers, on tapered square legs, c1935, 66in (168cm).
£1,000–1,500 *S(S)*

A George III mahogany, line inlaid satinwood and crossbanded bowfronted sideboard, with central frieze drawer flanked by cupboard door and cellaret drawer, on square tapering legs and spade feet, superstructure missing, 61in (155cm).
£2,000–2,500 *CSK*

A George III mahogany inlaid and bowfronted sideboard, with frieze drawer flanked by 2 cellaret drawers and 2 small cupboards, on square tapering legs, 71in (181cm).
£3,800–4,200 *MEA*

A George III Sheraton design serpentine fronted sideboard, the brass curtain rail to back with adjustable twin scroll candle branches at centre and urn finials, the top and shaped sides with wide kingwood banding, damaged, some later inlay, 54in (137cm). **£3,000–4,000** *CAG*

A late George III mahogany and ebonised line inlaid bowfronted sideboard, formerly with a back rail, restored, 72in (183cm).
£3,200–3,700 *CSK*

A George IV mahogany bowfronted sideboard, 35½in (90cm).
£2,000–3,000 *MEA*

A George III and later mahogany bowfronted sideboard, with satinwood crossbanding, 3 drawers, on tapered square legs and spade feet, 66in (168cm).
£2,000–2,500 *S(S)*

A mahogany and satinwood inlaid breakfront sideboard, the brass rail above crossbanded top, with one short drawer and 2 cupboards, late 19thC.
£800–1,000 *BIR*

A Regency mahogany and line inlaid bowfronted sideboard, with central frieze drawer and arched apron, flanked by deep drawers, on ring turned legs, some later inlay, 48in (122.5cm).
£1,200–1,700 *CSK*

A painted satinwood pedestal sideboard, with handpainted floral swags, cherubs and courting couples, 64in (162.5cm).
£3,000–3,500 *Mit*

A George III brass inlaid mahogany sideboard, crossbanded overall in kingwood, with a long frieze drawer simulated as 3 drawers, above an arched central tambour slide enclosing a green baize lined interior, flanked by a deep green baize lined drawer and a door, on convex fronted square tapering legs and splayed feet, restored, 85in (216.5cm).
£2,000–3,000 *C*

A Regency mahogany sideboard, inlaid with ebonised lines, on ring turned tapered legs and toupie feet, 70½in (179cm).
£2,500–3,000 *CSK*

A Regency style mahogany bowfronted sideboard, with fluted frieze, the central drawer flanked by a door and deep cellaret drawer, on square tapering legs with spade feet, stamped 'Gill & Reigate', 84in (214cm).
£1,700–2,200 *CSK*

Infilled Sideboards

In the Victorian period, the empty area between the pedestals was quite often infilled to provide extra storage space.

This type of sideboard was produced in large numbers and varied in quality.

Those with carved decoration and surmounted by a large mirror tend to be very fine quality.

A Victorian mahogany sideboard, 55in (140cm).
£530–600 *WIL*

A Victorian mahogany sideboard, with shaped back and 3 ogee outlined drawers, above 3 arch panelled doors, on plinth base, 59½in (151cm).
£650–750 *Bri*

An Edwardian mahogany line inlaid serpentine fronted sideboard, 73in (185.5cm).
£1,700–2,200 *CSK*

A George IV mahogany serpentine sideboard, crossbanded overall in kingwood and inlaid with boxwood lines, restored, previously with brass superstructure, the lock stamped 'Patent GRS' beneath a crown, 77½in (197cm).
£5,000–6,000 *C*

An Edwardian Adam style mahogany pedestal sideboard, decorated with drapery and bellflower hung urns, on plinth bases, with 'John Barker & Co. Ltd., Cromwell Crescent, W.' depository label, stamped 'Earl of Rosslyn', 84in (214cm).
£550–650 *CSK*

An Edwardian Sheraton revival serpentine fronted sideboard, the rail back supported on 3 square tapered uprights, the boxwood and chequer strung top above a central frieze drawer, flanked by cupboard doors with brass ring handles, raised on square tapered legs, 54in (137cm).
£850–1,000 *DMC*

A late George III mahogany and line inlaid bowfronted sideboard, on square tapering legs with spade feet, possibly associated, restored, 48in (122cm).
£1,500–2,000 *CSK*

Stands

A Yorkshire beech and brass umbrella stand, by A. K. Co., stamped and dated '1880', 20in (51cm).
£350–450 *DMT*

A William IV mahogany folio stand with one folding side, on turned supports, altered, 38½in (98cm).
£1,200–1,700 *MEA*

A William IV rosewood folio stand, with adjustable slatted supports on channelled uprights, dual splayed legs joined by a stretcher, 33in (84cm).
£2,200–2,700 *CSK*

A late Victorian black lacquer and decorated papier mâché music stand, the cartouche shaped adjustable rest with mother-of-pearl inlay, the extending support housed in a turned bulbous column, with shaped platform base and moulded legs, with a plaque 'Chinnock's patent', 17in (43cm).
£170–200 *CSK*

A William IV rosewood double-sided music stand, with adjustable height turned column support, circular base with 3 downswept scrolling feet.
£750–850 *Mit*

A Yorkshire umbrella stand, by A. K. Co., stamped and dated '1880', 9in (22.5cm).
£350–500 *DMT*

A Charles X mahogany folio stand, the tapered X-frame side supports with scroll top rails, on outswept legs, one support later, with stencil mark 'C. Talmy Jme', 28in (72cm).
£450–650 *P*

Steps

An Italian baroque walnut folding lectern, each double scrolled support headed by a female term continuing to foliage, with a tasseled velvet shelf joined by stretchers, on paw feet replacements, 64in (162.5cm).
£3,000–4,000 *CNY*

A set of commode steps, with original faux bamboo decoration, c1820. **£400–800** *CAI*

A set of Victorian mahogany three-tread folding library steps, the top with moulded edge, on splayed supports joined by side stretchers, 28in (71cm) high.
£1,800–2,000 *C*

A set of George IV mahogany metamorphic library steps, with 4 leather inset treads, converting to a low table with leather inset, on turned feet with brass casters, 35in (89cm) high.
£1,400–2,000 *DN*

A set of Georgian style mahogany library steps, formed as 4 graduated steps to a centre pole with ringed detail.
£350–400 *GAK*

Library Steps

Library steps were introduced in the middle of the 18thC, and continued to be made throughout the 19thC.

Most are small, the standard height being 36in (91.5cm), although the steps made in 1790 for Althorpe, the Princess of Wales' family seat, stands 108in (274cm) high, with a seat and book rest at the top.

Stools

A George II walnut stool, covered in later floral needlework on a brown ground, on cabriole legs and pad feet, 25in (64cm).
£2,300–3,000 *C*

A pair of 17thC style walnut stools, with gros point needlework upholstered tops, on spirally turned supports and bun feet, joined by spirally turned stretchers, minor variations, 19½in (49.5cm).
£3,700–4,200 *C(S)*

A George III design mahogany dressing stool, the gros point needlework upholstered top above a shaped rockwork and foliate carved frieze, on acanthus carved cabriole supports with claw-and-ball feet, 26in (66cm).
£500–600 *C(S)*

A George III mahogany window seat, with scrolled ends, covered in ivory floral silk damask, on reeded turned tapering legs and bun feet, 52in (132cm).
£1,500–1,800 *C*

A George III style mahogany serpentine window seat, 42in (107cm).
£700–800 *CSK*

A Regency simulated rosewood stool, with square tapestry seat, moulded X-shaped supports with central rosette decoration, joined by turned stretcher, on later bun feet, 15in (38cm) square.
£450–650 *CSK*

A Regency style mahogany stool, with gros point needlework upholstered top, on turned and fluted tapering supports, 21½in (54.5cm), and another similar.
£1,000–1,400 *C(S)*

A Victorian ottoman stool, the hinged top with a floral beadwork panel, the sides in red velvet, on a gilt plinth, 20in (51cm).
£400–500 *CSK*

A George IV rosewood X-framed stool, with a padded saddle seat, the moulded frame with gilt lines, with carved rosettes and a turned stretcher, on scroll feet, 22½in (57cm).
£700–800 *DN*

A pair of Victorian giltwood serpentine stools, from Buckingham Palace, each with a flower carved apron upholstered in contemporary but distressed silk needlework of roses, with cabriole legs, Buckingham Palace inventory mark 'VR BP No. 235 1866', with a paper label, written in pencil 'Room No. 234', one inventory mark obliterated and label removed, c1850, 17in (43cm).
£4,000–5,000 *S*

A pair of Edwardian line inlaid mahogany X-framed stools, with padded seats and roundel decoraion, 21in (53cm).
£1,200–1,700 *CSK*

An Italian 17thC style carved giltwood stool, with human and lion's masks, the gold velvet seat above acanthus clad legs and claw feet, c1870, 37in (94cm).
£1,500–2,000 *S(S)*

A pair of simulated rosewood and parcel gilt X-framed stools, each covered in yellow fringed red velvet, the legs with roundels and on bun feet, 28in (71cm).
£1,800–2,000 *C*

A pair of Regency mahogany stools in the manner of Gillows, covered in close nailed green velvet, on reeded turned tapering legs and splayed turned feet, the shape and seat rails altered, 18½in (47cm).
£2,000–2,700 *C*

A Turkish wicker window seat, by Heywood Brothers, c1880.
£500–700 *DMT*

An Edwardian inlaid mahogany piano stool, 21in (53cm).
£400–450 *SUL*

A mahogany piano stool, c1900, 23½in (60cm).
£250–275 *SUL*

An early Victorian mahogany stool, with padded seat, on X-framed supports with roundels joined by a baluster turned stretcher, 20in (51cm).
£500–800 *CSK*

A buttoned footstool, 30in (76cm) diam.
£100–125 *SUL*

Torchères

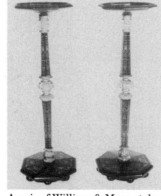

A pair of Regency style torchères, 27½in (70cm) high. **£300–350** *SUL*

A pair of William & Mary style ebonised and parcel gilt seaweed marquetry torchères, each with hexagonal stem, carved with fret collar and centre boss, on an octagonal inlaid platform with 8 bun feet, 44½in (112cm) high. **£3,000–3,500** *MEA*

A carved fruitwood cherub torchère, 42in (106.5cm) high. **£650–750** *SUL*

A pair of ebonised and gilt decorated torchères, each with simulated marble top on fluted tapering uprights, joined by stretchers with cross central paterae, on paw feet, 39in (99cm) high. **£850–1,000** *CSK*

A pair of carved beech torchères, each with octagonal top above a carved pheasant, the foliate carved column on naturalistic base, 40in (102cm). **£2,000–2,500** *CSK*

A pair of walnut torchères, each octagonal top inlaid with a central stellar design, on baluster turned and spiral twist column with splayed scroll legs, 14½in (37cm). **£1,500–1,700** *CSK*

A George III mahogany architect's table, with ratcheted top, above extending uprights, restored, 41in (104cm). **£1,200–1,800** *CSK*

Architects' Tables

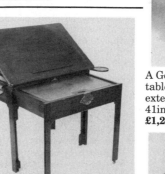

A George III mahogany architect's table, the adjustable top with a ratchet support, removable book or chart rest, above a shelf with rounded corners, on trestle supports, joined by a turned stretcher on sabre legs, c1810, 41in (104cm). **£3,000–3,500** *MEA*

A George III mahogany architect's table, the pull-out front revealing fitted interior. **£1,800–2,500** *BWe*

A south German mahogany and parcel gilt architect's table, with trellis pattern adjustable reading slope, on square tapering legs and block feet, late 18thC, 35½in (90cm). **£4,500–5,500** *C*

A late George III mahogany architect's table, with ratcheted top, on adjustable square section supports joined by turned stetcher with downswept legs, restored, 36in (91cm). **£900–1,200** *CSK*

Breakfast Tables

A late George III mahogany and rosewood crossbanded breakfast table, on turned column and ebonised line inlaid downswept legs, possibly associated, 57½in (146cm).
£1,200–1,700 *CSK*

Breakfast Tables

Most 18thC breakfast tables are rectangular with rounded corners. Round and oval examples from this period are rare, although from the early 19thC round examples on a pedestal or platform base are as plentiful as rectangular tables.

The finest examples incorporate crossbanded decoration, and may have cast gilt metal feet, intricate brass line inlay, or gilt metal moulding around the base of the frieze.

Large examples, to seat 8 or more, are rarer and considerably more expensive than smaller tables of equal quality.

A William IV rosewood breakfast table, with circular tip-up top, on faceted baluster turned shaft and trefoil platform with bun feet, 55½in (141cm) diam.
£1,500–2,000 *CSK*

A George III style mahogany and satinwood crossbanded tilt-top breakfast table, on quadruple splayed supports ending in brass paw feet and casters, 53in (135cm) diam. **£800–1,000** *S(S)*

A Napoleon III ebonised and gilt metal mounted breakfast table, with oval top, on fluted column and scroll feet, 54in (137cm).
£900–1,200 *CSK*

A Victorian walnut breakfast table, the top with matched burr walnut quarter veneered panels, inlaid with boxwood leaf scroll arabesque motifs and ebony stringings, on central column composed of 4 turned, fluted and lobed supports with turned circular centre tier, on 4 leaf capped scroll supports, 52in (132cm) long.
£1,700–2,000 *CAG*

A William IV rosewood circular breakfast table, with tip-up top, turned column with gadrooned collar, triform platform base with concave sides and reeded bun feet, 47½in (121cm) diam.
£1,200–1,500 *CSK*

A William IV mahogany breakfast table, with gadrooned edge, on foliate scroll carved triform column with concave sided platform base and hairy paw feet, 54in (137cm) diam.
£1,200–1,700 *CSK*

A Victorian walnut breakfast table, with figured quarter veneered top, plain apron and on turned central column with carved bulbous knop, 59in (149.5cm) long.
£1,000–1,500 *CAG*

A Regency mahogany breakfast table, with tip-up top, on ring turned shaft and 4 splayed legs, the top possibly re-used, 56in (142cm).
£700–1,000 *CSK*

A Regency mahogany breakfast table, with crossbanded top, on ring turned column and fluted downswept legs, repaired, 54in (137cm).
£1,500–2,000 *CSK*

A late George III mahogany breakfast table, with tip-up top, on turned tapering column with 3 splayed legs with brass terminals, 46½in (118cm).
£700–900 *DN*

A Regency mahogany breakfast table, the top with rounded corners, on reeded shaft with 4 channelled hipped splayed legs, 42in (107cm).
£2,500–3,000 *CSK*

A William IV rosewood breakfast table, with tip-up top, on foliate clasped turned column with concave sided platform base and turned feet, one later, bolts missing, 50in (127cm) diam.
£1,000–1,500 *CSK*

A rosewood crossbanded, line inlaid mahogany breakfast table, the circular radially veneered top on turned column with 4 splayed scroll legs, restored, early 19thC, 47½in (120cm) wide.
£2,200–2,500 *CSK*

A Regency line inlaid breakfast table, the crossbanded rounded rectangular top on ring turned column and 4 splayed legs, restored, 53½in (136cm) wide.
£1,200–1,500 *CSK*

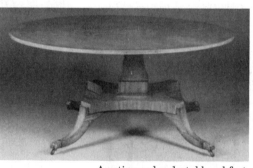

An early Victorian mahogany breakfast table, with moulded tip-up top and bulbous column with stylised collar, on quatrefoil platform base and foliate carved scroll feet, 62in (157cm) wide.
£1,200–1,800 *CSK*

Miller's is a price GUIDE not a price LIST.

A satinwood pedestal breakfast table, the banded circular moulded top on a square spreading support with concave sided platform base on splayed legs, lions' paw brass caps and casters, 66in (166cm) diam.
£1,800–2,200 *CSK*

A Victorian rosewood tilt-top breakfast table, on bulbous column with ovolo motifs, on leaf and scroll carved quadruple splay supports, 60in (152cm).
£800–1,000 *MCA*

A mid-Victorian burr walnut and marquetry breakfast table, with inlaid top, on ring turned uprights with central turned finial, on foliate headed cabriole legs with foliate scroll feet, 52½in (133cm).
£1,200–1,700 *CSK*

An early Victorian walnut breakfast table, with radially veneered top, on faceted tapering column and circular platform base with paw feet, 48in (122cm).
£1,500–2,000 *CSK*

Card Tables

A Regency mahogany and rosewood crossbanded line inlaid card table, with hinged top above a geometrically inlaid tablet, on ebonised turned baluster column, quadripartite platform with splayed legs, 36in (92cm).
£900–1,200 *CSK*

A mid-Georgian mahogany card table, with eared top, frieze drawer, on cabriole legs with pad feet, restored, 33in (84cm).
£1,500–2,000 *CSK*

A George III mahogany and crossbanded serpentine fronted card table, with fold-over top, the turned and stop fluted tapering legs surmounted by oval paterae, on leaf carved feet, restored, c1780, 36½in (93cm).
£2,000–2,700 *S(S)*

A George III mahogany card table, c1780, 34½in (88cm).
£1,000–1,500 *S(S)*

A George III mahogany and marquetry demi-lune card table, the crossbanded top with inlaid fan and boxwood lines, on square tapering legs with spade feet, 36in (91.5cm).
£1,000–1,200 *CSK*

A George III satinwood serpentine shaped fold-over card table, with mahogany crossbanded top and later painted floral decoration.
£2,500–3,500 *MEA*

A George III mahogany and parquetry D-shaped double gateleg action card table, crossbanded overall with amaranth and inlaid with boxwood lines, the trellis work headed square tapering legs inlaid with a needle, on block feet, brass caps and casters, the later lock stamped 'Secure Lever', restored, 40in (101.5cm).
£1,000–1,500 *C*

A George III mahogany semi-circular card table, with crossbanding and boxwood stringing, c1790, 36in (92cm).
£2,000–2,500 *S(S)*

A George II mahogany card table, opening to reveal baize inset, counter wells and candle stands, the frieze with a small drawer, on acanthus carved cabriole legs ending in claw-and-ball feet, c1745, 34in (81cm). **£2,000–2,700** *S(S)*

A George III satinwood and painted card table, the top crossbanded in amaranth, decorated overall with flowers and crossbanded in tulipwood, on block feet, later decorated, 36in (91.5cm).
£2,500–3,500 *C*

A Regency mahogany pedestal card table, the crossbanded and inlaid top with canted corners, on quadruple reeded splayed feet, warped, c1810, 36in (91cm).
£1,800–2,000 *S(S)*

A George IV mahogany pedestal card table, inlaid with satinwood banding and stylised motifs, c1825, 36in (92cm).
£1,200–1,700 *S(S)*

A Regency rosewood card table, the fold-over top with cut brass stringing, the twin turned pillars above quadruple splayed legs with ornate brass cappings and casters, damaged, c1810, 33in (90cm).
£1,000–1,400 S(S)

A Regency brass inlaid rosewood card table, with hinged top above turned column, on circular platform and 4 splayed legs, base detached, 36in (92cm).
£1,000–1,500 CSK

A Regency rosewood and brass inlaid pedestal card table, with tooled green leather inset, on quadruple base, c1810, 34in (87cm).
£3,000–3,500 S(S)

A George IV rosewood card table, with X-shaped supports joined by a reeded pole stretcher, 32in (81cm).
£1,200–1,500 S(S)

A late Regency rosewood card table, with crossbanded baize lined hinged top, 34in (87cm).
£1,500–2,000 P

A George III mahogany serpentine card table, with eared top, on square channelled legs with pierced spandrels, the back legs with concertina action, one hinge stamped 'H. Tibats', 35in (89cm).
£2,000–2,500 CSK

Numerous fine mid-18thC card tables are found stamped with this name on the concertina mechanism.

A pair of George IV rosewood card tables, with baize lined hinged tops, on tapering polygonal columns, quadripartite platforms with scroll feet and casters, 36in (92cm).
£1,800–2,500 P

A Regency rosewood D-shaped fold-over card table, with decorative brass inlay, supported on a tapered square section pedestal, with quadruple scroll legs terminating in brass claw feet and casters, 36in (91.5cm).
£1,800–2,200 MAT

A Regency rosewood card table, with gilt metal mounts, the fold-over top with cut brass inlaid stringing and spear motifs, on a knopped pillar and quadruple scroll legs with casters, c1815, 36in (91.5cm).
£2,000–3,000 S(S)

A mahogany patience table, with green baize inset, on turned barley-twist legs, c1830, 18½in (47cm) square.
£550–650 STA

A burr walnut, marquetry and
ebonised crossbanded and inlaid
card table, on turned tapering
fluted legs, with ormolu edging,
19thC, 34in (86cm).
£1,000–1,500 *MCA*

A Victorian burr walnut fold-over
card table, with inset green baize
playing surface, on quadripartite
base with casters.
£800–1,000 *BWe*

A late Victorian rosewood and
marquetry envelope card table,
with overall foliate scroll
decoration, frieze drawer and
scroll supports, centred with a
reeded column, on arched legs,
21½in (55cm).
£1,200–1,700 *CSK*

A rosewood card table,
36in (91.5cm).
£1,500–1,850 *SUL*

A Regency card table, with
crossbanded canted top above
turned column, on hipped splayed
legs, restored, 36in (91.5cm).
£800–1,200 *CSK*

A William IV rosewood veneered
card table, with baize lined D-
shape swivel top, the top flap with
rope edge, 36in (91.5cm).
£750–900 *WW*

A Dutch walnut, feather
banded and floral marquetry
card table, with profuse overall
floral and bird inlay, the hinged
top with concertina action, on
turned tapering legs with pad
feet, mid-18thC, restored and
repaired, 31in (78cm).
£2,000–2,500 *CSK*

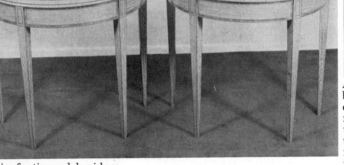

A pair of satinwood demi-lune
card tables, the crossbanded
folding tops with green baize
interiors, on tapering legs,
33½in (85cm).
£2,000–2,700 *JNic*

A pair of George III line inlaid
mahogany card tables, each with
crossbanded top, on square
tapering legs, restored, 34in (83cm).
£1,600–2,500 *CSK*

A mahogany card table, with
concertina action, mid-18thC
with later carving, restored,
34in (86cm).
£1,200–1,700 *CSK*

A walnut card table, with eared
line inlaid top above concertina
action and central frieze drawer,
on cabriole legs with pointed pad
feet, damaged, 34½in (87.5cm).
£2,500–3,000 *CSK*

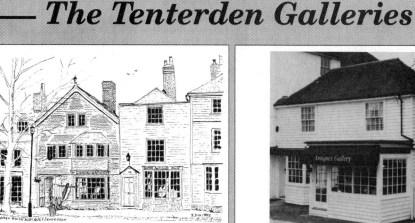

An Edwardian rosewood, mahogany and tulipwood banded card table, inlaid with chequer stringing, on square tapering legs, 20in (51cm).
£550–700 *CSK*

A pair of Regency rosewood brass mounted card tables, the crossbanded tops inlaid with satinwood banding, each opening to reveal a baize lined surface, above a frieze inlaid with brass anthemion decoration and beaded edge, on turned pedestal, with 4 splayed legs with similar brass decoration, brass paw feet and casters, 36in (91.5cm).
£5,000–6,000 *B*

An Edwardian inlaid mahogany envelope card table, the frieze drawer with a pair of gilt brass knob handles, on square tapering legs united by arched X-stretchers, on brown china casters, 31in (78.5cm).
£350–500 *MJB*

Centre Tables

A black lacquer and chinoiserie decorated tray top centre table, with overall decoration, with re-entrant corners, cabriole legs with pad feet, restored, early 18thC, 33in (84cm).
£3,000–3,500 *CSK*

An early Victorian rosewood serpentine centre table, with a drawer at each end, on reeded bulbous uprights and dual scroll legs, joined by a turned stretcher, 50in (127cm).
£1,000–1,400 *CSK*

A Victorian walnut topped centre table, 31in (79cm) diam.
£800–1,000 *DA*

A Victorian burr walnut centre table, on turned and carved end supports joined by a pole stretcher, with label on underside, 'George Spademan, Cabinet Maker and Upholsterer, Stamford', 47in (120cm).
£1,000–1,500 *S(S)*

A late Victorian mahogany, marquetry and mother-of-pearl inlaid centre table, on square channelled tapering legs, headed by bellflowers, with spade feet, 33½in (85cm).
£800–1,200 *CSK*

A mid-Victorian inlaid walnut and parcel gilt decorated centre table, the crossbanded top with central floral marquetry bouquet and floral border, above foliate carved bulbous column, on foliate carved splayed scrolled legs, restored, 52in (132cm) diam.
£3,600–4,200 *CSK*

A Continental gilt centre table, with circular specimen marble top, over trellis work arched frieze, 3 scroll supports headed with bearded masks, on square tapering legs united by a shaped stretcher with 3 masks, 32in (81cm) diam.
£3,200–4,000 *MEA*

A shaped rosewood centre table, on brass casters, united by shaped stretchers, mounted by a central carved urn, 19thC, 50in (127cm).
£900–1,200 *FLE*

An early Victorian rosewood centre table, with moulded brêche violette marble top, on foliate clasped end column supports with fluted and scroll decoration, on platform bases with paw feet, 59½in (151cm).
£3,000–3,500 *CSK*

A Victorian table, with quartered burr walnut top on 4 S-scroll supports, with central turned boss and final, splayed legs with scroll terminals and casters, 54in (137cm).
£1,700–2,200 *DN*

A Killarny yew wood veneered tip-up centre table, c1840, 49in (124cm) diam.
£5,500–6,500 *WIL*

An Edwardian rosewood veneered centre table, 31in (79cm) high.
£900–1,100 *WIL*

A Napoleon III boulle centre table, the serpentine top above a frieze drawer, the cabriole legs with caryatids and sabots, c1860, 50½in (128cm).
£2,000–2,500 *S(S)*

A Louis Philippe mahogany centre table, with white marble top, gadrooned shaft and foliate carved splayed legs with paw feet, 39in (99cm) diam.
£1,000–1,500 *CSK*

A Louis XVI style carved giltwood centre table, the shaped white marble top with a moulded edge, 19thC.
£1,700–2,000 *FLE*

A French walnut ebonised and marquetry centre table, the serpentine top with bevelled glass panel enclosing a central oval panel, decorated within marquetry panels, 19thC, 52in (132cm).
£3,300–5,000 *HSS*

A Italian baroque walnut centre table, with fluted edge, on later baluster turned legs joined by a flat stretcher, on bun feet, 39in (231cm).
£13,000–16,000 *CNY*

Console Tables

A Swiss elm, walnut and marquetry centre table, the top inlaid with rampant lions and geometric panels above a frieze drawer, on square tapering legs joined by stretchers, on block feet, 18thC and later, 40in (102.5cm).
£700–1,000 *CSK*

A pair of mottled grey-green and variegated green marble console tables, each on square stepped uprights, 47½in (120cm).
£1,500–2,000 *CSK*

An Anglo Indian ebonised and marquetry console table, mid-19thC, 30in (76cm).
£800–1,000 *CSK*

A late Victorian mahogany and parquetry centre table, the ten-sided tip-up top inlaid in geometric and stellar patterns with a variety of woods, 39½in (101cm).
£1,000–1,500 *CSK*

A rosewood and giltwood console table, with grained marble top above stiff-leaf decorated frieze, on female headed scrolled uprights with hoof feet, mirrored back and breakfront plinth base, mid-19thC, 29in (73cm).
£800–1,000 *CSK*

Miller's is a price GUIDE not a price LIST.

An Edwardian carved giltwood console table, the cabriole legs headed by shell carving, with trailing vines, terminating in scroll feet, 28in (71cm).
£700–800 *FLE*

A pair of Regency mahogany console tables, in the manner of George Smith. **£5,000–6,000** *B*

Dining Tables

A William IV mahogany console table, the green marble top above twin scroll cabriole supports, on concave plinth base, c1830, 51in (129.5cm).
£1,200–1,700 *S(S)*

A George II revival walnut and parcel gilt extending dining table, with an oval top, on carved cabriole legs with claw-and-ball feet, with 2 leaf extensions and winding key, 96in (244cm) fully extended. **£1,200–1,700** *S(S)*

A mahogany extending dining table, the top with a moulded edge resting on a replacement block, with ring turned column and splayed reeded quadripartite supports, with brass cappings and casters, 19thC, with one extra leaf, 60in (152cm) long extended.
£1,200–1,700 *P*

A mahogany three-section D-end dining table, including central drop flap section, the rounded top on square chamfered legs, late 18thC and later, 109in (277cm) fully extended.
£1,500–2,500 *CSK*

A Georgian mahogany twin pedestal dining table, with alterations, 90in (228cm) long.
£3,200–4,000 *MEA*

A mahogany dining table, the top with curved corners above shaped apron, on a stand of 4 turned column platform-design , on carved scrolled feet, with sockets and casters, 2 additional leaves, 19thC.
£2,000–3,000 *BWe*

A George III mahogany twin pedestal dining table, with 2 D-shaped end sections on turned shafts and downswept fluted legs with brass caps, reduced in size, each pedestal with one leg shortened, and one extra leaf, 81½in (207cm) extended.
£2,500–3,500 *C*

Dining Tables

- Large multi-pedestal dining tables with freestanding D-ends were common in 18thC and 19thC, but were broken up when considered to be unfashionable in the 20thC.

- Many items on the market are made up from various different pieces of furniture.

- Look for original square legs - later turned legs are less valuable.

- Any piece which has disguised screw holes, new fixings or unmatching timbers, is unlikely to be in original condition, so make further checks.

A George III mahogany extending dining table, with triple reeded edges to top, with D-shaped end section and a D-shaped drop end, on 8 turned legs, with unusual folding action, with 2 extra leaves, 84in (213cm) extended.
£2,800–3,500 *CAG*

A George IV mahogany triple pedestal dining table, with hipped splayed legs ending in brass paw feet and casters, with 2 extra leaves, 90in (228.5cm) extended.
£5,500–8,500 *S(S)*

A late Georgian mahogany dining table, 63in (160cm) diam.
£5,000–6,000 *WIL*

A Regency style mahogany line inlaid triple pedestal D-end dining table, on turned columns and splayed legs, 142in (355cm).
£2,500–3,000 *CSK*

A George IV mahogany dining table, with 2 D-shaped ends, the central section with 2 drop leaves, on 14 turned tapering legs with brass casters, 126in (320cm).
£6,000–8,000 *DN*

A Georgian mahogany dining table, with 6 loose leaves, 190in (480cm) extended.
£6,000–8,000 *HSS*

A mahogany dining table, on turned fluted legs, with fitted sockets and casters, with 2 additional leaves, 19thC.
£1,200–1,800 *BWe*

A late George IV mahogany dining table, in 2 sections, each with one drop leaf, raised on 12 ring turned legs, 104in (264cm) extended.
£5,000–7,000 *MEA*

A Regency mahogany 2 pedestal dining table, the underframe probably replaced, clips missing, 86in (219cm) extended.
£7,000–9,000 *C*

A William IV rosewood dining table, the tilt-top on a chamfered triangular spreading shaft, the tripartite platform with egg-and-dart moulding, on scrolled legs with casters, 54in (137cm) diam.
£1,500–2,500 *P*

A late Regency draw-leaf mahogany dining table, the top with a reeded edge, 2 end drawers, inlaid ebony string lines, gilt brass lion mask and ring handles and mounts, turned and spiral fluted legs, brass terminals and casters, 87½in (222cm) extended.
£2,500–3,500 *P(S)*

A Victorian mahogany dining table, 72in (182.5cm).
£1,000–1,500 *DaD*

A Regency style mahogany two pillar dining table, with D-ends, on vase turned columns, reeded triple splay bases, with brass toe caps and casters, with 2 spare leaves, 100in (254cm) extended.
£2,000–2,700 *RBB*

A mahogany D-end dining table, with 2 extra leaves, 120in (306cm) extended.
£5,200–5,700 *CSK*

An early Victorian mahogany dining table, on 8 turned and melon lobed legs, terminating with brass toe caps and casters, with leaf carrying case, 154in (390cm) extended.
£5,000–5,500 *WL*

An early Victorian mahogany dining table, with 2 extra leaves, 90in (229cm) extended.
£1,700–2,200 *CSK*

An early Victorian mahogany dining table, with rounded rectangular top above reeded tapering legs, top associated, 2 later extra leaves, restored, 99in (252cm) extended.
£2,000–3,000 *CSK*

A mahogany twin pedestal D-end dining table, on ring turned shafts and splayed legs, with 2 extra leaves, 110in (279cm) extended.
£2,300–3,000 *CSK*

A late Victorian walnut extending dining table, top associated, including 2 extra leaves and winder, 92in (234cm) extended.
£2,000–2,500 *CSK*

A Regency mahogany twin pedestal dining table, the top with panelled frieze, on ring turned column and foliate decorated quadruple supports, terminating in brass clasped paw cappings and casters, leaf supports adapted, with 3 additional leaves, 126in (320cm).
£4,500–5,500 *P*

A William IV mahogany twin pedestal dining table, the turned pedestals with 3 hipped supports, brass paw socket feet and casters, with one leaf, 68in (172cm).
£1,000–1,500 *Bri*

A mahogany dining table, the oval top with foliate carved edge above gadrooned frieze, on foliate scroll headed cabriole legs with claw-and-ball feet, including winder and 4 extra leaves, 146in (371cm) extended. £2,700–3,700 *CSK*

A mahogany and line inlaid D-end dining table, the crossbanded top and square tapering legs with spade feet, parts early 19thC, with one leaf, 72½in (184cm) extended.
£1,000–1,500 *CSK*

Display Tables

A mahogany kidney-shaped display table, with glazed hinged top, foliate marquetry border, on cabriole legs with shaped stretchers, 24½in (62cm).
£800–1,000 *DN*

A miniature tortoiseshell display case, with ormolu mounts and bevelled glass top, c1900.
£800–900 *AHL*

A Victorian walnut drum table, 29in (74cm) diam.
£1,800–2,000 *SUL*

Drum Tables

A George III style rosewood octagonal drum table, with foliate edged radially veneered top above 4 true and 4 dummy drawers, on triform foliate carved support centred with a finial, above foliate carved and pierced splayed legs terminating in scroll feet, one dummy drawer front loose, 23in (59cm) wide.
£1,500–2,000 *CSK*

A George III style mahogany drum table, the leather lined top above 4 true and 4 false drawers, on ring turned column and 4 channelled splayed legs, 48in (122cm) wide.
£2,500–3,000 *CSK*

A William IV oak drum table, the circular radially veneered top above 4 true and 4 false drawers, with reeded frieze and laurel leaf decorated turned column, on quadripartite platform base with scroll feet, veneer lifting, 51in (130cm) wide.
£2,000–2,500 *CSK*

A mahogany drum table, with revolving leather lined top, containing 4 frieze drawers and 4 dummy drawers, on turned column and reeded downswept legs, altered and restored, early 19thC, 46in (117cm) diam.
£2,000–2,500 *CSK*

An early Victorian mahogany octagonal drum table, the lined top above 2 true and 6 false drawers, on turned column with 3 splayed legs, some damage, 45in (114cm) wide.
£1,500–2,000 *CSK*

A Regency mahogany library drum table, inlaid overall with ebonised lines, the green leather lined top above 4 frieze drawers and 4 simulated drawers, on a turned shaft and panelled tripod base with downswept legs and brass caps, 35in (89cm) diam.
£4,500–6,000 *C*

A late George III mahogany and satinwood banded library drum table, the revolving circular moulded and lined top engraved with the numbers 1-4 above 4 frieze drawers, each fitted with a lock stamped 'J. Bramah' with 4 further false drawers, on a ring-turned support and 3 splayed legs with brass caps and casters, later ebonised handles, 40in (102cm).
£3,500–4,000 *CSK*

Dressing Tables

A mahogany bowfronted dressing table, with a three-quarter gallery, 2 frieze drawers, ebony stringing, and turned legs with casters, early 19thC, 37in (94cm). **£850–1,000** *DN*

A Regency mahogany drum table, the crossbanded top above 4 hinged triangular mahogany lined drawers, each simulated as 2 smaller drawers, on a ring turned baluster support and channelled hipped downswept legs with turned feet, variously inscribed, 19in (48cm) diam. **£3,500–4,000** *C*

A kidney-shaped dressing table, with oval mirrored superstructure flanked by gilt metal girandole, above frieze drawer, on tapering turned legs with gilt sabots, 40in (101cm). **£400–600** *CSK*

A 19thC style mahogany dressing table, **£550–650** *W*

Games Tables

A Regency period mahogany games or library table, the top with reversible centre panel and rounded corners, over 2 false and 2 frieze drawers, on reeded standards and splayed legs, 39in (99cm). **£2,500–3,000** *MEA*

A Regency mahogany games table, attributed to James Newton, the hinged rotating top enclosing a green and tan leather lined chessboard above a frieze drawer between diamond point end panels, on twin X-shaped end supports joined by turned baluster stretcher, the casters stamped 'BS & P Patent', 21½in (54cm) wide. **£1,500–2,000** *CSK*

A pair of walnut games tables, each with removable top decorated with kingwood banding, fitted with removable sections containing various games, including skittles, target shooting, a pinball game and billiards, with scoring mechanisms, the whole on channelled cabriole legs, joined by waved X-shaped stretchers, on scrolled feet, one with repair to stretcher, small variations in dimensions, some parts missing, mid-18thC, 45½ and 44½in (115.5 and 113cm). **£30,000–40,000** *C*

A Victorian burr walnut games or work table, the fold-over top inlaid with backgammon and chess boards, lacking a sliding well, 22in (55cm). **£950–1,200** *S(S)*

A Victorian red and gilt japanned and parcel gilt games table, enclosing a backgammon well and a chessboard, with frieze drawer, on baluster shaft and tripod base simulated as dragons, with dragon head feet, extensively restored and regilded, 35in (89cm). **£1,500–2,000** *C*

A Victorian walnut fold-over games or work table, 30in (76cm).
£1,200–1,700 *LT*

A Victorian walnut games or sewing table, with serpentine front fold and turn-over top, the interior inlaid with a backgammon and cribbage board, on twin baluster and carved supports, 21in (53cm).
£1,000–1,500 *HOLL*

A German mahogany games table, the baize lined hinged top with a reeded edge, above an apron drawer, on tapered legs with ball feet, early 19thC, 22in (56cm).
£450–650 *P*

A late Victorian burr walnut, walnut, inlaid games or work table, the canted top inlaid for chess, opening to a baize lined interior, above a fitted frieze drawer and tapering pull-out basket, on turned tapering legs joined by stretchers, 25½in (65cm).
£1,000–1,500 *CSK*

An Italian baroque walnut games table, with removable top panelled with a backgammon board, over a panelled frieze drawer, on baluster turned legs joined by straight stretchers and square feet, 51in (151cm).
£16,000–18,000 *CNY*

Gateleg Tables

A walnut gateleg table, early 18thC.
£3,500–4,500 *B*

A George I Virginian walnut gateleg table, the twin flap top above a frieze drawer, the turned block legs with plain stretchers and splay feet, 31⅛in (65cm).
£1,400–1,800 *WW*

Library Tables

A George III mahogany library table, the top with re-entrant corners, inlaid with wide rosewood banding and ebony stringings, fitted with one true and one dummy drawer to front and back, with gilt brass rosette mounts to sides, and on gilt brass ball feet, some damage, 45in (114cm).
£2,500–3,000 *CAG*

A mahogany library table, with leather lined top above a hinged fall, on reeded tapering legs, part early 19thC, 54in (137cm).
£2,000–2,500 *CSK*

A George III mahogany library table, with leather lined top above 3 frieze drawers, on square chamfered legs, 58in (147cm).
£1,700–2,200 *CSK*

A William IV mahogany partners' library table, with tooled leather lined top, above 4 frieze drawers, on baluster turned tapering legs, 54in (137cm).
£1,500–2,000 *CSK*

A Regency rosewood and brass inlaid library table, fitted with one true and one dummy drawer to front and back, on tapering rectangular centre column, the swept-in rectangular base with gilt brass paw pattern feet and casters, 42in (106.5cm).
£4,000–5,000 *CAG*

A Regency mahogany library table, with panelled sides and 2 panelled end frieze drawers, on ring turned column and reeded downswept legs, fitted with Bramah locks, 44in (112cm).
£1,200–1,800 *CSK*

An early Victorian rosewood library table, the top now with a tooled leather inset, the frieze with foliate carved tablets and a drawer, the turned and foliate carved supports on scrolled legs, drawer stamped 'T.Wilson, 68 Great Queen Street, London', c1840, 53in (134cm).
£2,200–2,700 *S(S)*

Loo Tables

A Victorian walnut loo table, with shaped top, on reeded cluster column base and 4 carved cabriole legs terminating in ceramic casters, 55in (140cm).
£750–850 *WL*

A Victorian mahogany loo table, the top with a moulded edge and plain frieze with beaded border, supported on a bulbous fluted column with 4 outswept, channelled, scrolled and carved legs, 52in (132cm).
£1,000–1,500 *FLE*

A Victorian figured walnut loo table, with oval quarter-veneered moulded edge top, raised on a cabochon carved stem, 4 floral carved downswept legs with scroll toes and casters, 53in (134.5cm).
£750–1,000 *DMC*

Nests of Tables

A nest of 4 George III style sycamore and mahogany quartetto tables, on ring turned supports and splayed feet, c1910, 19½in (50cm).
£1,000–1,300 *S(S)*

A nest of 3 quartetto tables, one
stretcher replaced, the largest
21in (53cm).
£2,000–2,500 *C*

A nest of 4 line inlaid mahogany
quartetto tables, each top with
central oval, on ring turned
uprights, joined by stretchers,
on bracket feet, the largest
20in (51cm).
£900–1,200 *CSK*

A nest of 4 rosewood quartetto
tables, each with rectangular
top, on turned end supports and
stretchers, the largest
20in (51cm).
£2,200–2,700 *C*

A nest of 4 plum pudding
mahogany and brass inlaid tea
tables, the tops with inlaid brass
string lines and brass bead edges,
on slender turned supports with
brass collars and splayed feet,
22in (56cm).
£850–950 *P(S)*

Occasional Tables

A Louis XV style occasional table,
in figured walnut, with gilt
mounts, 19thC.
£2,000–2,500 *McC*

A nest of 4 walnut tables, c1960,
the largest 24in (61cm).
£200–250 *APO*

An Edwardian satinwood and
marquetry occasional table, on
turned tapering legs joined by
stretchers, 29in (73.5cm).
£1,800–2,200 *CSK*

A mid-Victorian black lacquer and
parcel gilt papier mâché
occasional table, the serpentine
top inlaid with a central
mother-of-pearl and painted floral
bouquet, on baluster turned
column and hipped downswept
legs, some edges chipped,
27½in (70cm).
£550–700 *CSK*

A hardwood tip-top occasional
table, c1900.
£400–500 *W*

An Edwardian mahogany and satinwood banded occasional table, with vertical splats, on square legs joined by a serpentine undertier, on outswept feet, needs restoration, 30in (76cm) extended.
£420–500 *CSK*

A George IV rosewood occasional table, the snap-top and triangular plinth inlaid with a variety of woods, 19½in (48cm).
£600–700 *RID*

A snap-top occasional table, with marquetry chequered design, on curved supports.
£650–750 *BWe*

Pedestal Tables

A walnut inlaid tip-up table, on turned pedestal base, 27in (69cm).
£2,000–2,250 *SUL*

A Victorian rosewood pedestal table, the turned pillar above a triform base, on concealed casters, stamped 'Miles & Edwards, 134 Oxford Street, London, No. 32198', 54in (13cm) diam.
£2,700–3,200 *S(S)*

A Victorian burr walnut pedestal table, lacking casters, c1860, 54in (137cm) diam.
£1,200–1,500 *S(S)*

Pembroke Tables

A George III mahogany line inlaid Pembroke table, with rosewood crossbanded top above frieze drawer, on square tapering legs, 32in (81cm).
£850–1,000 *CSK*

A George III mahogany Pembroke table, the 2 drop leaves with rounded corners, one drawer with brass handle and escutcheon, on square tapering legs with leaf carved corner brackets, on block feet with casters, the top water damaged, 31½in (80cm) extended.
£650–800 *DN*

A George III mahogany line inlaid Pembroke table, with crossbanded top, restored, 30in (76cm).
£1,500–2,000 *CSK*

A Georgian satinwood Pembroke table, with drop leaf and a drawer.
£1,800–1,900 *SUL*

A late George III mahogany and line inlaid Pembroke table, with oval crossbanded top, frieze drawer and opposing dummy drawer, on square tapering legs, 38in (96cm).
£1,700–2,200 *CSK*

A rosewood and satinwood banded Pembroke table, with geometric line inlay, on square tapering legs, late 18thC, restored, 37½in (95cm) extended.
£800–1,200 *CSK*

A George III mahogany Pembroke table, the hinged top above frieze drawer, on chamfered channelled square legs, joined by a pierced X-stretcher, restored, 30in (76cm).
£800–1,200 *CSK*

A rosewood Pembroke table, the top with satinwood crossbanding, over a frieze drawer with writing slide, on square tapering crossbanded legs, 29in (73cm).
£3,000–3,500 *MEA*

Serving Tables

A George III mahogany serpentine serving table, the top with moulded edge above a plain frieze, the sides with slides, on square tapering legs with collared feet, 59in (84cm).
£2,500–3,000 *C*

A George IV mahogany serving table, with an arched ledge back and frieze drawer, on turned reeded tapered legs, 53in (134.5cm).
£900–1,200 *P*

Mahogany

There are several types of mahogany of which San Domingan, Cuban, Honduran and Spanish are the most important. Mahogany was imported into England from the Americas c1730 when it became very popular with cabinet makers, and has been used ever since.

Quality varies considerably; at best this wood has a beautiful rich golden colour; but it can look rather bland if of poor quality. Victorians tended to polish mahogany to a red colour. The natural finish is preferred today.

A Regency mahogany bowfronted serving table, the three-quarter galleried top with reeded edge, above a geometrically inlaid frieze, on reeded turned tapering legs, headed by lions' masks and ring handles, 91½in (232.5cm).   **£3,000–4,000** *C*

A William IV mahogany serving table, the top with bowed centre above a panelled frieze, with 2 drawers centred with foliate panel, on foliate headed reeded tapering legs, restored, 83in (212cm).
£2,300–3,300 *CSK*

A Regency mahogany serving
table, 102in (259cm).
£4,700–5,200 *C*

A Regency mahogany serving table, the inverted
breakfront top with three-quarter gallery, above
3 geometrically inlaid frieze drawers, on part fluted
baluster turned legs and brass paw feet,
replacements and restorations, 82in (208.5cm).
£4,000–5,000 *C*

Side Tables

A walnut and featherbanded
lowboy, with quarter-veneered,
crossbanded and moulded top,
waved apron above later cabriole
front, and later turned back legs,
early 18thC, 27in (68cm).
£500–700 *P*

A mahogany bowfronted side
table, with boxwood stringing and
one drawer, on square tapering
legs, early 19thC, 35in (89cm).
£300–400 *DN*

A mahogany side table, with
mottled white marble top, on
scroll headed cabriole legs with
pointed pad feet, 43in (109cm).
£1,200–1,700 CSK

A mahogany side table, with grey
veined white marble top above a
plain frieze, with moulded apron,
on square legs, marble chipped,
18thC, 84in (213cm).
£2,000–3,000 *C*

A pair of Georgian mahogany
demi-lune side tables, each plain
frieze with beaded edge, on square
chamfered legs, 44in (111.5cm).
£350–400 *FLE*

A mahogany and red walnut side table, with brass handles, shaped frieze, on cabriole legs and cut-away pad feet, slight damage, 18thC and later, 28in (71cm).
£950–1,200 *WL*

An inlaid mahogany side table, with kingwood banded top above line inlaid frieze drawer, on square legs headed by inlaid ovals, late 18thC, some later inlay, 30in (76cm).
£600–900 *CSK*

A Georgian mahogany lowboy, with rectangular moulded top above 3 drawers and shaped apron, on cabriole legs, some alterations, 30in (76cm).
£6,000–7,000 *MEA*

A Georgian mahogany hinged top side table, with one long frieze drawer, brass drop handle and shaped back plate, on tapered square legs with applied fretwork spandrels, 34in (86cm).
£700–900 *Mit*

A Georgian mahogany side table, with moulded edge and frieze drawer, on square chamfered legs, with later pierced spandrels, restored, 30in (76cm).
£750–850 *P*

A pair of Regency mahogany side tables, each with mahogany lined frieze drawer, on gadrooned bun feet, adapted from a sideboard, and partially re-veneered, 21in (51cm).
£1,200–1,700 *C*

Locate the source

The source of each illustration in Miller's can be found by checking the code letters below each caption with the list of contributors.

A burr elm, burr walnut and line inlaid lowboy, the top with re-entrant corners above 3 frieze drawers, shaped apron and cabriole legs with pad feet, 30½in (77cm).
£3,500–4,000 *CSK*

A wicker side table, by Heywood Brothers, 22in (56cm).
£220–300 *DMT*

A Dutch mahogany and floral marquetry serpentine lowboy, with dished top, 2 frieze drawers, on foliate scroll carved cabriole legs with claw-and-ball feet, adapted, needs slight restoration, 19thC, 28in (71cm).
£2,200–2,700 *CSK*

A George III mahogany serpentine side table, the eared top above a plain frieze, edged with geometric banding, one side drawer and one dummy drawer, on panelled square tapering legs and block feet, 42in (106.5cm).
£2,700–3,700 *C*

An Irish mahogany side table, the moulded top above a frieze and ornate apron, profusely carved with scrolling leaves and flower heads flanking a large centre carved basket of flowers, on leaf carved cabriole legs, with claw-and-ball feet, 48in (122cm).
£3,500–4,500 *MEA*

A Dutch side table, the top decorated with panels of marquetry on an ebonised ground within oyster veneered borders, 19thC, 42in (107cm).
£1,500–2,000 *DN*

A set of 4 Louis XIII style walnut side tables, each with demi-lune top, above a plain frieze, turned baluster legs joined by a stretcher, on canted square feet, 23in (59cm).
£7,000–8,000 *CNY*

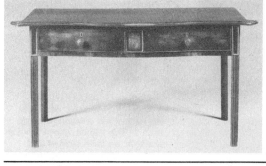

A pair of William IV Scottish mahogany serpentine side tables, each with later canted eared top, above 2 frieze drawers divided by a panel of burr elm, flanked by beaded panels, on channelled canted square legs, the drawers relined, repaired, 66in (168cm).
£2,500–3,500 *C*

Sofa Tables

A Regency mahogany sofa table, the top with reeded edge and rosewood crossbanding, 2 false and 2 frieze drawers, on 2 lyre supports with splayed legs, 60in (152cm) extended.
£5,500–6,500 *MEA*

A Regency mahogany sofa table, with twin-flap rounded top, crossbanded with rosewood and inlaid with boxwood and ebonised lines, the legs with brass hairy claw caps and casters, restored, base possibly later, 63in (160cm).
£2,500–3,500 *C*

A Regency mahogany sofa table, with hinged top above 2 frieze drawers, on reeded bulbous column with quadripartite platform base and reeded hipped splayed legs, 37in (94cm).
£1,700–2,300 *CSK*

A rosewood sofa table, the shaped top and side flaps with moulded edge, above a shaped frieze fitted with a drawer, on chanelled cabriole legs with acanthus carving, 19thC.
£1,200–1,700 *FLE*

A Regency rosewood brass strung sofa/library table, with 2 drop flaps, spring mechanism to the panelled extending frieze, side drawers, cast brass feet and casters, 58in (147cm) extended.
£4,500–5,500 *HSS*

A Regency rosewood pedestal sofa table, inlaid with cut brass, with frieze drawer above a pillar and platform, the 4 sabre legs with brass paw finials and casters, 36in (91cm) long.
£2,700–3,200 *S(S)*

A Regency mahogany and satinwood banded sofa table, with 2 frieze drawers and 2 false drawers, on rectangular end standards and splayed legs, joined by a stretcher, 61in (155cm).
£1,700–2,200 *CSK*

A late Regency period mahogany sofa table, the top with 2 flaps and rosewood crossbanding, above 2 false and 2 frieze drawers, on standard supports united by a turned and pineapple carved stretcher, on splayed legs, 58in (147cm).
£2,500–3,000 *MEA*

A Regency rosewood line inlaid sofa table, with mahogany crossbanded top above 2 frieze drawers flanked by 2 false drawers, on uprights with splayed legs joined by a stretcher, restored, 65in (165cm).
£4,200–5,000 *CSK*

A Regency rosewood sofa table, the satinwood crossbanded top with 2 drop leaves, above 2 frieze drawers, on twin turned end supports with turned spindle and splayed legs, brass terminals and a turned stretcher, 60in (152cm) long.
£2,000–2,500 *DN*

A pair of Regency mahogany sofa tables, now converted for use as a twin pedestal dining table, restored, 86in (219cm) extended.
£2,000–2,500 *CSK*

A rosewood inlaid and crossbanded sofa table, with 2 drop flaps and 2 frieze drawers, on inlaid standard supports with splayed legs, 67in (170cm) extended.
£3,000–4,000 *MEA*

A Biedermeier mahogany and gilt decorated sofa table, on quadripartite platform base with winged paw feet, mid-19thC, 51in (130cm).
£900–1,200 *CSK*

A rosewood and mahogany crossbanded drop-leaf sofa table, with 2 frieze drawers, raised on 4 square supports, with splayed legs united by 2 shaped flat stretchers and arched crossrails, 60in (152.5cm).
£2,800–3,500 *MEA*

A George IV mahogany sofa table, 57in (145cm) long.
£2,000–2,500 *DN*

A Regency rosewood and inlaid sofa table, the hinged top above 2 drawers, on a turned column with quatripartite platform and splayed legs with brass paw cappings and casters, the top needs restoring, 57½in (146cm).
£1,200–1,700 *P*

Tea Tables

An Edwardian mahogany and satinwood banded sofa table, on lyre shaped end supports, joined by a serpentine stretcher, with arched legs, later chequer strung, top needs restoring, 56in (142cm) extended.   £1,200–1,700 CSK

A mid-George III mahogany serpentine tea table, restored, 36in (92cm).
£1,000–1,500 CSK

A George III inlaid mahogany demi-lune tea table, the crossbanded top with oak leaf marquetry, above marquetry conch shells, on square tapering legs, restored, 39in (99cm).
£1,500–2,000 CSK

A George III mahogany demi-lune tea table, the top and interior fan veneered in rich curl grain with boxwood stringing and crossbanding, 36in (91cm).
£1,000–1,200 Bri

A Regency mahogany tea table, the fold-over top above a ring turned pillar, on quadruple splayed base, restored, c1810, 36in (91cm).
£800–1,000 S(S)

A Regency D-shaped fold-over top tea table.   **£1,200–1,700** P(S)

A George III serpentine shaped mahogany fold-over telescopic action tea table, raised on 4 moulded cabriole legs, 36in (92cm).
£2,500–3,500 MEA

A Regency mahogany swivel top folding tea table, with turned column above quadrifoil platform, and 4 shaped sabred legs with brass terminals, 45in (114cm).
£1,000–1,500 DaD

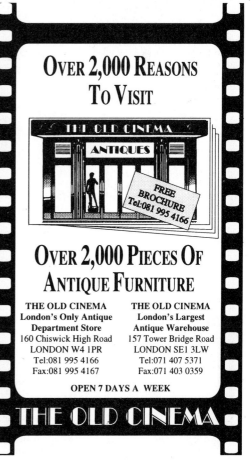

An early Victorian rosewood tea table, with folding swivel top, on a leaf carved baluster column, the 4 carved scroll legs with shell terminals, 36½in (93cm).
£1,000–1,200 *DN*

A George IV mahogany and rosewood crossbanded tea table, the hinged top above foliate carved reeded frieze, on reeded rectangular upright and quadripartite platform base, with reeded bun feet, 36in (92cm).
£600–900 *CSK*

A Regency mahogany tea table, the hinged top with a reeded edge and roundel decorated frieze, on a turned column and splayed quadruped supports, scroll feet with cappings and casters, 37in (94cm). **£1,000–1,200** *P*

A Regency mahogany turn-over top tea table, with applied edge moulding, on tapered reeded legs, 34in (86cm).
£650–800 *Mit*

> **Miller's is a price GUIDE not a price LIST.**

A Regency mahogany and inlaid tea table, the brass line inlaid bowed top crossbanded in bird's-eye maple and rosewood, on curved square section supports and central ring turned column, with platform base and anthemion scrolls, on quadripartite hairy legs, repaired, 36in (91cm).
£1,500–1,900 *CSK*

A mahogany tea table, inlaid with boxwood lines, the D-shaped hinged top crossbanded and inlaid with tulipwood, on square tapering legs, reduced in height and altered, mostly late 18thC, 18in (46cm).
£500–700 *P*

A Regency mahogany tea table, inlaid with ebonised lines, the hinged top banded in satinwood, with geometrically panelled frieze, on turned tapering fluted legs headed by fluted rectangular panels, on toupie feet, 36in (91.5cm).
£1,700–2,200 *C*

A George III ebonised mahogany and line inlaid tea table, on square tapering legs, later inlaid, 37in (94cm).
£700–1,000 *CSK*

A late Georgian mahogany fold-over top tea table, with reeded edge, above frieze inlaid with a boxwood line, on tapered reeded legs, 33in (84cm).
£700–900 *Mit*

A Victorian mahogany fold-over top tea table 36in (91cm).
£900–1,100 *Mit*

A George II red walnut concertina action tea table, the eared moulded rectangular hinged top above a plain frieze with sliding well to the interior, on cabriole legs and pad feet, restored, 36in (91.5cm).
£3,000–3,500 *C*

Tripod Tables

A mahogany pie crust table, 19thC, 30in (76cm) diam.
£750–800 *WIL*

A mid-Victorian walnut and marquetry tripod table, the ebony veneered top with central floral marquetry roundel, on spiral-twist shaft, shell headed splayed legs with scroll feet, 20in (51cm) diam.
£700–900 *CSK*

A Victorian mahogany carved table, 23in (59cm) diam.
£1,400–1,750 *SUL*

A mahogany tripod pie crust table, on a turned spiral gadrooned shaft and cabriole legs carved with acanthus and C-scrolls, on claw-and-ball feet, 19in (48cm) diam.
£4,000–5,000 *C*

A mahogany tripod table, with associated top above turned part gadrooned tapering shaft, with cabriole legs and pad feet, 10in (25.5cm) diam.
£500–700 *CSK*

A Victorian papier mâché tripod table, inlaid with mother-of-pearl, the tilt-top painted with a 17thC landscape and figures, gilt highlights, on baluster column and shaped base with 3 feet, 20in (51cm) diam.
£370–420 *L&E*

Work Tables

Work Tables

Work tables were introduced in the late 18thC, primarily for ladies to sew at. Usually fairly small and compact, they are fitted with a silk bag and compartments for needles, cottons and so on. Some have lift-up tops with fitted interiors.

Most of those from the late 18thC stand on 4 square tapering or slender turned legs. Pedestal supports and turned fluted legs are typical of the early 19thC as is the desirable type with lyre shaped supports.

As the 19thC progressed, work tables began to be produced in larger quantities and in a greater range of quality. Victorian work tables are characterised by their use of walnut. The pull-out 'bags' of this period are usually of solid form and veneered.

A burr walnut work table, the shaped and quartered hinged top enclosing a fitted interior, the frieze with applied mouldings above a sliding bag, on shaped and moulded supports with a central stretcher, 21½in (54.5cm).
£500–700 *DN*

A Victorian walnut work table, the hinged quartered top with tulipwood crossbanding and boxwood marquetry, enclosing compartments with fret covers and a central well, on turned end supports, with carved splayed legs and turned stretcher, 22½in (57cm).
£750–850 *DN*

An early Victorian mahogany work table, with 2 drop leaves and 2 drawers to one end, and false drawers to the reverse, with wood handles, on turned legs with casters, 30in (76cm).
£300–500 *DN*

A Victorian rosewood and satin walnut work table, the hinged top and sides decorated in marquetry with birds and leaf scrolls, the fitted interior with well, on three carved splayed legs with scroll terminals, 17½in (44cm).
£500–600 *DN*

A mahogany work table, the 2 drop leaves with a reeded edge, a fitted drawer above a deep double front drawer, on slender turned legs with casters, early 19thC, 19in (48cm).
£1,000–1,400 *DN*

A Regency rosewood work table, the hinged top enclosing a fitted interior above sliding well, on U-shaped support and faceted column, on quadripartite platform base with turned bun feet, 23in (58cm).
£800–1,200 *CSK*

A George IV rosewood work table, 24in (61cm).
£900–1,200 *CSK*

A Regency rosewood work and games table, the top with sliding cover and 2 hinged compartments, the apron with a chessboard inset slide and a pleated fabric well, on lyre shaped end supports, 27in (69cm).
£2,000–3,000 *S(S)*

A William IV mahogany drop-leaf work table, with 2 true and two opposing false drawers, the fabric well flanked by 4 scroll supports, on claw feet and casters, 17in (43cm). **£1,000–1,500** *S(S)*

A simulated rosewood and painted work table, with octagonal hinged top above central frieze drawer, on turned column with scrolling splayed legs on bun feet, redecorated, early 19thC, 18in (45.5cm). **£700–900** *CSK*

A late Regency rosewood work table, the frieze drawer with wooden knob handles, bag below, standing on turned end supports united by a turned stretcher, 24in (61cm). **£800–900** *Mit*

A Regency period burr walnut lady's work and games table, the reversible top within 2 bowed pierced galleries above a wool box, raised on 4 square supports and ebonised spindle splats and 4 splayed legs with urn feet, 31½in (80cm). **£3,500–4,000** *MEA*

A Victorian walnut and inlaid combined work and games table, the fold-over top revealing chessboard, backgammon and cribbage insets, the fitted frieze drawer above a well, on turned end supports, c1860, 25in (64cm). **£2,000–2,700** *S(S)*

A Victorian rosewood work table, c1840, 27in (69cm). **£1,500–2,000** *S(S)*

An French rosewood inlaid work table, 27in (69cm). **£1,200–1,450** *SUL*

A Louis XV style burr walnut, tulipwood and marquetry work table, the serpentine gilt metal edged top inlaid with floral bouquets, enclosing a fitted interior with inset mirror, on cabriole legs, headed with foliate cabochon mounts trailing to sabots, 21½in (55cm). **£1,000–1,500** *CSK*

Writing Tables

A late George III mahogany writing table, restored, 36in (92cm). **£1,000–1,500** *CSK*

A Victorian figured walnut kidney-shaped writing table, on turned and carved end supports, joined by a pole stretcher, 41in (105cm). **£900–1,200** *S(S)*

A Continental kingwood and tulipwood writing table, with inlaid designs and inset leather top, on 4 cabriole supports with gilt bronze mounts, 36in (91.5cm).
£1,400–1,600 *LRG*

A mahogany writing table, with rounded leather lined top, above 6 frieze drawers, on reeded tapering legs, part early 19thC, 47in (119cm).
£2,000–2,500 *CSK*

A mahogany writing table, with wide crossbanding and 3 drawers, on X-frame supports.
£800–1,200 *LRG*

An Edwardian mahogany and marquetry writing table, the raised superstructure with open compartment, fitted drawer, flanked by inlaid panelled doors above leather lined top, frieze drawer, on square tapering legs with spade feet, 36in (92cm).
£1,000–1,500 *CSK*

A George IV ormolu mounted bird's-eye maple folding writing table, the part-galleried rounded hinged top banded in calamander, on end supports headed by a mahogany lined narrow drawer, joined by a solid stretcher, on scroll mounted platform base and bun feet, 32in (81cm).
£1,000–1,500 *C*

A Regency rosewood lady's writing table, with satinwood crossbanding, enclosed leather writing surface, pen and ink compartments, a locking well and pull-up silk panel heat screen, over 2 frieze drawers, on square tapering legs, 21in (53cm).
£4,000–5,000 *MEA*

A mahogany and line inlaid writing table, with coromandel crossbanded leather lined top, early 19thC, 27in (68.5cm).
£700–1,000 *CSK*

A French walnut veneered writing table, late 19thC, 40in (101.5cm).
£350–400 *WIL*

An early Victorian rosewood writing table, on scroll mounted platform bases and bun feet, branded 'VR OC 1846', 42in (107cm).
£4,500–5,500 *C*

Supplied to Queen Victoria for Osborne House, Isle of Wight, which was completed and furnished in 1845-46 with much of the furniture being supplied by Holland and Sons.

A Regency mahogany writing table, with rounded corners, 2 frieze drawers, on end supports with reeded splayed legs and turned stretcher, restored, 41in (104cm).
£1,800–2,200 *DN*

A George IV rosewood writing table, with 2 frieze drawers, on turned end supports terminating in flutes, on bases with scrolls and paw feet, 47in (120cm). **£1,300–1,700** *DN*

An early Victorian rosewood writing table, the later red leather lined mahogany top above a pair of mahogany lined frieze drawers, on turned tapering legs with brass caps, branded and inscribed in ink 'Buckingham Palace Room 57', 50in (127cm). **£2,500–3,500** *C*

A Victorian mahogany writing table.
£600–1,000 *LRG*

Miscellaneous Tables

An Irish mahogany wake table, 18thC.
£2,800–3,500 *P(S)*

A mahogany reading table, with sliding top, 19thC, 35½in (90cm).
£750–850 *STA*

A Victorian burr walnut pedestal table, with quadruple foliate scroll carved supports, 54in (137cm).
£1,800–2,500 *S(S)*

A mahogany silver table, with moulded edge, shaped corners and inset plate glass, the oak turned frieze drawer with French style bronze rococo spray handles and open escutcheons, on cabriole legs to club feet, 36in (92cm).
£1,500–2,000 *WW*

A mahogany and bird's-eye maple banded adjustable bed table, the top with moulded edge, on a square column to one side over a rectangular base with a moulded edge, 19thC.
£350–450 *FLE*

A Venetian painted wood blackamoor table, with circular quartered simulated malachite top, the figure support with polychrome and gilded cap, holding a staff, on square base, 19thC, 18½in (47cm).
£900–1,400 *BWe*

A wooden camel table, late 19thC, 23in (59cm) high.
£760–900 *DUN*

Teapoys

A rosewood teapoy, with spring assisted mechanism for rising top, 20in (51cm) diam.
£2,000–2,260 *SUL*

A Regency kingwood gilt metal mounted teapoy, the hinged top with fleur-de-lys canted angles decorated with ribbon banding, fitted interior, on a bead carved tapered column, platform and hipped quadruped supports with foliate cappings and casters, 20in (51cm).
£1,400–1,900 *P*

An Anglo Indian rosewood teapoy, with profusely carved sarcophagus top, on reeded and gadrooned column, with concave sided platform base and scroll feet, converted to a work table, some beading lost, the lock stamped with a crown 'J. Bramah, 114 Piccadilly,' early 19thC, 19½in (49cm).
£1,000–1,500 *CSK*

Whatnots

A pair of Regency mahogany three-tier whatnots, on turned uprights, slight damage, restored, 18in (46cm).
£2,500–3,000 *CSK*

A mid-Victorian mahogany three-tier whatnot, with three-quarter pierced fretwork gallery, above frieze drawer, on fluted spiral turned uprights, stamped 'C. Hindley & Sons, late Miles & Edwards, 134 Oxford Street, London 42476', 34in (86cm).
£1,700–2,500 *CSK*

A George IV rosewood three-tier whatnot, with a three-quarter pierced gallery, on turned columns, fitted with a drawer, on turned legs, 18in (46cm).
£1,500–2,000 *P*

A mahogany four-tier whatnot, 19thC, 17in (43cm).
£700–900 *C(S)*

A mid-Victorian rosewood four-tier whatnot, with adjustable ledged top, spiral twist uprights and turned feet, 20in (51cm).
£1,300–1,700 *CSK*

A Victorian walnut canterbury/whatnot, with amboyna banding and boxwood stringing, spindle turned divisions, fitted drawer, on turned and fluted supports and casters, 24in (61.5cm).
£900–1,200 *RBB*

A Victorian walnut canterbury/whatnot.
£800–1,200 *W*

A stained fruitwood four-tier canterbury/whatnot, with ring turned uprights, 19in (48cm).
£850–1,000 *CSK*

A Victorian corner whatnot, 51in (130cm). **£400–500** *WIL*

Wine Coolers

A late George III mahogany and brass bound wine cooler, on later stand, the domed lid with later finial, the oval body with lions' mask handles, on square moulded legs with corner spandrels, restored, 24in (61cm) wide.
£1,000–1,500 *CSK*

A George III inlaid mahogany cellaret, 17in (43cm) wide.
£800–1,000 *Mit*

A George III mahogany octagonal wine cooler, adapted as a coal box, with hinged top and 2 brass handles on a stand with square tapering legs and brass casters, repaired, 18in (45cm) wide.
£400–600 *DN*

A George III brass bound wine cooler, with gilt brass lions' mask handles, later zinc liner for plants, the later stand on square tapering legs to spade feet, 24in (61.5cm) wide.
£1,200–1,700 *WW*

A late George III mahogany cellaret, with domed lid, enclosing a fitted interior and with a side drawer, with brass carrying handles, 18in (46cm) wide.
£600–800 *CSK*

A George III mahogany cellaret, the hinged coffered top enclosing a fitted interior, the sides with carrying handles, on square tapering legs, 18in (46cm) wide.
£1,500–1,900 *CSK*

A George III mahogany and brass bound hexagonal wine cooler, with brass loop handles, hinged lid revealing liner, on 3 moulded square tapering supports with brass toes and casters, 19½in (49cm) wide.
£1,700–2,000 *AH*

A mahogany wine cellaret, the gilt brass gadroon mouldings and brass bordered panels, the interior zinc lined, on brass mounted turned feet with casters, early 19thC, 34in (86cm) wide.
£3,500–4,000 *WW*

A figured mahogany domed top wine cooler, the lozenge-shaped body lead lined, raised on ring turned supports with original brass casters, early 19thC.
£1,800–2,200 *TM*

A mahogany hexagonal wine cooler, the top inlaid with stringing and crossbanded, the interior fitted, brass carrying handles, the frame with square moulded legs, on brass casters, slight restoration, late 18thC, 20in (51cm) wide.
£1,500–1,800 *WW*

A mahogany cellaret, with domed cover, stringing and brass carrying handles, the unlined interior with divisions, c1790, 21in (53cm) wide.
£800–1,200 *S(S)*

A Regency mahogany sarcophagus wine cooler, with lead lined interior, on turned feet and brass caps, 21½in (54.5cm).
£1,200–1,700 *C*

A mahogany decanter table, fitted to take decanters and glasses, with panelled sides and rounded end, on square tapering legs, 19thC, 29in (74cm) wide.
£700–900 *DN*

A mahogany and maple cellaret, the string inlaid domed lid enclosing a divided interior, over 2 cupboard doors on short bracket type feet, c1785, 19in (49cm) wide.
£2,500–3,000 *MEA*

An early Victorian mahogany wine cooler, of sarcophagus form, with compartmented interior, carrying handles, on turned feet, stamped Gillingtons, numbered '5999', 35in (89cm) wide.
£800–1,200 *CSK*

Miscellaneous

A Regency mahogany washstand, in the manner of Gillow, the top with apertures for basins, three-quarter gallery and tilting toilet mirror, on reeded baluster supports with brass candle sconces, the panel moulded frieze on spherical knopped reeded legs with casters, the underframe stamped with the number '79043'.
£700–900 *P*

A mahogany dinner gong and stand, supported on carved and turned central support, with 3 downswept carved and scrolling legs.
£550–600 *Mit*

A Georgian style staved mahogany log bin, with a later galvanised liner, 15in (38cm).
£500–550 *HSS*

A Georgian mahogany butler's tray, the turned folding stand with turned stretchers, 28in (71cm).
£550–650 *DA*

A Victorian mahogany butler's tray, with galleried top on folding X-framed support, with square legs, 36½in (93cm).
£750–900 *C*

ARCHITECTURAL ANTIQUES
Bronze

A bronze figure of Venus, after
Allegrain, on a square base cast
with shells and bullrushes,
stamped 'Gautier Editaur', c1870,
32½in (83cm).
£2,500–3,000   *S(S)*

A bronze fountain, probably Italian,
weathered green patination, mid-
20thC, 32½in (82cm) high.
£1,200–1,800   *S(S)*

A bronze fountain of a putto cherub,
holding a fish, after Verrochio, on
a circular base, weathered green
patination, plumbed for water,
29in (74cm) high.
£1,200–1,700   *S(S)*

A bronze fountain figure of a
cherub holding a fish, on circular
base, stamped 'G. Varlese Napoli',
weathered green patination,
c1900, 25in (64cm) high.
£750–1,000   *S(S)*

A bronze figure of a youth holding
a ball and a lamb, seated on a
pedestal, signed 'Luella Varney,
Ferrao 1926, Fond. Art. Lagana
Napoli', weathered green
patination, 28½in (72cm) high.
£1,700–2,200   *S(S)*

A bronze figure of Mercury, after
Giam Bologna, standing on an
allegory of the wind, weathered
green patination, 44in (111.5cm)
high, on associated square
moulded stoneware pedestal,
decorated with laurel wreaths,
20½in (52cm) high.
£1,700–2,200   *S(S)*

A bronze figure of the dancing
faun, after the antique, the
circular base signed 'Chiurazzi,
Napoli', weathered green
patination, 27in (69cm) high.
£900–1,200   *S(S)*

*The faun was discovered at
Pompeii on 26th October 1830,
and was taken to the Museo
Borbonico, (later Museo
Nazionale) Naples. It became
instantly famous, probably due to
its small scale which made copies
particularly attractive for gardens
and interiors. This figure appears
as Lot 92 in the Chiurazzi
Foundry catalogue, dating to the
turn of the century. The Chiurazzi
Foundry was the largest in the
area having incorporated a
number of other smaller foundries
in the Naples area. They were
largely producing Grand Tour
copies of antique originals, many
of which were discovered during
the excavations of Pompeii and
other sites.*

Iron

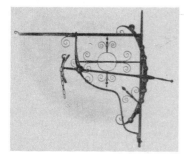

A wrought iron chimney crane, with foliate and twist turned decorative ironwork, the adjustable arm on a semi-circular ratchet, with mushroom-shaped buttons, early 18thC, 49in (124.5cm) high.
£750–900 *S(S)*

A cast iron 'Jubilee' seat, with wooden slatted back and seat, the 3 uprights cast with scrolls and foliage, a portrait medallion of Queen Victoria and stamped 'Victoria Die Gratia Britt 1887 Jubilee Reg.fd'.
£700–800 *S(S)*

A pair of wrought iron gates, early 19thC, 74in (188cm) high.
£700–1,200 *S(S)*

A reeded wrought iron seat, with segmented back and plain slatted seat, early 19thC, 72in (182.5cm).
£900–1,200 *S(S)*

A pair of wrought iron gates, with cresting in the form of seated cats, early 20thC, 86in (218.5cm).
£1,700–2,200 *S(S)*

A cast iron rainwater hopper, 18in (46cm) high.
£35–45 *GRF*

A pair of cast iron urns, late 19thC, 30in (76cm) high.
£700–1,000 *S(S)*

A cast iron lamp, the wrythen fluted and canted square column stamped 'Baker & Co., Ltd., Makers, Westminster Street', surmounted by a domed glazed lantern with scrolling brackets, c1860, 142in (360cm).
£1,000–1,500 *S(S)*

A Coalbrookdale Fern and Blackberry pattern cast iron seat, with wooden slatted seat, late 19thC, 75in (190.5cm).
£1,000–1,500 *S(S)*

This design is registered in the 1875 Coalbrookdale catalogue, section III, page 254, number 29.

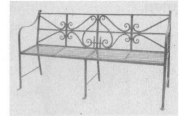

A reeded wrought iron seat, the back centred with scrolls and a lyre, on reeded legs joined by stretchers, 71in (180cm).
£1,500–2,000 *S(S)*

A cast iron chair, the arched back with central foliate panel, flanked by barley-twist columns, on X-framed supports, numbered '15', diamond registration stamp for 28th March 1859, together with a pair of cast iron tables, each with a circular tin top on 4 paw supports, 30in (76cm).
£400–600 *S(S)*

A Coalbrookdale cast iron seat with wooden slatted seat, the back decorated with Oak and Ivy, stamped 'C.B. Dale', and with diamond registration stamp for 'January 8th 1857', 72in (182.5cm).
£2,500–3,000 *S(S)*

This design is registered in the 1875 Coalbrookdale catalogue, section III, page 256, number 30. The oak and ivy pattern was designed by the sculptor John Bell, whose deerhound table made for the 1855 Exhibition is now in the Ironbridge Gorge Museum.

A Coalbrookdale Passion Flower pattern cast iron seat, painted in naturalistic colours, back altered, stamped 'Coalbrookdale No. 74, Registered No. 3511', 56in (142cm).
£1,800–2,200 *S(S)*

This seat is a variation on the more common curved seat registered in the 1875 Coalbrookdale catalogue, section III, page 263.

A pair of cast iron rainwater hoppers, 18in (46cm) high.
£35–45 each *GRF*

A pair of cast iron seats, each pierced with arabasques and foliage, the serpentine-shaped back cast with hoops, beneath foliate cresting, on cabriole supports, with foliate cast apron, c1870, 44in (111.5cm).
£2,000–3,000 *S(S)*

A pair of wrought iron gates, early 20thC, 104in (264cm).
£700–1,000 *S(S)*

Apart from the cabriole back legs, these seats are identical to a Carron Foundry design which was first registered on 16th March 1846. The original signed drawing for this seat is at the Public Records Office and is inscribed 'class N.1. Carron Company, Carron Warehouse, 15 Upper Thames Street, London Works at Carron Stirlingshire, Scotland'. Both the Carron and Falkirk Foundries are located on the Firth of Forth on the east coast of Scotland, but with warehousing and retailing premises close to each other in Upper Thames Street, London, to which the iron goods were transported by sea, and up the River Thames.

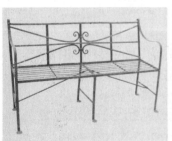

A reeded wrought iron seat, with plain slatted seat, the back centred with scrolls, on 6 legs with paw feet, joined by stretchers, early 19thC, 60in (152cm).
£1,000–1,500 *S(S)*

A reeded wrought iron games seat, with plain slatted seat and segmented back, on 4 supports with 2 wheels and 2 paw feet, joined by stretchers, early 19thC, 48in (122cm).
£1,000–1,500 *S(S)*

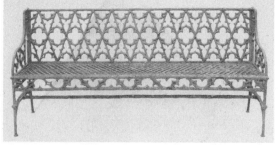

A Coalbrookdale Convolvulus pattern cast iron seat, the supports joined by stretchers, registration stamps obscured by paint, 60in (152cm).
£1,200–1,800 *S(S)*

This is the earliest pattern registered by Coalbrookdale at the Public Records Office, and illustrates a panel of convolvulus. The foundry adapted this into a garden seat shortly afterwards.

A Val'Osne foundry cast iron seat, with quatrefoil and tracery pierced back, and hexagon pierced seat, c1860, 71in (180cm).
£1,000–1,500 *S(S)*

This design is illustrated in the Société Anonyme des Haute-Fourneaux et Fonderies du Val d'Osne catalogue, Tome II, Fontes d'Art.

A cast iron plant stand, with 3 foliate pierced trays, arranged on 2 tiers, the end supports pierced with foliage, c1870, 37in (94cm).
£1,500–2,000 *S(S)*

A cast iron rainwater hopper, 18in (46cm) high.
£35–45 *GRF*

A pair of cast iron urns, on associated Vicenza stone panelled square pedestals, each carved with ribbon tied swags, mid-19thC, 41in (104cm).
£650–850 *S(S)*

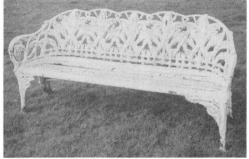

A Coalbrookdale Lily of the Valley pattern cast iron seat, with wooden slatted seat, registration stamps and foundry stamps obscured by paint, c1870, 74in (188cm).
£1,200–1,700 *S(S)*

A Coalbrookdale Lily of the Valley pattern cast iron seat, the back stamped 'C.B. Dale' and with diamond registration stamp, c1870, 62in (157cm).
£1,800–2,200 *S(S)*

This design is registered in the 1875 Coalbrookdale catalogue section III, page 255, number 36.

A pair of cast iron Medici and Borghese urns, late 19thC, 29in (74cm) high.
£2,500–3,000 *S(S)*

A Coalbrookdale cast iron fountain, stamped 'C.B. Dale & Co.,' and with diamond registration stamp, c1870, 38in (96.5cm) high.
£1,500–2,000 *S(S)*

This design is registered in the 1875 Coalbrookdale catalogue, section III, page 277, number 17.

A Coalbrookdale Horse Chestnut pattern cast iron seat, painted in naturalistic colours, stamped 'Coalbrookdale & Co.,' numbered '217568', and with registration stamps for 1868, 73in (185cm).
£2,000–3,000 *S(S)*

This design is registered in the 1875 Coalbrookdale catalogue, section III, page 256, number 46.

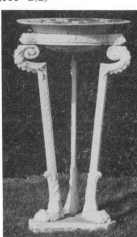

A pair of cast iron braziers, stamped 'Registered W. Addis, Leicester Road, Leicester Square, London', c1870, 54in (137cm).
£3,700–4,200 *S(S)*

A number of these braziers originally lined London Bridge, and are illustrated in a painting celebrating the marriage procession across London Bridge of Queen Alexandra and Edward VII.

A Coalbrookdale cast iron urn, with registration mark, 19thC.
£250–350 *GHA*

A pair of cast iron urns, mid-19thC, 45in (114cm) high.
£700–1,000 *S(S)*

A cast iron seat, with wooden slatted seat and arcaded foliate cast back, the end supports cast with serpents and grapes with dogs' head terminals, 60in (152cm).
£800–1,000 *S(S)*

A cast urn basket urn, late 19thC, 47in (119cm) high.
£1,100–1,500 *S(S)*

A Coalbrookdale Gothic pattern cast iron seat, stamped 'C.B. Dale Co. No. 99277', with diamond registration stamp for 5th February 1854 and numbered '22', c1860, 60in (152cm).
£1,500–2,000 *S(S)*

A cast iron water tank, of bolted construction, the panels cast with stylised flowerheads and leaves, early 19thC, 78in (198cm).
£1,000–1,200 *S(S)*

Lead

A lead cistern, the panelled front dated '1825', decorated with flowerheads and initials 'R.B.L.', 27½in (69cm) high.
£3,000–3,500 *S(S)*

A lead rainwater hopper, dated '1718'.
£200–220 *GHA*

A lead fountain, early 20thC, 22in (56cm) high.
£1,200–1,700 *S(S)*

A pair of lead stags, on rectangular bases and composition stone pedestals, early 20thC, 72in (182.5cm) high.
£6,400–6,800 *S(S)*

A pair of lead figures of a shepherd and shepherdess, in the style of John Cheere, he in early 18thC dress holding a crook, she holding a lamb, both on associated square Vicenza stone pedestals, mid-20thC, 71in (180cm) high.
£3,000–4,000 *S(S)*

A set of 4 lead figures of children representing the Seasons, each holding an attribute, 30in (76cm) high, on composition stone pedestals moulded with ribbon tied swags, 20in (50.5cm) high.
£1,800–2,200 *S(S)*

A lead rainwater hopper.
£130–150 *GRF*

A Georgian lead cistern, the front panel dated '1726' flanked by strapwork and armorials, 34in (86cm) high.
£3,200–4,000 *S(S)*

A lead figure of a dancing girl swirling drapery, 38in (96.5cm) high, together with a lead figure of a young boy, playing the pipes, mid-20thC, 31in (79cm) high.
£1,200–1,700 *S(S)*

Marble

A veined white marble table, the top on ogee section supports, on stepped plinths, 20thC, 62in (157cm). **£700–1,000** *S(S)*

A set of 4 white marble urns, mid-19thC, 37in (94cm) diam. **£4,000–5,000** *S(S)*
These urns were removed from Crystal Palace during the sales by tender in the 1950s and 60s.

An Italian white marble bath, with egg-and-dart moulded rim above stop fluted wrythen and foliate carved decoration, the lower section with geometric and rope-twist friezes, centred with flowerheads, c1900, 68½in (174cm), on associated stone brackets carved with masks. **£10,000–14,000** *S(S)*

An Italian white marble figure of a girl, the base indistinctly signed 'FI Firenze', arms missing, c1870, 51in (129.5cm) high. **£1,700–2,200** *S(S)*

A marble composite order capital, c1800, 29in (74cm) high. **£1,500–2,000** *S(S)*

An Italian white marble figure of a girl, c1900, 34in (86cm), on serpentine column pedestal, 40in (101.5cm) high. **£3,500–4,500** *S(S)*

A pair of white marble urns, mid-19thC, 45in (114cm) high. **£2,000–3,000** *S(S)*

A pair of white marble urns, late 19thC, 46in (116.5cm) high. **£2,000–2,500** *S(S)*

A white marble bench, the curved seat with egg-and-dart carved border, on double-sided sphinx supports, c1900, 57in (144.5cm). **£1,800–2,000** *S(S)*

An Italian white marble wellhead, carved in high relief with a frieze of putti, supporting festoons of flowers and playing musical instruments, c1870, 41in (104cm) diam., with associated octagonal surround. **£18,000–24,000** *S(S)*

A white marble fountain, in the form of a scantily clad boy holding a snake, on circular base, late 19thC, fitted with sprinkler attachment, 37in (94cm) high.
£1,200–1,700 *S(S)*

A marble mortar, 18thC, 14in (36cm) diam.
£90–110 *GHA*

A pair of white marble column pedestals, each of tapering fluted circular form, with stiff-leaf carved circular capital and square base, c1840, 47in (119cm) high.
£2,000–2,500 *S(S)*

An Italian pair of white marble urns, c1900, 32½in (83cm) high.
£5,000–7,500 *S(S)*

Stone

A pair of Vicenza stone figures of putti, early 20thC, 34½in (113cm) high. **£3,200–3,700** *S(S)*

A set of 4 carved stone urns, c1860, 25in (64cm) high.
£3,000–3,500 *S(S)*

A Vicenza stone figure of a donkey, early 20thC, 43in (109cm) high.
£2,000–3,000 *S(S)*

A pair of sandstone urns, each body carved in relief, with scrolling foliage flanked by putto herms, on associated terracotta circular foot, moulded with foliage, 27½in (70cm) high.
£2,000–2,700 *S(S)*

A carved stone monkey, c1870, 18in (46cm) high.
£600–800 *S(S)*

A modern composition stone fountain, in the form of a putto leaning over a lion's mask, with shell basin, on foliate cast base, drilled for water, 59in (149.5cm) high.
£2,000–2,500 *S(S)*

A Coade stone urn, on rising circular foot and square base, stamped 'Coade, London 1792', 30in (76cm) high.
£1,000–1,700 *S(S)*

A Vicenza stone sundial base, with stylised mask, square top, early 20thC, 36in (91.5cm) high.
£1,000–1,500 *S(S)*

A pair of carved stone Borghese and Medici urns, one damaged, 19thC, 32in (81cm) high.
£650–1,000 *S(S)*

A pair of composition stone urns, late 19thC, 55in (139.5cm) high.
£1,000–1,200 *S(S)*

A pair of carved sandstone heraldic lions, c1870, 49in (124.5cm) high.
£5,500–8,500 *S(S)*

A pair of Istrian stone busts of an Emperor and Diana, he in classical armour with robe draped shoulders, wearing a laurel wreath, the Goddess bare breasted, with flowers and a moon crescent in her hair, 28½in (72cm) high.
£4,500–5,500 *S(S)*

A composition stone figure of a girl, early 20thC, 53in (134.5cm) high, and on associated stone base, 18½in (47cm) high.
£1,200–1,500 *S(S)*

A Coade and Sealy urn, the body with stiff-leaf decoration and lion's mask handles, on raised oval foot and rectangular base, stamped 'Coade and Sealy London 1811', one handle missing, 24in (61cm) high.
£2,000–2,500 *S(S)*

A similar urn is illustrated in Etchings of Coade's Artificial Stone Manufacture, drawing No. 105.

A set of 4 Vicenza stone baskets, early 20thC, 16in (41cm) high.
£1,200–1,700 *S(S)*

A Portland stone sundial pedestal, the column on stepped base, the top inscribed 'Transeo sic praeteris', with associated later marble inclined twin dial, calibrated on both sides, angled gnomon ridge, 49in (124.5cm) high, with circular stone surround.
£1,000–1,500 *S(S)*

A pair of carved stone urns, each body carved in relief with acanthus and ribbon tied swags, on circular bases, 18thC, 25in (64cm) high.
£1,000–1,500 *S(S)*

A pair of composition stone caryatid figures, on fluted bases, early 20thC, 111in (282cm).
£3,000–3,500 *S(S)*

A Vicenza stone figure of a dog, early 20thC, 30in (76cm) high.
£1,500–2,000 *S(S)*

A set of 4 modern composition stone putti, playing musical instruments, each on square panelled pedestals, 58in (147cm) high. **£3,100–3,700** *S(S)*

A pair of carved sandstone urns, c1800, 27in (69cm) high. **£1,200–1,700** *S(S)*

A Portland stone sundial, of wrythen baluster form, supporting a bronze armillary sphere, calibrated with hours, surmounted by a flag, late 19thC, 61in (155cm) high. **£750–900** *S(S)*

A Portland stone seat, with plain rectangular back and replaced oak seat, the overscroll arms surmounted by ball finials, and on fluted supports, 19thC, 100in (254cm). **£3,500–4,000** *S(S)*

A carved limestone seat, with overscroll arms and strapwork carved apron, on shaped supports, early 19thC, 47½in (120cm). **£3,000–3,500** *S(S)*

A Vicenza stone figure of the infant Bacchus, on associated carved stone pedestal, early 20thC, 71in (180cm) high. **£2,000–2,700** *S(S)*

A French sandstone head of a maiden, 19thC, 30in (76cm) high. **£2,000–2,200** *DRU*

Two stone sinks, 22in (56cm) and 18in (46cm). **£80–95** *GRF*

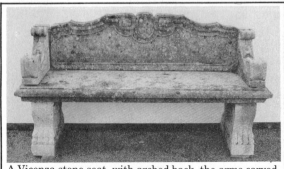

A Vicenza stone seat, with arched back, the arms carved with scrolls, on volute and paw carved supports, early 20thC, 67in (170cm). **£3,500–4,000** *S(S)*

A carved stone lion, c1900,
24in (61cm) high.
£600–800 *S(S)*

A pair of composition stone lions,
mid-20thC, 18in (46cm).
£1,100–1,500 *S(S)*

A stone corner trough,
37in (94cm).
£325–375 *GRF*

A white marble bench, the seat with egg-and-dart
carved border, on lion-headed sphinx supports,
c1900, 57in (144.5cm).
£1,800–2,200 *S(S)*

A limestone bench, the top on
seated Assyrian winged lion
supports, late 19thC, 62in (157cm).
£2,200–2,700 *S(S)*

A Portland stone figure of a putto,
clad in a robe holding a Minerva's
helmet on his head, on associated
canted square base, mid-18thC,
51in (129.5cm) high.
£10,000–12,000 *S(S)*

A Victorian sandstone sundial,
the top centred with a circular
dial, with scroll pierced gnomon,
bearing the date '1665', on
octagonal baluster column and
square base, 56in (142cm) high.
£1,200–1,700 *S(S)*

A pair of Victorian limestone
figures of angels, each wearing
robes, holding a shield, c1860,
50in (127cm) high.
£1,000–1,500 *S(S)*

Terracotta

A pair of terracotta griffins, c1870.
£1,700–2,200 *S(S)*

A pair of terracotta planters,
possibly by Liberty & Co., c1900,
19½in (50cm).
£1,400–1,700 *S(S)*

A pair of French terracotta
baskets, 19thC, 15in (38cm) high.
£1,200–1,700 *S(S)*

A pair of Blashfield terracotta
brackets, each moulded with
volutes and foliage, and a bearded
mask stamped 'J. M. Blashfield
1870', 44in (111.5cm) high.
£600–800 *S(S)*

*J. M. Blashfield purchased some
of the moulds from the Coade
factory when William Croggan,
Eleanor Coade's cousin, closed
down the original factory in 1836.
Blashfield opened his own 'Terra
Cotta' works at Poplar, before
moving to Stamford in 1858.
Although Blashfield called his
material terracotta from the Greek
'baked clay', it would be more
accurate to call it stoneware. The
clay was fired to a temperature of
more than 1,100°C, at which
temperature the clay vitrifies and
becomes non-porous, and thus
more resistant to frost and
the elements.*

A Blanchard terracotta urn, with
Medusa head handles, an everted
egg-and-dart moulded rim, on
rising circular foot, stamped
'Terra Cotta, Mark H. Blanchard
& Co., Blackfriars Road., London
S. CLAY, from the Estate of
Arthur H...', on square moulded
plinth, c1870, 35in (89cm) high.
£1,200–1,700 *S(S)*

*This model seems likely to have
been in production since 1862.
Sir Arthur Helps was Clerk to the
Privy Council and Private
Secretary to Queen Victoria. He
lived at Vernon Hill House, near
Bishops Waltham. In 1860
Blanchard is known to have taken
several samples from clay beds on
Mr. Helps' estate (he was later
knighted). However, after having
these samples tested, Mr. Helps set
up in business using the name of
Bishops Waltham Clay Company
in 1862. Despite his exalted
position at court, Helps lacked
business acumen and the company
went into liquidation in April
1867, finally closing in December
of that year. The business was
then taken over by Blanchard,
who is known to have renewed
the lease in 1871. In 1880
Blanchard left the Blackfriars
Road works in London and moved
to Bishops Waltham.*

A pair of terracotta urns, on
square panelled pedestals,
moulded with lions' masks, and
egg-and-dart borders, stamped
'W. Meeds & Son., Manufacturers,
Burgess Hill, Sussex', c1870,
25½in (65cm) high.
£1,500–2,000 *S(S)*

A Manifattura di Signa
terracotta group of wrestlers,
after the antique, on a shaped
plinth, bearing manufacturer's
stamp and numbered '1435',
36in (91.5cm) high.
£1,500–2,000 *S(S)*

*Manifattura di Signa was a
terracotta manufacturer
operating in Florence, Rome,
Turin and Purugia at the end of
the 19thC, producing a wide
variety of figures, urns and
architectural items and often
copying the antique.*

A French Régence style kingwood writing desk, overlaid with cherub musicians in the manner of Charles Cressent, bearing signature 'F Linke', c1910, 79in (200.5cm). **£22,000-25,000** *S*

A George III mahogany double-sided kneehole desk, c1800, 50in (122cm). **£3,800-4,500** *S*

A rosewood double-sided pedestal desk, the top with leaf-carved moulding and black leather inset, the other side with 3 drawers and a pair of panelled doors, early 19th, 60in (151cm). **£10,000-11,000** *S*

A mid-Georgian mahogany kneehole desk, the fascia with 3 dummy drawers, moulded base and bracket feet, 36in (91.5cm). **£2,000-3,000** *AH*

A South German walnut, birch and line inlaid gilt metal mounted kneehole desk, mid-18thC, 57in (145cm). **£5,800-6,500** *CSK*

A George III mahogany pedestal partners' desk, with leather lined top, on a reveneered plinth base, restored, 62½in (158cm). **£4,800-5,200** *C*

l. A George I burr walnut and walnut kneehole desk, the quarter-veneered top inlaid with feather banding above a baize lined slide, on shaped bracket feet, minor restorations, 30in (76cm). **£9,000-10,000** *C*

r. A George II burr and figured walnut kneehole desk, restored, 33in (83cm). **£9,500-11,000** *C*

A pair of Italian ivory and mother-of-pearl inlaid writing desks, the sides veneered in olivewood, probably Milanese, c1870, 58in (146cm). **£25,000-26,000** *S*

An Anglo-Indian ebony partners' pedestal desk, with mahogany lined frieze drawers to each side, early 19thC, 66in (167.5cm). **£29,000-31,000** *C*

A Regency mahogany
dumb waiter, c1810,
22in (56cm) diam.
£4,000–4,500 *S*

A George II mahogany
dumb waiter, 24in
(62cm) diam.
£2,600–3,000 *S*

A George II mahogany
dumb waiter, c1745,
20in (51cm) diam.
£2,800–3,200 *S*

A pair of George III carved
giltwood mirrors, c1760,
42in (108cm) high.
£15,000–16,000 *S*

A George II parcel gilt
walnut wall mirror,
38in (96cm) high.
£2,000–2,500 *S*

A carved giltwood
mirror, 18thC, 49in
(124cm) high.
£2,200–2,800 *S*

An Italian glass mosaic
mirror, with a view of
Venice, c1900, 59in
(150cm) high.
£4,800–5,200 *S*

A George I giltwood pier
mirror, the cresting apron
with leaves and plumes,
c1720, 70in (178cm) high.
£8,500–10,000 *S*

A giltwood wall mirror,
restored, c1765, 33in
(84cm) high.
£3,000–3,500 *S*

A William & Mary style verre
églomisé pier mirror, decorated
in Bérainesque style, 72in
(183cm) high. **£6,000–7,000** *S*

A gilt gesso carved
mirror, 46in
(116.5cm) high.
£1,500–2,000 *C*

A Spanish carved, gilded and painted frame, the
sides carved with cherubs holding attributes of
St. Barbara, 17thC, 30in (76cm) high.
£6,250–7,000 *C*

A pair of giltwood mirrors, each with rockwork encrusted aprons, 66½in (169cm) high.
£12,000–13,000 *C*

A George III giltwood pierced framed mirror, 44in (112cm) high.
£2,500–3,000 *C*

A French Provincial giltwood mirror, c1800, 70in (177cm) high.
£5,250–5,750 *S*

A German giltwood mirror, mid-18thC, 48in (122cm) high.
£2,250–2,750 *S*

A Spanish carved, gilded, silvered and painted frame, 24½in (62cm) high.
£3,250–3,750 *C*

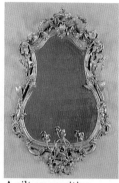

A gilt composition girondole, with 3 candle arms below, c1860, 74in (188cm) high. **£4,500–5,000** *S*

A pair of giltwood mirrors, 67in (170cm) high.
£7,000–7,500 *C*

A George II giltwood wall mirror, c1755, 47in (120cm) high.
£3,000–4,000 *S*

An Italian carved, gilded and painted frame mirror, 20in (51cm) high.
£1,000–1,500 *C*

An Italian carved and gilded frame, 17thC, 10in (26cm) high.
£2,500–3,000 *C*

A mahogany and parcel gilt mirror, 53in (135cm) high.
£3,500–4,000 *C*

A pair of Italian stained fruitwood mirrors, slight damage, 66in (168cm) high. **£6,000–7,000** *CSK*

A Holy Roman Empire carved ebonised frame, c1580, 15in (38cm) high.
£3,500–4,000 *C*

A pair of giltwood mirrors, 30in (77.5cm) high.
£3,500–4,000 *C*

A pair of George III mahogany cheval fire screens, with Regency silk embroidered sliding panels, glazed, 46in (117cm) high. **£4,000–5,000** *C*

A Victorian carved and gilt gesso framed three-fold screen, with floral needlework panels, c1850, 75in (190cm) high. **£3,000–3,500** *S(S)*

A George III mahogany urn stand, the fluted frieze with paterae, with a slide, 11in (28cm) square. **£6,000–7,000** *S*

An Edwardian satinwood semi-elliptical sideboard, c1910, 54in (137cm) wide. **£3,500–4,000** *S(S)*

A George IV ormolu mounted and brass inlaid plum pudding mahogany sideboard, inlaid overall with ebonised lines, restored, 91in (230.5cm) wide. **£5,500–6,500** *C*

A pair of rosewood veneered and brass wall shelves, c1815, 22in (55cm) high. **£7,750–8,500** *S*

A pair of rosewood and parcel gilt open bookshelves, with parcel gilt moulded edges, on turned leaf carved ball feet, c1835, 50in (127cm) high. **£8,500–9,000** *S*

A Victorian mahogany folio stand, on a baluster turned pillar, stamped 'Kane Patent', c1850, 44in (112cm) high. **£1,750–2,000** *S(S)*

A Portuguese or Dutch Colonial lacquer four-leaf screen, 18thC. **£26,000–28,000** *C*

A William IV mahogany library folio stand, with adjustable reading slopes, 42½in (108cm) high. **£4,500–5,000** *C*

A George III mahogany urn stand, with waved gallery and pull-out slide, 27in (68cm) high. **£1,000–1,500** *S(S)*

A mahogany, satinwood and line inlaid bowfronted sideboard, with crossbanded top, late 18thC, 45½in (115.5cm) wide. **£3,500–4,000** *CSK*

A George III solid satinwood and brass wall shelf, c1780, 31in (79cm) high. **£2,750–3,000** *S*

A George IV mahogany serpentine sideboard, with
brass gallery, c1820, 76in (194cm) wide.
£4,000–5,000 *S*

A George III mahogany serpentine sideboard, inlaid
with boxwood lines and partridge wood bands, the
eared top with brass gallery above central frieze
drawer, 66in (168cm) wide. **£7,000–7,500** *CSK*

A George III mahogany sideboard, with crossbanded
top, 6 square tapering legs, c1780, 50in (128cm) wide.
£4,000–5,000 *S*

A Regency mahogany and line inlaid broken
D-shaped sideboard, with central frieze drawer,
arched apron drawer flanked by cupboards, on turned
reeded legs, 67in (170cm) wide.
£3,750–4,250 *CSK*

A George III mahogany double chair-back settee, with padded drop-in seat, on claw-and-ball feet, 56in (137cm) wide. **£13,500–14,000** *C*

A George III mahogany French style sofa, with moulded arm supports, on cabriole legs headed by fan panels, c1775, 83in (211cm) wide. **£10,000–11,000** *S*

A Regency rosewood and cut brass inlaid chaise longue, on sabre legs with brass paw feet and casters, c1820, 72in (183cm) wide. **£3,000–3,500** *S(S)*

A George II style mahogany double chair-back settee, 56in (142.5cm) wide. **£5,800–6,200** *CSK*

An Italian rococo painted and parcel gilt window seat, with out-curved scrolled supports, mid-18thC, 95in (241cm) wide. **£8,000–8,500** *S(NY)*

A Regency ebonised sofa, with scrolled back and arms, on turned tapering legs and brass caps, 86in (219cm) wide. **£13,000–14,000** *C*

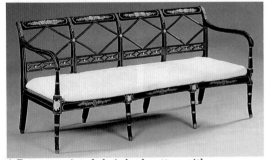

A Regency painted chair-back settee, with open diamond backs, decoration renewed in cream and gilt on black, c1805, 71in (180cm) wide. **£2,500–3,000** *S*

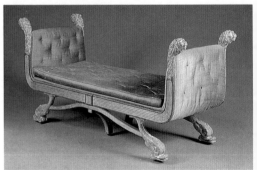

A Regency Sheraton design simulated mahogany and parcel gilt window seat, with twin lions' mask headed scrolled end supports and padded buttoned ends, 46in (117cm) wide. **£14,500–15,500** *C*

l. A pair of Regency holly inlaid brown oak sofas, by George Bullock, 76in (193.5cm) wide. **£25,000–30,000** *C*

A Regency brass inlaid rosewood breakfast table, 48in (121cm) diam. **£2,800–3,200** *C*

A George IV rosewood breakfast table, with bead-and-reel edge, 56in (143cm) diam. **£5,000–5,500** *C*

A George III mahogany and plum pudding mahogany breakfast table, crossbanded in kingwood, restored, 42in (107cm) diam. **£4,250–4,750** *C*

A Regency brass inlaid rosewood breakfast table, 52in (132cm) diam. **£8,000–8,250** *C*

A Regency calamander card table, with brass inlaid rosewood crossbanding, 36in (90cm) wide. **£4,500–5,000** *S*

A George II burr walnut concertina action card table, restored, 36in (91cm) wide. **£42,000–44,000** *C*

A pair of George III satinwood card tables, etched and tinted with flowers, with rosewood and satinwood inlay, c1780, 39in (100cm) wide. **£14,000–16,000** *S*

A pair of Regency brass inlaid rosewood fold-over card tables, the tops inlaid and crossbanded, 34in (86.5cm) wide. **£9,750–10,250** *MEA*

A mahogany breakfast table, with 'fiddle' figured top, reeded edge and sabre legs, c1805, 43in (110cm) wide. **£7,500–8,000** *S*

A George IV tulipwood veneered breakfast table, the hinged top on a beaded square pillar with concave square shelf and sabre legs, with brass stringing, c1820, 51in (130cm) diam. **£4,800–5,500** *S*

A pair of George III harewood, satinwood and marquetry fold-over card tables, 39in (99cm) wide. **£50,000–55,000** *MEA*

A George III strung rosewood card table, with maker's label for J. Taylor of Colchester. **£2,500–2,750** *SWO*

A George III satinwood and crossbanded card table, inlaid with stringing, the tapered square legs surmounted by oval medallions, restored, 37in (93cm) wide. **£1,750–2,000** *S(S)*

A Victorian rosewood card table, on 4 shaped and carved legs with central pillar, lined with green baize. **£1,250–1,500** *JH*

A George III satinwood, sabicu and marquetry card table, inlaid with boxwood and ebonised lines, restored, 38in (95cm) wide. **£6,500–7,000** *C*

An Edwardian mahogany, crossbanded and gilt metal mounted envelope card table, the moulded edged burr walnut top with mother-of-pearl and string inlaid trellis pattern panels, on chamfered legs with brass casters, 22in (56cm) wide. **£1,800–2,000** *AH*

A pair of walnut card tables, with plain feather-banded frieze, 24in (60cm) wide. **£8,500–9,500** *C*

A Louis XVI mahogany card table, with baize lined top above a well, panelled frieze and fluted tapering legs, c1785, 34in (87cm). **£1,800–2,000** *S*

A George III satinwood and marquetry card table, crossbanded in mahogany, reveneered, 41in (104cm) wide. **£2,250–2,500** *C*

A George III satinwood and marquetry card table, crossbanded and inlaid with boxwood and ebonised lines, later marquetry, on square tapering legs, 38in (95cm) wide. **£4,500–5,000** *C*

A Dutch mahogany, floral marquetry and line inlaid card table, with folding top, on square tapering legs, 19thC, 64in (162.5cm) wide. **£4,750–5,000** *CSK*

A Regency gilt metal mounted coromandel, satinwood banded and giltwood card table, 36in (91.5cm) wide. **£2,500–3,000** *CSK*

l. A serpentine mahogany card table, in the French style, with moulded top and fan carved cabriole legs, 37in (94cm) wide. **£2,750–3,000** *S*

A French marquetry centre table, in the manner of Joseph Cremer, c1855, 52in (132cm). **£3,500–4,000** *S*

A French tulipwood, purple heart, marquetry and ormolu mounted centre table, 28in (71cm) wide. **£2,500–3,000** *CSK*

A French marquetry centre table, with gilt bronze mounts, c1870, 51in (130cm) wide. **£3,800–4,200** *S*

An ormolu mounted, brass inlaid mahogany centre table, late 19thC, 26in (66cm). **£7,000–8,000** *C*

A Charles X ormolu and pietra dure centre table, the inlaid Florentine top with brèche violette border, 27in (68.5cm) diam. **£29,000–35,000** *C*

A rosewood marble topped centre table, c1830, 44in (111cm) diam. **£3,500–4,000** *S*

A Victorian marquetry centre table, in the manner of G. J. Morant, 33in (115cm) diam. **£5,250–6,000** *S*

A rosewood and giltwood centre table, with line inlaid crossbanded top, on 3 giltwood dolphin supports and gilt paw feet, 66in (168cm) diam. **£5,500–6,000** *CSK*

A walnut and parcel gilt centre table, with alabaster top, 37in (92.5cm) wide. **£2,500–3,000** *C*

An Italian walnut and marquetry centre table, c1820, 41in (104cm) diam. **£7,500–8,000** *S(S)*

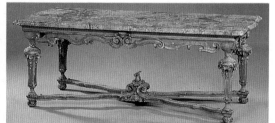

An Italian painted and parcel gilt centre table, with replaced marble top, on baluster legs, restored, mid-18thC, 84in (213cm) wide. **£6,000–7,000** *S*

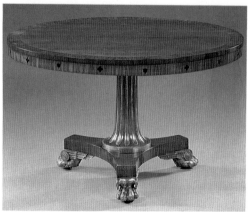

A Regency satinwood centre table, the hinged top with rosewood crossbanding, the frieze inlaid with quatrefoils, c1810, 47in (120cm) diam. **£9,500–11,000** *S*

A mahogany console table, with marble top above a rosette filled trellis frieze, the shaped apron with scrolling acanthus, on hairy claw feet, top repaired, 55in (140cm) wide. **£7,500–8,500** *C*

A George II style brown painted and parcel gilt console table, with marble top, Greek key pattern frieze supported by a splayed eagle on oak branches, on a flowerhead and rockwork base, 44in (112.5cm) wide. **£5,000–6,000** *C*

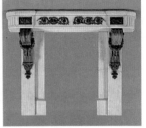

A French gilt bronze mounted Carrara and St. Anne marble console table, c1920, 43in (109cm) high. **£1,800–2,000** *S*

A carved giltwood console table, the frieze and inscrolled legs carved with flowers, 24in (62cm) high. **£1,400–1,800** *S*

A pair of French or Italian giltwood corner console tables, each with white marble top, the frieze with ribbon tied oak swags, the legs in the form of fasces, late 18thC, 33in (84cm) high. **£12,000–13,000** *S*

A pair of George III satinwood console tables, the tops crossbanded in purple heart and inlaid with stringing, c1790, 62in (158cm) wide. **£35,000–37,000** *S*

A pair of Neapolitan painted and giltwood console tables, each with a green mottled marble top, mid-18thC, 48in (122cm) wide. **£32,000–35,000** *S*

A pair of William IV giltwood console tables, with white marble tops, on reeded turned tapering legs, one marble inscribed 'B Horn', one damaged, 60in (154cm) wide. **£4,800–5,200** *C*

A George IV mahogany Pembroke dining table, with 2 flaps, round corners and 6 circular tapering reeded legs, c1820, 59in (150cm) open. **£1,600–2,000** *S*

A Regency mahogany three-pillar dining table, with 2 leaves, each baluster on 3 sabre legs, c1815 and later, 154in (393cm) extended. **£3,250–4,000** *S*

A George IV mahogany dining table, with 2 D-shaped end sections and 2 extra leaves, one associated, 107in (272cm) extended. **£3,500–4,000** *C*

A mahogany twin pedestal dining table, with D-shaped tilt-top end sections and an associated leaf, restored, 19thC, 102in (260cm) extended. **£3,500–4,000** *C*

A mahogany D-shaped dining table, with 4 extra leaves, inlaid with boxwood, 18thC and parts associated, 153in (389cm) extended. **£6,000–6,500** *C*

r. A Victorian mahogany dining table, the moulded top with rounded corners, on lotus carved baluster legs, with 4 leaves and winding handle, c1870, ·172in (436cm) extended. **£3,750–4,000** *S*

An Anglo-Indian padouk dining table, the hinged three-plank top with reeded frieze, on a leaf carved pillar, mid-19thC, 84in (213cm) diam. **£8,750–9,000** *S*

A mahogany three-pillar dining table, with ringed pillar on quadruple sabre legs, with later centre pedestal and 2 later leaves, c1815, 152in (386cm) extended. **£12,000–13,000** *S*

A mahogany two-pedestal D-shaped dining table, restored, top early 19thC, 111in (282.5cm) extended. **£4,800–5,200** *C*

A mahogany three-pillar dining table, on sabre legs, c1825, 84in (214cm). **£4,800–5,000** *S*

r. A mahogany dining table, 152in (386cm) extended. **£8,000–8,500** *MEA*

A George III mahogany dressing table, with fitted interior, probably by Gillows of Lancaster, c1770, 19in (48cm) wide. **£700–800** *S*

A French Louis XV style marquetry vitrine, with serpentine double glazed sides, inlaid with foliage, 34in (86cm) wide. **£3,800–4,000** *S*

A French rosewood and boulle display table, with foliage ormolu mounts, on slender tapering cabriole legs, late 19thC, 29in (74cm) wide. **£1,200–1,500** *E*

An Edwardian satinwood serpentine-shaped display table, with rosewood banding and boxwood and ebony line inlay, 24in (61cm) wide. **£1,800–2,000** *E*

A pair of French Louis XVI style kingwood display tables, with octagonal tapering legs and gilt bronze leaf-cast mounts, c1900, 38in (96cm) wide. **£5,000–6,000** *S*

A French ormolu mounted kingwood vitrine, with cabriole legs and gilt clasps trailing to gilt sabots, 30in (76cm) wide. **£2,500–2,750** *CSK*

A French Empire style mahogany veneered display table, on lion monopodia supports, c1860, 36in (91cm) wide. **£4,800–5,500** *S*

A French ormolu mounted kingwood vitrine, the glazed hinged lid enclosing velvet lined interior, the frieze with pierced mounts of putti with grapes and floral garlands, late 19thC, 25in (62cm) wide. **£2,500–3,000** *CSK*

A German Empire style ormolu mounted burr elm, burr thuya and mahogany dressing table, with later satinwood crossbanded writing surface, possibly reduced width, early 19thC, 41in (104cm) wide. **£4,250–5,000** *C*

l. A French vitrine, with plain top, on cabriole legs, c1870, 36in (90cm) wide. **£3,250–4,000** *S*

A Regency calamander games table, crossbanded in ebony and satinwood, 47in (119cm) wide. **£5,250–6,000** *C*

A mahogany gateleg table, the twin-flap top with moulded edge, on turned legs with fluted scroll feet, 35in (89cm) wide. **£3,750–4,500** *C*

A Russian mahogany and gilt bronze guéridon, c1800, 30in (77cm) diam. **£20,000–22,000** *S*

A Russian marquetry games table, the top with inlaid panel of Mars, c1785, 39cm (98cm) wide. **£17,000–19,000** *S*

A penwork games table, painted and ebonised, c1810, 19in (48cm) square. **£5,000–6,000** *S*

A figured walnut games table, c1860, 21in (53cm) square, closed. **£3,500–4,000** *S*

A mahogany spider gateleg table, with one flap, on turned legs, c1750, 24in (61cm) wide. **£2,000–3,000** *S*

A Georgian laburnum spider gateleg table, crossbanded with padoukwood, restored, 30in (76cm) wide. **£3,500–5,000** *C*

A Louis XV kingwood games table, with long money wells, 34in (85cm) wide. **£3,750–5,000** *S*

An Empire guéridon, with porphyry marble inset top, 22in (56cm) diam. **£3,000–4,000** *S(S)*

A pair of French style satinwood marble topped guéridons, the drawer with purple heart banding, one shelf re-veneered, c1785, 21in (53cm) wide. **£13,500–14,500** *S*

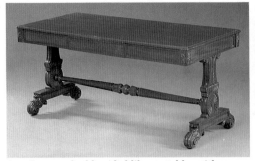

A mahogany double-sided library table, with a drawer in the front and back, carved end supports, pole stetcher, and carved scroll feet, c1840, 62in (156cm) long. **£3,750–5,000** *S*

A Regency rosewood, ebonised and parcel gilt library table, crossbanded in yew wood and kingwood, with decorated frieze, on pierced lyre-shaped end supports, restored, 51in (129cm) wide. **£80,000–85,000** *C*

A mahogany double-sided library table, with leatherette lined top, 3 drawers each to front and back, on slender ringed legs, c1805, 54in (137cm). **£3,000–3,500** *S*

A mahogany brass inlaid double-sided library table, the top with reeded edge, inset with leather, on shaped end supports on reeded sabre legs, c1825, 55in (140cm) long. **£5,750–6,750** *S*

A satinwood inlaid occasional table, the segmented veneered top with musical trophy, c1910, 40in (103cm). **£4,500–5,500** *S(S)*

An early Victorian rosewood occasional table, with engraved white marble top, 21in (53cm) diam. **£1,750–2,000** *C*

A late Victorian walnut octagonal library table, with moulded top above 4 true and 4 false drawers, stamped Gillow & Co., Lancaster, 54in (137cm) wide. **£3,000–3,500** *CSK*

A George IV rosewood library table, the frieze drawers with cedarwood lining, on acanthus carved scroll uprights, damage to veneer, no leather lining, 60in (152cm). **£4,500–5,500** *CSK*

A satinwood occasional table, with crossbanded top, c1910, 35in (90cm) wide. **£1,000–1,500** *S(S)*

An Italian pietre dure occasional table, c1860, 33in (83cm) wide. **£9,000–10,000** *S*

A George III mahogany and satinwood inlaid Pembroke table, with single frieze drawer, 32in (82cm) wide. **£2,500–3,500** *C*

A set of rosewood quartetto tables, each on 2 pairs of ringed legs, c1820, 18in (46cm) wide. **£3,500–4,500** *S*

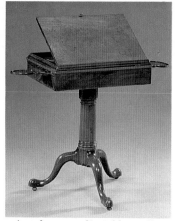

A mahogany adjustable reading table, with candle stands, c1740, 25in (64cm) wide. **£4,250–5,250** *S*

A Victorian coromandel Pembroke table, inlaid with banding, with brass mouldings, c1870, 24in (61cm) wide. **£2,750–3,500** *S(S)*

A set of 4 George III satinwood quartetto tables, the kingwood crossbanded tops with raised borders, on twin turned legs, restored, one with label, largest 18½in (47cm) wide. **£10,000–11,000** *C*

A late Victorian satinwood, mahogany and tulipwood Pembroke table, with frieze drawer, 34in (86cm) wide. **£2,500–3,000** *CSK*

A mahogany Pembroke table, with moulded crossbanded top, curved drawer, and square tapering legs, c1780, 41in (104cm) wide. **£4,500–5,500** *S*

A rosewood double-sided adjustable reading table, with a through drawer, c1825, 24in (61cm) wide. **£1,800–2,200** *S*

A painted Pembroke table, attributed to Henry Clay, Covent Garden, the drawer decorated with husk swags, restored, c1785, 32in (82cm) wide. **£4,500–5,000** *S*

A mahogany side table, with verde antico marble top above a Vitruvian scroll frieze, restored, 72in (183cm) wide. **£12,000–13,000** *C*

An Irish George II style mahogany side table, with marble and quartz top, 19thC, 61in (155cm) long. **£18,500–20,000** *C*

A pair of William IV mahogany mirror-backed side tables, c1830, 22in (57cm) wide. **£8,250–8,750** *S*

A pair of marble topped mahogany side tables, 19thC. **£5,250–6,000** *S*

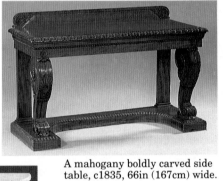

A mahogany boldly carved side table, c1835, 66in (167cm) wide. **£4,500–5,500** *S*

An Italian painted and parcel gilt side table, with later mottled green marble top, 53in (135cm) wide. **£6,000–7,000** *S*

A giltwood side table, c1800, 34in (86cm) high. **£6,000–7,000** *S*

A George IV mahogany serving table, with moulded carved frieze, scrolled legs on paw feet, 84in (213cm) wide. **£4,000–5,000** *C*

An oyster veneered walnut side table, with geometric inlay, above a frieze drawer, 37in (94cm) wide. **£2,250–3,250** *C*

A Louis XVI painted and carved side table, with marble top, c1790, 26in (66cm) wide. **£5,250–6,000** *S*

l. A Florentine giltwood side table, the frieze carved with leaves and flowers, with later faux marble top, on husk-filled fluted tapering legs, c1800, 49in (125cm) wide. **£4,500–6,000** *S*

A William IV mahogany side table, with later chequer pattern inlaid marble top, 84in (213cm) wide. **£9,000–12,000** *CSK*

A satinwood sofa table, crossbanded in rosewood and inlaid with burr yew, c1800, 63in (160cm) wide. **£15,000–20,000** *S*

A Regency mahogany sofa table, the twin flap top crossbanded in calamander, above a frieze drawer, 39in (98.5cm) wide. **£4,500–6,000** *C*

A Regency calamander sofa table, attributed to Gillows, with mahogany lined frieze drawers, restored, 62in (157cm) wide. **£10,500–12,000** *C*

A Regency rosewood sofa table, crossbanded and inlaid with boxwood lines, with 2 true and 2 false drawers, 59in (149.5cm) wide. **£13,500–16,000** *C*

A George IV japanned sofa table, with 2 drawers and double scroll supports, decorated throughout with gilt chinoiseries on black, c1820, 61in (154cm) open. **£5,750–7,000** *S*

A rosewood and parcel gilt sofa table, the top with crossbanded border and cut brass stringing, c1810, 38in (97cm) wide. **£6,000–8,000** *S(S)*

A rosewood and parcel gilt sofa table, the top with bands of cut brass, with gilt metal claw feet and casters, c1825, 37in (94cm) wide. **£12,500–15,000** *S(S)*

A Regency rosewood inlaid sofa table, restored, 58in (147cm) wide. **£4,500–5,500** *C*

A calamander and boxwood strung sofa table, with 2 drawers, on end supports and splayed feet, c1810, 38in (96cm) wide. **£14,000–16,000** *S(S)*

r. A Regency calamander sofa table, crossbanded in satinwood and ebony, with part cedar lined frieze drawers, restored, 60in (152cm) wide. **£8,500–10,000** *C*

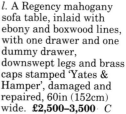

l. A Regency mahogany sofa table, inlaid with ebony and boxwood lines, with one drawer and one dummy drawer, downswept legs and brass caps stamped 'Yates & Hamper', damaged and repaired, 60in (152cm) wide. **£2,500–3,500** *C*

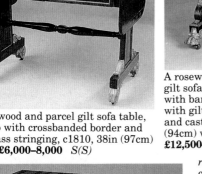

A pair of early Victorian ormolu and porcelain mounted, tulipwood, kingwood banded and line inlaid serpentine work/writing tables, 17½in (45cm) wide. **£6,800–7,500** *CSK*

A mahogany tripod table, the top with egg-and-dart carved edge, c1755, 11in (28cm) wide. **£2,500–3,000** *S*

A satinwood tripod table, the brass bound top on a slender pillar with sabre legs, c1800, 28in (71cm) high. **£3,500–4,000** *S*

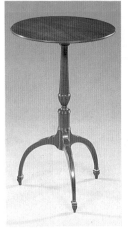

A pair of mahogany tripod tables, on slender baluster, mid-19thC, 18in (46cm) diam. **£2,750–3,750** *S*

A walnut games/work table, with boxwood stringing, c1860, 27in (68.5cm) wide. **£2,250–2,750** *S(S)*

A mahogany work table, inlaid with boxwood stringing, c1790, 19½in (49cm) wide. **£1,400–1,600** *S(S)*

A mahogany tripod table, with spindle galleried top, knopped stem, leaf-carved cabriole legs and claw feet, c1750, 12in (30.5cm) diam. **£3,750–4,250** *S*

A mahogany tripod table, with hinged pie-crust top, on plain stem, leaf-carved cabriole legs and claw-and-ball feet, c1750, 46in (116cm) diam. **£2,000–2,500** *S*

A Regency ormolu mounted mahogany and specimen marble work table, the inlaid top with central jasper panel above a panelled mahogany lined frieze drawer, by James Newton, 20in (51cm) wide. **£7,500–9,000** *C*

l. A George II mahogany tripod table, the circular tilt-top above a baluster turned pillar, restored, c1750, 31½in (80cm) wide. **£550–800** *S(S)*

A Regency brass inlaid and mounted rosewood work table, with lyre-shaped end supports, on scrolled legs and anthemion caps, 27½in (70cm) wide. **£3,750–4,750** *C*

A mid-Victorian burr yew, burr walnut and ebonised writing table, banded in sycamore, restored, 44in (111.5cm) wide. **£7,500–8,500** *C*

A George IV mahogany leather lined writing table, 53½in (136cm) wide. **£4,250–5,250** *C*

A William IV rosewood whatnot, the base with frieze drawer, raised on reeded bun supports, 42in (107cm) high. **£1,500–2,000** *Bri*

A mahogany writing table, possibly Irish, the top with 5 panels for leather, c1740, 89in (226cm) long. **£24,000–28,000** *S*

A Regency mahogany whatnot, 56in (142cm) high. **£3,500–4,500** *C*

A rosewood writing table, the leather lined top above 2 frieze drawers to each side, with downswept legs and brass paw feet, possibly originally with 4 legs, 54in (137cm) wide. **£8,500–9,500** *C*

A Regency mahogany whatnot, with galleried tiers, 39½in (100cm) high. **£2,750–3,250** *C*

A pair of Continental Empire style mahogany torchères, c1900, 50in (127cm) high. **£4,500–5,500** *S*

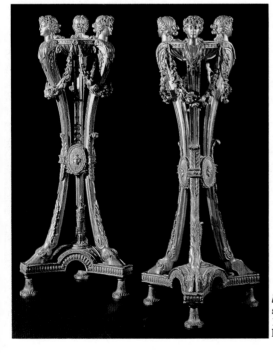

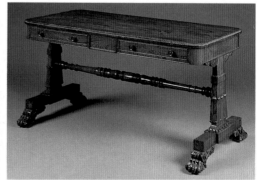

An early Victorian rosewood writing table, with 2 mahogany-lined frieze drawers, spreading end supports headed by scrolls and carved, paw feet, 57in (145cm) wide. **£4,800–6,000** *C*

l. A pair of George III giltwood tripod torchères, supplied by William Gates to the Prince of Wales in 1781, each with later red marble tops, 48in (122cm) high, excluding marble. **£145,000–150,000** *C*

An Italian marble group of Cupid asleep on a rocky outcrop, with Psyche, and an owl symbolising night behind his head, late 19thC, 29in (73.5cm) high. **£10,500–11,500** *S(S)*

A pair of white marble campana-shaped urns, 31½in (80cm) high. **£2,500–3,000** *S(S)*

A French cast iron fountain figure, c1870, 61in (155cm) high. **£6,750–7,250** *S(S)*

A Victorian composition stone figure of a nymph, 61in (155cm) high. **£3,500–4,000** *MSW*

A marble urn, carved with Apollo and Daphne, mid-19thC, 46in (116.5cm) high. **£2,800–3,200** *S(S)*

A set of Italian white marble figures of The Seasons, 66½in (170cm) high. **£7,500–8,000** *S(S)*

A Portland stone seat, with panelled back, the end supports in the form of seated lions beneath lobed finials, late 18thC, 72in (182.5cm) wide. **£12,250–13,000** *S(S)*

A bronze fountain, in the form of a scallop shell above fish and foliage, with a stylised dolphin, plumbed for water in front of the frog, late 19thC, 57in (144.5cm) wide. **£4,800–5,200** *S(S)*

A pair of bronze Oriental figures, the man and woman seated in robes holding a fan and a parasol, weathered green patination, c1950, 44in (111.5cm) high. **£16,000–16,500** *S(S)*

A Portland stone seat, with panelled back, the seated lions supports on paw feet, weathered, late 18thC, 72in (182.5cm) wide. **£11,000–12,000** *S(S)*

A pair of cast iron garden urns, with wavy borders, raised flowers and central ovals, on scrolled feet.
£350–400 *FLE*

A pair of Bath stone plain ovoid urns, each with lug handles, 18thC, 24in (61cm) high.
£1,200–2,000 *S(S)*

A cast iron group, stamped 'J.J. Ducel et Fils', late 19thC, 64in (163cm).
£8,000–9,000 *S(S)*

A bronzed cast iron group of a cherub, putto and water putto, after Mazière, the base stamped 'J. J. Ducel et Fils, Rue de Forges, Paris, late 19thC, 64in (163cm) high. **£8,750–10,000** *S(S)*

l. A white marble group of 'The Swan Girl', by George Simonds, damaged, signed and dated on reverse '1898', 66½in (168cm) high.
£20,000–22,000 *C*

A terracotta casting of the Warwick vase, the body with bearded masks and entwined branch handles, c1860, 25in (64cm) high. **£4,000–5,000** *MSW*

A Bath stone seat, carved in relief with Celtic designs, 18thC, 90½in (230cm) wide.
£6,500–7,500 *S(S)*

An Italian white marble group of Bacchus, c1860, on a composition stone pedestal.
£6,000–8,000 *S(S)*

A white marble group, inscribed 'Dorothea from Don Quixote, John Bell SC'.
£4,500–5,500 *S(S)*

A cast iron model of Diana the Huntress, stamped 'J.J. Ducel & Fils, Rue des Forges, Paris', c1870, 132in (653cm) high overall.
£13,000–18,000 *S(S)*

A pair of Portland stone figures of young satyrs, one standing playing the cymbals, the other a lyre, 18thC, 39in (99cm) high.
£5,500–6,500 *S(S)*

A white marble figure of a putto, circular base signed 'G Dupre Fece il 1871'.
£10,000–11,000 *S(S)*

A white marble figure of The Venus De Medici, on an associated stone pedestal, 102in (259cm) overall. **£5,000–6,000** *S(S)*

A white marble figure of Paride, c1800, 63in (160cm) high.
£9,000–10,000 *S(S)*

A white marble figure of Diana de Gabies, late 19thC, on associated pedestal.
£6,000–7,000 *S(S)*

A set of 4 carved stone urns, each lobed body with egg-and-dart carved rim, on ribbed circular foot, square base and square panelled pedestal, c1800, 55in (140cm). **£22,000–25,000** *S(S)*

A pair of urns, stamped 'Terracotta M.H. Blanchard & Co.', c1870, 49½in (125cm).
£2,750–3,500 *S(S)*

A matched pair of carved Bath stone urns, mid-18thC, 42in (107cm) high.
£6,000–7,000 *S(S)*

A set of 4 Vicenza stone statues, representing The Seasons, on composition stone pedestals, mid-20thC, 98½in (250cm) high.
£7,000–10,000 *S(S)*

A Restauration gilt bronze fender, in the form of a balustrade surmounted by 2 lionesses, c1810, 39in (100cm) wide. **£1,800–2,000** *S*

A Restuaration bronze and gilt bronze fender, the frieze decorated with berried leaves, c1825, 29½in (75cm) wide. **£1,300–1,800** *S*

A brass and iron serpentine fronted fire grate, with arched backplate decorated with ribbon tied swags, c1900, 32½in (82.5cm) wide. **£2,200–2,500** *CSK*

A polished steel serpentine fire grate, the railed basket above a pierced frieze, centred by an engraved oval, with arched backplate, 32in (81cm) wide. **£1,300–1,600** *CSK*

A French white Carrara marble gilt bronze mounted fireplace, the moulded shelf with gilt bronze beading, the frieze with 2 panels flanking a central cartouche, marble restored, c1870, 44in (111.5cm) wide. **£700–1,000** *S*

A Restauration bronze and gilt bronze fender, the plinths faced by profile medallions surmounted by lions, c1825, 47in (120cm) wide. **£2,800–3,000** *S*

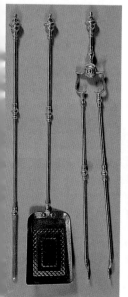

A set of 3 brass fire irons, the shovel with pierced steel pan, mid-19thC. **£850–950** *S*

A brass and steel fire grate, the serpentine basket with baluster supports above a rocaille cast frieze, 36½in (93cm) high. **£975–1,250** *CSK*

A brass serpentine fronted fire grate, the railed basket above a pierced frieze with engraved birds and scrolls, 30½in (77cm) wide. **£950–1,250** *CSK*

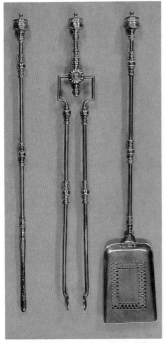

A French bronze and ormolu adjustable fender, the stepped uprights surmounted by seated lions, with railed frieze and moulded base, 53in (134.5cm) wide. **£1,500–1,750** *CSK*

A Restauration bronze and gilt bronze fender, each plinth surmounted by a recumbent sphinx and faced by female masks, c1820, 56in (142cm) wide extended. **£2,250–2,750** *S*

A Restauration bronze and gilt bronze fender, each plinth surmounted by winged griffons and faced by Zeus's attributes, c1820, 48in (123cm) wide extended. **£3,000–3,500** *S*

A set of brass mounted steel fire irons, the circular handles with inset beaded brass bands, c1790. **£2,800–3,200** *S*

A set of 3 brass fire irons, stamped with maker's mark 'JW', late 18thC. **£2,000–2,500** *S*

A pair of Louis XVI gilt bronze chenets, each in the form of a sphinx with a basket of fruit on her head, c1780, 13½in (34cm) wide. **£2,250–2,500** *S*

A pair of nickel alloy fire grates, with railed serpentine baskets, late 19thC, 29in (74cm) wide. **£3,600–4,000** *CSK*

An Empire bronze and ormolu adjustable fender, the uprights modelled with seated greyhounds, 53½in (136cm) wide. **£1,000–1,200** *CSK*

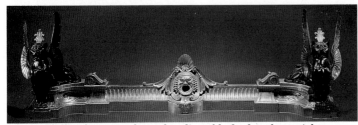

A Louis Phillipe bronze and ormolu adjustable fender, the uprights modelled with winged lions, the frieze centred by an Egyptian style 'tragic' mask, 49½in (126cm) wide extended. **£1,000–1,200** *CSK*

A set of 3 brass and steel fire irons, on a wrought iron tripod stand, mid-19thC. **£1,300–1,500** *S*

POTTERY
Bottles

A harvest flagon, the body with tooled border, short neck and strap handle, covered in a mahogany brown glaze, probably Sussex pottery, chips to rim, 19thC, 9½in (24cm).
£400–500 *S(S)*

A stoneware oviform bottle, covered in an apron of mottled dark brown glaze over grey, the body incised 'Jemaco Rumm 1728' and the neck inscribed 'Richd Niblin'?, damaged, perhaps Vauxhall, 18½in (47cm).
£950–1,200 *C*

A German salt glazed stoneware bellarmine, with loop handle, applied with 3 oval panels, each with a figure, a bird, leaves, the date '1670' and scattered flowerheads, the neck applied with the Cardinal's mask, c1670, 16in (40cm).
£1,800–2,200 *DN*

Busts

A creamware bust of Locke, decorated in coloured enamels, the titled socle decorated with puce bands, some flaking, c1815, 7½in (18cm).
£250–300 *DN*

A Ralph Wood Junior pearlware bust of George Washington, 1790–1800, with light grey curly hair tied in black en queue, brown eyes and ruddy cheeks, wearing a white jabot, a white patterned black waistcoat and a sponged pale blue coat, on a black marblised waisted plinth, impressed on the reverse 'Washington' and Ra. Wood Burslem mark, some damage, 10in (25cm).
£1,500–2,000 *S(NY)*

A Ralph Wood pearlware bust of John Milton, c1790, after the model by Jean-Michel Rysbrack, impressed 'R. Wood' and mould number '81', together with an Enoch Wood style bust of Rev. John Wesley wearing white bands and black clerical robes, on a waisted plinth marblised in grey, green and yellow, edged in gilding, some damage, 9 and 11½in (23 and 29cm).
£300–400 *S(NY)*

Cottages & Pastille Burners

A Staffordshire cottage, with green and floral decoration, c1855, 5in (13cm).
£240–265 *JO*

A Spode pastille burner and cover, modelled as an octagonal cottage, the roof applied with flowers and foliage, some damage, printed mark, c1820, 4½in (11cm).
£550–650 *CSK*

A Staffordshire cottage, with floral decoration and black base, c1835, 6in (15cm).
£400–500 *JO*

A pearlware pastille burner and cover, modelled as an octagonal cottage, with 'thatched' roof, decorated in black and iron red, 19thC, 4⅜in (11cm).
£100–120 *DN*

A Staffordshire pastille burner, 19thC, 5in (13cm).
£200–250 *DUN*

> In the Ceramics section when there is only one measurement it refers to the height of the piece, unless otherwise stated.

A Staffordshire cottage, with green and orange floral decoration, c1860, 7in (18cm).
£200–245 *JO*

A Staffordshire cottage, decorated in floral colours, c1860, 7in (18cm).
£175–200 *JO*

A Staffordshire cottage, with animals, decorated in orange, green and gilt, 6½in (16cm).
£350–400 *JO*

A Staffordshire cottage, decorated in orange, green, yellow, brown and pink, c1860, 4⅜in (11cm).
£125–150 *JO*

A Staffordshire pastille burner, decorated in green and orange, c1860, 8in (20cm).
£200–245 *DeA*

A Staffordshire cottage, with green and brown floral decoration, c1845, 5½in (14cm).
£140–160 *JO*

Cups

A Staffordshire salt glazed cup, c1750.
£400–465 *JHo*

A Quimper cup and saucer, c1915, cup 3in (7.5cm), saucer 7½in (19cm) diam.
£85–100 *VH*

Figures - Animals

A pair of Liverpool tea bowls and saucers, transfer printed in black with The Rock Garden and Rural Conversations, from the factory of Philip Christian, c1766.
£400–500 *C*

A Bristol delft polychrome loving cup and cover, painted in blue, iron red and yellow on the baluster shaped body and around the blue ringed mushroom knop on the cover, with panels of stylised flowering plants, the rim with a chain border, the neck with an iron red and blue border of leafage, blue striped strap handles, some damage, c1725, 7½in (19cm).
£4,000–5,000 *S(NY)*

A pearlware figure of a cockerel, after a Wood original, sponged in brown and ochre, perched upon a mound with green washed border, damaged, c1800, 5in (13cm).
£520–600 *S(S)*

A slipware model of a bear, holding a dog between it's forepaws, wearing a muzzle and chain, poured with cream slip streaked with brown, damaged, late 18thC, 10in (25cm).
£600–700 *CSK*

A majolica model of a heron, painted in pale grey and white with pink and yellow features, its tail feathers painted in yellow and white enriched in black, standing on a pierced tree trunk, impressed mark, damaged and restored, c1870, 21½in (54cm).
£700–900 *C*

A Staffordshire parakeet, decorated in green, ochre, brown and blue, 3½in (9cm).
£500–550 *JHo*

A Prattware figure of an eagle, with an ochre beak and legs, brown crest and plumage spotted in blue, yellow and ochre and sponged in brown, modelled with raised wings, on green rocky perch, above a base patterned with blue squiggles and ochre dots, on an incised ground between impressed bands of yellow and ochre lozenges, repaired, c1810, 9½in (24cm).
£2,500–3,000 *S(NY)*

A Staffordshire tortoisehell glazed figure of a hawk, with incised plumage on his wings and tail, the cream coloured body streaked in manganese and ochre, perched on a tree stump incised with bark and coloured in teal blue and manganese, restored, c1765, 8in (20cm).
£650–850 *S(NY)*

A Prattware figure of a hawk, with brown eyes, legs and tail tip, ochre sponged neck and breast, and yellow, ochre and blue wing and tail feathers, perched on a green mound, moulded on either side with a large ochre blossom above an ochre sponged square base, chipped, c1805, 6½in (16cm).
£1,700–2,000 *S(NY)*

A Staffordshire bird, decorated in cream, ochre, red, black and green, early 19thC, 3½in (9cm).
£200–220 *JHo*

A Prattware hen, possibly Staffordshire, 7½in (19cm).
£1,400–1,600 *JHo*

A Yorkshire pottery bird, decorated in brown and ochre, on green base, early 19thC, 5½in (14cm).
£1,200–1,350 *JHo*

A Rockingham figure of a recumbant cat, with orange collar and tortoiseshell markings, above a gilt band, c1830, 2in (5cm) wide.
£420–500 *DN*

A mid-Victorian Staffordshire dog group, c1860, 10in (25cm).
£250–300 *DeA*

A treacle glazed earthenware figure of a cat, seated on an oval base, the yellow ware body covered in a syrupy brown glaze, damaged, probably Staffordshire, c1880, 10½in (26cm).
£200–250 *S(NY)*

A Delft model of a seated cat, with a mouse caught in its jaws, some chips and flakes, 19thC, 8½in (21cm).
£500–600 *CSK*

A pair of St. Bernard dogs, painted with patches of black and brown, the features picked out in colours, the collars enriched in gilt, damaged and restored, c1885, 14in (35cm) wide.
£550–700 *CSK*

A Staffordshire creamware tortoisehell glazed figure of a lion, his body and the base splashed with manganese brown, the centre of his back with splashes of ochre, cracks, c1770, 7in (18cm).
£480–520 *S(NY)*

A Wood family creamware figure of a setter, his white curly coat with dark grey spots, one grey ear and black eyes, seated on the green glazed top of a waisted base, with a pale yellow cable moulded upper edge and a brown washed foot rim, cracked, c1785, 5in (13cm).
£1,000–1,200 *S(NY)*

A Staffordshire elephant, c1820, 4in (10cm).
£2,000–2,200 *JHo*

This is a rare size for a group of this type.

A Staffordshire creamware figure of a Suffolk punch, his cream coloured body with drippy brown spots, his eyes, incised mane and lightly moulded harness picked out in brown, on green washed base, cracked, c1800, 7½in (19cm).
£4,300–4,500 *S(NY)*

A Staffordshire lion, decorated in brown and ochre, c1830, 7in (17.5cm) wide.
£1,200–1,400 *JO*

A Staffordshire rabbit, early 19thC, 4in (10cm) wide.
£600–800 *JHo*

A Staffordshire tortoiseshell glazed figure of a lion, with a shaggy mane and an open mouth, baring his teeth and tongue, the cream coloured body splashed in brown, green and blue, some damage, c1765, 3½in (9cm).
£1,500–2,000 *S(NY)*

This model would appear to be adapted from a late 17thC Chinese porcelain (probably blanc-de-chine) figure of a fu lion.

A Staffordshire lion, wearing a crown, with background bocage, decorated in brown, ochre, green, red and blue, restored, early 19thC, 6in (15cm).
£1,200–1,350 *JHo*

A pair of Staffordshire deer,
c1820, 8½in (21cm).
£1,000–1,200 *JO*

A pair of 'comforter' spaniels,
painted with black patches,
the features picked out in
natural tones, their chains
enriched in gilt, minor damage,
each impressed with shape
number '3' to the base, c1850,
9in (22cm).
£300–400 *CSK*

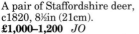

A Ralph Wood pearlware figure
of a ram, covered with Whieldon
type glazes in tones of grey,
brown, green and ochre, on a
naturalistic rocky base, minor
damage, c1790, 7in (18cm) wide.
£1,000–1,200 *S(S)*

A Staffordshire brown lion,
c1870, 9in (23cm).
£400–600 *JO*

A Continental pottery green
glazed flower holder, modelled
as a seated pig, the back pierced
with 3 lines of apertures,
damaged and repaired, 19thC,
8in (20cm) long.
£100–150 *CSK*

A Staffordshire poodle, on
base, c1830, 4in (10cm).
£140–160 *DeA*

A Ralph Wood type glazed goat,
c1790, 7in (17.5cm) wide.
£2,500–2,850 *JHo*

A Staffordshire squirrel,
decorated in cream, green and
ochre, c1770, 7½in (18cm).
£3,000–3,500 *JHo*

A Ralph Wood type Staffordshire
creamware figure of a ram, the
horns and hooves picked out in
brown, on green glazed mound
base, one horn damaged, c1790,
6in (15cm) wide.
£500–600 *DN*

A Staffordshire brown glazed
squirrel, on green base, c1770,
5in (13cm).
£2,000–2,200 *JHo*

Figures - People

A Staffordshire salt glazed stoneware seated figure, decorated in blue and grey, 2½in (6cm).
£3,000–3,650 *JHo*
This figure is ex-Gullanz Collection.

Two Staffordshire figures on square bases, from a set of The Four Seasons, the girl with wheat is 'Autumn', 18thC.
£150–200 each *DeA*

A Staffordshire figure of Nicodemus, decorated in green, pink, blue, cream, red and brown, early 19thC, 11in (28cm).
£750–850 *JHo*

A Staffordshire group of Madonna and Child, wearing brown gown and red cloak, on green base, c1800, 13½in (34cm).
£700–1,000 *JO*

A Staffordshire figure of a Turkish gentleman, wearing a green coat, c1800, 6in (15cm).
£200–245 *DeA*

A pair of Staffordshire figures, 'Anthony' and 'Cleopatra', decorated in mauve and orange, c1800, 12in (31cm) long.
£2,000–2,400 *JO*

A Staffordshire figure group, Flight From Egypt, c1820, 11in (28cm).
£1,400–1,600 *JO*

A pair of Staffordshire figures of Andromache and Hygeia, c1810, 10½in (26cm).
£1,200–1,400 *JO*

A Staffordshire figure of a maid, wearing a puce dress, c1810, 6in (15cm).
£300–400 *JO*

A pair of Staffordshire figures of Elijah and The Widow', by Obadiah Sherratt, c1830, 9½in (24cm).
£1,200–1,400 *JO*

A Staffordshire group of Abraham and Isaac, c1820, 7½in (19cm).
£1,200–1,350 *JHo*

A Staffordshire 'Friendship' group, c1800, 6½in (16cm).
£400–500 *JO*

A Staffordshire figure of Jeremiah, wearing a blue and gold cloak, c1820, 10in (25cm).
£1,800–2,000 *JO*

A Staffordshire group, Return of the Prodigal and Killing the Fatted Calf, with removable bocage, c1820, 13in (33cm).
£5,000–6,000 *JO*

A Staffordshire group, with dancing dogs, c1820, 9in (23cm).
£4,000–4,500 *JHo*

A Staffordshire portrait figure Tallis group, by Parr, representing Garibaldi standing by his horse, combed base, 19thC, 10in (25cm).
£400–450 *L&E*

A Staffordshire group of Abraham offering up Isaac, wearing a green and manganese robe, c1820, 10½in (26cm).
£900–1,400 *JO*

A Staffordshire group of the Welsh Tailor's Wife, c1830, 6½in (16cm).
£300–400 *JO*

A Ralph Wood Staffordshire group of The Vicar and Moses, the blue coated clerk reading a sermon below, the front with an impressed title between winged cherubs' heads, impressed model number '62', restored, c1775, 9in (23cm).
£250–350 *S(S)*

A Staffordshire Tythe Pig
group, c1830.
£1,600–1,800 *JO*

A Staffordshire pearlware group
of dandies, the gentleman
wearing a black hat and coat, tan
breeches and yellow gloves,
carrying a green purse, his
companion wearing a white
plumed pale blue hat, a lilac coat,
a rose striped white skirt, black
shoes and carrying a yellow
purse, behind them a green tree
stump, on a brown banded base,
repaired, c1820, 8½in (21cm).
£700–1,000 *S(NY)*

A Staffordshire pearlware group
of dandies, modelled as a
gentleman wearing a black hat
and coat and black striped salmon
breeches, strolling arm-in-arm
with his companion wearing a
yellow hat, turquoise coat, yellow
skirt and blue shoes, each
wearing yellow gloves and
carrying a yellow purse, before
a green tree stump, on a
rectangular base with an iron
red hatchwork border, damaged
and restored, c1820, 8½in (21cm).
£700–1,000 *S(NY)*

A Staffordshire figure of The
Reading Maid, by Obadiah
Sherratt, c1830, 12in (31cm).
£500–650 *JO*

A Staffordshire
figure wearing
an orange cloak
and blue
jacket, c1845,
19in (48cm).
£400–500 *JO*

A Wood family creamware group
of The Lost Sheep, the shepherd
wearing a dark brown hat and
shoes, light brown waistcoat and
coat and pale olive green
breeches, carrying the sheep
across his shoulders, walking by a
brown tree stump on a brown and
green rocky mound base, some
damage and restoration, c1780,
9in (22.5cm).
£850–950 *S(NY)*

A pair of Ralph Wood Staffordshire figures of St. Peter and St Paul, St. Peter wearing cream robe with green lining, St. Paul wearing wearing a pink robe with green lining, 14½in (37cm).
£700–800 each *JO*

An assembled set of pearlware Pratt type allegorical figures of The Four Seasons, 'Spring' and 'Summer', each standing on a grey and green mottled mound above a rose and black sponged low square base, c1830, Autumn and Winter later, 8½ to 9in (21 to 23cm).
£500–800 *S(NY)*

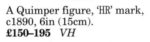

A Quimper figure, 'HR' mark, c1890, 6in (15cm).
£150–195 *VH*

A Staffordshire figure of St. Luke, c1820, 9½in (24cm).
£400–500 *JO*

A Wood family creamware pastoral group of The Flute Player, modelled as a shepherd wearing a blue plumed grey hat, a pale green coat, white waistcoat and pale yellow breeches, playing a flute and seated on a grassy cairn, beside his listening companion, wearing a green hat and skirt, pale yellow stomacher, grey dress and blue edged white apron, behind them a blue flowering tree and beneath their feet a recumbent goat and sheep, on the tan and green mound base, damaged and repaired, impressed mould number '88', c1780, 10½in (26cm).
£500–800 *S(NY)*

A Victorian Staffordshire group entitled 'Departure', c1830, 9½in (24cm).
£250–300 *DeA*

A Victorian Staffordshire group of The New Marriage Act, 'John Frill and Ann Boke both aged 21, That is right says the Parson, Amen says the Clerk', c1860, 6½in (16cm).
£350–400 *DeA*

An earthenware caricature figure of Benjamin Disraeli, damages and repairs, impressed marks and registration mark for 1876, 17in (43cm).
£350–450 *CSK*

A Staffordshire figure, Just a Peck, wearing a blue coat and yellow breeches, with removable hat, c1860, 13in (33cm).
£300–340 *DeA*

A Staffordshire equestrian figure, possibly portraying Garibaldi, c1860, 9½in (24cm).
£160–180 *RWB*

A mid-Victorian Staffordshire group, Tam-o'-shanter and Sooter Johnny, c1870, 13½in (34cm).
£240–285 *DeA*

A Staffordshire penholder, modelled as a man and a woman, possibly the Prince Regent and Mrs Fitzherbert, c1840, 6in (15cm).
£200–225 *RWB*

A Victorian Staffordshire figure of a seated judge, c1860, 9½in (24cm).
£225–260 *DeA*

A Victorian Staffordshire figure, entitled 'Sexton', c1860, 14½in (37cm).
£350–380 *DeA*

A Staffordshire 'Welch Goat' group, c1850, 11in (28cm).
£180–200 *RWB*

A Staffordshire figure of St. Winefride, the Patron Saint of Holywell in Clwyd, c1850, 13in (33cm).
£270–300 *RWB*

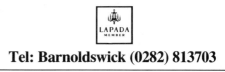

A two-sided figure, entitled
'Water' and 'Gin', c1890, 9in (23cm).
£150–185 *DeA*

A Prattware figure of a woman
and child, c1800, 10in (25cm).
£650–750 *JHo*

A pair of Victorian Staffordshire
figures of Queen Victoria and
The Prince of Wales, c1865,
17½in (45cm).
£550–600 *DeA*

Victorian Staffordshire Figures

A standing figure of a clergyman,
either Dr. Thomas Raffles or the
Revd. John Fletcher, wearing
typical dress, resting his hand on
a bible above a plinth, on a
circular gilt line base, sparsely
coloured, damaged, 19thC,
8½in (21cm), D41.
£150–250 *CSK*

A Staffordshire group portraying
King John signing the Magna
Carta, c1860, 12½in (32cm), E1(a).
£160–180 *RWB*

A Staffordshire figure of a sailor
figure dancing the hornpipe,
c1835, 8in (20cm), C258.
£500–550 *RWB*

Staffordshire Figures

The letters and figures at the end of
each caption refer to *Staffordshire
Portrait Figures*, by P.D Gordon
Pugh, pub. Antique Collectors' Club
Ltd., 1970.

A pair of Staffordshire figures of
Queen Victoria and Prince Albert,
c1845, 11in (28cm), A42, A7.
£380–420 *RWB*

A figure of
Jullien, c1847,
8in (20cm),
E162.
£500–550
RWB

A figure of Robert Burns, taking
snuff, wearing a blue long coat,
pink waistcoat and breeches, on a
shaped gilt line base, damaged,
c1848, 7½in (19cm), H56.
£600–700 *CSK*

Flatware

A Bristol delft plate, decorated in pale blue, blue, green and red, c1730, 8in (20cm) diam.
£600–660 *JHo*

A Bristol delft charger, painted blue, red, yellow and green on a pale blue ground, c1760, 13in (33cm) diam.
£2,000–2,200 *JHo*

A Bristol delft charger, with an Oriental design painted in blue, yellow, green and red on a pale blue ground.
£2,400–2,650 *JHo*

A delft blue and white plate, c1695, 9in (22.5cm) diam.
£1,400–1,850 *JHo*

A delft charger, painted in blue, green and yellow, probably London, c1710, 13½in (34.cm) diam.
£8,400–8,800 *JHo*

A Lambeth delft balloon design plate, painted in green, puce, blue and white, c1785, 8in (20cm) diam.
£1,000–1,100 *JHo*

An English delft plate, centrally decorated in blue within a stylised flower and scroll border, rim chips, c1725, 9in (23cm) diam. **£200–250** *DN*

A Bristol delft Adam and Eve dish, painted in colours, damaged, c1740, 13in (33cm) diam. **£1,000–1,500** *CSK*

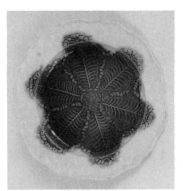

A Staffordshire cauliflower design plate, decorated in green on a cream background, c1770, 9½in (24cm) diam. **£1,700–1,950** *JHo*

An English delft dish, centrally decorated in blue and black with a bunch of grapes, the blue ground border with stylised flowers and emblems, cracks, c1700, 8in (20cm) wide. **£250–350** *DN*

A pair of delft dishes, each painted in blue with a chinoiserie scene of a figure crossing a bridge between a temple and an island, framed within a stylised floral border, London or Bristol, c1750, 4½in (11cm) diam. **£1,000–1,500** *S(S)*

A Staffordshire solid agate silver-shaped salver, the scalloped and barbed rim lightly moulded on the edge with shells, the underside raised on 3 waisted hemispherical legs, and the whole marbled in cream, teal blue and shades of brown, c1750, 6in (15cm) diam. **£3,500–4,000** *S(NY)*

A Staffordshire slipware plate, c1770, 14in (35.5cm) diam. **£6,500–6,800** *JHo*

A Staffordshire slipware dish, with pie crust rim, the upper surface combed with narrow brown lines across a ground of cream slip, slightly damaged, early 18thC, 17in (43cm) diam. **£400–500** *S(S)*

A Quimper dish, 'HR' mark, c1895, 7½in (19cm) diam. **£100–140** *VH*

A Sunderland lustre dish, with black transfer decoration, c1840, 8½in (21.5cm) diam. **£30–40** *STA*

A Sunderland lustre dish, c1850, 5½in (14cm) diam. **£18–20** *STA*

A Staffordshire slipware dish,
late 18thC, 13in (33cm) diam.
£2,200–2,650 *JHo*

A Quimper dish, 'HR' mark,
c1885, 9in (23cm) diam.
£150–185 *VH*

An English delft saucer dish,
centrally decorated in blue with
the birth of Venus, within a blue
line border, large rim chip, c1725,
9in (23cm) diam.
£250–350 *DN*

A pair of delft plates, each
painted in blue within a double
blue line, the rim with a blue line
and manganese band border,
London or Bristol, chips to glaze,
c1750, 9in (22.5cm) diam.
£1,500–2,000 *S(S)*

A blue and white pottery
warming plate, by Thomas
Higginbotham & Co.,
Dublin, c1840, 10in
(25cm) diam.
£150–185 *STA*

A Bristol delft Adam and Eve
charger, painted in orange, green,
yellow and underglaze blue, the
everted rim painted with blue
dashes and crescents, early
18thC, 13in (33cm) diam.
£3,500–4,500 *Bea*

A Bordeaux
faïence plate,
with green
design, c1780,
10½in
(26.5cm) wide.
£180–210 *VH*

A Rouen dish, c1750, 15in
(38cm) wide.
£500–525 *VH*

A Dutch Delft dish, centrally decorated in Chinese style in blue with a basket of flowers and leaves, the blue ground rim with a band of scrolls, inscribed number '33' verso, 18thC, 13½in (34cm) diam.
£150–200 *DN*

A pair of majolica chargers, each painted with Biblical scenes, damaged, c1900, 18in (46cm) diam.
£800–900 *CSK*

A Quimper dish, 'HR' mark, c1890, 6in (15cm) wide.
£45–55 *VH*

A Roanne faïence dish, decorated with a cockerel, 'The Bird of France', c1780, 9in (23cm) diam.
£240–260 *VH*

A majolica charger, painted in the Castelli style, damaged, c1880, 20in (51cm) diam.
£350–450 *CSK*

A pair of iron stone china soup plates, by Folch & Sons, c1820.
£200–220 *VH*

A pair of Italian faïence chargers, possibly Cantagalli, late 19thC, 24½in (62cm) diam.
£1,000–1,500 *S(S)*

A Quimper dessert set of 5 plates and one dish, c1920, 7½in (19cm) diam.
£300–325 *VH*

> **Miller's is a price GUIDE not a price LIST.**

A Hicks & Meigh platter, water lily pattern, No. 5 pattern mark, c1825, 20in (50.5cm) wide.
£450–500 *JP*

A Quimper plate, c1885, 9in (23cm) diam.
£100–120 *VH*

An Italian majolica charger, painted within an ochre rim, slight damage, 19thC, 24in (61cm) diam.
£800–1,200 *S(S)*

Jardinières

A majolica turquoise ground jardinière and circular stand, painted in colours with a pink interior, possibly Minton, damaged, c1875, 13in (33cm) high.
£800–1,100 *CSK*

A Mintons majolica jardinière, after an original by Thomas Longmore, modelled as a ship supporting 4 scantily clad figures holding swags of leaves, on stylised dolphins' head feet, painted in bright colours, damaged, impressed and painted marks, shape number '1864', date code for 1875, 22in (55.5cm) wide.
£2,000–2,500 *CSK*

A majolica jardinière, moulded with eagles' mask handles with foliate terminals, on a deep blue ground, the matched pedestal decorated with foliage and scrolls, probably Staffordshire, late 19thC, 38in (97cm) high.
£600–800 *S(S)*

Jars

An Italian maïolica wet drug jar, named for 'OL. D. SCORP. SEM.' in manganese, dated on reverse '1721', probably Savona, damaged, 9in (23cm) high.
£600–700 *CSK*

A Sicilian albarello, inscribed 'E. D. COMITSS', painted with a green and yellow cartouche on a dark and light blue ground, damaged, 8½in (21cm) high.
£500–600 *C(S)*

A Sicilian wet drug jar, inscribed 'O Ventisce' above a yellow and green cartouche containing a crest, damaged, 8½in (21cm) high.
£800–900 *C(S)*

A Dutch Delft tobacco jar and brass cover, painted in blue with a panel inscribed 'St. Vincent', flanked by 2 Indian figures smoking pipes, blue painted factory mark, c1740, 10in (25cm).
£450–550 *S(S)*

A Sicilian albarello, inscribed 'B. DFENSIV', enamelled in brown and yellow with a praying monk, damaged, 6½in (16cm) high. **£400–500** *C(S)*

A pair of Castelli albarelli, inscribed to the reverse 'P. B. 1760', damaged, 10in (25cm) high.
£2,000–2,500 *CSK*

A Deruta maïolica wet drug jar, painted with a plain banner on a ground of grotteschi and foliage, damaged, 8in (20cm) high, and a similar ewer.
£900–1,200 *CSK*

An Italian maïolica albarello, with 2 strapwork handles, inscribed 'Acorns Calami' in blue, on a scroll within a stylised dolphin, stylised cartoon and scroll border and surmounted by a grotesque mask, on a mottled yellow ground within blue stiff-leaf borders, possibly 16thC Faenza, mis-fired, 9in (22cm).
£1,600–2,000 *HSS*

A ceramic tobacco jar, 20thC, 6in (15cm) high.
£100–120 *JO*

A drug jar, decorated in blue dash style, London, c1680, late 17thC, 7in (17.5cm). **£900–1,200** *DaD*

A pair of Quimper sweet jars, marked 'HB', c1885, 3in (7.5cm).
£100–150 *VH*

An English delft ovoid drug jar, inscribed 'C:ABSINT:R:' in blue, above a cherub's head, tassel and floral garlands, the shaped cartouche surmounted by a bowl of fruit, birds and leaves, crack to base, c1700, 7½in (19cm) high.
£350–450 *DN*

A pair of Italian blue and white waisted storage jars, one painted with a scene of a duel and the other a stag hunt, within blue bands, possibly Naples, restored, c1740, 10in (25cm) high.
£700–800 *CSK*

Jugs

A Staffordshire salt glazed jug, c1765. **£1,000–1,250** *JHo*

A Staffordshire salt glazed cream jug, c1765.
£1,000–1,250 *JHo*

A pearlware puzzle jug, with mask moulded spout, printed and painted with Masonic emblems on one side, and a verse on the other, all within garlands of flowers beneath a yellow ground band with blue borders, inscribed 'W WOOD 1821', handle and base pierced for water retention and expulsion, restored, c1821, 7in (17.5cm) high.
£300–400 *CSK*

A creamware jug, decorated and inscribed with 'Aurora, Goddess of the Sun, 1775', probably Greatbatch, 9in (23cm) high.
£4,000–4,500 *JHo*

A pearlware ovoid jug and similar bowl, painted in underglaze blue with formal Chinese buildings in simple landscapes, within diaper borders, jug 10½in (27cm) high.
£200–250 *P*

A Staffordshire puzzle jug, with transfers of Cashmore the Clown, Harlequin and other figures, with painted details, hollow handle, 8½in (21cm) high.
£200–300 *RBB*

A Tudor earthenware jug, the upper part and the small looped handle partially coated with a green speckled glaze, possibly Surrey, slight damage, 16thC, 5in (13cm) high.
£500–600 *S(NY)*

A Prattware jug, 19thC, 9in (23cm) high.
£70–80 *STA*

A Yorkshire pottery painted jug, c1755, 6½in (16cm) high.
£3,500–4,500 *JHo*

A lustre jug, decorated and inscribed with 'Sir C.Cambell', mid-19thC, 8in (20cm) high.
£100–110 *STA*

A Turner flattened oviform stoneware jug, enriched with bands of brown glaze, slight damage, impressed marks, late 18thC, 9½in (24cm), and another similar, 8in (20cm).
£150–250 *CSK*

A Tudor green glazed jug,
5½in (14cm) high.
£500–550 *JHo*

A Tudor earthenware jug, the
upper part and the small looped
handle coated with a yellow green
glaze, small rim chip, probably
Cheam, Surrey, 16thC, 7in
(17cm) high.
£100–150 *S(NY)*

A Staffordshire salt glazed
stoneware jug, c1750, 4in
(10cm) high.
£700–850 *JHo*

A Nottingham pottery carved jug,
c1700, 4in (10cm) high.
£2,000–3,000 *JHo*

Toby Jugs

A Yorkshire pearlware Toby jug,
wearing a brown and ochre
decorated waistcoat and blue coat,
on blue, brown and ochre sponged
base, the leaf moulded handle
with 'Pan' moulded terminal,
c1800, 8in (20cm) high.
£800–1,200 *DN*

A Staffordshire Toby jug, wearing
a pink jacket, c1820, 10in (25cm).
£450–500 *JO*

Two Staffordshire creamware
Toby jugs, each wearing a dark
brown tricorn hat, a blue coat,
white waistcoat, yellow breeches
and brown shoes, one with
manganese hair and skin, some
damage and restorations, c1790,
6½in (16cm) high.
£550–600 *S(NY)*

A set of 4 Wilkinson Pottery jugs
from the First World War Series,
designed by Carruthers Gould,
each brightly coloured,
representing: Lloyd George, Earl
Haig, Marshall Foch and Admiral
Beatty, Lloyd George's hat
repaired. **£800–1,000** *Bea*

A Staffordshire Toby jug, wearing
an orange coat and pink
waistcoat, c1810, 9in (22.5cm).
£500–600 *JO*

Mugs

A blue and white pottery mug, English, c1840, 5in (12.5cm) high.
£60–70 *STA*

A delft blue and white mug, London, c1770, 5in (12.5cm) high.
£800–950 *JHo*

A Belleek pottery mug, printed in green with the factory mark of a hound and a harp before a tower, above 'BELLEEK' inscribed on a scroll within borders with ribbons entwined with blossom and shamrocks, an angular handle, damaged, First Period, 4in (10cm) high.
£70–90 *CSK*

A pearlware 'Constitution' mug, painted in brown, inscribed within an ochre beadwork frame, flanked by colourful sprays of flowers beneath a brown dart rim and continous border of fruiting vines between ochre lines, slight damage, c1790, 6in (15cm) high.
£600–800 *S(S)*

A set of 6 children's mugs, each printed in blue with titled scenes of adults and children, including 'Cherries Ripe', 'Dangerous Play', and 'Good Exercise', late 19thC, 3in (7.6cm) high.
£300–350 *DN*

Services

A Spode Landscape 53-piece dinner service, c1890, plates 10in (25cm) diam.
£1,400–1,500 *STA*

A George Jones 'monkey' part tea service, comprising: a teapot and cover, sugar bowl and cover, cream jug, 4 cups and saucers and a stand, with deep blue ground, the teapot and cream jug handles formed as monkeys, the cup handles and finials as buds, moulded with leaves and blossoms, enriched in colours, damaged, impressed marks and registration marks for 1875, pattern number 3465.
£4,200–5,000 *CSK*

Tankards

A stoneware tankard, with a silver rim, probably Fulham, London 1710, 7in (18cm).
£1,200–1,350 *JHo*

A Mortlake tankard, c1785.
£1,200–1,350 *JHo*

A Staffordshire redware tankard, c1740.
£1,200–1,350 *JHo*

Tea & Coffee Pots

A Staffordshire Prattware salt glazed teapot, with applied cobalt blue and white decoration, c1745, 4in (10cm) high.
£1,450–1,650 *JHo*

A Staffordshire creamware teapot, c1765, 7in (17.5cm) high.
£1,000–1,150 *JHo*

A Staffordshire salt glazed enamelled teapot and cover, painted in rose, turquoise, green, yellow and black, some chips and repairs, c1760, 4in (10cm) high.
£600–700 *S(NY)*

A Staffordshire teapot, moulded as a cauliflower, possibly Wedgwood, c1770, 5in (12.5cm) high.
£3,000–3,300 *JHo*

The development of new colours during the 1760s led to the introduction of exotic tea wares in the form of fruit and vegetables - cauliflowers being the most popular. A number of manufacturers produced these wares.

A Staffordshire salt glazed enamelled teapot and cover, painted in rose, green, turquoise, yellow, iron red and black, some damage, c1760, 4⅜in (11cm) high.
£800–850 *S(NY)*

A Staffordshire William Greatbatch creamware teapot and cover, transfer printed and coloured with Captain Cook being directed by Britannia, inscribed 'W.R., number 129', the reverse with Minerva protecting Telemachus, the domed cover printed and coloured with winged cherubs' masks flanking a puce sponged ground, c1780, 5½in (14cm) high.
£2,200–2,400 *S(S)*

A Staffordshire solid agate pecten shell teapot and cover, moulded on either side as a fluted scallop shell, affixed with a serpent spout and S-scroll handle, restored, c1750, 5⅓in (13.5cm) high.
£650–700 *S(NY)*

A Staffordshire or Derbyshire teapot, c1755, 6in (15cm) high.
£1,400–1,650 *JHo*

A Prattware figural teapot, modelled as a brown-haired lady wearing an ochre bonnet, its open crown threaded on the interior for a screw-on cover (missing), an ochre fichu, cobalt blue bodice, blue edged white skirt and brown shoes, seated on a green chair with her right arm raised to form the spout and her left akimbo to form the handle, slight damage, 8in (20cm) high.
£325–350 *S(NY)*

Locate the source

The source of each illustration in Miller's can be found by checking the code letters below each caption with the list of contributors.

A William Greatbatch printed and painted creamware teapot and cover, with flower finial, from the Prodigal Son series, repaired, c1775, 5in (12.5cm) high.
£350–550 *CSK*

A Victorian Mintons majolica teapot and cover, modelled as a monkey wearing a pink flower-decorated blue jacket, his head forming the cover, his tail the handle with a bamboo spout, damaged, impressed 'Mintons', incised '1844'.
£550–650 *HSS*

Tiles

A Bristol tile, decorated with a manganese bird, corner chipped, c1760, 5in (12.5cm) square.
£200–235 *JHo*

A Bristol manganese and grey tile depicting Jacobs ladder, 5in (12.5cm) square.
£100–120 *JHo*

A Bristol manganese and grey tile, mid-18thC, 5in (12.5cm) square.
£60–70 *JHo*

A Bristol blue and white tile, 18thC, 5in (12.5cm) square.
£45–55 *JHo*

A London blue manganese tile, c1740.
£40–60 *JHo*

A Liverpool manganese and grey tile, c1756, 5in (12.5cm) square.
£350–400 *JHo*

A London blue, white and manganese tile, 18thC, 5in (12.5cm) square.
£50–75 *JHo*

Eleven Liverpool delft tiles, painted in yellow, blue, green and manganese, with views of buildings in landscapes and river scenes, chips and damages, c1770, 5in (12.5cm) square. **£200–250** *CSK*

A London blue, red, green and yellow tile, c1740, 5in (12.5cm) square.
£150–185 *JHo*

A Liverpool manganese tile, c1780, 5in (12.5cm) square.
£50–85 *JHo*

A Bristol blue and white tile, 18thC, 5in (12.5cm) square.
£50–95 *JHo*

Tureens

A Dutch Delft blue and white tureen, with profuse floral decoration, 18thC, 14in (36cm) wide.
£1,500–2,000 *B*

A Niderviller faïence polychrome soup tureen, cover and stand, painted in shades of rose, purple, yellow, blue, green and grey, some damage, the stand with a large 'N.B.' mark in manganese, c1760, 12in (31cm) wide.
£1,500–2,000 *S(NY)*

A Dèsvres wall vase, by George Martel, c1920, chipped, 8in (20cm) wide.
£100–130 *VH*

A pair of Dèsvres cornucopia vases, c1890, 5in (12.5cm) high.
£100–115 *VH*

Vases

A pair of Staffordshire creamware vases, mounted as lamps, glazed in green, the sides with green winged wyvern handles spotted in brown, now drilled and fitted for electricity, one vase repaired, both with footrim chips, c1785, 10in (25cm) high.
£800–1,000 *S(NY)*

A Ridgways vase and cover, pattern no. 356, c1835, 13in (33cm) high.
£300–340 *VH*

An English delft flower vase, painted in blue with flying birds and floral sprigs, the everted wavy neck with alternating circular flower holders and scroll handles, on flared foot painted with foliage enclosed within a zig-zag and line border, damaged, c1730, 6½in (16cm) high.
£3,000–3,500 *S*

Use the Index!

Because certain items might fit easily into any number of categories, the quickest and surest method of locating any entry is by reference to the index at the back of the book.

This has been fully cross-referenced for absolute simplicity.

A pair of Dutch Delft blue and white vases, mounted as lamps, drilled and fitted for electricity, minor chips and abrasions, c1775, 12in (30.5cm). **£650–850** *S(NY)*

A Bristol delft campana-shaped vase, with frilled rim and sponged double entwined loop handles, decorated in blue with sprays of flowers and leaves, c1745, rivetted crack at rim area, foot chipped, 6in (15cm) high.
£450–550 *DN*

A maïolica vase, probably Caltagirone, painted in blue, chips and some flaking, mid-18thC, 12in (31cm) high.
£1,200–1,700 *S(S)*

Spill Vases

A Staffordshire elephant spill vase, c1845, 7in (17.5cm).
£700–900 *JO*

A Staffordshire spill vase, modelled as a reading maid, c1820, 8in (20cm).
£400–500 *JO*

A pearlware spill vase, the moulded base applied with 5 various models of recumbent rams, ewes and lambs, on beds of foliage and flower heads, painted in colours, minor damage, painted numerals, c1820, 9½in (23.5cm).
£700–800 *CSK*

A pair of Staffordshire elephant spill vases, painted in orange and green, on gilt lined serpentine bases, 6½in (16cm).
£1,250–1,500 *HSS*

A pair of Staffordshire horse group spill vases, c1865, 12in (30.5cm).
£1,000–1,200 *JO*

Miscellaneous

A pair of Staffordshire spill vases, c1860, 6in (15cm) and 5½in (14cm).
£300–400 *JO*

A Staffordshire saltglazed pierced dish, minor damage, c1760, 9½in (24cm) diam.
£2,000–2,500 *C*

A Sunderland pottery lustre bowl, c1830, 8in (20cm) diam.
£40–50 *STA*

A pair of Staffordshire figure spill vases, c1820, 8in (20cm).
£600–700 *JO*

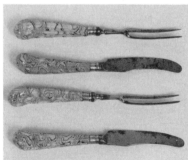

Two pairs of fruit knives and forks, with cream and brown agate pottery handles, c1750.
£1,600–1,800 *JHo*

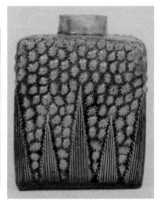

A Staffordshire green and ochre tea canister, c1765, 4½in (11.5cm).
£1,000–1,200 *JHo*

A George Jones majolica barrel-shaped garden seat, moulded in relief with cranes and swallows among lotus grasses, between bands of flower heads, with a wicker moulded seat pierced with an aperture, painted in colours on a deep blue ground, the interior with green and brown glazes, slight damage, late 19thC, 18in (46cm) high.
£2,500–3,000 *CSK*

A Minton majolica four-tier oyster dish, the bowls as oyster shells on a bed of seaweed, the loop finial formed as 3 fish and an eel, on a shaped base with metal mechanism, enriched in colours, impressed marks, date code for 1864, pattern No. 636, minor damage, 10in (25cm).
£2,000–2,500 *CSK*

A holy water font, 19thC, 13in (33cm).
£180–200 *STA*

A London or Bristol delft shoe, c1710, 6in (15cm) wide.
£3,300–3,850 *JHo*

Two Quimper menu cards, with menu written for 6th March 1921, damaged, c1890, 4½in (11cm).
£150–200 *VH*

A Pratt type model of a baby asleep in a wickerwork cot, wearing a bonnet and nightdress painted with flowerheads, restored, 4in (10cm) long.
£250–300 *CSK*

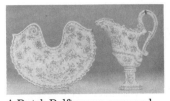

A Dutch Delft rococo ewer and basin, slight damage, pseudo 'ARK' monogram painted in blue, 19thC, ewer 13in (33cm).
£400–500 *S(S)*

A Pratt type coiled tobacco pipe, the elaborately moulded curling stem painted with dashes in blue and ochre, the pipe bowl moulded as a grimacing monkey's face, damages and repairs, c1800, 11in (28cm) wide.
£500–800 *CSK*

A pair of Continental glazed pottery pedestals, each moulded with 3 satyr's leg supports around a central pillar, raised on a waisted triangular base, covered in marbled green and brown running glaze, minor damage, late 19thC, 29in (74cm).
£500–600 *S(S)*

A delft blue and white brick, mid-18thC, 5in (12.5cm) wide.
£445–465 *JHo*

A Quimper book shaped snuff box, c1885, 3in (7cm).
£90–95 *VH*

Mason's Ironstone

A Mason's Ironstone vase, with centurion mask handles, impressed circle mark, c1820, 8in (20cm).
£480–550 *JP*

A Mason's Ironstone jardinière pattern pot pourri, early crown mark, **£750–800,** and matching dessert dish, impressed mark, 11in (28cm) wide.
£400–480 *JP*

A Mason's Ironstone part dessert service, painted in the Imari palette with stylised flowers, comprising: 2 two-handled sauce tureens and covers, 4 shaped service dishes, and 15 plates, damaged, impressed marks, c1820.
£1,200–1,700 *CSK*

A Mason's Ironstone bowl, decorated with the Sacrificial Lamb pattern, c1830, 24in (61.5cm) diam.
£2,250–2,350 *JP*

A Masons Ironstone Japan pattern footbath jug, printed crown and impressed mark, c1815. **£850–900** *JP*

A Mason's Ironstone jug and basin, impressed mark, bowl 13in (33cm) diam.
£700–750 *JP*

A Mason's Ironstone punch bowl, restored, c1820, 20in (51cm) diam.
£600–650 *JP*

A Mason's Ironstone dinner service, decorated in blue with flowers, butterflies and foliage on a white ground, comprising 109 pieces.
£600–800 *FLE*

The Trading Methods of the Mason's Ironstone Factory

The aggressive entrepreneurial style of Charles James Mason and his pressurised trading methods, might come as a surprise to collectors who perhaps imagine that the world of the Potteries at the beginning of the 19thC operated above the hurly-burly of the commercial world. His father, Miles Mason produced the gentlest of wares in porcelain, then later bone china, in no way reflecting the tightly protectionist atmosphere of the industry.

Indeed, one of the motives that spurred Miles Mason into the production of ceramics may have been the embargo in 1791 by the East India Company of the bulk import into England of Chinese export wares on which he and his fellow London retailers had until then illegally controlled prices. The combined effect of this, with the imposition of the heavy import duties in 1799 which ruined the livelihood of the Chinamen, spurred his initiative to collaborate with the Liverpool factory of Thomas Wolfe in producing wares to match the services of the gentry.

Such assuredness foreshadowed the wares that were yet to be made in the ironstone body, on which Miles was certainly experimenting in 1810, and patented by Charles in 1813. He had largely capitalised on the Turners' formula for Stone China patented by them in 1800, 6 years before their bankruptcy.

C. J. Mason's sales methods, by means of auctions all over the country, smack of urgent pressure and the consequent speed at which the wares had to be made would explain the many hastily produced examples so often seen now. Wage costs were kept down by employing pauper children. Contrasted with the superb workmanship of the specially commissioned pieces, or those of higher quality auctioned by Christie's and Phillips in 1818 and 1822 respectively, these seem incompatible.

During the 1820s and 30s Samuel Faraday, a relative of the scientist Michael, worked with the Masons as a travelling representative and was responsible for organising sales held all over the country. These sales disposed of huge quantities of ironstone china at a hectic pace and made the personal fortune of Charles James.

The early rumblings of industrial change and demands for better conditions for the potters were making themselves felt. At first, Charles James appeared to acquiesce to their demands, but resenting the loss of total control of his business, he worked to inhibit the power of the Potters Union.

A 6 month strike in 1843 against annual hiring and grievances, such as deductions for imperfect work and the attempted introduction of machinery, marked a turning point in his prosperity. In 1844, Faraday died, and Charles James lost his key associate responsible for the vital auction sales which turned over the massive output of the factory. Coupled with the added discomfort of his debt to the Potteries' bankers, in 1847 his luck ran out. He was declared bankrupt and his properties, house and factory were put up for auction.

A Mason's Ironstone storage jar, c1820.
£600–800 *CAI*

A Mason's Ironstone plate, impressed mark, c1817.
£100–110 *JP*

A Mason's Ironstone ewer and basin, c1820, jug 10in (25cm) high, bowl 13in (33cm) diam.
£650–725 *VH*

A Mason's Ironstone meat dish, printed in underglaze blue, and overpainted in burnt orange, yellow, green and pink, printed crown over fringed scroll mark in black, 19in (48cm) wide.
£300–500 *HSS*

A Mason's Ironstone soup tureen, decorated with Nanking pattern, repaired, impressed mark, 15in (38cm) wide.
£880–920 *JP*

A Mason's Ironstone bud vase, firing fault on rim, c1815, 8in (20cm).
£100–140 *VH*

A Mason's Ironstone part dinner service, transfer printed in underglaze blue, and enriched in gilding, with a chinoiserie scene depicting Oriental figures in a fenced garden, one crane on the ground and another flying above, comprising: a hexagonal soup tureen and cover, an oval meat dish, 4 serving dishes, 6 soup plates and 14 dinner plates, minor damage, impressed marks, c1825. **£2,000–3,000** *S(S)*

A Mason's Ironstone dessert sauce tureen stand, with deep foot rim, painted in enamels, c1815, 7in (17.5cm) wide.
£100–120 *VH*

A pair of Mason's Ironstone dishes, c1835, 24in (61.5cm) wide.
£245–265 *VH*

A pair of Mason's Ironstone ice pails, c1820, 9½in (24cm).
£1,200–1,500 *CAI*

A Mason's Ironstone two-handled vase and cover, reserved on a deep blue ground, and flanked by 2 gilt dragon handles, damaged, c1817, 26in (66cm).
£320–380 *S(S)*

A Mason's Ironstone cider jug, decorated with the Sacrificial Lamb pattern, slight damage, c1815, 5in (13cm).
£195–215 *VH*

A Mason's Ironstone mazarine blue ink stand, c1820, 7½in (19cm) wide.
£400–420 *VH*

A Mason's Ironstone School House pattern crocus pot, restored, c1815.
£150–175 *VH*

Wedgwood

A pair of Wedgwood blue jugs, c1870, 7½in (18.5cm).
£400–440 *DeA*

A Wedgwood Fairyland lustre circular bowl, Portland mark in gold, 9in (22.5cm) diam.
£2,500–3,000 *JNic*

A Victorian Wedgwood mug, inscribed 'Fill this cup and drink it up', c1880, 5in (12.5cm).
£100–175 *DeA*

A Wedgwood jasper bi-colour dip coffee can and saucer, the pale green ground applied with oval mauve ground medallions, within white relief moulded garlands, suspended from rams' heads, interspersed with trophies, slight damage, impressed upper case marks, 19thC.
£500–600 *CSK*

A Wedgwood and Bentley solid blue and white jasper plaque, with a portrait of Euterpe, slight damage, 3½in (8.5cm), and a blue dip and white jasper oval portrait plaque of a partially draped muse, leaning against a column, impressed marks, ebonised and giltwood frames, c1775, 3in (8cm).
£900–1,200 *C*

A Wedgwood creamware crested plate, from the Alexander I service, the border painted in black with the Russian crowned double-headed eagle, with the badge of the Order of the Holy Martyr of St. George, within a brown and gilt line rim, the well edged with a gilt line, c1817, 10in (25cm) diam.
£600–900 *C*

The service, made by Wedgwood in 1817 for Tsar Alexander I, was ordered by Count Lieven originally for the Palace at Gatchina. A small number of pieces from the service are now to be found in The Hermitage Museum, although apparently not on display.

A Wedgwood black basaltes 'famille rose' campana pot pourri vase and cover, decorated with sprays of enamelled flowers in bright colours, reserved between brown line borders, the flat circular cover pierced with holes, impressed 'Wedgwood' and comma mark, 19thC, 10½in (26cm).
£1,000–1,500 *S*

A Wedgwood majolica blue ground fumigator and pierced cover, enriched in colours, repaired, impressed mark and pad mark for 'Piesse and Lubins. Fumigating', 19thC, 9in (22.5cm).
£800–1,000 *CSK*

A Wedgwood coffee pot and domed cover, decorated in white relief with scenes from Domestic Employment, restored, impressed 'Wedgwood', c1786, 10in (25cm).
£2,200–2,700 *S*

Only 4 of these coffee pots and covers appear to have been produced.

A Wedgwood blue jasper copy of the Portland or Barberini vase, the two-handled vase, decorated in relief with a frieze of classical figures, said to represent the myth of Peleus and Thetis, impressed mark, 19thC, 10in (25cm). **£400–500** *DN*

A pair of Wedgwood blue jasper dip earrings, sprigged in white with classical figures, 19thC, 1½in (3.5cm).
£500–600 *S*

A Wedgwood jasper plaque, decorated in white relief with the Dancing Hours reserved on a deep blue ground, within a continuous floral border and outer powder blue ground, impressed factory marks, c1895, 10in (25cm) wide.
£700–900 *S(S)*

A set of 12 Wedgwood plates, with gadrooned borders, each printed in blue with birds, flowers and leaf scrolls, within a bird panelled border, 19thC, 10in (25cm) diam.
£360–420 *DN*

A pair of Wedgwood vases, painted by Emile Lessore, with garlands of stylised leaves in ochre and turquoise ground borders, slight damage, impressed upper case marks and 3 letter date code for 1861, 10in (25cm).
£850–1,000 *CSK*

A Wedgwood black ground oviform vase, with loop handles, damaged, impressed marks, 19thC, 15in (38cm).
£750–900 *CSK*

A Guide to Identifying Wedgwood Wares

Josiah Wedgwood I began to mark his wares consistently during the early stages of his career, perhaps as early as 1759. In July 1771 Wedgwood was writing to inform his partner, Thomas Bentley, of his intention to have letters made for a stamp '...we are going upon a plan to mark the whole if practicable'. One can therefore assume that from 1772 onwards, every item was marked before leaving the Wedgwood factory. For this reason, it is extremely rare to find an unmarked example. Exceptions may include the following cases:-

• When an object is composed of more than one part, for example, a vase which may consist of a plinth, lid and main body, and only one of these parts is marked.

• When the impressed marks are obscured by heavy glaze or restoration work.

• When the mark has been 'turned' out by the engine turner whilst completing an object.

A pair of Wedgwood pale blue jasper pot pourri oviform vases, with liners and pierced covers, restored, impressed marks, c1880, 12in (30.5cm).
£1,200–1,700 *CSK*

A pair of Wedgwood Victoria ware blue ground oviform vases, applied with pink and white decoration of classical devices, between swags of flowers suspended from rams' masks above a stiff-leaf band, enriched in gilt, worn, impressed mark, c1880, 7in (18cm).
£350–450 *CSK*

A Wedgwood creamware teapot and cover, transfer printed in black 'at Liverpool', with a portrait of John Wesley preaching, within an inscribed scrolling banner, the reverse with a pious verse within elaborate mantling, the cover with 3 winged angels' heads, damaged, 5in (13cm). **£800–1,200** *S*

A Wedgwood pearlware bough pot and pierced cover, moulded, incised and washed in dark brown to simulate a barrel, the cover with 2 large apertures and 6 smaller, slight damage, impressed mark, c1790, 7½in (18.5cm) wide.
£350–450 *CSK*

Wemyss

A Wemyss Earlshall slop bucket and cover, painted in black with rooks perched among nest-laden trees and windmills, restored, impressed R H & S mark, and painted Earlshall mark, 11in (28cm).
£800–900 *C(S)*

A Wemyss ewer, decorated with violets, restored, painted mark, 10in (25cm).
£470–520 *C(S)*

A Wemyss Gordon plate, decorated with strawberries, marked 'T. Goode & Co.', 8in (20cm) diam.
£100–150 *RdeR*

A Wemyss two-handled flower tub, painted by Karl Nekola, with cabbage roses, restored, impressed R H & S mark, and printed T. Goode & Co. mark, 10½in (26.5cm).
£550–850 *C(S)*

This flower tub, although painted with the most common floral decoration of cabbage roses, is unusual because the reverse of a rose can be seen, a rare occurence in the decoration of Wemyss pottery.

A Wemyss ewer and basin, painted with carnations, restored and slight damage, both with impressed R H & S mark, basin 15½in (39cm) diam.
£450–650 *C(S)*

Locate the source

The source of each illustration in Miller's can be found by checking the code letters below each caption with the list of contributors.

A Wemyss Gordon plate, decorated with brambles, marked 'T. Goode & Co.', 8in (20cm) diam.
£100–150 *RdeR*

A Wemyss dog bowl, c1920, 6½in (16cm) diam.
£300–400 *RdeR*

A Wemyss ewer and basin, decorated with cabbage roses, impressed R H & S mark, basin 15½in (39cm) diam.
£800–1,000 *C(S)*

A Wemyss ewer and basin, decorated with cabbage roses, restored, impressed R H & S marks, and printed T. Goode & Co. mark, basin 15in (38cm) diam.
£600–800 *C(S)*

A Wemyss Honeysuckle plate, 8in (20cm) diam.
£200–300 *RdeR*

A Wemyss plate, transfer printed in brown with Wemyss Castle, and the inscription 'Souvenir of the Randolph Wemyss Memorial Hospital Bazaar', within a green striped border, impressed mark, 8½in (21cm) diam.
£200–300 *C(S)*

A Wemyss Poppy plate,
8in (20cm) diam.
£200–250 *RdeR*

A Wemyss Gordon dessert plate,
restored, impressed mark, 8½in
(21cm) diam.
£170–220 *C(S)*

A Wemyss Gordon dessert plate,
decorated with strawberries,
restored, impressed marks,
8½in (21cm) diam.
£100–150 *C(S)*

A Wemyss heart-shaped inkwell,
6in (15cm) wide.
£200–250 *RdeR*

A Wemyss heart-shaped dish,
decorated with apples and leaves,
impressed R H.& S mark to base,
and transfer printed retailer's
mark, 12in (30.5cm).
£400–450 *L&E*

A Wemyss plate, painted with
bees buzzing around the hive,
restored, impressed Wemyss and
R H & S marks, 7½in (19cm).
£300–350 *C(S)*

A Wemyss tray, decorated with
violets and inscribed 'I looked for
something sweet to send you and
the violets asked if they would do',
restored, impressed and painted
Wemyss marks, 6in (15cm) wide.
£400–500 *C(S)*

A Wemyss Buttercup plate.
£200–250 *RdeR*

A Wemyss heart-shaped tray,
10in (25cm) wide.
£400–500 *RdeR*

A Wemyss preserve jar and cover,
painted with blackcurrants,
restored, impressed and painted
marks, 4½in (11cm).
£150–250 *C(S)*

A Wemyss three-handled tyg,
9½in (23.5cm) diam.
£700–800 *RdeR*

A Wemyss preserve jar and cover,
painted with brambles, restored,
impressed Wemyss R H & S
mark, 6in (15cm).
£150–200 *C(S)*

A Wemyss two-handled goblet,
painted with a pheasant,
damaged, 6½in (16cm).
£200–300 *RdeR*

A Wemyss mug, painted with
sweet peas, restored, impressed
Wemyss mark, 5½in (14.5cm).
£270–350 *C(S)*

A Wemyss five-sided ashtray,
decorated with thistles, painted
Wemyss mark, 6in (15cm) wide.
£200–300 *C(S)*

A Wemyss chamber stick, painted
with cabbage roses, painted
Wemyss mark, 5in (13cm) diam.
£400–500 *C(S)*

A Wemyss hatpin holder,
painted with lilac, impressed
Wemyss mark, 6in (15cm).
£500–700 *C(S)*

A Wemyss umbrella stand,
painted by Karl Nekola, with
flowering dock, slight damage,
restored, impressed Wemyss R H
& S mark, 25in (64cm).
£2,000–3,000 *C(S)*

A Wemyss mug, painted with
cabbage roses, restored,
impressed Wemyss R H & S
mark, 5½in (14.5cm).
£300–350 *C(S)*

A Wemyss chamber pot, painted
with cabbage roses, impressed
Wemyss mark and painted
T. Goode & Co. mark,
10in (25cm) wide.
£300–500 *C(S)*

A Wemyss mug, painted with
a brown cockerel and 4 hens,
restored, impressed Wemyss
mark and printed T. Goode & Co.
mark, 5in (14cm).
£250–350 *C(S)*

A Wemyss vase, painted as a thistle, 5½in (13.5cm).
£220–300 *C(S)*

A Wemyss early morning tea set, teapot 5in (12.5cm) high.
£300–350 *RdeR*

A Wemyss waisted vase, decorated with geese, restored, impressed Wemyss R H & S mark, 6in (15cm).
£220–300 *C(S)*

A Wemyss preserve jar and cover, painted with bees buzzing around a hive, restored, impressed and painted Wemyss marks, and printed T. Goode & Co. mark, 4½in (11.5cm).
£200–250 *C(S)*

A pair of Wemyss candlesticks, 9in (22.5cm).
£150–200 *RdeR*

A Wemyss Grosvenor vase, painted with carnations on a black ground, slight damage, impressed and painted Wemyss marks, 8in (20cm).
£200–300 *C(S)*

A Wemyss black and white pig, restored, impressed Wemyss mark and printed T. Goode & Co. mark, 18in (46cm).
£1,000–1,500 *C(S)*

A Wemyss pink piglet, 6½in (16cm) long.
£300–400 *RdeR*

A Wemyss black and white pig, 18in (46cm) long.
£1,000–1,500 *RdeR*

A Wemyss plaque, painted with plums, 5½in (13.5cm) wide.
£100–150 *RdeR*

A Wemyss waisted vase, painted with dragonflies, restored, painted Wemyss mark, 6in (15cm).
£300–350 *C(S)*

A Wemyss matchbox holder, painted with roses design, 3in (7.5cm) high.
£150–200 *RdeR*

PORCELAIN
Baskets

A Vienna pierced basket and 2 stands, the ground painted with scattered black and gold flowers within red-ground borders painted in black with stylised anthemion motifs, further enriched in green and gilt, minor damage, underglaze blue shield marks and 'Pressnummer 99' for 1799, stands 10½in (27cm) diam.
£200–300 *CSK*

A Vienna pierced porcelain basket and stand, the basket of pedestal form, each painted with a continuous colourful band of flowers and foliage within finely pierced scale borders decorated with alternate bands of blue and gilding, slight damage, shield marks in underglaze blue, painted and impressed numerals, c1820, stand 12in (31cm) diam.
£400–550 *S(S)*

A Belleek 3 strand basket and cover, the finial formed as a large spray of flowers, buds and leaves including a rose, shamrock and daisy, applied with scrolling branch moulded handles on a loop rim, slight damage, impressed pad, early 20thC, 10in (25cm) diam.
£1,500–2,000 *CSK*

A Copeland parian basket and associated blue glass liner, the pierced basket between leaf-moulded borders and a beadwork edged rim, raised on a circular pedestal base, the blue glass bowl with everted rim, slight damage, impressed 'Copeland', c1870, 9in (23cm) diam.
£200–300 *S(S)*

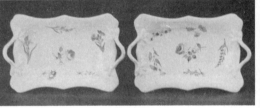

A pair of Swansea two-handled baskets, painted with sprays of summer flowers, minor cracks, printed marks 'Swansea' in red, c1820, 11in (28cm) wide.
£1,200–1,700 *S*

A basket, heavily encrusted with colourful flowers and foliage around a gilt scroll rim, the exterior with deep blue ground, the interior with floral sprays and gilt scrollwork, flower encrusted gilt scroll handle, some damage and restoration, possibly Coalport, c1840, 12½in (31.5cm) wide.
£300–400 *S(S)*

Bowls

A Lowestoft bowl, c1770, 3in (8cm) diam.
£40–50 *STA*

A Worcester First Period blue and white bowl, Dr Wall, c1750, 6in (15cm) diam.
£300–340 *DeA*

A Worcester yellow bordered and enamelled blue and white sugar bowl and cover, each piece spirally wrythen and painted in underglaze blue heightened in gilding, decorated in purple, iron red, yellow and turquoise insects beneath a yellow basket moulded border, some damage, workman's mark in underglaze blue, c1760, 4in (10cm) high.
£350–400 *S(NY)*

A Fürstenberg slop basin, the exterior finely painted in puce camaieu with harbour scenes within green and gilt scroll vignettes and flanked by delicate sprays of flowers, the interior with a single spray of flowers and foliage, gilt edged rim, some wear to rim, painted 'F' factory mark in underglaze blue and incised numerals, c1760, 7in (17.5cm) diam.
£1,700–2,200 *S(S)*

Boxes

A German snuff box and hinged cover, painted with figures in landscapes and harbour scenes within gilt scroll borders, enriched with gilt to the interior and inscribed 'Ich gratulire', slight wear, 19thC, 3in (8cm) wide.
£1,500–2,000 *CSK*

A Royal Worcester box and cover, possibly after an original model by James Hadley, modelled as a child falling backwards into a drum, enriched in colours and gilt, wear to gilt, puce printed and impressed marks, late 19thC, 4in (10cm) high.
£300–400 *CSK*

A Coalport ivory ground 'jewelled' box and cover, the cover painted in colours with a richly gilt border, enriched with turquoise enamels, the base gilt with C-scrolls and flowers, slight damage, printed and painted marks, c1900, 3in (7.5cm) square.
£250–300 *CSK*

A Berlin gilt metal mounted snuff box, slight damage, c1775, later gilt metal mounts, 3½in (9cm).
£2,800–3,500 *C*

A box, the interior painted with scattered sprays of flowers and insects, the exterior with figures in harbour landscape vistas alternating with sprays of flowers within scroll cartouches reserved on a powder blue ground of overlapping lappets, possibly Reichenstein, Prussia, impressed eagle factory mark, cover missing, rim chips, 19thC, 9½in (24.5cm) wide.
£250–350 *S(S)*

A German snuff box, painted with scenes of figures in 18thC dress, with gilt metal mount to the rim and fitted gilt metal four legged stand, each leg to the stand cast with a winged caryatid, cover missing, slight wear, porcelain mid-18thC, probably Meissen or Fürstenberg, the mounts slightly later, box 2½in (6cm) wide.
£700–1,200 *CSK*

Busts

A pair of Paris busts, each modelled as a lady in romantic Renaissance style dress, enriched in colours and gilt, damaged and repaired, each signed to the reverse 'Paul Duboy', with fluted wood pillar stands, 19thC, 61in (155cm) high overall.
£1,500–2,000 *CSK*

> **Miller's is a price GUIDE not a price LIST.**

A Sèvres bisque bust of a young girl by E. Houssin, impressed and inscribed marks, dated '1892', with wood stand, 9½in (24cm) high.
£400–500 *CSK*

Candlesticks

A pair of Continental flower encrusted four-branch figure candelabra, minor chips, c1900, 19in (48cm) high.
£400–500 *S(S)*

A pair of three-branch candelabra, Plaue, Germany, slight damage, impressed and painted factory marks, c1900, 14⅝in (37cm) high.
£350–550 *S(S)*

An assembled pair of Chelsea 'fable' candlestick groups, each depicting *'The Tygre and the Fox'* and modelled as a black spotted white leopard with salmon-lined ears, seated beside a recumbent russet fox before a flowering bocage, supporting a gilt heightened and pierced floriform candle nozzle and green edged leafy bobèche, moulded with iron red berries above a base encrusted with colourful flowers and raised on 3 elaborate gold and turquoise heightened scroll feet, the front foot draped with a gilt fringed banner, one group depicting the leopard pulling from his side a tan and purple arrow beneath a bocage of yellow-centred rose blossoms and green leaves, and the other with the open-mouthed leopard and white chested fox snarling at each other before a bocage of maroon-centred blue and white blossoms, damaged, gold anchor marks, c1765, 12in (30.5cm) high.
£3,500–4,000 *S(S)*

The Chelsea factory's pairs of 'fable' candlesticks were always intended to represent 2 different fables involving slightly different animals. Interestingly, these models appear to be painted as leopards but they are clearly intended as a pair. Each pair should involve one of each beast rather than 2 of the same, but most of the known examples of the models mysteriously have been mis-matched as 2 tigers or 2 leopards, the odd pairing possibly having occurred at the factory.

A Meissen blue and white chamber stick, c1860, 2in (5cm) high.
£100–150 *DAV*

A pair of Meissen three-branch candelabra, the stems moulded with 3 cherubs above small painted panels of birds, supporting scroll branches and a central sconce, minor chips, crossed swords in blue, c1870, 17in (43cm) high.
£2,000–3,000 *S*

Two Bow candlestick groups of gardeners, each modelled as a youth wearing a gilt edged rose and yellow costume, offering a posy to his companion wearing a gilt edged black hat, yellow and blue bodice, and a colourfully flowered apron or skirt, heightened in rose, gold and turquoise or blue, damaged and restored, the bobèches with impressed repairer's letter 'T.', c1765, largest 9in (23cm) high.
£700–750 *S(NY)*

Centrepieces

A table centre, probably by John Bevington, after a Meissen original, minor chips, restored, painted factory mark, c1882, 19in (47.5cm) high.
£550–650 *S(S)*

A Meissen blue and white chamber stick, c1880, 5in (12.5cm) diam.
£300–350 *DAV*

A pair of candlesticks, the details picked out in underglaze blue and gilding, pseudo factory marks in underglaze blue, probably French, late 19thC, 8in (21cm) high.
£300–400 *S(S)*

A Continental centrepiece, painted in pale green and pink, highlighted in gilding, all on a wave moulded base, c1900, 9in (23cm) high.
£250–300 *S(S)*

A Sitzendorf centrepiece, minor restorations, late 19thC.
£900–1,000 *RA*

A centrepiece, Plaue, Germany, the large pierced basket encrusted with branches of pink roses, raised on a pierced pedestal base with 3 scantily clad cherubs, on 3 scroll feet, slight damage, printed factory mark, early 20thC, 12in (30.5cm) high.
£350–550 *S(S)*

Cottages & Pastille Burners

A Staffordshire castle-shaped spill vase, encrusted with flowers and with coloured decoration, on a brown ground mound base, slight damage, 19thC, 4in (10cm) high.
£120–150 *DN*

A Staffordshire cottage-shaped pastille burner, the yellow and green thatched roof encrusted with flowers and coloured decoration, on a mound base, slight damage, 19thC, 4in (10cm).
£150–200 *DN*

A cottage pastille burner and tray, modelled as a 2 storey thatched house, painted in colours with climbing wall flowers and encrusted with flowers and foliage, on a shaped base, marblised to base, enriched in gilt, restored, c1825, 9in (23cm) wide.
£2,000–2,500 *CSK*

A pastille burner, modelled as a Gothic cottage, enriched in colours and gilt, repaired, c1830, 6in (15cm) high.
£200–250 *CSK*

Cups

A pair of Derby tea cups and saucers, inscribed on the bases, red painted mark, c1820.
£450–550 *WW*

A Meissen forget-me-not encrusted chocolate cup with cover, and saucer, cup 4in (10cm) high.
£650–750 *DAV*

A Miles Mason bone china cup and saucer, pattern No. 665, c1810, saucer 5in (12.5cm) diam.
£100–130 *VH*

A Miles Mason bone china coffee can and saucer, c1812, cup 2in (5cm) high.
£120–140 *VH*

A Miles Mason can and saucer, pattern No. 878, c1812.
£100–140 *VH*

Two German topographical cabinet cups and saucers, with scrolling handles, enriched in gilt, saucer damaged and restored, some minor wear, impressed numerals, possibly Fürstenberg, 19thC, 5in (12.5cm) high.
£1,000–1,400 *CSK*

A Chelsea octagonal tea bowl, and saucer, painted in the Kakiemon palette with the Flaming Tortoise pattern, saucer badly worn, c1752.
£1,500–2,000 *S*

The tortoise is emblematic of the Minogame or Raincoat tortoise, which lived a thousand years, and got its name after 500 years by acquiring on its shell a plantation of water weeds which streamed out behind.

A Sèvres cabinet cup, painted with a portrait entitled 'Hetteâ d'Angleterre', against a deep blue ground gilt with a trellis pattern and enclosing white 'jewelled' fleur-de-lys, minor loss of 'jewelling', blue interlaced 'L' mark, 19thC.
£250–350 *S(S)*

A Sèvres bleu nouveau coffee can and saucer, decorated with entwined ribbons of white, pink and red enamel 'jewels' on gilt circular discs, restored, gilt interlaced 'L' marks, gilder's marks 'LG' for Le Guay, incised '43' to can and '38A' to saucer, c1780.
£2,400–2,600 *C*

Etienne-Charles Le Guay worked at Sèvres 1778-82, and 1809-40.

An English cup and saucer, with gilt decoration, c1820, saucer 5½in (14cm) diam.
£30–35 *STA*

A Meissen tea bowl and saucer, painted in colours with deutsche Blumen amongst scattered sprigs below brown line rims, worn, blue crossed swords marks, impressed 'E', c1750, cup 2in (5cm) high.
£350–400 *CSK*

A Copeland and Garrett Felspar hound's head stirrup cup, with gilt rim, decorated in brown, hair crack, printed mark in green, 4in (10cm) long.
£400–500 *DN*

A Vienna blue ground coffee can and a matched Meissen (Marcolini) straight-sided saucer, painted in colours with townscapes of Pillnitz and Dresden within gilt borders, below scrolling gilt rims, titles to the reverse, gilt worn, impressed numerals on cup and blue beehive mark, saucer with blue crossed swords mark, 2½in (6cm) high.
£700–900 *CSK*

Ewers

A pair of Minton ewers, reserved on a yellow ground, gilt with flowerheads and foliage, repaired, puce printed globe mark, impressed factory mark and date codes, 10½in (27cm) high.
£1,200–1,700 *S(S)*

Figures - Animals

A pair of Sèvres pâte dure nouvelle models of a cock and hen, 1923, slight damage, largest 6½in (17cm) high.
£425–500 *WL*

A Derby group of a seated black striped cat and kitten, the cat with red and gilt collar, on green and gilt base, ears chipped, c1825, 3in (7.5cm) high.
£400–500 *DN*

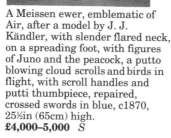

A Meissen ewer, emblematic of Air, after a model by J. J. Kändler, with slender flared neck, on a spreading foot, with figures of Juno and the peacock, a putto blowing cloud scrolls and birds in flight, with scroll handles and putti thumbpiece, repaired, crossed swords in blue, c1870, 25½in (65cm) high.
£4,000–5,000 *S*

A Vienna style green ground ewer and stand, painted with 2 classical roundels featuring Cupid and the Muse of painting, indistinctly titled to base, enriched with raised scrolls, on a broad claret and pink ground band, the base painted and gilt in similar style, slight damage and wear, blue beehive marks, c1900, 23in (59cm) high.
£1,400–2,000 *CSK*

A Royal Worcester white biscuit figure of a cockerel, Marguerite, modelled and incised by A. Azori, black printed marks, model No. 3582, date code for 1960, 9in (23cm) high.
£350–450 *C*

A pair of Continental models of Amazon parrots, perched on tree stumps, 10in (25cm) high.
£300–400 *C(S)*

A pair of Royal Worcester ewers, each decorated with sheep in a landscape, by H. Davis, signed.
£1,800–2,200 *Mit*

A Royal Worcester figure of Arkle, modelled by Doris Lindner, No. 484 of a limited edition of 500, with wood mount and certificate, black printed factory marks, c1967, 15in (38cm) long.
£400–500 *S(S)*

A Meissen figure group of 3 blue tits, crossed swords mark to base, 9in (23cm) wide. **£420–470** *Mit*

A Meissen cat and mouse, c1850, 7in (17.5cm) high.
£900–1,100 *DAV*

This was first modelled by J. J. Kändler c1741.

A pair of Bow blanc de chine lions, faintly incised with a combined circle and arrow marks, c1750, 12in (31cm) wide.
£5,000–7,000 *WW*

A Continental model of an Amazon parrot, perched on a tree stump with its wings outstretched, 10½in (27cm) high.
£600–700 *C(S)*

A Meissen model of a guinea fowl, with red wattle and comb, purple neck and black plumage with white spots, standing astride reeds on a mound base, slight damage, c1745, 2in (5cm) high.
£500–800 *C*

A Continental figure of a crouching rabbit, decorated in brown, repaired, pseudo blue crossed swords mark, late 19thC, 11in (28cm) wide.
£500–600 *DN*

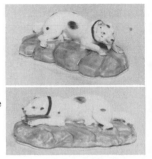

A pair of Samuel Alcock figures of mastiffs, each picked out in black and lying on green ground mound base, damaged and repaired, c1835, 5in (12.5cm) wide.
£400–500 *DN*

A Royal Worcester figure of Wellington, modelled by Bernard Winskill, from a series of famous military commanders, black printed marks, 1969, 15in (38cm) long, on a wooden stand.
£1,000–1,500 *S(S)*

A figure of a rhinoceros, by Rudolstadt, after a Meissen original by J. J. Kändler, naturalistically coloured in tones of brown, slight damage, impressed factory mark and numerals, late 19thC, 13½in (34cm) long.
£500–600 *S(S)*

A pair of Meissen figures of a lion and lioness, modelled by J. J. Kändler, damaged and restored, c1740, on later shaped giltwood bases, largest 15in (38cm) long. **£7,000–9,000** *C*

Figures - People

Two Belleek parian figures emblematic of Meditation and Affection, partially draped in classical robes, enriched with a lustrous glaze, on circular bases, slight damage, printed black marks, Second Period, 15in (38cm) high.
£500–800 *CSK*

A pair of Derby figures of Ranelagh Dancers, on scroll moulded bases picked out in turquoise, damaged, c1765, 10in (25cm) high.
£1,800–2,200 *S*

A Chelsea figure of a piper, Gold Anchor period, damage to bocage.
£850–950 *RA*

A pair of Bow figures of a hunter and his companion, enriched in colours, restored, c1758, 7in (17.5cm) high.
£1,000–1,500 *CSK*

A Derby figure of Sancho Panza, the bearded man wearing a brown hat, green jacket and yellow lined dark red cloak, standing on a grey base with gilt line rim, black printed title and blue printed factory mark, c1878, 8in (20cm).
£200–300 *S(S)*

Two Derby figures, one modelled as America as a Red Indian girl, standing beside an alligator, the other as Africa as a blackamoor wearing an elephant headdress, standing beside a lion, from a set of The Four Quarters of the Globe, each raised on flower encrusted bases, damaged and repaired, c1770, 9in (23cm).
£350–550 *S(S)*

A pair of Derby figures of a boy with a dog and a girl with a cat, the boy wearing a tricorn hat, blue coat and yellow breeches, the dog wearing a brown coat, the girl wearing a bodice and long skirt, holding a spoon to the cat, each on pierced scrolling bases, painted in colours and gilt, slight damage, restored, painted iron red marks, incised shape No. '362', early 19thC, 6in (15cm) high.
£900–1,200 *CSK*

A pair of Derby musicians, restored, incised factory mark No. '11', c1830, 6in (15cm) high.
£500–600 *S(S)*

A Copeland parian figure of The Dancing Girl Reposing, modelled by Calder Marshall for The Art Union of London, impressed factory marks, c1860, 18in (45.5cm) high.
£450–550 *S(S)*

Two Royal Worcester figures of boys holding wicker baskets, modelled by James Hadley, the children wearing Kate Greenaway style clothes, restored, purple and green printed marks, model No. 826, date code for 1881, 7in and 7½in (17.5 and 18cm).
£200–250 *C*

The incorrect No. '827' is impressed on one of the figures.

Two miniature Staffordshire figures of Elijah and The Widow, c1835, 3in (7.5cm).
£380–400 *JO*

A Royal Worcester white menu holder figure of Cairns, restored, impressed and green printed marks, date code for 1875, 6in (15cm), and a similar white parian figure of Disraeli, restored, model No. 512, 6in (15cm).
£520–600 *C*

The other politicians in the series were Mornington, Bright, Gladstone and Lowe.

A Derby figure of Neptune, standing with a dolphin on a mound of colourful shells and seaweed, complete with gilt metal trident, 11½in (29cm).
£800–1,000 *Bea*

A Royal Worcester figure of Colleen, after the original model by James Hadley, wearing an orange cloak, green dress and carrying a basket, standing barefoot on a paved base, puce printed marks and script, model No. 1874, date code for 1831, 6in (15cm).
£250–300 *C*

The script on the base incorrectly records the modeller as C. Evans.

A Royal Worcester figure of Bacchus, after an original by James Hadley, clad in a goat skin, with a ribbon-decorated wand, printed mark and date code for 1892, 29in (74cm).
£1,500–2,000 *Bea*

A Royal Worcester group of two ladies, both wearing lilac mob caps with black bows, black capes with lilac bows, flowered white skirts and black shoes, slight damage, green printed marks, model No. 2616, date code for 1918, 4in (10cm).
£200–300 *C*

A pair of Royal Worcester figures, after originals by James Hadley, emblematic of Music and Dance, wearing flowing robes enriched in blue and gilt on rocky moulded circular bases, minor restoration, printed puce marks, incised 'W', shape No. 1827 and 1828, date codes for 1924, 12½in (31cm).
£470–600 *CSK*

A pair of Royal Worcester figures, entitled Joy and Sorrow, draped in green and bronze, flecked in gold, pattern No. 2/57, printed mark and date code for 1916, 10½in (26.5cm).
£600–700 *Bea*

A Royal Crown Derby freestanding huntsman and hound group, 7in (17.5cm).
£75–100 *MJB*

A Grainger's Worcester white biscuit figure of Medora, wearing a turban, jacket, bodice and skirt adorned with lace, slight damage, reverse with incised script 'published November 1845', 12in (31cm).
£100–200 *C*

A Royal Worcester figure of a City Imperial volunteer, standing to attention with his rifle beside him, painted in shades of khaki and cream, enriched in gilding, top of rifle missing, green printed marks, impressed '111', model No. 2106, printed registration mark, date code for 1900, 7½in (18cm).
£550–650 *C*

A Royal Worcester figure of a gentleman, with an opera hat in his right hand, wearing a voluminous pale yellow lined lilac cape edged in black, and a black evening coat and trousers, slight damage, green printed marks, model No. 2633, indistinct date code, c1916, 5in (13cm). **£200–300** *C*

A Royal Worcester figure of an Irishman, modelled by James Hadley, wearing a green jacket, shaded orange waistcoat, light brown breeches, turquoise socks and brown shoes, on a shaped paved base, purple printed marks, impressed '50' and '31', date code for 1894, 7in (17.5cm).
£250–350 *C*

A Royal Worcester figure of The Seamstress, modelled by Freda Doughty, wearing a pale blue dress, black printed marks, model No. 3569, date code for 1957, 7½in (19cm). **£200–300** *C*

A Royal Worcester plaster group, modelled by Eileen Soper, painted in pale blue, pink and black, slight damage, incised marks, inscribed in black on base 'Pussy Cat, Pussy Cat, Where Have You Been?', c1940, 7in (18cm).
£260–300 *C*

A Royal Worcester coloured parian figure of a Welsh girl, modelled by James Hadley, wearing a tall black hat, orange shawl, pale brown blouse and apron, pale blue skirt and purple socks, holding a basket, on a paved base, slight damage, impressed 'Hadley', impressed and green printed marks, model No. 1875, indistinct date code, c1900, 7in (18cm). **£350–450** *C*

A Royal Worcester figure of Louisa, from the Victorian series, modelled by Ruth van Ruyckevelt, standing on a stairway with a book and flowers, No. 412 of a limited edition of 500, 7½in (19cm), with fitted box and certificate. **£250–350** *Bea*

A Royal Worcester figure of Cecilia reading a letter, modelled by Ronald van Ruyckevelt, end of ribbon missing, black printed marks, model No. 329, copyright for 1972, 7½in (19.5cm). **£300–400** *C*

Two Royal Worcester figures, c1899, 31in (79cm). **£3,000–3,500** *Mit*

A Royal Worcester group, entitled The Tea Party, modelled by Ruth van Ruyckevelt, depicting fashionably dressed ladies with a girl playing with a small dog, by a table set for tea, No. 160 of a limited edition of 250, 8in (20cm), with fitted box and certificate. **£800–1,200** *Bea*

A Royal Worcester figure of a Hindu, after an original by James Hadley, wearing an orange turban, blue robe with a yellow sash and orange shoes, on a paved base, puce printed marks and script, model No. 838, date code for 1931, 6½in (16cm). **£300–400** *C*

A Meissen group of putti, c1850, 5in (12.5cm). **£550–750** *DAV*

A Royal Worcester figure of Summer Day, modelled by Freda Doughty, wearing a green, dark pink and white dress, black printed marks, model No. 3547, date code for 1960, 9in (23cm). **£300–400** *C*

A Royal Worcester figure of a girl, modelled by Agnes Pinder-Davis, entitled Two's Company, Three's None, from the Chinoiserie Sayings series, wearing a leaf-shaped hat, blue flowered white tunic, blue trousers and red slippers, on a shaped base printed with black script, black printed marks, model No. 3499, date code for 1954, 5in (12.5cm). **£250–550** *C*

A Meissen group of Pluto and Persephone, picked out in gilt, restored, blue mark, late 18thC, 10½in (26.5cm). **£200–250** *DN*

A Meissen figure from a series of 16 putti, with an inscription in French, 'Te les accouple', on a triangular base, c1860, 5in (12.5cm).
£450–550 *DAV*

A Meissen figure of The Taylor and The Goat, the man wearing a yellow floral coat, c1860, 9in (23cm).
£900–1,100 *DAV*

A Meissen figure of Columbine, modelled by J. J. Kändler, enriched in colours and gilt, damaged and restored, c1745, 5in (12.5cm).
£600–700 *CSK*

A Meissen group, depicting a monkey rocking a goat in a cradle, with two putti, c1860, 6½in (16cm).
£600–800 *DAV*

A Meissen group of lovers, the man wearing a crimson jacket, decorated with pastel shades, c1860, 9½in (24cm).
£1,450–1,700 *DAV*

A Meissen group of putti, from the Industry series, c1880, 4in (10cm).   **£400–480** *DAV*

A Meissen figure of Count von Bruhl's Tailor, after a model by J. J. Kändler, wearing a pale pink floral coat, seated astride a goat with various accoutrements of his trade, and 2 young kids in a basket on his back, slight damage, crossed swords in underglaze blue, incised model No. '171', c1880, 8in (20cm).
£350–550 *S(S)*

A Meissen barrel Wine Festival group, modelled after Acier, 19thC.
£2,800–3,000 *RA*

A Nymphenburg white chinoiserie figure of a musician, modelled by Franz Anton Bustelli, restored, impressed shield mark to top of base, c1760, 7in (17cm).
£7,500–9,000 *C*

A Meissen group, c1860, 6in (15cm).
£1,000–1,200 *DeA*

A Meissen figure of a putto gardener, painted in colours and gilt, slight damage, blue crossed swords mark, incised No., Pressnummern, c1880, 5in (12.5cm), and a Meissen figure of a girl holding a basket of fruit, 20thC.
£450–550 *CSK*

A Meissen group of angel lovers, 19thC.
£800–900 *RA*

A pair of French coloured bisque figures of a gallant and companion, wearing brightly coloured costume, one base painted to simulate marble painted with a panel of instruments, damaged and restored, one impressed 'L&M' late 19thC, 17½in (44.5cm).
£600–800 *S(S)*

A pair of Vienna figures of a vintner and companion, he in a conical hat, yellow puce-lined jacket, white waistcoat with gilt frogging, pale green apron and puce breeches, she in a conical hat, yellow and pink bodice, green apron and white skirt with puce hem and zig-zag border, restored, blue beehive marks, he with incised 'Q', she with impressed 'E' and painter's 'W', c1765, the man 6½in (16.5cm).
£1,800–2,500 *C*

A Continental figure, blue crossed swords marks scratched through to underside, 9½in (24cm).
£200–250 *MJB*

A Continental figure group of a suitor giving unwanted attentions to a lady, 8½in (21cm).
£200–250 *Mit*

A German monkey band, comprising: a conductor and 10 instrumentalists, each standing on a scroll moulded base, slight damage, conductor 7in (17.5cm).
£1,500–2,000 *Bea*

Flatware

A Chelsea dish, decorated in the manner of Jefferyes Hamett O'Neale, with brown line rim, c1752, 4½in (11cm) diam.
£3,200–3,700 *WW*

A Bow fluted plate, decorated in coloured enamels with sprays of flowers and leaves, within a gilt border, slight damage, red anchor and dagger mark, c1760, 7in (18cm) diam.
£250–350 *DN*

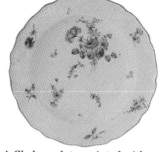

A Chelsea plate, painted with a loose bouquet and scattered flowers within a shaped brown line rim, red anchor and '2' mark, c1755, 9½in (23.5cm) diam.
£750–850 *C*

A Longton Hall strawberry leaf-moulded plate, the centre painted in colours with a loose spray of flowers among scattered sprigs, the border moulded with fruiting leaves, slight damage, c1755, 9in (23cm) diam.
£1,000–1,400 *CSK*

A pair of Chelsea plates, painted with a loose bouquet and scattered flowers within shaped brown line rims, c1755, 9in (23cm) diam.
£1,000–1,500 *C*

A Meissen open work plate, in the Watteau style, with a green, yellow and gold border, c1860, 10in (25cm) diam.
£500–800 *DAV*

A Caughley decorated plate, painted in shades of grey with the fable of the *Wolf & Crane,* within a gilt roundel below a band of gilt foilage, the blue ground shaped rim gilt with dot and wreath panels, between leaves and flowerheads, slight damage and wear, titled in iron red script to the reverse, c1795, 8in (20cm) diam.
£500–600 *CSK*

A pair of Minton shaped armorial plates, each printed and painted in colours and gilt, with a coat-of-arms above a banner, the rims gilt with C-scrolls and wreaths of flowers, slight wear to gilt, titled to the reverse for 'Lytham Hall', impressed marks, 20thC, 10in (25cm) diam. **£100–150** *CSK*

A Longton Hall strawberry moulded plate, the central panel decorated by the 'Trembly Rose' painter with loose bouquets and sprigs of summer flowers within a moulded border, unmarked, slight damage, 9in (23cm) diam.
£600–800 *HSS*

Two Caughley dishes, each decorated in bright blue with fishermen in a Chinese river landscape, within a diaper panelled key fret border, c1788, 11in (28cm).
£270–350 *DN*

A set of 6 Minton dessert plates, each decorated with a fan, the open leaf painted with a different bird subject signed by W. Mussill, all on a celadon ground within a gilt dentil rim, 2 restored, impressed 'Minton', and year cypher, painted pattern No. 'G1253', c1873.
£500–700 *S(S)*

A Stevenson & Hancock silver-shaped cabinet plate, the central panel painted in the style of W. E. Mosley, in polychrome enamels against a shaded grey ground, within a gilt ciselé decorated cobalt blue and gadroon moulded border, marked in burnt orange, 9in (23cm) diam.
£350–450 *HSS*

A Derby botanical dish, decorated with Love in the Mist and Yellow Horn poppy, named in blue on the reverse, with brown line rim, slight damage, crown, crossed batons, D marks and pattern No. 139 in blue, Wm. Duesbury & Co., c1795, 9in (23cm) diam.
£650–850 *C*

A Meissen dish, painted in a bright palette within a gilt band entwined with green ribbon, below a shaped gilt line rim, slight damage, blue crossed swords and 'Punkt' mark, 'Pressnummer' and impressed marks, 18thC, 10in (25cm) wide and a similar saucer.
£400–600 *CSK*

A Meissen dessert plate, with gilt border and floral centre, c1860, 8in (20cm) diam.
£200–230 *DAV*

A Meissen open work plate, c1860, 9½in (23.5cm) diam.
£500–800 *DAV*

A Meissen dish, painted in brown, green and yellow within a brown line rim, slight damage, blue crossed swords mark, 'Pressnummer 21, Dreher's ///' to footrim, c1740, 13½in (33.5cm) diam.
£2,000–2,500 *C*

A Worcester Flight, Barr and Barr, Worcester dish, the handles with leaf terminals, centrally decorated in coloured enamels, on a pale green and gilt ground, printed mark in brown, c1823, 5in (13cm) wide.
£450–550 *DN*

A Miles Mason dessert dish, with moulded cabbage leaf decoration, edged with gilt against a ground of solid gilding, restored, with 'Grey Wagtail' in red script on reverse, c1813, 10½in (26cm) wide.
£300–330 *VH*

A Worcester teapot stand, by Robert Hancock, printed in deep lilac with 2 maids carrying pails and a gentleman, before cattle, within a gilt line rim, slight damage, c1765, 5½in (14cm) wide.
£350–500 *CSK*

A Royal Worcester plate, centrally decorated by James Stinton, signed, printed marks in puce for 1917 and registration number '571649', 10in (25cm) diam.
£450–550 *DN*

A Worcester plate, small rim chip, c1775.
£500–550 *RA*

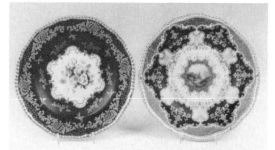

A Coalport topographical plate, painted with a view of the Ruins of Brunnenburg, indistinct signature, titled to the reverse, printed and impressed marks, c1900, and another painted by F. Howard, slight damage, printed and impressed marks, signed, 9in (23cm) diam.
£200–300 *CSK*

A Minton perforated plate, on 4 scroll feet, outlined in gold, slight damage, 8in (19.5cm) diam.
£900–1,200 *Bea*

Two Worcester plates, with blue mazarine ground and floral reserves, c1775.
£600–650 *RA*

A Miles Mason bone china dessert plate, with acanthus and cabbage leaf moulded decoration, restored, with 'Green Woodpecker' in red script on reverse, c1813, 8½in (21cm) diam.
£250–280 *VH*

Two Meissen dessert plates, one with greenfinch, the other with blue tit in the centre, c1880, 8in (20cm) diam.
£85–115 each *DAV*

Two Minton plates, signed by Gustav Leonce, one slightly damaged, impressed marks, date codes for 1879, 9½in (23.5cm) diam, and another painted with 2 ducks in a basket, unsigned, slight damage, impressed marks, date code for 1881.
£250–300 *CSK*

A Royal Worcester dessert dish, the centre painted by John Stinton with a view of Chepstow Castle, within a gold decorated blue border reserved with sprays of flowers, inscribed and printed marks, date code for 1916, 9in (23cm) wide.
£600–800 *Bea*

A Meissen leaf-shaped dish, c1870, 8in (20cm) wide.
£200–300 *DAV*

Three Meissen dinner plates, and 4 soup plates, each painted within a border of scattered insects and flowers and a waved rim, slight damage to one plate, blue crossed swords mark, 9in (23cm) diam.
£1,200–1,500 *C(S)*

A Doccia tin glazed deep dish, painted en camaieu rose, with a vignette of buildings in an Italianate landscape, slight damage, c1780, 14in (36cm) diam.
£300–350 *CSK*

A bone china dessert plate, with scroll pattern edge, c1813, 8in (20cm) diam.
£80–100 *VH*

A set of 6 Berlin dessert plates, each finely decorated in coloured enamels, picked out in green, slight damage, blue and red marks, impressed numerals, 19thC, 9in (23cm) diam.
£550–700 *DN*

A Doccia fluted dish, with shell-moulded terminals, painted in colours, enriched in puce and gilt, slight damage, c1770, 10½in (26cm) wide.
£400–600 *CSK*

A Meissen dish with elaborately gilt foliate border and shaped gilt edged rim, minor damage, cancelled crossed swords in underglaze blue and impressed number '5', late 19thC, 11½in (29cm) wide.
£300–400 *S(S)*

Two Vienna style plates, painted with Classical scenes, entitled to the reverse 'Psyche beschenkt ihre Schwestern' and 'Aglaia' within gilt borders with panels of scrolling foliage, slight damage, blue beehive marks, c1900, 10in (25cm) diam. **£600–800** *CSK*

Four Sèvres turquoise ground plates, painted in colours within oeil de perdrix borders, below rims enriched with gilt, slight damage, interlaced 'L' marks, 18thC with later decoration, 9½in (23.5cm) diam.
£600–800 *CSK*

Ice Pails

A Davenport ice pail, with moulded raised band, heightened in gilt and floral sprigs, gilt scroll side lifts, each side painted with a floral bouquet, gilt rims and bands, puce printed mark, c1820, 8in (20cm).
£600–700 *WW*

A pair of English pink ground ice pails and covers, with pine cone finials, painted in colours, the ground painted with quatrefoil flowerheads reserved with gilt flowers, between gilt bands, on 3 feet, with 2 liners, damaged and restored, the liners replaced, 19thC, 14½in (37cm).
£1,200–1,700 *CSK*

A pair of Ridgway ice pails and covers, with bud finials, painted in colours, enriched in gilt, one cover damaged and restored, some slight wear, c1815, 11in (28cm).
£2,700–3,200 *CSK*

A Meissen ice pail, cover and liner, outside decorated, the two-handled pail raised on 3 bun feet and painted with panels of harbour scenes within gilt scroll borders, the cover with pierced gallery rim and plum knop, cancelled crossed swords in underglaze blue, 19thC, 8in (20cm).
£700–900 *S(S)*

Inkwells

An English inkstand of tripartite form, on geometric gilt foliate ground, damages and minor restorations, c1815, 7in (18cm) wide.
£500–600 *CSK*

An English pen stand and stopper, modelled as a winged putto leaning on a shell-moulded bowl with 3 apertures, on a bed of shells and seaweed above an octagonal base, painted in colours and gilt, slight damage, gilt mark, possibly Chamberlain's Worcester, c1825, 5in (12.5cm) wide. **£200–300** *CSK*

A Derby inkwell and cover, painted in bright colours with flowers on a black band between gilt rims, the shoulder with 3 pierced holes, slight damage, painted iron red mark, c1810, 2½in (6cm) diam. **£450–550** *CSK*

A 'Sèvres' gilt metal mounted inkstand, comprising a pair of inkwells and hinged covers and a fitted oval tray, the pots painted with panels of birds, the tray with winged cherubs on a richly gilt ground, minor damages and repairs, blue painted interlaced 'L' mark, 19thC, 9½in (24cm) wide. **£750–850** *S(S)*

An inkwell, possibly French, c1840, 7½in (18.5cm) wide. **£300–335** *STA*

A Staffordshire drum-shaped inkwell and liner, the sides decorated in puce with a continuous landscape, the liner with flowers and leaves within gilt borders, early 19thC, 4in (10cm) diam. **£270–350** *DN*

A Paris inkwell with liners, modelled as a recumbent hound wearing a collar, on a rectangular shaped green ground base, pierced with 3 apertures and enriched with gilt scrolling foliage, the footed base moulded with scrolls, 2 liners replaced and restored, damaged, 19thC, 11in (28cm) wide. **£300–400** *CSK*

Jugs

A Worcester small sparrow beak baluster-shaped jug, with reeded loop handle, decorated in blue with the Cormorant pattern, damaged, decorator's mark, c1757, 3in (7.5cm). **£1,000–1,200** *DN*

A Spode double inkwell, with 2 lift-out wells and pen holes, rope twist borders, the sides painted with river landscapes and bouquets of flowers in reserves, between a basket weave moulded ground, painted in blue and pink, with later gilt highlights, 5in (12.5cm). **£150–250** *WW*

A cream jug, painted with colourful sprays of flowers between rope twist rims, on a blue tinted glazed ground, damaged, probably Liverpool, Seth Pennington's factory, c1775, 5in (12.5cm). **£120–180** *S(S)*

A Derby baluster mask jug, with scrolling handle, painted in colours below a brown line rim, damaged and restored, c1765, 8in (20cm). **£350–450** *CSK*

A cream jug, decorated in coloured enamels with Chinese style figures, the interior with an iron red band, on round foot, damaged, c1800, 5in (12.5cm). **£200–250** *DN*

A Worcester reeded barrel-shaped sparrow beak jug, with loop handle, decorated in coloured enamels with flowers and leaves, within a puce lobed cartouche, and with scattered flowers and insects, c1780, 3in (7.5cm).
£750–850 *DN*

Mugs

A Derby mug, slight damage, crown, crossed batons, 'D' and '62' marks in iron red, Robt. Bloor & Co., c1815, 5in (12.5cm).
£1,500–2,000 *C*

A Derby ornithological mug, painted in the manner of Richard Dodson, slight damage, crown, crossed batons, 'D' and '18' marks in iron red, Duesbury & Kean, c1810, 4½in (11cm).
£1,000–1,500 *C*

A Royal Worcester reticulated jug, the body pierced with a band of stylised ornament between honeycomb bands, enriched with gilding, the gilt scroll handle with dragon mask terminal, the top of the body with a single white and turquoise gilded band, the whole coloured in pale tones of pink, cream and ivory, printed crowned circle mark, registered number '44622' and shape number '1143', almost certainly the work of George Owen and gilded by Samuel Radford, signed 'SR', 6in (15cm).
£4,000–4,500 *S*

A Worcester blue and white mug with groove handle, painted with 2 quail by fencing, below a gnarled tree and an Oriental in a boat, minor damage, c1754, 2½in (6cm). **£4,000–4,500** *CSK*

A John and Robert Godwin jug, printed in blue, with a view of Crystal Palace, beneath a flower and cell diaper rim, printed title mark 'A View of the Great Exhibition Palace', c1855, 7½in (19cm).
£80–120 *DN*

This version of the pattern appears to be unrecorded.

A Sèvres jug, the rim painted with a panel of gilt festoons on a blue du roi ground, minor damages, blue enamel interlaced 'L' marks, with date letter 'MM' for 1790, and painter's mark 'DT' for Du Tanda, 6in (15cm).
£300–400 *CSK*

A Chelsea white beaker, the sides moulded with prunus sprays, c1750, 3in (8cm).
£1,000–1,500 *C*

Two Meissen beakers, from the Swan Service, c1860.
£350–450 each *DAV*

Salts

A Meissen cruet, c1860, 4in (10cm) diam.
£250–350
DAV

Two Chelsea white crayfish salts, after the silver gilt models by Nicholas Sprimont, the crayfish with one claw resting on a shell-moulded dish, among coral and shells, the rockwork bases applied with seaweed and further shells, damages, parts lacking, incised triangle marks, c1747, 4½in (11cm) wide.
£7,500–9,000 *C*

A pair of Meissen salt cellars, in the form of a young boy and a girl, each seated between 2 oval flower decorated and encrusted baskets, on scroll moulded mound base, marks in blue and incised numerals, 5in (12.5cm).
£650–750 *DN*

Sauceboats

A Bow fluted sauceboat, painted in colours to the exterior and interior with flowersprays and sprigs, the rim and foot enriched in puce, slight damage, c1765, 5in (12.5cm) wide.
£300–400 *CSK*

A Meissen leaf-moulded sauceboat and ladle, the handles formed as stalks, enriched in shades of green and purple, painted in colours, slight damage, repairs, blue crossed swords mark, c1745, the sauceboat 7½in (18.5cm) wide, the ladle 8in (20cm) long.
£600–800 *CSK*

Services

A Grainger's Worcester cream boat, modelled as a swimming duck with incised feathers, sparsely coloured, with a gilt dentil rim, slight damage, printed puce mark, c1850, 5in (12.5cm).
£200–300 *CSK*

A Derby dinner service, all Imari decorated with flowering trees to the centre and gilt lion masks, comprising 57 pieces, early 19thC.
£3,000–4,000 *HCH*

A Bow silver-shaped sauceboat, moulded with swags of flowers and gilt, with flowersprays, above a spreading oval foot, slight damage, paper label for 'Toppin', c1750, 5in (12.5cm). **£600–750** *CSK*

A Coalport orange ground part tea service, painted in bright colours, the gilt handles reserved with leaves, comprising: a London-shape teapot, cover and stand, sugar bowl and cover, 2 cream jugs, and 2 slop basins, slight damage, c1815. **£800–1,000** *CSK*

A Coalport type tea service, each piece well-painted with colourful flowers against a white ground enriched in gilding, gilt dentil rim, comprising: a teapot and cover, sucrier and cover, milk jug, plate, 7 cups and saucers, teapot with crack, gilt pattern number '830', c1820.
£1,500–2,000 *S(S)*

A Derby composite Imari pattern part dinner service, painted in underglaze blue, iron red, pink and enriched in gilding, various iron red marks, some damage, c1825. **£3,000–5,000** *CSK*

A Miles Mason bone china trio, pattern number 743, c1813, 5in (12.5cm) diam.
£200–220 *VH*

A Royal Crown Derby tea service, each piece decorated in Imari style with panels of flowers and leaves, within flower panelled borders, comprising: oval teapot and cover, milk jug, two-handled sucrier and cover, hot water jug, 6 tea cups and saucers, slop bowl, 12 tea plates in 2 sizes, and a pair of bread and butter plates, printed marks for 1917 and pattern number 2541.
£1,200–1,700 *DN*

A Minton type dessert service, decorated in coloured enamels within turquoise and gilt borders, comprising: 12 plates, 9½in (14cm) diam, and 4 round stands, in 2 sizes, pattern number '7/766' in gilt, c1855.
£600–700 *DN*

A Coalport part tea service, painted after a New Hall pattern 426, in underglaze blue, iron red and gilt, comprising: an oval teapot, cover and stand, milk jug, slop basin, 2 dishes, and 8 cups and saucers, slight damage, c1800.
£1,200–1,700 *CSK*

A William Brownfield botanical dessert service, each piece brightly painted within a pink border and shaped gilt saw tooth rim, comprising: 2 tall comports, 4 low comports, 12 dessert plates, minor wear to gilding, impressed factory marks, painted pattern numbers '519', impressed numerals '2/78', c1875.
£500–700 *S(S)*

A Davenport Japan pattern dessert service, comprising: 9 plates, 3 low pedestal tazzas and high pedestal 'dolphin' tazza, printed crown over Davenport Longport Staffordshire and inscribed pattern number '1392' in iron red. **£600–800** *HSS*

Eight Meissen tea cups and 6 saucers, minor damage, blue crossed swords marks, cups with 'Pressnummern 14' and '67', saucers with '37', painted numbers '37' and '64', c1880.
£1,200–1,800 *C*

In the Ceramics section when there is only one measurement it refers to the height of the piece, unless otherwise stated.

A Chamberlain's Worcester tea and coffee service, decorated in gilt, within blue and gilt borders, comprising: oval teapot, cover and stand, milk jug, sucrier and cover, with fixed ring handles, 12 tea bowls, 12 coffee cans, 12 saucers, slop bowl, 2 saucer dishes, some damage, the teapot and sucrier with painted marks in puce, pattern number '273', c1800.
£400–600 *DN*

A set of 6 Royal Worcester bone china cups and saucers, painted by Moseley, signed, the cups with gilt exteriors, small chip to one cup, puce printed marks, c1939.
£1,300–1,700 *S(S)*

A New Hall teapot, cover and boat-shaped milk jug, painted in colours with flowers issuing from baskets below a mazarine blue line, the spout richly gilt with sprig within oval panels, and a circular deep dish, slight wear, painted pattern No. '611', c1805.
£1,000–1,500 *CSK*

A Chamberlain's Worcester Flight period part tea service, damaged and repaired, blue crescent and 'Flight' marks, late 18thC.
£1,700–2,000 *CSK*

A Sèvres cabaret service, painted on a turquoise ground, comprising: a shaped square tray, teapot and cover, sugar bowl and cover, jug, 2 cups and 2 saucers, minor damage and repair, blue painted interlaced 'L' mark, gilt titles, late 19thC. **£650–800** *S(S)*

A Limoges cabaret set, decorated within gilt borders, comprising: teapot and cover, sucrier and cover, milk jug, 2 cups and saucers, and a round two-handled tray, printed marks in green, in a silk lined case. **£900–1,200** *DN*

Sweetmeats

A Bow sweetmeat figure of a seated Turkish lady, wearing purple headdress, a yellow lined coat patterned with iron red, blue and green, a white sashed rose robe, iron red and purple striped white pantaloons and iron red shoe, left shoe missing, c1760, 5½in (13.5cm).
£950–1,200 *S(NY)*

A pair of Meissen sweetmeat figures of a Turk and companion, modelled by J.F. Eberlein, he in white, red, pink and blue, she in white, pink and yellow, damaged and repaired, blue crossed swords marks to back of bases, c1750, 6½in (16.5cm).
£2,500–3,500 *C*

Tea & Coffee Pots

A Worcester baluster coffee pot, and a domed cover with flower finial, painted in colours with Orientals in gardens, minor damage, c1770, 9½in (24cm) high.
£500–700 *CSK*

A Meissen coffee pot, in Streu blumen pattern, c1850, 10½in (26cm) high.
£250–350 *DAV*

A Bow porcelain teapot and cover, printed and painted in underglaze blue, the domed cover similarly decorated beneath the pear-form knop, 5½in (14cm) high.
£400–600 *S(S)*

A Sèvres teapot and an associated cover, painted in colours within blue enamel bands and gilt dentil rims, the cover with gilt peach finial, minor damage, interlaced 'L' marks to the base, decorator's marks and incised marks, c1765, 4in (10cm) high.
£350–450 *CSK*

A Derby miniature blue and white teapot and cover, printed with pagodas in a landscape below blue lines, slight damage, c1765, 3in (7.5cm) high.
£1,000–1,400 *CSK*

Tureens

A Derby botanical sauce tureen, cover and stand, attributed to William Pegg, with named botanical specimens from *Curtis Botanical Journal* in English and Latin, gilded borders, minor damage, crown, crossed batons and script 'D' in blue enamel, c1800, the stand 9½in (24cm) wide. **£1,200–1,700** *S*

A pair of Fürstenberg tureens and covers, with pear finials and pierced scrolling handles, supported by 4 scroll feet, painted in colours with vignettes of wild fowl among shrubs and grasses within scrolling foliate moulded panels alternating with panels of flowers, the ground painted with song birds in branches, enriched in gilt, minor damage and restorations, blue 'F' and incised marks, c1770, 11in (28cm) wide. **£3,500–4,000** *CSK*

A pair of Miles Mason bone china dessert sauce tureens and stands, printed in black with scroll pattern, painted in enamel colours, the ox head handles and cow finial solid gilt, rim painted cerulean blue, c1813, stand 7in (17.5cm) wide. **£1,000–1,250** *VH*

A pair of Worcester chestnut tureens with domed lids, rustic loop handles, gilded, pierced and applied flowers and leaves on white ground, matching stands, late 18thC, 10½in (26cm) wide. **£1,500–2,000** *AH*

Vases

A pair of Royal Worcester two-handled vases, each painted with red and gilt foliage on a yellow ground, with pierced rims, repaired, green printed crown and circle mark, c1884, 15in (38cm) high. **£400–500** *S(S)*

A pair of Coalport vases, painted with Loch Tummel, on an apple green ground, marked, c1870, 5½in (14cm) high. **£200–280** *DeA*

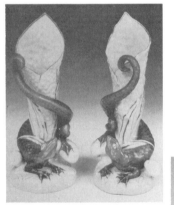

A pair of Belleek First Period lizard vases, enriched in bronze and gilt, slight wear, black printed marks, 9in (23cm) high. **£1,500–2,000** *CSK*

A Worcester Flight, Barr and Barr vase, decorated in coloured enamels, on a lime green ground, on square base, minor rim chips, impressed mark and painted address mark, c1820, 10in (25cm). **£600–700** *DN*

A Coalport vase garniture, decorated with scenes in the Grampian Hills and Mount Venue, Perthshire, pattern No. 283570, signed, 8 and 10in (20 and 25cm) high. **£800–1,000** *Mit*

A garniture of 5 H & R Daniel porcelain vases, with gilt twig handles, each ribbed baluster body painted on one side with a Chinese figure in a garden and on the other with exotic birds, reserved on a gold decorated green and cream ground, damaged, pattern No. 196/200, 8½ and 9½in (21 and 24cm). **£300–500** *Bea*

A pair of Derby double-walled octagonal vases, each with continuous bands of colourful flowers and gilt foliage, black printed factory marks and incised numerals '213', red painted 'R', c1885, 3in (8cm) high. **£300–400** *S(S)*

A Grainger's Worcester two-handled vase and cover, of Eastern inspiration, the pierced domed cover with pierced acorn finial, minor chips, brown printed and impressed factory marks and red painted pattern number, c1880, 7in (17.5cm) high. **£500–600** *S(S)*

A Continental porcelain thistle-shaped jar and cover, painted in a Meissen style, worn and restored, gilder's marks, 19thC, 7in (17.5cm). **£1,000–1,500** *CSK*

A Staffordshire porcelain spill vase, modelled on the fable of the *Fox and the Stork*, enriched in colours and gilt, minor damage, c1830, 6½in (16cm) high. **£150–200** *CSK*

A Rockingham blue ground vase, with a turnover lip, painted in colours, within a gilt panel, on a circular spreading foot, minor damage, printed red griffin mark, painted numbers, c1830, 6in (15cm) high. **£1,500–2,000** *CSK*

A pair of Meissen vases, painted in colours on a deep blue ground between gilt rims, crossed swords in underglaze blue and impressed numerals, late 19thC, 9in (23cm). **£700–900** *S(S)*

A Bloor Derby campana-shaped vase, with gold satyrs' head and loop handles, decorated in gold with scrolling foliage, some damage, 17in (43cm) high. **£850–1,200** *Bea*

A Royal Worcester vase, painted by Sedgley, with sprays of pink and red roses reserved on a matt silk ground beneath a gilt upper rim, signed, printed factory marks and shape number '2472', c1922, 9½in (24cm) high. **£350–500** *S(S)*

A garniture of 3 Coalbrookdale vases, applied with brightly coloured flowers, slight damage, early 19thC, 11½ and 13in (29 and 33cm) high.
£400–500 *Bea*

A pair of Sèvres style vases and covers, painted in colours, within bleu celeste ground ribbons, gilt with leaves and oak branches, on circular feet above square section bases, wear and repairs, painted blue marks, 19thC, 14in (36cm).
£1,700–2,000 *CSK*

A Russian vase, possibly Moscow, decorated in underglaze blue with stylised flowers and foliage picked out in tooled gilding between burnished gilt borders, gilt factory marks, early 20thC, 14in (36cm) high.   **£300–400** *S(S)*

A Paris Rue Thiroux vase and cover, painted alternately with orange and gold ground lozenges, with roses, trophies and birds en grisaille between pink roses, suspended on blue ribbons from gilt loops and sepia paterae hung with purple swags, between gilt foliage swags and above sepia paterae suspending green foliage swags, the shoulders striped with diagonal sepia foliage between gilt bands, the stem and cover with green stiff-leaves and a pink band reserved with foliage scrolls, on a circular foot and simulated green marble square base, damaged and restored, gilt crowned 'A' mark, c1790, 19½in (49cm) high.
£2,000–3,000 *C*

A Hadley's Worcester onion-shaped pot pourri vase and cover, painted in colours by A. Schuck, with pheasants perched and flying amidst fir trees, within gilt decorated shaded green borders, signed, printed mark in green, numbered 'F130' over '11567' in burnt orange, 10in (25cm) high.
£550–700 *HSS*

A pair of Sèvres style blue ground urn-shaped vases and domed covers, with gilt metal mounts, painted in colours, slight wear and chip, blue interlaced 'L' marks to the covers, 19thC, 11in (28cm) high.   **£1,500–2,000** *CSK*

A Royal Worcester vase, decorated by James Stinton with pheasants in a landscape, beneath a gilt line rim, signed, printed marks in green for 1912, shape number 'G461', 4in (10cm) high.
£250–300 *DN*

A Berlin bisque two-handled Empire style vase, chips and damages, wear to gilt, red printed orb mark and indistinct blue printed mark, 19thC, 16in (41cm) high.   **£400–500** *CSK*

A pair of French vases, brightly painted with a continuous band of flowers and fruit reserved on a graduated mottled pink ground beneath gilt line rims, one damaged, late 19thC, 13in (33cm) high. **£200–250** *S(S)*

Miscellaneous

A Meissen watering can with screw lid, replaced silver gilt handle, c1750, 6in (15cm) high. **£1,250–1,450** *DAV*

A George Jones and Minton ashtray, the lobed oval bowl modelled with a cat creeping over the edge of the bowl to catch a bird, impressed Minton year mark for 1873 and impressed registration diamond for George Jones 22 January 1876, 5in (12.5cm) wide. **£2,500–3,500** *S*

This most unusual ashtray may well have been made by George Jones using a Minton blank, this would explain the marks for both George Jones and Minton.

A Royal Worcester vase, painted by William Ricketts, with apples, berries and blossom on a mossy ground, printed mark and date code for 1924, 9in (23cm) high. **£400–500** *Bea*

A set of 8 two-pronged forks with Bow pistol-shaped handles, damaged, c1755, the handles 3½in (9cm) long, and a knife. **£200–250** *DN*

A knife and fork with Worcester blue and white pistol-shaped handles, painted with sprays of roses among scattered sprigs of flowers, c1760, 8½ and 10in (21 and 25cm) long. **£550–650** *CSK*

A Nantgarw Masonic tumbler, probably painted by William Billingsley, decorated in gilt with a sunburst face between gilt lined rims, c1820, 3in (7.5cm). **£2,500–3,500** *S*

A Ridgway foot bath, c1840. **£500–600** *CAI*

An English boat-shaped eyebath, on tapering stem and round base, decorated in gilt with swags and pendant leaves, within puce line borders, small chips, c1800, 2in (5cm) high. **£350–400** *DN*

A pair of Derby butter tubs and covers, painted with sprigs and sprays of summer flowers, each cover applied with a strawberry finial, lug handles and scroll feet, minor chips, c1758, 4in (10cm). **£1,800–2,200** *S*

Goss & Crested China

A gramophone horn by Willow Art.
£25–30 *G&CC*

A Shetland collie by Swan China.
£25–30 *G&CC*

A statue of Peter Pan by Willow Art.
£75–85 *G&CC*

A Goss bust of the Duchess of Devonshire, known as The Beautiful Duchess, enriched in colours, with square section plinth moulded with laurel garlands and with 4 volute feet, chipped and restored, the bust with impressed marks, 15in (38cm) high with plinth.
£1,100–1,700 *CSK*

A clown candle snuffer by Clifton.
£35–40 *G&CC*

A baby in a bootee, British manufacturer.
£6-12 *G&CC*

A yacht by Carlton.
£12–15 *G&CC*

A snail by Grafton
£12–15 *G&CC*

Pups in a basket, made in Saxony.
£15–20 *G&CC*

A roller skate by Carlton.
£35–45 *G&CC*

A Staffordshire spill vase group, 10in (25cm) high. **£1,500–2,000** *JO*

A Sunderland lustre jug, depicting Sunderland Bridge and the Mariner's Arms, c1840, 9½in (24cm) high. **£400–500** *RP*

A Staffordshire spill vase group, 8in (20cm) high. **£1,500–2,000** *JO*

A slipware tile, trailed and incised with the initials 'I R M' and dated '1727', and 4 spotted stylised flowerheads, 7½in (19cm) square. **£1,750–2,000** *S*

A Whieldon dovecote, raised on a conical base, one side moulded with 2 figures in an open door above the sign 'A NEW PAVILION', restored, 8½in (21cm) high. **£9,000–12,000** *S*

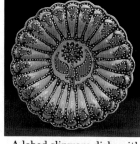

A lobed slipware dish, with central floral motif and scalloped border, restored, c1700, 11½in (29cm) diam. **£4,000–5,000** *S*

An early Southwark tin glazed mug, the silver die-cast band around rim with initials 'AH MG', damaged, c1630, 5½in (14cm). **£28,000–30,000** *S*

A Mason's Ironstone Neapolitan ewer, richly gilded, restored, 27in (69cm) high. **£3,750–4,550** *JP*

Ten Wilkinson Ltd., WWI character jugs, designed by F. Carruthers Gould, retailer's mark for 1914-18, and a Copeland Spode Toby jug modelled as Winston Churchill. **£5,000–6,000** *C*

Two Mason's Ironstone cider mugs, in Japan pattern, c1820, 5in (12.5cm). *l.* **£400–450** *r.* **£350–400** *JP*

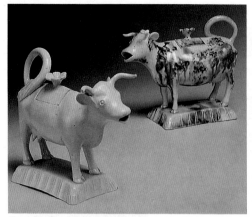

Two Staffordshire saltglazed stoneware cow creamers, c1765, 5½in (14cm) long.
l. **£3,300–3,500**
r. **£1,300–1,500** *JHo*

A Staffordshire figure of 'The Prince of Wales', 14½in (37cm) high.
£450–500 *JO*

A Staffordshire group, c1820, 10in (25cm) high.
£1,500–1,700 *JHo*

A Wood family pearlware figure of a lion, underside unglazed, some damage, c1780, 11in (28cm) long. **£1,600–1,800** *S(NY)*

A Staffordshire group, depicting a tiger hunt, 10½in (27cm) high.
£650–700 *JO*

A Staffordshire polychrome salt glazed model of a hawk, on a rockwork base, beak chipped, c1755, 7½in (19cm) high.
£28,000–30,000 *C*

A pair of Staffordshire earthenware figures of a fox with a chicken, and a hound with a hare, decorated in enamel colours, early 19thC, fox 7in (18cm). **£1,300–1,500** *JHo*

A pair of Staffordshire figures, The Poor Labourer, and The Poor Soldier, 6½in (16.5cm) high.
£800–900 *JHo*

A Staffordshire pink lustre cow creamer, c1820, 6in (15cm) long.
£300–400 *RP*

A Staffordshire bust of Nelson, 19thC, 7½in (19cm) high. **£180–200** *PCh*

A tin glazed inscribed barber's bowl, the indentation on the rim is either for a bar of soap or for the barber to lather his shaving brush, the footrim pierced with 2 holes for suspension, c1715, 10in (25cm) diam.
£7,000–7,500 *JHo*

A Lambeth caster, inscribed 'December 16 E H 1696' and on base 'December the 16 Day', 4½in (11cm).
£15,000–16,000 *S*

A Bristol delft blue dash 'Adam and Eve' charger, with serpent behind, cracked, c1710, 13in (33cm) diam.
£2,000–3,000 *S*

A Pennington's Liverpool porcelain coffee can, painted in underglaze blue with Oriental figures in a garden, late 18thC.
£30–40 *PCh*

A Bristol 'Adam and Eve' dish, inscribed 'S B 1740', with serpent, rim with scrolling foliage, repaired, 13in (33cm).
£11,000–12,000 *S*

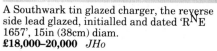

A Southwark tin glazed charger, the reverse side lead glazed, initialled and dated 'R N E 1657', 15in (38cm) diam.
£18,000–20,000 *JHo*

A Bristol delft flower brick, decorated with birds, flowers and rockwork, in Chinese style, chipped, c1760, 6in (15cm) wide.
£2,000–3,000 *DN*

A Bristol delft 'Adam and Eve' charger, with sponged blue rim, restored, c1740, 13in (33cm).
£750–850 *S*

A Liverpool tin glazed dish, decorated with a portrait of Simon Fraser, Lord Lovat, taken from Hogarth's original 1746 etching, c1750, 13in (33cm) diam. **£7,000–7,500** *JHo*

Two English delft tulip chargers:
l. early 18thC, 12in (30cm) diam. **£2,000–2,500**
r. cracked, c1680, 14in (35cm) diam.
£1,500–1,700 *SWO*

An Urbino Istoriato Armorial dish, painted in the Fontana workshop with Hannibal and his soldiers, the border with a coat-of-arms and motto 'VICI SSI TVDO', c1560. **£11,000–15,000** *C*

A Famiglia Gotica waisted albarello, Italian, c1500, 12in (31cm) high. **£7,000–8,000** *C*

An Urbino Istoriato tazza, painted by Francesco Xanto Avelli, inscribed on base, dated '1541', 10½in (27cm) diam. **£21,000–25,000** *C*

An Urbino Istoriato low tazza, painted by Francesco Durantino with the birth of Adonis, Lucina nursing the infant and nymphs surrounding the Goddess Myrrha, cracked, 1545, 10½in (27cm) diam. **£14,000–15,000** *C*

A Castelli drug bottle, of Orsini-Colonna type, inscribed 'A.FARFARE', restored, 16½in (42cm). **£14,000–16,000** *S*

A Sicilian maiolica albarello, painted with a medallion of a Roman bust against a ground of scrolling foliage, late 17thC, damaged, 8½in (22cm). **£1,000–1,200** *S*

A Sicilian maiolica albarello, damaged, 17thC, 12in (31cm). **£2,000–2,500** *S*

An Urbino crested tondino, the centre painted with Cupid and inscribed 'ARDET ÆTERNUM', Patanazzi workshop, damaged and restored, 1579, 9in (23cm) diam. **£5,000–7,000** *C*

An Urbino Istoriato dish, the underside inscribed, dated '1533', 10½in (26cm) diam. **£24,000–30,000** *C*

l. A Castelli plaque, painted in the Grue workshop, damaged, early 18thC, 10½in (26cm) wide. **£5,500–6,500** *C*

A Wemyss Cherry basket, c1900, 12in (30.5cm) wide.
£500–600 *RdeR*

A Wemyss commemorative mug, decorated with linked hearts, roses, thistles, and shamrocks, inscribed 'Fear God, Honour The King', c1906, 5½in (14cm).
£500–600 *RdeR*

A Wemyss Gordon Brambles plate, c1900, 8in (20cm) diam.
£150–200 *RdeR*

A Wemyss Coomb pot, painted with roses, 10in (25cm) high.
£400–500 *RdeR*

A Wemyss violet plate, 4in (10cm) diam.
£100–150 *RdeR*

A Wemyss Beehive plate, 8in (20cm) diam.
£200–300 *RdeR*

A Wemyss mug, painted with daffodils, 5½in (14cm) high.
£300–400 *RdeR*

A Wemyss black and white pig, left ear restored, impressed Wemyss Ware R H & S mark, 18in (45.5cm).
£2,250–2,500 *C(S)*

A Wemyss Iris plate 8in (20cm) diam.
£200–250 *RdeR*

A Wemyss Bovey Tracey smiling cat, painted with pink roses, painted 'Wemyss Ware' and initials for Joseph Nekola, 12½in (31.5cm). **£2,000–2,200** *CSK*

A Wemyss Strawberry quaiche, 10½in (26.5cm) wide.
£200–300 *RdeR*

Two Wemyss bowls, one inscribed, both impressed and with painted marks, largest 11in (28cm) diam.
top. **£1,000–1,500**
bottom. **£700–900** *C(S)*

A pair of Meissen candlesticks, mid-19thC. £1,200–1,500 *DeA*

A Chelsea fluted tea bowl, painted in the manner of J. H. O'Neale with the fable of The Lion and the Mouse, c1752. £5,000–6,000 *C*

A Royal Naples box, c1880, 5½in (14cm) wide. £400–450 *DeA*

A Thuringian pear-shaped painted coffee pot and cover, damaged and restored, c1770, 10in (25cm) high. £6,000–7,000 *C*

A Berlin can and saucer, hand painted and gilded, c1812, saucer 5in (12.5cm) diam. £150–200 *DeA*

A Worcester barrel-shaped jug, decorated in coloured enamels, c1765, 4⅓in (11cm) high. £450–600 *DN*

A Worcester lobed oval chestnut basket, with pierced cover and stand, damaged, c1770, 11in (28cm) wide. £600–800 *DN*

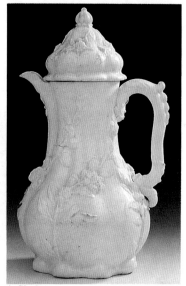

A Chelsea white tea plant baluster coffee pot and cover, chipped, incised triangle mark, c1745, 9in (23cm) high. £11,000–12,000 *C*

A Böttger Hausmalerei beaker, painted at Breslau by Ignaz Bottengruber with Neptune, a hippocamp, fish, sea birds and shells, c1730. £10,000–11,000 *C*

A pair of Spode beaded pot pourri baskets, with pierced covers and loop handles, decorated in Imari style, marked in red and pattern number '1645', c1817, 6in (15cm) high. £2,500–3,000 *DN*

A Royal Naples box, c1885, 5in (12.5cm) wide. £350–400 *DeA*

A Bow rococo coffee pot and shell-shaped cover, painted with exotic birds, restored, impressed 'To', c1755, 12in (30cm) high. £15,500–16,000 *S*

A Dresden group, c1860,
9in (22.5cm) high.
£650–700 *DeA*

A Meissen group of lovers,
probably modelled by J. F.
Eberlein, restored, traces of
crossed swords in blue, mid-
18thC, 6in (15.5cm).
£3,800–4,200 *S*

A pair of German cupid figures,
c1880, 8in (20cm) high.
£550–600 *DeA*

A Meissen figure of a pug and
puppy, c1850, 7½in (19cm) high.
£1,400–1,600 *DAV*

A Meissen 'Broken Egg'
group, c1860, 9½in (24cm)
high. **£1,450–1,750** *DAV*

A Meissen
figure of a lady
with a gun and
a dog, c1860, 6in
(15cm) high.
£400–425 *DeA*

A Royal Worcester
figure of a man in
Spanish clothes,
19thC, 11in (28cm).
£250–300 *PCh*

A Worcester figure of an elephant, by
James Hadley, c1850, 8in (20cm) high.
£650–700 *DeA*

A pair of Meissen figures of badgers, modelled by J. J. Kändler, on
contemporary ormolu mounts cast as a row of stiff-leaves, on paw
feet, damaged, 18thC, 5in (13.5cm).
£9,500–10,500 *S*

Two Bow figures of Earth and Water,
one with red anchor and dagger mark,
c1760, 17in (43cm) high.
£2,200–2,500 *AG*

A pair of Worcester figures,
by James Hadley, c1865,
10in (25cm) high.
£750–800 *DeA*

A Meissen dancing group,
c1850, 9½in (24cm) high.
£2,200–2,700 *DAV*

A Meissen partridge,
after a model by Kändler,
c1850, 8in (20cm) high.
£1,500–1,700 *DAV*

A Meissen hoopoe
bird, after a model by
Kändler, c1850, 12in
(30cm) high.
£600–900 *DAV*

A Meissen figure of
a card player, c1860,
6½in (16cm) high.
£600–850 *DAV*

A Sèvres écuelle, cover and
stand, painted by Chappuis
aîné, interlaced 'Ls' enclosing
date letters 'ff' and painter's
mark, c1783. **£4,000–5,000** *S*

A Meissen figure,
The Racegoer's
Companion, c1860,
8in (20cm) high.
£700–1,000 *DAV*

A Bow figure of a cook,
after a Meissen model by
J. J. Kändler and
P. Reinicke, from the
Cris de Paris series,
c1756, 6in (15cm) high.
£5,000–6,000 *S*

A Meissen figure of a
Bulgar, by J. J. Kändler
and P. Reinicke, from the
Nations of the Levant
series, c1745, 9in (23cm).
£4,000–5,000 *C*

A Meissen figure of a
potter, c1850, 8in (20cm)
high. **£900–1,000** *DAV*

A Höchst vegetable tureen
and cover, puce wheel mark,
'IN' incised, c1765, 8in (20cm)
diam. **£6,000–7,000** *S*

A Meissen
figure of a
snuff taker,
c1745.
**£7,000–
8,000** *C*

A pair of Chelsea porcelain
figures, c1860, 9in (23cm)
high. **£600–700** *DeA*

l. A gilt metal mounted
bonbonnière of 'Girl in a
Swing' type, modelled as a
pagoda figure, damaged,
c1755, 2½in (6cm) high.
£3,000–3,500 *C*

Three Meissen figures
allegorical of The
Seasons, crossed
swords in blue and
underglaze blue, c1750,
10½in (26.5cm).
£4,000–5,000 *S*

A Meissen group of The
Listener At The Well,
c1860, 9in (23cm) high.
£1,800–2,200 *DAV*

A pair of Royal Crown Derby hand painted cabinet plates, with cobalt blue glaze and gilded decoration, 9in (22.5cm) diam. **£650–700** *DeA*

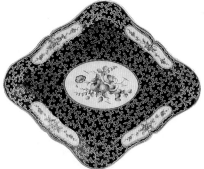

A Sèvres tray, from the Duchess of Bedford service, blue interlaced 'L' marks, incised script 'J', possibly 1762, 12in (30cm) wide. **£5,750–6,000** *C*

A set of 10 Minton pâte sur pâte plates, with pierced borders, signed by Alboine Birks, c1900, 9½in (24cm) diam. **£12,000–12,500** *CB*

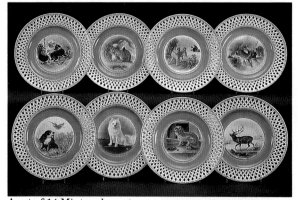

A set of 14 Minton dessert plates, attributed to Henry Mitchell, impressed and printed marks, date cyphers, retailers mark for T. Goode & Co., c1877, 10in (25cm) diam. **£2,500–3,500** *S*

A Worcester plate from the Duke of Gloucester service, painted with fruit, insects and butterflies, gold crescent mark, c1775, 9in (22.5cm) diam. **£10,500–11,500** *C*

A Royal Worcester dessert service, mostly painted by A. Schuck, marks, date code, c1912, 7½in (19.5cm). **£3,000–4,000** *S*

A Meissen dish, crossed swords mark and star, c1775, 9in (22.5cm) square. **£700–950** *DAV*

A pair of famille rose decorated plates, c1890, 11½in (29cm) wide. **£350–400** *DeA*

A Minton tray, decorated with a painting of The Virgin and Child, raised gilding, 12in (30.5cm) wide. **£1,000–1,250** *CB*

A Meissen plate, with floral decoration, pierced border and gilded, c1880, 10in (25cm). **£500–700** *DAV*

A Meissen cabaret set, crossed swords in underglaze blue, c1860, tray 14in (36cm) wide. **£5,300–5,800** *S*

A Royal Worcester vase
and cover, with bud finial,
painted by H. Davis
depicting Highland sheep,
15½in (39cm) high.
£1,500–1,800 *AH*

A Worcester Flight, Barr &
Barr garniture of 3 two-
handled vases, damaged and
restored, impressed and
script marks, c1815.
£5,500–7,000 *C*

A Royal Worcester
vase, signed
'A. Schuck', some
damage, late 19thC,
9in (23cm) high.
£80–100 *PCh*

A pair of Sèvres gilt and
enamel vases, with
ormolu mounts.
£900–1,200 *Sim*

A Royal Worcester
vase, 19in (48cm).
£550–650 *LT*

A Derby pot pourri
vase, and lid, c1840,
13½in (34cm).
£750–850 *DeA*

A Royal Worcester vase,
decorated by Chivers, late
19thC, 5½in (13.5cm).
£400–600 *PCh*

A Derby hand painted
and gilded vase, c1810,
6½in (16cm) high.
£500–600 *DeA*

A Vienna porcelain
vase and cover, with
gilt metal finial,
signed 'J. Fenner',
20½in (52cm) high.
£600–800 *AH*

A pair of Dresden vases
and covers, late 19thC.
£700–900 *DeA*

A pair of Paris porcelain vases, decorated in
coloured enamels, the loop handles with
swans' head terminals, c1825, 9½in (23.5cm)
high. **£800–1,000** *DN*

A Worcester vase, with
pierced lid, painted by
James Hadley, c1885.
£450–550 *DeA*

A Transitional Wucai painted and enamelled baluster jar, small crack, c1650, 18in (46cm) high. **£2,800–3,500** *C*

A Wucai wine jar, painted with a continuous frieze of carp, six-character mark and period of Jiajing, 1522-66, neck restored, 13½in (34cm). **£450,000–500,000** *S*

A Canton bowl, c1870, 15½in (39cm) diam. **£1,000–1,200** *CAI*

A Japanese porcelain bowl, c1880, 16in (40.5cm) diam. **£1,200–1,500** *CAI*

A polychrome box and cover, some wear, mark and period of Wanli, 1573-1620, 9½in (24cm). **£35,000–36,000** *S*

A Shonzui style serving dish, the base with a 'fu' mark in a double square, Chonghzen, 6in (15cm) diam. **£4,000–4,500** *C*

A famille verte enamelled dish, the reverse with a band of formal lotus scrolls, rim slightly chipped, Kangxi, 17½in (45cm) diam. **£4,800–5,200** *C*

A famille verte incised 'pomegranate' jar, possibly Kangxi, 7in (17.5cm) high. **£3,000–3,500** *C*

A famille rose dish, slight damage to enamels, Yongzheng six-character mark and of the period, 8in (10cm). **£2,500–3,000** *C*

An export punchbowl, the centre painted with 2 long-tailed birds, damaged, Qianlong, 15in (38cm) diam. **£4,000–4,800** *C*

An armorial dish, with the full arms of Hohenzollern encircled by the collar and badge of the Order of the Black Eagle, monogrammed and inscribed 'Gott Mit Uns', Qianlong, 1750-56, 13in (31cm). **£24,000–26,000** *S*

A Sancai phoenix head ewer, slight damage, Tang Dynasty, 618–907, 11in (28cm) high. **£16,500–18,500** *S*

A pair of Ming Fahua Buddhistic lion dogs, small chips and minor restorations, 16thC, 19in (48cm) high.
£7,000–8,000 *C*

A Sancai glazed flask, Tang Dynasty, 618-907, 6in (15cm) high.
£55,000–60,000 *S*

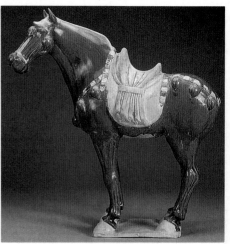

An amber glazed pottery figure of a caparisoned horse, restored, Tang Dynasty, 618-907, 19½in (49.5cm).
£14,000–15,000 *S*

A pair of famille rose boar's head tureens and covers, Qianlong, 8⅜in (21.5cm) long.
£18,000–20,000 *C*

A Ko-Imari figure of Hotei, restored, c1700, 9⅛in (23.5cm) high.
£7,000–8,000 *S*

Two Kakiemon figures of boys seated on Go boards, with later European ormolu caps, late 17thC, 10in (25cm). **£90,000–95,000** *S*

A famille rose group of a lady and a seated child, restored, Qianlong, 9in (22.5cm) high.
£3,500–4,000 *C*

A pair of figures of spaniels, one slightly damaged, one restored, Qianlong, 9½in (23.5cm) long.
£7,000–8,000 *C*

A famille rose boar's head tureen and cover, restored, Qianlong, 16in (41cm) wide.
£17,500–18,500 *C*

A pair of Sancai glazed pottery figures of Earth spirits, Tang Dynasty, 618-907, restored, 26in (66cm).
£4,000–5,000 *S*

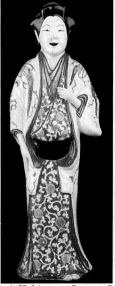

A Kakiemon figure of a bijin, old damage and restoration, late 17thC, 14½in (36.5cm) high.
£15,500–16,500 *C*

A set of 12 kraak porselein dishes, slight damage, Wanli, 8½in (21.5cm) diam. **£5,800–6,500** *C*

A set of 10 kraak porselein dishes, each painted with a pair of deer in a landscape, slight damage, Wanli, 8½in (21cm) diam. **£2,000–2,500** *C*

A Nabeshima dish, decorated with flowers and a fence post, on a tall, tapering foot with 'comb' design, 18thC, 8in (20.5cm) diam. **£12,000–14,000** *S*

A Ming style pear-shaped vase, Qianlong seal mark and of the period, 12in (30cm) high. **£24,000–28,000** *C*

A meiping, the base painted with a lingzhi scroll, Ming Dynasty, c1430, 13in (33.5cm). **£17,500–18,500** *S*

A Ming style moon flask, each shoulder with a scroll handle, Qianlong seal mark and of the period, 19½in (49.5cm) high. **£68,000–75,000** *C*

A Ming style moon flask, with ruyi-head handles, some damage, Qianlong seal mark and of the period, 9½in (24cm) high. **£5,200–6,000** *C*

A Ming style pear-shaped vase, body crack, Qianlong seal mark and of the period, 11½in (29cm) high. **£3,000–3,500** *C*

A Ming style bottle vase, restored, Qianlong seal mark and of the period, 14½in (37cm) high. **£2,000–3,000** *C*

A pear-shaped faceted vase, decorated with panels of flowers, Yuan Dynasty, 11½in (24.5cm) high. **£9,000–10,000** *S*

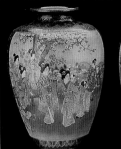

A pair of painted and gilt vases, signed 'Ryuun Fuzan', 12½in (31.5cm) high.
£800–900 *CSK*

A pair of Imari vases, c1880, 18in (46cm).
£1,200–1,500 *CAI*

A Guan type hu-shaped vase, Yongzheng seal mark and of the period, 22in (55.5cm) high.
£8,500–9,500 *C*

A bottle vase, with black ground and green glazed enamel, Kangxi/Yongzheng, 9½in (23.5cm) high.
£5,500–6,000 *C*

A glazed and carved lantern vase, impressed Qianlong seal mark and of the period, 17½in (44cm).
£135,000–140,000 *C*

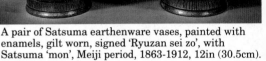

A pair of Satsuma earthenware vases, painted with enamels, gilt worn, signed 'Ryuzan sei zo', with Satsuma 'mon', Meiji period, 1863-1912, 12in (30.5cm).
£5,000–6,000 *S*

A coral glazed vase, blue enamel Yongzheng four-character mark, 12½in (32cm) high.
£4,500–5,000 *C*

A pair of painted and heavily gilt vases, signed 'Hattori sei zo', 6½in (16cm) high.
£1,000–1,500 *CSK*

A famille verte enamelled rouleau vase, Kangxi period, 18½in (47cm).
£28,000–30,000 *C*

A ruby ground famille rose vase, with gilded rim, glazed turquoise base and interior, six-character iron red seal mark and period of Qianlong, 1736-95, 13½in (34cm).
£110,000–120,000 *S*

l. A pair of painted and gilt vases, signed 'Seizan', 9in (22.5cm).
£1,000–1,500 *CSK*

A Jiangxi saucer dish, decorated in famille rose enamels, six-character iron red mark, 7in (18cm) diam. **£600–800** *Wai*

A semi-eggshell ovoid vase, decorated in famille rose enamels, four-character Hongxian nian zhi mark, 11in (27.5cm) high. **£2,000–3,000** *Wai*

A pair of Wang Yunshen vases. **£1,800–2,000** *Wai*

A bottle vase with flared neck, unenclosed four-character iron red Hongxian nian zhi mark, 16in (40cm) high. **£2,500–3,500** *Wai*

A brushwasher, inscribed, qi zhen () yu mark, dated 1936, 4½in (11cm) diam. **£1,200–1,600** *Wai*

An eggshell ovoid vase, Ya wan zhen cang mark, 6in (16.5cm) high. **£1,200–1,600** *Wai*

An 18thC style altar vase, decorated with Buddhist emblems in iron red enamel, unmarked, 9in (22cm) high. **£1,200–1,500** *Wai*

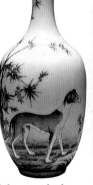

A long necked vase, four-character Qianlong seal mark, 8in (20.5cm) high. **£1,400–1,600** *Wai*

A pair of vases, decorated in famille rose enamels, Hongxian nian zhi mark, 11in (29cm) high. **£1,400–1,600** *Wai*

An ovoid vase, the reverse inscribed with a poem, four-character Qianlong seal mark, 8in (20cm) high. **£800–1,500** *Wai*

An eggshell garlic necked vase, with Zhong guo Jingdezhen zhi mark, 10in (25cm) high. **£1,200–1,500** *Wai*

A garlic necked bottle vase, inscribed with a poem, with Qianlong seal mark, 8in (20cm). **£1,600–1,800** *Wai*

A lozenge-shaped vase, four-character iron red Qianlong seal mark, 6½in (16cm) high. **£1,000–1,400** *Wai*

A pair of two-handled vases and stands, with overlaid decoration, probably French, late 19thC, 19in (48cm).
£6,500–7,500 *S*

A set of 3 Bristol blue decanters, with lozenge stoppers and gilded labels, in a silver plated stand, c1800, 11in (28cm) high.
£1,200–1,400 *CB*

A green decanter and stopper, with white overlay, c1870.
£250–280 *CB*

A lily vase, overlaid with fruiting vine, c1880, 20in (51cm).
£850–920 *MJW*

A French ruby glass carafe and tumbler 'up-and-over' on a stand, c1870, decanter 8in (20cm) high. **£300–350** *CB*

A pair of north Bohemian blue overlay vases, attributed to Franz Zach, c1860, 11in (28cm) high.
£6,000–7,000 *S*

A Whitefriars bottle and stopper, probably 19thC, 6in (15cm). **£250–300** *SWB*

A French opaline déjeuner set, by Jean-Baptiste Desvignes, c1820, decanter 11in (28cm) high.
£3,000–3,500 *S*

A Bohemian amber glass goblet and cover, engraved with a deer and a hunter, c1870.
£3,500–4,000 *CB*

An amber glass facet-sided decanter, c1870, 14½in (36.5cm).
£200–250 *CB*

A pair of Baccarat enamelled and gilt opaline vases, attributed to Jean-François Robert, c1845, 19in (48cm) high.
£12,000–15,000 *S*

A Bohemian ruby overlay cut glass comport, c1880, 9in (22.5cm) diam.
£350–380 *CB*

A mercury glass goblet, c1880, 11in (28cm) high. **£1,200–1,400** *ARE*

A pair of etched brandy and whisky presentation decanters, with carved wooden stoppers, c1858, 15½in (39.5cm). **£300–450** *ARE*

A cranberry glass oil lamp, with ormolu base, c1880, 38in (96.5cm) high. **£1,400–1,800** *ARE*

A vaseline glass épergne, with silver plated base, c1880, 13½in (34.5cm) high. **£400–500** *ARE*

A Victorian cranberry glass épergne, c1880, 17in (43cm) high. **£700–800** *ARE*

A glass oil lamp, with intricate glass detail, c1880, 18in (46cm) high. **£2,000–3,000** *ARE*

A rainbow spangle glass vase, c1890, 11in (28cm) high.
£200–220 *CB*

A double-overlay armorial part dessert service, with the crest of John Campbell, 5th Marquess of Breadalbane, French or Bohemian, c1840, carafe 6½in (16.5cm) high. **£2,200–2,500** *S*

A pair of French hand painted opaline vases, c1840, 9in (22.5cm) high.
£2,000–3,000 *MJW*

A transparent enamelled beaker, painted with an interior scene, signed by Gottlob Samuel Mohn, Vienna, dated 1812, 4in (10cm) high.
£22,000–24,000 *S*

A cased façon de Venise beaker, with milled footrim, south Netherlands, c1600, 7in (18.5cm) high. **£14,000–16,000** *S*

A pair of Val St. Lambert blown white opaque glass vases, with translucent ox blood red casing, painted by La Barré, and gilded in the style of Japanese lacquer work, by Camille Renard and Léon Fuller, 12in (30.5cm).
£1,500–1,800 *MJW*

A ceremonial goblet and domed cover, with flared funnel bowl, crown finial, the stem formed as 4 wrythen moulded loops, late 17thC, 18in (45.5cm) high.
£68,000–72,000 *C*

A cameo glass vase, by Webb, c1885, 5½in (13.5cm) high.
£950–1,000 *MJW*

A French cobalt blue cut and gilded decanter, with original stopper, c1775.
£3,000–3,500 *CB*

A Venetian enamelled mug, possibly made for the Turkish market, c1730, 4½in (11cm).
£2,300–2,500 *S*

An intaglio cut claret jug, with silver top, c1894.
£1,200–1,400 *CB*

r. A coraline bowl, c1890.
£350–400 *CB*

A Paul Ysart paperweight, the dark glass decorated with a flower and double garland, c1930, 3in (7.5cm) diam. **£250–300** *SWB*

A Baccarat paperweight, with spaced millefiori on muslin and silhouettes, dated '1847', 3in (7.5cm) diam. **£1,400–1,600** *SWB*

A Whitefriars faceted paperweight, 1953, 3in (7.5cm) diam. **£145–165** *SWB*

A Baccarat 'scrambled' paperweight, c1845, 3in (7.5cm) diam. **£375–450** *SWB*

A Baccarat paperweight, with close-pack mushroom and blue torsade, star cut base, c1845, 3in (7.5cm) diam. **£1,000–1,250** *SWB*

A Clichy spaced millefiori paperweight, c1845, 3in (7.5cm) diam. **£600–700** *SWB*

A set of 4 Baccarat sulphide paperweights, depicting some members of The Royal Family, by John Pinches Limited, stamped to reverse, 1976. **£400–500** *GH*

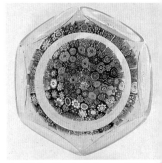

A Clichy faceted close millefiori mushroom paperweight, mid-19thC, 3½in (8.5cm) diam. **£4,200–4,500** *C*

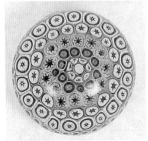

A Bacchus concentric millefiori paperweight, mid-19thC, 3½in (9cm) diam. **£1,800–2,000** *S*

A Baccarat pansy paperweight, with star cut base, c1852, 2in (5cm) diam. **£200–250** *SWB*

A Paul Ysart paperweight, marked 'H' on cane, c1970, 2½in (6cm) diam **£185–210** *SWB*

A Baccarat faceted double clematis, paperweight, c1845, 2in (5cm) diam. **£800–900** *SWB*

A St. Louis crown paperweight, mid-19thC, 3in (7.5cm) diam. **£700–1,000** *C*

A St. Louis diamond faceted paperweight, c1845, 3in (7.5cm). **£600–650** *SWB*

l. A concentric paperweight, c1850, 3½in (8.5cm) high. **£150–165** *SWB*

A Victorian flowerpot paperweight made from bottle glass, 3½in (8.5cm) high. **£50–70** *SWB*

A set of 4 Caithness abstract paperweights, depicting the Elements, all monogrammed 'CT/PH', and numbered '180/1000', trade label, 1973/74, boxed. **£550–750** *GH*

A Paul Ysart aventurine paperweight marked 'PY' on a cane, c1970, 3in (7.5cm) diam. **£400–450** *SWB*

A St. Louis crown paperweight, mid-19thC, 3in (7.5cm) diam. **£1,400–1,800** *C*

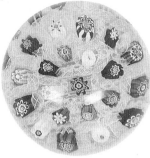

A Clichy 'Magnum' chequer paperweight, mid-19thC, 4in (10cm) diam. **£3,000–3,500** *S*

A paperweight, designed by Colin Terris, from a limited edition of 750, issued 1981, 3in (7.5cm) diam. **£100–130** *Cai*

A Venetian paperweight, in the form of an inkwell and stopper. **£550–600** *AAV*

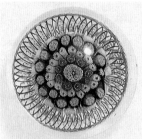

A St. Louis concentric millefiori mushroom paperweight, slight bruising, dated '1848', 3in (7.5cm) diam. **£2,600–3,000** *C*

A St. Louis concentric millefiori paperweight, dated 'SL1848', 3in (7.5cm) diam. **£2,800–3,200** *S*

A Clichy apple green ground patterned millefiori paperweight, mid-19thC, 3½in (9cm) diam. **£700–900** *S*

An opaque white taperstick, decorated in famille rose enamels with Oriental figures, south Staffordshire, c1760, 7in (17cm) high.
£12,250–12,750 *C*

A German Bohemian goblet, c1840, 9½in (24cm) high.
£1,600–1,800 *MJW*

An enamelled Kurfurstenhumpen, possibly Franconia, late 17thC, 8in (21cm) high.
£16,500–17,500 *S*

A Viennese transparent enamelled gilt ground beaker, attributed to Anton Kothgasser, c1825, 5in (12.5cm).
£13,000–15,000 *S*

A pair of French opaline vases, with flared crenellated rims, on knopped stems and spayed feet, c1850, 20in (50.5cm).
£2,500–3,000 *S*

A Potsdam/Zechlin goblet, engraved and gilt decorated, c1750, 7in (18.5cm) high.
£3,800–4,500 *S*

A Viennese transparent enamelled beaker, painted with 3 Tarot cards, inscribed on reverse, on an amber stained star-cut base, c1820, 4½in (11cm) high.
£7,000–7,500 *S*

A Baccarat vase, c1860, 11½in (29cm) high.
£600–680 *MJW*

A Bohemian amber stained goblet and cover, attributed to Franz Hansel, minute repairs, c1840, 18in (46cm).
£9,500–10,500 *S*

A Webb faux cameo vase, with amethyst decoration, c1910, 9½in (24cm) high.
£950–980 *MJW*

A Bohemian ruby overlay vase and cover, probably by Harrach Glasshouse, c1850, 25in (64cm) high.
£4,250–4,750 *S*

An engraved blue stained decanter and stopper, signed August Böhm, c1845, 15in (37.5cm).
£4,500–6,000 *S*

A Venetian enamelled flask and stopper, from the atelier of Osvaldo Brussa, c1730, 5½in (35.5cm) high.
£4,000–5,000 *S*

Chinese dynasties and marks

Earlier Dynasties

Shang Yin, c.1532-1027 B.C.
Western Zhou (Chou) 1027-770 B.C.
Spring and Autumn Annals 770-480 B.C.
Warring States 484-221 B.C.
Qin (Ch'in) 221-206 B.C.
Western Han 206 BC-24 AD
Eastern Han 25-220
Three Kingdoms 221-265
Six Dynasties 265-589
Wei 386-557

Sui 589-617
Tang (T'ang) 618-906
Five Dynasties 907-960
Liao 907-1125
Sung 960-1280
Chin 1115-1260
Yüan 1280-1368

Ming Dynasty

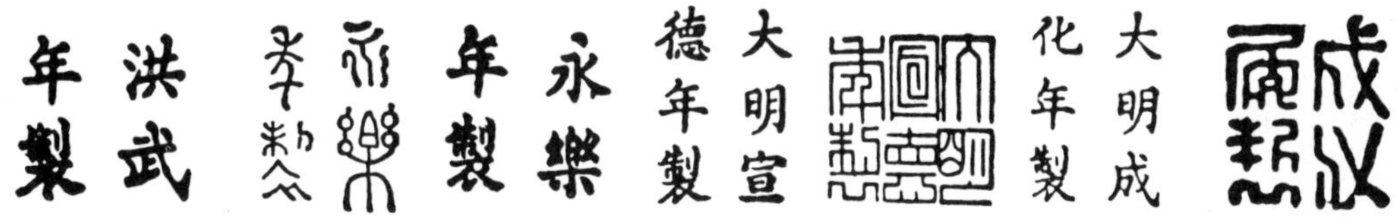

Hongwu (Hung Wu)
1368-1398

Yongle (Yung Lo)
1403-1424

Xuande (Hsüan Té)
1426-1435

Chenghua (Ch'éng Hua)
1465-1487

Hongzhi
(Hung Chih)
1488-1505)

Zhengde
(Chéng Té)
1506-1521

Jiajing
(Chia Ching)
1522-1566

Longqing
(Lung Ching)
1567-1572

Wanli (Wan Li)
1573-1620

Tianqi
(Tien Chi)
1621-1627

Chongzhen
(Ch'ung Chéng)
1628-1644

Qing (Ch'ing) Dynasty

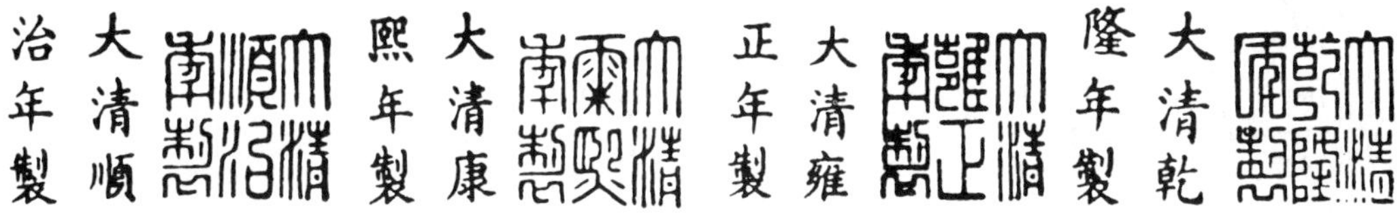

Shunzhi
(Shun Chih)
1644-1661

Kangxi (K'ang Hsi)
1662-1722

Yongzheng (Yung Chêng)
1723-1735

Qianlong (Ch'ien Lung)
1736-1795'

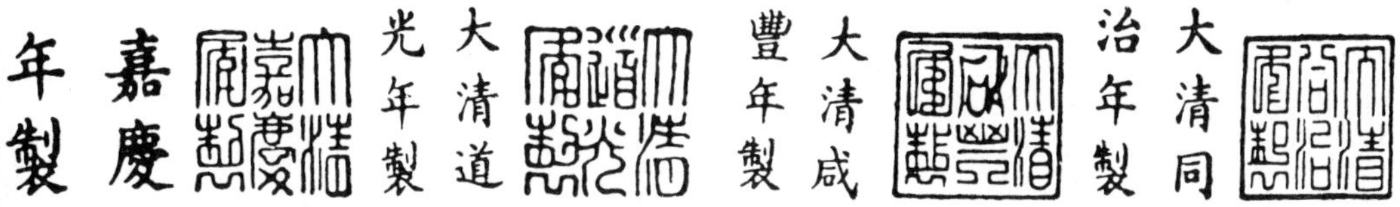

Jiaqing (Chia Ch'ing)
1796-1820

Daoguang (Tao Kuang)
1821-1850

Xianfeng (Hsien Féng)
1851-1861

Tongzhi (T'ung Chih)
1862-1874

Guangxu (Kuang Hsu)
1875-1908

Xuantong
(Hsuan T'ung)
1909-1911

Hongxian
(Hung Hsien)
1916

CHINESE CERAMICS

Bowls

An underglaze blue and copper red bowl, the interior plain, slight fritting to rim, underglaze blue Qianlong seal mark and of the period, 8in (20cm) diam.
£400–500 *CSK*

A famille rose deep bowl, slight cracks, underglaze blue Qianlong seal mark and of the period, 7in (18cm) diam.
£450–500 *CSK*

A peach bloom bowl, on short foot with slightly everted rim, the mottled glaze covering the interior and exterior, underglaze blue Xuande six-character mark, probably 18thC, 9in (22.5cm) diam.
£470–600 *CSK*

Four Ming blue and white bowls, damaged, 5½in (14cm) high.
£350–450 *CSK*

A famille rose export ware punch bowl, painted inside and out with panels of figures between flowers and precious objects, the borders with birds and bats on a flower decorated ground, slight damage, Canton, Qing Dynasty, 19thC, 16in (40cm) diam.
£1,200–1,700 *S(S)*

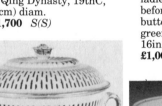

An export armorial reticulated bowl and domed cover, with flowerhead finial and pierced handles, painted in coloured enamels and gilt, slight damage, Qianlong, 8in (20cm) diam.
£1,000–1,500 *CSK*

A doucai bowl, damaged, Chenghua six-character mark, Yongzheng, 3in (7.5cm) diam.
£350–450 *CSK*

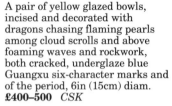

A pair of yellow glazed bowls, incised and decorated with dragons chasing flaming pearls among cloud scrolls and above foaming waves and rockwork, both cracked, underglaze blue Guangxu six-character marks and of the period, 6in (15cm) diam.
£400–500 *CSK*

A Cantonese bowl, painted and gilt inside and out with alternating panels of dignitaries, ladies and attendants on terraces before a screen and birds and butterflies beside flowers, on green and gold scroll grounds, 16in (40.5cm) diam.
£1,000–1,500 *CSK*

A famille rose bowl, the interior painted in underglaze blue with a roundel depicting figures with an ox and birds, seal mark and period of Daoguang, Qing Dynasty, 6in (15cm) diam.
£2,000–3,000 *S(S)*

Drinking Vessels

A pair of Imari tankards painted and gilt with shaped panels of peony spray, on a ground of lotus heads and trellis pattern, early 18thC, 5in (12.5cm).
£1,000–1,200 *CSK*

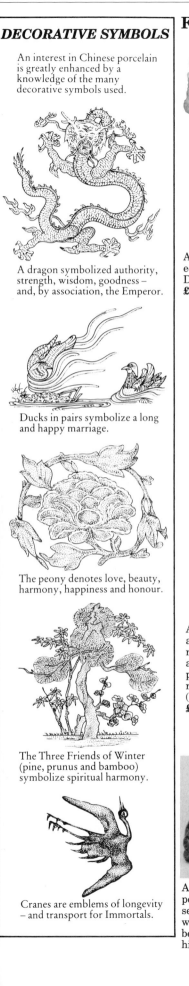
Figures

A buff pottery model of an equestrian rider, restored, Tang Dynasty, 13in (33cm) high.
£500–800 *CSK*

A pair of green, ochre and aubergine glazed models of Buddhistic lions, the female with a cub under her left paw, the male with a brocade ball, on pierced rectangular bases, 16in (41cm).
£600–700 *CSK*

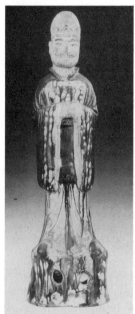

A Sancai glazed pottery figure of a bearded official, in long sleeved robes and a cap, his arms folded across his chest, standing on a pierced rockwork base, glaze rubbed, Tang Dynasty, 26½in (67.5cm) high.
£3,500–4,000 *CSK*

Two glazed pottery figures of bearded Immortals, enamelled in green, black, blue, red, white and pink, damaged, Qianlong, 8½in (21.5cm) high.
£450–550 *CSK*

A pair of export coral glazed porcelain models of hounds, seated on their haunches, each with a green glazed collar and bell, glaze rubbed, 6½in (16.5cm) high. **£500–600** *CSK*

A buff pottery model of an equestrian rider, restored, Tang Dynasty, 14in (35.5cm) high.
£500–800 *CSK*

A pair of green, yellow, aubergine and black glazed pottery figures of attendants, 19in (48cm) high.
£200–300 *CSK*

A pair of famille rose models of attendants, wearing lilac robes decorated with cloud scrolls, each holding a jar of peaches, restored, Qianlong, 9½in (24cm) high.
£1,500–2,000 *CSK*

A pair of ochre glazed pottery models of recumbent dogs with their heads turned to left and right, the tongues in aubergine, 5in (12.5cm) long.
£1,500–2,000 *CSK*

A copper red and cream glazed model of a bird, underglaze blue Kangxi six-character mark, 10in (25cm) high.
£150–250 *CSK*

Flatware

A blue and white dish, damaged, Wanli, 17in (43cm) diam.
£500–700 *CSK*

A blue and white dish painted overall with phoenix, the underside with precious objects, slight damage, Kangxi, 15in (38cm) diam.
£500–550 *CSK*

A Ming style blue and white saucer dish, restored, 20in (50.5cm) diam. **£3,500–4,000** *CSK*

An export armorial dish, painted and gilt with a coat-of-arms within a gilt rim, the underside plain, enamels rubbed, Qianlong, 15in (38cm) diam.
£1,500–2,000 *CSK*

The arms are of a Dutch family De Heere van Holy of Dordrecht.

A blue and white dish, the interior painted with 2 ladies seated at a table with a qin, within a fenced garden of plantain and rockwork, within a border of the Three Friends, the underside with bamboo sprays, Yongzheng six-character mark and of the period, 8in (20cm) diam.
£1,000–1,500 *CSK*

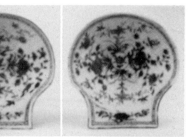

A pair of blue and white meat dishes, painted with precious objects on rockwork among peonies and willow, within borders of butterflies and geometric patterns, Qianlong, 12in (30.5cm) wide.
£400–500 CSK

A pair of Imari scallop-shaped dishes, painted and gilt with various flowers, rim fritting, 18thC, 6in (15cm) wide.
£600–700 CSK

A blue and white dish, the centre painted with a dragon chasing a flaming pearl, the underside similarly decorated, slight damage, Guangxu six-character mark and of the period, 7in (17.5cm) diam.
£250–350 CSK

A Doucai dish, the centre painted with a writhing dragon among cloud scrolls, the underside with a phoenix and a dragon among cloud scrolls, underglaze blue Chenghua mark, Yongzheng, 6in (15cm) diam.
£700–800 CSK

A set of 10 famille rose plates, painted and gilt with scattered flowersprays within spearhead borders, slight damage, Qianlong, 9in (22.5cm) diam.
£1,000–1,200 CSK

Jars

> **Miller's is a price GUIDE not a price LIST.**

A blue and white saucer dish, the interior painted with the Three Friends around a rocky outcrop, the exterior with a narrow continuous band of figures at leisure beneath silk awnings and on terraces, slight damage, Tongzhi six-character mark and of the period, 7in (17.5cm) diam.
£750–850 CSK

A blue and white jar, damaged, Transitional, 10in (25cm) high.
£400–500 CSK

A famille rose dish, the centre painted and gilt with a chrysanthemums flowerhead, within a border of interlacing peonies and further chrysanthemums within further bands of flowerheads on geometric grounds, chipped, Qianlong, 16in (40.5cm) diam.
£500–600 CSK

An export plate, painted in sepia and gilt with a castle before a bridge crossing a river in a hilly landscape of trees and shrubbery, Qianlong, 9½in (24cm) diam.
£450–550 CSK

A blue and white jar, damaged, 17thC, 16in (40.5cm) high.
£1,000–1,200 CSK

A blue and white ginger jar and pierced wood cover, painted with interlocking chrysanthemums heads and shou symbols between lappet border, Kangxi, 8½in (21.5cm) high. **£170–220** *CSK*

A baluster jar and cover, decorated in underglaze blue, damaged, 18thC, 23in (58.5cm) high. **£800–1,200** *DN*

A jar and domed cover, with knop finial, decorated with a marbled ochre and brown glaze, cover restored, Tang Dynasty, 4in (10cm). **£1,500–2,000** *CSK*

A blue and white baluster jar, with short neck and 6 lug handles, damaged, 16/17thC, 15in (38cm) high, on a copper mount. **£800–900** *CSK*

Pots

A Ming blue and white water pot, with short flaring neck, moulded spout and handle modelled as a cockerel, painted overall with scrolling flowers and foliage, firing faults, 3in (7.5cm) high. **£600–700** *CSK*

A blue and white jar and related domed cover with bronze Buddhistic lion finial, painted with a continuous scene of ladies at literary pursuits in a fenced garden of prunus, bamboo and willow, the cover with boys playing in a garden, jar damaged, finial replaced, 17thC, 25½in (65cm) high. **£1,500–2,000** *CSK*

A brushpot, with fluted corners and flattened rim, painted in iron red and gilt, slight damage, Qianlong seal mark, 6½in (16.5cm) high. **£700–900** *CSK*

Tureens

A blue and white export ware tureen and cover, painted with a pagoda under a pine tree and figures on a bridge, between animal heads handles, the cover with a lion dog knop, Qing Dynasty, Qianlong, 12in (31cm) wide. **£400–600** *S(S)*

A blue and white tureen and domed cover, with pomegranate finial and boars' head handles, painted with figures before buildings in a rocky river landscape within a border of interlocking flowers and foliage, finial chipped, Qianlong, 13in (33cm) diam. **£1,500–2,000** *CSK*

A famille rose tureen and domed cover, with boars' head handles and pomegranate finial, painted and gilt, damaged, Qianlong, 13in (33cm) wide. **£3,000–3,500** *CSK*

A blue and white tureen, cover and stand, with boars' head handles and pomegranate finial, painted with deer in a rocky landscape of pine and flowers, stand damaged, Qianlong, stand 15in (38cm) wide.
£1,000–1,200 *CSK*

A famille rose octagonal tureen and domed cover, with pomegranate finial and hares' head handles, damaged, Qianlong, 11½in (28cm) diam.
£3,000–3,500 *CSK*

A cloisonné bottle vase, decorated on a dark blue ground reserved with S-scrolls, a band of stiff-leaves to the shoulder, and ruyi heads to the neck, 16in (40.5cm) high.
£250–300 *CSK*

Vases

A pair of export inverted baluster shaped vases and covers, with dog of Fo knops, decorated in famille rose enamels with flowers, butterflies and bamboo within applied fruiting vine borders, each rim modelled with 4 beasts, slight damage, late 18thC, 12in (31cm) high. **£2,000–2,500** *DN*

A celadon ground vase of archaistic form, finely carved with stiff-leaves, beneath a thick glaze, decorated with butterflies, birds and scattered flowers, with a central band of blue key fret decoration on a gold ground, c1850, 13½in (34cm) high.
£600–800 *DN*

A pair of blue and white square bottle vases, some glaze fritting, 17thC, 10½in (26.5cm) high.
£1,800–2,200 *CSK*

A pair of Cantonese vases, with pierced handles, painted and gilt with panels of dignitaries on terraces, on a ground of lychee, birds, butterflies and flowers, both damaged, 12½in (31cm) high.
£400–500 *CSK*

A famille rose mallet-shaped vase, with pierced handles, iron red Qianlong seal mark, 8½in (21.5cm) high.
£600–700 *CSK*

A pair of Cantonese vases, with gilt mask handles, one damaged, 12in (30.5cm) high.
£800–1,000 *CSK*

A blue and white yanyan vase, painted with prunus and pine issuing from rockwork, on shaded grounds, neck cracked, Kangxi, 18½in (47cm) high.
£400–600 *CSK*

A blue and white tulip vase, painted overall with scrolling flowers and foliage below bands of lappets, 10in (25cm) high.
£600–700 *CSK*

A pair of ochre ground double gourd vases, incised and painted with bats among clouds and flames within horizontal bands, Jiajing six-character marks, 31in (78.5cm) high.
£400–600 *CSK*

A pair of Cantonese rouleau vases, slight damage, 24½in (62cm) high.
£1,500–2,000 *CSK*

A famille rose bottle vase, painted with 2 iron red bats in flight beside fruiting and flowering peach branches, iron red six-character Qianlong mark, 21in (53cm) high.
£1,800–2,500 *CSK*

A blue and white yanyan vase, restored, Kangxi, 18in (45.5cm) high.
£1,500–2,000 *CSK*

A Cizhou cream glazed vase, painted in brown slip, early Ming Dynasty, 8in (20cm) high.
£300–400 *CSK*

A pair of blue and white Dutch influenced vases, with flattened globular bases, tall flaring necks and pierced foliate handles, painted with dense flowers and foliage, the necks with birds among scrolling flowers, Kangxi, 9½in (24cm) high.
£5,000–6,000 *CSK*

20thC Chinese Ceramics

On February 12th 1912, the Chinese Imperial family abdicated, thus ending centuries of uninterrupted rule by the Chinese monarchy. For 250 years the production of the best porcelain had been subject to tight Imperial control; designed and approved at court before being sent to Jingdezhen for careful reproduction in the Imperial kilns. The ending of the Imperial patronage brought a relaxation of rigid control and the potters and artists started to produce individual wares. The artistry and quality of some of these wares have recently become a revelation to serious collectors. Wares which were previously dismissed as being 'modern' are now keenly sought by collectors all-over the world.

On December 12th 1915, the first republican President, Yuan Shikai, was persuaded by the National Council to assume the 'Mandate of Heaven', thereby establishing a new dynasty. Some 82 days later, after countrywide resistance, Yuan Shikai was forced to decree the abolition of his dynasty, formally reinstating the Republican government. It is known that during his brief reign Yuan Shikai ordered 40,000 ceramic pieces at a total cost of 1,400,000 yuan. How many of these pieces were made and how they are marked is the subject of much current scholarly debate.

The 20thC has been one of the most tumultuous in Chinese history. The political and economic upheavals have resulted in a demanding time for the potters of Jingdezhen. War and civil unrest, loss of patronage, diminishing exports due to fierce overseas competition and scarcity of resources have all taken their toll on output and quality. The finest output from this brief period, although small in quantity, stands alongside that of any previous century.

Peter Wain

(See page 289 - Colour Section)

Miscellaneous

A blue and white ovoid vase, cover missing, Transitional, 9½in (24cm) high, with a stand.
£1,400–1,800 *CSK*

A blue and white candlestick, restored, Transitional, 13in (33cm) high, on a wooden base, drilled.
£4,500–5,500 *CSK*

A blue and white kendi, painted with alternating panels of horses above foaming waves and peonies, the neck with prunus, some fritting, Wanli, 8½in (21cm) high.
£700–800 *CSK*

An armorial teapot and cover, with coat-of-arms of Edward Southwell, the shoulder painted with an encircling vine, slight damage, Qianlong, 5in (12.5cm) high.
£650–750 *Bea*

A famille verte biscuit ewer, with cabriole spout and 2 mask handles, the body divided into 3 moulded bands enamelled with horses leaping over waves on a whorl pattern ground embellished with prunus blossoms, restored, Kangxi, 17½in (45cm) high.
£1,500–2,000 *C*

A blue and white bidet, the interior painted with fishing boats before pagodas and pavilions in a rocky river landscape, the exterior with peonies, chrysanthemums and lotus sprays, metal spout, Qianlong, 24in (61cm) wide.
£600–800 *CSK*

A Kinrande green glazed and gilt fluted kendi, decorated with bands of scrolling foliage, gilt rubbed, Ming Dynasty, 8in (20cm) high.
£1,000–1,200 *CSK*

A famille rose part tea and coffee service, comprising: a coffee pot and cover, 3 cups and 6 saucers, 6 smaller cups and 7 saucers, and 3 tea cups, all painted and gilt with scattered flowersprays within diaper borders, damaged, Qianlong, pot 7½in (19cm) high.
£300–500 *CSK*

A pair of Cantonese joss-stick holders modelled as recumbent dogs, each with a vase on its back, and with mouths slightly open and tongues protruding, one restored, 7in (17.5cm) wide.
£1,700–2,000 *CSK*

JAPANESE CERAMICS
Bowls

An Imari bowl and cover, painted in typical palette with landscapes in scrolling panels reserved on a ground of peony and other flowers, knop restored, c1700, 10in (25cm) diam.
£1,800–2,200 *S*

A Fukugawa fluted shallow bowl, with foliate rim, painted and gilt with panels of chrysanthemums and orchids on a ground of ho-o roundels, blue bird mark, 10in (25cm) diam.
£300–400 *CSK*

An Arita deep bowl, painted in underglaze blue, coloured enamels and gilt, cracked, 17th/18thC, 14½in (37cm) diam.
£1,200–1,700 *CSK*

A Fukugawa bowl, painted and gilt with panels of carp and fan-shaped cartouches of bamboo on an iron red ground of ho-o and floral designs, Mount Fuji mark, 12in (31cm) diam.
£500–700 *CSK*

An Imari monteith style deep bowl, painted and gilt with panels of chrysanthemums and lotus, 16½in (42cm) diam.
£1,400–2,000 *CSK*

A Kakiemon bowl, decorated in iron red, green, yellow, black and blue enamels and gilt, rim restored, late 17thC, 10½in (27cm) wide.   **£7,000–8,000** *C*

An Imari barber's bowl, painted and gilt, with a central vase of peonies on a fenced terrace, within a border of further flowerheads, chipped and rubbed, c1700, 11in (28cm) wide.
£500–600 *CSK*

A set of 3 Imari graduated fluted bowls, variously painted and gilt, all slightly damaged, underglaze blue running fuku marks, largest 13½in (34cm) wide.
£1,500–1,800 *CSK*

Japanese Periods

c7000BC: Jomon culture; first recorded pottery with simple design.
c300BC: Yayoi culture; bronzes and more sophisticated pottery.
C1 to C4AD: Haniwa culture bronzes and distinctive red pottery. 220AD, first influence from Korea.
Asuka: 552-645.
Hahuko: 672-685.
Nara: 710-794.
Heian: 794-1185.
Kamakura: 1185-1333.
Muromachi (Ahikaga): 1338-1573.
Momoyama: 1573-1615.
1598: Immigrant Korean potters begin kilns at Kyushu, producing the first glazed pottery to be seen in Japan.
Edo (Tokugawa): 1615-1867.
1616: First porcelain made by Ninsei (1596-1666).
1661-1673: Great age of porcelain; Arita, Nabeshima, Kutani and Kakiemon.
1716-1736: Popularity of lacquering and netsuke as art forms.
Meiji: (1868-1912). Strong influence of Western cultures developing and growing. Japanese art appears to decline in many respects. Much trading with the West.

Drinking Vessels

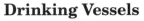

An Imari mug, with loop handle, decorated in underglaze blue, iron red and gilt, on a blue ground further decorated with scattered flowerheads, rim chipped, late 17thC, 8½in (21.5cm) high.
£1,700–2,200 *C*

An Hirado cup stand, decorated in underglaze blue with 3 aoi-mon, with a tall foot with lappet design, damaged, 19thC, 7in (17.5cm).
£550–650 *S*

An Arita blue and white tankard, with loop handle, late 17thC, 8½in (21.5cm) high. **£1,000–1,200** *C*

Figures

A pair of Kutani models of eagles, each decorated in iron red, black enamels and gilt, 19thC, 7in (18cm) high. **£900–1,200** *C*

An Hirado white glazed model of a cockerel, 19thC, 8in (20.5cm). **£500–800** *C*

Arita Wares

The earliest recorded Japanese porcelain was made in the Arita district of northern Kyushu Island from c1610. Japanese potters learnt the techniques from craftsmen who settled there in the late 16thC after Hideyoshi brought them back from his expedition to Korea. Blue and white was one of many kinds of porcelain made at the Arita kilns for the export trade as well as the domestic market. During the second quarter of the 17thC, the Arita porcelain industry grew rapidly until there were about 30 kilns operating in the area. As well as blue and white, polychrome, Imari, Kakiemon, Nabeshima, Hirado, Fukugawa and Makuzu wares were all produced at kilns in and around Arita.

Flatware

A blue and white Kakiemon style foliage rimmed dish, chocolate rim, restored, kin mark, late 17thC, 9½in (24cm) diam. **£800–1,000** *C*

A Imari charger, brightly decorated with figures by a garden pavilion, within a panelled border of scrolling flowerheads, reserved with shaped panels of lotus, c1800, 18in (46cm) diam. **£900–1,200** *DN*

Use the Index!

Because certain items might fit easily into any number of categories, the quickest and surest method of locating any entry is by reference to the index at the back of the book.

This has been fully cross-referenced for absolute simplicity.

A Satsuma earthenware dish, by Kozan, painted with a bijin and attendants beside a vase filled with peonies and wisteria, surrounded by a flower and textile decorated border, six-character mark, Meiji period, 8½in (22cm) diam. **£600–700** *S(S)*

A Satsuma dish, painted and gilt with a multitude of chrysanthemums, signed, 7½in (19cm) diam. **£250–300** *CSK*

A pair of Imari reticulated dishes, painted in underglaze blue, iron red and gilt, damaged, 12½in (32cm) diam. **£400–500** *CSK*

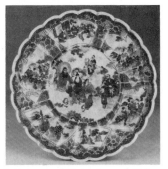

A Satsuma foliate rimmed dish, painted and gilt with Buddhist figures, within a border of panels of warriors and strolling figures, signed, 7in (17.5cm) diam. **£200–250** *CSK*

An Imari charger, with radial flower decoration in blue and iron red with gilt embellishments, 19thC, 24½in (62cm) wide.
£500–600 *AH*

Jardinières

An Arita jardinière, on tripod feet, decorated in underglaze blue with kirin, ho-o and Buddhistic emblems, damaged, mid-19thC, 29½in (75cm) diam.
£1,800–2,200 *C*

An Imari jardinière, with flattened rim, painted and gilt with shaped panels of birds above baskets of flowers on a ground of kiku heads and foliate stems, slight damage, 15in (38cm) diam.
£550–700 *CSK*

A Fukugawa jardinière, painted to the interior with a ho-o among pawlonia, the exterior with prunus on an iron red ground, Mount Fuji mark, 15½in (39.5cm) wide.
£450–550 *CSK*

A pair of Arita fluted leaf-shaped dishes, painted and gilt with leafy sprays of prunus, early 18thC, 9in (22.5cm) wide.
£1,200–1,600 *CSK*

An Imari baluster jar, painted and gilt with panels of confronting dragons and ho-o chasing flaming pearls above foaming waves on a ground of peonies, brocade balls and quatrefoil panels of pawlonia, slight damage, 24in (61.5cm) high.
£1,000–1,500 *CSK*

Vases

An Imari bottle vase, slight damage, 18thC, 9in (22.5cm) high.
£900–1,200 *CSK*

Jars

An Arita jar, painted in underglaze blue with panels of chrysanthemums and peonies, reserved on a floral ground, the shoulder with floral medallions on a brocade ground, late 17thC, slight damage, 14in (36cm).
£3,000–3,500 *S*

A Kutani jar and domed cover with a rat and nut finial, damaged, 16½in (42cm) high.
£900–1,200 *CSK*

An Arita blue and white baluster vase, neck chipped and possibly reduced, 18thC, 10in (25cm) high.
£500–700 *CSK*

A Fukugawa vase, painted and gilt with a continuous scene of cranes and young in a bamboo grove, between formal borders, blue bud mark, 10in (25cm) high.
£350–450 *CSK*

An Imari bottle vase, painted and gilt with shaped panels of trees and flowers, bordered by ho-o on a geometric and floral ground, 16½in (42cm) high.
£500–600 *CSK*

A pair of Kutani vases, with pierced handles and reticulated necks, painted and heavily gilt with panels of legendary scenes, signed, 10in (25cm) high.
£2,000–2,500 *CSK*

A Fukugawa vase, painted and gilt with a scroll style dragon below a neck of scrolling flowers, Mt. Fuji mark, 12in (30.5cm) high.
£200–300 *CSK*

A pair of Kutani vases, iron red marks, Meiji period, 12in (30.5cm) high.
£1,000–1,700 *S(S)*

A porcelain vase, by Makuzu Kozan, painted with pale maroon irises outlined in white on a shaded leaf green ground, underglaze blue six-character mark, slight damage, Meiji period, 7in (18cm) high.
£750–850 *S(S)*

A pair of porcelain vases, 12½in (31.5cm) high.
£500–550 *Bea*

A pair of Imari vases and covers, 19thC, 20in (51cm) high.
£3,000–3,500 *S*

An Imari beaker vase, painted and gilt on a ground of chrysanthemums heads below a border of floral lappet heads, ormolu mounted with fruiting grape vines, the porcelain 18thC, 15in (38cm) high.
£600–700 *CSK*

A pair of Kutani vases, on a fern decorated ground, iron red marks, Meiji period, 14½in (37cm) high.
£1,800–2,200 *S(S)*

A Satsuma vase, painted and gilt with a panel of ladies and children at leisure before trees and beside a lake, the reverse with pigeons in a flower strewn landscape, all between formal borders, signed, 10½in (26.5cm) high.
£2,200–2,700 *CSK*

An Imari baluster vase, painted and gilt with shaped panels of birds among flowers issuing from behind banded hedges, on a ground of confronting ho-o and scattered ferns and foliate, restored, 30in (76cm) high.
£800–900 *CSK*

A pair of Satsuma vases, with mask loop handles, painted and heavily gilt with panels of dignitaries and attendants before river landscapes, 30in (76cm) high.
£2,000–2,500 *CSK*

A blue and white baluster vase, 18½in (47cm) high.
£150–200 *CSK*

A pair of Satsuma vases, painted and gilt with Immortals and boys at leisure between formal borders, signed, 14in (35.5cm) high.
£530–600 *CSK*

A cloisonné pear-shaped vase, decorated with shell-shaped cartouches of flowers and maple on a grey-brown netting style ground decorated with flowerheads and scattered shells, 10in (25cm) high.
£300–350 *CSK*

Miscellaneous

A Kakiemon style blue and white tureen and cover, the domed cover surmounted by a karashishi finial, cover damaged, late 17thC, 12in (31cm) diam.
£3,500–4,000 *C*

An Imari box and domed cover, with shishi lion finial, painted and gilt with floral and geometric designs, 8in (20cm) high.
£450–500 *CSK*

An earthenware bell-shaped teapot and cover, decorated with figures and flowers, within shaped panels, on a flower and gilt dot ground, signed Kozan, 4in (10cm) high.
£450–500 *DN*

GLASS
Bowls

A sugar bowl, with cut diamond, flute and prism cutting, fan cut rim, short knopped stem and circular foot star cut underneath, c1825, 5in (13cm) high.
£450–520 *Som*

An Irish cut bowl, with faceted sides beneath a waved bevelled rim, on a short stem and oval foot with facet cut rim, c1800, 8½in (21.5cm) wide.
£700–800 *C*

A canoe shaped bowl, the castellated rim above diamond pattern bands, on an inverted baluster stem, damaged, 19thC, 13½in (34cm).
£450–550 *CSK*

A Davenport cut glass bowl, the shallow bowl cut with alternate panels of flutes and fine diamonds, serrated wavy rim, prismatic cut base, short faceted stem above a wide circular foot, star-cut base, minor rim chips, 5in (13cm) high.
£650–750 *S*

A set of 6 cut and etched glass finger bowls, c1890, 5in (12.5cm) diam.
£240–280 *DUN*

A set of 6 cut and engraved glass finger bowls, c1900, 4⅜in (11cm) diam.
£140–160 *DUN*

A set of 6 finger bowls, engraved and highlighted in gilt, with a crest of a double-headed eagle enclosing a shield, and the motto 'Tuum Est' ('It is Thine'), with a border of fruiting vine, 4½in (11.5cm) diam.
£300–350 *HSS*

The crest is possibly Cowper.

Decanters

A cruciform decanter, the body of deeply indented section, the neck with an applied collar beneath an everted rim, 11in (28cm).
£500–600 *S*

A club form decanter, with a quatrefoil simulated wine label inscribed 'Madeira', with faceted lozenge stopper, c1770, 11½in (29.5cm) high.
£500–600 *S*

A spirit decanter, with flute cut base and neck, slice cut lozenge stopper, c1780, 8½in (21cm).
£150–200 *Som*

A pair of decanters, the bodies with 2 raised bands, the necks with 3 raised rings and bull's-eye stoppers, c1800, 10in (25cm).
£600–700 *S(S)*

A pair of mallet-shaped decanters, the bodies cut with base flutes and a band of small diamonds, 3 neck rings and lunar cut target stoppers, c1810, 9⅓in (23.5cm).
£600–900 *Som*

DECANTER SHAPES

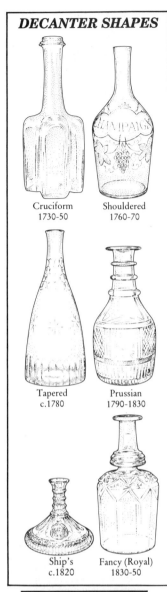

Cruciform
1730-50

Shouldered
1760-70

Tapered
c.1780

Prussian
1790-1830

Ship's
c.1820

Fancy (Royal)
1830-50

A mallet-shaped decanter, the tapered body cut with base fluting and band of looped stars, above a band of egg and printy decoration, scale cut neck with round lunar cut disc stopper, c1770, 9½in (24cm).
£600–900 *Som*

A pair of mallet-shaped decanters, with star cut base, the sides cut with a series of large diamond facets beneath a waisted hexagonal neck, with faceted club stoppers, c1840, 13½in (34cm).
£300–400 *S(S)*

Three opaque white decanters, named in gilt for 'Gin', 'Rum' and 'Brandy', within scrolling panels gilt with fruiting vines suspended by gilt chains from bands, with cork stoppers and metal mounts, 19thC, 14in (36cm).
£400–500 *CSK*

Stoppers

It is difficult to guarantee that a stopper is original except on Victorian clear glass decanters, which often have matching numbers etched on the stopper and decanter neck. Coloured glass decanters often have the number painted on the stopper and underside of the decanter. Generally a stopper is acceptable when it is the same cut and colour as the decanter, and of the right style and period.

Decanters often become damaged by the careless replacement of the stopper or by being knocked over. Chipped surfaces or edges can be restored, which may alter the proportions of the lip, but will not greatly affect the value. Broken stopper pegs can be replaced by glueing on a replacement and then grinding and polishing the whole peg. A very thin radial line will indicate where this has been done.

A club-shaped decanter, engraved with a label named for 'Mountain', above a spray of stylised fruiting vine, lacking stopper, 9½in (24cm).
£750–800 *S(S)*

A pair of mallet-shaped decanters, with reeded base and engraved shoulders, a continuous arrangement of fruiting vines, beneath 3 tooled double neck rings, moulded bull's-eye stoppers, 11½in (28.5cm).
£500–600 *S(S)*

A pair of Bohemian amber-flash flask-shaped decanters, engraved with continuous scenes of deer in woodland, the ball stoppers with a hound and game birds, slight damage, 19thC, 11in (28cm).
£400–500 *CSK*

A pair of mallet-shaped decanters, with puce and amber flashing, 3 neck rings, the bodies cut with lenses engraved with sprays of flowers and foliage, with octagonal stoppers, c1900, probably Bohemian, 11in (28cm). **£700–800** *S(S)*

A pair of mallet-shaped decanters, engraved with the monogram 'RHA', with 3 neck rings and target stoppers, c1800, 8½in (21.5cm) high. **£900–1,200** *Som*

A pair of Irish club-shaped decanters, with moulded radials and flutes around the base, below engraved stylised hops and barley, with 2 milled neck rings and moulded bull's-eye stopper, probably Cork, 11½in (29.5cm). **£500–700** *S*

A pair of ship's decanters, with star cut base, the body cut with gadroons above a band of sunray medallions and stylised foliage, with 3 collars to the neck and gadrooned cut ball stopper, damaged, possibly Perrin Geddes and Co, Warrington, c1820, 11in (28cm). **£3,200–4,000** *S*

A pair of decanters, the shoulders cut with horizontal rows of facets between slatted shoulders and a star cut base, the necks with 3 slat cut rings, faceted and star cut cushion stoppers, one rim chipped, mid-19thC, 13½in (34cm) high. **£470–520** *S(S)*

Drinking Glasses

A German beaker, enamelled in colours with The King of Sweden on horseback, and the inscription 'Gustavus Adolphus Konig in Schweden, Cum deo ef Victoribus Armis, Anno Domini 1631', late 19thC, 6in (15cm). **£350–450** *C(S)*

Two goblets, each with ovoid bowl raised on a single blade knop, short stem and circular foot, one engraved with 2 panels of figures and animals, the other inscribed 'I & M Wilson' within a laurel wreath, the reverse with a flower-spray, 19thC, 6½in (16cm). **£250–350** *S(S)*

An opaque twist cordial glass, with a thick funnel bowl, the stem with a laminated corkscrew core, on a conical foot, c1765, 7in (17.5cm) high. **£700–800** *C*

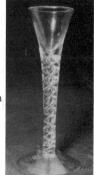

A cordial glass, the drawn stem with a pair of medium air-twist corkscrews, on a plain conical foot, c1740, 7½in (18.5cm). **£750–800** *Som*

Three wrythen ale glasses, with rudimentary knopped stems and plain conical feet, c1810.
£250–275 *Som*

A set of 6 dwarf ale glasses, engraved with hops and barley motifs, with capstan stems and plain conical feet, c1810, 5in (13cm).
£450–500 *Som*

A George I Royal commemorative goblet, the funnel bowl with teared solid base and engraved with a crown and cypher 'GR' direct and indirect, set on a teared inverted baluster stem and folded domed foot, c1715, 10in (25cm).
£5,000–6,000 *S*

The cypher is that of King George I (reigned 1714–27).

A Beilby opaque twist goblet, the bucket bowl enamelled in white with a border of fruiting vine, the rim with traces of gilding, the stem with a gauze corkscrew core within 2 spiral threads, on a conical foot, footrim chipped, c1770, 7in (18cm).
£2,000–2,600 *C*

William and Mary Beilby

The brother and sister duo, William and Mary Beilby, produced some of the finest enamelling on English drinking glasses from 1762–78. William is considered the greater exponent; Mary's precise contribution is unknown.

Although working mainly with white enamel, William is particularly noted for his coloured coats-of-arms on large goblets.

An ale glass, the funnel bowl with flammiform edged wrythen moulded lower part, set on a wrythen knop above a plain section and basal knop, on a folded conical foot, early 18thC, 5in (13cm) high.
£500–600 *C*

A Dutch goblet, the funnel bowl stipple engraved with a scene of 2 draped putti shaking hands, set on a multi-knopped facet cut stem, on a conical foot, attributed to Alius, c1775, 8½in (21cm).
£6,000–7,000 *S*

A baluster shaped cordial glass, the straight sided funnel bowl with solid lower part enclosing a tear, the stem with a large quadrangular shoulder knop, moulded with pronounced lugs and with stars at the angles, above a plain section and melon basal knop and enclosing a large elongated tear, above a folded conical foot, c1705, 6in (15cm).
£5,500–6,500 *C*

The Withens goblet, a Façon de Venise diamond point engraved winged goblet, inscribed on one side in diamond point 'Francis Withens', and '10 Maie 1590' on the other, set on a merese, the stem composed of symmetrically coiled tubing enclosing white and brick red threads terminating in opposed heads with applied pincered clear trails, folded conical foot engraved with flutes, Lowlands, 17thC, 10in (25cm).
£10,000–12,000 *S*

The inscription possibly records the birth of Francis Withens on the 10th May 1590. The aristrocratic family of Withens is recorded in Leiden, near Amsterdam. Coincidentally, Sir Francis Withens (or Wythens) 1634-1704, was an English High Court Judge who lived at Eltham, London.
The form of this glass is typical of the production of the Low Countries in the 2nd half of the 17thC. It is interesting to note the combination of foliate scroll with spiral threads between double line borders on both glasses. However, it is probable that this piece was made as an anniversary goblet and that the style of engraving copies that of the 16thC.

Locate the source

The source of each illustration in Miller's can be found by checking the code letters below each caption with the list of contributors.

A set of 6 goblets, with square cut bases, c1890, 5¼in (13.5cm).
£240–270 *DUN*

A Richardson's of Stourbridge enamelled goblet, stencilled 'Richardson's Vitrified Enamel Colours' in black, c1850, 6½in (16.5cm). **£700–750** *S*

A Bohemian amber stained goblet, the octagonal stem with flared octagonal foot with scalloped rim, with a star and diamond cut base, c1850, 8½in (22cm) high.
£600–700 *S*

A Venetian enamelled goblet, the green tinted waisted globular bowl with everted rim, painted possibly by Leopoldo Bearzotti, with a portrait of Venus and Cupid, after Titian, within a gilt scallop frame, the reserve with formal gilt leaf scroll between lappet and bead borders, set on a hollow ribbed knop with aventurine inclusions, the folded conical foot with gilt scroll band edged in white beads, inscribed 'Tiziano/Venere Benda Amore', probably by Salviati and Co, Murano, 10½in (26cm).
£800–1,000 *S*

A Bohemian goblet, on an inverted baluster and basal knop, with translucent red spiralling threads flanked by collars, the conical foot engraved with scroll, 8½in (20.5cm).   **£650–750** *S*

A Bohemian engraved armorial goblet, the bowl engraved with a coat-of-arms and the initials 'C.M.' and 'V.F.', set on a tall slender multi-knopped stem and wide folded conical foot engraved with crossed leaf fronds, c1690, 9½in (23.5cm).
£1,000–1,500 *S*

The arms are those of von Frankenberg of Silesia.

Stipple Engraving

This type of engraving used a diamond needle, which was lightly tapped and drawn against the surface of glass to create a series of dots or small lines. By varying the density of the dots and lines, areas of light and shade were produced.

This is the most difficult engraving technique, and consequently good examples are rare. Most stipple engraving originates in the Netherlands where, during the 18thC, some of the best work was executed by Aert Schouman, David Wolff and Frans Greenwood.

A Saxon point engraved goblet, the thistle-shaped bowl engraved with 2 oxen in a field, with an indistinct Dutch inscription above, with facet cut lower part and on a faceted knopped and teared inverted baluster stem and folded conical foot, indistinct initials on the pontil, 7½in (19.5cm).
£800–1,000 *S*

A Dutch engraved goblet, inscribed 'T' Welvaren Van Land en Kerk', supported on a ball knop above a tapering hexagonal stem, set into a baluster basal knop on a conical foot, engraved in diamond point with the initials 'F', c1750, 8½in (21.5cm).
£900–1,200 *C*

A pair of rummers, with double ogee bowls, capstan stems and plain feet, c1825, 6in (15cm).
£100–120 *Som*

A Bohemian engraved goblet, the funnel bowl with gadrooned lower part engraved with a leopard and a bird in continuous woodland, set on a collar above a flattened ball knop and merese with plain section and basal knop, with a wide folded conical foot, 7in (17.5cm). **£650–750** *S*

A Silesian goblet and cover, the double ogee bowl engraved with a continuous scene, the conical foot with faceted rim, gilt line rim, the domed cover with faceted bud finial, engraved with scroll between gilt line border, c1750, 9in (22.5cm). **£3,000–4,000** *S*

A wine glass, with a bell-shaped bowl, raised on an annular knopped baluster stem and conical folded foot, c1720, 7in (17.5cm).
£500–600 *S(S)*

A pair of rummers, with straight sided bowls, each finely etched with a two-masted vessel in full sail, and inscribed 'Success to the Telemachus', the reverse inscribed 'Edwd. and Ann Kenny', above floral emblems, on tapering stem and moulded square foot, early 19thC, 5in (12.5cm).
£600–700 *DN*

Despite extensive research, including reference to all Lloyd's Registers of Shipping from the first issue of 1764 to 1830 inclusive, no Edward Kenney has been traced as either owner or master of any of the numerous brigs named 'Telemachus' which are listed during this period.

Two wine glasses, with multiple spiral air-twist stems and plain conical feet, c1750, 6 and 6½in (15 and 16cm).
£460–600 each *Som*

Three engraved goblets, the ogee sided bowls with fluted lower sections below Imperial Russian eagles holding an orb and sceptre, below Romanov crowns flanked by sprays of flowers, the reverse with oval panels inscribed 'N I', supported by facted stems on conical feet, c1900, 6in (15cm).
£850–950 *CSK*

A rummer, the cup-shaped bowl engraved with scrolling flowers and foliage, merging into a hollow cylindrical stem applied with 2 rows of raspberry prunts beneath a milled band and with kick-in base, on a spreading folded foot, from The Netherlands or Germany, 18thC, 8½in (21cm). **£2,000–2,500** *S*

A green tinted rummer, the ovoid bowl merging into a cylindrical stem, with trailed collar above 3 rows of applied raspberry prunts, on a high conical spun foot, from Lowlands or north Germany, c1800, 7in (17.5cm). **£1,500–2,000** *S*

Two wine glasses, with multiple spiral air-twist stems and plain conical feet, c1750, 6½in (16.5cm) and 7⅓in (18.5cm). **£580–630 each** *Som*

A rummer, with cup-shaped bowl merging into a hollow cylindrical stem applied with 2 rows of raspberry prunts beneath a milled band, and with kick-in base, on a spreading folded foot, from Germany or The Netherlands, base cracked, 17thC/18thC, 8½in (21cm). **£1,200–1,700** *S*

A pair of rummers, the straight sided bowls each etched with a two-masted vessel in full sail, the reverse with monogram 'JRW', beneath a hatched band on plain stem and moulded square foot, 19thC, 5in (12.5cm). **£450–500** *DN*

A wine glass, with pan top bowl, multiple spiral air-twist stem with shoulder and central knops, and plain conical foot, c1750, 6in (15cm). **£620–670** *Som*

A wine glass, with trumpet bowl on a drawn stem section with multiple spiral air-twist stem, above a beaded air knop and plain section, with a plain domed foot, c1720, 7in (17.5cm). **£660–700** *Som*

A Silesian goblet, the straight sided quatrefoil bowl engraved with the monogram 'J.A.' beneath a coronet and above the motto 'Fructus Laboris', on a faceted inverted baluster stem with a double basal knop, the spreading foot etched to the rim and cut with flutes to the underside, mid-18thC, 7in (17.5cm).
£500–600 *CSK*

A 'Historismus' Façon de Venise winged goblet, by C. H. F. Müller, Hamburg, c1875, 9in (23cm).
£600–700 *S*

A Jacobite 'Boscobel oak' wine glass, the drawn trumpet bowl engraved with an oak tree, the branches enclosing 3 crowns and a face in diamond point, the stem with tear, conical foot, c1740, 6½in (16cm). **£11,000–14,000** *S*

The tree probably represents the so called 'Boscobel oak' in which Charles II hid from the Parliamentarians after the Battle of Worcester on 3rd September 1651. The trunk of the oak may represent the Church as the foundation of the state, supported by 3 crowns representing the kingdoms of England, Scotland and Ireland. The oak tree, and in particular the oak leaf, remained a popular symbol of the Stuart cause.

It has been suggested that glasses of this type may be centenary glass, and that the crowns could represent James, the Old Pretender, and his 2 sons, Prince Charles Edward and Henry, later Cardinal of York.

Jacobite Glasses

Jacobite glasses were used by secret societies who supported the claim to the throne of the descendants of the Roman Catholic Stuart King, James II of England, who abdicated in 1688 in favour of the Protestants, William and Mary. The glasses were engraved with a variety of Stuart mottoes and emblems. The most frequently found Jacobite symbol is the rose, representing the English crown. One or two buds beside the rose stand for the Pretenders - James II's son, James Francis Edward Stuart, known as the Old Pretender, and his son, Charles Edward Stuart (Bonnie Prince Charlie), the Young Pretender.

A trumpet bowl wine glass, engraved with fruiting vine and a bird in flight, a double series opaque twist stem, and a plain conical foot, c1760, 7½in (18.5cm).
£580–620 *Som*

A facet stemmed wine glass, the funnel bowl engraved with a bird in flight flanked by trees and foliage issuing from a tree stump, c1780, 6in (15cm) high.
£750–850 *C*

A Jacobite wine glass, the bell-shaped bowl engraved with a portrait medallion of Prince Charles Edward Stuart, the motto 'Audentior ibo', and a rose and thistle, foot lacking, 4½in (10.5cm).
£1,500–2,000 *C(S)*

A Dutch 'Newcastle' baluster wine glass, inscribed ''S' Lands Welvaren', set on a multi-knopped stem including a slender inverted baluster and basal knop, with conical foot, c1740, 7in (18cm).
£4,400–5,500 *S*

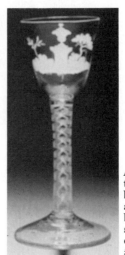

A Beilby enamelled opaque twist wine glass, the funnel bowl decorated in white with an urn on a pedestal flanked by trees, supported on a double series stem and conical foot, c1765, 6in (15cm).
£1,800–2,200 *C*

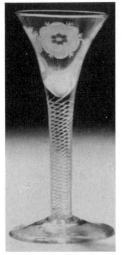

A Jacobite wine glass, the drawn trumpet-shaped bowl engraved with a rose, a bud and half-opened bud, the reverse with the motto 'Fiat', the air-twist stem filled with spiral threads above a conical foot, engraved with an oak branch, its foliage flanking the motto 'Redi', c1750, 6½in (16cm).
£1,700–2,200 *C*

A Dutch engraved armorial light baluster wine glass, the funnel bowl engraved with the arms of Holland, c1740, 7in (17.5cm).
£750–950 *S*

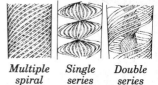

A Jacobite wine glass, engraved with a rose, bud and a half-opened bud, the reverse with an oak leaf and the motto 'Fiat', the air-twist stem filled with spiral threads, on a conical foot, c1750, 6½in (16cm) high.
£1,000–1,400 *C*

A Dutch wine glass, engraved in the manner of Jacob Sang, with the name 'D. Vrindschap', raised on a dumb-bell knop above an inverted baluster stem, the shoulders enclosing 2 rows of beads, on plain conical foot, c1745, 8in (19.5cm).
£1,300–1,700 *S(S)*

A Dutch engraved armorial light baluster wine glass, set on a teared swollen section, flanked by 2 teared cushion knops and a teared basal knop, on a conical foot, c1750, 7in (18cm).
£750–950 *S*

A Dutch 'Newcastle' baluster wine glass, inscribed 'Het.Aanstaande.Huwelyk', set on a beaded cushion knop and baluster knop flanked by an angular knop and plain section with basal knop, with conical foot, c1740, 7in (18cm).
£1,700–2,200 *S*

An engraved facet stemmed wine glass, c1780, 6in (15cm).
£750–850 *C*

A Dutch 'Newcastle' baluster wine glass, inscribed 'S' Lands Welvaren', set on a teared slender section with central swelling flanked by cushion knops and basal knop, with conical foot, c1750, 7½in (18.5cm). **£1,200–1,700** *S*

A Dutch 'Newcastle' baluster wine glass, inscribed 'De Inclenaatie', set on a beaded inverted baluster stem flanked by a dumb-bell knop and basal knop, with conical foot, c1750, 7½in (18.5cm).
£1,400–1,700 *S*

A funnel bowl wine glass, engraved with a building flanked by a fruit tree and a row of hops, the air-twist stem with a gauze core entwined by 2 spiral threads, on a conical foot, mid-18thC, 5⅓in (14cm) high.
£500–600 C

David Wolff

Stipple engravings by David Wolff are sometimes confused with those of an anonymous stippler, who may have been employed in Wolff's workshop. Both worked to a high standard. However, the stippled areas in Wolff's work are more delicately executed, with more contrasts of light and shade, than on the work of his colleagues.

A Dutch 'Newcastle' baluster wine glass, possibly engraved by David Wolff, stipple engraved with 2 coats-of-arms suspended from a ribbon above the date '1788', inscribed in Dutch in diamond point, set on an inverted baluster stem with dumb-bell knop, the conical foot also inscribed, 7⅓in (18.5cm) high.
£2,800–3,800 S

The inscription reads 'On the wedding day of Pieter Leeuenburgh and Geertruy van der Syde, Good health. May you live long as a united and blessed couple. May you not be afflicted by misfortune but with the Lord's protection may your House always be cared for'.

A Dutch light baluster wine glass, the funnel bowl engraved with a pair of mating fowl flanked by shrubs, inscribed above 'Utinam sic semper', set on an inverted baluster flanked by a triple annulated knop and a basal knop, with a domed foot, 7in (18cm).
£1,000–1,500 S

A Williamite colour-twist wine glass, the ovoid bowl engraved with an equestrian figure within the inscription 'The Glorious Memory of King William', the reverse inscribed 'Boyne 1 July/1960' within branches of tied berried foliage, the stem with an opaque entwined ribbon core within opaque and yellow spiral threads, on a plain foot, perhaps 19thC and the glass Low Countries, 6in (15cm).
£500–800 C

Williamite Glasses

Williamite glasses dating from c1750, commemorated the victory of King William III over James II at the Battle of the Boyne in Ireland in 1690.

A Dutch armorial 'Newcastle' baluster wine glass, the funnel bowl finely engraved, in the manner of Jacob Sang, with a monogram 'FTR', within an elaborate coroneted cartouche, the reverse with a building and garden, inscribed above 'Floreat Pastoratus', and the date '1786', set on a multi-knopped stem including 2 beaded knops, on a conical foot, 7⅓in (18.5cm).
£5,000–6,000 S

A German engraved armorial wine glass, Lauenstein or Hesse, the funnel bowl engraved with a coat-of-arms with initials 'HW' within an oval line panel surmounted by a coronet and flanked by leaf fronds, beaded base above a teared large angular knop, basal knop and folded domed foot, 6in (15cm).
£500–700 S

The arms are those of Winckler von Dölitz, of Leipzig, Bavaria. They were created nobles of the Holy Roman Empire in 1650, confirmed in 1781.

Epergnes

A cranberry glass épergne, the frilled bowl fitted with a tall trumpet vase flanked by 2 cranberry glass handkerchief vases, with clear glass spirals, late 19thC, 23in (59cm).
£450–550 *S(S)*

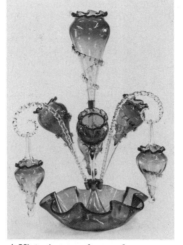

A Victorian cranberry glass épergne, with bulbous central vase and 3 smaller vases, 3 twisted cane arms supporting conforming baskets, all with crimped rims and with trailing ornaments, crimped circular base, central vase repaired, 22in (56cm) high.
£450–550 *CAG*

A three-branch glass épergne, the central trumpet vase cut with diamonds raised on a gilt metal stem, flanked by 2 tusk-shaped vases, above a star cut petal base, minor chips, central vase possibly matched, 19thC, 15½in (39cm).
£180–220 *S(S)*

A four-branch cranberry glass épergne, fitted with a central fluted trumpet vase, surrounded by 3 smaller trumpets above a crimped circular base, late 19thC, small chips, 21in (53cm).
£500–600 *S(S)*

Ewers

An engraved claret ewer, possibly Stourbridge for Dobson and Pearce, the scroll handle engraved in the form of a snake with a cherub mask terminal, c1860, 10½in (27cm).
£2,000–2,500 *S*

A Stourbridge green flash slender oviform ewer, with hinged silver cover, engraved with lilies issuing from stylised foliage, with a clear notched handle supported by a circular foot, early 20thC, 12½in (32cm).
£600–700 *CSK*

A trailed glass épergne vase, possibly by Powell, c1900, 12in (30.5cm) high.
£200–240 *DUN*

An engraved claret ewer, probably Philip Pargeter, Stourbridge, the flattened ovoid form deeply engraved on one side, probably by James O'Fallon, with a pair of classical figures seated on an elaborate raft drawn by a pair of swans and cherubs, the reverse with monogram 'RAH' within a circular cartouche with palmettes and ivy, applied scroll hand and drip ring, rim repaired, c1875, 9in (23cm).
£1,500–2,000 *S*

Flasks

A central European enamelled pewter mounted amber flask, with lobed angles, decorated in shades of yellow, blue, green and white with stylised flowersprays and foliage, divided by dash ornament, the rim with a pewter mount, mid-18thC, 5½in (13.5cm).
£1,000–1,500 *C*

A Bohemian enamelled and painted flask, inscribed 'Gottes namen...Anno 1777', the shoulder with an iron red and yellow foliate band, the short neck with folded rim, 8in (20cm).
£2,500–3,500 *C*

A Bohemian enamelled flask, painted in black, green and yellow, the reverse with an inscription and the date '1792', with a stylised foliage spray, the shoulder with radiating iron red and yellow dash ornament, the short neck with folded rim, 8½in (21cm).
£4,500–5,500 *C*

A central European spirit flask, with canted corners, enamelled in colours with a milkmaid, sprays of flowers to the reverse and sides, slight damage, 18thC, 5in (12.5cm).
£300–330 *CSK*

A central European spirit flask, and a pewter cover, with canted angles, enamelled in colours, the shoulder and sides with bands of stylised foliage, cover replaced, slight damage, mid-18thC, 7in (17.5cm).
£400–500 *CSK*

Jugs

A baluster stemmed cream jug, the flared funnel bowl with pouring lip, set on a cushion knop above a teared inverted baluster and folded domed foot, applied scroll handle, c1710, 6in (15cm).
£2,500–3,000 *S*

A claret jug, the body with broad cut flutes and 2 annulated neck rings, a heavy strap handle and notched rim, with cut mushroom stopper, c1830, 11½in (28.5cm).
£475–550 *Som*

An engraved glass claret jug and 2 glasses, possibly Stevens and Williams, each piece finely engraved with oval panels of flowers, reserved on a muslin ground with stylised leaf designs between formal acanthus borders, c1870, jug 12in (30.5cm).
£350–450 *S(S)*

A pair of Dobson and Pearce claret jugs, of globular form with stepped shoulder and flared rim applied with an angular handle, engraved with a boar's head crest above the monogram 'HGT', between star and dot borders, 13in (33cm).
£1,500–2,000 *S*

The crest is that of the Gordon family.

A cut glass jug, early 19thC,
6½in (16cm) high.
£140–180 *DUN*

Lighting

A cranbrerry glass water
jug, c1880, 9in (23cm) high.
£150–180 *DUN*

A marbled Milchglas jug, the
ovoid form with slender neck and
everted trefoil rim with spout, set
on a pincered circular foot and
with applied scroll handle, the
pale cream glass marbled with
cobalt blue, iron red and white,
17thC, possibly north Italian or
south German, 5in (12.5cm).
£1,500–2,000 *S*

A water jug, the cut body with
base fluting, a band of strawberry
diamonds, printy cut neck, a
scalloped rim and strap handle,
c1825, 7in (17.5cm).
£475–550 *Som*

A heavy cut glass oil lamp,
c1880, 17in (43cm) high.
£850–1,050 *DUN*

A pair of cut glass lustres,
c1820, 9½in (23.5cm) high.
£500–600 *DUN*

A cut glass oil lamp,
with original shade, c1880,
30in (76cm).
£1,000–1,200 *DUN*

A cut glass bird candle lamp,
on an ormolu branch, c1880.
£1,750–2,000 *DUN*

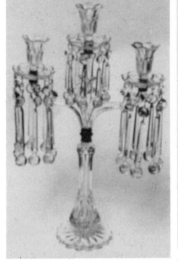

A Victorian cut glass three-branch candelabra, c1860, 22½in (57cm).
£1,000–1,200 *DUN*

A cut glass oil lamp, with original etched glass shade, c1880, 30in (76cm) high.
£1,200–1,500 *DUN*

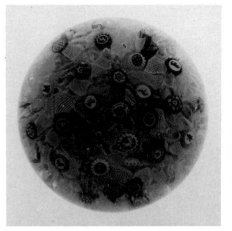

A Baccarat magnum paperweight, containing scattered canes with animals, flowers and the date '1847' on a tumbled muslin ground, damaged, 3½in (9cm) diam. **£3,500–4,000** *DN*

A candle jar, 19thC, 8in (20cm).
£140–180 *DUN*

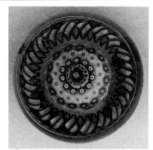

A St. Louis concentric millefiori mushroom weight, composed of a central florette cane within 5 rows of white, red, blue and green coloured millefiori canes, with an outer row of hollow white cog wheel canes lined in red, divided by a single dark blue cane signed and dated 'S.L. 1848', with a torsade at the periphery composed of a white corkscrew cable, within a cobalt blue spiral thread, and with star cut base, chipped, 3in (7.5cm) diam.
£2,500–3,000 *HSS*

A St. Louis pelargonium weight, the flower with a yellow, brown and green centre, surrounded by 5 pink heart-shaped petals edged in white and with 4 green sepals between, the stalk with 2 slender green leaves, mid-19thC, 3in (7.5cm) diam.
£1,800–2,400 *C*

Paperweights

A St. Louis salamander weight, the richly gilt reptile lying coiled on the top of a green tinted hollow sphere, mid-19thC, 3½in (9cm) diam.
£2,000–2,500 *C*

A scrambled paperweight, the clear glass set with candy stripes and other coloured cut canes and gauzes, chipped, unmarked, 2⅜in (6cm) diam. **£150–200** *HSS*

A Baccarat 'mushroom' paperweight, with central millefiori canes within a blue and white spiral twist band, star cut base, damaged, 19thC, 2⅜in (6cm) diam.
£600–700 *DN*

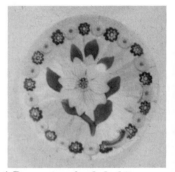

A Baccarat garlanded white double clematis weight, the flower with 12 ribbed petals about a red, white and blue centre and with 5 green leaves showing behind, the stalk with 2 further leaves, set within a garland of alternate blue centred white and claret canes, on a star cut base, damaged, mid-19thC, 2½in (6.5cm) diam.
£650–750 *C*

A Clichy swirl paperweight, the clear glass set with alternating turquoise and white spiral threads, radiating from a central pink and red pastry mould centre cane, lined in white with a ring of green and white inner canes, scratched, 3in (7.5cm) diam.
£600–700 *HSS*

A multi-faceted glass paperweight, designed by Colin Terris, limited edition of 1,000, issued 1977, 76mm diam.
£100–135 *Cai*

A pair of glass dumps, c1850, 3½in (9cm) high.
£250–300 *DUN*

Contemporary Paperweights

Contemporary paperweights are often overshadowed by their 'loftier cousins' the antique weights who, because of their age, lay claim to a superiority which may not be justified by better craftsmanship. Modern weights on the other hand are not only as beautiful but more available and within the reach of the collector's pocket. Thus they are widely collected and very much sought after.

Modern paperweights are produced in many parts of the world. The French Baccarat and St. Louis factories produced some of the finest antique specimens and are still producing weights today. In the U.K., Caithness and Perthshire are probably the best known, although Whitefriars, now a subsidiary of Caithness, still produces a small range and some of the crystal manufacturers also make a few weights. It could be argued that some of the best weights now come from America where the trend is towards small workshops.

The form of modern weights has developed widely since the war. Traditional millefiori designs are still produced, largely by Perthshire and the French factories. Caithness and some of the Continental artists also produce a large range of abstract designs in both limited and unlimited versions. There has also been a substantial move towards lamp-work design, led by Paul Ysart, the 'father' of modern Scottish paperweights. Many self-employed glass artists, particularly in the USA, produce wonderful examples of this work.

Contemporary paperweight makers identify their work with an initial cane or an etched logo. Other artists engrave their signature on the weight. However, care should be taken when buying as there are many fakes.

A multi-faceted lamp-work paperweight, designed by Colin Terris and William Manson, a limited edition of 500, issued 1981, 78mm diam.
£125–150 *Cai*

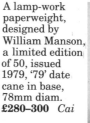

A green glass dump, c1880, 5in (12.5cm) high.
£120–140 *DUN*

A glass engraved paperweight of Silver Jubilee Fleet Review, designed by Colin Terris, a limited edition of 100, issued 1977, 85mm diam.
£180–200 *Cai*

A glass paperweight, designed by Colin Terris, limited edition of 500, issued 1971, 78mm diam.
£300–325 *Cai*

A lamp-work paperweight, designed by William Manson, a limited edition of 50, issued 1979, '79' date cane in base, 78mm diam.
£280–300 *Cai*

Vases

A ruby and white cameo vase, carved with bees flying amongst foxgloves, the neck with zig-zag border, c1880, 8½in (21cm).
£1,000–1,500 *P(S)*

A pair of Bohemian engraved blue stained vases, the rims cut with flutes, late 19thC, 13in (33cm).
£1,200–1,800 *S*

A pair of cut oviform vases and covers, the bowls with a band of diamonds, on fluted stems and square bases, the domed covers with bands of diamonds and flutes and with fluted mushroom finials, damaged, possibly Irish, early 19thC, 7½in (19cm).
£400–500 *C*

A pair of gilded glass vases, c1900, 6in (15cm) high.
£75–95 *DUN*

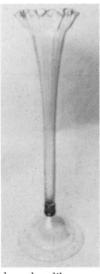

A clear glass lily vase, c1870, 41in (104cm) high.
£750–1,000 *DUN*

A pair of Italian bottle vases, the straw-tinted glass set on a rib moulded blue tinted cushion knop, above a folded conical foot, 5in (12.5cm).
£700–900 *S*

An enamelled opaline vase, ovoid with everted rim, painted and gilt with a bird amidst a flowering branch, between zig–zag borders, 2 scroll handles and flared foot, slight damage, 'E' above spider's web in red, by Edward Webb, White House Glass Works, Wordsley, c1880, 6in (15cm).
£300–500 *S*

Miscellaneous

A heavy cut glass box and cover, c1920, 7in (17.5cm) wide.
£120–140 *DUN*

A Venetian glass comport, c1890.
£180–220 *DUN*

A silver mounted cut glass tea caddy, c1800, 4⅓in (11cm) high.
£700–1,100 *CB*

A green glass witch's ball, c1860, 12in (30.5cm) diam.
£200–250 *DUN*

A glass candlestick, with a cylindrical sconce above a square tapered stem and ringed domed foot, 8in (20cm).
£600–700 *C(S)*

A dark blue witch's ball, c1880, 5in (12.5cm) diam.
£100–120 *DUN*

A Silesian stemmed tazza, the 8 sided stem on a collared and high domed fold-over foot, c1740, 13½in (34cm) diam. **£400–600** *WW*

A Bohemian or Venetian cranberry tinted punchbowl, cover, stand and 12 beakers, of globular quatrefoil form with footring, the stand with raised centre, the domed cover with rasberry prunt finial and shell handles, gilt rims, the globular beakers with gilt rims, traces of burnished gilding, one beaker damaged, late 19thC, the stand 18in (45.5cm) diam.
£700–800 *S*

A pair of Webb's pinched posy holders, engraved with flowersprays and foliage, flanked by diaper pattern panels, on everted feet with star cut bases, one marked, 20thC, 3in (8cm) high.
£200–300 *CSK*

A Stourbridge millefiori ink bottle and domed stopper, the base and stopper each centred by a blue and white cane within radiating bands of purple, apricot, white, red and blue canes, 3 solid white canes, stopper chipped, indistinct date, possibly 1868, 5½in (14cm) high. **£180–250** *HSS*

An oval cut tea caddy, the body cut with a band of flutes below a band of diamonds, with flute cut neck and rim, diamond cut mushroom stopper, c1810, 6in (15cm) high.
£340–375 *Som*

A set of 6 cut glass wine glass rinsers, c1840, 5in (12.5cm) wide.
£210–250 *DUN*

A cranberry flash and cut scent bottle case, with metal mounts, hinged cover and lock, enclosing a gilt metal frame holding 2 square section scent bottles, each with stopper and hinged gilt metal covers, chased with flowers in full bloom, wear to gilt, key to lock lacking, minor chips, 19thC.
£300–500 *CSK*

CLOCKS
Bracket Clocks

An ebonised bracket clock, by William Allam of London, with original verge escapement to the 8-day striking movement, the engraved backplate signed by the maker and signed again on the brass dial with visible beat aperture, strike/silent and calendar apertures, original ebonised and gilt case, 11in (28cm) high.
£9,500–11,000   B

A burr walnut and gilt metal striking bracket clock, dial signed 'Sam. Clay Gainsborough', silvered chapter ring with pierced blued hands, the matted centre with calendar aperture, the 5-ringed pillar twin fusee movement now with anchor escapement and strike on bell and with repeat, signature to the foliate engraved backplate, the movement c1700, later dial and case, 15in (38cm) high.
£2,000–3,000   C

A Victorian ebonised chiming giant bracket clock, the dial signed 'Cook Bros., London', on silvered chapter ring with pierced blued hands, Indian mask-and-foliate spandrels, subsidiary chime/silent ring in the arch, the 5 pillar triple chain fusee movement with anchor escapement chiming on 4 bells with hour strike on gong, pendulum holdfast to the foliate engraved backplate, 36½in (93cm) high.
£2,500–3,000   C

A George III fruitwood striking bracket clock, dial signed 'John Fladgate, London', on a silvered sector in the foliate engraved arch flanked by subsidiary rings for strike/silent and regulation, narrow silvered Roman and Arabic chapter ring with pierced blued hands and calendar aperture in the finely matted centre, foliate spandrels, the 6 pillar twin fusee movement with verge escapement and steel suspended pendulum with cam adjusted regulation bar, strike on bell, pendulum holdfast to the foliate engraved backplate with similarly engraved securing brackets to case, 18½in (47cm) high.
£1,800–2,500   C

An mahogany chiming bracket clock, the painted 7½in (19cm) convex dial signed 'Denne, Lambs Conduit St., London', strike/silent lever, the triple fusee movement chiming on 8 bells and striking on a further bell, the lancet case inlaid with brass stringing, c1820, 20in (50.5cm) high.
£1,700–2,200   S(S)

A Regency rosewood and brass inlaid bracket clock, with 8-day movement by Bruger, Holborn, London.   **£900–1,200   Mit**

Bracket Clock Cases

- The earliest English bracket clock cases were usually veneered with ebony often featuring an architectural top.
- Walnut veneer became popular from the early 18thC.
- Mahogany took over as the standard veneer c1740.
- Early cases often have elaborate metal mounts.
- From c1725 the arched dial replaced the square dial. Arched dial brackets became increasingly decorative in the 18thC. However, the bell top remained the most common style.
- Lacquer finishes were popular from 1730 - 1780. Ebonised cases, typically with a bell top (or inverted bell), were also produced in the late 18thC.
- In the Regency period, rosewood became fashionable, and English makers produced a great variety of case shapes.
- From the 1840s inexpensive shelf clocks were imported from the USA.
- The French were also prolific makers, favouring cases of gilt metal, often combined with marble or other materials.

A Victorian mahogany striking bracket clock, signed 'Charles Frodsham', c1870, 18in (46cm) high. **£900–1,200** *WIL*

A George III ebonised striking bracket clock, the dial signed 'Wm. Ward, London' on the silvered Roman and Arabic chapter ring with finely pierced blued hands, mock pendulum and calendar apertures to the finely matted centre, foliate spandrels, strike/silent ring in the arch, the 5 pillar twin fusee movement with strike on bell and original verge escapement, the backplate also signed, 19in (48cm) high. **£3,000–4,000** *C*

An ebonised repeating bracket clock, by Christopher Gould, with 6 pillar double fusee movement with crown wheel escapement, striking the hours on a single bell and repeating the hours and quarters on 5 graduated bells, the back cock with pierced foliate engraved apron, the backplate richly engraved with maker's name, mounted with the set up ratchets, click spring and pendulum keep, in ebony veneered domed case, late 17thC, 16in (41cm) high. **£11,000–13,000** *HSS*

A German 'ting-tang' bracket clock, with brass finials and caryatids, in a simulated tigerwood case, restored. **£600–650** *HAW*

A late Victorian double fusee bracket clock, by Webster, Queen Victoria Street, London, c1890, 20in (51cm) high. **£2,000–2,500** *Mit*

A Victorian Gothic style bracket clock, with silvered dial, the movement chiming and striking on 8 bells and a gong, in carved oak case, 25in (64cm) high, with bracket 12in (31cm) high. **£300–400** *Bea*

A George III mahogany striking bracket clock, the painted Arabic dial signed 'Leplastrier, London', with pierced blued hands, the 5 pillar twin fusee movement with anchor escapement and strike on bell, pendulum holdfast to foliate engraved backplate, securing brackets to case, 15in (38cm) high. **£1,000–1,400** *C*

An walnut and gilt brass mounted chiming bracket clock, the 6in (15cm) dial with silvered chapter ring and foliate pierced centre, levers for strike/silent and 8 bells/4 bells, signed 'Chas. Frodsham, New Bond Street, London, No. 1751', the substantial movement with triple fusees, chiming on 8 bells and striking on a gong, signed and numbered on the backplate with address at 84 Strand, c1885, 22in (56cm) high. **£3,000–3,500** *S(S)*

A Regency mahogany bracket clock, the white enamel dial in arched case with brass stringing, 8-day striking movement, dial requires restoration, Gothic side grilles and ring handles, ball feet, and a matching bracket, 15in (38cm) high. **£750–850** *L&E*

A George III bracket clock, by Raymond, London, the 8-day movement with repeat and alarm, backplate engraved with scrolling foliage within a geometric border, 2 circular subsidiary dials for strike/silent and minutes, the main dial with alarm ring and foliate surround, in gilt brass mounted mahogany case, damaged, 14½in (37cm) high. **£9,000–11,000** *Bea*

A satinwood bracket clock, the 8-day repeating 3 train movement with 6 screwed plate pillars, striking the quarters on a choice of 4 or 8 bells with a gong for the hour, c1890, 21in (53cm) high. **£5,000–6,000** *PAO*

Locate the source

The source of each illustration in Miller's can be found by checking the code letters below each caption with the list of contributors.

A Victorian ormolu mounted ebonised quarter-chiming bracket clock, the dial signed 'Chas. Frodsham & Co., Clockmakers to the Queen, 84 Strand., No. 1440' on the silvered chapter ring with finely matted centre and blued hands, winged cherub spandrels, strike/silent lever above XII, the massive 5 baluster pillar movement with triple chain fusees, blued overcoiled spring to the cut bi-metallic compensated balance of the lever platform, chiming on 4 gongs and with hours strike on larger gong, similarly signed plain backplate with securing brackets to case, 19in (48cm) high. **£3,200–4,000** *C*

A Regency fruitwood striking bracket clock, signed 'John Harper, 65 Goswell Street London', with blued steel pierced spade hands, the 5 pillar twin fusee movement with anchor escapement, with steel suspended calibrated pendulum, strike on bell on border engraved backplate, similarly engraved securing brackets to case, 16½in (42cm) high. **£1,200–1,700** *C*

A French contra boulle bracket clock, with 5in (12.5cm) 12-piece enamel cartouche dial, square plated bell striking Vincenti movement No. 100, glazed case veneered with brass inlaid with tortoiseshell, mother-of-pearl and stained bone, outline with gilt brass mounts, c1860, 19in (48cm) high, bracket 7in (18cm) high.
£1,200–1,800 *S*

A French red boulle bracket clock, with 12-piece enamel cartouche dial, gong striking movement with anchor escapement, the waisted case veneered with brass and tortoiseshell, outlined with ormolu mounts, putto finial, c1880, 16in (40.5cm) high.
£800–1,000 *S*

A bracket clock, by Johnson, Grays Inn Passage, the brass dial with silvered brass chapter ring, spandrels and strike/silent to the arch, the 8-day movement striking the hours on a bell and repeating at will, the verge escapement with bob pendulum and with backplate engraved with maker's name, in mahogany broken arched case, c1775, 15in (38cm) high.
£7,000–8,000 *PAO*

> • All bracket clocks are spring driven.
> • The most collectable bracket clocks on the market are mahogany veneered examples, with either bell or arched top, produced during the second half of the 18thC.

A Regency brass inlaid mahogany striking bracket clock, the Roman dial with black painted moon hands, the 5 pillar twin wire fusee movement with anchor escapement, strike on bell above, plain backplate, securing brackets to case, 19in (49cm) high.
£800–1,200 *C*

A Victorian red walnut single fusee bracket clock, with pagoda shaped door and top, pierced brass side screens and panels, 16in (41cm) high.
£500–700 *CoH*

Carriage Clocks

A silver cased carriage clock, with round enamel dial, French lever movement, swing handle and bun feet, Chester 1906, 4½in (11cm) high. **£700–900** *DN*

A gilt brass carriage clock, with mother-of-pearl 1¾in (4.5cm) dial with foliate engraved gilt mask, the earlier watch movement signed 'Tho Mudge and Wm Dutton, London', 4½in (11cm) high. **£700–800** *S(S)*

A gilt brass carriage clock, with 2½in (6cm) enamel dial, signed 'F. Dent, Chronometer Maker to the Queen 1442', the signed fusee and chain movement with maintaining power, under-slung ratchet-tooth lever escapement with compensation balance and helical spring, free-sprung, rectangular moulded glazed case with shuttered back, with a safety ratchet winder, c1850, 6in (15cm) high.
£7,000–7,500 *S*

A rare striking and repeating carriage clock, with silvered case, gilded Atlantes to the 4 corners, solid ebony moulds and base, 6½in (16.5cm) high without handle.
£5,000–6,000 *DRA*

A French repeating carriage clock, with 2½in (6.5cm) dial and silvered annular chapter ring with Roman numerals, in a blue mask decorated with scrolling foliage, the movement with bi-metallic compensated balance wheel with lever escapement striking and repeating the hours on a gong, in a gilt brass case, 6in (14.5cm) high.
£700–900 *L*

A French brass carriage clock, with white enamel dial, the bell striking movement signed 'Moser A Paris, 1824', with outside count wheel and replaced platform escapement, in a plain case with front and rear doors, c1850, 4in (10cm) high. **£650–750** *S(S)*

A carriage clock, with 1¼in (3cm) white enamelled dial, Roman numerals and parcel gilt blued steel hands, the movement with compensated balance wheel and lever escapement, 3in (8cm) high, with winding key and travelling case. **£350–450** *L*

Carriage Clocks

Few people today would think of packing a carriage clock for a journey even though, as one of the earliest types of travelling clock, this was their purpose. Carriage clocks usually have brass cases and are fitted with handles so they can be easily carried - hence their name - many also came with leather travelling cases. Nearly all carriage clocks were made in France during the 19thC and early 20thC; a few were also produced in England.

The ingenuity of the French carriage clock maker was almost limitless, involving case and dial manufacturers, gilders, bronzers, enamellers, chasers, engravers, and those who produced highly decorative porcelain panels. The height of the clocks varied from under 2in to over 10in and a vast array of different styles were produced.

A French repeating carriage clock with alarm, the movement with compensated balance wheel and lever escapement mounted on the backplate, striking and repeating on a bell, in gilt brass case with borders of foliage and flowerheads, 5½in (14cm) high. **£750–800** *L*

A gilt metal striking carriage clock, with later lever platform, strike/repeat on gong, white enamel Arabic chapter disc with blued hands, 7in (17cm) high. **£500–700** *C*

A brass 8-day repeating carriage clock, by Dent, Paris, striking on a single bell, 4⅓in (11cm) high, with original fitted case. **£700–900** *HOLL*

A shibayama carriage clock, by E. Maurice & Co., the 1in (2.5cm) dial with silvered chapter ring and pierced centre, the gong striking movement with lever platform escapement, 'E M & Co' stamp, No. 4529, the ivory case inlaid with hardstones and mother-of-pearl, Japanese or French, c1870, 4⅓in (11cm) high. **£750–850** *S(S)*

A French carriage clock, with fluted columns, yellow dial with Arabic numerals, gilt and silvered mask of flowers and leaves, single train movement, restored, 7in (17.5cm) high. **£400–450** *HAW*

A French gilt brass miniature carriage clock, by H. Jacot, No.12730, with white enamel dial, the movement stamped, lever platform escapement, c1900, 3in (8cm) high. **£700–800** *S(S)*

A French gilt brass miniature carriage timepiece, the gilt dial with pierced centre, the movement with lever platform escapement, the case cast with caryatids and foliate scrolls, c1900, 3½in (8.5cm) high. **£650–750** *S(S)*

A French gilt bronze and champlève enamel mantel clock garniture, the brass 3½in (8.5cm) dial with foliate engraved centre, the bell striking movement stamped 'Leroy & Fils A Paris, N8038', Brocot suspension, the architectural case surmounted and flanked by cupids, enamelled in polychrome flowers and simulated quatrefoil tiles in the manner of the Barbedienne foundry, 10½in (53cm) high, together with a pair of matching cupids formerly holding candle branches, 10½in (27cm) high. **£1,200–1,700** *S(S)*

A French brass quarter repeating carriage clock, the white enamel dial with subsidiary alarm dial, the movement chiming on 2 gongs, lever platform escapement, in a corniche case, c1880, 5½in (13.5cm) high. **£500–700** *S(S*

A French repeating carriage clock, the 2in (5cm) annular chapter ring with Arabic numerals in pierced gilt mask, the movement with compensated balance wheel and lever escapement striking and repeating the hours on a gong, in brass case with wrythen columns, 6½in (16cm) high. **£750–800** *L*

Garnitures

A French gilt and patinated bronze elephant clock and a pair of candlesticks, with 4in (10cm) enamel dial, Japy Frères bell striking movement No. 5697 in a drum case, surmounted by a chinaman with a parasol and carried on the back of an elephant standing on a rocaille plinth, 16½in (42cm), with a pair of candlesticks in the form of male and female native figures, c1885, 13in (33cm) high. **£3,300–3,700** *S*

A Second Empire ormolu and white marble striking clock garniture, with classical figures, on a foliate cast plinth set, with an alabaster dial with gilt spade hands, the twin-going barrel movement with anchor escapement and strike on bell, on D-ended marble base and ormolu bracket feet, and 2 figures of classical ladies holding a lyre and harp, 15½in (39cm) high. **£1,500–2,000** *C*

Lantern Clocks

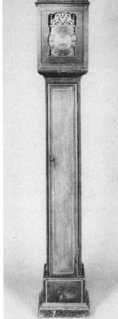

A Charles II striking lantern clock, the movement with verge escapement and short bob pendulum, count wheel strike on bell above, with iron straps to the 4 corner finials, with pierced frets, the dial signed 'James Delance Froome Fecit', within the centre with tulip engraving, silvered Roman chapter ring with single pierced steel hand, 15½in (39cm).
£2,000–2,500 *C*

A brass lantern clock, by Francis Forman, the 6in (15cm) chapter ring set on an engraved dial plate, central alarm disc, posted weight driven movement with verge and balance wheel escapement, later chains, the case with metamorphic frets, the front one signed 'Francis Forman at St. Paules' gate', slender corner columns, ball feet, urn finials, wall spikes and top mounted bell, restored, alarm work removed, c1635, 14in (35.5cm).
£4,700–5,500 *S*

A Queen Anne oak longcased striking lantern clock, with later decorated case, the clock with verge escapement and centre swinging bob pendulum, countwheel strike on bell above, damaged, the dial signed 'William Speakman Londini Fecit' on the brass chapter ring, with steel hour hand, lacking alarm disc, 67in (170cm).
£2,000–3,000 *C*

A brass lantern clock, the 6in (15cm) chapter ring set on a tulip engraved plate, formerly with an alarm disc, the posted weight and rope driven movement with early conversion to anchor escapement, the case with later finial, alarm work removed, with an oak wall bracket, 16in (40cm) high.
£2,200–2,700 *S*

A Charles II brass striking lantern clock, with verge escapement, countwheel strike on bell above, the brass bell straps supported by urn finials, pierced and engraved dolphin frets, the front fret signed 'Henry Montlon London', brass Roman chapter ring with single steel hand, foliate engraved centre with alarm disc, alarm assembly lacking, 15in (38cm).
£2,800–3,400 *C*

Longcase Clocks

A George III mahogany longcase clock, with arched dial, signed 'Thomas Barton, Manchester' on a silvered arc above the moon phase in the arch, silvered chapter ring with silvered matted centre having subsidiary seconds and calendar aperture, pierced black painted hands, the 4 pillar rack striking movement with anchor escapement, 89in (226cm).
£3,000–4,000 C

A George III mahogany longcase clock, with painted dial signed 'Philip Bromyard' within the centre with subsidiary seconds ring, Roman and Arabic chapter ring, rolling moonphase in the arch, and 4 pillar rack striking movement with anchor escapement, 97in (246cm).
£2,000–2,500 C

A mahogany longcase clock, with silvered 12in (30.5cm) break arch dial, signed 'Henry Adams', Hackney, subsidiary seconds and date dials, strike/silent dial in the arch, the 8-day movement striking on a bell, c1800, 85½in (217cm).
£2,500–3,500 S(S)

A longcase clock, by Andrews, Dover, with 8-day duration 5 pillar movement striking the hours on a bell, silvered brass dial showing both seconds and date, mahogany case with frame veneers and inlaid with shells and oak leaves, the hood with Kent cresting and 3 brass finials, c1790, 85in (216cm) high.
£5,750–6,250 PAO

A small country oak longcase clock, by R. Alexander, Chippenham, with 8-day duration movement striking the hours on a bell, white dial showing both seconds and date, plain oak case with canted corners to the trunk veneered with mahogany, the hood with swan's neck top and brass finial, c1830, 82in (208cm).
£1,500–2,000 PAO

A satin burchwood longcase clock, by James Common, Coldstream, with 8-day duration movement, striking the hours on a bell, the dial showing date and seconds, c1810, 81in (205.5cm).
£4,500–5,000 PAO

An oak longcase clock, with 10in (25cm) chapter ring, subsidiary seconds and calendar dials, well pierced steel hands, scalloped edge, raised gilt foliate decoration and signed 'Thos. Brown, Birmingham', rack and bell striking movement, engraved on the backplate with a monogram, c1800, 90in (228.5cm).
£2,000–3,000 S

A longcase clock, by David Ferris, Calne, the 8-day duration movement striking the hours on a bell, with square dial showing both seconds and date, c1840, 81in (205.5cm) high.
£2,750–3,250 PAO

A Scottish mahogany longcase clock, by John Bryson, Dalkeith, with 8-day movement striking the hours on a bell, painted dial with both seconds and date, c1840, 85in (216cm).
£2,700–3,300 PAO

PARTS OF A CLOCK

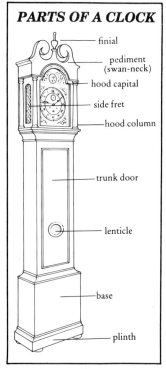

- finial
- pediment (swan-neck)
- hood capital
- side fret
- hood column
- trunk door
- lenticle
- base
- plinth

A George I quarter chiming longcase clock movement, the dial signed 'Jos. Boult London' on a silvered plaque within the matted centre, with subsidiary seconds ring, lacking hand, decorated calendar aperture, silvered chapter ring with pierced blued hands, female mask and foliate spandrels, the arch with penny moonphase with matted centre and silvered chapter ring, the 7 ringed pillar triple train movement with anchor escapement, count wheels planted on the backplate with a quarter wheel carrying a pin to trip linkage connecting to the hour count wheel, the chime on 6 bells via 6 hammers with hour strike on further bell, dial 12in (30.5cm) high.
£1,500–2,000 C

A Georgian mahogany longcase clock, with 11½in (30cm) arched brass dial, raised chapter, cherubs' head spandrels and subsidiary seconds dial signed 'Cyrus Crew, Tetbury', 8-day movement, bell strike, original painted dial by Walker and Hews, Birmingham, 84½in (214cm).
£1,400–2,000 WL

A mahogany longcase clock, with 14in (35.5cm) painted dial signed 'Jno. Chambley W. Hampton', with calendar dial and unusual central moon disc, 92½in (234cm).
£2,000–2,500 S

A Georgian oak longcase clock, with brass dial, moon phase, second hand, date aperture, silvered chapter ring and 8-day movement by John Clark, quarter striking, with either 4 or 8 bells, flanked on either side by turned columns with conforming trunk door and base, 86in (218.5cm).
£2,000–2,500 Mit

A Provincial oak chiming longcase clock, the 12in (30.5cm) dial with foliate scroll spandrels, seconds dial, calendar aperture, strike/silent dial in the arch, and signed 'John Best, Padstow', 5 pillar 3 train movement chiming on 8 bells with a further hour bell, c1780, 88½in (224cm).
£2,000–3,000 S

A George III oak longcase clock, with a swan's neck pediment above the silver chapter ring and 30 hour movement by Barwise, Cockermouth, flanked on either side by plain pillars above a shaped trunk door flanked by reeded quarter column corners, the base on shaped bracket feet.
£900–1,200 *Mit*

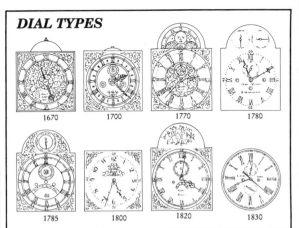

DIAL TYPES

1670 · 1700 · 1770 · 1780
1785 · 1800 · 1820 · 1830

A mahogany longcase clock, by W. D. Fenwick, Dundee, with 8-day duration movement striking the hours on a bell, the mahogany veneered case with quarter columns to the trunk with panelled door and base, the hood with swan's neck top and brass central finial, c1850, 85½in (216.5cm).
£3,000–3,500 *PAO*

A green lacquered longcase clock, the 11½in (29cm) dial with added arch, the silvered chapter ring signed 'John Cotsworth, London', subsidiary seconds dial and date aperture, the 8-day 6 pillar movement with external locking plate and striking on a bell, the associated case with pagoda top and break arch trunk door, part late 17thC, 96½in (244cm).
£1,500–2,000 *S(S)*

A Regency mahogany longcase clock, with 12in (30.5cm) square silvered and engraved dial signed 'Chas. Haley, London' within the Roman chapter ring, subsidiary seconds and calendar rings lacking hands, strike/silent lever, the 5 pillar movement with anchor escapement and rack strike on bell, 79in (200.5cm) high.
£1,700–2,200 *C*

A mahogany longcase clock, with painted 14in (35.5cm) break arch dial, signed 'John Cooke, Runcorn', subsidiary seconds dial and date aperture, moonphase in the arch, the 8-day movement with bell striking, Wilson falseplate, the case with blind swan's neck pediment, double fluted columns, shaped trunk door and freestanding columns, inlaid trunk and base, c1790, 96in (243.5cm).
£2,000–2,500 *S(S)*

An white dial longcase clock, by Beverley, Caistor, with 8-day duration movement striking the hours on a bell, and painted dial showing both seconds and date, c1795, 84in (213cm).
£3,000–3,250 *PAO*

An automata longcase clock, by Aquila Barber, Bristol, with 8-day duration movement striking the hours on a bell, white dial painted with roses to the corners, and a Father Time automata to the arch, c1795, 92in (234cm).
£5,000–5,500 *PAO*

A mahogany longcase clock, by Carter, Salisbury, with signed 12in (30.5cm) arched brass dial with Roman numerals, subsidiary seconds dial with Arabic quarter hour intervals, strike/silent lever in the arch and engraved spandrels, the 4 pillar 3 train movement with anchor escapement striking on a bell and chiming on 8 bells, with pendulum, weights and keys, 88½in (225cm).
£2,500–3,000 *L*

Anchor Escapement

Anchor escapement, supposedly invented c1670 by Robert Hooke or William Clement, is a type of anchor-shaped escape mechanism, which engages at precise intervals with the toothed escape wheel. The anchor permits the use of a pendulum (either long or short) and gives greater accuracy than was possible with earlier verge escapement.

A small mahogany longcase clock, by Thomas Aldridge, Deal, with 8-day 5 pillar movement striking the hours on a bell, engraved brass silvered dial with sunken seconds and square date aperture, mahogany case with long trunk door and double plinth to base, the hood with reeded pillars, brass capitals and blind fret, c1785, 76½in (194cm).
£4,000–4,250 *PAO*

Small mahogany clocks are very rare and desirable.

A George III mahogany musical longcase clock, by Farley of Southwark, London, 12in (30.5cm) brass dial with recessed plaque bearing the maker's name, strike/silent and tune selection dials either side, engraved and silvered dial centre, with a seconds ring and date aperture, with substantial movement playing Auld Lang Syne, Home Sweet Home, Chimes or Annie Laurie at each hour, employing 10 bells and hammers, 3 brass cased weights and massive cased bob to the steel rodded pendulum, c1780, 94½in (238cm).
£20,000–25,000 *DRA*

An oak longcase clock, by William Horn Hale, Devizes, with 8-day duration movement striking the hours on a bell, brass dial with cast brass spandrels, silvered brass chapter ring, seconds, date aperture and strike/silent feature to the arch, c1775, 81in (205.5cm) high.
£4,200–4,700 *PAO*

An 8-day oak longcase clock, with engraved and silvered dial signed Chaffey, Sherborne, c1770, 76in (193cm) high.
£2,250–2,500 *ALS*

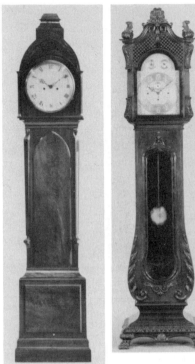

A mahogany chiming longcase clock, the 13in (33in) silvered dial with applied gilt Arabic numerals, overlaid with a gilt filigree mask signed 'Finnigans Ltd., Manchester', with seconds dial, strike/silent lever and subsidiary dials in the arch, substantial 3 train movement with deadbeat escapement maintaining power and playing one of 3 chimes on 8 tubular bells with a further hour bell, c1910, 98½in (250.5cm).
£6,000–7,000 *S*

A Scottish oak longcase clock, by Charles Lowe, Arbroath, with 8-day duration movement striking the hours on a bell, the painted dial showing both seconds and date, the hood with brass capped reeded columns each side and swan's neck top, c1800, 81in (205.5cm).
£2,850–3,250 *PAO*

A George III mahogany longcase clock, by Richard Chater of London, with 12in (30.5cm) painted dial, 8-day striking 5 pillar movement, with heavy shaped topped brass plates, contained in Gothic pattern case inlaid with ebony stringing, a Lancet pattern hood with triple cluster columns to sides, Lancet topped trunk door with Egyptian style columns with sphinx pattern heads and matching feet, panelled base, 86in (218.5cm).
£3,000–4,000 *CAG*

A West Country longcase clock, by Richard Maggs, Wells, with 8-day duration movement striking the hours on a bell, white dial showing seconds, date and phases of the moon to the arch, mahogany case with flame veneers inlaid with boxwood and stringing, the hood with cresting and 3 brass finials, c1840, 92in (233.5cm).
£4,250–4,650 *PAO*

A West Country longcase clock, by Hayward, Ashley, with 8-day duration movement striking the hours on a bell, painted dial showing seconds, date and moonphase to the arch, the mahogany case with flame veneers to trunk and base with rosewood crossbanding, the hood with twisted pillars capped with Corinthian brass capitals and surmounted by cresting and 3 brass finials, c1840, 89in (226cm).
£3,850–4,250 *PAO*

A mahogany longcase clock, with pagoda hood, the brass face with silver chapter ring and moonphase to arch, inscribed 'James Thomas, Chester', flanked by fluted columns, with arched trunk door.
£2,700–3,200 *BWe*

A Scottish longcase clock, by Joseph McIntyre Crieff, with 8-day duration movement striking the hours on a bell, with seconds and date, the painted dial showing chinoiserie scenes to the arch and corners, c1835, 82in (208cm) high.
£2,200–2,800 *PAO*

A longcase clock, 11in (28cm) dial with silvered chapter ring signed 'Jo Jackman, London Bridge', with 8-day duration movement, subsidiary seconds dial and date aperture, the 5 pillar movement with internal locking plate and striking on a bell, the later William and Mary style walnut and marquetry case inlaid with flowers and birds, c1700, 85in (216cm).
£3,500–4,000 *S(S)*

An early Victorian Scottish mahogany longcase clock, signed 'W. McEwan, Auchterarder', the 8-day striking movement with anchor escapement, arched painted dial with 2 subsidiary dials, the case with decorative stringing, 82in (208cm).
£900–1,200 *MCA*

William McEwan is recorded in Auchterarder from 1840–60.

An inlaid mahogany longcase clock, by L. Wyatt, Macclesfield, with 8-day duration, enamel dial with seconds ring, gilt calendar aperture and bird design gilt hands, the case decorated with boxwood stringing and feather banding, early 19thC, 90in (228.5cm).
£650–750 *CoH*

An automata longcase clock, by Richard Herring, Newark, with 8-day duration movement striking the hours on a bell, with both seconds and date features, white dial with flowers to the corners and an Adam and Eve automata to the arch, oak and mahogany case with canted corners to the trunk, inlaid with mahogany and boxwood, the hood with twisted pillars, pagoda top and brass finials, c1800, 86in (218.5cm).
£2,750–3,350 *PAO*

A mahogany inlaid longcase clock, by Samuel Richie, Forfar, with 8-day duration movement striking the hours on a bell, with dial showing seconds and date, the trunk with inlaid quarter columns to the sides and boxwood stringing and rosewood crossbanding to the trunk door, the hood with inlay and swan's neck top, c1830, 82in (208cm) high.
£3,500–4,000 *PAO*

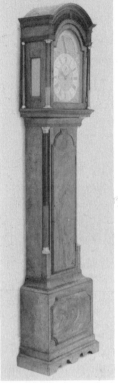

A West Coast Scottish longcase clock, by Charles Lyon, Hamilton, with 8-day duration movement striking the hours on a bell, brass dial seconds, date and phases of the moon to the arch, mahogany veneered case with rosewood and boxwood inlay, c1780, 87in (221cm).
£5,250–5,750 *PAO*

A mahogany musical longcase clock, signed by Jonathan Marsh, London, 90in (229cm).
£4,000–4,500 *L*

A mahogany chiming longcase clock, by Morgan, London, 99in (252cm) high.
£3,000–3,500 *L*

A walnut and marquetry longcase clock, the 10in (25cm) chapter ring signed 'Thos. Smith, Leighton', foliate engraved centre, the later 8-day movement striking on a bell, the altered case with formerly rising flat top hood, the trunk door and base inlaid with flowers and birds, part late 17thC, 82in (208cm).
£2,500–3,500 *S(S)*

A Queen Anne walnut longcase clock, with 12in (30.5cm) dial, signed 'Rich. Medhurst, London' on the silvered chapter ring, the matted centre with subsidiary seconds ring and decorated calendar aperture, ringed winding holes, pierced blued hands, crown and putti spandrels, 5 ringed pillar movement with anchor escapement and inside countwheel strike on bell, 96in (243.5cm).
£2,600–3,500 *C*

A Georgian mahogany longcase clock, c1800.
£3,000–3,500 *Mit*

An mahogany longcase clock, by James Whitelaw, Edinburgh, with 8-day duration movement striking the hours on a bell, the silvered dial with Roman hour chapters and Arabic seconds, the case with round drumhead hood and brass concave bezel, the trunk door and base with mahogany flame veneers, c1830, 82in (205.5cm). **£2,500–3,000** *PAO*

A George III mahogany longcase clock, with 12in (30.5cm) engraved brass dial, signed 'Puckridge, Snow Hill, London', with seconds and calendar dials and a strike/silent dial in the arch, 5 pillar movement with rack and bell striking, c1800, 84in (213cm) high. **£3,000–4,000** *S*

A George III oak longcase clock, by Thomas Pringle, St. Ninians, with 8-day movement, second and day counter, over a panel door, on a rectangular plinth. **£1,500–2,000** *FLE*

An oak longcase clock, by Joshua Square, with arched brass dial, 8-day movement with date and second hand, silvered sunburst between dolphin spandrels in the arch, the hood with moulded pediment and arched glass window sides, 18thC, 88in (223.5cm). **£1,500–2,000** *DA*

A late Edwardian longcase clock, with 3 train Westminster chimes movement and 5 gongs, arched brass and silvered dial, hood with turned Corinthian columns and arched top, glass door and fluted quarter columns and ogee feet. **£2,000–3,000** *WIL*

A mahogany longcase clock, the break arch silvered 12in (30.5cm) dial, signed 'Robt. Mawley, London', subsidiary seconds dial, date aperture, strike/silent in the arch, the 8-day movement striking on a bell, the case with pagoda top, break arch trunk door and panel base, c1780, 94½in (239cm) high. **£2,000–2,500** *S(S)*

A longcase clock, by
J. Slade, Trowbridge,
with 8-day duration
movement striking the
hours on a bell, the dial
with seconds, date and
moonphase to the arch,
the mahogany case with
flame veneers and
boxwood string inlay,
c1825, 92in (233.5cm).
£4,250–4,600 *PAO*

A George III walnut
longcase clock, the dial
signed 'Richard Peckover,
London' on the silvered
chapter ring, the matted
centre with subsidiary
seconds ring and
calendar aperture,
pierced blued hands,
female mask and foliate
spandrels, subsidiary
strike/silent ring in the
arch, the 5 pillar rack
striking movement with
anchor escapement,
93½in (238cm).
£2,500–3,000 *C*

A walnut marquetry
longcase clock, with 12in
(31cm) dial signed 'Jonat,
Marsh, London', with
seconds dial, calendar
aperture, double cherub
and crown spandrels,
movement with inside
countwheel, flat top case
with brass balustrade
cresting, Corinthian hood
pilasters, the trunk door
with a lenticle, bordered
with brass moulding and
profusely decorated with
foliate marquetry, the
sides divided into panels
by chequered stringing,
altered, c1705, 86½in
(219cm) high.
£4,000–5,000 *S*

A walnut longcase clock,
by Andreas Mülner,
Eisenstadt, the 10in
(25cm) dial with central
calendar, arcaded
minutes, leaf engraved
centre and fan spandrels,
similarly engraved arch
with a signed silvered
boss, flanked by
subsidiary dials for
'repetirt/nicht' and
'schlagt/nicht', the 3 train
weight driven movement
with anchor escapement,
front mounted pendulum
and striking on 2 bells,
c1800, 95in (242cm).
£3,000–4,000 *S*

A mahogany longcase
clock, the 12in (30.5cm)
break arch dial signed in
the arch 'Samu.
Townson, London', with
silvered chapter ring,
subsidiary seconds dial
and date aperture, the
8-day 5 pillar movement
striking on a bell, the
later associated case with
swan's neck pediment
and rectangular trunk
door, part 18thC, 83in
(211cm) high.
£1,400–2,000 *S(S)*

A George III mahogany
quarter chiming longcase
clock, the dial signed
'Brandreth Middlewich'
on the silvered chapter
ring, the matted centre
with foliate cherub
spandrels, rolling painted
moonphase in the arch,
the 6 pillar rack striking
movement chiming on
6 bells with hour strike
on further bell, anchor
escapement, 90in
(228.5cm) high.
£2,500–3,500 *C*

A walnut and marquetry
longcase clock, with 12in
(30.5cm) dial signed
'George Raby, Falmouth',
subsidiary seconds dial
and date aperture,
wheatear border, the
later 8-day movement
part early 18thC, 81½in
(207cm) high.
£3,400–5,000 *S(S)*

An inlaid mahogany musical and chiming longcase clock, by S. Smith & Son, Strand, London, with signed 17⅛in (44.5cm) silvered dial, seconds dial, leaf and flower engraved centre, engraved spandrels representing music, subsidiary dials in the arch for music selection, chime selection and chime and music/silent, massive 4 train 6 pillar movement with deadbeat escapement, mercury pendulum and maintaining power, one of 2 chimes sounded at the quarters on 8 tubular bells with a large hour gong, and one of 6 tunes played by a 14in (36cm) pinned cylinder on 12 tubular bells, c1900, 106in (269cm).
£7,000–9,000 *S*

A walnut chiming longcase clock, the 12in (30.5cm) break arch dial signed 'E. Tregent, London', silvered chapter ring, subsidiary seconds dial, strike/silent in the arch, the massive 3 train 8-day movement chiming on 8 bells and striking on a gong, 90in (228cm).
£1,500–2,000 *S(S)*

A walnut longcase clock, by Windmills, London, with 8-day duration 5 pillar movement striking the hours on a bell, the brass dial with silvered brass chapter ring, seconds and date feature to the arch, c1730, 90in (228.5cm).
£13,000–13,500 *PAO*

A mahogany longcase clock, with 13in (33cm) painted dial signed 'Peter Evers, Chester', with well pierced steel hands, central calendar, subsidiary seconds and a moon disc in the arch, the corners painted with flowers and strawberries within gilt borders, the falseplate signed 'Osborne's Manufactory Birmingham', rack and bell striking movement, c1780, 88in (223cm).
£2,700–3,500 *S*

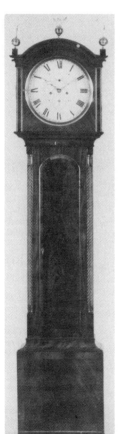

A George III Scottish mahogany longcase clock, with 13in (33cm) silvered dial, signed 'Wllm. Ross Huntly', with seconds and calendar dials, rack and bell striking movement with deadbeat escapement, maintaining power and wood rod pendulum, c1820, 86in (218.5cm) high.
£2,200–2,700 *S*

Mantel Clocks

An oak mantel clock, with 5in 12.5cm) silvered engraved arched dial, signed 'Fairer Maker to the Queen London', bordered with leaf scrolls, fusee and chain movement with anchor escapement, Gothic pointed arch case flanked by spiral columns with obelisk finials, carved leaf cresting and glazed sides, c1860, 14½in (37cm) high.
£400–500 *S*

An ebonised mantel clock, the silvered 3in (7.5cm) dial with foliate engraving and signed 'Frodsham, Gracechurch Street, London', the fusee movement also signed and with anchor escapement, c1840, 8in (20cm).
£800–1,000 *S(S)*

A gilt metal cased mantel clock, by T. Moss, Ludgate Street, the gilt dial with black Roman numerals and engine turned decoration to centre, strike and silent movement, supported on gilt metal Ionic scroll, the white marble base with applied gilt metal decoration, 19thC.
£1,200–1,800 *LANG*

A mahogany mantel clock, the 5½in (14cm) dial with silvered chapter ring, signed 'Payne & Co, 163 New Bond Street, London, No. 3562', the fusee movement also signed and numbered, striking on a gong, the case with bell top and gilt brass mounts, c1890, 18in (45.5cm).
£900–1,200 *S(S)*

An ormolu mantel clock, the 5in (12.5cm) enamel dial signed 'Bunon A Paris', the drum case signed 'Viel', c1775, 15in (38.5cm).
£6,000–7,000 *S*

A mahogany mantel clock, the painted convex 5½in (14cm) dial signed 'Purvis & Bishop, North Audley St., London', the fusee movement with shaped plates and anchor escapement, the lancet case with brass inlay, side handles and ball feet, 19thC, 14in (36cm) high.
£950–1,200 *S(S)*

A mahogany Gothic revival mantel clock, the silvered arched 6½in (16cm) dial engraved with foliate scrolls, the twin fusee movement striking on a gong, with anchor escapement, c1850, 26½in (67cm).
£800–1,200 *S(S)*

Condition of Clock Cases

All clocks should have their original finish and decorative features intact. Some restoration is acceptable, if carried out sympathetically. Cases in need of extensive repair and reconstruction should be avoided. Changes in temperature and humidity cause veneers to lift and for longcase clock trunk doors to warp. All mouldings may loosen as the original glue dries out and bubbles may appear under the lacquer on lacquered cases. This is caused by excessive heat and humidity. No clock should be kept in direct sunlight, as this causes the finish to bleach. Other problems include:

• Missing finials.
• Damaged mouldings.
• Broken glass on the hood.
• Scratching or damage to polish.

A mantel clock, by Japy Frères, Paris, with white enamel dial, black Roman numerals and inscribed 'Muirhead à Paris', the 8-day movement with outside countwheel and striking on a bell, with the Muirhead mark, in an ormolu case surmounted with figures, late 19thC, 21in (53cm).
£800–1,000 *Bea*

A gilt bronze and white marble mantel clock, with 2in (5cm) enamel dial, the fusee movement with anchor escapement, altered pendulum, the drum surmounted by an eagle, and supported by 4 columns with gilt finials and mounts, alterations to eagle, 16in (41cm) high.
£400–600 *S(S)*

A French white marble and ormolu mantel clock, with enamel convex dial, restored, 7in (18cm).
£350–400 *HAW*

A French striking mantel clock, with enamel dial, by Jacob Petit, Paris, in a porcelain case, 19thC, 15½in (39cm) high.
£900–1,200 *McC*

A French mantel clock, with porcelain dial and columns, in a spelter case, restored.
£350–400 *HAW*

A French ormolu and bronze striking mantel clock, with white enamel Roman chapter ring, blued moon hands, pierced gilt centre, twin going barrel movement with Brocot escapement and foliate cast pendulum, strike on bell on backplate, with stamp for 'Samuel Marti', 19½in (49.5cm).
£2,000–2,500 *C*

A French mantel clock, with silk suspension and silvered dial, in a rosewood case inlaid with satinwood, restored.
£550–600 *HAW*

A French gilt bronze and black marble mantel clock, the dial formed by gilt numerals mounted on the case, the bell striking movement with outside count wheel and silk suspension, signed 'Laguesse & Farrett A Paris', c1835, 15½in (39.5cm).
£700–900 *S(S)*

A French World Time mantel clock, the movement strikes on a bell stamped 'Marti et Cie Paris', and 'Brevete of Dutot, S.B.D.G.', the main chapter ring of the dial has I-XII twice in Roman numerals, with outer Arabic minutes, in a 4-glass case, with glazed panel to the top, 14in (36cm) high. **£3,000–4,000** *DRA*

Within the chapter ring is a rotating centre displaying the time at some 70 places throughout the world.

A French bronze and marble mantel clock, the 3½in (8.5cm) dial with serpent hands, bell striking movement 'No. 4921', with jewelled lever platform escapement, signed 'Ed. Minart', c1875, 20in (51cm).
£1,500–2,000 *S*

A French perpetual calendar polished bronze 4-glass mantel clock, the 4¼in (11cm) enamel dial with central month hand and subsidiary dials below for date and day of the week, the bell striking movement signed 'Frennele Bté. S.G.Du.' with Brocot escapement, c1875, 14in (35cm).
£2,000–3,000 *S*

A French ormolu mantel clock, the 4½in (11cm) enamel dial decorated with garlands of flowers, bell striking S. Marti movement 'No. 154' with Brocot escapement, elaborate leaf cast case surmounted by an urn with cockerel term handles, flanked by cast corbels with leaf finials, c1890, 21in (53cm).
£2,000–3,000 *S*

A French ormolu, bronze and marble mantel clock, with 3½in (8.5cm) gilt dial, bell striking movement with pinwheel escapement and silk suspension, the fluted drum case carried on the head of a seated putto with pipes and a tambourine, on a circular Siena marble plinth with ormolu mounts, c1825, 18in (45.5cm).
£1,200–1,800 *S*

A French perpetual calendar ormolu and marble mantel clock, with 2-piece enamel dial signed 'W.C. Shaw Paris', bell striking movement with Brocot escapement, a lever connected to the calendar which records day, date, moonphase and month with equation of time, marble cracked, c1860, 19in (48cm).
£2,000–3,000 *S*

A French bronze and ormolu automaton windmill mantel clock, the 3½in (8.5cm) silvered dial with engine turned centre and gilt bezel, bell striking silk suspension movement, the windmill case concealing a subsidiary mechanism for driving the sails, windmill sails and some animals replaced, c1835, 23½in (60cm).
£1,400–1,700 *S*

A Louis XV gilt bronze mantel clock, the 5⅓in (13.5cm) enamel dial signed 'Ate.Wolff A Paris', with central calendar and pierced gilt hands, the bell striking movement with circular flat bottomed plates, verge escapement, silk suspension and outside count wheel, the case re-gilded, c1770, 14⅓in (36.5cm).
£3,700–4,500 *S*

A French mantel clock, by Jacob Petit, with an engraved silvered metal dial, the striking movement inscribed 'Dupont à Paris 2371', the case decorated in gilt, blue and white with a trellis pattern, having brass pineapple finial and ormolu bezel, on a fitted matching stand, marked 'J.P.', 12in (30.5cm).
£500–600 *MCA*

A French porcelain mounted gilt brass mantel clock, with Japy bell striking movement 'No. 1125', c1880, 16in (41cm) high.
£800–1,000 *S*

A French red boulle mantel clock, with 5⅓in (13.5cm) 13-piece enamel cartouche dial, gong striking square plated movement 'No. 42013' with Brocot escapement, sunburst pendulum and the stamp of 'A. D. Mougin', the Régence style case veneered with red shell inlaid with brass and outlined with gilt bronze mounts, c1885, 23⅓in (60cm).
£1,000–1,200 *S*

A French gilt bronze and porcelain mantel clock, the 3⅓in (8.5cm) dial signed Raingo Fres, A Paris', the bell striking movement with outside count wheel and Brocot suspension, with 'Raingo' stamp, c1880, 21⅓in (54.5cm).
£1,500–2,000 *S(S)*

A French gilt brass mantel clock, with 3⅓in (8.5cm) enamel dial, the gong striking movement with Brocot suspension, the Louis XV style waisted case cast with rococo scrolls, 20⅓in (52cm) high.
£800–1,000 *S(S)*

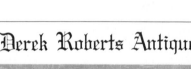

A French ormolu mounted bronze mantel clock, with 4⅓in (11cm) dial, formerly silvered, bell striking silk suspension movement, c1820, 18in (45cm).
£400–600 *S*

A French revolving chapter ring mantel clock, the altered movement with lever escapement, and lacking strike train driving 2 enamel chapter rings contained in a globe, flanked by Venus with a lyre and Cupid, the bow ended red marble plinth applied with ormolu mounts, c1880, 19½in (49cm) high.
£3,000–4,000 *S*

A French beam engine industrial mantel clock, with 2¼in (5cm) enamel dial, 8-day movement 'No. 204', with the stamp of 'Guilmet', the escapement connected to a beam pendulum above the weights concealed in the cylinders, on a black marble plinth, 7in (18cm) high.
£900–1,200 *S*

A French ormolu and silvered bronze mantel clock, with bell striking Vincenti movement 'No.194', contained in a silvered globe applied with Gothic Roman numerals and with serpent hands, the young Bacchus seated above, the leaf cast plinth decorated with a fruiting vine, c1850, 14in (36cm).
£750–950 *S*

Pinwheel Escapement

A type of escapement mechanism in which the pallets of a narrow anchor or arm engage semi-circular pins on the side of the escape wheel, rather than the usual teeth. Commonly used on 18thC French clocks.

A French gilt, silvered and patinated bronze automaton mantel clock, the 3in (7.5cm) silvered dial with serpent bezel, bell striking movement with altered pendulum suspension, c1840, 17in (43.5cm).
£650–950 *S*

A French ship's quarterdeck automaton mantel clock, with gong striking Guilmet movement 'No. 2195', connected to the rocking helmsman above, the quarterdeck case set with a compass and a mariner on the lower deck with a coil of rope, the marble plinth applied with a presentation plaque for Christmas 1889, helmsman replaced, 12in (30.5cm).
£2,000–2,700 *S*

A French marble and gilt bronze portico mantel clock, with 4in (10cm) enamel dial, the bell striking movement with outside count wheel and silk suspension, sunburst pendulum, the portico surmounted by ribbon tied swags, c1790, 19½in (49cm).
£1,200–1,700 *S(S)*

A French year-going 4-glass mantel timepiece, the 4in (10cm) 2-piece enamel dial with visible Brocot escapement, 2-tier movement with high count train, a massive spring barrel mounted on the backplate, glazed Ellicott gridiron pendulum, in a moulded gilt brass case, c1870, 14in (36cm).
£2,000–2,500 *S*

Portico Clocks

A German marquetry cuckoo mantel clock, the 6in (15cm) dial with bone numerals and hands, the wooden plated fusee movement with outside count wheel, the case surmounted by a carved eagle above the cuckoo doors, with foliate carved decoration and geometric marquetry base, c1880, 26in (66cm) high.
£1,500–2,000 *S(S)*

An Empire mahogany striking portico clock, with silvered Roman chapter disc, blued moon hands, twin going barrel movement with anchor escapement and count wheel strike on bell, stamped 'Le Roy A Paris' on the backplate, the case with rectangular plinth applied with foliate ormolu mounts, and 4 columns with ormolu capitals supporting the stepped pediment, 20in (50.5cm).
£800–1,000 *C*

A French mahogany portico clock, the 5in (13cm) dial signed 'Le Roy Hr. Du Roi A Paris', with centre seconds, the movement with pinwheel escapement, knife edge suspension, gridiron pendulum, outside count wheel cut for the quarters and striking on 2 bells, the 4 pillar case with engine turned ormolu capitals, c1810, 21½in (54cm) high.
£2,500–3,000 *S*

A French gilt bronze and porcelain mantel clock, the 3⅓in (8.5cm) dial with floral painted porcelain centre, cast chapter ring with enamel cartouche numerals, the bell striking Japy movement signed 'Robin A Paris', with outside count wheel and Brocot suspension, in Louis XVI style case, c1860, 16in (40.5cm).
£1,600–2,000 *S(S)*

A mahogany mantel clock, the 6½in (16cm) dial signed 'Nickisson, Chester', the fusee movement with anchor escapement, bell striking with repeat, chord missing, strike/silent lever on the backplate, c1820, 15in (38cm).
£1,600–2,000 *S(S)*

Skeleton Clocks

A month duration skeleton clock, signed 'B. Parker of Bury' and numbered '30', with deadbeat escapement and Arabic numerals, on a replaced velvet covered mahogany base, c1835, 16in (41cm) high.
£4,000–5,000 *DRA*

A skeleton clock, attributed to Smiths of Clerkenwell, based on the Brighton Pavilion, the chain fusee movement wheelwork with 5 crossings, half hour strike on a bell mounted vertically between the plates with a halbard for the hammer, hours struck on a 3 rod gridiron pendulum gong, with a silver plaque inscribed 'Presented to the Revd. Andrew Pope. M. A. by his Parishioners and Friends on leaving Cusop, July 30th 1873', 18½in (47cm) high.
£8,000–9,000 *DRA*

A French skeleton alarm clock, the 2in (5cm) enamel annular chapter ring with central alarm disc, 8-day going barrel movement 'No. 4203', with anchor escapement and silk suspension, in a scissor-shaped frame on a bow-ended brass base and an ebonised plinth concealing the pull/wind alarm mechanism, with a glass dome, c1850, 9in (22cm).
£700–800 *S*

A brass skeleton clock, with passing strike, with a 4⅓in (11cm) silvered chapter ring, the movement with going barrel, large great wheel, half deadbeat escapement and passing strike on a gong in the base, the scrollwork frame supported on a rectangular base with applied plaque signed 'James Condliff Liverpool', 15in (38cm) high.
£5,000–6,000 *S*

A skeleton clock, in the form of Lichfield Cathedral, with 5in (12.5cm) pierced chapter ring, 2 train fusee and chain repeating movement, with deadbeat escapement, half hour strike on a bell and hour gong, the frame on a stepped brass plinth and rosewood base applied with carved leaves, spires reduced, c1850, 17in (43cm) high.
£1,500–2,000 *S*

A skeleton clock based on Westminster Abbey, attributed to Evans of Handsworth, chiming the quarters on 8 bells, replacement macassar ebony base, c1865, 27in (69cm).
£9,000–10,000 *DRA*

Imposing clocks of this type, which were extremely time consuming and expensive to make, were only ever produced in small numbers. Much of their appeal over other 8 bell skeleton clocks is that they have, in effect, 4 frames instead of the usual 2, which adds depth and perspective to the clock. Besides the 2 movement frames, there is a third for the dial and an additional smaller one represents the porch of the Abbey.
The very substantial triple chain fusee movement is of the highest quality with 6-spoke wheelwork and 8 turned plate pillars. The bells are mounted transversly in 2 nests of 4 between the towers with a gong for the hours. A mercurial pendulum with 2 glass jars is employed, and the silvered brass chapter ring has engraving between the Roman numerals.

A brass skeleton clock, with silvered and pierced 6in (15cm) chapter ring, the single fusee movement with passing strike on the top mounted bell, anchor escapement, the Gothic frame with a later oak base, 17½in (45cm) high. **£700–900** *S(S)*

A mid-Victorian rosewood cased quarter chiming musical exhibition skeleton clock, the massive triple fusee movement with 6 double screwed pillars, engraved at the base of the scroll frame 'J. R. Losada, 105 Regent Street, London', all wheels with 6 crossings, deadbeat escapement with Graham type jewelled pallets, quarter chiming on 8 bells via 8 hammers and hour strike on gong, trip lever to set off the musical movement in the base signed 'Nicole Frères A Geneve', '26165' on the frame, massive 12in (30.5cm) long pin barrel, the steel comb with similar signature, some teeth missing, 3 levers to the side for the 4 tune selection/manual trip or continuous play and stop, c1860, 43in (109cm) high.
£20,000–25,000 C

A Victorian brass Cathedral style skeleton clock, with a silvered open dial, the 8-day movement striking on a bell, on a stepped rosewood veneered base, with brass marquetry inlaid front, shallow bun feet, glass dome cracked, 15½in (39cm) high.
£600–800 WW

Quality
The quality of skeleton clocks is of paramount importance. The wheelwork should be finely executed and the better clocks may have 5 or 6 spokes to each wheel instead of the usual 4 found on a bracket clock. Other signs of quality are well executed pendulums, finely turned pillars, decorative collet work, clickwork and well laid out dials.

A brass 'One-at-the-Hour' skeleton clock, with 7½in (18cm) brass chapter ring, Roman numerals, chain fusee going train with anchor escapement striking one at the hour on a bell, with ebonised wood stand, brass pendulum with lenticular bob, winding key and glass dome, 15½in (39cm) high.
£600–700 L

Table Clocks

A brass mounted mahogany chiming table clock, the 7½in (18.5cm) dial signed 'Bennett Bros. Liverpool', with shell and leaf spandrels and subsidiary dials in the arch for chime/silent, regulation and chime selection, 3 train fusee and chain movement chiming on 8 bells and a gong, c1900, 26in (66cm) high.
£1,800–2,200 *S*

A Victorian walnut and gilt brass striking table clock, the engraved silvered Roman dial signed 'Chas. Frodsham, Clockmaker to the Queen, 84 Strand, London 1880', blued spade hands, the 5 pillar twin chain fusee movement with anchor escapement and strike on gong, pendulum holdfast to the signed plain backplate, 13in (33cm).
£3,000–3,500 *C*

A brass inlaid mahogany musical table clock, the 9in (22.5cm) dial signed 'John Cross, Trowbridge', with seconds dial, engraved leaf spandrels and subsidiary dials in the arch for music/silent and tune selection, the 3 train fusee and chain movement bell, striking and repeating movement with deadbeat escapement, and playing one of 7 tunes on 13 bells, 28in (71cm) high.
£2,700–3,200 *S*

A German stained beech talking table clock, the 4½in (11cm) Arabic chapter ring set on a gilt surround stamped 'D.R.P.', and signed 'Henry Rüttimann Watchmaker, Lucerne Switzerland', the 8-day Gustav Becker movement 'No. 2225739' with pin pallet escapement attached to the large talking mechanism, with massive spring barrel and a spoked barrel driving a continuous loop film type record, controlled by a gramophone type governor, the sound box with cellulose diaphragm fitted to a papier mâché horn above, the mechanism released by the clock every half hour or at will, in a stained beech case flanked by double columns with plain brass capitals and brass fret around the top, film record broken, c1915, 16in (41cm) high.
£1,400–2,000 *S*

A mahogany chiming table clock, the 8½in (21cm) silvered chapter ring set on an engraved gilt surround, signed 'Maple & Co. Ltd., London', with subsidiary dials in the arch for chime/silent, regulation and chime selection, massive 3 train fusee and chain movement with anchor escapement and chiming on 8 bells or 4 gongs, with a further hour gong, in Chippendale revival case, c1910, 39½in (100cm).
£3,500–4,500 *S*

A mahogany table clock, with alarm, the 5in (12.5cm) painted dial signed 'Robt. Roskell Liverpool', with alarm dial in the arch, similarly signed fusee movement with anchor escapement, pull/wind alarm and engraved border to the backplate, c1820, 13in (33cm).
£1,200–1,700 *S*

A German silvered table clock, with 3 chapter rings, the centre ring showing minutes and inner quarters, flanked by 12 and 24 hour rings, linear fly back hour sector below signed 'Joseph Laminit', with steel arrow head hand, front swinging pendulum to the verge escapement, with automaton connection to a painted eye at the top, the movement with 4 ringed pillars and going barrel with later cover and stand, c1715, 13in (33cm).
£5,200–5,800 *C*

A French ebony veneered table clock, the 7in (17.5cm) gilt chapter ring set on a black velvet surround with flower spandrels, signed 'Baltazar Martinot A Paris', a hinged pendulum aperture cover below, the similarly signed movement with tandem drive from a single spring barrel, verge escapement with altered cycloidal cheeks, outside numbered count wheel and well pierced steel striking gates, the moulded case applied with cast brass mounts around the door, distressed, c1670, 14in (36cm).
£2,500–3,000 *S*

A copper gilt, brass and iron table clock, with alarm dial, blued metal lunar dial, subsidiary seconds dial and calendar dial, the spring driven movement with balance escapement, the drums richly engraved, striking the hours and quarters on 2 graduated bells, probable conversion and re-conversion from pendulum, early 17thC, possibly Dutch or German, 8in (20cm).
£17,000–19,000 *HSS*

A gilt brass mounted ebonised musical table clock, the 8in (20cm) dial with silvered and patterned chapter ring, with calendar aperture to the matted centre, the arch inset with a plaque signed 'Prior London', below a tune selection arc and flanked by subsidiary dials for strike/silent and chime/silent, the 3 train fusee and chain movement with verge escapement, bell striking and playing one of the 4 tunes at every hour, or at will, on 10 bells, c1780, 24in (61cm).
£7,500–8,500 *S*

An ormolu mounted red tortoiseshell table clock, the 6in (15cm) silvered arched dial with strike/silent dial below, 5 pillar 2 train fusee and chain bell striking movement, with anchor escapement and arched footed plates, the case veneered with red stained shell, c1800, 20in (50.5cm) high.
£2,000–2,500 *S*

A mahogany table clock, the 7½in (18.5cm) silvered break arch dial signed 'John Pollard, Plymouth Dock', with date aperture, strike/silent dial in the arch, the 5 pillar movement with twin fusees and verge escapement, 20in (50cm) high.
£1,200–1,700 *S(S)*

Wall Clocks

A late George III mahogany wall clock, the 11½in (29cm) dial signed 'John Good, London', with glazed brass bezel, engraved silvered Roman and Arabic dial, with black painted spade hands, the 4 pillar single fusee movement with A-shaped plates and verge escapement, 15½in (39.5cm) diam.
£1,500–2,000 *C*

A mahogany trunk dial wall clock, the 8¼in (20cm) painted wood dial signed 'J. Thwaites London', with cast brass bezel, fusee movement, ogee shouldered footed plates and anchor escapement, the case with moulded wood dial surround and under curved trunk incorporating a door, c1820, 14in (36cm) high.
£1,300–1,700 *S*

A mahogany wall clock, the 14in (35.5cm) dial signed 'T. R. Russell, Liverpool', with double fusee half hour striking movement, restored.
£1,500–1,700 *HAW*

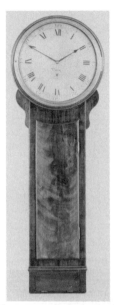

A mahogany wall clock, the 14in (35.5cm) brass dial signed 'John Gudgeon, Bury', with cast brass moulded concave bezel incorporating the lock, weight driven movement with large great wheel and anchor escapement, c1810, 49in (124.5cm).
£1,700–2,200 *S*

A George III green lacquered Act of Parliament clock, the 29in (74cm) white painted dial with Roman and Arabic chapters, pierced blued spade hands, the 4 pillar movement with tapered plates and anchor escapement, the case with raised gilt chinoiserie decoration, 58½in (148cm) high.
£1,700–2,200 *C*

The Tavern or Act of Parliament Clock

These terms are used virtually synonymously and refer to the large wall clocks made for the coaching inns and taverns throughout the country from c1740-1800. Their prime purpose was to provide local time and in particular to regulate the arrival and departure of the stage coaches which kept to surprisingly reliable schedules.

The diameter of the dials of these clocks was generally between 20in and 30in (50.5 and 76cm), and their overall length from 53in to 72in (134.5 and 182.5cm) and were not usually protected by any glazing.

Traditionally the cases were painted with black lacquer and decorated with ornamental scenes, but sometimes they were just left black and occasionally enlivened with gilt lines. It was only towards the end of the 18thC that mahogany cased clocks started to appear, frequently with glazed doors to the dial. The majority of tavern clocks had round dials but other shapes such as the octagonal and shield shapes were also used.

There is much debate as to why they were nearly always decorated with black lacquer and probably the simple answer is tradition. However, this finish would also have been far more practical in the smoke laden atmosphere of a pub than a finely polished mahogany case.

The term 'Act of Parliament clock' arose from the Act which was passed in 1797 putting a tax on all clocks and watches. This was two shillings and sixpence for a silver watch, ten shillings for a gold watch and five shillings for each clock.

The net result of this tax was that people stopped buying clocks and watches and concealed those they already had, thus producing an increased need for public clocks. This is exactly what tavern clocks had been made for in the first instance and is why they acquired the name 'Act of Parliament clock'.

Because of the dramatic fall in the sale of clocks and watches many makers faced bankruptcy. The King was petitioned and within a year of its introduction the Act was repealed.

A full striking black lacquer Act of Parliament clock, by Perinot, Paddington, with cream coloured dial and brass hands, Roman hour and Arabic minute numerals, with unusual full hour striking on a bell, substantial movement fitted with barrels, in oak case, c1770, 44in (111.5cm). **£8,000–9,000** *DRA*

A solid mahogany wall clock, the 14in (35.5cm) painted wood dial signed 'Walter Rowland, Berwick', with moulded mahogany bezel, weight driven movement with inverted Y-shaped plates, anchor escapement and double pulley arrangement, the narrow trunk with shaped top to the door and bombé plinth, with sliding front panel, c1800, 47in (119cm). **£2,000–3,000** *S*

A walnut cased drop dial wall clock, by J. Maple & Co., London. **£300–350** *JH*

A German drop trunk wall clock, half striking on a gong, in a walnut case with boxwood stringing, restored. **£500–550** *HAW*

A Victorian ebonised combination wall clock and barometer, the moulded case with panelled front displaying an aneroid barometer signed 'Cary, 181 Strand, London, 601' on the silvered dial, with steel hand and brass recorder, the flanking dial blued similarly signed, with Roman chapter ring and blued spade hands, regulation slide above XII, the 4 pillar single chain fusee movement with cut bi-metallic balance to lever platform, mercurial thermometer in the centre with silvered scale, frame 24in (61cm) wide. **£1,000–1,200** *C*

A French tôle peinte wall clock, the 5in (12.5cm) enamel dial signed 'Guillaume à Paris', bell striking silk suspension movement, the octagonal case of stepped form with scalloped upper section, the whole painted with flowers on a simulated wood ground, with ring handle, c1810, 15in (38cm) high. **£500–600** *S*

A French 2-day advertising clock, the 6in (15cm) dial inscribed 'Grand Magazins du Louvre, Paris', ribbon wound, restored.
£300–350 *HAW*

Miscellaneous

A French religieuse clock, by Marti et Cie, inlaid with brass and pewter with ormolu mounts, restored, 21in (53cm) high.
£2,250–2,500 *HAW*

A Swiss or English silver rhomboid desk compendium, retailed by Asprey, in a silver engine turned case containing an 8-day clock with enamel dial, an aneroid barometer, a hand set calendar indicating day, date and month, a hand set appointments dial with two 12 hour dials with dates, a compass, casemakers' initials 'M & Co. Ltd', hallmarked '1910', 3in (7.5cm) high.
£3,000–3,500 *S*

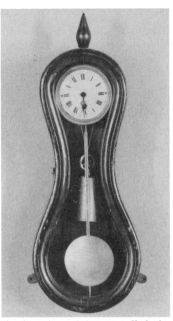

An Austrian miniature wall clock, with 2½in (6cm) enamel dial, weight driven movement, in a simulated rosewood waisted case, with a glazed door, weights replaced, 14in (35.5cm) high.
£1,200–1,700 *S*

A German carved beech cuckoo clock, the 5in (12.5cm) chapter ring with carved bone hands, 8-day 2 train fusee movement with posted wood movement, gong striking and sounding a cuckoo call at the hour, the carved case with 'tiled' roof applied with a fruiting vine and a bird, the front and base decorated with similar carving, a pair of doors above the dial opening to reveal a wooden bird with automaton wings and beak, the backboard with a 19thC label for 'Camerer Kuss & Co.', c1865, 18in (46cm) high.
£1,500–2,000 *S*

This clock came from W. T. Spencer, an antiquarian bookseller who had many dealings with Georgina Hogarth, Charles Dickens' sister-in-law. It is reputed to have been in the Swiss chalet built by Dickens in the grounds of Gads Hill Place. Mr. Spencer's name appears in pencil on the backboard together with repairers' marks dating from 1889.

An Austrian giltwood musical wall clock, with 6½in (16cm) enamel dial, 8-day spring barrel movement with circular plates, anchor escapement, silk suspension, sunburst pendulum and gong striking, a hand operated 2 tune musical mechanism below with 2in (5cm) pinned cylinder plucking a comb, comprising 18 separate screwed sections, in a giltwood picture frame case, with egg-and-dart moulded border surmounted by a carved eagle, c1830, 19½in (49.5cm) high.
£1,200–1,700 *S*

Cuckoo Clocks

Cuckoo Clocks were made in the Black Forest from c1850 until WWII.

Carefully inspect cases to ensure that all carvings are intact.

A bronze clock in the form of Big Ben, with 4 working dials, c1880, 35in (89cm) high.
£3,000–3,200 *ARE*

A battery powered pendulum clock, by Frank Holden, the 3½in (8.5cm) silvered chapter ring signed 'Apollo Patent' with visible hour wheel, the ratchet and pawl movement with 'free' pendulum oscillating over a permanent magnet with pivoted trailer contact, the whole supported on a brass column support rising from a walnut stand concealing the battery, with a glazed cover applied with a plaque engraved 'Frank Holden, pat.1909', 11⅓in (29cm).
£600–800 *S*

A Dutch marquetry staartklok, the arched dial with spandrels symbolising the seasons and painted with a canal scene, the alarm movement striking on a bell and in a posted frame, in floral marquetry case with Corinthian columns to the hood and pierced brass pendulum aperture, 39½in (100cm).
£1,200–1,700 *Bea*

A French falling ball gravity clock, with 7in (17.5cm) dial, the movement with Brocot escapement, the driving power produced by a supply of steel balls fed onto a large paddle wheel by an endless chain, driven by a concealed spring barrel movement, the rate supply controlled by a counter-balanced locking lever released by a ratchet wheel, mounted behind the paddle wheel, a grooved channel at the front for returning the used balls to the chain, the gilt brass frame applied with a thermometer and an aneroid barometer, the black marble plinth with gilt industrial mounts, c1890, with a later ebonised base and later cracked glass dome, 22½in (57cm) high.
£7,500–8,500 *S*

A French industrial automaton boiler clock, with 2½in (6.5cm) silvered dial, 8-day movement 'No. 2230', with platform cylinder escapement, the boiler case inset with an aneroid barometer and applied with a thermometer, a separate mechanism causing the governor to revolve above, on a black marble plinth, c1880, 14in (36cm) high.
£1,000–1,500 *S*

A French ormolu cartel clock, the 6½in (16.5cm) enamel dial signed 'F. Barbedienne A Paris', with bell striking movement and Brocot escapement, the case cast with garlands of berried leaves and trellis fretwork, surmounted by an urn, with later painted decoration, c1870, 28in (71cm).
£1,000–1,400 *S*

Cartel Clocks

Cartel clocks are a type of decorative spring-driven clock, usually with verge escapement.

They were produced in France during the late 18thC.

A French musical picture clock, the 8-day Raingo Frères gong striking movement with anchor escapement, releasing the independent musical movement on the hour, playing a tune on a pinned cylinder and a 71-tyne comb, c1840, 23 by 28in (58 by 71cm) overall.
£2,500–3,000 *S*

A hooded lantern clock, the brass 7in (17.5cm) break arch dial signed in the arch 'Geo. Lumley, Bury', with foliate engraving, single hour hand, the 30 hour movement of conventional posted construction with anchor escapement, top mounted bell, the associated mahogany bracket and hood with pagoda top, part 18thC, 30in (76cm) high.
£1,000–1,200 *S(S)*

This lantern clock would appear to have been converted to hooded form as there is evidence of side frets and a rear hanging hoop. The feet are later replacements leaving no sign of spurs.

A French bronzed spelter revolving movement mystery clock, the movement contained in a black painted sphere applied with Roman numerals and suspended from 3 chains pendant from an elaborate suspension held aloft by a cast figure of a girl, standing on a leaf cast and ebonised circular plinth, the upper pinion extended to engage with a fixed rod causing the movement to revolve, arm cracked, c1880, 27½in (70cm).
£3,500–4,000 *S*

Mystery Clocks

One of the most popular novelties of the 19thC is the mystery clock. The most common style shows a female figure holding a pendulum, which seems otherwise unconnected to the clock.

The movement causes the figure to rotate almost imperceptibly to the left and right. The motion set up causes the pendulum to swing, apparently unaided.

An George III ormolu quarter striking automaton, organ and carillon pagoda clock, attributed to James Cox, with 6½in (16cm) enamel dial, paste set bezel, centre seconds, 2 train movement with fusee and chain for the going train, standing barrel for the strike, cylinder escapement beating half seconds and striking on 2 bells, the massive automaton and musical movement stamped 'BWC' with double fusee and chain driving a 12in (30.5cm) long, brass cylinder 11in (28cm) diam, pinned for 3 tunes playing on 18 bells and/or a 35 pipe organ, a series of cams causing the jewelled 9 tier pagoda to rise, while 4 simulated waterfalls play below, with purpose-built ormolu mounted kingwood display cabinet, raised on slender feet. An invoice for the clock and the cabinet dated July 10th 1835 is included, c1775, 93in (236cm) high overall.
£350,000–400,000 *S*

An English or French miniature mahogany and inlaid longcase clock, with 2in (5cm) enamel dial, the movement with replaced platform escapement, the case with domed top and inlaid paterae, 12in (30.5cm).
£400–600 *S(S)*

Regulators

A regulator, by George Tight, London and Reading, with 8-day duration 5 pillar movement, deadbeat escapement and maintaining power, the 12in (30.5cm) silvered brass dial showing seconds, date and strike/silent, c1815, 82½in (209cm) high.
£7,350–8,350 *PAO*

A Georgian mahogany cased regulator, by Thomas Morgan of Edinburgh.
£2,000–2,500 *Mit*

A Georgian mahogany cased regulator, c1820.
£1,800–2,200 *Mit*

A late Victorian mahogany regulator, by George Wilson of Edinburgh, the silvered dial with subsidiary hours and seconds dials, the case carved with foliate scrolls and acanthus, fitted with a glazed door enclosing a mercury filled pendulum, the panelled base on a plinth, 82½in (209cm) high.
£4,000–5,000 *C(S)*

A mahogany regulator, the 11in (28cm) silvered dial with subsidiary seconds and hour dials, the 8-day movement with deadbeat escapement, the case with carved pediment, glazed trunk door and panel base, c1830, 82in (208cm) high.
£1,200–1,700 *S(S)*

A month-going domestic regulator, with annual calendar and passing quarter strike, two 14in (36cm) painted dials, the upper dial with a chapter ring enclosing subsidiary dials for seconds, date, day of the week and month, the lower dial signed 'John Woodwiss, Birmingham, 1862', 88½in (224cm) high.
£7,500–8,500 *S*

Regulators

The regulator is an extremely accurate weight-driven clock, either wall hung or free-standing, used as a standard of timekeeping for other clocks. Regulators were produced in England and France from the mid-18thC until around the end of the 19thC.

A regulator was usually found in the workshop of a clockmaker and in the shop of an important retailer. Large private houses with many clocks would also have owned at least one regulator. If the size of a collection justified it, a local clockmaker would visit every week to wind the clocks and adjust the settings, using the time indicated by the household's regulator.

A mahogany table regulator, by Tarault Jeune, Rue St. Denis Paris, the enamelled dial with centre sweep seconds, minute, hour and date hands, a substantial movement with external count wheel strike on a bell, pinwheel escapement and a 9 rod gridiron pendulum resting on a knife edge suspension, on replacement brass feet, early 19thC, 19in (48cm).
£10,000–12,000 *DRA*

Tarault Jeune is recorded in Tardys' register of French clockmakers as working in Paris from 1810-1820.

A weight-driven ebonised table regulator, by Robert Gibson, the 6in (15cm) painted dial with centre seconds, the hours and minutes dials contained within the seconds ring, the substantial movement signed 'Robert Gibson, Fecit London, No. 2,' with 4 fixing brackets, half deadbeat escapement, maintaining power and 6 spoke wheels, the steel rod pendulum with roller suspension, the flat lead weight with an integral pulley and suspended from the gut line carried on a pair of rollers above the movement and travelling down the back of the case, the arched case with a brass framed pendulum aperture, 15in (38cm).
£2,500–3,000 *S*

An early Victorian mahogany domestic regulator, with glazed gilt bezel to the circular silvered Roman dial with seconds ring at XII, the 4 pillar movement with deadbeat escapement and maintaining power, lacking pendulum and weight, 70in (178cm) high.
£1,700–2,200 *C*

Vienna Regulators

A German walnut and ebonised Vienna wall clock, with 3in (7.5cm) 2-piece enamel dial, 8-day open spring lantern pinion movement with wood rod pendulum, glazed case with shaped cresting and flanked by ebonised pilasters, restored, c1895, 20in (51cm).
£500–600 *S*

A rosewood Vienna regulator, the 8in (20cm) one-piece enamelled dial with blue Roman numerals and gilt decoration between and a pie-crust bezel, the 8-day movement with grande sonnerie striking on 2 gongs and with repeat and strike/silent regulation, the pendulum just less than seconds beating, c1845, 50in (127cm) high.
£11,000–12,000 *DRA*

Vienna Regulators

Vienna regulators are some of the most decorative wall clocks produced in the Austro-Hungarian Empire. Their unique style is a result of several different factors including an influx of Swiss craftsmen from 1780 onwards and the strong influence of the French which was reinforced by the marriage of Napoleon to Marie Louise of the House of Hapsburg in 1806. This gave rise to a renewed appreciation of classical proportions of which the Vienna regulator is an excellent example.

The first half of the 19thC might be considered as the golden age of Austrian clockmaking. The ingenuity of the clockmakers during that period was, on many occasions, quite exceptional, with clocks being produced with grande sonnerie striking, compensated pendulums, complex calendar work and often of long duration.

By 1860 the Vienna regulator had lost its finer classical proportions, being far more fussily decorated. By 1876 mass production had begun, spelling the death knell to the beautifully hand crafted pieces which had been produced until this time.

Watches

A silver quarter repeating verge pocket watch, with concealed erotic scene, 54mm dial.
£1,000–1,500 C

An English cylinder pocket watch, signed 'Thos Mudge/W. Dutton London, 1156', in a gilt consular case, full plate fire gilt movement with signed gilt dust cover, square baluster pillars, pierced and engraved masked cock, diamond endstone in a polished steel setting, fusee and chain with worm and wheel barrel setup between the plates, plain 3 arm polished steel balance, blue steel spiral hairspring, polished steel cylinder, large brass escape wheel, fitted in a contemporary gilt metal case covered with black leather, circular shutter to the winding aperture at the rear, c1770. £750–850 PT

A George III 18ct gold cased pocket watch, engine turned dial with matt chapter ring and wavy hands, Arabic numerals, keywind fusee verge movement with diamond endstone, signed 'Hawleys, London No. 1075', the case London 1810.
£300–400 DN

This watch is probably by J.T. Hawley & Co., watchmakers to the King, 1796-1825.

An 18ct gold free-sprung hunter pocket watch, by D. Glasgow, 20 Myddelton Square, London, No. 798, the dial chased and engraved and engine turned silvered, signed in a sector, gilt floral mounts, Roman numerals, subsidiary seconds, blued steel halberd hands, frosted gilt three-quarter plate jewelled to the centre with screwed chatons, free-sprung bi-metallic balance with flat blued steel hairspring and terminal curves, English lever escapement signed and numbered, with gold swivel key inset with semi-precious stone, hallmarked London 1869, 48mm, with original presentation box and spare glass.
£1,700–2,200 C

A late 17thC gilt oignon verge pocket watch, by Prevost à Paris, in plain gilt case, with gilt dial, inner enamelled half-hour ring, unusual winding through the single blued steel hand, signed movement, fusee chased and engraved cock showing mock pendulum, pierced Egyptian pillars, 55mm diam.
£2,000–2,500 C

A gentleman's silver pair cased open faced pocket watch, the silvered champlevé dial with Roman hour numerals, Arabic minute numerals, steel hand, the gilt fusee movement with a verge escapement, squared architectural pillars with scrolls at intervals, engraved and scroll pierced balance cock, the backplate signed 'HENY DEEME, HONITON, 2886', the inner case back initialled 'T.H.', plain outer case, minute hand missing, replacement base metal post and bow fittings, London 1759.
£400–500 S(S)

A Movado silver purse watch, with automatic wind, matt white dial with raised gilt numerals, gilt hands, inscribed 'Cartier', the movement signed 'Movado' with 15 jewels, screwed chatons and 4 adjustments, winding on ribbed and numbered '4256' opening case, with Cartier presentation box, 47 by 21mm.
£1,000–1,200 C

A pocket watch, the parcel gilt champlevé dial with Roman hour numerals and Arabic 5 minute markers, blued steel hands, fusee verge movement with engraved balance cock and elaborate leaf-shaped pierced pillars, signed 'R Colston, London, No. 780', the case with maker's mark 'SB' and numbered '780', the outer case missing, early 18thC.
£500–600 DN

An English gold and gilt metal pair cased cylinder pocket watch, the white enamel dial with Roman and Arabic numerals, gold beetle and poker hands, full plate fire gilt movement, signed gilt dust cover, turned pillars, pierced and engraved masked cock, diamond endstone in polished steel setting, silver regulator disc, fusee and chain with worm and wheel barrel set-up between the plates, Harrison's maintaining power, plain 3 arm polished steel balance, blue steel spiral hairspring, polished steel cylinder, large brass escape wheel, push pendant half quarter repeating on a bell in the case, gold inner case, push pendant and bow, purpose made engine turned gilt metal outer case, c1796.
£1,500–2,500 *PT*

Matthew and Thomas Dutton: in partnership 1796-9, sons of William Dutton who worked earlier in the century with Thomas Mudge. The Dutton family appears to have continued to use the worm and wheel barrel set-up longer than other watchmakers of the period. The original outer case would probably have been of gilt metal covered in shagreen pierced with round holes to allow the sound of the bell to escape.

An Irish verge watch, signed 'May & Son Dublin', in a very large silvered open face case, white enamel 116mm dial with Roman numerals and gilt hands, full plate fusee watch movement with round pillars, pierced and engraved round cock, steel regulator on top plate below the plain 3 arm steel balance, substantial plain silvered open face case, c1810.
£700–800 *PT*

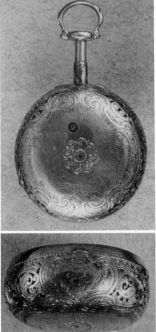

A gold and enamel verge pocket watch, by Vaucher à Paris No. 9584, signed white enamel dial, with Roman numerals and Arabic 5 minute divisions, gold decorative hands, signed and numbered frosted gilt fusee verge movement, painted enamel case with seed pearls to the rim and bezel, the band decorated with a gold and seed pearl twist design, late 18thC, 36mm diam.
£1,000–1,200 *C*

A gold open face keyless cylinder pocket watch, by Patek Philippe & Co., Geneve, No. 71737, the signed white enamel dial with Arabic numerals and blued steel hands, frosted gilt bar, jewelled to the third with wolf-tooth winding and cylinder escapement, the case signed and numbered to the back cover and cuvette, the reverse and band chased and engraved, 32mm diam.
£700–900 *C*

A silver verge pocket watch, by Louis Prevost, silver dial, signed on chased and engraved cartouche, single blued steel hand, frosted gilt fusee signed movement, finely pierced cock and chased foot, pierced Egyptian pillars, with green synthetic material pinwork case, early 18thC, 52mm diam.
£1,000–1,500 *C*

A minute repeating gold full
hunter Swiss lever watch, signed
'Fernand Bonnet Chaux-de-Fonds,
Watch Manufacturers, Hong
Kong Shanghai TienTsin
Repetition a Minutes, London',
gilt split three-quarter plate
keyless movement with going
barrel, plain cock with polished
steel regulator, uncut
bi-metallic balance with overcoil
hairspring, club foot lever
escapement, slide minute
repeating on 2 polished steel
gongs, visible repeating train
regulator, blue steel hands,
engine turned 18ct full hunter
case with ribbed middle, signed
gold cuvette, c1885.
£1,700–2,200 PT

A pocket watch, with verge escapement, by
George Fowler Horncastle, No. 54310.
£300–350 W

An English silver pair cased verge
watch, with champlevé dial
signed 'Hen. Perry, St Annes,
Soho, London, 319', deep full plate
fire gilt movement, Egyptian
pillars surmounted by a gallery,
fusee and chain with worm and
wheel barrel set-up between the
plates, pierced and engraved
winged cock with pierced and
engraved foot, plain steel balance,
silver regulator disc, matching
silver pair cases, silver pendant
and bow bearing the number
corresponding to that on the
movement, maker's mark 'CW'
under a crown, c1705.
£1,000–1,500 PT

A large Swiss
lever
chronograph,
with minute
recording split
seconds, in a
nickel open face
case, signed
'Lemania', c1940.
£700–800 PT

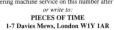

A gold half quarter repeater
pocket watch, by Frodsham, in
a gold full hunter case, with
maker's mark 'LC' in an oval,
with 12in (30.5cm) gold chain,
acking buttonhole bar,
hallmarked London 1845.
£1,000–1,500 PT

An 18ct gold cased open faced pocket watch, the gilt dial with Roman numerals on an engine turned ground in a foliate border, plain gilt hands, the gilt fusee movement with a verge escapement, mask engraved balance cock, the backplate signed 'E.J. & W. Marshall, North Bridge, Edinburgh, 1163', the case with foliate moulded rims, otherwise engine turned, London 1823.
£300–350 *S(S)*

A silver gilt and glass panelled octagonal verge pocket watch in 17thC style, with engraved dial plate with floral motifs, raised silvered chapter ring with Roman numerals and shaped blued steel hour hand, with turned pillars, engraved top plate with floral decoration, inscribed 'Simon Bartram fecit', pierced and engraved cock and foot, fusee with gut line, balance wheel and staff lacking, 19thC.
£1,500–2,000 *C*

A Swiss lever watch, signed 'A Kaiser Patent' with digital dial, in a nickel open face case, keyless gilt bar movement with going barrel, plain cock with polished steel regulator, uncut bi-metallic balance with blue steel overcoil hairspring, signed engine turned gilt dial with a border of engraved decoration, digital indication of hours, minutes and subsidiary seconds, the minutes change instantaneously as the seconds hand passes 60, fitted in a contemporary plain nickel open face case with screw back and bezel, c1890, 51mm diam.
£400–500 *PT*

A gold hunter cased keyless pocket watch, by Vacheron & Constantin, the brushed gilt dial with Arabic numerals, subsidiary seconds, frosted gilt bar with mono-metallic balance, signed and numbered '380609' movement, the case with maker's mark and numbered '241727', 50mm diam.
£1,500–2,000 *C*

A gold and enamel cylinder open face pocket watch, by LeRoy & Fils, Hgers du Roi à Paris, No. 16316, with frosted gilt bar with cylinder escapement and ruby endstone movement, the case signed and numbered to the cuvette '47482', early 18thC, 42mm diam.
£1,000–1,200 *C*

A gold quarter repeating open face cylinder pocket watch, by Milleret à Geneve, the dial with Roman numerals, blued steel moon hands, signed frosted gilt bar with cylinder escapement, repeating on 2 gongs operated by a slide in the band, 34mm.
£750–950 *C*

A Swiss calendar lever, signed 'Quantième Suisse B^te S. D. G. E.' in a silver open face case with a faded monogram on the back cover, signed white enamel dial with subsidiaries for day, date and seconds, gilt hands, keyless nickelled bar movement with going barrel, plain cock with blue steel regulator, uncut bi-metallic balance with spiral hairspring, club foot lever escapement, fully restored, c1880, 50mm diam.
£200–300 *PT*

A Continental gilt and enamel and paste set verge pocket watch, with white enamel dial, with Roman numerals and Arabic 5 minute divisions, blued steel hands, frosted gilt fusee movement with bridge cock, 41mm diam.
£750–950 *C*

A Swiss verge watch, in a silver open face case, full plate gilt fusee movement, finely pierced and engraved bridge cock with steel coqueret, plain 3 arm gilt balance with blue steel spiral hairspring, silver regulator dial with blue steel indicator, round pillars, winding through the white enamel dial, Roman numerals, blue steel hands, purpose made engine turned silver open face case, maker's mark 'ROJE' in an oval and London hallmark for 1850, 27mm diam.
£400–500 *PT*

A Swiss double-sided verge watch, signed 'Jn Ls Bourquin', with calendar and fly back hour hand, the minute hand is offset and rotates as normal once every hour, the hour hand unusually travels from 6 o'clock on the left to 6 o'clock on the right and then flies back again, plain silver case glazed on both sides, silver pendant and bow, full plate gilt fusee movement, c1780.
£4,000–4,500 *PT*

A Swiss verge pocket watch, in a fine gold and enamel consular case with matching chatelaine, key and seal, full plate gilt fusee movement, finely pierced and engraved bridge cock with steel coqueret, plain 3 arm gilt balance with blue steel spiral hairspring, silver regulator dial with blue steel indicator, c1780.
£500–550 *PT*

Complete matching chatelaines and watches are rarely found, especially in such outstanding condition. The condition, and the blank seal suggest this watch may have remained unsold as part of a retailer's stock.

An 18ct gold fob/pocket watch, half hunter, with enamelled chapter ring on front cover, in working order, dated 'Birmingham 1894'.
£250–300 *DA*

A slim gold open face cylinder pocket watch, the engine turned silvered 38mm dial with polished chapter ring and Roman numerals, regulation above the XII, blued steel moon hands, frosted gilt bar with cylinder escapement and ruby endstone movement, engine turned snap-on back with aperture for the male key revealed by pressing a button in the pendant, engine turned band and bezel, with presentation box inscribed 'Comte Diedrichstein', early 19thC.
£700–900 *C*

A silver quarter repeating automata open face pocket watch, with blue enamel dial plate with central white dial and Arabic numerals, mounted with 2 gilt jacquemarts apparently striking on bells, frosted gilt, fusee, verge with bridge cock repeating quarter hours on 2 gongs operated by the pendant, 55mm diam.
£1,000–1,200 *C*

Wristwatches

A Rolex Oyster 9ct gold wrist gentleman's watch, 1945.
£1,500–2,000 *HOLL*

A Rolex Oyster Perpetual lady's 18ct gold wristwatch, the dial with gilt Arabic and arrow-shaped numeral indicators, plain hands and subsidiary seconds, domed bubble milled case back, with a black strap and gilt Rolex buckle, with fitted case.
£1,200–1,700 *S(S)*

An Omega 9ct gold gentleman's wristwatch, with Swiss 17 jewel manual wind movement and integral 9ct gold bracelet.
£270–320 *DA*

A Rolex Oyster 18ct gold automatic wristwatch, with day/date function, matching 18ct gold bracelet.
£2,000–2,750 *DA*

A gentleman's 18ct gold wristwatch, signed by Vacheron & Constantin, Geneva, with silvered dial, gilt baton numeral indicators, subsidiary seconds and gilt hands, on a brown strap.
£950–1,300 *S(S)*

A Bueche Girod lady's gold wristwatch, malachite dial, movement jewelled to the third with 17 jewels, signed, with matching integral flexible gold bracelet.
£800–900 *C*

A gold wristwatch, by International Watch Co., the matt white dial with raised Arabic quarter-hour numerals and baton 5-minute divisions, sweep centre seconds, the case with maker's mark and numbered '1320458', jewelled movement signed and numbered '1318856'.
£800–900 *C*

A Rolex Cellini 18ct gold wristwatch, brushed gilt dial with raised baton numerals, the signed movement jewelled to the third with 19 jewels, the case with maker's mark and numbered '757 7 85 4292176', with integral flexible gold bracelet, maker's presentation box and guarantee.
£1,200–1,700 *C*

A Rolex Oyster gentleman's steel and silver wristwatch, the signed white enamelled dial with black Arabic numerals, subsidiary seconds and blued steel hands, the jewelled movement detailed 'Rolex Ultra Prima', the screw-off milled case back import marked 'Glasgow 1928', apparently rhodium plated inside, the case frame steel, the milled front bezel rhodium plated silver, hour hand damaged, on a textile strap.
£800–1,000 *S(S)*

A gold Rolex chronometer wristwatch, the silvered dial with Roman numerals and outer 5 minute ring, movement timed to 6 positions, the case with maker's mark and numbered 4497, with maker's mark and numbered 'E 22348'.
£2,200–2,700 *C*

A gold wristwatch, by International Watch Co., brushed silvered dial with raised Arabic quarter-hour marks and dagger 5-minute divisions, sweep centre seconds, the case with down-turned lugs, snap-on back, maker's mark and numbered '1185712', jewelled movement signed and numbered '1163124'.
£650–800 *C*

A lady's gold and diamond set wristwatch, by Baume & Mercier, Geneva, movement with 17 jewels, signed and numbered 'BM777', the case with maker's mark and numbered '38393 9 1065238', with integral gold woven bracelet.
£1,200–1,500 *C*

A steel triple calendar and moonphase wristwatch, by Universal, Geneva, two-tone silvered dial with Arabic numerals, day aperture, subsidiary dials for running seconds, date and month, sector for phases of the moon, movement jewelled to the third, with 17 jewels, signed and numbered '231776', the case with maker's mark and numbered.
£700–900 *C*

Miscellaneous

A Jaeger-LeCoultre gold alarm Memovox wristwatch, the silvered dial with raised dagger numerals, recessed centre with alarm ring, sweep centre seconds, the case with maker's mark and numbered '595231', the jewelled movement signed and numbered '851012'.
£1,000–1,200 *C*

A Continental brass watch stand, in the form of a snake with open jaws, its tongue forming the hook for a watch, 19thC, 4½in (11.5cm) high. **£750–900** *S*

An Indian ivory and steel inlaid watch stand, the domed arch supported by 4 pillars with ivory filigree decoration, finials and watch stand, the stepped base with ivory and steel inlay, on 4 brass ball feet, c1850, 12in (30.5cm) high. **£340–440** *S*

BAROMETERS

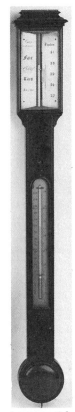

A mahogany bowfronted cased barometer, by Dollond, London, with ogee top moulding and ebonised cistern cover, the silvered brass scale reading from 27in to 31in, the vernier with ivory key, the centrally mounted thermometer with both fahrenheit Reaumur scales, maker's name engraved with cross-hatching, c1825.
£5,400–5,800 *PAO*

A walnut stick barometer, by Bennett, London, the scale showing weather notations, and reading from 27in to 31in operated by brass setting key, c1850.
£1,200–1,400 *PAO*

A Georgian mahogany stick barometer, by Thos. Blunt & Son, London, c1810.
£2,800–3,000 *W&W*

A mahogany stick barometer, the silvered plates signed 'Cary, 181 Strand, London', mid-19thC, 38½in (97cm) high.
£1,400–1,700 *S(S)*

A Victorian stick barometer, the rosewood veneered case with a glazed domed ivory dial, with vernier scale and thermometer, inscribed 'F. A. Pizzola, Optician, 7 Charles Street, Hatton Garden', the base with a half ball cover to the well.
£550–600 *WW*

A mahogany flame veneered stick barometer, by J. Jenkins, Swansea, signed under scales 'Tagliabue & Casella, London', the bone scales reading from 27in to 31in, with vernier operated by original ivory key, the thermometer showing both fahrenheit and centigrade scales, c1840. **£1,000–1,250** *PAO*

This barometer was made by the London partnership of Caesar Tagliabue and Louis Casella, and supplied to Jenkins of Swansea who would have sold it as their own make.

A mahogany stick barometer, the ivory plates signed 'Chadburn Brothers, Sheffield, Registered Oct 14th 1851, No. 2980, No. 168', mercury thermometer, the case with flat top and half-turned cistern cover, c1855, 38in (96cm) high.
£500–700 *S(S)*

A Victorian mahogany marine barometer, signed 'Elliott Brothers, Charing Cross, London' on a plaque above the register plates, with hinged door, the plain shaft terminating in a brass mercury bulb, 37½in (95cm) high.
£1,000–1,500 *C*

A provincial mahogany stick barometer, by Smith, Kington, the case with fan and star inlay and boxwood string edging, the brass silvered scale engraved 27in to 31in, and 10°-100°F with weather notations, c1780.
£1,650–1,850 *PAO*

A mahogany stick barometer, by Dollond, London, the top with ivory paterae and finial, the silvered brass scale reading 27in to 31in, with access to vernier by lockable glazed door, c1800.
£1,650–1,850 *PAO*

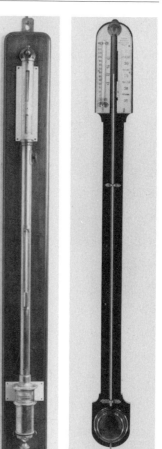

A brass cased Fortin stick barometer, on a mahogany backboard, c1890.
£800–900
W&W

An oak carved bowfronted stick barometer, by Chamberlain, London, c1865.
£1,200–1,400 *W&W*

A mahogany model barometer, with ivory plates, c1870.
£600–700 *W&W*

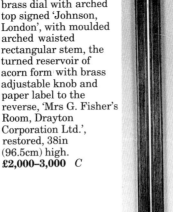

An Admiral Fitzroy's oak cased barometer, with arched carved top, fitted interior with Victorian lozenge marked 'No 367815', 19thC, 42in (106.5cm) high.
£250–350 *GH*

A walnut double angle stick barometer, with wooden and paper scales, the cistern adjusted by a screw to give weather indications, in a plain case with carved pediment, c1900, 41½in (105cm) high.
£300–400 *S(S)*

A Regency mahogany stick barometer, signed 'Cary, London'.
£700–900 *LT*

A George III stick barometer, by T. Naylor, Halifax, with flower painted plates, and bulb cistern, in mahogany, crossbanded and marquetry inlaid case, with scrolled pediment, glazed door, and oval cover with paterae, 38½in (97cm) high.
£1,200–1,400 *AH*

A George III mahogany stick barometer, the brass dial with arched top signed 'Johnson, London', with moulded arched waisted rectangular stem, the turned reservoir of acorn form with brass adjustable knob and paper label to the reverse, 'Mrs G. Fisher's Room, Drayton Corporation Ltd.', restored, 38in (96.5cm) high.
£2,000–3,000 *C*

A Dutch walnut barometer, the pewter plate inscribed 'J. Stopanni Fect Amsterd', with thermometer and mercury U-tube, in typical chequer inlaid case with architectural pediment surmounted by a wood urn finial, 50in (127cm) high.
£400–600 *C*

A mahogany wheel barometer, by A. Tacchi, Bedford, the case with ebony edge stringing, crossbanded sides, the thermometer engraved brass scale reading from 10°-110°F, c1800.
£650–850 *PAO*

A shell inlaid mahogany wheel barometer, by Stampa, London, c1815.
£780–880 *W&W*

A Regency mahogany clock barometer, with hygrometer dial, detachable mercurial thermometer below, the spirit level below signed on the silvered plaque 'G. Rossi Norwich', 51in (130cm) high.
£3,000–4,000 *C*

A mahogany cased barometer, by Stanislao Catteli, London, with fan inlay and triple boxwood and ebony stringing, 2in crossbanded sides, the 8in (20cm) silvered brass dial reading 28in to 31in, and 0°-100°F, with weather indications around outer edge, glazed brass concave bezel, c1790.
£1,450–1,650 *PAO*

A mahogany wheel barometer, by Josh. Somalvico, London, c1790.
£1,800–2,000 *W&W*

A bird's-eye maple '5 dial' wheel barometer, by Evans, Carmarthen, c1850.
£600–800 *W&W*

A satinwood wheel barometer, by Saltery, London, c1825.
£900–1,200 *W&W*

A mahogany 10in (25cm) dial wheel barometer, by Dollond, London, c1840.
£1,200–1,500 *W&W*

A mahogany 6in (15cm) wheel barometer, by Northen, Hull.
£1,200–1,600 *W&W*

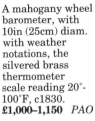

A mahogany wheel barometer, with 10in (25cm) diam. with weather notations, the silvered brass thermometer scale reading 20°-100°F, c1830.
£1,000–1,150 *PAO*

A wheel barometer, by Corti & Son, London, the 8in (20cm) silvered brass scale reading from 28in to 31in,
£1,000–1,350 *PAO*

A Regency rosewood cased brass inlaid banjo barometer, by M. Barnascone of Leeds, the humidity, temperature, barometer and levelling dials all silvered, with convex mirror, 37in (94cm) high.
£300–375 *DA*

A William IV brass inlaid rosewood wheel barometer, the case with swan's neck cresting and set with a hygrometer, the 8in (20cm) silvered dial signed 'F. Amadio & Son, 118 St. John St. Rd. London', an alcohol thermometer and spirit level, the whole outlined in brass stringing and inlaid with brass foliage, c1840, 39in (99cm) high.
£900–1,200 *S*

A mahogany wheel barometer, with broken pediment, hygrometer, thermometer box, 10in (25cm) silvered dial, butler's mirror, 19thC, 42in (106.5cm) high.
£200–300 *GH*

A miniature barometer, c1890, 13in (33cm) high.
£400–500 *ARE*

A Victorian carved giltwood barometer, signed 'Watt, London', c1870, 36in (91.5cm) high.
£2,000–2,500 *ARE*

A recording aneroid barometer, with enamelled dial and blued steel needle, over silvered scale divided into days of the week and various pressures, with rack-and-pinion daily pointers, in ebonised case with brass handle, 9in (22cm) high.
£450–500 *CSK*

Barographs

A barograph, by C. W. Dixey & Son, with dial, mechanism and recording drum, in glazed mahogany case with drawer in base containing spare charts, ink bottle missing, c1910, 14½in (37cm) wide.
£900–1,000 *S*

A barograph, by Negretti & Zambra, with clockwork revolving graph barrel, inking armature and mercury thermometer, in glazed oak case with graph storage drawer in the base, early 20thC, 19in (49cm) wide.
£800–900 *S*

A mahogany banjo barometer, by A. Maspoli of Hull, ebony and boxwood string inlaid, with silvered humidity and thermometer dials over a convex mirror and silvered barometer and levelling dials, 19thC.
£300–400 *DA*

A barograph, by Horne & Thornthwaite, with mechanism, recording pen, bevelled glazed cover, on oak plinth base with drawer, 14in (35cm) wide.
£350–450 *CSK*

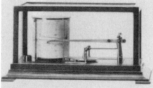

A lacquered brass barograph, with mechanism, drum and recording pen, in glazed oak case with plinth base, retailer's label 'A. J. Harrison, Birmingham', 14in (36cm) wide.
£300–400 *CSK*

A barograph, in a moulded oak case with drawer, c1890.
£900–1,000 *W&W*

A Victorian mahogany wheel barometer, the case with swan's neck cresting, set with a thermometer, 8in (20cm) silvered dial signed 'Thos Jones, 62 Charing Cross', the whole veneered in well-figured wood outlined in ebony stringing, c1845, 41in (104cm) high.
£600–700 *S*

Thomas Jones, an eminent instrument maker, was working at 62 Charing Cross between 1816-50.

A barograph/thermograph, by Negretti & Zambra, with lacquered brass mechanism, drum, recording pen and ink bottles, in glazed oak case with drawer in base containing instructions and charts, 14½in (37cm) wide.
£580–620 *CSK*

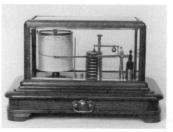

A miniature barograph, with
laterally mounted capsules, in a
mahogany case, c1890.
£1,000–1,500 *W&W*

A barograph, with thermometer,
in an oak case, c1900.
£600–700 *W&W*

A lacquered brass barograph,
with drum, recording pen and ink
bottle, in glazed mahgoany case
on plinth base, 13in (33cm) wide.
£300–400 *CSK*

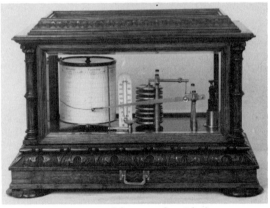

A barograph, with thermometer,
in a carved oak case, c1890.
£1,200–1,800 *W&W*

A barograph, with lacquered
brass mechanism, drum,
recording pen, ink bottle and pen
adjustment, in glazed oak case on
plinth base, 10in (26cm) wide.
£250–350 *CSK*

A barograph, by Negretti &
Zambra, the lacquered brass
instrument with drum, recording
pen and glazed oak case on plinth
base, ink bottle missing, 13in
(34cm) wide, with a quantity
of graphs.
£300–400 *CSK*

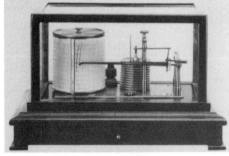

A lacquered brass barograph, by
Casella, London, with clockwork
mechanism, recording pen and
ink bottle, in glazed mahogany
case with drawer in base, 14½in
(37cm) wide, with instructions,
spare cylinder, charts and pen.
£500–600 *CSK*

A barograph, with twin capsules,
in an ebonised case, c1890.
£900–1,200 *W&W*

SCIENTIFIC INSTRUMENTS
Dials

A brass inclining dial, signed 'G. Adams London', with engraved compass rose, hinged hour ring, gnomon and latitude arc, the base engraved with 11 European capitals and their latitudes, late 18thC, 4½in (11cm) wide.
£600–800 *S*

A brass mining dial, by A. Abraham & Co., Liverpool, with silvered dial, edge bar needle, level, cross bubble, folding sights, cover and staff mount, 12in (30.5cm) wide.
£200–250 *CSK*

A brass mining dial, by Bate, London, with cover engraved with scales for 'Diff of Hypo & Base', silvered dial, edge bar needle, clamp, removable sights and staff mounting, in fitted wood case, 8in (20cm) wide.
£200–250 *CSK*

A bronze sundial, signed in cartouche 'Cary London' the plate divided with hour scale VIII-XII-IIII, months and cardinal point, the outer ring divided in degrees in 6 sectors, the hour ring sub-divided with 32 locations for countries and cities, including Boston, Amer., Constantinople, Siam and Mexico, with engraved compass rose and monogram, gnomon replaced, late 18thC, 18in (46cm) diam.
£2,000–2,500 *CSK*

A brass mining dial, by Bleuler, London, with edge bar needle and replacement sights, 11in (28cm) long, in part shaped, fitted wood case.
£160–200 *CSK*

A lacquered and silvered brass compass/sundial/thermometer, by C.W. Dixey, with folding gnomon, the hour ring divided IIII-XII-VIII, the latitude arc engraved 0°-60°, the compass with paper dial, with edge bar needle on pivot, the base with silvered dial divided into Fahrenheit and Reaumur, with top and bottom covers, 3in (7.5cm) diam.
£600–700 *CSK*

A Universal Equinoctial ring dial, signed 'E. Nairne, London', the engraved instrument for northern and southern latitudes, the meridian ring with 2 latitude arcs reading to 30°, the reverse and the hour ring with nautical ring reading to 1°, with reversed graduation of the double scale, the bridge engraved with zodiac calendar scale and fitted with sliding cursor, with adjustable suspension mount with swivel and steel ring, late 18thC, 6in (15cm) diam.
£2,700–3,200 *S*

A lacquered brass mining dial, by J. Davis, Derby, with silvered dial, edge bar needle, level, cross bubble, folding sights, cover and staff mount, 10in (25cm) wide, in fitted woodcase, and a tripod.
£250–300 *CSK*

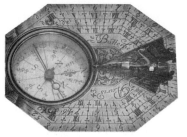

A French silver dial signed 'Butterfield à Paris', the plate with inset compass rose, mounted with shaped gnomon with bird pointer, 4 hour scales for latitudes 43, 46, 49 and 52°, the base engraved with 30 European cities and their latitudes, 3in (7.5cm) long, in green velvet lined leather covered base, early 18thC.
£1,200–1,700 *S*

A Müller gilt brass universal equinoctial dial, engraved with initials 'L.T.M.', the octagonal plate with inset compass well and mounted with hinged latitude arc, hour ring and gnomon, Augsberg, mid-18thC, 2in (5cm) diam, in leather case.
£350–400 *S*

A brass universal equinoctial ring dial, the meridian ring divided 90°-0°-80°, the pivoted equinoctial ring divided XII-I-XII hours, the reverse divided 0°-90°, the bridge with sliding pinhole sight against calendrical, zodiacal and declination scales, with suspension ring, 9in (23cm) diam.
£2,200–2,700 *CSK*

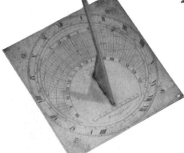

A brass double horizontal dial, signed 'H. Sutton fecit 1660', the square dial with engraved hour scale divided III-XII-VII reading to 10 minutes, the concentric inner degree scale reading to 1° within which is engraved an horizontal projection of the sphere for 56° 30 minutes latitude and engraved with the arcs of the ecliptic, 8in (20cm) square.
£6,000–7,000 *S*

This is a rare type of dial of which less than 20 examples are known to survive. The latitude of this dial is appropriate for places in central Scotland, the most likely being Dundee or perhaps Arbroath.

A gilt brass and silver universal equinoctial dial, signed on the base 'Johann Willebrand in Augspurg 48', the plate with inset compass well, mounted with hinged latitude arc, plumb-bob and support and hour arc with gnomon, the base engraved with 40 European cities and their latitudes, c1725, 2in (5cm) diam.
£2,500–3,500 *S*

A German gilt brass and silver sun and moon string gnomon dial, signed 'Johann Martin in Aigspurg', the base carrying an applied circular hour scale reading to 30 minutes, within this an age of the moon scale and within this an adjustable hour scale without sub-divisions, at the centre is mounted an underslung compass with 4 point wind rose and magnetic declination mark, the underside of the compass box engraved with the names and latitudes of 17 European towns, a folding plumb holder attached to one side of the plate and serves as a support for the upper end of the string gnomon, which may be adjusted for latitudes between 45° and 50°, late 17thC, 2⅓in (6cm) diam, in original octagonal metal box. **£5,000–6,000** *S*

When used as a lunar dial the hour is taken from the main hour scale by the position of the shadow of the gnomon by moonlight. The rotatable hour scale is then turned until this value is opposite the value of the age of the moon for the night of observation. The value on the main outer hour scale opposite the age of the moon then gives a direct reading of the time in solar reckoning.

A Troughton & Simms brass mining dial, with silvered dial, edge bar needle, bubble level, cross bubble and folding sights, in fitted pine case, 12½in (31.5cm) wide.
£300–500 *CSK*

A French lacquered and silvered brass universal equinoctial compass/sundial, the brass ring with spring gnomon and folding latitude arc, the silvered compass with part blued needle, jewelled cap and clamp, the horizontal plate engraved with the names and latitudes of 5 French cities, with level, cross bubble and 3 adjustable feet, in fitted mahogany case, late 19thC, 6in (15cm) wide.
£500–600 *CSK*

An F.L. West lacquered and silvered brass compass dial, with folding gnomon, the hour ring divided IIII-XII-VIII, the latitude arc engraved 0°-60°, the compass with paper dial and blued needle, engraved on the underside 'Tibetexpedition Schlagintweit', in plush-lined leather case with applied paper calendar, 3in (8cm) diam.
£800–900 *CSK*

A white metal imitation nocturnal dial, the face with inset rotatable disc within a decorative border, carrying a month scale, second toothed disc with hour scale and spurious Latin inscriptions, index arm at the centre, reverse with pictorial zodiac signs and central adjustable aspectarium, 20thC, 7in (17.5cm) diam.
£500–600 *S*

A French pattern lacquered and silvered brass universal equinoctial compass/sundial, signed on the underside of the compass box 'Solomons & Co., Calcutta' the compass dial with part blued needle with jewelled cap and clamp, the hour ring with spring loaded pin gnomon and folding latitude arc, the base plate engraved with the latitudes for Canton, Calcutta, Bombay, Pekin and Yedo, with level, cross bubble and 3 adjustable feet, in fitted mahogany case, 19thC, 7in (17.5cm) wide.
£650–800 *CSK*

A brass universal equinoctial ring dial, the meridian ring with sliding suspension ring, engraved on one face with scale for northern and southern latitudes, 83°-0°-90° by 1°, for use as an altitude quadrant with plumb line originally secured to the pivoted equinoctial ring with hour scale twice marked 12 hours in Roman numerals divided to ⅛th of an hour, the bridge with sliding pinhole sight, with scale of months and zodiac scale with declination, divided to 1°, the Vernal Equinox given as 10 March, 4in (10cm) diam.
£1,200–1,500 *CSK*

The form of the engraved numerals resembles those found on instruments signed by Thomas Wright (1686-1748), Mathematical Instrument maker to George, Prince of Wales from 1718.

A French ivory magnetic azimuth diptych dial, signed on the lower brass disc, 'Charles Bloud à Dieppe', the upper outer dial with pin gnomon dial, upper inner face with volvelle, lower inner face with analemmatic magnetic dial with eliptical hour scale adjusted from lower face, the base well-engraved and decorated with calendar scale, late 17thC, 2⅜in (6cm) wide when closed.
£2,000–2,500 *S*

A French horizontal dial and noon gun, the gilt and silvered brass instrument signed 'Lafontaine 18 Palais Royal Galerie, Paris', with black painted cannon, quadrant supports to lens with altitude adjustment, the base with inset compass and bubble levels and engraved single latitude horizontal dial, in maker's leather covered case, c1840, 3in (7.5cm) diam.
£2,000–2,500 *S*

Globes

A 1½in terrestrial globe, coloured gores printed 'Newton & Son's New Terrestrial Globe', in turned mahogany stand under domed lid, mid-19thC. **£1,500–2,000** *S*

A 2in terrestrial pocket globe, the coloured gores printed 'Newtons New Terrestrial Globe 1818', contained in fishskin case with print of the moon and earth phases applied to the interior.
£3,000–3,500 *S*

A Cary celestial globe,
for the year 1800.
£800–1,000 *CAI*

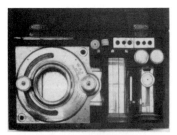

A Johann Bernard Bauer terrestrial and celestial 2¾in
pocket globe, the outer wooden sphere applied with
hand coloured gores of the heavens, opening at the
equator to a smaller sphere applied with terrestrial,
some damage, 1821, celestial sphere.
£1,000–1,200 *S*

A 4½in terrestrial globe, by Alex
Donaldson of Edinburgh,
mounted in a brass meridian
within horizontal ring of calendar
and zodiac scale, on turned
ebonised supports, early 19thC,
8in (20cm) high.
£1,700–2,200 *CAG*

A 2¾in pocket terrestrial globe,
the sphere applied with hand
coloured gores and printed with
Anson's Tract and within
cartouche 'A New Terrestrial
Globe by Nath Hill 1754', in
fishskin covered case with
coloured print of the heavens
applied to the 2 inner surfaces,
scratches and scuff marks, 1754.
£3,300–3,700 *S*

A 12in (30.5cm) Dudley Adams
terrestrial globe on brass stand,
the solid sphere applied with
hand coloured gores, printed
within floral bordered cartouche
with inscription to George III,
the sphere mounted with brass
armilliary sphere with equator
engraved with circle of degrees
and named Arctic Circle, Tropic
of Cancer, Tropic of Capricorn
and Antartic Circle, meridians
engraved with degrees of latitude
and broad ring engraved with
calendar and zodiac scales, the
whole raised on later brass stand
with horizontal ring engraved
with calendar, zodiac and degree
scales, the later stretchers
centred by compass rose and
needle, late 18thC, 27in (69cm)
high. **£13,000–18,000** *S*

Microscopes

A W. & S. Jones, London,
lacquered brass solar microscope,
with coarse screw mirror
adjustment, condenser body tube,
barrel with rack-and-pinion
focusing and screw mounted wood
handle, in fitted mahogany case
containing objective bar 1-6,
3 condenser bars numbered '1 &
2', '3 & 4' and '5 & 6', ivory talc
box, stage forceps and other items.
£900–1,200 *CSK*

A pocket microscope, the
mahogany case with racked
column screwing into the front,
signed 'Cary, London', with
reflector, forceps, 2 objectives and
live box, c1830, 6in (15cm) high.
£400–500 *S*

A brass compound monocular
microscope, the culpeper-form
with single draw tube and
circular stage engraved
'G. Adams, London', on circular
base with reflector, 10½in (27cm)
high, in pyramid mahogany case
on stand, with drawer of
accessories including 4 objectives,
live box, Bonanni stage, fish plate
and stage forceps, early 19thC.
£1,800–2,200 *S*

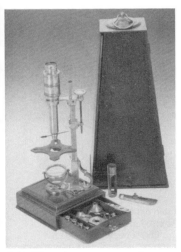

A Cuff type brass compound monocular microscope, focusing by long thread screw, shaped stage with concave reflector below, on mahogany base with 6 objectives, live box, Bonanni stage, cone, Lieberkuhn, set of bone mounted slides, stage forceps, fish plate and other accessories, in mahogany carrying case with loop handle, late 18thC, 13in (33cm) high, the case 16½in (42cm) high.
£2,200–2,800 *S*

A Beck oxidised brass and black enamelled compound monocular microscope, No. 18646, with a Cooke, Troughton & Simms camera attachment set in a Prontor shutter, rack-and-pinion focusing, micrometer fine focusing, electric alternative light source, mechanical square stage and plano-concave mirror on Y-shaped base, 12in (30cm) high, with accessories in a fitted mahogany case.
£150–200 *CSK*

A brass Cuff pattern compound monocular microscope, with eyepiece, dust slide, long nosepiece graduated 3-6, screw rod focusing, pillar graduated 1-4, cruciform shaped stage, and plano/concave mirror, on large mahogany base with drawer containing 6 objectives, fish plate, cone, Lieberkuhn and carrier and other items, 17in (43cm) high.
£900–1,200 *CSK*

A Henry Crouch brass compound binocular microscope, with rotating 4 lens nosepiece, circular stage and rack-and-pinion focusing, 14in (36cm) high, in mahogany case with 5 objectives, 4 oculars, analyser and polariser, bench condenser and other accessories, late 19thC.
£600–900 *S*

A Miller & Adie compound chest microscope, with eyepiece, slide tube and rack-and-pinion focusing, objective, square stage and mounting bracket, in fitted mahogany chest with Lieberkuhn and 2 circular slides, 13in (33cm) wide. **£200–300** *CSK*

A lacquered brass Culpeper type compound microscope, with draw tube focusing and circular stage on mahogany plinth base with accessories drawer containing 5 objectives, Lieberkuhn in can, carrier, cone diaphragm, stage forceps, slides, fish plate, live box, talc box and other items, in pyramid shaped mahogany case with carrying handle, early 19thC, 17in (43cm) high.
£2,500–3,000 *CSK*

A simple/compound aquatic microscope, by Negretti & Zambra, London, with eyepiece, draw tube and rack-and-pinion focusing, swivelling limb, circular glass stage and plano mirror on sliding collar, on tripod legs, 9in (23cm) high, with 2 objectives and 3 simple lenses, in fitted mahogany case. **£400–500** *CSK*

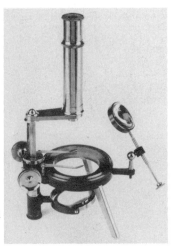

A brass Culpeper type compound monocular microscope, signed on the stage 'Wm Harris & Co., 50 High Holborn, London', focusing by rack-and-pinion, circular stage with concave reflector below, on mahogany base containing 5 objectives, stage forceps and condenser, fish plate, live box and cone, in original oak pyramid case, late 18thC, 15in (38cm) high.
£1,700–2,200 *S*

A lacquered brass portable microscope, No. 4048, by Ross, London, with eyepiece, draw tube and rack-and-pinion focusing, square stage and concave mirror, on folding tripod legs, 11½in (29cm) high extended, with spare eyepiece in leather covered case.
£400–500 *CSK*

A Ross binocular compound microscope, No. 5115, with dividing eyepieces, rack-and-pinion and fine focusing, prism and housing, double nosepiece, circular mechanical stage, sub-stage condenser with wheel stops and plano/concave mirror on sliding tube, on large trunnions supported by twin pillars, on an A-shaped foot, 16½in (42cm) high, with bench condenser and a circular brass stand.
£1,000–1,200 *CSK*

A lacquered brass Society of Arts Prize type compound monocular microscope, by M. Pillischer, London, No. 644, with eyepiece, screw mounted body tube, rack-and-pinion and fine focusing, single nosepiece, square stage with ball-and-joint movement and plano/concave mirror, on Y-shaped foot, 12in (30.5cm) high, with live box, stage forceps and 2 objectives, in fitted mahogany case, with slides in base and presentation plaque to door inscribed 'The Middlesex Hospital, Prize in Clinical Medicine, Presented to Mr. Daniel Devereux, Session 1857-8'.
£300–400 *CSK*

A lacquered brass monocular microscope, unsigned, with rack-and-pinion coarse and micrometer fine focusing, with accessories, in mahogany case, late 19thC.
£270–350 *DA*

A Swift & Son, London, lacquered and oxidised brass binocular compound petrological microscope, with dividing eyepieces, rack-and-pinion and fine focusing, polarising analyser, prism, circular mechanical stage with silvered scales, mechanical sub-stage condenser and plano/concave mirror on sliding collar, on raised horseshoe-shaped foot, 14in (36cm) high, with bench condenser, stage forceps, various eyepieces and objectives, in fitted mahogany case.
£1,100–1,500 *CSK*

A simple folding microscope, with lens, forceps and ivory handle, 3in (7.5cm) high, in pressed card case.
£300–400 *CSK*

A Ross monocular aquarium and physiological compound microscope, No. 3670, with replacement W.G. Pye, Cambridge body tube on pillar with vertical and horizontal movement, on flat tripod foot, 13½in (34cm) high.
£300–500 *CSK*

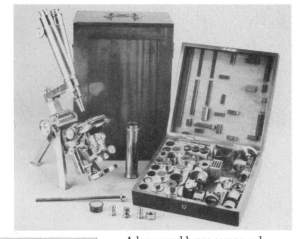

A compound monocular microscope, signed on the foot 'A. Ross London No. 440', the bar limb construction with rack-and-pinion, lever and screw focusing, mechanical stage and sub-stage with large plano/concave mirror below, 18in (46cm) high, in mahogany case with brass carrying handles at the sides and fitted with 4 drawers of accessories including a Ross 1½ & 2in Lieberkuhn, a wheel of stops, 5 oculars, ⅛, ¼, ½in and 1in Ross objectives together with other accessories. **£2,000–2,500** *S*

A lacquered brass compound binocular microscope, signed 'Powell & Lealand, 170 Euston Road, London, 1876', with binocular body tube attachment, prism and cover, rack-and-pinion focusing, the limb with micrometer fine focusing, concentric rotating stage divided 0°-360°, mechanical sub-stage and condenser with rotating and concentric movement and plano/concave mirror on double jointed swivel arm, 18½in (47cm) high, in replacement mahogany case, with accessories including monocular body tube, objectives, eyepieces, bench condenser, stage forceps and condenser and other items in fitted mahogany case. **£8,500–10,000** *CSK*

A Carl Zeiss black enamelled and lacquered brass compound monocular microscope, No. 76548, with eyepiece, rack-and-pinion and fine focusing, jug handle triple nosepiece, circular mechanical stage, sub-stage condenser with iris diaphragm and plano/concave mirror, on horseshoe-shaped foot, 12½in (32cm) high, with accessories, in fitted mahogany case. **£800–900** *CSK*

A lacquered brass compound monocular microscope, the body tube held in cradle, with eyepiece, rack-and-pinion focusing, nosepiece, square stage, slot for sub-stage and plano/concave mirror below, the trunnion on turned pillar on Y-shaped foot with label 'W. Hall, 54 Olsutton St., Somers Town, London', 15in (38cm) high, with accessories in fitted mahogany case. **£350–450** *CSK*

A Watson lacquered brass compound binocular microscope, No. 1082, with twin dividing eyepieces, rack-and-pinion and fine focusing, twin nosepiece, Lister limb, circular mechanical stage and sub-stage condenser with iris diaphragm and plano/concave mirror on sliding collar, mounted on tripod foot, 17in (43cm) high, with accessories, in fitted mahogany case. **£1,000–1,200** *CSK*

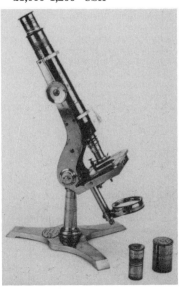

A Smith & Beck brass compound monocular microscope, No. 838, with eyepiece, graduated draw tube, rack-and-pinion and micrometer focusing, twin nosepiece, mechanical square stage with collar below for parabolic illuminator and plano/concave mirror on sliding collar, mounted by large trunnions, on twin supports on revolving disc, on flat tripod foot, on mahogany base, 19½in (49cm) high, in mahogany case, with separate case of accessories including 5 objectives in cans, live box, stage condenser, camera lucida, Lieberkuhn, parabolic illuminator, and other items. **£1,700–2,200** *CSK*

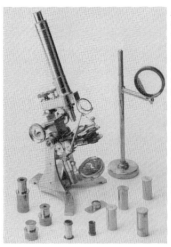

A Swift type lacquered brass compound, monocular microscope, with eyepiece, draw tube, rack-and-pinion and micrometer focusing, single nosepiece, square mechanical stage, sub-stage wheel stops and plano/concave reflector on sliding collar, mounted by large trunnions, on flat tripod foot, signed 'E.R. Watts, Maker, Old Kent Rd., London', on wood base, 18½in (47cm) high, with 3 additional eyepieces, 3 additional objectives, stage forceps and condenser, bull's-eye condenser, live box and tweezers, in fitted mahogany case.
£650–800 *CSK*

A lacquered brass simple microscope, with ivory handle, in leather case, 3¾in (9cm) long, and a Zeiss cased centreglass. **£150–200** *CSK*

A part-set of microscope accessories, by Smith & Beck, London, including parabolic illuminator, polarizer, analyser, limb condenser, centering condenser, Lieberkuhn, 3 objectives in cans, micrometer slide and other items, in fitted mahogany case, 10in (25cm) wide.
£400–500 *CSK*

Telescopes

A Primavesi Bros. 3¾in lacquered brass refracting telescope, with eyepiece, rack-and-pinion focusing, starfinder with cross hairs, 44in (111cm) body tube, front and back caps, located by plate on universal joint to tapered pillar, on folding cabriole legs, with 3 telescopic steadying rods, in fitted mahogany case with accessories, 45½in (115cm) wide.
£1,200–1,500 *CSK*

An H. Fritz, New York, 4¼in astronomical telescope, with 54in (137cm) wood body tube, brass lens cap and rear mounting, rack-and-pinion focusing extension tube and star finder telescope, raised on an alt-azimuth mount with tangent screw gear adjustment, the mahogany tripod with shaped legs and vertical adjustment by open gear, with mahogany accessories case containing additional eyepieces to the power of 30, 60, 120, 180 and 240, with Newtonian mount and colour filters.
£2,000–2,500 *CSK*

A combined telescope, compass and walking stick, the Malacca cane with top section bound in fishskin, and containing a 2-draw telescope with turned horn cap to the objective fitted in the inside, with a small magnetic compass, early 19thC.
£1,000–1,200 *S*

A Storer 1½in 3-draw The Subscription Telescope, with brass eyepiece, rack-and-pinion focusing and shagreen covered front body tube, the rear body tube engraved with the Royal coat-of-arms and signed 'Storer', focusing knob and dust slide missing, 7in (17.5cm) long when closed.
£700–900 *CSK*

A walking stick telescope, with 1in objective, 2 plated draws, folding to store in the stem of a walking stick, with lacquered wood stem, late 19thC, 36in (92cm).
£1,000–1,200 *S*

A paper card and vellum ¾in 3-draw telescope, stamped on the outer body tube 'Leonardo Semitecolo', with horn mounts and objective lens cap, the outer tube stained orange and decorated with geometric patterns, eyepiece lens missing, 12in (30cm) long when closed.
£400–500 *CSK*

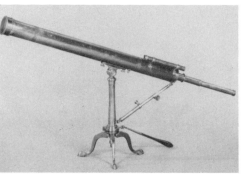

A 3¼in brass refracting telescope-on-stand, signed on the tube 'Troughton & Simms, London', the tube with star finder mounted in parallel, supported by a bracket above tapering brass column and folding tripod base, complete with adjustable steadying strut, with slow motion azimuth adjustment by turned mahogany handle, mid-19thC, length of tube 43in (109cm).
£1,000–1,500 *S*

A George Dollond 3in brass astronomical refracting telescope, the tube with star finder mounted in parallel supported by a bracket at the side, on a trunnion with counter weight above equitorial mount, with slow motion adjustment by 2 turned mahogany handles, in mahogany case, complete with 6 eyepieces, oil lamp, eyepiece extension, tapering brass column and other accessories, mid-19thC, the tube 43in (109cm) long.
£3,000–4,000 *S*

A 2in reflecting telescope, with screw rod focusing, speculum mirrors and leather covered body tube, late 18thC, 15½in (39.5cm). **£300–350** *CSK*

A 1¼in 5-draw vellum bodied telescope, with turned wood eyepiece and horn mounts, the body tube with gilt tooling including Royal coat-of-arms, lacks object lens, c1700, 21½in (54.5cm) long.
£2,000–2,500 *CSK*

Surveying & Drawing Instruments

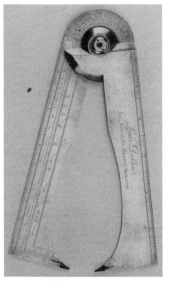

A French brass graphometer, signed 'blondeau', the instrument with frame cut from a single piece of brass, with decorative supports engraved with floral decoration to the central compass, the limb engraved with a double reversed scale of 180°, sub-divided by transversals to 12 minutes, the alidade is fitted with vertical bar sights, replacing the original silk thread sights, the whole raised on universal joint mount for staff head, mid-17thC, later compass rose and needle, 17in (43cm), wide, 7¼in (18cm) radius.
£3,500–4,500 *S*

A pair of Spear's brass gunner's callipers, with scales for 'Iron Guns Proof Service' and 'Brass Guns Proof Service', with twin iron pointers, 7in (18cm) long.
£500–550 *CSK*

A French brass graphometer, signed 'Lennel Eleve et Successeur de Mᵣ Canivet à Paris 1774', the alidade moving over double 180° arc and compass rose, engraved with 8 cardinal points, dated 1774, in embossed shaped leather case, 11½in (29cm) wide.
£2,000–3,000 *S*

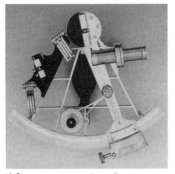

A brass sextant, signed
'G. Whitbread, London', and
owner's name 'F.S.H. Webber',
silver scale and vernier,
magnifier, 2 sets of coloured
filters and rosewood handle,
6in (15cm) radius, in shaped
mahogany case with 3 telescopes,
magnifier in guard and
screwdriver, mid-19thC.
£1,800–2,200 *S*

A mahogany Hadley's quadrant,
signed on ivory plaque 'Made by
Spencer and Browning London',
the ivory scale and vernier with
central zero, peephole eyepiece
with fore and back mirrors, late
18thC, 16in (41cm) radius.
£600–700 *S*

A French surveying compass,
with printed paper dial,
blue/silver needle, indicator and
brass scale, in fitted mahogany
frame with sliding cover and
tripod bush.
£175–220 *CSK*

An American pattern oxidised
brass transit theodolite, signed
on the silvered compass dial
'Troughton & Simms, London'
and engraved on the horizontal
tangent screw bracket 'Harrison
& Co., Montreal, Canada, Agents',
the telescope with rack-and-
pinion focusing, cross wire
adjusters and graduated bubble
level, the axis located on twin
trunnions and supported by A-
frames from the horizontal plate,
the vertical half-circle with
silvered scales divided in
2 quadrants 0°-80°, with vernier,
the compass box with rack
adjustment, the enclosed
horizontal circle with silvered
scale and twin verniers and
reflectors, on 4 screw tripod
mount, in fitted mahogany case,
the base with leather cover,
13½in (34cm) high.
£750–850 *CSK*

A brass transit theodolite, by Otto
Fennel Sohne, Cassel, No. 11820,
the telescope with rack-and-
pinion focusing, cross wire
adjusters, bubble level and ray-
shade, under cross bubble, the
axis with vertical scale with
enclosed silvered scale and
verniers marked 'A' and 'B', twin
magnifiers with reflectors, over
compass, bubble level and cross
bubble, enclosed silvered scale
with verniers marked 'I' and 'II',
with twin magnifiers and
reflectors ,on 3 screw tripod
stand, restored 15in (38cm) high.
£2,000–3,000 *CSK*

A lacquered and silvered brass
noon gun, with twin latitude arcs
supporting the burning glass,
inset compass with blued/silvered
needle, the twin dial with sprung
bird gnomon and divided VI-XII-
VI and inscribed '44-46-44-46',
bubble level and cross bubble, on
tapered pillar on revolving, 3
screw tripod foot, 3½in (9cm) high.
£2,500–3,000 *CSK*

A brass miniature theodolite, the
1in telescope with eyepiece
focusing, bubble level and cross
hairs, vertical half-circle divided
110°-0°-110°, horizontal scale
with twin verniers on 4 screw
tripod bush, 6½in (16cm) high.
£300–400 *CSK*

A German brass transit
theodolite, signed 'Pister &
Martins, BERLIN, No. 608', the
vertical and horizontal circles of
degrees with silver scales,
verniers and magnifiers, spirit
level with telescope mounted
adjacent, the whole raised on 3
levelling screws, 8½in (21cm)
high, in mahogany case with top
inset with 3 brass recesses for
mounting the tripod, 19thC.
£3,000–3,500 *S*

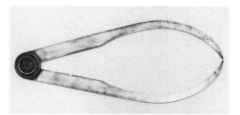

A pair of brass gunner's callipers, by J. Sisson, London, engraved with various scales, the ends with iron tips, repaired, c1750, 22½in (57cm) long.
£500–550 *CSK*

An Irish set of Walker drawing instruments, presented to the Marquis of Kildare, the mahogany and oak Freedom Box with lid carved in relief, with various coats-of-arms velvet lined and fitted with silver compass and dividers, accessories, the ivory sector and the ivory and silver mounted parallel rule stamped 'WALKER DUBLIN', the base with pine box for watercolours and brushes, with handwritten presentation note dated 1st October 1767, 10in (25cm) wide.
£1,500–2,000 *S*

A lacquered brass theodolite, by J. Davis, Derby, the telescope with 1¼in lens, cap, rack-and-pinion focusing and bubble level, located in twin clamps over vertical half-circle, with silvered scale and vernier, the opposite side divided with 'Diff of Hypo & Base' mounted by trunnion on twin A-supports, over horizontal plate with compass box with silvered dial, edge bar needle and clamp, bubble level, cross bubble, chamfered silvered horizontal circle with twin verniers and single magnifier, on 4 screw tripod mount, in fitted mahogany case, 10in (25cm) high.
£700–800 *CSK*

An ivory quadrant, for the measurement of elevation, with engraved 0-90° scale, numbered every 10°, complete with original brass sights and plumb bob, 3in (8cm) radius, in pink silk lined case with fishskin covering, late 18thC. **£3,000–4,000** *S*

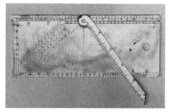

A lacquered brass proportional protractor, with pivoting arm and punched and engraved scales, 8in (20cm) wide.
£300–350 *CSK*

This instrument was possibly constructed for use with a Mercator chart or other architectural use.

A brass protractor, divided 10°-180°-10°, signed 'T. Wright fecit', c1740, 4in (10cm), and an ivory sector, rule and ebony parallel rule.
£300–350 *CSK*

A rare cast aluminium surveyor's level, by C. Baker, London, No. 3028, with graduated bubble level, cross bubble, rack-and-pinion focusing and detachable ray-shade/lens cap on 4 screw tripod mount, in fitted mahogany case, 14½in (38cm).
£150–200 *CSK*

A set of brass drawing instruments, with ivory sector and wood rule, in shagreen covered wood case, with maker's paper label 'Made by Thomas Harris, Paradise Row, Bethnall Green, London', 7½in (19cm) wide.
£280-350 *CSK*

A set of drawing instruments, including ivory sector and rule, brass semi-circular protractor and other instruments, in fitted fishskin covered case, with manuscript dated '1817', 6½in (16.5cm) high.
£400–450 *CSK*

Medical & Dental Instruments

A pair of gilt copper ear trumpets, signed in the bells 'Rein & Son, Patentees, sole inventors & only makers, 108 Strand, London', further marked 'E' probably indicating size, with ivory ear pieces, one earpiece replaced, c1865, 3in (7cm) wide.
£400–550 *CSK*

A black painted metal bodied ear trumpet, with scrollwork cover, 2in (5cm) diam.
£100–150 *CSK*

A glass ear trumpet, 10in (25cm) long.
£420–470 *CSK*

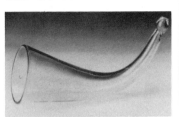

A glass ear trumpet, with handblown earpiece and curved funnel, 8in (21cm) long.
£450–500 *CSK*

A pair of tortoiseshell framed spectacles, with round blue tinted lenses, arched bridge and folding sides, in shagreen case, 5in (13cm).
£100–150 *CSK*

A French simulated mother-of-pearl ear trumpet, with brass tube, signed 'Ardente, 309 Oxford St., London', 6in (15cm) long.
£200–300 *CSK*

A black painted tin ear trumpet, with maker's label 'Arnold & Sons, Surgical Instrument Manufacturers, Giltspur Street London', 5½in (13.5cm) high.
£170–200 *CSK*

A pair of tortoisehell framed pale blue tinted 'railway' spectacles, with folding sides, and a pair of silver sliding-sides spectacles, 19thC, both in later cases.
£150–200 *CSK*

An imitation tortoiseshell ear trumpet, with pierced cover, 2in (5cm) diam.
£125–150 *CSK*

Medical Instruments

The collecting of medical instruments may seem initially to be rather an unusual pastime, especially as many of the instruments appear to be implements of torture rather than healing. However, this relatively new collecting field has, over the last few years, shown a marked increase in interest and, therefore, value. Collectors are predominantly from the medical profession but the associated decorative pharmaceutical jars, ceramic phrenology heads and medicine chests have a much wider appeal.

The Napoleonic Wars created a demand for surgeons to operate on those injured on the battlefield or at sea. They carried their amputation saws, torniquets, knives and associated instruments in brass bound and velvet lined mahogany cases. The instruments are normally of high quality steel with carved and hatched ebony handles. It is important that the pieces are original to the set. This can be determined by the signature often found on each piece and whether or not they fit snugly into the spaces provided in the case.

Other popular cased sets are those instruments used by general practitioners for trepanning (operating on the skull) and blood letting, which was popular throughout the 19thC. Leeches were kept in decorative ceramic jars and applied to the surface of the skin to relieve pain or cure almost any ailment. Alternatively there were a number of brass mechanical leeches, or scarificators, which efficiently and without too much pain cut the skin using several sharp blades. A small glass bell jar or cupping glass was placed over the wound and the blood drawn out. These were normally housed in lined fitted cases.

Other instruments and associated decorative collectables which are currently popular are ceramic or ivory phrenology heads, turned wood monaural stethoscopes and the various shaped designs of hearing trumpets. The scope for collecting medical instruments is vast, with prices ranging from a few pounds to thousands of pounds for the rare and early examples.

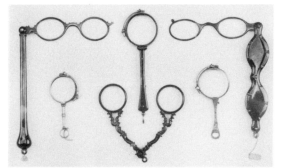

A carved tortoiseshell scissor spectacle frame, 4⅓in (11cm), a gilt metal and tortoiseshell long folder, a Viennese pattern tortoiseshell hand case, a short handle tortoiseshell lorgnette, and 2 metal folders.
£700–800 *CSK*

A double-sided domestic medicine chest, the front opening to reveal 7 bottles, above a drawer containing scales with mother-of-pearl pans, weights and other utensils, lower compartment containing glass mortar and pestle and 6 further bottles, the rear with 5 further bottles, with inset brass handles and key, 9in (23cm) wide.
£2,000–2,500 *S*

An optician's shop display, comprising various spectacles and pince-nez, with prices, guarantees and other advertising slogans, framed and glazed, 27⅓in by 36in (69.5cm by 92cm).
£700–900 *CSK*

This display was recently discovered in the loft of a shop in south London.

A painted plaster model of the human eye, sectioned and numbered, with detachable cornea, lens and anterior chamber, on plinth base, damaged, 9in (22.5cm) wide.
£200–300 *CSK*

A pair of Chinese tortoiseshell framed sunglasses, with round smoked lenses, decorated bridge, folding sides with decorated pads, in brown lacquered case with incised characters and bamboo shoots, 6½in (16cm) long.
£300–350 *CSK*

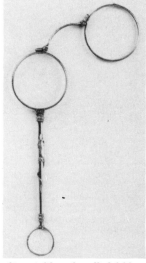

A gilt metal long handled folder, the handle modelled with a gold salamander, 6in (15cm) long.
£400–450 *CSK*

A mahogany domestic medicine chest, opening to reveal compartments for 16 bottles, with 2 drawers containing scales, mortar, pestle, eye bath, burnisher and 5 additional bottles, the rear with poison compartment containing 4 bottles, some missing, mid-19thC, 10½in (27cm) high.
£800–900 *S*

A part set of opthalmic scalpels, by Laundy, London, 3 replacement ivory handled instruments, one by Bigg & Milikin, with carved ivory handles, and a bleeding lancet, in velvet lined fitted leather covered case, with tooled decoration and plaque inscribed 'Edward Cock', c1820, 7in (17.5cm) wide.
£100–120 *CSK*

A walnut veneered homeopathic domestic medicine chest, by Ashton & Parsons, the top with 63 fitted bottles and compartment for medical book, the base with 29 fitted bottles and compartment for other accessories, lacking 2 bottles, 15½in (39cm) wide.
£500–600 *CSK*

A mahogany domestic medicine chest, by Thomson, with hinged lid and fall front, the interior with 13 fitted bottles, some with retailer's label for 'Hardy & Co, 42 Fenchurch St., (corner of Mincing Lane), London', the central section with twin lift-out trays, containing 8 further bottles and other items, mid-19thC, 13in (33cm) wide.
£1,000–1,200 *CSK*

An oak travelling medicine chest, by Ch. Delacre, Brussels, with compartments for 12 bottles and other items, with instructions, c1905, 13in (33cm) wide.
£350–450 *CSK*

A delft blue and white plaque, with the arms of The Apothecary Company, restored, London, mid-18thC, 10 by 8½in (25 by 21cm).
£2,000–2,200 *JHo*

A Dutch blue and white ointment jar, named for 'U. Populeun', within a scroll bordered cartouche surrounded by peacocks, above a spreading foot, 19thC, 6in (15cm) high.
£250–300 *CSK*

A glass specie jar, decorated with painted and gilded Royal coat-of-arms, flanked by lion and unicorn on a white ground, with gilded lid, base damaged, 29½in (75cm) high.
£300–350 *CSK*

A Spanish faience waisted drug jar, named for 'R. Gentiana' on a banner before figures in a landscape, 19thC, 12in (30.5cm) high.
£600–650 *CSK*

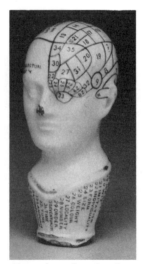

A pottery phrenology head cane handle, slightly chipped, 2½in (6cm) high.
£700–900 *S*

A mahogany domestic medicine chest, the lid rising to reveal compartments for 14 bottles, over a drawer with 2 lead containers, velvet lined with brass fittings, early 19thC, 8 by 7in (20 by 18cm).
£500–550 *CSK*

A pair of mahogany drug-runs, with inset gilt and black labels and glass knobs, one with maker's paper label 'From Richard Tomlinson & Sons, Bond Street, Birmingham, Druggists' Shop Fitters and Dealers in Druggists' Sundries', 41½in (105.5cm).
£600–700 *CSK*

A mahogany domestic medicine chest, the upper compartment with 6 fitted bottles and one other compartment, the front with 2 fitted bottles, over double drawers, one with 4 compartments with sliding covers, the lower part containing a balance, with brass carrying handles, lacking 2 bottles, 7in (18cm) wide.
£600–700 *CSK*

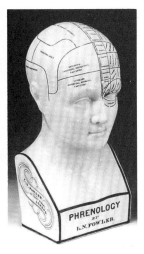

A porcelain phrenology head, by
L. N. Fowler, 12in (30cm) high.
£700–1,000 *CSK*

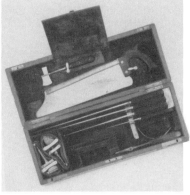

A part set of Hutchinson
amputation instruments,
including bone saw, skull saw and
4 Liston knives, all with chequer
grip ebony handles, bone forceps
and tourniquets, in velvet lined
brass bound mahogany case,
16in (41cm) wide.
£850–1,200 *CSK*

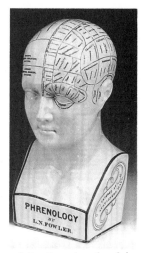

A porcelain phrenology head, by
L. N. Fowler, 12in (30cm) high.
£600–800 *CSK*

A German part amputation set,
by H. Schmidt, Giessen,
comprising bone saw with
chequer gripped ebony handle
and 2 spare blades, finger saw
and 6 Liston knives, 4 knives
by W. Lony, in velvet lined
fitted leather covered case,
15in (38cm) wide.
£350–450 *CSK*

An ivory phrenology head,
engraved on the back
'LEVESLET', together with
engraved lines on the skull and
numbers referring to a list of
characteristics around the stem,
slight damage, mid-19thC, 3½in
(9cm) high.
£750–950 *S*

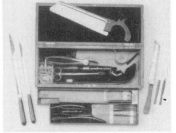

A set of field surgeon's
instruments, by Evans &
Wormall, including large bone
saw with smooth ebony handle,
finger saw, bone forceps, bullet
forceps, trephine with handle
tourniquet, 3 Liston knives,
various scalpels and probes and
other items, in a velvet lined
brass bound mahogany case, with
lift-out tray, 18in (45cm) wide.
£1,000–1,500 *CSK*

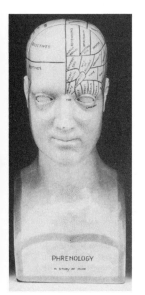

A porcelain phrenology head,
the base with blue lining,
18in (46cm) high.
£1,400–1,700 *CSK*

A surgeon's tool kit, by Wood &
Co., of York, in original mahogany
case, 19thC, 11½in (29cm).
£700–800 *RBB*

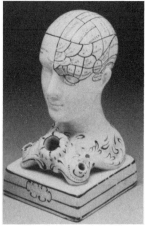

A porcelain phrenology inkwell,
by Bridges, the cranium divided
into several areas of character,
emotions and characteristics,
with 3 inkwells below, white
glazed overall with blue lining
and highlights, 19thC, 5½in
(14cm) high.
£700–850 *S*

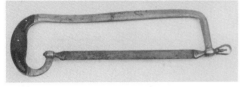

A Rust's pattern bow saw, with steel frame adjustable blade and G-shaped handle with part chequered ebony grip, 15½in (39cm) long.
£200–250 *CSK*

A quantity of dental instruments, by Reymond Frères, C. Ash & Sons, Collin & Co., and others, including elevators, pluggers, forceps and denture preparation instruments, some with ebony and other wood handles.
£250–300 *CSK*

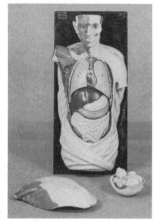

An anatomical model of the human male torso, by Alexander & Fowler, the painted plaster torso with removable cranium and chest, opening to models of interior organs, mounted on ebonised wood base, in original pine carrying case, c1910, 38½in (97cm).
£600–900 *S*

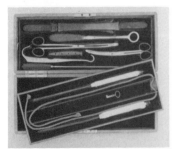

A cased set of lithotomy instruments, including 4 ebony handled instruments and 8 others, in fitted mahogany case, mid-19thC, 16in (41cm) wide.
£1,000–1,200 *S*

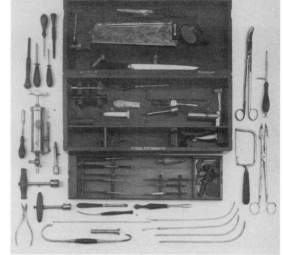

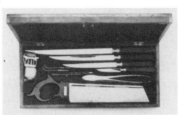

An amputation set, by Mackenzie, Edinburgh, comprising bone saw with smooth ebony handle and detachable spine, 4 Liston knives with ebony handles, bone forceps, tourniquet and other items, in brass bound mahogany case with presentation plaque engraved 'Edinburgh University, Class of Surgery 1870-71, Senior Division 1st Prize, Awarded To William Stirling B. Sr., James Spence, Professor', 18in (46cm) wide.
£1,500–2,000 *CSK*

A coloured rubber anatomical model of the human torso, with spine, rib cage, pelvis and internal organs, on metal stand, 36in (91.5cm) high.
£200–400 *CSK*

A set of surgeon's instruments, by W. B. H. Hillard & Sons, Glasgow, including a bone saw with smooth ebony handle, a Liston knife with chequer grip ebony handle, an obstetric scissor perforator, craniotomy forceps and crochet, various Weiss instruments including trephines, skull saw, trocar and cannulae, and other instruments including finger saw, scalpels, dental forceps and other items, in fitted mahogany case with lift-out tray and maker's label, 19½in (49.5cm) wide.
£1,200–1,700 *CSK*

It would appear that this set of instruments was intended for use by a ship's doctor or a similar physician.

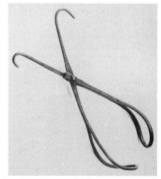

A pair of wrought iron Chamberlin pattern obstetric forceps, with curved and fenestrated blades, riveted pivot and loop handles, 17thC, 12½in (31cm) long.
£1,800–2,500 *CSK*

Although known to have been used by the Arabs circa 1000BC, obstetric forceps appear to have been introduced in the West by Dr William Chamberlin around 1610-20. Wrapped in cloth to prevent them rattling, they were brought into the chamber in a large box, which was placed under the bedclothes. All onlookers were sent from the room, and even the patient was blindfolded. In this way, the forceps could be used without anyone seeing.

A William and Mary silver mounted ebonised striking bracket clock, the later dial inscribed 'Francis Robinson, London', with pierced blued hands and 5 ringed pillar twin fusee movement, 15½in (39cm).
£6,500–7,500 *C*

A George III mahogany striking bracket clock, dial signed 'Judah Jacobs, London', strike/silent ring in the arch, 5 pillar twin fusee movement with verge escapement and strike on bell, engraved backplate, 18in (46cm) high.
£4,500–5,500 *C*

An ebony and ebonised striking bracket clock, dial signed 'Dan Delander, London', the movement with bob escapement, engraved backplate, on a moulded plinth, 16½in (42cm).
£4,500–6,000 *C*

A George III mahogany automaton table clock, dial with calendar aperture signed 'John Darke, Barnstaple', strike/silent lever, 5 pillar fusee movement, 21in (53cm).
£3,000–3,500 *S*

l. A Regency brass mounted ebonised striking bracket clock, glazed white painted enamelled dial signed 'Grant, Fleet St., London', with a ripple moulded brass mounted base and lions' mask carrying handles, signed backplate, 19in (48cm) high.
£3,500–4,000 *C*

A George III ebonised striking bracket clock, the dial signed 'Michl. Roth, London', strike/silent ring in the arch, 5 pillar twin chain fusee movement, 16in (41cm) high.
£3,000–4,000 *C*

A George III mahogany chiming table clock, dial signed 'John Abchurch, London', 5 pillar fusee movement with verge escapement, 23½in (60cm) high.
£8,500–9,500 *S*

r. A Louis XV brass inlaid and brown tortoiseshell boulle bracket clock, with ormolu dial engraved with foliate arabesques and central cockerel, Roman blue and white enamel dial and further Arabic numeral dial to the outside, the movement stamped to the reverse 'De Lorme A Paris', the backboard inlaid with Berainesque figures of musicians and dancers, case inlaid with scrolling foliage surmounted by a figure of Minerva, 64in (163cm).
£7,500–8,500 *C*

A George II ebony veneered table clock, 7in (17.5cm) dial signed 'Fra. Mayhew, Parham', 6 pillar 2 train bell striking fusee movement, 18½in (47cm).
£2,000–2,500 *S*

l. An oak longcase clock, by Phillip Averell, Farnham, with engraved silvered brass dial and 8-day movement, c1770, 79in (201cm) high.
£2,500–3,200 *PAO*

A mahogany longcase clock, by S. Passmore, Plymouth, with flame veneers and boxwood string inlay, brass silvered dial and 8-day movement, c1840, 87in (221cm) high.
£2,000–3,300 *PAO*

A George III mahogany longcase clock, with 8-day rocking ship movement.
£1,500–2,500 *SWO*

A mahogany longcase clock, by J. MacGregor, Edinburgh, with flame veneers and boxwood inlay, the painted dial with seconds and date, 8-day movement, c1830, 79½in (201cm) high.
£2,000–3,250 *PAO*

A mahogany longcase clock, by John Richardson, London, the brass dial with matted centre, the 8-day, 5-pillar movement striking the hours on a bell, c1765, 100in (254cm) high.
£8,000–9,250 *PAO*

A mahogany longcase clock, by Francis Hobler, London, the brass dial with silvered chapter ring, the 8-day, 5-pillar movement striking the hours on a bell, c1770, 95in (241cm) high.
£7,000–9,000 *PAO*

A mahogany longcase clock, William Carter, Hampstead, with brass dial, silvered brass chapter ring, 8-day movement, c1790, 84in (213cm) high.
£7,000–8,500 *PAO*

A mahogany longcase clock, by M. Michael, Bristol, the white dial painted with shells to the corners and flowers to the arch, 8-day movement striking the hours on a bell, c1820, 88in (224cm) high.
£3,000–4,000 *PAO*

An oak longcase clock, by Thomas Furnival, Taunton, with brass dial and silvered brass chapter ring, with 8-day, 5-pillar movement, c1750, 80in (203cm) high.
£3,500–4,500 *PAO*

r. An oak longcase clock, by Martin, Faversham, with painted dial and 8-day movement, c1810, 84in (213cm) high.
£2,000–3,000 *PAO*

An oak longcase clock, by Thomas Mear, Dursley, with mahogany banding, painted dial, the 8-day movement striking the hours on a bell, c1820, 78in (198cm) high.
£1,500–2,250 *PAO*

l. An oak longcase clock, by John Sterland, Nottingham, the arched brass dial with silvered chapter and well, 8-day movement striking the hours on a bell, engraved centre showing both date and seconds, maker's name on a cartouche in the arch, long trunk door, c1780, 81in (205.5cm). **£3,000–3,500** *PAO*

A mahogany longcase clock, by John Breakenrig, Edinburgh, 8-day movement, engraved dial, c1790, 85in (216cm) without finial. **£6,000–6,400** *PAO*

A mahogany longcase clock, by Bell, St. Andrews, the 8-day movement striking the hours on a bell, c1790, 87in (221cm). **£4,750–5,250** *PAO*

r. A mahogany longcase clock, by James Rowland, Bristol, the 8-day movement striking the hours on a bell, white dial showing both seconds and date and phases of the moon in the arch, c1790 and later, 88in (223.5cm). **£4,750–5,250** *PAO*

l. An oak longcase clock, by John Stokes, St. Ives, brass dial with silvered chapter ring, date, strike/silent in the arch, the 8-day movement striking the hour on a bell, long trunk door, c1750, 83in (210.5cm). **£3,500–4,000** *PAO*

A mahogany longcase clock, by John Anderson, with 8-day 5 pillar movement striking on a bell, strike/silent in the arch, c1765, 101in (256.5cm).
£6,700–7,300 *PAO*

A mahogany longcase clock, by James McCabe, London, with 3-train movement on 4 graduated bells, early 19thC.
£4,500–5,500 *BWe*

An olive wood parquetry month-going longcase clock, signed 'Robert Thompson', 5 ringed pillar movement, restored, 78in (198cm) high.
£3,500–5,000 *C*

A mahogany longcase clock, signed 'Saml. Collier, Eccles', c1790, 93in (236cm) high.
£5,000–5,500 *S*

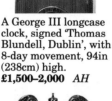

A George III longcase clock, signed 'Thomas Blundell, Dublin', with 8-day movement, 94in (238cm) high.
£1,500–2,000 *AH*

A mahogany and inlaid longcase clock, signed 'George White, Bristol', c1790, 100in (254cm).
£6,000–7,000 *S(S)*

A William and Mary walnut marquetry and ebony longcase clock, signed 'Thomas Lumpkin, London', 77in (195cm) high.
£6,500–8,000 *C*

A George III mahogany and rosewood cross-banded longcase clock, signed 'J. Dankin, Grassington', 93in (236cm) high.
£1,500–2,000 *AH*

An Edwardian Gothic quarter chiming longcase clock, with 4 pillar 3-train movement with dead-beat escapement and mercury pendulum, 93in (236cm) high.
£4,000–6,000 *C*

A George II walnut and burr walnut longcase clock, signed 'Michael Gibbs, London', with gilt metal mounted dial, and silvered chapter ring, associated, 87in (221cm) high.
£4,500–5,500 *C*

l. A George III mahogany longcase clock, the dial signed 'Feniller Liverpool', the gilt centre engraved with foliage and dragons' heads, 95in (242cm) high.
£2,800–3,200 *C*

r. A burr walnut longcase clock, the dial inscribed 'Dan. Quare, London', composite and restored, 103in (262cm) high.
£3,500–4,000 *C*

r. A William & Mary walnut and seaweed marquetry longcase clock, the dial signed 'John Finch, London', 76in (193cm) high.
£5,500–6,000 *C*

A George III mahogany and satinwood inlaid longcase clock, the dial signed 'John Snow, Frome Fecit', restored, 87in (221cm) high.
£3,200–3,500 *C*

l. A Queen Anne marquetry inlaid walnut and ebony month-going longcase clock, the dial signed 'Dan Quare, London', 99in (250cm) high.
£17,500–20,000 *C*

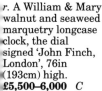

A walnut 8-day longcase clock, the brass dial with silvered Roman and Arabic chapter ring, inscribed 'Dan. Quare, London', 88in (224cm) high.
£3,000–3,500 *CSK*

A Charles II burr walnut month-going longcase clock, the dial signed 'Daniel Quare, London', 86in (218cm) high.
£10,500–13,500 *C*

A Dutch walnut and marquetry longcase clock, the case on carved claw-and-ball feet, the dial signed 'Gerit Bramer, Amsterdam', 114in (289.5cm) high.
£6,000–6,500 *C*

A Regency mahogany 8-day longcase clock, the brass dial with Roman and Arabic chapter ring, foliate engraved centre, the trunk with fluted canted angles, on a stepped panelled plinth, 92½in (235cm) high.
£1,400–1,800 *CSK*

An Edwardian mahogany quarter chiming longcase clock, 4 pillar movement with jewelled deadbeat escapement, 113in (287cm) high.
£6,000–7,000 *C*

l. A walnut month-going longcase clock, the dial signed '234, Dan. Quare & Ste. Horseman, London', the case with domed caddy cresting and 2 ball and spire finials above a fret, 100in (254cm) high.
£17,500–18,500 *S*

A Charles II olive wood oyster and floral marquetry grande sonnerie quarter striking longcase clock, the dial signed 'Eduardus East Londini', the case on bun feet, 73½in (186cm) high.
£11,000–12,000 *C*

r. A japanned longcase clock, the dial signed 'William Kipling, London', the oval boss engraved 'Tempus Fugit', c1715, 103in (262cm).
£15,000–16,000 *S*

A William & Mary walnut and marquetry longcase clock, the dial signed 'Luke Wise, Reading', 83in (211cm) high.
£7,000–8,000 *C*

Samuel Orr
Antique Clocks

36 High Street, Hurstpierpoint
West Sussex BN6 9RG

Telephone:
Hurstpierpoint (0273) 832081
(24 Hour Answerphone)

The Pantiles Spa Antiques
Tunbridge Wells
(0892) 541377
Car Phone: 0860 230888

ANTIQUE CLOCKS · BAROMETERS
RESTORATION CLOCKS PURCHASED

**FINE SELECTION OF ANTIQUE CLOCKS
FOR SALE**

Exhibitor at Olympia

OVER 200 CLOCKS ALWAYS IN STOCK

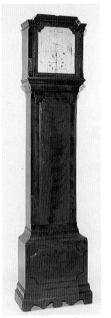

A Georgian mahogany regulator clock, with silvered dial, minute dial, seconds and hours indicators, 75in (190cm) high.
£12,500–14,000 *BWe*

A Regency mahogany sidereal and mean time month-going longcase regulator, signed 'Margetts, London', 74½in (189cm).
£35,000–38,000 *C*

A Regency mahogany longcase regulator, dial signed 'Webster, London, No.6096', 77in (196cm).
£7,000–8,000 *C*

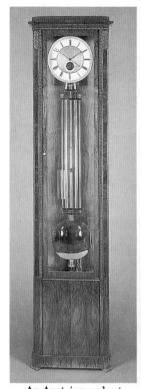

An Austrian walnut year-going longcase regulator, signed 'V. Bittner in Komotau No. 5. 1856', 76in (193cm) high.
£25,000–30,000 *C*

A Victorian ormolu mounted walnut month-going wall regulator, signed 'Chas. Frodsham, No. 1702', 62in (157cm).
£70,000–72,000 *C*

r. A Louis XV ormolu mounted tortoiseshell, ebony and boulle astronomical and musical regulator.
£600,000–700,000 *C*

A Louis Philippe mahogany 6 month-going longcase regulateur, signed 'Ame. Jacob', 85in (216cm).
£55,000–60,000 *C*

A Regency mahogany longcase regulator, the dial signed 'Matthews Leighton', with 6 pillar movement, 75½in (192cm) high.
£4,500–5,500 *C*

A Viennese rooftop style regulator, in a mahogany veneered case with maple stringing, the enamel dial with engine turned bezel, c1830, 35in (89cm) long.
£5,500–7,500 *GeC*

A Viennese regulator, in a lantern style mahogany veneered case with ebonised stringing, month-going precision movement, the dial signed 'Brandl in Wien', c1810, 54in (137cm) long.
£24,000–28,000 *GeC*

A Viennese grande sonnerie striking regulator, in a rosewood case, with applied decorations and stringing, two-piece enamel dial, c1845, 48in (122cm) high.
£6,500–8,500 *GeC*

A Viennese regulator, in a burr walnut veneered lantern style case with marquetry inlay, precision month-going movement, c1825, 46in (117cm) high.
£24,000–28,000 *GeC*

A French Empire ormolu mantel clock, with 3¼in enamel dial, bell striking silk suspension movement, with Cupid and a maiden viewing him through a zograscope, c1810, 14in (36cm) high. **£1,500–2,000** *S*

A French bronze, ormolu and red marble mantel clock, bell striking movement signed 'Hemon A Paris', in a bronze and ormolu star-studded globe with an equatorial ring cast with the signs of the Zodiac and supported by an eagle, the figure of Zeus to the side holding aloft a bolt of lightning, the marble plinth applied with chased ormolu mounts, c1815, 28in (71cm). **£10,000–11,000** *S*

A French ormolu mantel clock, 3¼in enamel dial, bell striking movement with silk suspension, the case in the form of a Centurian's plumed helmet, with the figure of Cupid seated at the opening, c1805, 13½in (34cm) high. **£3,000–4,000** *S*

A French ormolu mounted 'jewelled' porcelain mantel clock, bell striking S. Marti movement No. 2365 with Brocot escapement, dial painted with putti and a border of flowers and butterflies, c1880, 20in (50cm). **£3,000–3,500** *S*

A French ormolu musical mantel clock, the 3¼in enamel dial signed 'Commingea, Palais Royal No. 62 A Paris', bell striking silk suspension movement releasing the music every hour, with young woman standing to one side with a winged putto, c1810, 21in (53cm) high. **£4,500–5,000** *S*

A French porcelain mounted ormolu singing bird automaton mantel clock, the enamel dial with visible Brocot escapement, stamped 'H & F Paris', c1875, 26½in (67cm). **£10,500–11,500** *S*

An Empire ormolu mounted bronze and white marble mantel clock, the glazed enamelled dial with Arabic numerals and signed 'Revel', surmounted by a winged cupid caressing Venus, on a stiff-leaf moulded stepped plinth and red griotte marble base, the movement numbered '135490', 31in (79cm). **£4,500–6,000** *C*

A French gilt and patinated bronze mantel clock, the enamel dial signed 'Maniere à Paris', bell striking movement with silk suspension, the case surmounted by Cupid playing with a butterfly, c1815, 15in (38cm) high. **£2,000–2,500** *S*

A William and Mary ormolu
mounted ebony grande
sonnerie table clock, the dial
signed 'Thomas Tompion
Londini Fecit', the backplate
engraved and punch-numbered
'217', 27in (68cm) high.
£300,000–350,000 *C*

A George III ormolu mounted and
lacquered quarter chiming bracket
clock, the dial signed 'Recordon,
Spencer & Perkins, London', 28½in
(72.5cm) high.
£9,000–10,000 *C*

A Regency brass inlaid mahogany
striking bracket clock, signed
'Dulin, Cornhill, London', with
detailed and figured mahogany
case, c1820, 18½in (47cm) high.
£5,000–6,000 *DRA*

l. A Regency ormolu
mounted marble Weeks'
Museum mantel clock, the
case on gadrooned toupie
feet, a four pillar chain
fusee movement with
deadbeat escapement, on
velvet lined ebonised wood
base and with glass dome,
12in (30.5cm) high.
£8,500–9,000 *C*

A Victorian ebonised
quarter chiming table clock,
surmounted by a cupola with
8 gilded brass moulds,
female figures on all four
corners, the dial with a
silver plaque inscribed
'Elkington, Regent St,
London', 36in (91.5cm) high.
£11,000–12,000 *DRA*

A walnut quarter repeating table
clock, signed 'Joseph Knibb, London',
the backplate signed and engraved
with tulips and scrolling leaves, the
domed case veneered with richly
figured wood, with brass carrying
handle, c1685, 12in (31cm) high.
£40,000–45,000 *S*

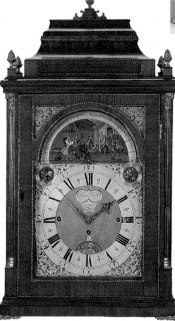

l. A George III mahogany
musical and automaton
table clock, the dial
signed 'Daye Barker,
London', the inverted bell
top surmounted by
pineapple finials, 34in
(87cm) high.
£13,000–14,000 *C*

A French ormolu and bronze cartel clock of Louis XVI style, enamelled dial with Roman and Arabic numerals, signed 'BAGUES FRERES FABRTS DE BRONZES, PARIS, 19thC, 32in (81cm) high. **£2,500–3,000** *C*

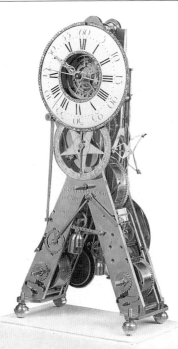

A Directoire long duration quarter striking equation skeleton clock, the Y-form plates signed 'Bouchet Horloger du Roy Paris', beneath the engraved silvered year calendar ring, with gilt arrowhead pointer, 18in (46cm). **£26,000–30,000** *C*

A mahogany dial clock, the painted dial signed 'Wm. Carter, Hampstead', outer zodiac indication above the automaton scene of 2 conjurors with others looking on, c1770, movement and case late 19thC, 15in (38cm) diam. **£2,000–2,500** *C*

A copper lustreware clock, in the shape of a two-handled ornament, 8in (20cm) high. **£25–35** *PCh*

A French marble and bronze band clock, in late Louis XVI style, the movement contained in a vase and cover supported by 2 cherub terms, on marble plinth, c1870, 22in (56cm). **£4,000–5,000** *S*

A French Empire ormolu and bronze pendule au 'Negre', with 3in enamel dial, bell striking silk suspension movement, the case in the form of a barrel of coffee beans flanked by a palm tree and a negro figure, c1805, 11in (29cm). **£9,000–10,000** *S*

A south German gilt metal quarter striking Türmchenuhr, transverse alarm train lacking, c1600, later verge escapement, 13in (33cm). **£10,500–15,000** *C*

A brass repeater carriage clock, by Elkington & Co., 6½in (16cm) high. **£600–700** *LT*

l. A silver cased astronomical, calendar and alarm carriage timepiece, the silver dial signed 'Breguet', with calendar indicating day, date, month and year, the going barrel movement numbered on the gilt backplate 'B. No. 1624', 1928, 6in (16cm). **£35,000–40,000** *C*

An 18ct gold keyless half hunter pocketwatch, with up-and-down indicator, by Charles Frodsham, 84 Strand, London, No. 03418, AD FMSZ, casemaker's mark JB, hallmarked London 1866. **£2,000–2,500** *C*

An 18ct gold half hunter dumb repeating ruby cylinder pair case pocketwatch, by Dwerrihouse, Carter & Son, London 1807. **£1,800–2,200** *C*

An early silver waterproof free sprung deckwatch, with up-and-down indication, by Herbert Blockley & Co., London No. 31629, and signed mahogany box. **£3,000–4,000** *C*

l. A gilt, enamel and seed pearl erotic automata pocketwatch, playing music on 5 bells, the reverse with painted landscape, the section of castle in the foreground opening to reveal an erotic scene, 18thC. **£10,000–11,000** *C*

A gold quarter repeating automata verge pocketwatch, the dial plate with floral decoration to the rim. **£4,000–5,000** *C*

A gold and enamel open face virgule pocketwatch with gold and enamel chatelaine, dial signed 'Breguet à Paris'. **£3,500–4,000** *C*

r. A gold quarter-repeating and musical double-dialled pocket-watch, the engraved gilt dial with Alpine scene in centre. **£2,000–3,000** *C*

A gold and enamel seed pearl set duplex open face signed pocketwatch, for the Chinese market, by Ilbery, London, No. 6805, the reverse painted with pastoral scene. **£3,500–4,500** *C*

A gold and enamel keyless hunter pocketwatch, Eterna, No. 2415364. **£1,500–2,000** *C*

A gold open face split second chronograph keyless pocketwatch, by C.H. Meylan, Brassus. **£2,000–2,500** *C*

A gold, enamel and seed pearl quarter repeating musical cylinder pocketwatch, by Piguet & Meylan, No. 2116, the white enamel dial signed 'Le Roy'. **£14,000–15,000** *C*

A gold and enamel and seed pearl set open face pocketwatch, reverse with painted portrait, early 19thC. **£1,800–2,200** *C*

A gold and enamel musical cylinder open face pocket-watch, early 19thC. **£3,000–4,000** *C*

An Audemars Piguet
18ct gold ultra-thin open
face dress watch, with
nickel lever movement,
with silver dial, signed,
c1965, 4.1cm diam.
£1,400–1,600 *S(G)*

A Patek Philippe & Co. 18ct gold
hunter minute repeating watch,
with nickel lever movement, wolf-
tooth wind, highly jewelled, white
enamel dial, signed, No. 65010,
c1880, 5.1cm diam.
£9,500–10,000 *S(G)*

A gold open face minute
repeating watch, with gilt
cylinder movement, plain 3 arm
gold balance, gold Breguet
hands, cuvette missing, dial
signed 'Longlois', in an engine
turned case, 5.4cm diam.
£2,500–3,000 *S(G)*

A verge pocket watch,
with painted enamel
scene on copper, dial and
movement inscribed
'Quare, London', early
18thC, 4.6cm diam.
£5,600–7,000 *C*

A 14ct gold and mother-of-
pearl open face Masonic
watch, by V. Piguet, Le
Sentier, with signed gilt
lever movement, c1900,
4.8cm diam.
£2,000–2,500 *S(G)*

A Patek Philippe & Co.,
18ct gold open face
5 minute repeating watch,
with nickel lever
movement, 31 jewels,
signed, c1910, 4.7cm
diam. **£4,800–5,200** *S(G)*

A Patek Philippe
& Co., 150th
Anniversary pink
gold tonneau jump
hour wristwatch,
c1988, with case.
£19,000–20,000
S(G)

A Rolex 18ct pink gold
chronograph wristwatch,
with registers,
tachometer, and
telemeter, nickel lever
movement, 17 jewels,
signed, c1945, with
associated bracelet.
£4,500–5,000 *S(G)*

A stainless steel
chronograph wristwatch,
with registers for 30
minutes and 12 hours,
dial and movement
signed 'Universal Geneve
Tri-Compax', c1935.
£700–1,000 *S(G)*

A Rolex Oyster
Perpetual 18ct pink
gold self-winding
sweep seconds
wristwatch, nickel
lever movement,
with associated
bracelet, c1945.
£3,800–4,200 *S(G)*

A Rolex Oyster Perpetual
18ct gold self-winding
calendar wristwatch, with
moon phases, nickel lever
movement, Super Oyster
crown, dial and movement
signed, c1950.
£18,000–19,000 *S(G)*

A Patek Philippe & Co., 18ct gold perpetual calendar chronograph wristwatch with moon phases, nickel lever movement, the dial and movement signed.
£45,000–50,000 *S(G)*

A Rolex Oyster Perpetual stainless steel and gold self-winding chronograph wristwatch, with register and tachometer, dial and movement signed, with Rolex Oyster bracelet.
£6,000–7,000 *S(G)*

A Cartier Calandre 18ct gold wristwatch, quartz movement, signed, with fitted leather-covered box.
£3,800–4,200 *S(G)*

A Rolex Oyster Perpetual 18ct gold self-winding sweep seconds wristwatch, with cloisonné enamel map of India, presented to the first Prime Minister of India, c1949.
£25,000–26,000 *S(G)*

A Rolex Oyster Perpetual 18ct gold self-winding sweep seconds wristwatch, with cloisonné enamel dial, signed, c1955.
£7,000–8,000 *S(G)*

A Patek Philippe & Co., 18ct white gold self-winding perpetual calendar wristwatch, with moon phases, signed, c1972.
£16,500–17,500 *S(G)*

A Patek Philippe & Co., 18ct gold self-winding perpetual calendar wristwatch, with moon phases and display back, dial and movement signed.
£12,000–13,000 *S(G)*

A Cartier 18ct gold backwind bracelet lady's wristwatch, movement signed 'Jaeger Le Coultre', c1940, with integral rope twist bracelet.
£3,000–3,500 *S(G)*

A Patek Philippe & Co., platinum perpetual calendar chronograph wristwatch, with register, moon phases and leap year, nickel lever movement, signed.
£42,000–45,000 *S(G)*

A Ulysse Nardin 18ct two-colour gold self-winding astronomical wristwatch, Planetarium Copernicus, limited edition No. 26-65.
£9,000–10,000 *S(G)*

A Patek Philippe & Co. 18ct gold square watch, with integral bracelet, dial and movement signed, c1975.
£5,500–6,500 *S(G)*

A mahogany round top wheel barometer, with wooden bezel, by Domenico Gatty, London, c1780.
£2,500–3,000 *W&W*

A mahogany stick barometer, by Dollond, London, c1835.
£2,500–2,800 *W&W*

A mahogany 10in dial wheel barometer, by Matthew Woller, Birmingham, c1800.
£1,500–1,900 *W&W*

A mahogany stick barometer with waisted door, by Francis Pelegrino, London, c1800.
£1,500–1,900 *W&W*

A rosewood and brass inlaid wheel barometer, by Francis Amadio, London, c1830.
£2,000–2,500 *W&W*

A satinwood 12in dial wheel barometer, with pagoda top, by Gabalio, London, c1810.
£3,500–4,500 *W&W*

A flame mahogany 'two-dial' wheel barometer, by King, Bristol, c1830.
£700–900 *W&W*

A mahogany inlaid wheel barometer, with Masonic symbols, by Peter Caminada, Taunton, c1820.
£800–900 *W&W*

A flame mahogany 6in dial wheel barometer, by John Braham, Bristol, c1830.
£1,200–1,800 *W&W*

A flame mahogany scroll top wheel barometer, by Cox, Devonport, c1860.
£400–600 *W&W*

A pair of library globes, by Smith, each on a mahogany frame with 3 square tapering legs and compass stretcher, early 19thC, 25in (64cm) diam.
£25,000–30,000 *C*

A pair of Regency celestial and terrestrial table globes, by J. and W. Cary, on oak and mahogany stands, globes 12in (30cm) diam. **£5,000–6,000** *C*

A pair of mahogany table globes, by Newton, the terrestrial dated 1860, the celestial dated 1840, 17in (43cm) diam.
£6,500–7,500 *S*

A gilt and lacquered brass mechanical calculator, the cover plate signed within a reserve 'Rechnungs Maschine von Johann Christoph Schuster zu Ansbach in Franken angefangen 1820 vollendet 1822', 8½in (21cm) diam, with later mahogany case.
£7,700,000+ *C*

A manuscript celestial globe, by C.A. Hoffmann, made up of 14 paper gore strips and 2 polar calottes pasted over a wood and plaster base, c1730, 18in (46cm) diam. **£35,000–38,000** *C*

A lacquered brass English drum-type planetarium with tellurium and lunarium attachments, signed 'W. & S. Jones, Holborn, London', 17½in (44cm) high overall, the orrery contained in original fitted mahogany case, c1800.
£16,000–20,000 *C*

A pair of terrestrial and celestial pocket globes, by Newton's, 66 Chancery Lane, London, each globe with 12 hand coloured engraved gores over a plaster base, c1817, 3in (7.5cm) diam.
£7,000–8,000 *C*

A glass celestial globe, by Sholbergs Himmelsglob, Stockholm, the sphere made up of 2 hemispheres joined along the ecliptic and engraved, mounted and clamped at each pole, c1870.
£8,000–9,000 *C*

A pair of large library globes, by Thomas Malby and Son, terrestrial 1867, celestial 1870, each made of 2 sets of 12 lithographed gores with polar calottes, 18in (46cm) diam.
£25,000–30,000 *C*

Two table globes, terrestrial by W. & J. Newton, 1784, the celestial by Cary, 1800, 17in (44cm) diam.
£3,500–4,500 *S*

A pair of French bronze and ormolu three-light candelabra, after a model by the Caffieri workshop, on marmo rosso antico stands and toupie feet, mid-19thC, 20in (51cm) high.
£4,000–5,000 *CSK*

A pair of giltwood and gilt composition four-light girandoles, each backplate centred by a mirror with a beaded frame, 18thC, 36in (92cm) high.
£4,000–5,000 *C*

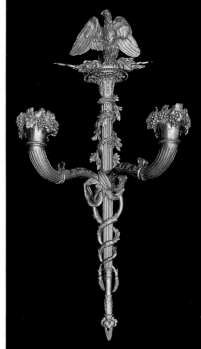

A pair of Louis XVI ormolu twin branch wall lights, with two tone gilding, each with laurel entwined reeded tapering quiver backplate, fitted but not drilled for electricity, one branch repaired, 19in (48cm) high.
£44,000–48,000 *C*

A set of 4 cut glass and gilt metal three-branch wall lights, the dished sconces hung with pendant drops, adapted for electricity, late 19thC, 26in (66cm) high.
£5,000–6,000 *CSK*

A pair of German ormolu and rock crystal five-light candelabra, each with finial above 6 tiers hung with flowerheads, drops and lozenges, damaged and restored, mid-18thC, 36in (92cm). **£8,000–12,000** *C*

A pair of French parcel gilt candelabra, c1860, 40in (102cm) high.
£6,000–7,000 *S*

l. A Louis Philippe ormolu ten-light chandelier, 32in (81cm) high.
£2,500–3,500 *CSK*

A Regency bronze and parcel gilt sinumbra lamp, labelled 'Bright & Co., Late Argand & Co., Bruton St.', 35½in (90cm) high.
£8,500–9,500 *CSK*

A pair of French ormolu five-branch candelabra, with central candle holder, black slate in base, mid-19thC.
£2,000–2,500 *CAI*

A pair of Empire ormolu twelve-light candelabra, by Pierre-Philippe Thomire, each with stiff-leaf cast central nozzle enclosed by one tier of 5 acanthus cast reeded scrolling arms with lotus leaf cast drip pans, both signed, one drip pan replaced, 47½in (120cm) high.
£42,000–45,000 *C*

A Regency bronze lantern, the tapering glazed body with anthemion plumed rams' masks and the base with a removable candle nozzle, c1810, 12in (31cm) high.
£900–1,200 *S*

A pair of Victorian brass and copper lanterns, each hexagonal body with bevelled glass, repoussé decoration and copper canopy, c1880, 29½in (76cm) high.
£2,500–3,500 *S*

A pair of French gilt bronze wall lights, in Louis XV style, the 3 candle arms cast with acanthus overlaid with acorn and oak leaves, fitted for electricity, c1850, 25in (64cm) high.
£3,000–4,000 *S*

A Victorian green and clear glass chandelier, with a circlet of 6 lights divided by obelisks hung by glass rods with gilt bronze mounts, c1850, 29in (74cm) diam.
£3,000–4,000 *S*

l. A set of 10 French brass wall lights, in the Gothic Revival style, with an arched lamp holder, fitted for electricity, c1910, 13½in (34cm).
£4,000–5,000 *S*

An Edwardian glass chandelier, in the Georgian style, the scrolled candle arms hang from a cascading tier of icicles, c1910, 29½in (76cm).
£2,000–3,000 *S*

A lady's tortoiseshell workbox, the moulded hinged lid centred by a silver plaque and enclosing a velvet lined fitted interior, with mother-of-pearl notecase, drawer with slide, pen tray and inkwell, c1820, 12in (31cm) wide. **£1,200–1,500** *S*

A Victorian rosewood and floral marquetry stationery box, with brass loop handles and hinged top, the fall front revealing fitted satinwood interior with a red morocco writing slope and blotter, letter racks, small drawers and leatherbound books, 17in (43cm) wide. **£2,000–2,500** *AH*

An Anglo-Indian ivory veneered sandalwood workbox, the hinged lid enclosing a tray of lidded compartments, with a drawer below, etched scroll decoration and silver mounts, early 19thC, 15in (38cm) wide. **£1,800–2,000** *S*

A Regency walnut and marble inlaid tea caddy, with inset lozenge panels of various marbles and hardstones, the interior with 2 lidded compartments, on paw feet, c1810, 9½in (24cm) wide. **£3,200–3,500** *S*

A George III satinwood and marquetry tea caddy, with ebony and boxwood stringing, inlaid with flowers and foliage, c1790, 8½in (22cm) wide. **£1,000–1,500** *S*

A pair of George III cutlery urns, each of half-octagonal vase form, with rising urn topped lid, turned socle and square base, c1785, 25in (63.5cm) high. **£4,000–5,000** *S*

A Regency penwork and satinwood tea caddy, the moulded lid decorated with a tulip, roses and convolvulus, the sides with flowers and foliage, on leaf-cast scrolled feet, c1820, 9in (23cm) wide. **£3,300–3,600** *S*

A Victorian papier mâché tea caddy, painted with flowers, foliage and peacocks within a scrolling gilt border, on turned feet, c1850, 8½in (22cm) wide. **£1,200–1,500** *S*

r. A pair of inlaid mahogany dining room cutlery urns, crossbanded in kingwood and inlaid with flutes and paterae, c1775, 29½in (75cm) high. **£6,000–7,000** *S*

John Edwards, *A Collection of Flowers drawn after Nature...,* pub. London 1797, 79 etched plates coloured by hand, dated 1783-95.
£21,000-25,000 *C*

C.-L. L'Heritier de Brutelle, *Cornus. Specimen Botanicum...,* pub. Paris 1788, 6 engraved plates, plain and coloured.
£33,000-35,000 *C*

James Edward Smith, *A Specimen of the Botany of New Holland,* pub. London 1793, 16 hand coloured plates by James Sowerby.
£4,000-6,000 *C*

Philip Miller, *Figures of the most Beautiful...,* pub. London 1760, 300 hand coloured engraved plates.
£6,000-8,000 *C*

Mark Catesby, *The Natural History of Carolina, Florida and the Bahama Islands...,* pub. London 1731, Vol I, 100 hand coloured etched plates.
£30,000-33,000 *C*

THROCHILUS PYRA

E. Mulsant and E. Verreaux, *Histoire Naturelle des Oiseaux-mouches ou Colibris,* pub. Lyon 1873-79, 117 hand coloured lithographic plates.
£4,000-5,000 *C*

l. Aimé Bonpland, *Description des Plantes Rares Cultivées à Malmaison et à Navarre,* pub. Paris 1812-14, 64 stipple engraved plates.
£17,500-18,500 *C*

r. I. Alessandri and P. Scattaglia, *Descrizione degli Animali,* pub. Venice 1771-75, 200 hand coloured engraved plates, 4 hand coloured engraved section titles.
£20,000-25,000 *C*

BISON GIUBATO

Robert John Thornton, *New Illustration of the Sexual System of Carolus von Linnaeus ...*, London 1807, 167 various plates.
£38,000–40,000 *C*

Jean-Théodore Descourtilz, *Ornithologie Brésilienne ou Histoire des Oiseaux du Brésil,* Rio de Janeiro c1852, 48 hand finished chromolithographic plates.
£9,000–10,000 *C*

Robert John Thornton, W. Ward, engraver, after Reinagle, *The Superb Lily,* June 1 1799, bound in original part II, no text.
£3,600–3,800 *C*

Sarah Bowdich, *The Fresh-water Fishes of Great Britain,* London 1828, 45 original watercolours and 3 pencil sketches.
£19,000–20,000 *C*

George Brookshaw, *Pomona Britannica,* London 1817, 60 stipple engraved plates, 2 vols.
£5,500–6,000 *C*

François Levaillant, *Histoire Naturelle des Perroquets,* Paris 1801-05, 2 vols, 145 engraved plates, printed in colours and finished by hand.
£123,000–128,000 *C*

Moritz Balthasar Borkhausen, *Teutsche Ornithologie oder Naturgeschichte aller Vögel ...* Darmstadt 1800-11, 126 hand coloured etched plates, l vol.
£6,000–6,500 *C*

Christoph Jacob Trew and Georg Dionysius Ehret, *Plantae Selectae,* 1750-73, 3 uncoloured mezzotint portraits, 10 engraved titles and 100 hand coloured etched plates, 1 vol.
£12,000–15,000 *C*

L. A. Reeve and G. B. Sowerby, *Conchologia Iconica...,* London 1843-78, 2,722 coloured lithographic plates, hand finished, 5 plain plates, 20 volumes in 21.
£22,000–24,000 *C*

A field surgeon's set, by John Weiss & Son, including a Butcher's bone saw with chequer gripped composition handle and 3 blades, bone saw with hinged spine, finger saw, 6 Liston knives with smooth ebony handles, bullet forceps, 2 hook forceps, 2 trephine heads with composition handle, lenticular, bone brush, various elevators, chain saw with handles, rib cutters and other instruments, contained in a velvet lined brass bound mahogany case. the lid with inset brass cartouche signed 'A.M.D. RESECTION INSTRUMENTS', one scissor missing, c1850, 18in (46cm) wide.
£3,000–3,500 *CSK*

A set of 6 ivory handled dental scalers, with burnished steel heads, in velvet lined red leather case, 19thC, 5½in (13.5cm) wide.
£200–300 *CSK*

A mahogany domestic medicine chest, with hinged lid, front and rear opening doors, the lid obverse with inset ivory trade label 'DALMAHOY LONDON', the reverse with paper label entitled 'A CAUTION', the upper tray divided into compartments, the reverse divided vertically into 12 compartments for bottles, with 2 brass carrying handles, on damaged plinth base, early 19thC, 13in (33cm) wide.
£600–700 *CSK*

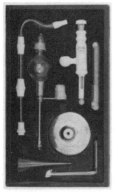

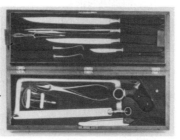

A French iodine inhalation apparatus, stamped 'IODOMETRE CHARTROULE BREVETE (S.G.D.G.), in glass, brass and turned ivory, complete with oil lamp on brass stand and ivory and glass inhaler, in fitted carrying case, 10½in (27cm).
£1,600–2,000 *S*

The use of iodine internally was advised for illnesses related to tuberculosis (scrofula, generated adenosis, tuberculosis of the bones, etc.), and the use of inhalations of iodine was specifically advocated by P. A. Piorry for pulmonary tuberculosis.

An amputation set, by T. Fenton, comprising bone saw with secondary blade, 4 Liston and other knives, finger saw and 2 ligatures, all with chequer grip ebony handles, bone forceps, tourniquet and tweezers, all in brass bound mahogany case with fitted velvet lined lift-out tray, lacking one tweezer, 16in (41cm) wide. **£1,700–2,200** *CSK*

An electroplated ladies' fainting wand, with mask finial on barley-twist stem, the end with fitted red feathers, 12½in (32cm).
£250–300 *CSK*

When the feathers were ignited and allowed to smoulder under the nose, the fumes were found to revive the patient.

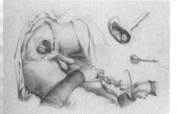

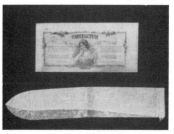

A French print, 'D'après nature par Leveille', 19thC, 13 by 17in (33 by 44cm).
£150–250 *CSK*

A T2M enema pump, by J. L., France, with brass fittings and clockwork motor, mainspring defective, 9in (22.5cm) high.
£25–30 *CSK*

A Contactum contraceptive device, of animal membrane, with yellow silk pull string, in maker's envelope with printed instructions, 8½in (21cm) long.
£200–300 *CSK*

A sycamore monaural stethoscope, by Allen and Hanbury, 7in (17.5cm) high, and a lignum vitae part stethoscope, 2in (5cm) diam.
£120–180 *CSK*

A Clarke's Pyramid Food Warmer, the ceramic vessel with spout and lid, on tin stand with ceramic candle holder, repaired, c1890, 10in (25cm), with printed instructions, and a creamware food warmer, repaired.
£150–180 *CSK*

A group of items relating to a pair of Siamese twins, Daisey and Violet Hilton, comprising an X-ray photograph of the young girls, a postcard photograph of the girls as infants, 2 publicity photographs of the girls as performers, a newspaper cutting reporting their birth and a newspaper cutting printed after their death.
£125–140 *CSK*

Daisey and Violet were born in Brighton in February 1908. Their mother was described at the time as 'a servant girl', and was presumably unmarried. Due to the circumstances of both their condition and her position, it is not surprising that they were adopted almost immediately. The midwife who assisted in their birth, Mrs. Hilton, adopted the girls and took them to live with her husband at the family pub. It was decided not to risk separating the girls due to the dangers to one or both.

As young women, Violet and Daisey became performers on the music hall and Vaudeville circuit. They toured throughout the U.K. and the U.S., where they eventually settled and married. Both marriages ended in divorce. They were found dead in bed in 1969.

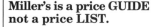

Miller's is a price GUIDE not a price LIST.

A Merlin pattern invalid's or 'gouty' chair, with upholstered back, wings, seat and removable arms, on a mahogany frame, with brass tyred wooden wheels, propelled by a crown wheel and pinion gears from hand cranks in the arms, brake lever in the seat and folding foot rest, 47in (119cm) high.
£900–1,200 *CSK*

John Joseph Merlin was born in Huys, part of present day Belgium, in 1735, and served his apprenticeship in Paris. In 1760 he came to London as a member of the court of the Conde de Fuentes, Ambassador to England. He later went to work for the famous goldsmith James Cox, where he was much appreciated. By 1773 he was self-employed and began inventing and obtaining patents for, amongst other things, a rotisserie, harpsichord and money scale. In the late 1780s, he opened a successful mechanical museum, following the example of Cox.

A metal bodied enema, finished in green with gilt lining, with folding brass arm, ivory plunger and tip, 8⅓in (21cm) high.
£140–170 *CSK*

A French phrenology patch box, the fruitwood case with 3 aspects of the human skull in relief, inscribed 'SYSTEME DES ORGANES CEREBREAUX DU DOCTEUR GALL', the base with list of numbers and corresponding human characteristics, mid-19thC, 3in (8cm) diam.
£750–900 *S*

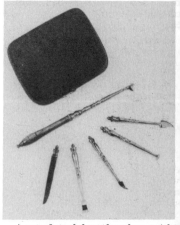

A set of steel dental scalers, with turned steel universal handles in oval, plush lined shagreen covered case with mirror in lid, mid-18thC, 4in (10cm) long.
£600–700 *CSK*

A steel dental chisel, with fruitwood handle, late 18thC, 2½in (6cm) long.
£180–200 *CSK*

A pair of bullet forceps, by Weiss, with chequered grip, 7½in (19cm).
£300–350 *CSK*

A steel dental chisel, with ivory handle and baluster stem, the blade stamped 'S', 3½in (8.5cm) long.
£450–500 *CSK*

A white metal dental mirror, by Charrière, with an octagonal ebony handle, the mirror supported in a yoke, 5in (13cm) long.
£150–200 *CSK*

A burnished steel dental chisel, the shaped head with engraved floral spray, turned stem with finger grip and mushroom shaped ivory handle, slight damage, mid-18thC, 4in (10cm) long.
£700–800 *CSK*

Miscellaneous

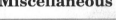

A Biram's Patent miner's airflow meter, by Davis, Derby, with lacquered brass frame, 6 blade copper fan, silvered dial, blued needle and suspension ring, in maker's leather covered card case, c1835, 4in (10cm) diam.
£200–250 *CSK*

An early 'Teasmade', the nickel plated mechanism comprising: an alarm clock, spirit burner, spring loaded match striker and automatically tilting kettle, on wooden base, c1903, 11in (28cm) wide.
£3,000–4,000 *S*

Patent 15,170 was awarded to Frank Clarke, a gun manufacturer of Snow Hill, Birmingham on 8 July 1903. An advertisement for this apparatus, reproduced in 'Collecting Mechanical Antiques' by Ronald Pearsall, gives the manufacturer as the Automatic Water Boiler Co., 26a Corporation Street, Birmingham, with London office and showroom at 31 George St. Hanover Square. The advertisement states that it is 'Invaluable to Ladies, Nurses, Professional and Businessmen'. It was priced between 25 and 70 shillings.

A French pocket compendium, the barometer with silvered dial, the opposite side with fahrenheit thermometer and compass with part blued needle, black dial, silvered scale and indicator, hinged to reveal a silvered signalling mirror, in nickelled case with suspension loop, 2in (5cm) diam, in a chamois pouch, c1915. **£200–300** *CSK*

A wind recorder, by A. Casella, with gravity driven clock mechanism in mahogany housing, single hand enamelled dial operating a cam and lever for time recording, separate belt driven trains for wind speed and direction, on slate base, and a Casella electric anemometer, in mahogany case.
£500–550 *CSK*

A Kelvin Bottomley & Baird Ltd., sunshine recorder, the glass sphere supported by brass mounts in a metal arc, adjustable for latitude, complete with curved mount for sunshine recording cards, on heavy black marble base, 20thC, 10in (25cm) high.
£600–700 *S*

CAMERAS

A brass mounted mahogany plate camera, with plaque, with 2 lenses, 'Optimus' Rapid Euryscope, by Perken Son and Rayment, Hatton Garden, London, and a Rapid Rectilinear lens 'No. 49394', by J. H. Dallmeyer, London, No. Plates 6, 2 and 3, and a brass exposure meter by R. Field & Co., Birmingham, and a folding tripod.
£350–400 *RBB*

A German 'Rolleidscope' stereoscopic camera by Franke & Heidecke, 'No. 15108', with a Zeiss Sucher-Triple f4.2 7.5cm viewing lens and a pair of Tessar f4.5 7.5cm taking lenses, in maker's shaped leather case, c1930 2½ by 5¼in (6 by 13cm).
£750–900 *S*

l. A mahogany plate camera, bearing the label of 'London Stereoscopic Co. 106-108 Regent St. W and 54 Cheapside, E.C.' with folding base, rising front and tilting back, rack and pinion focusing with crank, and Ross 'Rapid Symmetrical' f8 lens, one plate holder and focusing screen, the lens board replaced 7½ by 9½in (19 by 24cm).
£100–150
r. An ICA mahogany cased stereoscopic viewer with automatic slide feed and 6 magazines, contained in a cupboard.
£200–250 *DN*

A Newman & Guardia 'Trellis' camera, No. TI55, with Ross Combinable f11 10¼in lens, 'No. 98374', set in an Accurate shutter, with magazine back, c1920 3 by 4in (7.5 by 10cm), in a leather case.
£200–300 *S*

A French sliding box camera, the mahogany body with a brass bound Alexis Millet lens No. 2415, with removable ground glass screen, mid-19thC, 5½ by 7½in (13.5 by 17.5cm) .
£700–1,000 *S*

A Wrayflex 35mm precision camera, No. 2116, with Wray 'Unilite' f2 50mm lens, with case.
£200–250 *WIL*

A German Steineck 25mm ABC wristwatch camera, with Steineck f2.5 12.5mm lens and red wrist strap, in maker's presentation box, c1950.
£1,000–1,500 *S*

A Japanese Canon VI-T 35mm camera, 'No. 617210', with black finish, f1.4 50mm lens 'No. 27612', with trigger wind, c1958-60.
£900–1,200 *S*

A German Leica IIIc camera, 'No. 369225', with a Summitar f2.5cm lens 'No. 527926', the top plate engraved 'Fl. No. 38079', in a IIIg ever ready case, synchronised for flash, 1940.
£600–800 *S*

A William Storer type camera obscura, the sliding box focusing with rack-and-pinion, with double lens unit, angled mirror, and large diameter condenser, in mahogany case with sliding lid, slight damage and handle lacking, early 19thC, 13½in (34cm) long.
£500–600 *S*

A French 5 by 4½in sliding box reflex camera obscura, the walnut body with 1¾in lens and hinged ground glass cover, mid-19thC, 11in (28cm) long.
£700–800 *S*

A W. C. Hughes magic lantern-on-stand, the mahogany body with carved front panel, massive brass lens, maker's plate, twin access doors with blue glass inspection windows and original illuminent, converted to electricity, on a Marion & Co., mahogany lantern stand, with height and angle adjustment, restored, c1878, 58in (147cm) high.
£3,000–3,500 *S*

A French Secretan 6 by 5in sliding box camera obscura, the walnut body with inset lens, hinged ground glass screen cover, on turned stand, lacks ground glass, c1840, 11½in (29cm) high.
£800–1,000 *S*

SILVER
Baskets

A late Victorian cake basket, repoussé decorated with flowers, leaves, scrolls and shell motifs, on oval foot, having scrolled and chased swing handle, Sheffield 1898, maker's mark 'F.Bs.Ltd.', 12in (30.5cm) long, 27oz.
£400–500 *MCA*

A Victorian oval sugar basket, with shaped border, panelled with embossed flowers, birds, snakes and fruits, on a lobed oval foot, with swing handle, by R. Martin and E. Hall, London 1868, 6½in (16cm), 7oz.
£400–500 *DN*

A George III basket, by Christopher Haines, Dublin 1785, 5in (12.5cm) high.
£900–1,150 *WELD*

An Edward VII basket, chased and pierced with birds and animals amongst scrolls, flowers and foliage, with vine pattern edging, London 1909, 10in (25cm) diam, 10.4oz.
£350–400 *Bea*

A George III fruit or bread basket, by John Sherwin, Dublin 1812, 15½in (39cm) wide.
£2,000–2,500 *WELD*

A fruit basket with chased flowers and scroll borders, pierced and engraved sides, by the Goldsmiths and Silversmiths Co. Ltd., London 1905, 9½in (24cm) wide, 19¼oz.
£800–900 *DN*

A George V silver gilt fruit basket, with later presentation inscription, the pierced sides and base with chased vine pattern edging, Mappin and Webb, Sheffield 1919, 4⅜in (11cm) long, 22.8oz.
£600–700 *Bea*

A George III basket, the central panel engraved with a crest and motto 'Coelum Non Solum', with a ribbon tied foliate border and stiff-leaf chased rim, with bead cast twisted wire work double handle, tied by flowerheads and leaves, with circular box hinges and matching flowerhead and rope twist everted border, raised upon a stiff-leaf chased and bead cast rectangular foot, the base engraved 'Presented to Elizabeth Sophia Dawes By Her Uncle Joshua Horton on her Marriage', by Benjamin Smith, London 1814 14in (36cm) wide, 1805g.
£3,000–4,000 *HSS*

A cake basket, with rope twist borders, pierced sides, handle and foot, by Charles Stuart Harris, London 1914, 9½in (24cm) 17.5oz.
£600–700 *DN*

A George III swing-handled sweetmeat basket, with thread edging, bright cut band and rim base, by Thomas Wallis, London 1801, 7½in (19cm) long, 9.5oz.
£700–800 *Bea*

A George III bread basket, by John Moore Jr., Dublin 1795, 14in (36cm) wide.
£3,500–4,500 *WELD*

A graduated set of 3 Victorian shaped sweetmeat baskets, with chased and pierced sides and foliate scroll edging, on similarly cast supports, by James Dixon & Sons, Sheffield 1896-97, 21.6oz.
£600–700 *Bea*

A pair of George V two-handled oval baskets, the sides pierced and bright cut, with foliate trelliswork and reeded handles, by D. & J. Wellby Ltd., London 1910, 10in (25cm) long, 23.7oz.
£1,700–2,000 *Bea*

A George III sugar basket, with beaded borders and swing handle, embossed with fluting, swags of husks and paterae, with rams' head handles and oval base, foot repaired, the mark of George Gray overstriking that of Peter and Anne Bateman, London 1792, 5½in (14cm), 5oz.
£350–450 *DN*

Bowls

A George III bowl, by Matthew Walsh, Dublin 1780, 5in (12.5cm) diam.
£1,200–1,450 *WELD*

A rose bowl, with wrythen and embossed decoration, on pedestal base, 10in (25cm) diam, 18.5oz.
£350–400 *LF*

A George III swing-handled sugar basket, with thread edging, pierced and bright cut sides, on spreading pedestal base, with blue glass liner, by William Plummer, London 1786, 7in (17.5cm) wide, 7.6oz.
£400–500 *Bea*

A Victorian punchbowl, with presentation inscription and armorials amongst a profusion of scrolls, flowers and foliage, on spreading base, by C. S. Harris, London 1899, 11½in (29.5cm) wide, 38.9oz.
£1,000–1,200 *Bea*

An Edwardian part panelled tapering circular rose bowl, with a moulded rim, on a rising foot, by Martin Hall & Co., Sheffield 1907, 8in (20cm), 19.75oz.
£400–500 *CSK*

A George III sugar bowl, by Matthew West, Dublin 1786, 5in (12.5cm) diam.
£900–1,100 *WELD*

A graduated set of 3 pedestal boat shaped bonbon dishes, chased and pierced with flowers, scrolls and foliage with tongue, bead and shell edging, in fitted case, by Ball Brothers, Birmingham 1898, 6½ and 8⅓in (16 and 21cm) long, 14.5oz. **£450–550** *Bea*

Boxes

A Continental enamelled dressing table box, import mark for London 1904, 3½in (8.5cm) long.
£450–500 *Bea*

A George III cowrie shell box, by James Kennedy, Dublin 1785, 3½in (8cm) long.
£350–450 *WELD*

A Victorian tea caddy, with reeded sides and hinged cover, by Thomas Munday, London 1890, 3½in (8.5cm) high, 9.5oz.
£600–700 *Bea*

A George II tea caddy, with gadroon edging and shell motifs, the detachable cover with artichoke finial, by Charles Aldridge and Henry Green, London 1759, 5½in (13.5cm) high, 10oz.
£650–750 *Bea*

A snuff box, by William Currie, Dublin 1760, 3in (7.5cm) wide.
£1,000–1,250 *WELD*

A Victorian novelty vesta case, in the form of a padlock, with engraved decoration, by Nathan and Hayes, maker's mark worn, Birmingham 1888, 2½in (6.5cm) long.
£300–350 *Bea*

A George II Irish snuff box, by Bart Stokes, c1750, 3in (7.5cm) wide.
£1,300–1,650 *WELD*

A George III silver snuff box, the cover engraved with a hunting scene, by John Death, London 1806, 3in (7cm), 2oz.
£260–300 *DN*

A Russian silver cigar box, the cover, sides and base engraved to simulate a wood grain finish with tax bands, the cover also with internal inscription dated '1911', maker's mark 'N.K.', 6½in (16cm) long, 485g.
£800–1,200 *Bea*

A pagoda-shaped table matchbox, with 3 engine turned swivel doors, cylindrical columns, on square base, by Asprey & Co., London 1926, 7in (17.5cm) high.
£700–800 *DN*

A Victorian fox's head snuff box, with risqué engraving inside, 3in (7cm) long.
£2,500–3,500 *CRA*

A George IV engine turned snuff box, with leaf and flower chased thumbpiece, the cover inscribed 'J.A.' beneath a coronet, by Charles Rawlings and William Summers, London 1833, 3in (7cm) long, 3oz.
£150–200 *DN*

Candlesticks

A pair of George II candlesticks, by John Letablere, Dublin 1748, 7in (17.5cm) high.
£3,700–4,500 *WELD*

A pair of early George III rococo candlesticks, with semi-fluted baluster sockets on waisted knopped stems and wrythen fluted swept circular bases, cast with scrolls and acanthus leaves, repaired, maker's mark 'TE', London 1767, 11⅛in (28.5cm) high, 1222gm, together with a pair of plated on copper detachable sconces.
£1,000–1,500 *HSS*

A George III small chamberstick, with thread edging, initialled with detachable nozzle and extinguisher on chain, by John Emes, London 1807, 4in (10cm) diam, 3.6oz.
£400–500 *Bea*

A pair of George III Corinthian column table candlesticks, on square bases chased with rams' masks and pendant husks, with detachable square nozzles, by John Carter, 1733, 13in (33cm) high.
£2,500–3,000 *C*

Casters

A pair of George II casters, each on moulded foot, the covers pierced with stylised foliage and with baluster finial, by Samuel Wood, 1731, 6in (15cm), 11oz.
£1,200–1,700 *C*

A silver gilt hammered baluster caster, with fluted finial, embossed with bands of lion masks, flowers, leaves and strapwork, by George Dimmer, London 1926, 6½in (16cm), 10oz.
£300–350 *DN*

A pair of Regency candlesticks, with detachable sconces, the stems cast with shells, floral festoons, stiff acanthus and reeding, on hexagonal bases, the bases weighted with wood, old repair to one stem, Sheffield marks for John Roberts & Co., 1813, 10½in (26cm) high.
£1,000–1,500 *MJB*

Cups

A late Victorian sugar caster, engraved with a crest, by Samuel Watton Smith, London 1896, 8in (20cm), 9.75oz.
£350–400 *CSK*

A George II Provincial two-handled cup, with leaf capped scroll handles, engraved with a coat-of-arms, within a rococo cartouche, on moulded circular foot, by John Langlands and John Goodrick, Newcastle, 1755, 7in (18cm) high, 31oz.
£1,500–2,000 *C*

The arms are those of Cookson impaling another.

A George III Provincial loving cup, by Daniel McCarthy, Cork 1775, 7in (17.5cm) high.
£1,500–1,850 *WELD*

A pair of George III loving cups, by Matthew West, Dublin 1786, 6in (15cm) high.
£2,000–3,000 *WELD*

A Queen Anne Irish dram cup, by Joseph Walker, Dublin 1702, 1½in (3.5cm) high.
£1,800–2,200 *WELD*

Cutlery

Twelve Victorian Vine pattern dessert knives and forks, with engraved blades and tines, the loaded handles chased with fruiting vines, by Aldwinckle and Slater, London 1889, in fitted rosewood case.
£700–900 *Bea*

A George III fish server, by Samuel Neville, Dublin 1812, 11½in (29cm) long.
£300–400 *WELD*

A George III server, Dublin 1819, 13½in (34cm) long.
£850–950 *WELD*

Seven James I Apostle spoons, by Daniel Covey.
£1,500–2,000 *AAV*

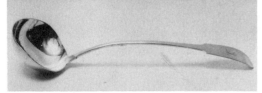

A George III soup ladle, by Samuel Neville, Dublin 1808, 13½in (34cm) long.
£375–475 *WELD*

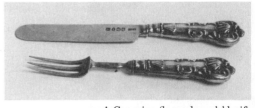

A Georgian 'leprechaun's' knife and fork, 3½in (8.5cm) long.
£100–120 *CRA*

A caddy spoon, by Samuel Neville, Dublin 1810, 4in (10cm) long.
£150–165 *STA*

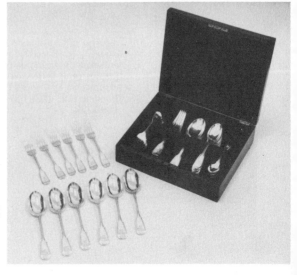

A Victorian 60-piece cutlery service, comprising: 12 table spoons, 12 dessert spoons, 12 teaspoons, 12 table forks and 12 dessert forks, London mark 1858, 129oz, in fitted mahogany cutlery box, and with a case of 24 bone handled stainless steel knives by Grant & Son, Carlisle.
£3,500–4,000 *Mit*

A double struck Fiddle, Thread and Shell pattern table service, comprising: 19 forks, 40 spoons, 2 sauce ladles and a soup ladle, each engraved with the initial 'C', retailed by Brook & Son of Edinburgh, hallmarked Sheffield 1938, 122oz, in walnut canteen.
£1,000–1,500 *C(S)*

An Apostle spoon.
£70-90 *W*

A George IV King's pattern table service, each piece additionally cast with foliage and a crest, comprising: 282 spoons, 204 forks, 195 knives, 2 soup ladles, 2 pairs of asparagus tongs, 4 marrow scoops, 4 fish slices, 2 mustard spoons, 4 ice shovels, one pair of salad servers, 6 meat skewers, 8 sauce ladles, all contained in 3 fitted wood boxes, by John and Henry Lias, 1821, 1406oz.
£20,000–30,000 *C*

The service was commissioned for the wedding in 1821 of William John Legh, Esq. (d.1834) of Brymbo Hall, Co. Denbigh and of Hordle, Co. Hants and Mary Ann, (d.1838), eldest daughter and heir of John Wilkinson Esq., of Castlehead. Each piece is either cast or engraved with the crest of arms of Newton.
Their fourth and eldest surviving son William John Legh (1828-1898) succeeded to his father's estates in 1834 and to those of his uncle in 1857. He was later created 1st Baron Newton of Newton-in-Makerfield in 1892.

A set of 10 French silver gilt crested teaspoons, the handles chased with baskets of flowers, ribbon ties and beading, maker's mark 'PQ' flanking an axe head, retailer Odiot, Paris marks c1850, 2 unmarked.
£200–250 *DN*

A pair of George III asparagus tongs, by William Law, Dublin 1785, 10in (25cm) long.
£400–500 *WELD*

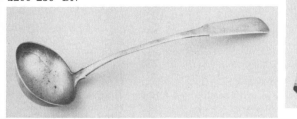

A George IV Fiddle pattern soup ladle, by John Pringle, Perth, c1827, 8oz.   **£300–400** *DN*

A Dutch spoon, with inscription on the reverse and dated '4th March 1769', 7in (17.5cm) long.
£120–140 *STA*

Ewers

A Victorian three-piece Communion set, with large baluster ewer and 2 goblets, each engraved with armorials and with gadroon edging, the ewer with presentation inscription to 'The Rev'd Joseph Arkwright M.A.', and with leaf-capped scroll handle on spreading pedestal base, Elkington and Co., Birmingham 1856, the ewer 16in (42cm), 84.7oz.
£3,500–4,500 *Bea*

A Renaissance style wine ewer, the lip and cover with masks and the handle formed as a female figure, by James and Nathaniel Creswick, London 1854, 12in (30cm) high. **£1,200–1,700** *DN*

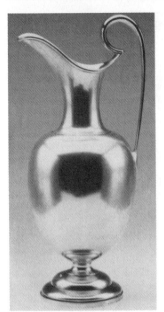

A Victorian baluster ewer, engraved with a mermaid crest, with plain loop handle on spreading base, by John S. Hunt, London 1863, the base rim inscribed 'Hunt & Roskill, Late Storr and Mortimer', 12in (30.5cm) high, 22.2oz.
£800–900 *Bea*

A Victorian baluster ewer, on a rising foot and with applied scroll rim and handle, the body decorated with rococo flowers, foliage, C-scrolls, scale and trellis work, the front with a vacant cartouche, engraved above the shoulder within a garter cartouche, probably John Mitchell, Glasgow 1854, 14in (36cm), 30.25oz.
£900–1,200 *CSK*

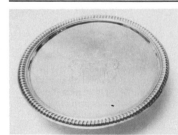

Flatware

A George III waiter, with shell and scroll border, on 3 feet, by Elizabeth Cooke, London 1763, 6½in (16cm) diam, 6¼oz.
£350–400 *DN*

A George III salver with beaded borders and an engraved shield-shaped armorial, on 4 anthemion chased feet, by John Scofield, London 1778, 14in (35.5cm), 41oz.
£1,500–1,800 *DN*

A pair of George II salvers, by Samuel Walker, Dublin 1752, 6in (15cm) diam.
£3,000–3,500 *WELD*

A pair of Queen Anne silver tazzas, by Edward Workman, Dublin c1710, 8½in (21cm) diam, 25oz.
£15,000–17,000 *WELD*

A two-handled tea tray, the edges gadrooned and with foliate and shell moulding at the corners, the handles moulded with foliage, shells and fruiting vines, the centre engraved within an elaborate rectangular cartouche with the arms of Sir Charles Johnston and a presentation inscription to Lady Johnston, by the Members of the Corporation of London, Mappin & Webb, Sheffield 1915, 146oz.
£1,500–2,000 *P(S)*

A George II mazarine, pierced and engraved with scrolls and shells, later engraved with a coat-of-arms, by Paul De Lamerie, 1745, 17½in (44cm) long, 26oz.
£2,500–3,500 *C*

The arms are those of Duncombe, Earls of Feversham.

A George II salver, the moulded border with a shell and scroll edge, engraved with an armorial within a band of scrolls, flowers and foliage, with 3 leaf scroll feet, maker probably George Methuen, London 1754, 15in (38cm), 48oz.
£1,200–1,500 *P(S)*

A George III salver, with gadrooned border and engraved crest, on 3 leaf scroll and paw feet, by Richard Sibley, London 1817, 9in (23cm), 16¾oz.
£450–500 *DN*

Inkstands

A Victorian salver, crested above presentation monogram and dated '1860', within a surround of scrolling foliage and chased scroll and acanthus border, on 3 shell and acanthus feet, London 1856, 14in (35.5cm) diam, 41.5oz.
£600–700 *Bea*

A salver, with Chippendale style border, standing on 3 short scrolling feet, Birmingham 1937, 14in (36cm) diam.
£370–400 *Mit*

A Victorian inkstand, the border stamped with trailing flowers, the 2 amber glass pots with flower embossed covers, on oak leaf bracket feet, damaged, by Yapp and Woodward, Birmingham 1846, 8in (20cm) long. **£500–600** *DN*

An inkstand, with 2 crystal inkwells, by Carrington, London 1893 and 1895.
£1,300–1,700 *LRG*

A Victorian inkstand, with 2 silver mounted cut glass pots and a central chamber taperstick with scroll handle and snuffer, on bracket feet, by Henry Wilkinson & Co., London 1891, 10½in (27cm) wide, 16¼oz. **£1,200–1,700** *DN*

A late Victorian desk standish, with undulating three-quarter gallery, pierced with scrolling foliage, with a pair of slice cut clear glass inkwells with silver mounts and hinged circular covers, and a well for pens to the front, raised on 4 slender knurl supports, the base engraved 'Charles Desprez Manufacturing Silversmiths, Bristol', London 1890, 8in (20cm) wide, 400g.
£500–600 *HSS*

A Victorian novelty inkstand, modelled as an envelope, the inkwell with clear glass liner and pen rests, a smaller rest holding a seal with uncut matrix, a match holder and a taper holder engraved 'The Gift of the Queen to William Boyd, Bishop of Ripon, Xmas 1893', also engraved with a patent registration number, by Heath & Middleton, Birmingham 1892, 7½in (18cm), 16.75oz.
£750–850 *CSK*

A George III inkstand, by John Thomas Settle, Sheffield c1818, 5in (12.5cm) long.
£1,000–1,250 *WELD*

An Edwardian desk standish, on 4 pad feet, by Martin Hall & Co. Ltd., Sheffield 1908, 14in (36cm) long, 1116g.
£400–550 *HSS*

A silver gilt four-piece desk set, each piece pavé set with small ruby coloured stones and a split seed pearl with the Persian crescent moon and star, and comprising rocker blotter, seal, pen and small clear glass inkwell, in a cream and velvet lined and fitted case, stamped '935', c1928.
£550–650 *HSS*

A George II inkstand with 3 divisions, engraved with armorials with reeded border, supporting a cylindrical pounce pot and inkwell and central combination bell/taperstick/seal, each engraved with a crest, the seal with armorial intaglio, by Paul Crespin, London 1728, the bell without maker's mark, the taper sconce unmarked, the seal and clanger with lion passant only, 12in (30.5cm) long, 47.9oz.
£6,500–8,500 *Bea*

The arms and crest are those of Cary.

Jugs

A George IV Provincial plain fluted cream jug, with scroll handle, on a circular foot, by J. Barber & Co., York 1821, 4½in (11.5cm) high, 9oz.
£1,500–2,000 *C*

A Victorian silver mounted and engraved glass claret jug, the hinged cover with crested shield and lion finial and presentation inscription, by John Figg, London 1860, 10½in (26.5cm) high.
£1,500–2,000 *Bea*

A George II cream jug, by James Douglas, Dublin 1752, 4in (10cm).
£850–950 *WELD*

A cut glass claret jug, with flower and leaf embossed mounts and presentation inscription, by The Goldsmiths and Silversmiths Co. Ltd., London 1916, 11in (28cm).
£700–900 *DN*

A late Victorian small jug-on-stand, with burner, lift-off swept cover, melon fluted ebony finial and right angled ebony handle, on a plain circular stand, engraved with a crest, maker's mark 'G.N.' over 'R.H.', Chester 1897, 403g.
£200–400 *HSS*

A Victorian hot water jug, with reeded and fluted lower body, beaded edging, leaf spout, wrythen finial and wood scroll handle, on spreading base, by C. S. Harris, London 1886, 9in (23cm) high, 13oz.
£250–300 *Bea*

Kettles

A silver kettle-on-stand, with cane covered scrolled loop handle, scroll decorated spout and chased rococo scroll and cartouche decoration, the stand with scrolled legs and pierced mask and flower decorated frieze, by William Kidney, London 1739, 14in (36cm) high, 70oz 10dwts.
£3,000–3,500 *AH*

A George III tea kettle, with leather covered swing scrolling foliate handle, the kettle engraved with an armorial, the stand and lamp engraved with crests, by William Plummer, London 1789, 15in (38cm), 88.25oz.
£1,800–2,200 *CSK*

A Victorian tea kettle, stand and burner, by John Bodman Carrington, London 1893, 14in (36cm) high, 43oz.
£700–800 *P(S)*

Mugs

A George III baluster mug, later chased with a hunt scene, maker's mark 'I.S.', possibly that of John Swift, London 1759, 11.9oz.
£500–600 *Bea*

A Victorian christening mug, embossed with leaf scrolls and fruits, with scroll handle and shell chased foot, by Martin Hall & Co., Sheffield 1855, 5in (12.5cm), 5oz.
£250–300 *DN*

An early Victorian tea kettle-on-stand, in George II style, the scroll engraved body with presentation inscription, ivory swing handle, the stand with spirit burner and 3 shell supports, maker's mark 'RK', Edinburgh 1842, 16in (40cm), 70oz.
£1,000–1,500 *Bri*

A George III mug, by John Nicholson, Cork 1790, 2½in (6cm).
£600–800 *WELD*

A George II baluster mug, with later all-over fluted decoration and engraved initials, with leaf-capped scroll handle, on spreading base, by Thomas Whipham, London 1743, 5in (12.5cm) 12.1oz.
£350–450 *Bea*

A George III mug, decorated with horizontal bands of reeding and with a bracket handle, the front engraved with a vignette of a running fox with an inscription 'Success to Newton Hunt and the Lancashire Fox Hounds', Peter and Ann Bateman, London 1792, 3½in (8.5cm), 6.75oz.
£300–400 *CSK*

A George III reeded coffee biggin, with polished wood scroll handle, the domed detachable cover with acorn finial, on a stand with curving supports with a burner, each component engraved with the same crest, by Henry Chawner & John Emes, London 1796, 12in (31cm), 33.25oz.
£1,000–1,400 *CSK*

Pots

A George I small bullet-shaped teapot, by Thos. Bolton, Dublin 1717, 8½in (21cm) wide.
£4,000–4,500 *WELD*

A George II chocolate pot, with turned finial, subsequently fixed to cover, wood scroll handle on spreading base, marks worn, by Peter Archambo II and Peter Meure, London c1753, 9in (23cm), 20.8oz. **£750–850** *Bea*

A George III monogrammed coffee pot, with thread edging, ivory finial and scroll handle, on spreading pedestal base, with presentation initials under the base, by Peter, Anne and William Bateman, London 1800, 10in (25cm) high, 25.7oz.
£1,000–1,400 *Bea*

A George III teapot, crested and initalled, with thread edging, bright cut decoration, green stained ivory pineapple finial and wood scroll handle, by Peter, Anne and William Bateman, London 1800, 6½in (16cm) high, 15.2oz.
£620–700 *Bea*

A German gilt lined coffee pot, with polished wood scroll handle and flattened rising cover with foliate baluster finial, one side engraved with a monogram, 19thC, 6in (15cm), 17.50oz.
£600–700 *CSK*

A Victorian coffee pot, with leaf-capped scroll handle and spout, on spreading base, by Robert Gray and Son, Glasgow 1843, 11in (28cm) high, 32.5oz.
£750–800 *Bea*

A George IV teapot and matching milk jug, with fluted and reeded lower bodies, leaf capped scroll handles and spreading bases, by T. Johnson, London c1822, 28.9oz.
£550–750 *Bea*

A George III bright cut teapot, by J. Le Bass, Dublin 1815, 11in (28cm) wide.
£1,200–1,500 *WELD*

A George III coffee pot, by John Lloyd, Dublin 1773, 13in (33cm).
£3,750–4,500 *WELD*

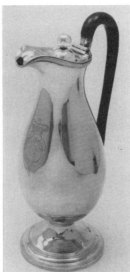

A George III hot water pot, with hinged cover and ebonised handle, engraved with the coat-of-arms of George III, surrounded by the Garter motto and a crown, maker's mark 'I.S.', by John Schofield, London 1787, 11in (28cm), 23oz 15dwts.
£1,600–2,000 *MCA*

A George III part fluted teapot, with shell and scroll border, silver knob and handle with cornucopia, on shell and scroll bracket and paw feet, by Solomon Royes and John East Dix, London 1818, 23¼oz. **£550–600** *DN*

An early George III coffee pot, by J. West, Dublin 1765, 10½in (26cm) high.
£4,000–4,500 *WELD*

A Victorian teapot, with richly embossed decoration, on 4 mask and scroll feet, 9½in (23.5cm) high, 30oz. **£650–700** *LF*

A Victorian coffee pot, with urn-shaped finial to hinged lid, beaded decoration and engraved body, on pedestal base, 10in (25cm), 24oz.
£500–550 *LF*

Services

A George V four-piece tea and coffee service, together with a pair of sugar tongs, by James Dixon & Sons, Sheffield c1918, 56.6oz, in a fitted mahogany case.
£900–1,200 *Bea*

A Victorian four-piece tea and coffee service, sugar bowl handle loose, maker 'R.G.', Edinburgh 1851 and 1853, 78oz.
£2,000–2,500 *DN*

A matched four-piece tea and coffee service, the teapot, milk jug and sugar basin by Jonathan Hayne, London 1827, the coffee pot, sugar basin lid and milk jug lid by Samuel Hayne and Dudley Cater, London 1836, 90.6oz.
£2,000–2,700 *Bea*

A Victorian Melon pattern monogrammed three-piece tea service, by Joseph and Albert Savory, London c1845, 49.3oz.
£1,200–1,700 *Bea*

Miller's is a price GUIDE not a price LIST.

A George IV teapot and matching two-handled sugar basin, by William Eley II and William Fearn, London c1823, 41½oz.
£700–800 *DN*

A Victorian four-piece tea and coffee service, by Joseph II and Albert Savory, London c1838, 73oz.
£1,600–2,000 *WW*

A Victorian four-piece tea and coffee set, by Daniel and Charles Houle, London 1855, 81¾oz.
£2,000–2,500 *P(S)*

A Victorian three-piece tea service, makers 'GR' and 'GS', London 1839, 46oz.
£750–950 *RBB*

A William IV three-piece teaset.
£850–900 *LT*

An Edward VIII four-piece
tea and coffee service, with
maker's mark 'S' and 'W',
Sheffield 1936, 54.7oz.
£550–600 *Bea*

An Edwardian silver four-piece
tea service, London 1901, the
teapot 10½in (26cm) wide, 74oz.
£900–1,200 *AH*

Tureens

A George III soup tureen, lacking
the cover, with nulled border,
2 lions' mask ring handles, on bird
claw feet, by William Fountain,
London 1806, 12in (30cm), 77oz.
£1,500–2,000 *DN*

A George III soup tureen,
by John Lloyd, Dublin 1775,
15in (38cm) wide
£10,000–12,500 *WELD*

A mid-Victorian entrée dish, cover
and detachable handle, of plain
oval form with bead cast borders,
the cover engraved with 2 oval
panels, one engraved 'T' within
foliate strapwork, by Martin Hall
& Co., Sheffield 1863, 12in (30cm)
wide, 1630g.
£450–650 *HSS*

A pair of Edwardian gadrooned
entrée dishes and covers, in the
19thC style, each with a scrolling
foliate handle, by Walker & Hall,
Sheffield 1902 and 1904, 11in
(28cm), 114oz. **£1,500–2,000** *CSK*

A revolving plated bacon dish,
with drainer and liner, on 4 legs
with rams' head masks, on bun
feet, damaged, 19in (48cm) wide.
£320–400 *LF*

Miscellaneous

A George II kitchen pepper,
by John Hamilton, Dublin
1730, 2in (5cm) high.
£900–1,150 *WELD*

A George III silver sugar vase,
possibly by Joseph Jackson,
Dublin 1775, 9in (23cm) high.
£1,000–1,350 *WELD*

A pair of George III buckles,
by John Niddin, Dublin 1788,
3in (7.5cm) wide.
£400–450 *WELD*

A pair of George III beaded sugar
vases, on rising circular bases,
each applied with 2 scrolling
foliate handles, and engraved
with an armorial within an oval
cartouche surrounded by paterae
and bow and foliate swags, the
waisted covers engraved with
crests and balustroid finials, by
James Young, London 1777,
7in (17.5cm), 23.25oz.
£1,000–1,500 *CSK*

A George III cruet stand, containing 8 silver topped cut glass bottles, by Robert & David Hennell, London c1800, 8in (20cm) wide, with a George III mustard spoon.
£1,000–1,200 *P(S)*

A Victorian 3 bottle decanter frame, the 3 faceted blue glass decanters with vine leaf spirit labels, pierced for 'Rum', 'Gin' and 'Brandy', by Henry Wilkinson & Co., Sheffield, London, 1839, 17in (43cm) high, 30oz.
£1,700–2,200 *S(S)*

A Victorian silver gilt sugar vase, the domed fluted cover with pineapple finial, the sides pierced and chased with scrolls, rams' head masks, medallions and swags of husks, on trefoil supports with rope twist decoration and hoof feet, triform platform base, with presentation inscription dated '1928', by Samuel Whitford, London 1867, 8½in (21cm), 21oz.
£750–850 *DN*

An Edwardian silver mounted green leather desk blotter, with a matching silver mounted simulated green leather stationery box, by W. H. Haseler, Birmingham 1906, 12 and 13in (30.5 and 33cm). **£800–1,000** *CSK*

A silver gorget, engraved with a royal coat-of-arms, by Irvine of Fermanagh, c1765, 4½in (8.5cm).
£650–750 *WELD*

A pair of silver napkin rings, by G. Angell, London 1860, 1½in (3cm) high.
£150–250 *WELD*

An Edward VII miniature model of a sofa, with chased and pierced decoration and padded velvet cusion, Birmingham 1901, 3⅓in (8.5cm) long, together with 5 miniature chairs and a footstool.
£400–500 *Bea*

A Burmese silver and buffalo horn centrepiece, on an ebonised wooden stand, with 3 dog of Fo supports, presented in 1877 to Henry Montague Matthews CIE, Chief Engineer, South Burma Railway, 22½in (57cm) high.
£1,000–1,400 *Bea*

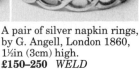

A George V enamelled silver mounted cut glass scent bottle, 4⅓in (11cm) high, and matching panelled dressing table box, 5in (13cm) long, each decorated with a river landscape, by Daniel Manufacturing Co., Birmingham 1934.
£350–400 *Bea*

A Georgian extending toast rack, 3½in (8cm) long closed.
£450–500 *CRA*

A George II snuffer tray, by Alexander Brown, Dublin 1740, 7½in (18.5cm) wide.
£1,200–1,400 *WELD*

A George II tankard, engraved with armorials above a reeded girdle, the domed hinged cover with scroll thumbpiece, the scroll handle with heart-shaped terminal, by Richard Gurney and Co., London 1744, 7½in (18.5cm) high, 27oz.
£1,500–2,000 *Bea*

A pair of George III bright cut sauceboats, by R. Williams, Dublin c1785, 8in (20cm) wide.
£3,500–3,750 *WELD*

A matched pair of Georgian vases and covers, London 1777 and 1782, 14in (36cm) high.
£3,000–3,700 *HOLL*

A George III goblet, with bands of etched lines and a monogram within a cartouche, on round reeded foot, inscribed beneath 'MB to TB', by Henry Chawner, London 1792, 5½oz.
£350–400 *DN*

An Edward VII épergne, fitted with 4 trumpet vases, on scroll supports, with inscription to base, Chester 1907, 13in (33cm), 39oz.
£500–600 *RBB*

A George III crested beaker, by Rebecca Emes and Edward Barnard I, London 1813, 3½in (8cm), 4½oz.
£350–400 *DN*

A late George III mustard pot, with chased border and crest, by Michael Starkey, London 1817, and a Fiddle and Thread pattern spoon by William Chawner II, 1826.
£250–300 *DN*

A George III punch strainer, by Michael Smith, Dublin 1793, 11½in (29cm) wide.
£1,200–1,500 *WELD*

A set of 6 Victorian salt cellars, with beaded borders and rams' head handles, the pierced sides with swags and husks and paterae, on oval fluted bases, with blue glass liners, by Charles Stuart Harris, London 1880, 5in (12.5cm) wide.
£1,000–1,200 *DN*

A suite of hunting buttons, by Jane Stone, Dublin 1786.
£2,400–2,900 *WELD*

SILVER PLATE

An electroplated épergne, complete with drip pans and nozzles, with cartouche and scroll borders, c1860, 23in (59cm).
£1,700–2,000 *S(S)*

A pair of Old Sheffield plate fluted candlesticks, applied with rococo shell, floral and C-scroll decoration, each with campana-shaped socket and detachable nozzle, probably re-plated, 11in (28cm).
£200–250 *CSK*

A set of 4 Sheffield plate candlesticks, 2 with detachable three-light candelabra branches, with acanthus leaf decorated reeded arms and central flambeaux finials, all with detachable sconces, tapering stems on shaped circular bases, decorated with scroll and gadrooned borders, and double star marks, lacking 2 sconces, 13in (33cm) high and 21in (53cm) high overall. **£650–700** *MCA*

A Sheffield and other plate composite tea and coffee service, by Elkington & Co., engraved with the initials 'JM' and 'JBB', numbered '8023' and '8072'.
£700–800 *HSS*

An argyll, with domed cover and wood side handle, beaded borders and round foot, 8½in (21cm).
£160–200 *DN*

A pair of Victorian silver plate comports, the latticed tops with grape and leaf borders, supported by vine stems on stepped bases, by Elkington & Co., bearing date codes for 1856, 10½in (26cm) diam.
£1,200–1,700 *HOLL*

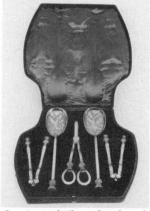

A plated salver, c1860, 11in (28cm) diam.
£60–75 *STA*

A Continental silver plate boxed set of nutcrackers, grape scissors and ladles, 10½in (26cm) wide.
£300–400 *ARE*

An electroplated four-piece tea and coffee service, the tray 24in (60.5cm) **£700–900** *Bea*

An Italian Empire style four-piece tea and coffee set and tray, with loop side handles, 20thC, 3740g.
£1,400–1,700 *S(S)*

WINE ANTIQUES

A pair of two-handled campana-shaped wine coolers, part fluted below bearded mask reeded handles and applied with fruiting bands, engraved with crests, 12in (30cm) high.
£1,800–2,200 *P(L)*

An unrecorded sealed wine bottle, of onion form with string ring, the dark green tinted glass applied with a seal inscribed 'IA 1720', with kick-in base, string ring chipped, 6in (16cm) high.
£2,500–3,000 *S*

The seal on this bottle appears to be unrecorded, but may represent the initials of I. Ayliffe of Hampshire, for whom later dated seals are known.

A pair of Old Sheffield plate wine coolers, collars and liners, each formed as a pail with reeded bracket handles, engraved with 2 crests beneath the Earl's coronet, c1820, 8in (20cm) high.
£5,000–6,000 *C*

The crests are those of Byng, for the Rt. Hon. John Byng, 1st Earl of Stafford, G.C.B., G.C.H., F.M., (1772-1860).

A pair of George III Sheffield plate wine coolers, by M. Boulton and Co., of campana shape with shell, leaf and gadroon chased borders, part fluted bodies and round bases, each with 2 leaf chased handles and engraved with armorials, 10in (25cm) high.
£2,500–3,000 *DN*

A bottle of 1893 Château d'Yquem château bottled Sauternes, 1er Grand Cru Classé, with original label, good level, label and colour.
£750–1,000
Five bottles of Château d'Yquem château bottled Sauternes, 1er Grand Cru Classé, 1929-40.
£260–360 each *S*

A Victorian silver wine jug, by R. Sawyer Jnr., Dublin 1842, 14½in (36.5cm) high.
£3,500–4,000 *WELD*

A George III silver brandy saucepan, by Robert Breading, Dublin 1810, 8½in (21cm) long.
£900–1,150 *WELD*

A selection of Château d'Yquem château bottled Sauternes, 1er Cru Classé, 1945-67.
£250–600 each *S*

A George III brandy warming saucepan, with hinged lid and spout cover, ball finial and turned wood side handle, by Joseph Hicks, Exeter 1822, 9in (23cm) long overall, 7.5oz.
£600–800 *Bea*

Two matching silver cast leaf decanter labels, inscribed 'Sherry' and 'Madeira', by Joseph Willmore, Birmingham 1841, and George Unite, 1854.
£150–200 *DN*

A George III silver wine funnel, by William Bond, Dublin 1802, 4in (10cm) high.
£600–750 *WELD*

A pair of George III silver coaster, by John Sherwin, Dublin 1812, Dublin 1812, 6½in (16cm) diam.
£2,000–2,500 *WELD*

A Victorian silver folding corkscrew, London 1876, 3in (7.5cm) long.
£175–225 *WELD*

A patented corkscrew, with ivory handle and brush, original condition, 7½in (18.5cm) long. **£250–280** *DUN*

A patented corkscrew, with ivory handle and brush, 7½in (18.5cm) long. **£150–200** *DUN*

A pair of George III crested coasters, pierced and bright cut with festoons and foliate motifs below undulating rims with thread edging, on turned mahogany bases, marks worn, possibly by Peter and Ann Bateman, London 1791, 4½in (11.5cm) diam.
£800–900 *Bea*

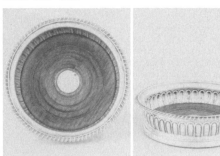

A pair of George III coasters, with gadrooned borders and fluted sides, on turned wood bases with silver plaques, by Rebecca Emes and Edward Barnard I, London 1814, 6in (15cm) diam.
£1,200–1,700 *DN*

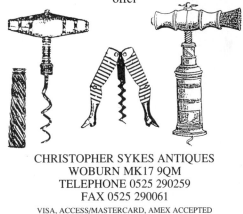

POSY HOLDERS

A Victorian posy holder, mirror set with various scenes, with mother-of-pearl handle, 6in (15cm).
£300–350 *CRA*

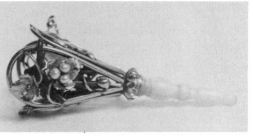

A Victorian posy holder, inset with coral and pearls, with mother-of-pearl handle, 5in (13cm).
£300–350 *CRA*

A gilt metal posy holder, in the form of a curved trumpet, overlaid with stamped husk and flower motifs, with a pocket hook, 2½in (7cm) long.
£120–170 *Bea*

A Victorian posy holder, mounted with turquoise, with mother-of-pearl handle, 4in (10cm).
£250–300 *CRA*

A gilt metal posy holder, with a scrolled tubular base applied with matted foliage, set with green and red pastes, with mother-of-pearl handle, 6½in (16.5cm).
£300–400 *Bea*

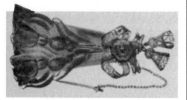

A filigree and blue glass brooch posy holder, decorated with a ribbon tied bunch of flowers with pendants, and chained pin, stamped label 'Registered/Feby 8 1850', 3in (7.5cm), in later case.
£270–320 *Bea*

Posy Holders

Posy holders were invented by the Victorians simply because they liked to wear small bunches of flowers on their clothes.

The job of the posy holder is to prevent the moisture from the flower stem marking clothing. Some holders contained a recepticle for water to keep the posy fresh, and others had tripod stands to allow the wearer to remove his or her flowers whilst dining.

Unlike most Victorian jewellery, the posy holder started off being made in gold for the society ladies, but was soon being manufactured in all kinds of metal to make them available to the masses.

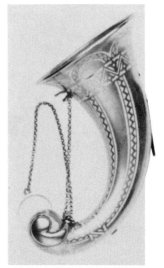

A gold plated, gilt metal posy holder, inlaid with panels of white enamel in Celtic style, complete with chains, finger ring and pin, 5in (12.5cm).
£300–400 *Bea*

A die-stamped posy holder, with slender handle and 3 small folding leaf supports, the bowl decorated with sprays of roses, chain and pin, 6in (15.5cm).
£250–300 *Bea*

A silver gilt posy holder, in the form of a flared cornucopia, with 2 folding supports, frilled lip, decorated with panels of flat chased scrolling foliage, complete with chain and pin, 5in (12.5cm).
£300–400 *Bea*

A bell-shaped posy holder, with faceted handle, the body encircled with a snake and chains, finger ring and pin, the latter with cairngorm set head, maker's mark of Fergusson and McBean of Inverness, 5½in (13cm).
£1,200–1,700 *Bea*

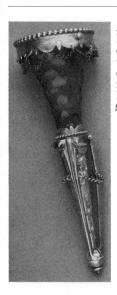

A silver mounted tripod posy holder, with folding supports and cut blue glass bowl, engraved with foliage, the beaded lip decorated with festoons of chains, maker's mark of Thomas Stapleton, London 1874, 5in (12.5cm).
£800–900 *Bea*

A spirally fluted posy holder, in the form of a cornucopia, terminating in a crowned eagle's head, embossed on both sides with scroll cartouches, one enclosing a crest, the other the initials 'A.S.' in monogram below a coronet, 5in (14cm).
£300–400 *Bea*

A Russian gold posy holder, decorated with a spiral of engraved foliage, the top with a complicated action opening into 4 leaves, chain and finger ring, label '56 Standard, Moscow 1851', in contemporary fitted case, 6½in (16.5cm) long.
£1,500–2,000 *Bea*

A die-stamped posy holder, with scrolling foliate handle, the bowl decorated with the fable of the Fox and Grapes, maker's mark 'M. B.', Chester 1900, 6½in (15.5cm).
£250–350 *Bea*

Locate the source

The source of each illustration in Miller's can be found by checking the code letters below each caption with the list of contributors.

A silver gilt trumpet shaped posy holder, with folding tripod support, engraved with foliate anthemions and decorated with chain festoons set with turquoises, maker's mark 'W.N.', London 1864, 4½in (11cm).
£600–800 *Bea*

A French silver gilt and blue posy holder, the flared bowl pierced and flat chased with beaded lattice work enclosed fleur-de-lys, the tubular stem similarly decorated with blue enamel and split pearls, the terminal of flattened form also set with pearls, one pearl missing, 6½in (16cm).
£1,800–2,200 *Bea*

A mother-of-pearl posy holder, with silver gilt mounts, the bowl applied at lip and base with chased sprays of flowers, the handle curved and similarly set with chain and pin, 5in (12.5cm), in contemporary fitted case, with label 'Parkes/12 Vigo Street/Regent Street/W', and incised maker's mark.
£2,500–3,000 *Bea*

A suite of silver filigree and shot work, comprising a posy holder, with 5 chained tassels with fringes, a pair of earrings with wire fittings, with boss and pendant bead, a flexible bracelet of 9 graduated beads covered with shot and wirework as rosettes, a brooch, cruciform covered in wire rosettes, a stiff hinged bracelet with flower foliate motifs, and a necklace composed of 11 Maltese crosses, all contained in original fitted blue velvet lined and leather covered case.
£1,200–1,700 *Bea*

A Bohemian millefiori gilt metal and ivory posy holder, the gilt metal pierced holder moulded and chased with C-scrolls, flowerhead and ribbon ornament, and set with three oval medallions of closely packed coloured millefiori canes, with turned ivory handle, mid-19thC, 5½in (14cm).
£400–500 *C*

METALWARE
Brass

A Georgian brass tobacco box, the lid engraved with floral motifs and inscribed 'William Burd 1715', the base with an engraved pseudo armorial, 4in (10cm).
£550–600 *S(S)*

A Georgian brass tobacco box, engraved with the arms of the Worshipful Company of Carpenters of the City of London, and inscribed 'John Williams, 1718, Pray keep the lid when you me lend. To fill a pipe unto your friend', 3½in (9cm) wide.
£1,000–1,200 *S(S)*

A Georgian brass and copper tobacco box, the lid inscribed 'James Rouse, London 1737', the base later pierced with holes and inscribed 'ER', 3½in (9cm).
£400–500 *S(S)*

A Georgian brass tobacco box, the lid engraved with the arms of The Worshipful Company of Turners of the City of London, the base inscribed 'George Wise 1735', the inside of lid with ink inscription, 4in (10cm) wide.
£700–800 *S(S)*

A pair of Georgian brass candlesticks, each with shell cast base, rising to double knopped stem, drip pans missing, c1750, 9in (22cm).
£450–550 *S(S)*

A pair of Georgian brass candlesticks, each with shell cast base rising to double knopped stem, drip pans missing, c1750, 9½in (23.5cm).
£450–500 *S(S)*

A pair of German brass candlesticks, each with domed octagonal base rising to vase knopped baluster stem, 18thC, 7½in (19cm).
£300–400 *S(S)*

A trumpet base brass candlestick, with ribbed stem, wide drip tray decorated with an engraved circle, on plain domed foot, 1655, 8in (20.5cm) high.
£1,500–2,000 *S(S)*

A pair of Dutch or English gilt brass candlesticks, each stop fluted column stem on gadrooned octagonal base, maker's mark 'A.D.' in a row of hallmarks, and each engraved with a crest of a hog's head, c1690, 10½in (26cm).
£17,000–20,000 *S(S)*

A pair of brass twin branch candelabra, each with a canted stepped base, engraved with a heraldic lion rising to knopped vase stem and nozzle, with slip-in branches and matching crests to drip pans, c1740, 15½in (39cm).
£5,400–5,800 *S(S)*

A pair of brass candlesticks, c1770, 11in (28cm).
£300–350 *KEY*

A pair of French brass
candlesticks, each with double
domed petal base and reeded
baluster stem, drip pans missing,
18thC, 9½in (24cm).
£200–300 *S(S)*

A pair of French brass
candlesticks, each with domed
petal base and baluster stem,
engraved all-over with flowers,
drip pans lacking, stamped 'P31'
under the base, 8in (20cm).
£200–300 *S(S)*

Two Dutch 'Heemskerk' brass
candlesticks, each with wide mid-
drip pan and baluster stems on
domed base, 9in (23cm).
£1,000–1,200 *S(S)*

A pair of Georgian brass
candlesticks, each with dished
square gadrooned base rising
to double knopped stem, beaded
nozzle and drip pan, c1755,
10in (24.5cm).
£2,000–2,500 *S(S)*

A pair of 17thC style brass
candlesticks, c1890, 15in (38cm).
£800–900 *ARE*

A French brass snuffer stand and
candlestick, the octagonal nozzle
above open work stem and domed
foot, the handle engraved with a
crest, 18thC, 6in (15cm), together
with a pair of brass snuffer scissors.
£350–400 *S(S)*

A brass snuffer tray, of double
ended form with reeded rim, a
scroll side handle, on 4 oval feet,
c1740, 8in (20cm).
£500–550 *S(S)*

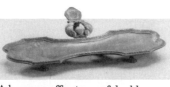

A brass snuffer tray, of double
ended form with beaded rim, shell
and flower cast side handle, on
4 paw feet, probably French,
c1740, 8in (20cm), and a pair of
snuffer scissors, c1820.
£350–400 *S(S)*

A brass snuffer tray, with angular
shaped end and long handle, on
3 ball feet, c1720, 10in (25cm).
£210–240 *S(S)*

A brass snuffer tray, the shaped
end with foliate handle, on 3 ball
feet, damaged, 18thC, 9in (23cm),
and a pair of snuffer scissors,
stamped 'B' over 'HW', 3in (7.5cm).
£220–250 *S(S)*

A brass snuffer tray, with trefid
handle, on 3 ball feet, damaged,
early 18thC, 8½in (21cm).
£100–200 *S(S)*

A pair of brass Colza oil lamps, each with classical urn reservoir and a single branch stamped 'Smethurst manufacturer 138 New Bond St', on associated marblised wood plinths, converted to electricity, mid-19thC, 16in (41cm).
£400–500 *S(S)*

A brass twelve-branch chandelier, the ball and baluster vase stem supporting 2 tiers of dolphin mask scroll branches, terminating in wide drip pans with turned nozzles, the ring stamped 'T. Smith', c1900, 33in (81cm).
£900–1,200 *S(S)*

A Georgian brass beer jug, the pear-shaped body with spout and scroll handle on a domed foot, hallmarks including crowned 'D', spout tipped, c1760, 9in (22.5cm).
£5,000–5,500 *S(S)*

A Georgian design brass snuffer stand, on canted rectangular domed foot, 4in (10cm), and a pair of Georgian brass snuffer scissors, 5½in (13.5cm). **£170–220** *S(S)*

A French brass ewer, the body with 2 girdles, and cut-card decorated base with a scroll handle, on domed beaded foot, engraved with a coat-of-arms, probably 'Mordon' or 'M'Beath', 11in (28cm).
£1,700–2,000 *S(S)*

A French brass ewer, with scroll handle and tapering body with raised bands and cut-card decoration, on knopped stem and foot, early 18thC, 7½in (19cm).
£600–900 *S(S)*

A Victorian gilt brass lamp, of classical form with fluted column on acanthus leaf base, with paw feet, supporting a bar with 2 downswept branches, converted to electricity, c1840, 31in (79cm).
£850–1,000 *S(S)*

A Georgian brass lidded tankard, the baluster body with a single girdle, scroll thumbpiece and handle, maker's stamp of 2 fleur-de-lys under base, c1760, 8in (20cm).
£4,000–4,500 *S(S)*

A Georgian brass coffee pot, hallmarks indistinct, c1750, 10in (25cm).
£4,400–4,800 *S(S)*

A Georgian brass baluster tankard, with scroll handle and domed foot, traces of maker's hallmarks, c1760, 5in (13cm).
£1,700–2,000 *S(S)*

A brass coffee pot, with domed lid and ball finial, wood side handle, maker's marks indistinct, early 18thC, 9½in (23.5cm).
£4,000–5,000 *S(S)*

A Georgian brass tankard, with domed lid and scrolled thumbpiece, the baluster body with a reeded girdle and engraved monogram, silvered interior, c1760, 8in (20cm).
£3,000–3,500 *S(S)*

A Georgian brass coffee pot, with a double domed lid, wood finial and scroll handle, row of hallmarks of the maker 'A.C.', 10⅛in (26cm).
£2,800–3,200 *S(S)*

A French brass coffee pot, the body with domed lid and plume thumbpiece, on 3 raised feet with turned wood side handle and engraved monogram, mid-18thC, 10½in (26.5cm).
£600–800 *S(S)*

A pair of French brass soap and sponge boxes, each of hinged circular form on domed petal base, now mounted on associated tray, with scalloped rim, on ball feet, c1740, 11½in (29cm) wide.
£700–1,000 *S(S)*

An engraved brass quill case, by Madin of Sheffield, decorated with animal heads and foliage, and inscribed 'I was in Sheffield made & many can witness I was not made by any man', 1655, 5in (13cm).
£3,000–3,500 *S(S)*

A brass and wrought iron down hearth cooking pan, 18thC, 24in (61cm).
£250–300 *KEY*

A brass door stop in the form of a bear, late 19thC, 14in (36cm).
£350–400 *ChC*

A set of 3 Georgian brass tea caddies, with stepped lids and reeded bases, shell handles and engraved crests, 18thC, 4¼in (11cm), and 2 brass pots with wood side handles, late 19thC.
£2,000–2,500 *S(S)*

A brass letter clip in the form of a duck's head, 19thC, 6in (15cm).
£75–100 *RdeR*

Bronze

A bronze cooking pot, 17thC,
5½in (14cm).
£300–400 *KEY*

Three bronze mortars, 17thC.
£120–400 each *KEY*

A Regency patinated bronze
inkwell, in the form of an
armadillo, c1820, 5in (12.5cm).
£1,000–1,200 *ChC*

A pair of French bronze and
parcel gilt candlesticks, each
with fluted tapering stem on
acanthus leaf triform base,
c1830, 10in (25cm).
£420–460 *S(S)*

An Indian cast bronze
candlestick, in the shape of a
cobra, 9in (22.5cm).
£250–280 *ChC*

A bronze inkwell, in the form
of a cat as illustrated in
Christopher Payne's 'The
Animalier', c1870, 7in
(17.5cm) long.
£750–850 *ARE*

A cast bronze and patinated
figure of a bull, after the model by
Giambologna, north European,
17thC, 11in (28cm) high.
£5,250–5,500 *ChC*

A cast bronze candlestick in the
form of a dragon, on marble base,
19thC, 8in (20cm) high.
£450–480 *ChC*

A gilt bronze inkwell, in the form
of an ostrich, c1880, 8in (20cm).
£450–480 *ChC*

A Vienna cold painted bronze
horse's head letter clip,
unmarked. 19thC, 7in
(18cm) long.
£600–700 *RdeR*

A pair of silvered and gilt bronze
hooks, in the form of donkeys,
heads, c1870, 9in (22.5cm) long.
£850–950 *ChC*

A Dove of Peace bronze finial
from a 17thC chandelier, on a
modern base, 6in (15cm) high.
£600–700 *ChC*

A French cast and patinated bronze figure of the Florentine boar, on a rouge marble base, c1820, 9in (22.5cm) wide.
£1,800–1,950 *ChC*

A pair of patinated bronze lions, after a model by Donatello, 17thC, 10in (25cm) high.
£3,200–3,500 *ChC*

A cast bronze model of a dog, 16thC, 6in (15cm).
£1,800–2,000 *ChC*

An Italian bronze of group Hercules and the Namean stag, c1820, 8in (20cm) high.
£850–950 *ChC*

A Vienna bronze figure of a kingfisher, original paint, unmarked, 19thC, 2½in (6cm) high.
£200–250 *RdeR*

A Vienna bronze figure of a squirrel, 19thC, 3in (7.5cm) high.
£200–300 *RdeR*

An Austrian bronze figure of a lizard, by Bergman, marked, 19thC, 8in (20cm) long.
£100–200 *RdeR*

A French goat and satyr, c1830, 11in (28cm) high.
£1,200–1,450 *ChC*

Three Austrian cold painted bronze figures of hares, c1870, 2in (5cm).
£200–220 each *ChC*

A bronze ashtray, in the form of a scallop shell, with a frog with glass eyes, c1920, 6in (15cm) wide.
£300–350 *ChC*

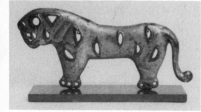

A gilt bronze copy of a Han tiger, c1900, 6in (15cm) wide.
£300–380 *ChC*

A cast bronze elephant's head, c1900, 8½in (21.5cm) high.
£850–950 *ChC*

A Vienna bronze figure of a bird, signed Bergman, 19thC, 6in (15cm) wide.
£700–800 *RdeR*

A bronze figure of General Gordon, cast from a model by Hamo Thornycroft, signed and dated '1888', inscribed 'CHARLES GEORGE GORDON', 14½in (37cm) high.
£1,000–1,200 *C*

The model of General Gordon was originally commissioned in 1885 and on completion was to be erected in Trafalgar Square. Sculpting his model, Hamo Thornycroft was anxious to obtain personal descriptions of his subject. Such descriptions proved to be rather contradictory, General Gordon being described as 'rather hump-backed' by one acquaintance but as someone who 'sat up well' by another. The General's brother urged Thornycroft to make the model 'as little military as possible'.

A Georgian bronze 14lb wool-weight, cast in relief with the Royal coat-of-arms, initialled 'G.R.', the border stamped with a crowned 'G', 2 ewers, a dagger and 2 capital 'A's', early 18thC, 7in (18cm).
£600–700 *S(S)*

A bronze group of 2 whippets, playing with a tortoise at their feet, on an oval base, 7in (17.5cm) long.
£70–100 *LF*

A bronze figure of a tiger, 17in (43cm) long.
£160–200 *LF*

A bronze model of The Duke of Wellington on horseback, by Mathew Cotes Wyatt, black brown patination, on a white marble oval plinth, mid-19thC, 10in (25cm).
£500–800 *S(S)*

A bronze figure of a Greek discus thrower, 15in (38cm) high.
£55–80 *LF*

A French gilt bronze model of a shepherdess on a rock, with a sheep and a spindle, by Suzanne Bizard, signed, on an oval green striated marble base, late 19th/early 20thC, 9in (23.5cm).
£400–600 *S*

Suzanne Bizard was born in Saint-Amand (Cher), and specialised in children, groups and portrait busts which she exhibited at the Société Perpetuelle des Artistes Français until 1936.

A pair of bronze figures, The Land and The Sea, by Etienne Henri Dumaige, mid-brown patina, signed, dated '1869', numbered '18448' and '18449', 19½in (49.5cm).
£2,200–2,700 *S*

A bronze figure of The Boy Blacksmith, by Antoine Bofill, light brown patina, signed, foundry stamp 'F. B. Sanson Succr. Hamburg u. Neuerwall, E.V.10', Spanish, late 19thC, 15in (38cm).
£1,000–1,200 *S*

A bronze group of St George and the Dragon, pale brown patination, late 19thC, 16in (41cm).
£550–850 *S(S)*

A bronze model of The Republic of France, by Albert-Ernest Carrier Belleuse, dark brown-gold patina, signed, 19thC, 18in (45.5cm).
£1,400–1,700 *S*

A bronze figure of Hercules wrestling with the Nemean Lion, by Edouard Drouot, with 3-colour gilt, green and brown patina, signed, foundry mark 'LN' and 'JL Paris', 27in (69cm).
£2,000–3,000 *S*

A bronze portrait bust of Nikolaus I, by Friedrich August Théodor Dietrich, golden patina, signed, foundry stamp of 'H. Gladenbeck', on black marble half column with silver presentation label, Bosnian, 19thC, 20in (51cm) high overall.
£1,800–2,200 *S*

This commemorative bust shows Tsar Nikolaus I (1825-55) in the uniform of the Regiment of the Imperial Guard, which was founded by Peter the Great. The silver plate on the front of the socle is inscribed with a list of German officers who, presumably, contributed to the bust. Friedrich Dietrich was born in Bosnia in 1817, studied in Berlin and specialised in portrait busts of Royalty, especially Russian and Prussian.

A bronze group of a kitten and sparrow, by Emmanuel Fremiet, red/brown patination, signed, Barbedienne foundry stamp, c1880, 15in (38cm) wide.
£1,700–2,200 *S(S)*

A bronze relief of a bull, by Christophe Fratin, very dark brown patina, signed, dated '1864', 19thC, 10in (25cm) wide.
£1,000–1,500 *S*

An Austrian bronze figure of a leaping bull, by Otto Hofner, dark brown patina, signed, on a bronze base, 12in (31cm) overall.
£1,500–1,800 *S*

A bronze model of 'Jiji', a greyhound with a ball, by Pierre Jules Mêne, dark brown patina, 19thC, 6in (15cm).
£600–900 *S*

A bronze figure of a child rescued by a St Bernard dog, by Adrien-Etienne Gaudez, dark brown patina, signed, inscribed label on base, late 19thC, 17in (43cm).
£800–1,200 *S*

A bronze entitled 'Ecole de Filles', by Pierre-Eugène-Emile Hébert, high and low relief, dark brown patina, signed, dated '1874', 13½in (34cm).
£800–1,000 *S*

This relief panel shows a scrawny figure peeking through the girls' school door which bears the label 'Ainsi seront traités touts rodeurs témeraires', (That's what happens to cheeky prowlers). Cupid cries on the outside as the girls remain behind bars.

A pair of bronze Arab stallions, after the model of Ibrahim, by Pierre Jules Mêne, rich brown patina, stamped, one indistinctly, 19thC, 4in (11cm). **£750–850** *S*

A bronze entitled 'Ecco il Moccolo', by Johann Eduard Müller, weathered brown patina with substantial traces of oxidisation, stamped 'Eduard Müller/aus Coburg Rom 1877', with foundry seal 'A Neli Fuse Roma', on a marble base, cracked, 67in (170cm). **£6,500–9,000** *S*

'Ecco il Moccolo' litrally translates as 'Here it is, candlestick - or light'. This unusual figure is extolling the virtues of electricity as a recently discovered source of light.
Müller began his life as a scullion in the palace kitchens of Coburg, and then went to study at the Antwerp Academy, and on to Rome where he ultimately became a professor at the Academy of St Luke.

A bronze figure of a female diver, by Fernand Lorrain, mid-brown patina, signed, late 19thC, 24in (61cm).
£350–550 *S*

A French bronze group entitled 'The Combat', cast from a model by Philippe Poitevin, depicting a battle between a Cimbrian and Roman warrior, each with stylised helmets, their unbridled charges rearing and falling respectively, signed 'Poitevin' and inscribed 'Boy', on a stepped rocky base with title plaque, with a modern black painted wood plinth, 19thC, group 28in (71cm) wide.
£4,000–6,000 *C*

Philippe Poitevin (1831-1907) studied at the Ecole des Beaux-Arts in Paris and remained there for a period of 10 years, before returning to Marseille, where he worked mainly for the Palais de Longchamp. His works were exhibited in the Paris Salon from 1855, among them busts, plaques, figures and genre scenes.
Boy was the name of a foundry, active during the 2nd half of the 19thC.

A bronze figure of Ondine, by Mathurin Moreau, mid-brown patina, signed, on a base with bronze title cartouche, inscribed 'Médaille d'Honneur', late 19thC, 21in (53cm). **£2,500–3,000** *S*

A bronze figure of young man, by Emile Louis Picault, black patina, signed 'E. Picault', inscribed in Latin on base 'Virtutes Civicae Ense et Labore', c1900, 23½in (60cm).
£950–1,200 *S*

A bronze figure of a seated pointer with a hare, by Ferdinand Pautrot, dark brown patina, signed, late 19thC, 19in (48.5cm). **£1,700–2,200** *S*

Copper

A Georgian copper tobacco box, the lid engraved with a coat-of-arms, the base inscribed 'Henry Clarson, Wine Cooper 1732', 4in (10cm) wide.
£700–800 *S(S)*

A copper weather vane, in the form of a cockerel, c1800, 22in (56cm) high.
£700–800 *KEY*

A copper chalice, the bowl inscribed 'The gift of Richard Keat to Thomas Keat. Katherine wife 1700', monogrammed 'RK' on a ball knopped brass stem and domed foot, traces of gilding, 9in (22cm).
£300–500 *S(S)*

A copper warming pan, c1800, 46in (116.5cm) long.
£170–200 *KEY*

A copper ale jug, late 18thC, 10in (25cm) high.
£150–200 *KEY*

A copper two-handled hot water bed warmer, 23in (58.5cm) long.
£55–75 *LF*

Iron

Two wrought iron rushlight holders, 18thC, 6 and 8in (15 and 20cm) high.
£150–200 *KEY*

A wrought iron adjustable pot hook, early 18thC, 48in (122cm) long.
£150–200 *KEY*

A German strong box, with original painted decoration, c1630, 23in (58cm) wide.
£1,500–2,000 *KEY*

A cast iron relief plaque, decorated with the arms of the Worshipful Company of Armourers and Braziers of the City of London within a foliate shield, 16in (41cm) high.
£1,200–1,700 *S(S)*

A sheet iron and horn lantern, c1830, 12in (30.5cm) high.
£80–120 *KEY*

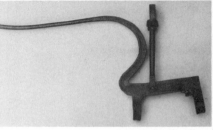

A wrought iron kettle tilter, c1800, 16in (41cm) long.
£90–120 *KEY*

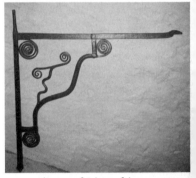

A wrought iron chimney crane, c1700, 40in (102cm) wide.
£200–250 *KEY*

Pewter

A pewter wavy edged plate, c1760, 9in (23cm) diam.
£70–90 *KEY*

A Georgian pewter domed lid tankard, the straight sided tapering drum with a single raised girdle, plain scroll thumbpiece, ownership 'E.B.' stamped under lid, touch indisctinct in base, c1740, 6½in (16.5cm).
£500–650 *S(S)*

A pewter broad rimmed plate, by James Taudin, with reeded rim, engraved crest, touch adverso 'O.P.4651', c1670, 10in (25.5cm).
£300–350 *S(S)*

A pewter triple reeded charger, c1690, 16½in (42cm) diam.
£200–250 *KEY*

A Scottish pewter communion cup, the tapering cup on a vase knopped stem and wide foot, c1780. 8in (20cm).
£100–150 *S(S)*

A pair of Scottish pewter chalices, each with swelling stem with central girdle on domed foot, late 18thC, 9in (23.5cm).
£250–350 *S(S)*

A Charles II style pewter flat lid tankard, with love bird thumbpiece and denticulated brim, row of 4 hallmarks to tapering body, on reeded domed foot, touch of John Slough 'O.P.4320A' in base, 6in (16cm).
£500–600 *S(S)*

A pair of Scottish pewter chalices, each with baluster stem and domed foot, c1800, 9in (23.5cm).
£320–400 *S(S)*

A German pewter flagon, c1790, 11in (28cm) high.
£200–250 *KEY*

A pewter flagon, by John Harrison, acorn finial replaced, cover bent, c1725, 13½in (34cm).
£2,500–3,000 *S(S)*

A Scottish pewter lidded flagon, c1790, 10in (25cm) high.
£300–400 *KEY*

A pewter 'bud' measure, c1720, 4½in (11cm) high.
£250–300 *KEY*

A Scottish pewter tappit hen, with plain domed lid and erect thumbpiece, c1800, 11in (28cm).
£300–400 *S(S)*

A Scottish pewter laver, by Graham & Wardrop, c1800, 10in (25cm). **£350–400** *S(S)*

A pewter inkwell, in the form of an elephant's head, c1840, 6in (15cm) high.
£350–400 *ChC*

A pewter cider jug, c1870, in (18cm) high.
150–180 *KEY*

A pair of pewter fox candlesticks, c1870, 7in (18cm) high.
£1,000–1,100 *ChC*

A pewter double domed lid tankard, by Thomas Willshire of Bristol, tulip shaped with open chairback thumbpiece, touch 'O.P.5202' in base, 7½in (19cm).
£450–500 *S(S)*

ALABASTER

A white and grey veined alabaster goblet, 6in (15cm) high.
£200–250 *HSS*

An alabaster bust of George III, on a grey and rouge marble column, the swept plinth with nulled frieze, damaged, 19thC, 69in (175cm) high overall.
£3,700–4,200 *HSS*

An Italian alabaster model of the Medici lion, after the antique, 19thC, 26in (66cm) high.
£4,000–4,500 *S(S)*

An alabaster group of Ariadne and the Panther, after Dannecker, late 19thC, 27in (69cm) high.
£950–1,200 *S(S)*

An Italian white alabaster figure of a young boy playing a flute, restored, late 19thC, 24in (61.5cm) high.
£2,000–3,000 *C*

An Italian alabaster group of Romeo and Juliet, late 19thC, 40in (102cm) high.
£2,000–2,500 *S(S)*

An Italian alabaster group of lovers, with stylised clouds behind, signed 'F. Vichi, Firenze', damaged, c1900, 23in (58.5cm) high.
£3,000–3,500 *C*

An alabaster bust of Clytie, on a marble socle base with carved hardwood stand, 19thC, 13⅜in (34cm) high.
£350–400 *PCh*

IVORY

An ivory panel, carved with bacchanalian figures revelling, after Ignatius Elhafen, 18thC, 8½in (21.5cm) wide.
£4,200–5,000 *HSS*

An ivory figure of George Washington, holding a sword, 19thC, 8in (20cm) high.
£1,000–1,500 *S(S)*

A pair of French ivory and boxwood figures, on waisted cylindrical ivory socles, damaged and repaired, 19thC, 12in (31cm) high. **£1,800–2,200** *HSS*

An ivory figure of Christ crucified, probably south German, minor losses, 17thC, 9in (23cm) high.
£1,200–1,700 *S(NY)*

MARBLE

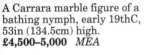

A Carrara marble figure of a bathing nymph, early 19thC, 53in (134.5cm) high.
£4,500–5,000 *MEA*

A pair of French marble busts of dignitaries, in late 17thC style, minor chips, 31½in (80cm) high, on marble columns and bases, some damage, 52in (132cm).
£13,000–15,000 *S(NY)*

A white marble bust of Evangeline, by Felix Martin Miller, signed, inscribed and dated '1860', 21in (53.5in) high.
£600–800 *S*

A white marble bust of a gentleman, in a classical toga, on a waisted socle, c1800, 16in (40cm) high.
£450–600 *S(S)*

A white marble portrait bust of a lady, signed and dated 'Mary Grant Sc. 1875', 24in (61cm) high.
£500–600 *S*

A Florentine marble bust of a gentleman, on an integrally carved socle, c1700, 25½in (65cm) high.
£4,000–5,000 *S(NY)*

This bust, said to be of Giovanni Gastone de Medici, has been attributed to Giuseppe Piamontini. Another bust of Gastone in later life, also by Piamontini, is in the Museo Mediceo, Florence, No. 48.30.

A white marble bust of Sir John Evelyn, by Joseph Durham ARA, inscribed, dated '1877', 30in (76cm) high.
£1,500–2,000 *S*

A white marble bust of a young man in the classical manner, by William Ewing, signed and dated 'Ewing, Rome 1829', on a turned socle, on a porphyry composition column, bust 28in (71cm) high.
£1,500–2,000 *S*

William Ewing, a neo-classicist in the style of Chantrey, worked in Rome in the first half of the 19thC, but exhibited in London at the Royal Academy. This marble is known to have come from a country house in the Earlham area of Norfolk, which was demolished after WWII.

An Italian bust of a girl in a mantilla, by Cesare Lapini, signed and dated '1888', 21in (53cm) high.
£3,000–3,500 *S*

A Continental white marble bust of a lady, 28in (71cm) high.
£1,000–1,500 *S*

A marble bust of a bearded man, after the Antique, worn, 20in (51cm) high.
£1,200–1,700 *S(NY)*

A Belgian marble and bronze bust of a young woman, with gilt patina, signed 'G. V. Vaerenbergh', marble socle, late 19thC, 25in (64cm) overall.
£3,500–4,000 *S*

An Italian marble baroque holy water stoup, carved with 3 cherubim among clouds supporting the basin below, damaged, 8in (20cm) high, mounted on an ebonised wood board.
£800–1,200 *S(NY)*

Miller's is a price GUIDE not a price LIST.

A white marble group of cherubs, after Thomire, repaired, c1900, 18in (45cm) high.
£1,500–2,000 *C*

An Italian marble bust of Caesar, after the Antique, on a salmon coloured turned marble socle, damaged, 16in (41cm) high.
£800–1,000 *S(NY)*

A pair of Italian white marble baroque putti supports, slight damage, 37in (94cm) high.
£27,000–30,000 *S(NY)*

An Italian white marble group of Cupid and Psyche, restored, late 19thC, 23in (58.5cm) high.
£2,000–3,000 *C*

An English white marble figure of Rebecca, signed 'J. Warrington Wood/Roma, damaged, with associated yellow and verde antico marble pedestal with stepped top and base, c1877, 88in (223cm) high overall.
£30,000–40,000 *C*

John Warrington Wood (1839-86) was born and studied in England, exhibiting at the Royal Academy in 1868, but spent much of his working life in Rome. He specialised in Biblical subjects, using them for studies of his ideal of feminine beauty rather than religious meaning.

A pair of Italian marble figures of putti, each originally holding an attribute, damaged and repaired, 18thC, largest 29in (74cm) high.
£4,000–6,000 *S(NY)*

A carved marble figure entitled 'Pensive', on a green and flecked marble column with egg-and-dart ormolu mounts, 19thC, 35in (89cm) high.
£2,000–2,500 *RID*

A white marble figure of a nude, seated on a rocky outcrop, by Henry Ryley, signed and dated 'Bristol, 1868', damaged, 22in (56cm) high.
£1,000–1,200 *S(S)*

An Italian white marble group of a girl feeding doves, by I. Possenti, on a circular base inscribed 'Peschke Fecit', signed 'IEM POSSENTI Sculp', damaged and repaired, late 19thC, 23½in (59.5cm) high, on a marble pedestal.
£13,000–17,000 *C*

A French white marble group of Venus and Cupid, signed 'Auguste Moreau', damaged, on a gilt metal mounted verde antico stepped rotating socle, c1900, 33½in (85cm) high overall.
£7,500–9,000 *C*

A white marble figure of a hunter, restored, c1900, 62½in (159cm) high, on a square base.
£4,700–6,000 *C*

A Venetian marble allegorical figure of Winter, in the manner of Antonio Corradini, repaired, 18thC, 69½in (177cm) high.
£5,500–6,500 *S(NY)*

An Italian marble figure of a nymph, signed to the reverse 'A. Bartacchi/Florence', c1900, 47in (119.5cm) high.
£10,000–15,000 *C*

A white marble figure of 'The Reaper and the Flowers', signed 'L. A. Malempré Sculp. 1878', on base, late 19thC, 34in (86cm) high.
£1,700–2,200 *S*

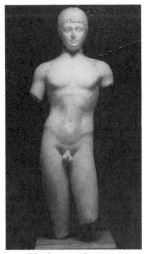

A marble figure of a youth, after the Antique, damaged, 37in (94cm) high, on a beige marble base.
£3,000–3,500 *S(NY)*

A Franco-Italian relief of Apollo and Daphne, c1700, minor damage, some cracks repaired, 24in (61.5cm) wide.
£35,000–45,000 *S(NY)*

This work may have been executed by a French or Italian apprentice to a Roman or Florentine studio, inspired by Bernini's famous group of Apollo and Daphne, carved for the Borghese Gallery, Rome, in 1625.

A white marble portrait plaque of Queen Victoria, in profile, wearing a lace veil, signed 'Frank Theed.SC/ 1883', carved in high relief, 24in (61cm) high.
£1,000–1,500 *C*

E. Frank Theed exhibited regularly at the Royal Academy 1873-88.

An Italian green marble pedestal, 19thC, 46½in (118cm) high.
£1,000–1,400 *S(S)*

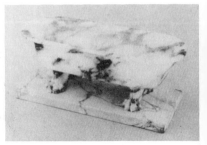

A Regency white veined marble pen tray in the form of a Roman sarcophagus, carved with a lion's head and raised on claw feet, on a Siena base, 9in (23cm) wide.
£700–900 *DN*

ORMOLU

An ormolu fox gondolier inkwell, c1870, 7½in (19cm) high.
£1,000–1,300 *ARE*
This inkwell is illustrated in Christopher Payne's book, Animaliers.

An ormolu elephant, c1880, 5in (12.5cm) high.
£250–350 *ARE*

An ormolu tortoise candle holder, with a lifting shell revealing matches, c1880, 7in (17.5cm) wide.
£1,000–1,500 *ARE*

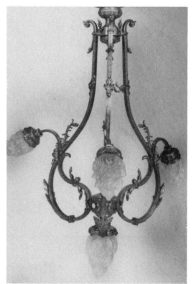

A three-branch light fitting, with scrolled and leaf carved design, embellished with animal masks, finials, and flamed globes, 19thC.
£650–700 *FLE*

TERRACOTTA

A figure of a pug, marked, c1880, 14in (35.5cm) high.
£800–1,000 *ARE*

A terracotta figure of a monkey, c1890, 7½in (18.5cm) high.
£1,000–1,200 *ARE*

An ormolu bear card holder, c1870, 5½in (14cm) high.
£1,000–1,300 *ARE*

A Continental Terracotta life size figure of a boy, holding a jardinière, 19thC.
£1,500–2,000 *DMT*

A terracotta figure of a fox, c1870, 29½in (75cm) long.
£2,200–3,200 *ARE*

A mid-Victorian terracotta figure of a spaniel, seated on a cushion, 15in (38cm) wide.
£1,000–1,600 *ARE*

A Victorian terracotta figure of a
dachshund, 7in (17.5cm) high.
£1,000–1,200 *ARE*

A pair of Scottish terracotta
jardinières, 19thC.
£600–800 *DMT*

A pair of French terracotta
figures, by Gossin Frères, Paris,
each in 18thC costume, on
naturalistic bases, signed
'GOSSIN. Frs/ PARIS', impressed
'131' and '130', repaired, late
19thC, the woman 52in
(132cm) high.
£9,000–14,000 *C*

*Louis and Etienne Gossin were
brothers working in Paris at the
end of the 19thC. Mainly genre
sculptors, their works were
exhibited at the Salon from 1877
onwards, and won bronze
medals at the Expositions of
1889 and 1990.*

WOOD

A Spanish gilt and painted
wood figure of Christ crucified,
slight damage, 16thC, 28½in
(72cm) high.
£2,000–3,000 *S(NY)*

A pair of Spanish Colonial gilt
and painted wood figures of the
Madonna and Joseph, both
kneeling, each clad in elaborately
embroidered gowns, their heads
set with glass eyes, some minor
damage, 18thC, Joseph 12½in
(32cm) high.
£4,000–5,000 *S(NY)*

A Spanish Colonial painted wood
group of the Visitation, both set
with glass eyes and originally
with wigs, damaged, 18thC, 35in
(89cm) high.
£2,000–2,700 *S(NY)*

A Spanish Colonial gilt and
painted wood figure of St.
Michael, the tunic elaborately
stippled and embroidered with
floral designs, his arms
outstretched and standing on a
bank of clouds with cherubim,
some losses, head re-attached,
18thC, 28in (71cm).
£3,000–4,000 *S(NY)*

A Spanish painted wood figure of
Christ crucified, on an ebonised
wood cross with stepped base, a
scroll with 'INRI' above, 18thC,
figure 17in (43cm) high.
£2,000–3,000 *S(NY)*

A north Italian painted wood figure of Christ crucified, slight damage, late 15thC, 14in (35.5cm) high.
£1,500–2,000 *S(NY)*

A north Italian gilt and painted wood relief of God the Father, with a cherub below, some damage, 16thC, 29in (73.5cm) high.
£2,500–3,000 *S(NY)*

A Spanish painted wood figure of Christ crucified, the eyes downcast and set with glass, some damage, 22in (56cm) high, mounted on a later ebonised cross.
£600–700 *S(NY)*

A south German painted linden wood group of Anna Selbdritt, Anna enthroned and supporting the Christ Child on her right knee, and the young Virgin on her left, paint restored, minor damage, some repair, 20in (50cm), early 16thC, mounted on a later stepped wood base.
£4,500–5,500 *S(NY)*

A Spanish Colonial gilt and painted wood group of the Madonna and Child, originally holding an attribute, the Child in her left hand, the Madonna with silver crown and the Child with silver rays, some damage, 18thC, on a later circular gilt wood base, 38½in (98cm) high.
£1,500–2,000 *S(NY)*

A south German wood figure of God the Father, holding the orb in His left hand, some repair and damage, 15thC, 27in (69cm) high.
£1,800–2,200 *S(NY)*

A south German limewood figure of St. Christopher, with traces of paint, early 17thC, 43in (109cm).
£2,500–3,500 *S(NY)*

A south German gilt and painted wood group of Anna Selbdritt, probably Franconian, the veiled figure of Saint Anne standing and supporting the Christ Child bearing an orb in her right arm, the praying Virgin in her left, some minor damage, extensive losses to paint, early 16thC, 33⅓in (85cm) high.
£14,000–17,000 *S(NY)*

A fruitwood figure of Hercules, probably south German, draped with a lion's skin, minor losses, 18thC, 13½in (34cm).
£2,000–2,500 *S(NY)*

A pair of Italian painted wood candle bearing angels, extensively repaired, some losses and refreshed paint, c1600, 32⅛in (82.5cm) high.
£3,500–4,000 *S(NY)*

A pair of Italian painted wood candle bearing angels, on later moulded wood plinths, some losses and flaking paint, 17thC, 53in (134.5cm).
£6,000–7,000 *S(NY)*

A Spanish Colonial gilt and painted wood figure of St. Anthony, originally holding the Christ Child, with tonsured head, wearing a long gown and elaborately embroidered cope with foliate designs, on later shaped wood base, hands replaced, damage and losses to paint, head re-attached, c1700, 61½in (156cm) high.
£2,000–2,500 *S(NY)*

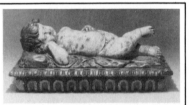

A Spanish gilt and painted wood figure of a reclining child, the sleeping child with legs crossed, resting his head on a tasselled cushion, his right hand supporting his head, some minor losses and flaking paint, 22in (56cm) long.
£2,000–2,500 *S(NY)*

A Spanish gilt and painted wood figure of St. Joseph, draped in an elaborately embroidered gown, his arms originally holding the Child, his head set with glass eyes and mounted with embossed metal halo, upon gilt and painted scrollwork base, minor losses, 21in (53cm) high.
£700–1,000 *S(NY)*

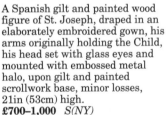

Two carved oak figures, one of a seated gentleman with a wide rim hat and beard, and a seated lady with a book, both on a Gothic carved panel seats, 15in (38cm) high.
£1,500–2,000 *RBB*

An Austrian painted wood figure of the Virgin, the veiled figure with her arms crossed at her chest, clad in long, windswept robes and standing on a serpent holding an apple in its mouth, losses to paint, 18thC, 18in (45cm) high.
£700–900 *S(NY)*

An Italian gilt wood figure of a putto holding a mirror, some losses and flaking paint, 18thC 32⅛in (82cm).
£3,000–3,500 *S(NY)*

A Spanish gilt and painted wood figure of St. Roch, a sick child pointing to his wound on his left, some flaking paint and losses, c1700, 45in (114cm).
£1,200–1,700 *S(NY)*

A Sienese painted wood figure of the Virgin of the Annunciation, clad in a long red gown belted at the waist, her right hand touching her stomach, the left holding a book, some damage and repair, c1500, 40½in (103cm) high, on a later wood stand.
£27,000–30,000 *S(NY)*

A gilt pine wood group of a couple, probably Austrian, both clad in contemporary dress, 18thC, on later ebonised wood base, 6in (15cm) high.
£1,200–1,700 *S(NY)*

A Spanish gilt and painted wood group of St. John the Evangelist and the Christ Child, the elaborately clad figure supporting the Child, their heads set with glass eyes, standing upon a cloud resting on a giltwood scrollwork base, some losses and repair, 18thC, 22in (56cm).
£600–800 *S(NY)*

A pair of Spanish or south Italian painted wood figures, probably from a Crèche, both kneeling, some minor losses and repair, 18thC, 26in (66cm) high.
£3,500–4,500 *S(NY)*

A Spanish painted wood group of St. Anthony and the Christ Child, both set with glass eyes, his right hand originally holding a crucifix, on later circular gilt and painted wood base, some flaking and minor losses, 18thC, 23½in (60cm).
£700–1,000 *S(NY)*

A south German painted wood figure of a bishop saint, the mitred figure standing and holding an open book in his right hand, left hand missing, some losses and flaking paint, early 16thC, 23in (59cm) high.
£2,000–2,500 *S(NY)*

A polychrome carved wood figure of Field Marshal Lord Kitchener, on a box base, possibly used for shop advertising, 62¼in (158cm) high.
£1,200–1,700 *Bea*

An Italian gilt and painted wood bust of a lady, some restoration and flaking paint, probably early 16thC, 20½in (52cm) high.
£1,700–2,500 *S(NY)*

A French wood head of a king, in Romanesque style, carved with curly hair, beard and large almond-shaped eyes, his lips pursed, losses, on later red marble base, 10½in (27cm) high.
£1,700–2,000 *S(NY)*

An Italian gilt wood bust of a saint, clad in a monk's habit, mounted on an ebonised wood base, 17thC, 22½in (57cm).
£1,200–1,700 *S(NY)*

A Spanish gilt and painted wood figure of a Saint, the bearded man clad in a cope over a long gown, the right arm raised in blessing, minor losses and some flaking paint, 37in (94cm) high.
£3,500–4,500 *S(NY)*

A carved oak figure of a sheep, c1750, 18in (46cm).
£2,400–2,600 *ChC*

A south German walnut bust of a saint, carved with long curly hair and beard, some damage and repair, 16thC, 13in (33cm).
£2,500–3,000 *S(NY)*

A pair of Italian giltwood and painted pricket altar candlesticks, some losses, worming and cracks, 18thC, 39in (99cm).
£5,000–6,000 *S(NY)*

A south German gilt, silvered and painted wood relief of God the Father, the bearded and heavily draped figure reclining on a bank of clouds incorporating a cherub, his left arm supported by an orb, his right hand raised in blessing, some losses of paint, Munich School, 18thC, 37in (94cm).
£6,500–7,500 *S(NY)*

A pair of Norwegian burr wood tankards, the handles with couchant lion knops, the plain drums with hinged lid, one carved with rampant lion and the other with scrolling foliage, minor losses, 18thC, 9in (22.5cm) high.
£1,700–2,200 *S(NY)*

A carved oak newel post, early 18thC, 21in (53cm).
£3,000–3,200 *ChC*

A south German walnut relief of the Agony in the Garden, repaired, some damage and losses, 16thC, 31in (79cm).
£6,500–8,000 *S(NY)*

A Norwegian wood skala, of traditional form, with traces of original decoration, the interior with bold flowers and leaves in white, blue, green, yellow and black on a pale orange field, the exterior with swags of flowers on a pale blue field, traces of an inscription below the lip, a square aperture in the base, slight damage, early 19thC, 14in (36cm).
£400–500 *DN*

A Tyrolian gilt and painted wood triptych, some minor losses, paint refreshed, early 16thC, 33½in (85cm) wide when open.
£6,000–7,000 *S(NY)*

A south German fruitwood relief of Adam and Eve, the couple embracing in the centre while Adam hands her the apple, surrounded by various flora and fauna, minor losses, 17thC, 7in (17.5cm), within later glazed marquetry frame.
£2,200–2,800 *S(NY)*

A Spanish gilt and painted wood reliquary, with Latin inscription below the top, mounted with 2 iron rings for suspension, some refreshed paint, 17thC, 30in (76cm) high.
£2,000–3,000 *S(NY)*

A south German gilt, silvered and painted wood relief of the Annunciation, the angel standing to the left holding a staff entwined by a banderole in his left hand, the Virgin kneeling, her left hand turning the pages of her book, some paint refreshed, minor damage and losses, early 16thC, 20in (51cm).
£6,000–7,000 *S(NY)*

A carved gilt wood figure of a paschal lamb, resting on a book with gilt tooled edges and clasps, late 15thC, 6½in (16cm).
£250–300 *DN*

A carved wood hanging sign, finished in dark colours and varnish, damaged, mid-19thC, 23in (59cm) wide.
£1,800–2,200 *CSK*

A Flemish boxwood relief of the Assumption of the Virgin, the Virgin, seated on a large bank of clouds, some minor losses, 17thC, 5½in (14cm) square.
£500–700 *S(NY)*

Two Flemish walnut reliefs of the Resurrection, both probably originally tabernacle doors, one with Christ standing on the tomb within a recessed niche, the other standing on the tomb flanked by soldiers below and cherubim above, a key escutcheon to the right, some damage and losses, c1600, 14in (36cm) high.
£750–850 *S(NY)*

ICONS

A Spanish gilt and painted wood relief, depicting the Nativity, some losses to paint and gilding, early 17thC, 32½in (82cm).
£6,000–7,000 *S(NY)*

An Italian gilt and painted wood relief of the Assumption of the Virgin, paint refreshed, some damage and losses, 16thC, 37in (94cm) high.
£3,500–4,000 *S(NY)*

An icon of the Apparition of the Mother of God, 17thC, 11in (28cm) wide.
£1,500–2,000 *CSK*

An icon of the Mother of God, 'Vzygranie Mladentsa', (The Playful Child), on cream ground, late 16thC, 10in (25cm) wide.
£3,500–4,000 *CSK*

An icon of the New Testament Trinity, on gilt ground, early 19thC, 10in (25cm) wide.
£550–750 *CSK*

A diptych panel of the Old Testament Trinity, and the Descent of the Holy Spirit, early 19thC, 23in (59cm) wide.
£1,500–2,000 *CSK*

An icon of the Mother of God of the Burning Bush, with the Lord Sabaoth and 11 Prophets on the borders, and further Old Testament scenes in the corners, early 19thC, 12in (31cm) wide.
£1,000–1,500 *CSK*

An icon of the Pokrov, on gilt ground, with the Guardian Angel and St. Catherine on the borders, with silver oklad, 19thC, 10½in (26cm) wide.
£950–1,200 *CSK*

An icon of the Mother of God, Joy to the Afflicted, Saints Maron and Evdokia on the borders, 10½in (26cm) wide.
£550–750 *CSK*

A quadripartite icon of the Mother of God of Unexpected Joy, St. Nicholas, the Archangel Michael and Saints Boris and Gleb, with Saint Feofelakt on the borders, on gilt ground, late 19thC, 12in (31cm) wide.
£600–800 *CSK*

An icon on 2 registers, the lower with 11 chosen saints, above the Mother of God of Unexpected Joy, flanked by the Three Handed Mother of God and Comforter of Souls, 19thC, 10in (25cm) wide.
£450–650 *CSK*

An icon of Saints Antipii and Dmitrii of Thessalonica, with the Mother of God of the Sign above, in silver gilt oklad, 18thC, 18in (46cm) wide.
£2,000–3,000 *CSK*

An icon of the Fiery Ascent of the Prophet Elijah, with scenes from his life, 19thC, 28in (71cm) wide.
£3,000–3,500 *CSK*

A Greek icon of the Descent of the Holy Spirit, 19thC, 13½in (34cm).
£900–1,200 *CSK*

An icon of the Nativity, on gilt ground, 19thC, 15in (38cm) wide.
£1,000–2,000 *CSK*

An icon of the Mother of God of Kazan, in silver oklad with gilt halo, 18thC, 17in (43cm) wide.
£2,000–2,500 *CSK*

A quadrapartite icon of the Crucifixion, with the Mother of God Ovsepetyia, the Pokrov, the Mother of God of Kazan and the Birth of the Mother of God with 8 saints on the borders, 19thC, 11in (28cm) wide.
£800–1,000 *CSK*

An icon of the Three Hierarchs of Orthodoxy, Saints Basil the Great, Gregory the Theologian and John Chrysostom, the Mandylion above, overlaid with a silver oklad, 10½in (31.5cm) wide.
£1,500–2,000 *CSK*

An icon of St. George and the Dragon, on gilt ground, with 4 Saints on the borders, 19thC, 12in (31cm) wide.
£1,500–2,000 *CSK*

An icon of the Mother of God
Bogoliubskaya, in silver oklad,
early 19thC, 11½in (29cm) wide.
£1,400–1,800 *CSK*

An icon of St. Sophia, the Wisdom
of the World of God, on gilt
ground, with the Guardian Angel
and St. Anna on the borders,
19thC, 12½in (32cm) wide.
£1,000–1,200 *CSK*

An icon of the Mother of God of
the Sign, with gilded haloes,
18thC, 14in (36cm) wide.
£2,000–2,500 *CSK*

An icon of Christ Enthroned, in
silver oklad with gilt halo, late
19thC, 17in (43cm) wide.
£1,200–1,500 *CSK*

An icon of the Archangel
Michael, by Gavriil Efimovich
Frolov, stamp on the
reverse, late 19thC,
10½in (26.5cm) wide.
£1,200–1,700 *CSK*

An icon of the Baptism of Christ,
18thC, 19½in (49cm).
£1,800–2,200 *CSK*

A double icon of
the Virgin and
Child and Christ
Pantocrator,
late 19thC.
£400–600 *LRG*

An icon of the Mother of God
of Vladimir, overlaid with
a silver gilt oklad, dated
'1884', 10in (25cm) wide,
framed and glazed.
£800–1,000 *CSK*

An icon of the Guardian
Angel and St. Anastasia,
with 4 saints on the borders,
19thC, 12in (31cm) wide.
£1,000–1,200 *CSK*

An icon of the Baptism,
within a brass riza,
18thC, 11in (28cm) wide.
£1,500–2,000 *CSK*

A painted coal scuttle, with brass fittings, the shovel fitted on the reverse, 19thC, 16½in (42cm) wide.
£200–300 *STA*

An Edwardian metal coal box, with painted decoration and brass trim.
£200–250 *SUL*

A gentleman's crocodile dressing case, one side fitted with brown leather boxes and tortoiseshell mounted brush set, the other with gilt topped monogrammed flasks and bottles, by Hermès, Paris, with monogrammed foul weather cover, some flasks damaged, c1930, 12in (30.5cm) wide.
£900–1,200 *CSK*

A rosewood and brass bound dressing box, the interior with cut glass and silver gilt monogrammed fitments, comprising: cosmetic jars, fitted mirror and correspondence file, with monogrammed lid and side carrying handles, marked 'Edwards, No. 21 King Street, Bloomsbury Square', complete with original leather case, hallmarked by Douglas, London 1826, 13in (33.5cm) wide.
£2,500–3,500 *WL*

A Continental gilt lined book-shaped tobacco box, the top and reverse bright cut with urns of flowers, 5in (13cm).
£500–600 *CSK*

A Victorian dressing case, fitted with cut glass bottles, engraved silver gilt mounts, by Hunt and Roskell, London 1858, in a brass bound box bearing inscription 'F. West, Manufacturers to Her Majesty, 7 St. James' Street', 10½in (26.5cm) wide.
£3,000–3,500 *WL*

A Victorian card case, each side stamped with studies of Windsor Castle, scrollwork and flowers above and below, by Nathaniel Mills, Birmingham 1845, 4in (10cm).
£600–700 *CSK*

A silver gilt snuff box, the movement by Duocommun Girod, playing 2 airs, the engine turned case with an oak leaf bordered lid and micro-mosaic scene of a classical building, with presentation inscription, the case by Alexander J. Straham, London 1830, 3½in (8.5cm).
£4,000–4,500 *CSK*

A Victorian rosewood and brass inlaid vanity box, with velvet lined fitted interior, containing various glass bottles and boxes with pierced metal covers and lift-out tray, with a jewellery drawer fitted to one side, 13in (33cm).
£300–500 *WIL*

A tortoiseshell snuff box, the movement with one piece comb playing 2 airs, the lid inset with a glazed painting, inner cover replaced, repaired, 3½in (8.5cm).
£3,000–3,500 *CSK*

A late Georgian mahogany
knife box.
£300–350 *Mit*

A French tobacco box, the lid
engraved with a scene of an
arrest, the reverse with a sea
battle, early 19thC, 5½in
(13.5cm). **£300–400** *CSK*

A Victorian dressing box, the
interior comprising lift-out trays
with 12 cosmetic jars with
engraved silver lids, and
manicure sets, the coromandel
case brass bound and inlaid with
mother-of-pearl, bears
manufacturers plaque 'Turrill
Dressing and Writing Case
Maker, 250 Regent Street',
London 1845, 13½in (34cm) wide.
£3,500–4,000 *WL*

A snuff box, by Bordier, the
sectional comb movement playing
2 airs, in a pressed horn case with
diamond-shaped silver inset in
lid, case repaired, 3in (7cm).
£1,500–2,000 *CSK*

An Edwardian card case, one side
stamped in high relief with a
view of Philae on the Nile, within
a keyhole shaped cartouche, the
reverse stamped with scrollwork
and flowers, by Crisford and
Norris, Birmingham 1904,
4in (10cm).
£370–420 *CSK*

A snuff box, the sectional comb
movement playing 2 airs, in a
pressed horn case inlaid with
engraved silver bands and
simulated handles, repaired,
4in (9.5cm).
£600–700 *CSK*

A George III snuff box,
the hinged cover richly
chased with a classical
scene with rocaille and
foliage borders,
unmarked, c1760.
£250–300 *C(S)*

A black composition musical
snuff box, with one piece comb
movement playing 3 airs, the
case with integral hinge and
embossed view of the Tir Federal,
Geneva, lacks male stopwork,
1851, 4½in (11cm).
£450–500 *CSK*

A tortoiseshell veneered tea caddy,
the hinged top decorated in mother-
of-pearl with a flower, and enclosing
2 covers, 6in (15cm) wide.
£700-800 *DN*

An Austrian snuff box, the hinged
cover chased with a view of
Vienna, on a matted ground, with
fluted base, mid-19thC, 3in (4cm).
£300–400 *C(S)*

A Continental coquilla nut snuff
box, forming 2 halves joined by a
threaded section, each carved
with multiple figures depicting
scenes from the life of Christ,
c1900, 4½in (11cm) high.
£950–1,200 *S(NY)*

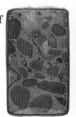

A gold mounted hardstone snuff
box, formed as 2 panels of flint
conglomerate, with moulded
borders, struck with a Dutch
control mark, 3in (7cm).
£550–600 *C(S)*

A Dutch brass tobacco box, engraved overall with allegorical figures, text and scrolling foliage, 18thC, 6½in (16.5cm).
£370–420 *Bea*

A Regency brass inlaid rosewood tea caddy, the fitted interior with 2 lidded canisters and later glass mixing bowl, with brass lions' mask ring handles and foliate feet, 13½in (34cm) wide.
£500–700 *Bea*

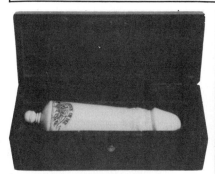

A snuff box, made by Napoleonic prisoners of war, inscribed 'Think of me', in fitted case, 5in (12.5cm) long.
£650–750 *CRA*

A Victorian gold mounted leather cheroot case, richly chased with entwined foliage and strapwork.
£200–300 *C(S)*

A tortoiseshell tea caddy, inlaid with mother-of-pearl, c1820, 7in (17.5cm) wide.
£700–800 *RdeR*

A rosewood and mother-of-pearl tea caddy, c1840, 8in (20cm) wide.
£200–300 *STA*

A Dutch gold mounted hardstone snuff box, with moulded borders and shaped thumbpiece, 2½in (6cm).
£700–800 *C(S)*

A box containing a decanter and glasses, 19thC, 15½in (39cm). **£600–700** *STA*

A tortoiseshell tea caddy, the domed hinged top with a plated urn finial, with plated escutcheon and ball feet, early 19thC, 4½in (12cm) wide.
£1,500–2,000 *DN*

A Tartan ware tea caddy, decorated with the tartan of the Stuart clan.
£150–200 *RdeR*

A burr yew tea caddy, with boxwood strung borders and 2 interior walnut covers, early 19thC, 7½in (18.5cm) wide.
£250–300 *DN*

A box with boulle decoration, 19thC, 7in (18cm) wide.
£200–250 *STA*

A snuff box, with one piece comb playing 4 airs, stamped 'SMG', in black composition case with integral hinge and internal trade mark 'H.F.V. à Paris', the lid inlaid with floral sprays in mother-of-pearl and white metal, repairs and slight damage, 4in (10cm).
£850–950 *CSK*

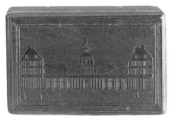

A black composition snuff box, with sectional comb movement playing 2 airs, the lid embossed with a view of the Palais de Luxembourg, 4in (10cm).
£500–600 *CSK*

A papier mâché tea caddy, with floating lid, the body painted with classical decoration after Flaxman, c1805, 6in (15cm).
£600–700 *RdeR*

A polychrome marquetry and oyster-cut walnut writing box, the top with moulded edge and inlaid with a flowerspray within an oval, with foliate spandrels, the interior with 2 divisions and a leather envelope, the sides inlaid with floral panels, on a moulded base, marquetry and oyster veneers late 17thC, and re-used in the 19thC, with printed paper label of 'L. M. E. Dent', 19in (48cm).
£1,000–1,200 *C*

A mahogany box, the hinged lid and sides decorated in marquetry with classical figures, chariots and animals, with a border of leaf scrolls, 13in (34cm) wide.
£250–300 *DN*

An Austro-Hungarian enamelled box, with engraved silver mounts, the lid depicting the Rape of the Sabine Women, the sides with vignettes of female figures and cherubs, on a pale pink ground with winged masks, flowers and scrolls, the interior and base with wooded landscapes with classical ruins, probably Vienna, maker's mark 'KB', slight damage, c1870, 3½in (8.5cm).
£700–800 *DN*

A rosewood and mother-of-pearl tea caddy, c1840, 9½in (23.5cm) wide.
£300–350 *STA*

A rosewood box, the lid decorated with a shamrock encrusted coronet, 19thC, 18½in (46.5cm).
£300–450 *STA*

A lady's cigarette box, the Berlin metal case with diamond decoration and sapphire clasp spring loaded hinge, 3in (7.5cm).
£100–150 *CRA*

A burr yew box, with boxwood stringing, the hinged top with a printed panel, chased brass handles and feet, early 19thC, 10in (25cm) wide.
£200–300 *DN*

MUSIC
Mechanical Music

Mechanical musical instruments cover a wide range of types, sizes and, of course, prices. Instruments were initially devised to produce musical entertainment in the home saving the owner the expense of either hiring a musician or learning to play an instrument.

The earliest types were barrel organs with pinned wooden barrels operating the keys to play on a series of wooden and metal pipes. They were produced either for home use or for street musicians who used them to entertain crowds on the pavement or at a private party.

The craftsmen in the early 19thC Swiss watch industry made small cylinder musical movements that initially were housed in snuff boxes, watches and seals, but later in the century the movements grew in size and complexity with interchangeable cylinders, accompanied by an organ, bells and drums contained in large bureaux. Such complex and large boxes range in price from £5,000 to well over £12,000.

The disc musical boxes introduced in the latter part of the 19thC by a predominantly German industry had the distinct advantage over the cylinder boxes by having a very wide range of discs available from stockists, while the cylinder boxes were restricted to the number of tunes on the cylinder. The size of the boxes grew until some were over 6ft high with attractively decorated glazed doors at the front through which the movement could be seen working. Many were made for public use and were installed in public houses where for the price of one penny a popular tune of the day could be played. The two largest manufacturers were Symphonion and Polyphon of Germany, but soon production spread to Switzerland and the U.S.A. Small boxes can be bought for as little as £200–300 but the larger examples are rare and command prices well in excess of £10,000.

The tone of the disc box tends to be of better depth than that of the cylinder. However, some of the best types of cylinders, termed overture boxes, have an outstanding display of musical arrangement and delicacy of sound. Such pieces, if in outstanding original condition, can be worth in excess of £10,000. The more standard type of cylinder box can still be acquired for less than £1,000. The better makers were Nicole Frères, Paillard, Vaucher Fils and Ducommun Girod, all located in or around Geneva.

Production of the individual wax cylinder playing phonograph and disc playing gramophone at the turn of the century sounded the death knell for the disc and cylinder musical box industry since they could not compete with the spoken voice. The so called talking machines were relatively inexpensive and there was a wide repertoire of music available. The decorative horn gramophones by makers such as HMV can fetch over £1,000 at auction while examples made on the Continent with painted metal horns can still be acquired for a few hundred pounds.

Condition is an all important factor when buying a mechanical musical instrument since restoration can be both lengthy and expensive. Listen carefully to the instrument before purchasing it as any problems can normally be heard rather than seen.

Musical Boxes

A Swiss cylinder musical box, playing 4 airs, No. 1030, the key wind movement with exposed controls, in a flamed mahogany veneered case with domed lid, damaged, mid-19thC, cylinder 8in (20cm).
£600–700 *S*

The serial number appears in the normal position in the upper left hand corner, however, it is surrounded on 4 sides by stamped stars. The domed lid is another unusual feature of this box.

An organ musical box, playing 6 airs with 14 key organ, nickel plated motor stamped 'MP & Co.' on the governor, the rosewood case with burr maple banding, inlaid front and lid, tune sheet, repaired, cylinder 7in (17.5cm).
£1,800–2,000 *CSK*

The organ keys are unusual in that they extend downwards below the pivots, instead of the normal bell crank arrangement. The space normally occupied by the horizontal levers is enclosed by a plate incorporating a tune indicator. The tune sheet, which is intended for a 12 air drum, bell and castanet box, is associated with Ducommun Girod and has also been seen on French musical box of L'Epee type.

A Swiss bells and drum in sight cylinder musical box, serial No. 1762, playing 6 airs, accompanied by snare drum and 6 saucer bells, contained in walnut veneered case with marquetry inlaid lid, c1800, cylinder 11in (28cm).
£2,000–3,000 *S*

A forte piano musical box, by Nicole Frères, No. 25952, playing 6 airs, with key wind 2 comb movement, tune sheet and grained case with end flap and inlaid lid, cylinder 13in (33cm).
£2,500–3,000 *CSK*

A cylinder key wind musical box, by Nicole Frères, No. 29696, playing 3 overtures, contained in rosewood veneered case with lid inlaid with boxwood stringing and boxwood and stained wood scrolling design, Swiss, c1835, cylinder 9in (23cm).
£3,000–4,000 *S*

A Swiss hidden drum and bells cylinder musical box, playing 6 airs, accompanied by bells and optional drum, in grained case with inlaid lid, c1860, cylinder 11in (28cm).
£1,800–2,200 *S*

A Swiss cylinder musical box, by Reymond-Nicole, No. 131, playing 8 airs, 2-per-turn, in fruitwood case with exposed controls, c1840, 7in (17.5cm) cylinder. **£1,000–1,500** *S*

A mandolin musical box, playing 4 airs, with unusual winding lever, hand written tune sheet signed 'A. Golay-Leresche - Geneva', grained case with inlaid and strung rosewood veneered lid, the cylinder 13in (33cm).
£2,500–3,500 *CSK*

Ord-Hume in Musical Box *refers to this box as bearing the stamp and tune sheet of Golay-Leresche. In fact, no stamp is visible, but the front edge of the comb base is inscribed 'L. Kimmerling'. Kimmerling is referred to by Ord-Hume, quoting Grosclaude, as joint inventor, with Ducommun, of the flutina musical box. The winding lever is not, as Ord-Hume suggests, hinged in the middle: it is cast in one piece in a cranked form, so that the hand grip end is central within the end compartment, rather than on the right as normal. In practice, this design offers no obvious advantage over the conventional form of lever. The box is illustrated in* The Cylinder Musical Box Handbook 1968, *by Graham Webb. The comb has approximately 187 teeth.*

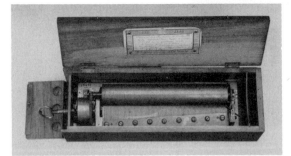

A Swiss cylinder musical box, by Ducommun Girod, No. 16416, playing 6 airs, with key wind movement and tune card, in fruitwood case with end flap, c1850, cylinder 11in (28cm).
£1,000–1,200 *S*

A Swiss cylinder musical box, by Nicole Frères, No. 24318, playing 6 airs, with key wind movement, in grained case with tune card, end flap and veneered lid, c1845, cylinder 11in (28cm).
£900–1,200 *S*

A Swiss forte piano cylinder musical box, by Moulinie Aine (Langdorff), No. 1849, playing 4 overtures, with key wind movement, cylinder signed '44' in rosewood veneered case with tune card, end flap and brass and mother-of-pearl inlay, the front with brass cartouche with maker's signature, wood handled winding key, repaired, dated 1844, cylinder 11in (28cm).
£5,000–6,000 *S*

The main comb contains approximately 98 teeth and the piano comb approximately 62.

A Swiss cylinder musical box, possibly by Bruguier, No. 5078, playing 6 airs, with key wind movement, in veneered case with tune card, end flap and inlaid lid, c1845, cylinder 11in (28cm). **£1,000–1,500** *S*

A Swiss 6 cylinder mandolin revolver musical box, by Nicole Frères, No. 43192, playing 6 airs, each as listed on tune card, approximately one half cylinder length in mandolin form, with 3-piece comb, capstan cylinder advance wheel, combination on/off and cylinder release lever and large single spring motor, in rosewood veneered case with brass stringing, the front with central cartouche with printed celluloid picture of a ship, the lid with similar portrait, restored, c1875, cylinders 16½in (42cm). **£45,000–60,000** *S*

The bass comb contains approximately 49 teeth, the middle approximately 32 and the mandolin comb approximately 81. Amedée Paillard's patent for a 'revolver' musical box was granted in the U.S. on 2 August 1870. It was an attempt to simplify the procedure of changing cylinders as on an interchangeable musical box, but due to the complication of the mechanism and the improvements in interchangeable movements, very few were produced.

A Swiss musical box, by Nicole Frères, No. 46419, playing 8 airs, with trimmed Keith Prowse tune card, in rosewood veneered case with inlaid front and lid, brass carrying handles, one bass tooth missing, c1878, cylinder 13in (33cm). **£1,200–1,800** *S*

A Swiss mandolin piccolo interchangeable cylinder musical box, playing 8 airs as listed on tune sheet, the comb covered in part by a zither applicable at will, contained in walnut veneered case with boxwood stringing and kingwood banding, with cylinder storage drawer in the base, c1880, cylinders 16in (33cm). **£3,500–5,500** *S*

A Swiss cylinder musical box, by Nicole Frères, No. 45481, playing 8 airs, with tune indicator, in grained case with tune card, carrying handles and inlaid lid, c1875, cylinder 13in (33cm). **£2,000–2,500** *S*

A Swiss hidden drum, bell and castanet cylinder musical box, No. 19133, playing 6 airs, with optional accompaniment, the comb stamped 'J', in stained case, damaged, c1860, cylinder 14in (36cm). **£1,500–1,800** *S*

A mandolin musical box, by L'Epee, No. 7421, for Thibouville Lamy, playing 8 popular airs, with nickel plated cylinder, zither attachment, tune indicator and grained case with tune sheet, carrying handles and inlaid rosewood veneered lid, cylinder 8in (20cm). **£850–950** *CSK*

A Swiss musical box, by Nicole Frères, No. 50181, playing 12 sacred airs as listed on tune card, with double spring motor in grained case with inlaid lid, late19thC, cylinder 13½in (34cm). **£600–700** *S*

A Swiss mandolin interchangeable cylinder musical box on stand, playing 8 airs as listed on original tune sheet, contained in walnut veneered case, on matching stand with 2 cylinder storage drawers in the front, on matching chamfered legs, some damage, c1880, each of 6 cylinders 13in (33cm). **£7,000–9,000** *S*

A Swiss single comb mandolin quatuor expressive accord parfait musical box, probably by Paillard, playing 6 operatic airs, two thirds cylinder length in mandolin form, in walnut veneered case with kingwood banding to all sides and carrying handles, c1880, cylinder 18in (46cm).
£5,000–6,500 *S*

Quatuor movements are usually associated with one utilizing 4 combs in sublime harmony effect.

A Swiss orchestral interchangeable cylinder musical box-on-stand, by George Bendon & Co., with twin spring barrels, tune indicator, snare drum, 6 saucer bells with 3 gilt metal mandarin strikers, castanets and 24 note organ, contained in burr walnut veneered case, the lid with boxwood stringing and brass and mother-of-pearl decoration, on matching stand with writing slope mounted in top drawer, with 5 cylinders playing 8 airs, the whole raised on 4 ebonised cabriole legs, restored, c1800, cylinders 14in (36cm).
£15,000–20,000 *S*

A Swiss mandolin cylinder musical box, by AMI Rivenc playing 10 airs, in grained case with inlaid lid, c1880, cylinder 13in (33cm).
£1,000–1,500 *S*

A Swiss forte piano mandolin cylinder musical box, by Bremond, No. 3245, playing 4 operatic airs, with tune card, in grained case with inlaid lid, c1860, cylinder 15in (38cm).
£4,500–5,000 *S*

The main comb contains approximately 155 teeth and the piano comb approximately 53.

A Swiss cylinder musical box, No. 3095, playing 8 airs, in grained case with tune card and lid key, late 19thC, cylinder 13in (33cm).
£750–850 *S*

An overture box, by Nicole Frères No. 41333, playing 4 overtures, with lever wind, brass comb washers, tune sheet with Keith Prowse & Co., labels, grained case with inlaid and strung rosewood veneered lid, cylinder 12in (31cm).
£8,500–10,000 *CSK*

A Swiss orchestral cylinder musical box, playing 8 airs as listed on tune sheet, accompanied by 5 saucer bells, castanets and brass drum, contained in brass and marquetry inlaid walnut and kingwood case, on stepped base with cast brass carrying handles, c1880, cylinder 16in (41cm).
£3,000–4,000 *S*

A Swiss 9in disc musical box, by Britannia, the single comb movement with ratchet wind motor, now in walnut case with glazed door with applied pilasters and disc storage drawer, c1900, 19in (48cm) high, together with 32 discs.
£720–1,000 *S*

A German 13¾in Kalliope disc musical box, the centre wind movement with single comb and 10 optional bells, in oak case, with 'Otto Pohland, Denmark' retailer's label, together with 25 discs, lid possibly replaced, c1900, 19in (48cm) wide.
£2,000–3,000 *S*

A sublime harmony piccolo musical box, No. 7132, playing 8 dance tunes, mainly from opera, with double spring motor, 2-piece comb, right hand sublime harmony and piccolo in one, tune indicator and tune sheet, in thuya veneered case with box stringing, ebony banding and carrying handles, cylinder 15in (38cm).
£9,500–11,000 *CSK*

A Swiss musical box, by Allard, with 3 interchangeable cylinders, playing 6 airs, fast/slow regulation and manual tune change, an engraved zither attachment and original sheet with diagram and instructions, c1890, on matching later base, cylinders 15in (38cm).
£14,000–15,000 *DRA*

A Swiss cylinder musical box, by Nicole Frères, No. 37779, playing 3 operatic and one dance air, with tune card and fruitwood handled winding key, in fruitwood case with stringing to front and lid and end flap, damaged, c1855, cylinder 8in (20cm).
£1,000–1,500 *S*

A Swiss 6 bell cylinder musical box, by Langdorff & Fils, playing 10 airs, with optional bells and tune card, in grained case with veneered front and inlaid lid, c1880, cylinder 13in (33cm).
£1,000–1,500 *S*

A Swiss music box, by Nicole Frères, signed on backplate, playing 12 airs, with 6 bells, comb and original song sheet and numbered 45298, c1881, cylinder 14½in (37cm).
£4,000–5,000 *DRA*

A German singing bird box, the cast brass case enamelled in blue and white, the bird with moving wings and metal beak, with key, early 20thC, 4in (10cm) wide.
£1,200–1,700 *S*

A German 5¾in symphonion 'monkey cyclist' automaton disc musical box, No. 258209, the single comb movement contained with ratchet wind, in walnut veneered case with a cam operated figure of a monkey on a penny-farthing bicycle riding around a circular track and through a classical façade, c1905, 7½in (19cm) wide, together with 5 discs.
£2,500–3,500 *S*

A Swiss cylinder musical box on stand, by Junod, No. 40110, playing 12 airs, with double spring motor, zither attachment, tune indicator and tune card, in ebonised case with turned legs and shaped undertier with transfer decoration, 2 teeth missing, late 19thC, cylinder 13in (33cm).
£1,500–2,000 *S*

A Swiss overture cylinder music box, by Nicole Frères, No. 51073, with 2 spring barrels, signed on the comb and numbered on baseplate, original song sheets, c1890, cylinder 13in (33cm).
£9,000–10,000 *DRA*

An oiseau chantant musical box,
playing 12 airs accompanied by
6 bells with bird finials and bee
strikers, 20 key reed organ and
singing bird with 10 note wood
pipe organ and moving axis, neck,
wings, tail and beak, in a bocage
of grass and flowers, with
separate engagement lever for
bass and treble bells, tune sheet
and burr walnut case with ebony
banding and brass stringing,
cylinder 19in (48cm).
£15,000–18,000 *CSK*

*No serial number or maker's mark
is visible on this movement, but
the tune sheet, No.150, is of a style
found on Bremond and Heller
boxes. The bird movements are
controlled by 4 keys between the
reed and pipe sections of the
key frame.*
*One bell tooth is broken, possibly
a non-functional one, as its
position does not seem to
correspond with the one non-
working striker and one bass
comb tooth. There is also a tip off
at the bass end, and series of tips
at the upper end of the bass comb.
These, however, appear to be filed
off rather than broken, and
alternate with whole tips,
suggesting a maker's intention, a
part alternate tips comb? The
corresponding section of the
cylinder is the most heavily
pinned, and the comb teeth are
abnormally closely-spaced for a
12 tune arrangement.*
*The movement appears to have
been fitted originally with a tune
indicator and a tune selector, but
neither is present.*

A German singing bird box, in
cast brass case with filigree
decoration on the top, the bird
with moving wings and metal
beak, with key, early 20thC,
4in (10cm) wide.
£900–1,200 *S*

A German gilt metal singing bird
box, the case with foliate
decoration, the lid with cherubs,
the bird with rotating perch,
wings and bone beak, the base
stamped 't' under a crown, early
20thC, 4in (10cm) wide.
£1,000–1,500 *S*

A German double singing bird box
with flute player, the front
opening to reveal a moving figure
when the bird-type mechanism is
activated causing a melody to be
performed, on bun feet, 20thC,
9in (23cm) wide.
£8,000–10,000 *S*

A Griesbaum German silver
singing bird box, the case cast
with cherub, birds and musical
instruments amidst foliage, the
bird with rotating perch, wings
and bone beak, early 29thC,
4in (10cm) wide.
£1,200–1,800 *S*

A Swiss mandolin harpe tremolo
musical box, by Bremond, No.
20006, playing 8 airs on 3 combs
laid out in sublime harmony style,
with zither attachment, double
spring motor, tune selector and
indicator in walnut veneered
case with tune card and original
instruction card over controls,
with key to lid, c1885, cylinders
17in (43cm).
£3,300–3,700 *S*

A German silver gilt singing bird
box, the serpentine case cast with
lovers in rural scenes, musical
instruments and birds, with rear
compartment, the bird with
rotating perch, wings and bone
beak, late 19thC, 4in (10cm) wide.
£1,500–2,000 *S*

A German Libellion book playing
musical box, the 54-note
movement with spring motor, in
walnut veneered case with
panelled lid and key, together
with 5 'books', one in maker's slip
case with printed instructions,
early 20thC, 20½in (52cm) wide.
£8,000–9,000 *S*

Gramophones

An HMV re-entrant gramophone, Model No. 163, in oak case, with 5a soundbox and tone chamber enclosed by fret and doors, with 'Naylor, Rochester' dealer's plaque, HMV speed tester and BCN thorn sharpener, 1929, 40½in (103cm) high.
£800–1,000 *CSK*

A Junior Monarch gramophone by the Gramophone & Typewriter Ltd., with single spring motor, oak case with transfer and large 'Imhof & Mukle' plaque, japanned back bracket with blue and gilt lining, G & T Exhibition soundbox No. 33616, gooseneck tone arm and brass horn, record clamp replaced, 15in (38cm) diam.
£1,200–1,800 *CSK*

A Monarch mahogany gramophone, with brass morning-glory horn, G & T Exhibition soundbox and gooseneck tone arm, double spring worm drive motor and mahogany case with fluted pilasters flanking panels, 'Gramophone & Typewriter Ltd' transfer and suppliers plaque 'R.W. Pentland, Edinburgh', turntable cracked, speed control screw replaced, c1907, the horn 24in (61cm) diam.
£2,000–2,500 *CSK*

The brass morning-glory horn is seldom found, partly because from 1908 it was effectively replaced by the wood horn as a deluxe option, and some existing brass horned machines were re-equipped with wood horns. Mahogany cases were apparently made by British cabinet makers, unlike standard oak versions imported from Victor in the USA.

A Dulcephone horn gramophone, with Dulcephone soundbox, back bracket and double spring motor with 12in turntable, mahogany case with oval panels and Dulcephone transfer, and brass flower horn with Art Nouveau embellishments to the rim, the horn, 22½in (57cm) diam.
£2,200–2,700 *CSK*

An Academy cabinet gramophone, the mahogany cabinet in the form of a cellaret, with Academy soundbox, internal horn covered by double doors, with transfer 'inlay' decoration, 1920s, 32in (81cm) high.
£300–400 *S*

This machine is more commonly seen with the Tyrella label.

A Klingsor gramophone, with Klingsor soundbox, in wood cabinet of typical form with sloping front to the turntable compartment, overhead internal horn enclosed by tuned strings, wood doors carved with Art Nouveau lily motifs, 33½in (85cm) high.
£900–1,200 *CSK*

An HMV gramophone, Model No. 202, in oak cabinet, the lift-up lid with moulded edge, Gothic panelled door front, fitted steel hinges, on baluster supports, 29in (74cm) wide.
£9,000–12,000 *RBB*

A Style 6 gramophone, by The Gramophone Company Ltd., 31 Maiden Lane, with Concert soundbox, No. 12727, side wind motor with 7in (17.5cm) turntable, aluminium horn, fielded panel oak case with maker's transfer and trade plaque of 'Archer & Sons, Liverpool', in fitted black leathercloth covered case with a Gramophone Co., 7in (17.5cm) album containing one cracked Berliner record, record clamp replaced, c1900, horn 14in (36cm) long.
£1,500–2,000 *CSK*

Phonographs

A Style 4 gramophone, with fielded panelled oak case, G & T Exhibition soundbox, No. 12562, top wind motor, 10in (25cm) turntable, brass horn, 'Gramophone & Typewriter City Road' transfer and trade label of 'Harry Tompkins, Newcastle', record clamp, winder and escutcheons replaced, 1904, the horn 17in (43cm) long.
£1,700–2,200 *CSK*

An HMV Intermediate Monarch mahogany horn gramophone, with Gramophone Co. Exhibition soundbox, No. 470040, gooseneck tone arm, single spring motor with bolt brake and Denison speed control, in mahogany case with Nipper and Intermediate Monarch transfers, with smooth mahogany horn 18in (46cm) diam.
£1,700–2,000 *CSK*

An Edison 'suitcase' Standard phonograph, Model A, No. S1229, with Standard speaker, shaving device and 'Edison-Bell' licence plaque, in oak case with 14in (36cm) witch's hat horn.
£400–450 *CSK*

A Kastenpuck phonograph with embossed tinplate flower horn, floating reproducer, typical key wind motor and gilt lined, japanned steel bedplate with colour transfer of Britannia, on wood box base.
£500–550 *CSK*

A French openworks phonograph, with standard and slip-on intermediate mandrels, nickel-plated mechanism on japanned iron base, movable support rail and small aluminium horn, on baseboard with flat topped walnut cover, replaced reproducer.
£500–600 *CSK*

An Edison Standard phonograph, Model D, No. 758445, with O reproducer with turn-over stylus bar, Combination gearing and oak case with No. 10 Cygnet horn with crane 19in (48cm) diam.
£1,200–1,700 *CSK*

An Edison Home Phonograph, Model A, No. H31765, with automatic reproducer, shaving device and oak case with banner transfer on lid, with large conical horn 8in (20cm) diam.
£600–700 *CSK*

A bronze, La Défense Nationale, by Louis-Christophe-Paul-Gustave Doré, on marble base, c1877. **£11,500–13,000** *S*

A bronze, Jeune Fille De Bou Saada, signed by 'E Barrias', on marble base, 15½in (38cm) high overall. **£5,500–6,000** *S*

A bronze, Victory, by Sir Alfred Gilbert, with turned bronze baluster base and oriental hardwood stand, c1912, 16in (41cm). **£3,500–4,000** *S*

A pair of Venetian bronze putti, from the workshop of Niccolo Roccatagliata, late 16thC, 23in (59cm) high. **£11,500–13,000** *CNY*

A bronze, La Toilette d'Atalante, signed by Jean Jacques Pradier, with mid-brown patina, on marble base, c1850, 14in (35cm). **£3,000–3,500** *S*

A French bronze, Suzon, signed by Auguste Rodin, mid-brown patina, bronze socle, inscribed 'Cie des Bronzes', c1871, 16in (40cm) high. **£11,000–13,000** *S*

A bronze, Comedy and Tragedy: Sic Vita, by Sir Alfred Gilbert, cast by The Compagnie des Bronzes, with black patina, on ebonised base, c1912, 31in (79cm) high overall. **£30,000–35,000** *S*

A French bronze figure, cast from a model by Edouard Drouot, the rotating socle with label inscribed 'Hippocrène', late 19thC, 27½in (70cm) high. **£3,500–4,000** *CSK*

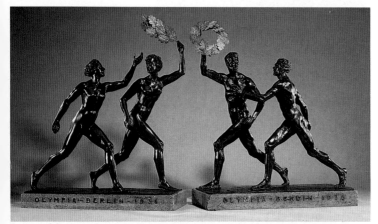

A pair of German bronze groups of Olympic athletes, signed and dated, by Eberhard Encke, each mounted on a marble base with applied bronze inscription, c1936, 32 by 30in (81 by 76cm). **£20,000–25,000** *C*

An Elizabeth I silver chalice, maker's mark 'G' above 'IV', late 16thC, 7½in (18cm) high, 8oz 17dwt.
£3,000–3,500 *S*

A George II cast taperstick, the knopped column on shaped and moulded base, engraved with crest and initials 'P*T', with snuffer, London 1739, 4in (10cm), 4¼oz.
£900–1,000 *DN*

A pair of silver shell-shaped salts, with gilt interiors, with a pair of matching spoons, Birmingham 1916, boxed.
£75–95 *PCh*

An Elizabeth I silver chalice and paten, maker's mark 'IP' in a shield, London 1573, 6½in (16cm), 5oz 4dwt.
£6,500–7,500 *S*

Four Continental silver gilt and 2 gilded white metal models of knights, on pierced bases, 5 with carved faces, 4 with English import marks, largest 9in (23cm) high, 3,213g.
£6,000–7,000 *C*

A Charles II silver beaker, engraved with plants and scrolls, maker's mark 'RD', a mullet below, London 1664, 4in (10cm), 5oz 8dwt.
£4,500–5,500 *S*

A Queen Anne cup, by J. Younghusband, scratched initials 'H' over 'AE', Newcastle, 1712, 2in (5cm) high, 2oz.
£800–1,200 *DN*

A Victorian heavily embossed repoussé plated four-piece tea and coffee set, jug with bird of prey finial.
£180–220 *PCh*

A pair of James II silver flasks, inscribed 'Ex-Dono Jacobus II', unmarked, c1685, 5in (13cm) high, 32oz 10dwt.
£4,500–5,000 *S*

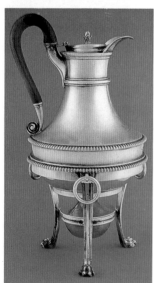

A George III coffee jug, by Paul Storr, engraved with an armorial, wood handle, on stand with 3 reeded lions' paw supports and burner, London 1803, 12in (30cm), 45oz.
£3,000–4,000 *DN*

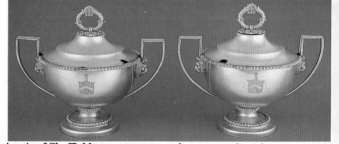

A pair of Sheffield sauce tureens and covers, each with an armorial, gadrooned borders, 2 angular handles with lions' masks, on round bases, 19thC, 6in (15cm) diam. **£650–700** *DN*

A George II silver gilt ewer and basin, by Aymé Videau, chased with floral swags and grotesque masks, London 1746, basin 15in (38cm) wide, 76oz 11dwt.
£35,000–40,000 *S*

A knop stemmed silver Christening spoon, decorated with a fish, cockerel and lion, early 12thC, 7in (18cm) long.
£3,500–4,000 *CSK*

A Victorian silver group, after a model by Pierre-Emile Jeannest, Birmingham 1852, 18½in (47cm) high, 353oz 17dwt.
£16,500–18,000 *S*

A George II silver salver, the border chased with alternating scale and shell motifs, the centre engraved with an armorial, London 1744, 10in (25cm) diam, 22oz 10dwt. **£25,000–27,000** *S*

A German silver and silver gilt beaker, incised 'IVL 1653' above a blank baroque cartouche, Cologne, c1600, 3½in (9cm) high.
£6,500–7,000 *ABB*

An early George III cup and domed cover, by Thomas Whipham and Charles Wright, London 1763, 14in (36cm) high, 63oz.
£3,000–3,500 *DN*

A Georgian bullet-shaped silver teapot, by A. Nelme, London, Britannia mark, 1720. **£9,000–10,000** *S&S*

An Empire style silver gilt breakfast service, the fan-shaped dishes and covers each with detachable seated dog finial, by Puiforcat, Paris, 16in (41cm) diam.
£13,000–15,000 *C*

A set of 4 George II cast candlesticks, by John Hugh Le Sage, engraved with owl crests, London 1739, maker's mark '1680' on bases and '1681' on nozzles, 10in (25cm) high. **£7,000–10,000** *DN*

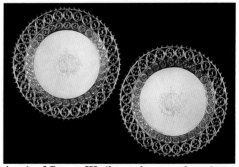

A pair of George III silver salvers, each on 3 cast scroll panel supports, the centres engraved with armorials, James Graham, Dublin, c1770, 9in (23cm) diam, 32oz 8dwt. **£14,000–16,000** *S*

A gold rosary, the links of the decades with 9 pairs of quatrefoils, gold floriate crucifix, 24in (61cm) long. **£2,000–2,500** *C*

An ornamental bronze inkstand, on 4 paw feet, 19thC, 13in (33cm) wide. **£220–250** *PCh*

A gold rosary, the links of the decades separated by 8 pairs of Pater Noster bead caps and quatrefoils, 27½in (70cm) long. **£3,000–3,500** *C*

A pair of French cast iron Egyptian figures, cast by Durenne of Sommeviore, one with founder's mark, light fittings missing, c1860, 51in (130cm) high. **£3,500–4,000** *S*

An Empire ormolu and patinated bronze centrepiece, with associated diamond-point cut glass tapering bowl, possibly Viennese, 24in (61cm) high. **£27,000–30,000** *C*

A Scottish pewter pot-bellied lidded measure, with domed lid and erect thumbpiece, c1700, 10in (25cm) high. **£2,000–2,500** *S(S)*

A pewter christening spoon, the handle inscribed, 'IESVS NAZARENVS REX IVDA' with acorn finial, 13thC, 5½in (14cm) long. **£2,750–3,000** *CSK*

A pair of Empire ormolu and patinated bronze centrepieces, one bowl modern, possibly Viennese, 19in (49cm) high. **£20,000–22,000** *C*

l. A gold engraved snuff box lid, Spanish Colonial work, early 18thC, 2½ by 2in (6 by 5cm). **£1,200–1,500** *C*

A James I pewter 'bun' lid flagon, with button finial and erect thumbpiece, on domed foot, c1610, 11½in (29cm) high. **£2,750–3,000** *S(S)*

A gold child's rattle, Ashanti, with English additions, unmarked, retaailed by R & S Garrard & Co., c1874, 4in (10cm) long. **£2,200–2,500** *S*

A 'gold' tumbaga cut bar, cut from a neatly formed bar, 2 royal tax stamps, 2 numerals 'VIIs' in incuse squares, Certificate no. 1001: gold 27.6%, silver 4.9%, copper 67.5%, 16.78oz, 6in (15cm) long. **£2,800–3,000** *C*

A French brass Gothic Revival bird cage, in the manner of Viollet-le-Duc, the roof supporting a tower, flanked by crocket finials above 4 lancet arches on columns set with 'jewels', c1870, 62in (157.5cm). high. **£6,250–7,250** *S*

A pair of Charles X ormolu centrepieces, each with pierced oval foliate basket above a gadrooned boss, on dolphin supports, on a plinth with lotus leaf cast rim and acanthus cast feet, stamped, 18in (45.5cm) high. **£15,500–16,000** *C*

A gilt bronze group of Hebe and Jupiter, by Albert Ernest Carrier Belleuse, on a rotating marble plinth, 23in (58.5cm) high. **£16,000–18,000** *Bon*

A pair of cast iron dogs, by Alfred Henri Jacquemart, each on a rectangular base, one stamped 'Val d'Osne', the other 'Barbezat & Cie, Val d'Osne', c1855, 32in (81cm) high. **£9,000–10,000** *S(S)*

A 'gold' tumbaga cut bar, with traces of 7 royal tax stamps, 6 numerals 'VIs' in incuse squares, one double punched, Certificate No. 1016: gold 38.1%, silver 7.9%, copper 54%, 9.9oz, 5in (12.5cm) long. **£2,250–2,750** *C*

A 'gold' tumbaga cut bar, cut from a neatly formed bar, 2 royal tax stamps, 2 numerals 'VIIs' in incuse squares, Certificate No. 1023: gold 43.5%, silver 6.9%, copper 49.6%, 11.52oz, 4½in (12cm) long. **£2,250–2,750** *C*

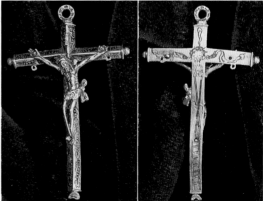

A German gold crucifix, the Saviour shown with perizonium tied to his left, the Cross incised with foliate ornament, with traces of enamel, the reverse chased with the Symbols of the Passion, 15thC, 3in (7.5cm) high. **£3,500–4,000** *CSK*

A white marble group
of Cupid and Psyche,
signed and dated 'C.
Finelli. F. Roma AD
1830', 54in (137cm).
£5,000–6,000 *S*

A white marble group of
Flora and Zephyr, by
Giovanni Maria Benzoni,
signed and dated '1867',
96½in (243cm).
£50,000–55,000 *S*

A marble bust of a girl
with a viper, on an Art
Nouveau bronze socle,
signed and dated 'Leo
Koch 1893', 25in (64cm).
£2,000–2,500 *S*

A white marble figure of
The Crouching Venus,
after the Antique, Italian
School, 19thC, 35in
(89cm) high.
£11,000–12,000 *S*

A set of 4 Empire brèche violette
marble columns, with gilt bronze
Ionic capitals, French or American,
c1885, 37in (94cm) high.
£11,000–12,000 *S*

A pair of Victorian veneered marble
columns, each drilled with a hole
for a vase or bust, c1850, 48½in
(123cm) high.
£3,500–4,500 *S*

A white marble group of an
Indian Brave and Squaw,
English, c1900, 50in (127cm).
£6,000–6,500 *S*

An Italian white marble
figure of a girl caught in a
storm, by Pietro
Guarnerio, signed, c1870,
47½in (120cm) high.
£7,000–10,000 *S*

A white marble
figure of The
Venus Italica,
signed 'Bartolini',
39½in (100cm).
£4,000–4,500 *S*

An Italian white
marble figure of a
dancer, signed 'T.
Zbrana', c1900, 32in
(81cm) high
including base.
£2,000–3,000 *S*

A pair of faux marble mottled
brown, grey and white urns, each
with flared circular rim and
moulded base, 48in (122cm) high.
£3,000–4,000 *CSK*

A pair of Italian white marble torchères, with carved baluster stems, c1800, 81in (205.5cm) high.
£15,000–18,000 *S*

An Italian white marble figure of The Athlete, by Donato Barcaglia, inscribed 'VENI NEC RECEDEM', signed and dated '1898', on a veined green marble base, 83½in (213cm) high overall.
£108,000–112,000 *C*

A Continental grey marble sphinx, with elaborate headdress, on a base with stylised meander and foliage pattern border, c1905, 62½in (158cm) long.
£17,500–20,000 *S*

A Florentine white marble group of The Infant Beggars, the boy signed 'F. Vichi', 26 and 27in (66 and 69cm) high.
£6,000–7,000 *S*

A white marble figure of Danaide, after the Antique, signed 'P. Barzanti, Florence', 79in (200cm) high overall.
£10,500–12,000 *S*

A white marble figure of Susannah After The Bath, signed and dated 'G.B. Lombardi f. Roma 1872', 84in (213cm) high overall.
£27,000–30,000 *S*

A white marble group of The Lady of the Lake, signed 'B.E. Spence Ft. Romae 1865', 46in (117cm).
£5,000–7,000 *S*

A white marble group of Cupid Whispering to Venus, signed and dated 'C.P. Summers Rome 1875', on a white marble column, 70in (178cm) high.
£32,500–35,000 *S*

A Louis XIV mottled brown marble cistern, with a lion's mask at each end, on a moulded base, repaired, 35½in (90cm) wide. **£16,500–18,000** *C*

A Wedjat-eye plaque, opaque yellow and red detail, with dark amethyst 'body', in translucent cobalt blue matrix, 3rd Century B.C.-1st Century A.D., 1.3cm square. **£3,000–3,500** *C*

Four architectural plaque fragments of Nilotic birds, opaque yellow matrix inset with fused mosaic goose, partridge and desert magpie (?), circa 1st Century A.D. or later, 2in (5.5cm) high. **£12,500–13,000** *C*

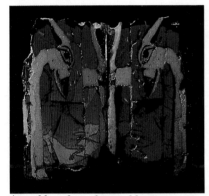

l. A half Bes head, with small triped 'shrine' headdress, translucent cobalt blue and opaque red border, blue matrix, 3rd-1st Century B.C., and another similar fragment, 1in (2.5cm) high. **£4,250–4,750** *C*

An ankh and was bar, ankh sign between 2 Seth headed was sceptres, and 2 halves of the same joined, 3rd-1st Century B.C., 1⅛in (3.5cm) wide. **£7,000–7,500** *C*

An Hetaira half mask, turquoise matrix, circa 1st Century B.C., 1in (3cm) high. **£6,500–7,000** *C*

A plaque, depicting a lion devouring a Nubian prisoner tied to a post, wearing white braces, red and white kilt and white boots, 3rd-1st Century B.C., 1in (2cm) wide. **£16,250–16,750** *C*

An Horus falcon, opaque white with translucent cobalt blue markings, red and blue 'striped' tail feathers, circa 1st Century B.C. **£9,500–10,000** *C*

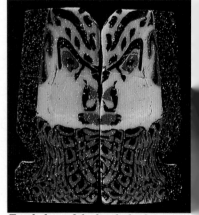

A half Bes head, wearing a 'shrine' headress, on amber brown surround, 3rd-1st Century B.C., 1in (2.2cm) high. **£6,500–7,000** *C*

A wagtail, with opaque white body, yellow and brown 'striped' wings, and yellow feet, 3rd-1st Century B.C., 1in (2cm) wide. **£4,250–4,750** *C*

Two halves of the head of a daimon, with pointed ears and eyebrows, translucent cobalt blue and opaque white snake scales below the face, hairline crack, circa 1st Century B.C., 1⅛in (3.2cm) high. **£9,500–10,000** *C*

An Attic black figure kyathos, attributed to the Group of Vatican 57, 525-500 B.C., depicting Dionysos offering a kantharos to a dancing satyr, 4½in (11cm) diam. **£17,500–25,000** *C*

An Attic black figure white ground lekythos, attributed to the Theseus Painter, circa 500 B.C., repaired, 12½in (32cm) high. **£11,000–15,000** *C*

An Attic black figure neck-amphora, attributed to the Affecter Painter, 530-520 B.C., lid slightly later, 20½in (52cm) high overall. **£90,000–95,000** *C*

An Attic red figure hydria, in the manner of the Meidias Painter, late 5th Century B.C., circa 420 B.C., depicting 2 dancing maenads, 8in (20cm) high. **£26,000–30,000** *C*

An Attic white ground black figure lekythos, attributed to the Athena Painter, 500-490 B.C., 11in (28cm). **£19,000–25,000** *C*

An Attic janiform kantharos, Class G of the head vases: the London Class, circa 470 B.C., in the form of the heads of a negress and white woman, restored, 8in (20cm) high. **£17,000–20,000** *C*

An Attic bi-lingual eye cup, attributed to Epiktetos, circa 520-510 B.C., with running figure of Hermes, 13in (33cm) diam excluding handles. **£128,000–135,000** *C*

l. An Attic red figure lekythos, attributed to the manner of the late Berlin Painter, circa 470 B.C., depicting Poseidon holding a trident, restored, 15½in (39cm) high. **£50,000–55,000** *C*

An Attic black figure eye cup, Kylix Type A, 525-500 B.C., interior decorated with a Gorgoneion, repaired, 8½in (21cm) diam excluding handles. **£13,000–15,000** *C*

An Italo-geometric buffware askos, Bisenzio Class, circa late 8th/early 7th Century B.C., in the form of a stylized bird, columnar filling hole and triple handle on the back, 17in (43cm) long. **£65,000–70,000** *S(NY)*

Three Mixtec polychrome terracotta effigy vessels, Postclassic, circa A.D. 900-1200, in the form of owls, their heads as lids, 5, 7 and 8in (12.5, 18, and 20cm) high. **£13,000–15,000** *S(NY)*

l. A bronze oinochoe, 10in (25cm) high. **£6,500–7,500**
r. A bronze olpe, both Greek or Etruscan, early 5th Century B.C., 8in (20cm) high. **£2,500–3,500** *S(NY)*

A wood statuette of a lady, early 12th Dynasty, circa 1938-1850 B.C., the base inscribed, 11in (28cm) high. **£320,000–330,000** *S(NY)*

A Mayan creamware two-part effigy vessel, Pacific Slope, Classic, circa A.D. 450-650, moulded as an armadillo, grasping his snout, incised with bands of cross-hatched triangles, 10in (25cm) high. **£15,000–18,000** *S(NY)*

An Achaemenid granite footed bowl, reign of Xerxes, 484-465 B.C., the shallow body with broad flat rim, on splayed stem hollow foot, 8½in (21cm) diam. **£17,000–20,000** *S(NY)*

A marble portrait head of a youth, Roman Imperial, 2nd Century A.D., perhaps a member of the Antonine family, 11in (28cm) high. **£10,000–12,000** *S(NY)*

Six Seljuk lustre tile panels, Kashan, circa first half of the 13th Century, each moulded in relief and painted with inscriptions, against white reserved ground. **£7,000–9,000** *S(NY)*

A marble child's sarcophagus, Roman Imperial, circa 2nd Century A.D., the front carved with the tale of Phaedra and Hippolytus, 12 by 45 by 16in (30 by 114 by 40cm). **£29,000–35,000** *S(NY)*

An indurated limestone ushabti fragment of Akhenaten, holding a crook and flail, 18th Dynasty, 1353-1336 B.C., 5½in (14.5cm) high. **£14,000–14,500** *S(NY)*

A monumental granite head of the Horus falcon, with eye rims in relief and crescentic markings flanking the beak, the underside carved at a later date, 19th/20th Dynasty, 1292-1075 B.C. 14in (36cm) wide. **£27,000–30,000** *S(NY)*

A Safavid polychrome dish, with low foot ring, a scale pattern to the rim, Kubachi, early 17thC, 15in (38.5cm) diam. **£2,500–3,000** *S(NY)*

A Roman Giallo Antico herm of an Hellenistic ruler, circa 1st Century A.D., 8½in (22cm) high. **£6,250–6,750** *S(NY)*

A limestone votive relief or sculptor's model, carved in shallow relief on 2 sides, Ptolemaic Period, 304-30 B.C., 10in (25. 5cm) high. **£4,800–5,800** *S(NY)*

A faience vase, moulded in relief with an animal frieze, early 1st Century A.D., 7in (18cm) high. **£3,000–3,500** *S(NY)*

A wood votive ushabti of Ken-Amun, 18th Dynasty, 13in (33cm) high. **£9,000–9,500** *S(NY)*

A Safavid dish, the interior painted with a foliate-tailed winged dragon, late 17thC, 18in (46cm) diam. **£2,000–2,500** *S(NY)*

A marble head of a goddess, circa 3rd-2nd Century B.C., 15in (38cm) high. **£4,000–4,500** *S(NY)*

A bronze head of a cat, with an ancient gold hoop earring in the left ear, the scarab on the forehead missing, 944-525 B.C., 4in (10cm) high. **£30,000–35,000** *S(NY)*

A quartzite relief fragment, depicting 3 falcon headed genii kneeling in the gesture of jubilation, the last genius with the signs for Buto in the Delta, 570-526 B.C., 38in (96.5cm) long. **£14,000–14,500** *S(NY)*

A marble relief fragment, carved with horses from a racing quadriga, Roman Imperial, probably Severan, circa late 2nd Century A.D., 13in (33cm) long. **£22,000–23,000** *S(NY)*

An Italian terracotta group of Cupid and Psyche as infants, late 17th/early 18thC, restored, 24½in (62cm) high. **£5,000–6,000** *CNY*

A Vizigapatnam engraved ivory miniature bureau, late 18th/early 19thC, decorated with colonial style villas and trees, iron handles and escutcheons, 22in (56cm) wide. **£2,000–2,500** *CSK*

Two giltwood and polychrome reliefs of St. Margaret and St. Joanna, probably north German, c1510, 23in (59cm) high. **£33,000–35,000** *S*

A pair of Spanish polychrome and giltwood columns, 17thC, 62½in (159cm). **£3,000–4,000** *CNY*

A Spanish parcel gilt and polychrome wood figure of St. Francis, damaged, 17thC, 51½in (131cm) high. **£10,000–12,000** *CNY*

A German carved fruitwood group of a pedlar and his dog, by Georg Zürn, signed 'GZ' and dated '1610', 11½in (29cm) high. **£44,000–48,000** *C*

A south German carved wood photograph stand, in the form of a bear standing painting at an easel, 16in (41cm) high. **£400–500** *E*

A Tibetan carved wood dragon panel, late 19thC. **£120–160** *GRG*

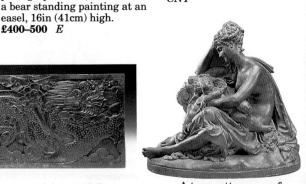

A terracotta group of Venus with Cupid asleep on her lap, signed 'Carrier Belleuse', 21in (53cm). **£2,000–2,500** *S*

l. A giltwood and plaster centrotavola, inset with glazed, painted foliate panels, mid-18thC, 70in (178cm) long. **£2,000–2,500** *CSK*

A south German terracotta figure of St. Sebastian, late 18thC, 17in (43cm) high. **£9,000–11,000** *C*

A Chinesco seated female figure, Proto-classic, circa 100 B.C.-A.D. 250, of Type C variety, painted overall 19in (48cm) high. **£18,500–20,000** *S(NY)*

A Nazca polychrome head vessel, circa A.D. 200-500, face marked with sacrificial flames to lower half, painted in deep red, brown and tan, 7in (17.5cm) high. **£5,500–7,000** *S(NY)*

A limestone pyramidion, 19th-20th Dynasty, 1292-1075 B.C., carved in sunk relief on all 4 sides, 16in (41cm) high. **£10,000–12,000** *S(NY)*

A Sinú gold finial of a bird, circa A.D. 500-1000, standing on an expanding shaft, 4in (10cm) high. **£35,000–40,000** *S(NY)*

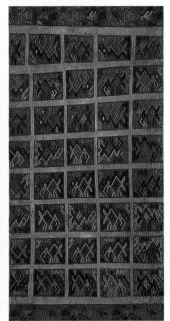

A Nazca shirt panel, circa A.D. 300-600, probably half of a cushma or unku, 67½ by 34in (171 by 86cm). **£35,000–40,000** *S(NY)*

An early/middle Mochica wood portrait mask, North Coast, circa 100 B.C.-A.D. 300, portraying the mature face of a lord, 10½in (26cm) wide. **£70,000–75,000** *S(NY)*

A pair of Inca silver and spondylus clothed figurines, circa A.D. 1470-1532, the faces almost obscured by parrot feather headdress, 6in (15cm) high. **£25,000–28,000** *S(NY)*

A Colima double-headed effigy vessel, Proto-classic, circa 100 B.C.-A.D. 250, in the form of an ocelot's body, skin indicated by incised lozenges, 15½in (39cm) high. **£18,000–20,000** *S(NY)*

A Greek bronze figure of a bird, Geometric Period, circa 750-700 B.C., with hollow cast navicella body, 5½in (14cm) high. **£20,000–22,000** *S(NY)*

A wooden figure of a cat, Late Period, 716-30 B.C., hollowed out to contain the mummy, 18½in (47cm) high. **£22,000–25,000** *S(NY)*

A burr walnut grand piano, the case with regilt foliage, keyboard signed 'Erard Patent London', stamped 'C. Martin', c1830.
£4,500–5,000 *S*

A Broadwood grand piano, the rosewood case with pie-crust edging, c1870, 101in (256.5cm).
£1,000–1,500 *PEx*

A guitar, by Antonio de Torres Jurado, with label, dated '1892', body 17in (42.5cm) long, with case.
£16,500–17,000 *S*

A Beulhoff baby grand piano, the mahogany case with painted scenes, Berlin, c1910, 62in (157cm).
£3,000–5,000 *PEx*

A Gebunden clavichord, the walnut case with tulipwood stringing, the lid with chequered stringing in various woods, probably German, mid-18thC, 51in (129.5cm). **£10,500–11,500** *S*

An upright overstrung burr walnut piano, by Carl Hardt, the centre panel carved with instruments, c1891. **£700–800** *PEx*

A concert guitar, by Ignacio Fleta, the two-piece back and sides of quarter-cut flamed maple, No.20, 1936, body 18½in (47cm) long, with case.
£14,000–16,000 *S*

A guitar, by Giovanni Hanggele, the back of pine veneered with strips of ivory and kingwood, engraved and inlaid, inscribed, dated '1639', 18½in (47cm) long.
£19,000–20,000 *S*

A Blüthner grand piano, the rosewood case with boxed ivory inlay, c1905, 76in (193cm) wide.
£3,000–5,000 *PEx*

r. A Steinway upright piano, the rosewood case with inlaid front panels, original good condition c1900. **£2,500–3,500** *PEx*

A rosewood cased pipe organ.
£3,500–4,000 *LT*

A Gothic satinwood and giltwood double-action harp, decorated with vine leaves, by Sebastian and Pierre Erard. **£2,000–2,500** *LT*

A Longman & Broderip grand piano, the mahogany case with boxwood stringing, facia board of maple painted with floral garlands and stained fruitwood stringing, 5½ octave keyboard with ivory naturals and ebony accidentals, 104in (264cm) long.
£13,500–15,000 *S*

An Eavestaff mini piano, the ebonised case with chrome binding, with matching stool, c1930.
£600–800 *PEx*

A Joseph Böhm grand piano, with mahogany case, 6⅓ octave keyboard, with ivory naturals and stained fruitwood accidentals, c1825.
£15,000–20,000 *S*

A French guitar, by Selmer, labelled 'M. Maccaferri/Orchestre/No.200', the back and ribs of rosewood, the front of spruce, back 18½in (47cm) long, in a fitted case.
£7,000–7,500 *CSK*

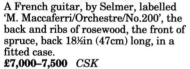

A Cramer portable piano, with mahogany case, 5 octave keyboard, overhauled action.
£400–500 *PEx*

An F.A. Klein lyre piano, the main front panel of veneered mahogany, with 6¾ octave keyboard, ivory naturals and ebony accidentals, Berlin, c1835, 83½in (211cm) high.
£9,000–10,000 *S*

A Michael Rosenberger pyramid piano, with cherry wood case, Vienna, c1820, 77in (196cm) high.
£13,000–14,000 *S*

A Chinese Export black and gilt lacquer decorated cabinet-on-stand, on a Charles II giltwood stand, with naturalistic legs headed by putti, stand re-gilt and previously ebonised, 66in (168cm) high. **£8,500–9,500** *C*

A finely carved early cinnabar lacquer stand, with bowed and incurved legs carved with foliage, Yuan Dynasty, c1300, 8½in (22cm). **£10,000–15,000** *S*

A gold lacquer shodana, with shelves and 3 compartments, the central compartment with hinged doors, the others with sliding doors, 19thC, 34in (87.5cm) wide. **£31,500–33,000** *S*

A Chinese pinewood storage cabinet, mid-19thC, 49in (125cm) high. **£1,500–2,000** *ORI*

A roironuri decorated ground tobacco set, with 4 drawers, brazier and an ashtray, each with a silver cover, 19thC, 10½in (27cm) high. **£4,500–5,000** *C*

A decorated gold lacquer kodansu, or perfume cabinet, the 2 doors opening to reveal 4 drawers, carved with scrolling foliage, Meiji period, 10in (26cm) wide, with 2 storage boxes, each inscribed, one signed. **£12,000–13,000** *S*

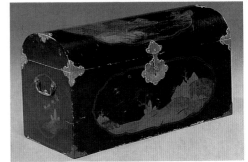

A Japanese coffer, decorated with landscapes and flowers, with copper mounts, 17thC, on later stand, 35in (89cm) high. **£3,750–4,250** *S*

A Momoyama period Christian folding missal stand, decorated with a sunburst halo with monogram of the Society of Jesus, restored, late 16th/early 17thC, 13½in (34cm) high. **£32,500–35,000** *C*

A Japanese cabinet-on-stand, with pierced apron and square shaped legs, c1720, 70in (177.5cm) high. **£5,500–6,500** *S(S)*

A Sage-Jubako or picnic box, with copper carrying handle, early Meiji period, 12in (30cm). **£4,750–5,250** *S*

A silhouette agate snuff bottle, carved with a bird on a tree, framing the bird silhouette, c1800-80. **£6,000–6,500** *S(NY)*

An inside-painted glass snuff bottle, depicting rabbits beneath a soaring bat, the base carved as a basket stand, c1800-80. **£1,200–1,400** *S(NY)*

A four-case inro, by Koma Kansai, signed, 19thC, 3½in (8.5cm). **£18,500–20,000** *S*

A five-case inro, by Shunsho, decorated with a scene of Sojobo, the reverse with 2 tengu fighting, signed, 19thC, 3½in (9cm). **£26,000–28,000** *S*

l. A four-case inro of sharkskin, by Koma Kyui, decorated with a dragonfly in gold, possibly 17thC, 2½in (6.5cm). **£4,800–5,200** *S*

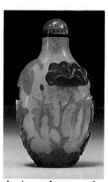

A nine-colour overlay glass snuff bottle, depicting a bat, butterfly and peony, c1760-1820. **£16,000–16,500** *S(NY)*

A two-colour jade snuff bottle, carved as a recumbent water buffalo, 18thC. **£5,500–6,000** *S(NY)*

A black lacquer, four-case inro with metal inlay, by Hara Yoyusai and Haruaki Hogen, signed, 19thC, 3½in (8.5cm). **£52,500–55,000** *S*

A gold lacquer four-case inro, by Shojosai, decorated with a mandarin duck, slight damage, signed, early 20thC, 3½in (9cm). **£13,000–13,500** *S*

A collection of 10 miniature snuff bottles, including a flask-form ruby bottle, 2 chalcedony bottles, and a metal eggplant-form bottle. **£1,800–2,200** *S(NY)*

A carved jade marriage bowl, the interior carved with 2 butterflies, one ring restuck, mark and period of Qianlong, 10⅓in (26cm).
£10,000–12,000 *S*

A white jade table screen, carved with 3 scholars, a stream, fruiting peach and a pavilion in the distance, Qing Dynasty, Qianlong, on wood stand, 9½ by 6in (24 by 15cm). **£12,000–13,000** *S*

An ivory okimono of an umbrella seller, damaged, unsigned, Meiji period, 9in (23cm) high.
£1,000–1,500 *S*

A carved jade teapot and cover, with 2 Daoist Immortal figures standing on clouds, dragon mask and phoenix head handle, Ming Dynasty, 7in (18cm).
£3,000–4,000 *S*

An ivory okimono of a fisherman, struggling to prevent his catch falling from a broken basket, by Ryuho, Meiji period, signed, 8in (20cm) high.
£2,000–2,500 *S*

A carved ivory model of a barge, with a clinker hull and pierced panelled cabins with hanging doors and windows, painted ivory figures playing cards, with crew members, flags and lanterns, minor damage, c1820, 16½in (42cm) long. **£12,000–13,000** *C*

A white jade koro and cover, carved and pierced with flowering peony on intertwining leafy stems, the footring with 4 ruyi feet, slight damage, Qing Dynasty, Qianlong, 7in (18cm). **£12,000–13,000** *S*

A set of 8 ivory figures of luohans, Xin Fingdeng, Wu Daxiang, Futuomiduo, Yi Xianchang, Bu Dong, You Boju Duo, Jiao Xingjie, Yinianjiegong, 19thC, 16½in (42cm) high.
£5,500–6,000 *C*

l. A set of 6 ivory figures of luohans and La Zu, including Bao Jian, De Guang, Yinianjiegong, A Naxi, and 2 others, 19thC, 22in (56cm) high.
£8,500–9,500 *C*

A bronze ritual dish, the interior with wide rounded sides encircled by 3 raised fillets below the lipped rim, the interior with a 'cartwheel' pictogram, late Shang Dynasty, 11th Century B.C., 14in (35cm). **£13,000–14,000** *S*

A carved grey stone figure of a bodhisattva, with slightly polished surface, chipped, Tang Dynasty, 12in (31cm) high. **£17,500–18,500** *C*

A bronze ritual food vessel, with 2 handles, supported on 3 cylindrical legs, late Shang Dynasty, 13th–12th Century B.C., 6in (15cm). **£4,500–5,000** *S*

A gilt silver cup, of hu shape, the gilt handle comprising a studded ring and thumb flange, the neck gilded, Tang Dynasty, 11in (28cm) high. **£14,000–18,000** *C*

A bronze ritual wine vessel, the 2 handles with taotie masks, a third taotie mask and loop handle set just above the base, Shang Dynasty, 12th–11th Century B.C., 13in (33cm). **£37,000–38,000** *S*

A bronze ritual vessel, cast with pairs of stylised dragons, the interior with a pictogram, late Shang/early Western Zhou Dynasty, 11th Century B.C., 10in (25cm). **£34,000–38,000** *S*

A bronze covered vessel, with a figure pictogram on the interior of the lid, early Western Zhou Dynasty, 11th–10th Century B.C. **£3,500–4,500** *S*

A bronze ritual vessel and cover, inscribed on the interior and cover 'Gou zi', early Western Zhou Dynasty, 10th Century B.C., damaged, 9½in (24cm). **£26,000–28,000** *S*

l. A cast bronze ritual vessel, with stylised horned dragons against a leiwen ground, pictogram on the interior, late Shang/early Western Zhou Dynasty, 11th Century B.C., 9in (23cm). **£19,000–25,000** *S*

A bronze wine vessel, the mid-section cast in shallow relief on a leiwen ground with taotie masks, Shang Dynasty, 11in (28cm) high. **£10,000–11,000** *C*

A silver and shibayama koro and cover, decorated with cloisonné enamel, mother-of-pearl and horn, signed Yoshietsu, damaged, Meiji period, 9in (23cm).
£4,000–5,000 *S*

A pair of painted bronze vases, probably Japanese, decorated with a cockerel and other exotic birds, insects and bamboo, mid-19thC, 41in (104cm) high. **£7,000–9,000** *S*

A repoussé iron kabuto, in the form of a coiled dragon, the horns added as well as the mabezashi with a silver fukurin, in the style of Miochin Ryoei, 18thC.
£5,000–6,000 *C*

A repoussé iron kabuto, in the form of a conch shell, with diagonal striations, the large mabezashi without decoration, the shikoro lacking, 18thC.
£5,500–6,500 *C*

A pair of cloisonné enamel vases, each decorated in gold and silver wire with sprays of chrysanthemums, by Namikawa Sosuke, slight damage, signed, Meiji period, 6in (15cm) high.
£20,000–22,000 *S*

A lacquer and wicker picnic basket, Chinese or Japanese, the lid and 3 removable trays decorated with figures and flowers, with loop handle, mid-19thC, 28in (71cm) high.
£1,000–1,500 *S*

A pair of silver candlesticks, chased and worked in repoussé, impressed on base 'Arthur & Bond, Yokohama' and 'yogin', Meiji period, 11in (28cm) high.
£2,000–2,500 *C*

An Oriental bronze incense burner, inlaid with gilt, depicting a god figure seated on a carp, 19thC, 9½in (24cm) high.
£100–115 *PCh*

An inlaid shibuichi and silver tripod koro and cover, the body carved in shishiaibori and inlaid with silver, copper and gold, slight damage, by Ozeki and others, c1896, 7in (18cm).
£26,000–28,000 *S*

A model of 2 wrestlers, by Chokichi Suzuki, Kawazu no Saburo Sukeyasu lifting up Matano no Goro Kagehisa by his belt, on a wooden base carved as dohyo, unsigned, Meiji period. **£26,000–28,000** *C*

A censer and cover, painted in famille-rose enamels with large stylised lotus, scrolling leaves and stems, detachable handles, damaged and restored, mark and period of Qianlong, 22½in (57cm). **£6,000–10,000** *S*

A gilt bronze mounted cloisonné enamel bowl, decorated with multi-coloured flowers, Ming Dynasty, 16th and 17thC, 7in (18cm) diam.
£5,000–6,000 *S*

A polychrome stone figure of a lohan, traces of pigmentation overall, Song Dynasty, 15in (38cm) high.
£5,000–6,000 *S*

A cast bronze censer, decorated around the exterior with mythical sea creatures, with traces of gilding, 17thC, 9in (23cm).
£3,000–3,500 *S*

A gilt bronze model of a cockerel, with gilt plumage and red patinated comb, on wood rockwork base, signed 'Masatsune', Meiji period, 17½in (44cm) high excluding base.
£5,000–6,000 *S*

A cast bronze tripod censer, of low bombé form, with loop handles, Xuande mark within a recessed cartouche, 17thC, 10in (25cm).
£5,000–6,000 *S*

A cloisonné censer and cover, Ming Dynasty, early 17thC, 21½in (54cm).
£5,000–6,000 *S*

A cloisonné enamel mythical beast, with a horn and beard, the rump overlaid with an armour-like shell, multi-cloven feet, slight damage and restoration, Qianlong four-character mark, 10in (25cm) long.
£16,500–18,000 *C*

A seated gilt bronze figure of Buddha, wearing a gilded loose robe with engraved floral borders, Ming Dynasty, 11in (28cm) high.
£2,500–3,000 *S*

A carved stone head of Guanyin with large long-lobed ears, on fitted stand, repaired, Tang Dynasty, 11½in (29cm).
£11,000–15,000 *S*

A gilt bronze figure of a lohan, dated 'Da Ming Zhengtong', 4th year, 3rd month, AD 1439. **£14,000–18,000** *C*

A carved wood figure of a lohan, Song Dynasty, 11th-12thC. **£10,500–12,000** *S*

A bronze sculpture of Benten, on a high stepped stand, supported by 4 demon head legs, signed 'Joun' with kao, Meiji period, 38½in (98cm). **£8,000–9,000** *S*

A carved limestone figure of a Bodhisattva, Northern Qi/Sui Dynasty. **£58,000–60,000** *S*

An inlaid iron charger, cast in relief with 2 rakkan in a central medallion, in gold and silver, by Komai, Meiji period, 19in (48cm). **£14,000–16,000** *S*

A gold lacquer and shibayama koro and cover, decorated in mother-of-pearl, ivory and horn, dragon handles, slight damage, signed 'Kaneko', Meiji period, 11in (29cm) high. **£10,000–12,000** *S*

A Ming cloisonné yenyen vase. **£8,500–10,000** *S*

A Namban export inlaid lacquer escritoire, damaged and restored, Early Edo period, c1600, 17½ by 12in (44 by 31cm). **£7,000–8,000** *S*

A Longmen relief limestone carving of Maitreya, a pair of recumbent lions flanking his knees, damaged and repaired, Northern Wei Dynasty, 13⅜in (34cm) high. **£8,500–9,500** *S*

l. A carved three-colour marble figure of a monkey, Qing Dynasty, Qianlong, 8in (20cm) high. **£19,000–21,000** *S*

A gilt lacquered bronze figure of a crowned Buddha, his loose robe with incised floral borders, Ming Dynasty, 29in (74cm) high. **£15,000–18,000** *S*

56 copies of *The Flintstones*, Nos. 7-60, 1962-70, and *Bigger and Boulder,* Nos. 1 and 2, based on the Hanna-Barbera television series, published by Gold Key.
£750–800 *CNY*

All Start Comics, No. 3, Winter Issue 1940, published by Periodical Publications, spine restored.
£2,000–2,500 *CNY*

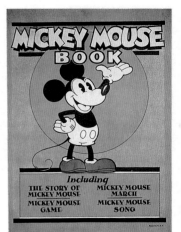

Mickey Mouse Book, 1930, cover art by UB Iwerks, featuring the first appearance of Mickey Mouse and Minnie Mouse in the first Disney book.
£3,500–4,000 *CNY*
© *Walt Disney Productions*

Superboy, No. 1, March-April 1949, published by National Periodical Publications.
£2,000–2,500 *CNY*

32 copies of *Yogi Bear,* Nos. 10-42, 1962-70, based on the Hanna-Barbera cartoon series, published by Gold Key.
£350–400 *CNY*

62 copies of *Mickey Mouse Magazine,* Summer 1935/ September 1940, published by K. K. Publications.
£8,500–9,000 *CNY*
© *Walt Disney Productions*

Weird Fantasy, No. 13 (No. 1), May-June 1950, published by E. C. Publications.
£200–250 *CNY*

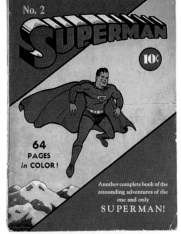

Superman No. 2 and *Superman* No. 11 *comic books,* published by D. C. Comics.
£500–550 *CNY*

Bulletman, No. 1, Summer 1941, published by Fawcett Publications.
£1,000–1,500 *CNY*

l. Archie, No. 1, Winter 1942, published by MLJ.
£1,000–1,500 *CNY*

An Edison Standard phonograph, with 2 speeds for 2 or 4 minute cylinders, in original oak case, together with nine 4 minute cylinders, c1906. **£400–500** *JH*

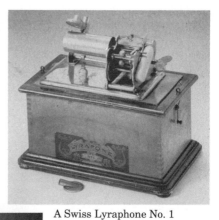

An Edison red Gem phonograph, Model D, No. 321189D, with K reproducer, Combination gearing and oak case with 'G.J.A. Turner & Co., London' retailer's label, and maroon 19in (48cm) 2-piece Fireside horn with crane. **£850–950** *CSK*

A Pathé Gaulois phonograph, in blue case with Pathé ebonite reproducer on over-mandrel carrier and glass horn, 16in (41cm) long. **£1,000–1,200** *CSK*

A Swiss Lyraphone No. 1 phonograph, by Barnes & Mullins, with open works mechanism, speed regulator, floating reproducer and recorder and walnut 'reversible' case, together with approximately 24 cylinders, c1905. **£300–400** *S*

Barnes & Mullins were music publishers as well as banjo and sheet music retailers, at 3 Rathbone Place, London W1, from c1900.

A Pathé Le Menestrel phonograph, the blue cast iron body with gilt decoration, 'J. Girard, Paris' retailer's label and matching lid, with black composition reproducer, lacking diaphragm and stylus, and original spun aluminium horn, French, c1905, 12in (31cm) wide. **£700–900** *S*

An Edison Bell Standard phonograph, No. S5048, with New Model reproducer, shaving device and 'Bell' medallion, in oak case with banner transfer and reproduction witch's hat horn. **£550–600** *CSK*

An Edison Fireside phonograph, Model A, No. 90789, with K reproducer, Combination gearing, oak case and maroon 19in (48cm) 2-piece Fireside horn with crane. **£850–950** *CSK*

Polyphons

An Excelsior phonograph, with open works mechanism, 'E.W.C.' transfer, boxed floating reproducer and recorder, oak case and large spun aluminium horn with cloth bag. **£450–500** *CSK*

A German 24½in Polyphon folding top Style 49C disc musical box, with twin comb movement, in mahogany case with carrying handles and 'Imhoff & Muckle, London' retailer's label, c1900, 29in (74cm) wide, together with 20 discs. **£25,000–30,000** *S*

An Edwardian table top Polyphon, in carved walnut case inlaid with floral marquetry, the lid inset with coloured scenic view, 21½in (55cm) square, together with 17 steel discs of late Victorian popular airs. **£2,000–3,000** *WL*

Musical Instruments

A 19¾in Polyphon, in original walnut banded case with drawer beneath, together with 12 original discs in original screw holder, 19thC. **£2,000–2,500** *B*

A German 8⅛in Polyphon disc musical box, with single comb movement, in walnut veneered serpentine case with colour print in lid, together with 31 discs in a wooden box and 2 Polyphon disc catalogues dated 1905 and 1907, 20thC. **£2,000–2,700** *S*

A 56-button English system accordion, by Lachenal, branded 'The Edeophone, No. 60245' on the endplate, and 'Rd. 129662' on the side, with pierced ebonised endplates, 17in (43cm) diam, in original box. **£500–700** *CSK*

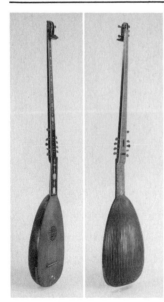

An archlute, by Magno Tieffenbrucker III, the body of 43 snakewood ribs with ivory stringing between, the back of both the main and subsidiary necks overlaid with mosaic of small kingwood and ivory triangles, the fingerboard and face of the subsidiary neck overlaid with ebony and inlaid with ivory stringing and plaques of mother-of-pearl diminishing in size towards the top, later table with pierced and carved inset rose, the main peg box pegged for one single and 5 double courses of strings, the secondary peg box pegged for 8 single courses of strings, labelled 'Magno Dieffopruchar', Venice, c1700, 24in (61cm) long, in contemporary wooden case. **£15,000–20,000** *S*

A Tanzbar 16-note automatic accordion, with lever operated mechanism, in stained wood case, together with 19 rolls, all in a plush lined leather covered carrying case with luggage tag inscribed 'Percy Honri', German, c1910. **£3,000–3,500** *S*

The accordionist Percy Honri was one of the great music hall stars in Britain at the turn of the century. He was one of the earliest artists to record with the fledgling Gramophone Co.

An English chamber barrel organ, the 22 key action with 6 stops including drum and triangle and 3 barrels playing 10 tunes each, in mahogany case with simulated gilt pipes, on matching base with tapered reeded legs and storage for 2 barrels, the barrels with label of 'W. Phillips, Manor Road, Tower Hill', the front also with maker's name in painted cartouche, 60in (152cm) high. **£3,500–4,000** *CSK*

A Bruder automaton barrel organ, No. 130, the 22 note instrument playing 11 airs, the lid and front section opening to reveal 6 painted automaton figures, contained in mahogany case with floral inlay on base, tulipwood and ebony stringing, on bracket feet, restored and in good working order, German, c1850, 24in (61cm) wide. **£27,000–35,000** *S*

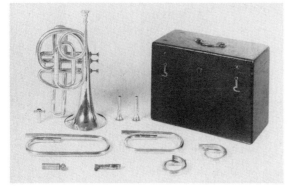

A cornopean, with silver plated tubing, with 3 Stölzel valves, 5 crooks, one bit and 3 mouthpieces, 10in (25cm) long, in original wooden case.
£600–800 *S*

A 56-button English system Aeola concertina, No. 29363, with nickel mounted endplates, 6 fold black leather bellows, wrist straps stamped 'C. Wheatstone & Co./London' and extended lower register, 7in (18cm) diam, in original square leather box.
£850–950 *CSK*

A 38-button Anglo-German system concertina, stamped 'C. Jeffries, Maker' with hexagonal nickel plated fretted endplates and 6 fold black tooled leather bellows, 6in (15cm) diam, with receipt signed 'C Jeffries' and dated '18/6/1898', with leather case.
£1,500–2,000 *CSK*

A 4 or 6-keyed ebony flute, by Carl August Grenser, with ivory mounts, silver keys with bevelled square covers, 2 foot joints, one with one key, the other with 3, an additional upper middle joint by another maker, in ebony with 2 silver keys with bevelled square covers, stamped 'A. Grenser' with the device of crossed swords on all joints, the foot joints also stamped 'Dresden' and the one keyed foot joint stamped '1798', the upper middle joint numbered '2', sounding lengths with each foot joint 21⅛in (53.5cm), and 23in (59cm), and sounding length of additional upper middle joint 5½in (14cm), in contemporary mahogany flute case.
£17,000–22,000 *S*

It can only be surmised as to why this flute, although bearing August Grenser's stamp is dated 2 years after he handed over his workshop to his nephew Heinrich Grenser. Possibly the instrument had been made at an earlier date and only sold after the transfer had taken place.

A 7-keyed bugle, by Charles-Joseph Sax, with original mouthpiece, engraved 'C. Sax a Bruxelle' on bell, in shaped case veneered with rosewood and decorated in marquetry with foliage and a keyed bugle, the latter bearing within its coil the name of the first owner now partly obscured by a later iron handle 'L. Honbert ***lerin*', also with a small square plaque bearing the date '1842', 57in (144cm) long.
£5,000–7,000 *S*

This instrument was built to the very best specification by a maker already renowned for his craftsmanship. The case was also built to special order but lacks the perfection of craftsmanship present in the bugle.

A one-keyed rosewood flute, by Adam Martin, with ivory mounts, the single key of silver with square cover, stamped 'Martin, No. 2, Cheapside, London', the key engraved 'D.M.' c1795, sounding length 22in (55cm), in original mahogany case,.
£950–1,100 *S*

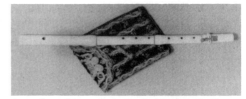

A one-keyed ivory flute, probably French, the single key of silver with square cover, in contemporary black velvet wallet embroidered in gold and silver thread with running foliage, the flap embroidered with a musical trophy of trumpets, kettle drums and horns, the latter incorporating the initials 'S' and 'L', late 18thC, sounding length 21⅛in (54cm).
£3,500–5,500 *S*

A walking stick fife, in 3 rosewood joints, with silver mounts and ferrule, the knob incorporating a small recess with screw lid, late 19thC, sounding length 13in (33cm).
£400–600 *S*

A one-keyed ebony flute, by Johann August Crone, with ivory mounts, the single key of silver with square cover on a silver saddle mount, 3 corps de réchange, stamped 'I.A. Crone' on all the joints except the foot joint, all joints stamped with an 8 pointed star, the upper middle joints further stamped with a pair of crowns and the figures '1', '2' and '3' respectively, late 18thC, 2 sounding lengths 21in (53cm) and one 20½in (52cm), in a padded wallet.
£3,500–5,000 *S*

A 6-keyed boxwood flute, by William Milhouse, with ivory mounts, silver keys with bevelled square covers, graduated stopper, 3 corps de réchange, stamped 'W. Milhouse, London, 337 Oxford St.', sounding lengths one 23½in (60cm), and 2 each 23in (59cm), in original mahogany case with Milhouse's trade card.
£1,700–2,200 *S*

A French guitar, labelled 'Goudot-Mollot, 1831, No. 213', the back and ribs of bird's-eye maple, the front decorated with mother-of-pearl and ebony, the head inset with a mother-of-pearl shield bearing the initials 'D.F.', the length of back 17½in (45cm).
£350–550 *CSK*

A 8-keyed ivory flute, by Louis Drouet, stamped 'Drouet, London', the silver keys with salt spoon covers, silver machined decorative mounts, sounding length 23in (58.5cm), in a fitted case.
£2,000–3,000 *C*

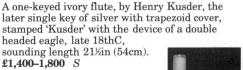

A guitar, by D & A Roudhloff Fils Aîné, London or Mirecourt, the one-piece back and sides of rosewood with blackwood edge bindings, pin bridge, ebonised neck and head, tuning pegs, stamped internally 'Roudhloff fils aîné a Mirecourt', c1800, body length 17½in (45cm), in a case.
£1,500–2,000 *S*

A one-keyed ivory flute, by Henry Kusder, the later single key of silver with trapezoid cover, stamped 'Kusder' with the device of a double headed eagle, late 18thC, sounding length 21½in (54cm).
£1,400–1,800 *S*

A guitar, after the syle of Panormo, the back and ribs of satinwood, the sound hole decorated with multiple purfling and mother-of-pearl, c1830, length of back 17½in (50cm), in a case.
£400–600 *CSK*

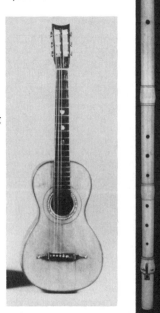

A guitar, by Giuseppe Filano, labelled 'Giuseppe Filano/Figlio di Donato Filano/Abita alla Strada di S. Chiara/A.D. 1794', the back and ribs of plain wood, the table and sound holes edged with mother-of-pearl and red mastic decoration, the neck with ebony lines, the fingerboard with mother-of-pearl, tortoiseshell and red mastic decoration, the figure of 8 head with 6 reverse pegs, the length of back 17in (43cm), in box.
£2,500–3,500 *C*

A one-keyed ivory flute, with 3 corps de réchange, lacking key, unstamped, sounding lengths 22in (55.5cm) and 22½in (58cm).
£2,800–3,200 *C*

A guitar, circle of Johann Georg Stauffer, Vienna, the one-piece back and ribs of rosewood, the ribs edged with decorative dogtooth inlay of stained wood, the table and soundhole edged with floral inlay in mother-of-pearl, ebony pin bridge with pearl inlay with inlaid embellishments at the extremes, ebony fingerboard with nickel silver frets, with an inlaid floral motif of pearl in the upper bass register, scroll-shaped head with metal machined and engraved cover plate, c1830, 18in (45cm) long, in contemporary veneered wooden case.
£900–1,500 *S*

A Continental 3-keyed boxwood oboe, the upper joint with onion and cotton reel finial, the latter with stamped decoration, the keys of silver, the C key with fishtailed touchpiece and oval cover, the duplicate E♭ keys with trapezoid covers, twinned G and F holes, stamped 'Klenig' with the device of fleur-de-lys on each joint, the E♭ keys engraved 'Anno' and '1720' respectively, the C key engraved 'Hein Garrleffs', 1720, 22½in (57cm) long.
£2,500–4,000 *S*

The stamped decoration around the upper part of the finial comprises a simple ring of circles. They are very shallowly stamped and probably a later addition. The maker's stamp on the bell joint is upside down.

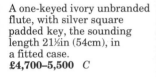

A one-keyed ivory unbranded flute, with silver square padded key, the sounding length 21½in (54cm), in a fitted case.
£4,700–5,500 *C*

A double action pedal harp, by Sebastian Erard, the arm inscribed 'Sebastian Erard/Patent N. 1437', the body, arm and soundboard with gilt lines, the fluted column surmounted by 4 gilt caryatids, 43 strings and 8 pedals.
£2,500–3,000 *CSK*

A crochet action pedal harp, by Henri Naderman, indistinctly stamped at the top of the soundboard, the body of 7 staves, the arm with floral mouldings, 37 strings, 7 pedals, c1820, 64½in (163.5cm) high.
£3,500–4,500 *C*

A mandore, by Francesco Plesber, labelled 'Francesco Plesber, in Milano, nella Contrada della Dogana, al Segno del Sole, 1769', the body of 15 yew ribs interleaved with ebony stringing, the table with inset rose pierced with a design of scrollwork and foliage, tie bridge, rosewood fingerboard inlaid with ivory strapwork, ebonised neck and peg box, the latter edged with tortoiseshell and terminating in a square finial overlaid with tortoiseshell and edged with ivory, 6 double courses of strings, 22in (56cm) long.
£3,500–4,500 *S*

A 2-keyed boxwood oboe, by Jakob Frederich Grundmann, Dresden, with onion and cotton reel finial, the keys of silver with octagonal covers, the C key with fishtailed touchpiece, a later nickel G# key added to the middle joint, stamped 'Grundmann, Dresden, 1768' on the bell joint, the other 2 joints stamped 'Grundmann, Dresden', the upper joint also stamped with the number '3', all joints stamped with the crossed swords device, 1768, 23⅓in (59cm) long.
£3,500–4,500 *S*

An organ built by Henry Holland, containing 5 ranks of pipes played from a single manual in a mahogany case, c1790, 96in (243.5cm) high.
£5,000–5,500 *McC*

A George IV square piano signed 'Astor and Horwood, Cornhill, London', the mahogany case with crossbanding, ebony stringing and chased brass mounts, green and gilt painted sound board, above 3 drawers, on ring turned legs with brass key mounts and rosettes, 68in (173cm) wide.
£1,700–2,200 *DN*

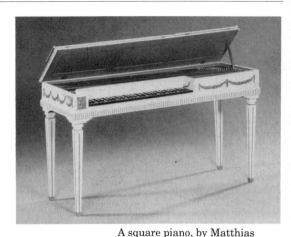

A square piano, by Matthias Christian Baumann, Zweibrücken, the case with later decoration, the 5 octave keyboard FF to f^3, with ebony naturals and ivory overlaid accidentals, prellmeckanic action, with 2 hand levers controlling damper lifts from c^1 upwards and b downwards, labelled on the soundboard 'Christian Baumann, Orgel-und Instrumentmacher, In Zweibrücken, 1777', 19½in (49.5cm) wide.
£6,000–8,000 *S*

A 12-keyed boxwood oboe, by Carl Golde, Dresden, with ivory mounts, nickel keys mounted on blocks, saddles and pillars, Brille key for F#, duplicate touchpiece for B♭ key, twin G holes, onion and cotton reel finial with tuning slide, integral thumb rest, stamped 'C. Golde, Dresden', with 2 stars, c1840, 22in (56cm) long.
£2,500–3,500 *S*

A Steinway Model K upright piano, No. 129161, overstrung and underdamped, in a rosewood case with satinwood and tulipwood crossbanding and inlay in the Sheriton style, 1907.
£5,000–6,000 *CSK*

A 6-valve trombone, by Désiré and Pierre Lebrun, Brussels, the tubing silver plated and forming an L-shape, Périnet valves, inscribed on the bell 'Medaille d'Or & P. Lebrun, R. de la Prevoyance, Bruxelles and Jules Springael, Loth', with a mouthpiece, c1910.
£3,700–4,200 *S*

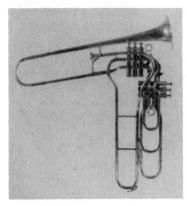

A Bechstein Boudoir grand piano, No. 18643, 90in (229cm) wide.
£1,400–1,900 *Bea*

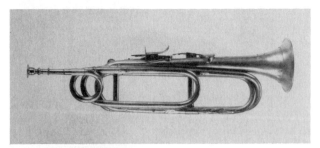

A 3-keyed trumpet, by James Cowlan, Liverpool, the tubing of brass coiled twice, the keys of brass with circular covers, the central key surmounted by a finger rest, with 2 crooks, one of them from another instrument, one shank and a brass mouthpiece with silver rim, engraved on a crescent shaped plaque on the bell 'Made by J. Cowlan, 39 Whitechapel, Liverpool', c1825.
£2,200–2,700 *S*

A symphonium, by Charles Wheatstone, the trapezoid nickel body on 4 outcurved feet engraved with scrolling foliage, ivory bushed oval mouth hole, 11 ivory tipped buttons giving the diatonic scale g^1 to c^3 with a further button mounted externally for f#² silver reeds, inscribed 'By His Majesty's Letters Patent. C. Wheatstone, Inventor, 20 Conduit St. Regent St. London', 2⅛in (5.5cm) high, in a case.
£2,500–3,000 *S*

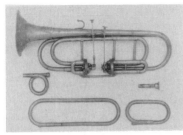

A trumpet, by John Augustus
Köhler, London, the tubing and
mounts of brass, the garland
embossed with scrolling foliage,
the mouthpiece socket mount
embossed with the national
flowers of Great Britain, the rose,
thistle and shamrock and spiral
turning, 2 Shaw disc valves, with
3 crooks, one bit and a silver
plated mouthpiece by George
Butler, London, inscribed on an
embossed plaque on the bell and
embossed on the garland, c1845.
17in (43cm) long, in case.
£4,500–5,500 *S*

An Evestaff walnut cased
pianette, the rectangular top
with fold-out music rest, on
cabriole legs.
£600–800 *BWe*

A 'Coinola' upright player piano,
electrically operated, the keys
accompanied by mechanism
including xylophone, drum,
tambourine visible in glazed
lower portion of case, early 20thC,
63½in (161cm) wide, complete
with 11 paper rolls.
£3,000–3,500 *S(NY)*

A pochette, possibly Austrian, the
body of 7 rosewood ribs with bone
and stringing, and alternately
inlaid with bone and mother-of-
pearl segments, the neck, head,
fingerboard and tailpiece also
inlaid with bone and mother-of-
pearl, the peg box surmounted by
a carved lion's head with bone
tongue, the table pierced by
2 f-holes and a geometric rose,
19thC, 20½in (52cm) long, and a
pochette bow with pike head and
open frog.
£1,800–2,500 *S*

A viola, attributed to Michael
Platner, Rome, the 2-piece back
of faint medium curl descending
from the joint, the ribs of
narrower curl, the head plain,
the table of medium grain in the
centre opening out towards the
flanks, the varnish of reddish
brown colour, labelled 'Michael
Platner fecit, Romae Anno 1740',
length of back 15½in (39cm),
in case.
£6,000–8,000 *S*

A Cabinet Roller Organ, by the
Autophone Co., Ithaca, N.Y., in a
gilt stencilled walnut case with
glass lid and 4 'cobs'.
£1,000–1,200 *CSK*

A bass viola da gamba, probably
by Richard Meares, London,
labelled twice, the flat back of 3
panels of medium curl maple, the
central panel inlaid with a
geometrical design in purfling,
the ribs of similar curl, the later
head of medium curl with open
scroll, the table of medium grain
inlaid below the fingerboard with
a floral design in purfling and
point d'aguille, with golden brown
coloured varnish, c1700, length of
body 26in (66cm).
£10,000–15,000 *S*

A viola d'amore, by Johann Georg
Thir, Vienna, 7 bowed strings and
7 sympathetic strings, labelled
'Johann George Thir, Lauten und
Geigenmacher • in Wein Anno
175*', with golden brown varnish,
length of body 16in (40cm),
in case. **£7,000–8,000** *S*

Music Stands

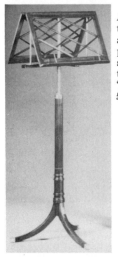

A double music stand, the lattice supports on an adjustable brass pole, with reeded pole support on splayed tripod base, branded 'Erard, London'.
£1,200–1,700 *CSK*

A copper music stand, with green patination, the scrolling music support on an adjustable pole and tripod base, c1860.
£550–650 *CSK*

Miscellaneous

A German Amorette 'Chalet' automaton organette, the 16-note mechanism contained in a painted wood case in the form of a chalet, with a pair of doors at the front, opening to reveal 2 small dancing china dolls, with mirror background, together with ten 8½in zinc discs, restored, c1905, 12½in (31.5cm) wide.
£650–1,000 *S*

A musical nécessaire, with movement by F. Nicole, playing 2 airs, near complete Palais Royale implement set, in mulberry wood case with bevelled lid, 8in (20cm) wide.
£1,000–1,200 *CSK*

A singing bird in a cage, of typical Bontems pattern, with coin mechanism and drawer in mahogany base, with ormolu mounts and canted corners, 21in (53cm) high.
£1,200–1,700 *CSK*

A musical seal, with barillet movement in gold case, with enamel inlaid floriate relief.
£1,500–2,000 *CSK*

RECEIVERS

A Marconiphone Type RB3 crystal set, with one wave length plate and cell cover, in black Rexine covered case with BBC transfer and instructions in lid, 1920s, 12in (31cm) wide.
£600–800 *S*

A telegraph outfit, by C. Lorenz A.G., Berlin, No. 26751, the mahogany base mounted with clockwork printer, key receiver No. 24442, galvanometer and cast iron bridge, the base containing tape spool, late 19thC, 21in (53cm) long.
£950–1,200 *S*

A vintage Marconiphone V-2 valve radio, in original mahogany case.
£300–400 *DA*

BOOKS & BOOK ILLUSTRATIONS

The market for rare and secondhand books has remained buoyant with more book fairs and auctions being held over the last year than ever before. One of the hallmarks of this season has been the number of private collections for sale. These fine collections such as John Merriam's collection of 19thC and 20thC illustrated books fetched premium prices. Other collections built around a theme, such as railways, economics, fireworks, angling, dogs or authors such as P.G. Wodehouse, were also very much in demand.

Children's books have, once again, proved to be popular. They are not only a good area for new enthusiasts to begin collecting but also providing some highly sought after rarities for the more seasoned collector. Beatrix Potter books, as ever, are still highly sought after. In particular, copies in good condition of her first book *The Tale of Peter Rabbit,* published in 1901 and 1902, sold for £20,000–30,000. The rarity of these books is partly due to the fact that Beatrix Potter could not find a publisher willing to print her first book so she had to finance the first and second issues of 250 and 200 books respectively on her own. Also, the early

books published by John Harris and the Newbery family have become increasingly hard to find in good condition and consequently are demanding higher and higher prices.

Books on mountaineering are always highly sought after, whether they be priced at a few pounds per copy or in the thousands. Louis Baume, a member of the Alpine Club and the Swiss Alpine Club, converted his passion for mountains into books and set up Gaston's Alpine Books. His large collection of books, mostly of Alpine and Himalayan interest, sold exceptionally well and provided like-minded enthusiasts with a rich hunting ground of mountaineering adventures and stories.

Another area of special interest for collectors is material based on the City of London. Maps, engravings, prints, panoramas and books which feature London, its bridges and buildings are always in demand as are books on the Thames. Many fine examples were to be found in Geoffrey Gollin's collection, the majority of which were sold in multiple lots and priced under £50.

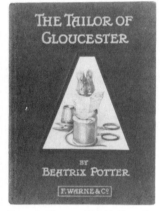

Beatrix Potter, *The Tailor of Gloucester,* first published edition, 27 coloured plates by Beatrix Potter, original boards, pictorial label on upper cover, 16mo, 1903.
£150–250 *S*

Hans Meyer, *Der Kilimandjaro,* first edition, plates and illustrations, folding maps, original pictorial cloth, 8vo, Berlin 1900.
£400–600 *BBA*

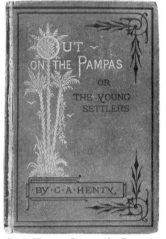

G. A. Henty, *Out on the Pampas,* first edition, 1871.
£200–220 *DW*

Dorothy Marion Wheeler, *A Fairy Retreat, Elfin Dance,* and *Through the Woods,* all signed with initials 'D.M.W.', inscribed as title, pencil and watercolour heightened with white, unframed, 20thC, 9 by 6in (22.5 by 15cm).
£720–800 *CSK*

J.M. Barrie, *Peter Pan in Kensington Gardens,* No. 211 of 250 copies, signed by the artist, 50 coloured plates by Arthur Rackham, original pictorial vellum gilt, 4to, 1906.
£800–1,200 *CSK*

The Bible, Oxford, 1759, Scottish tooled binding.
£300–320 *DW*

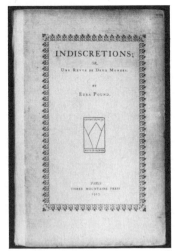

Ezra Pound, *Indiscretions,* one of 300 copies, first edition, 1923.
£250–270 *DW*

Virginia Woolf, *Monday or Tuesday,* first edition, 1921.
£250–270 *DW*

John Wilkins, *An Essay Towards a Real Character, and A Philosophical Language,* first edition, 1668.
£300–320 *DW*

Frederick Accum, *Description of the Process of Manufacturing Coal Gas,* second edition, 1820.
£250–270 *DW*

A World Cup Football programme, England-v-West Germany, 1966.
£70–90 *DW*

H. Rider Haggard, *Colonel Quaritch, V.C.,* 3 vols., first edition, 1888.
£450–470 *DW*

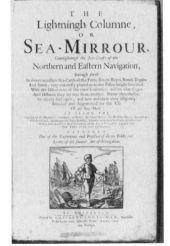

Kaspar Jacobsz, *The Lightningh Columne, or Sea-Mirrour,* 1711.
£1,700–2,000 *DW*

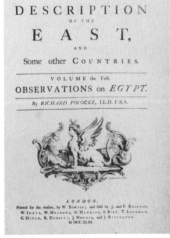

Richard Pococke, *A Description of the East, and Some other Countries,* 2 vols., first edition, 1743 and 1745.
£750–770 *DW*

Adrianus Metius, and Guglielmus Blaeu, *Rimum Mobile, Astronomice, Sciographice, Geometrice, & Hydrographice, et Instrumentis Mathematicis,* Amsterdam, apud Guilielmum Blaeu, 1633, 3 parts in one, 4°, editio nova, engraved additional title, woodcut astronomical diagrams and illustrations, some dampstaining to inner margins, 2F4 torn across, not affecting text, 3R1-3 slightly stained at outer margin, lightly browned, 19thC half calf, extremities rubbed, **£350–450** *CSK*

Giovanni Battista Cipriani, *Monumenti della Grecia,* Rome, no imprint, 1798, 4°, first edition, engraved title, plate list, and 25 hand coloured plates after Julien David Le Roy, occasional light spotting, modern half calf. **£600–700** *CSK*

Edgar Allan Poe, *A Dream within a Dream,* London, John Blockley, c1850, 2°, 5pp. musical score, small marginal tears, light soiling and spotting, original pale blue wrappers, upper wrapper with a lithographed illustraiton of a female spectre on a balcony overgrown with dark foliage, small fragment lacking from top of upper wrapper, lightly spotted, slight marginal tears. **£170–220** *CSK*

Herman Moll, a *Set of Thirty-Two New and Correct Maps of the Principal Parts of Europe,* 1727. **£740–780** *DW*

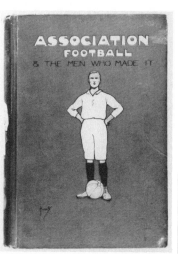

Alfred Gibson & William Pickford, *Association Football & The Men Who Made It,* 4 vols., 1905-6. **£300–350** *DW*

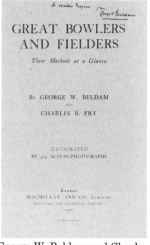

George W. Beldam and Charles B. Fry, *Great Bowlers and Fielders,* first edition, signed presentation copy, 1906. **£220–250** *DW*

An original design book, probably John Northwood, Stourbridge, dated 1860-68, contemporary blocked sheep leatherbound folio, 86 leaves carefully delineated either in pen and ink or in pencil, mostly on both sides, with designs for vases, jugs, bowls, decanters etc., with pattern numbers, and a loose leaf from another sketch book, working copy, distressed. **£8,500–9,500** *S*

Glass design books are extremely rare, particularly those dating from the 1860s. This example is signed 'J&JN 1860' on the flyleaf and several of the drawings are precisely dated, the latest date being June 1868. The signature probably stands for John and Joseph Northwood who supplied designs to several glassmakers in the Stourbridge district, notably Richardsons and Stevens and Williams. However, the designs appear to indicate the work of several hands and a lot of the later patterns reveal the use of hydrofluoric acid and work for template machines.

Speed's Map of Sussex, 1627. **£480–500** *DW*

William Golding, *Lord of the Flies,* London, Faber & Faber, first edition, 1954. **£320-360** *CSK*

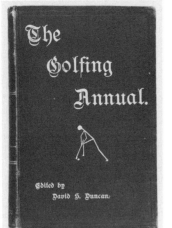

The Golfing Annual, vol. 3, 1890.
£250–270 *DW*

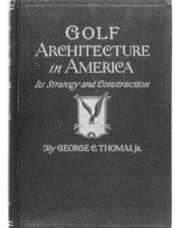

George C. Thomas, Jr., *Golf Architecture in America*, first edition, 1927.
£500–520 *DW*

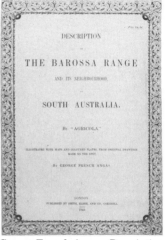

George French Angas, *Description of the Barossa Range and its Neighbourhood, in South Australia*, 1849.
£3,000–3,200 *DW*

Jean Baptiste Tavernier, *Collections of Travels through Turky into Persia, and the East-Indies*, 2 vols., 1684.
£1,000–1,200 *DW*

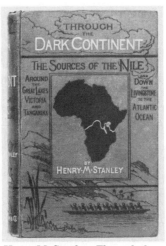

Henry M. Stanley, *Through the Dark Continent*, 2 vols., first editions, 1878.
£560–580 *DW*

Bernard Darwin, *The Golf Courses of the British Isles*, first edition, 1910.
£280–300 *DW*

Rudolph Akermann, *Microcosm of London*, vol. 1 of 3, first edition, 1808.
£1,400–1,600 *DW*

Official Report of *The Fourth Olympiad, London*, 1908.
£550–650 *DW*

Robert Rawlinson, *Designs for Factory Furnace and Other Tall Chimney Shafts*, 1858.
£1,200–1,400 *DW*

Charles Darwin, *On The Origin of Species*, contemporary half morocco, first edition, 1859.
£2,100–2,500 *DW*

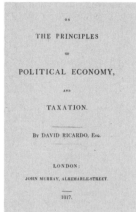

David Ricardo, *On The Principles of Political Economy, and Taxation,* first edition, 1817.
£4,400–4,600 *DW*

Walter Harrison, *A New and Universal History, Description and Survey of the Cities of London and Westminster, London,* for J. Cooke, 1775-6, 2°, engraved frontispiece and 100 engraved plates, 2 folding, contemporary calf-backed marbled boards, slight damage.
£700–800 *CSK*

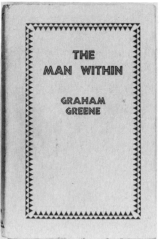

Graham Greene, *The Man Within,* first edition, 1929, original cloth in dust jacket.
£800–1,000 *DW*

C. W. Wilson, and H. S. Palmer, *Ordnance Survey of the Peninsula of Sinai,* 3 parts in 5 vols., 1869, mounted albumen photos.
£6,500–6,700 *DW*

Johan Michael Probst, *Sphaerae Artificiales,* part coloured engraving showing terrestrial and celestial globes and armillary sphere, late 18thC, 20 by 23in (51 by 59cm), framed.
£250–300 *P(S)*

Ferdinando Ruggieri, *Studio d'Architettura Civile,* 3 vols., 1722-28.
£2,000–2,500 *DW*

John Austen, *The Amorous Embrace,* signed, pencil, pen, black ink and grey wash, 7 by 5in (18 by 12.5cm).
£300–400 *CSK*

Isaac Robert Cruikshank, *King of Concord, Queen of Plenty,* initialled 'RCk', and inscribed as title, pen and brown ink and watercolour, unframed, 4½ by 4in (11.5 by 10cm), and 6 unframed illustrations, on 3 sheets.
£700–800 *CSK*

Eugene Atget, *Photographe de Paris,* first edition, 1930.
£220–250 *DW*

A collection of 19 books, with cloth bindings, designed by Charles Rennie Mackintosh, Glasgow, Blackie & Son Ltd. **£700–800** *C*

Fred Mason, *The Story of Duke Huon of Bordeaux,* including various chapter headings and Illustrations, 4 signed with monogram and many inscribed, pen and black ink, unframed, 8 by 6in (20 by 15cm), 14 in 3 mounts.
£400–500 *CSK*

Published as Huon of Bordeaux, *translated into English by Sir John Bourchier, Lord Berners, retold by Robert Steele, London, George Allen, 1895.*

Sidney Harold Meteyard, *But in peace hung over her sweet Basil evermore and moisten'd it with tears,* inscribed as title, pencil and watercolour with touches of white heightening, unframed, 8 by 6in (20 by 15cm).
£2,000–2,500 *CSK*

Louis William Wain, *Playtime,* signed, watercolour and bodycolour, 11 by 14in (28 by 36cm).
£2,000–2,500 *CSK*

Edmund Dulac, 'For some we loved, the loveliest and the best That from his Vintage rolling Time has prest, Have Drunk their Cup a Round or two before, And one by one crept silently to rest', from *The Rubaiyat of Omar Khayyam,* published by Hodder & Stoughton, London, 1909, pl. 7, signed, pencil and watercolour, 12½ by 9in (32 by 23cm).
£10,000–15,000 *CSK*

In June, 1909, Hodder & Stoughton announced the publication of their gift book of the year, The Rubaiyat of Omar Khayyam, *as a centenary tribute to its translator Edward Fitzgerald, with 20 colour plates from watercolours by Edmund Dulac. Dulac's illustrations are considered amongst his finest, his style more evocative with a studied exoticism. Here for the first time Dulac created depth, as perhaps nowhere else. The work marked his success and at just 31 he was now considered one of the most gifted and highest paid illustrators of his time. His watercolour illustrations were issued in a deluxe edition of 750 copies which was oversubscribed before publication. The original watercolours were exhibited soon after publication at the annual exhibition of Dulac's work at the Leicester Gallery, where Arthur Rackham also exhibited and enjoyed enormous popularity.*

Graham Laidler, *The British Character, Curiosity,* signed 'Pont', inscribed as title, pencil, pen and black ink, unframed, 9 by 12in (22.5 by 31cm).
£1,200–1,500 *CSK*

David Loggan, *Oxonia Illustrata,* first edition, 1675.
£1,700–1,800 *DW*

English School, *When Cradling Lilies Rocked my Sleep,* and *Where Mortal Things Might Never Breathe,* both inscribed as title on reverse and one further inscribed, pencil and watercolour, 19thC, 13 by 9in (33 by 23cm).
£600–700 *CSK*

Cecil Aldin, *'Just the Present for your Best Boy. They never upset you',* signed and inscribed as title, coloured crayons, 22 by 18½in (56 by 47cm).
£1,200–1,700 *CSK*

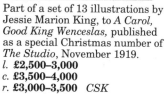

Part of a set of 13 illustrations by Jessie Marion King, to *A Carol, Good King Wenceslas,* published as a special Christmas number of *The Studio,* November 1919.
l. **£2,500–3,000**
c. **£3,500–4,000**
r. **£3,000–3,500**   *CSK*

Cyril Cowell, *Stores from the Stores* and *All A-Blowing,* both signed, pencil and watercolour heightened with white, unframed, 20thC, 6½ by 11in (16 by 28cm).
£400–600   *CSK*

Cyril Cowell, *Lettuce for Tea* and *Gardening,* both signed, pencil and watercolour heightened with white, unframed, 20thC, 7 by 11in (18 by 28cm).
£300–500   *CSK*

Charles Altamont Doyle, *The Fairy Tree,* pencil, pen and black ink and watercolour, unframed, c1880, 11 by 15in (28 by 38cm).
£6,500–7,500   *CSK*

Charles Altamont Doyle (1832-93), an Edinburgh civil servant, was the youngest son of the political cartoonist John Doyle, father of Sir Arthur Conan Doyle, and brother of the fantasy artist Richard Doyle. He suffered from alcoholism and later epilepsy, and spent his later years in various hospitals where his most memorable work was done. He died in a mental hospital in Dumfries on 10th October 1893.

Margaret Winifred Tarrant, 8 illustrations to *Peter Pan,* all signed twice, once with initials 'MWT', variously numbered, pencil, unframed, largest 9 by 6½in (23 by 16.5cm).
£1,500–2,000   *CSK*

Margaret Tarrant was a prolific illustrator, her first work being for Kingsley's Water Babies *in 1908. She also illustrated Browning's* Pied Piper, *1912 and Lewis Carroll's* Alice, *1916. Some of her best work can be seen in her* Flowers and Fairies *books.*

Louis William Wain, *The Vile Din,* signed, pencil and watercolour heightened with bodycolour, 10 by 14in (25 by 36cm).
£2,000–2,500   *CSK*

Locate the source

The source of each illustration in Miller's can be found by checking the code letters below each caption with the list of contributors.

Charles Altamont Doyle, *Playmates,* pen and brown ink and watercolour, 10 by 24in (25 by 61cm).
£3,000–5,000   *CSK*

G. J. W. Winter, *Butterfly's Burlesque,* signed and dated 1884, numbered '6' and inscribed as title on artist's label attached to backboard, oil on panel, 19thC, 10 by 17in (25 by 43cm).
£4,000–4,500   *CSK*

Cyril Cowell, *Goodness! ... He's 72 round the Chest,* and *The Glee Singers,* both signed, pencil and watercolour heightened with white, unframed, 20thC, 6½ by 11in (16 by 28cm).
£400–600 *CSK*

Cyril Cowell, *First Stop the Rookery,* and *The Squirrelquins bring home the Coconut from the Fair,* both signed, inscribed as title, pencil and watercolour heightened with white, unframed, 20thC, 6½ by 11in (16 by 28cm).
£400–600 *CSK*

Tony Sarg, *'Regarding themselves in a large Mirror',* signed and dated '08', pencil, pen and black ink and watercolour heightened with white, unframed, 10 by 7in (25 by 18cm).
£800–1,200 *CSK*

Published in John F. MacPherson's Children for Ever, *London, John Long, 1908, p26. Sarg was an American painter, illustrator and caricaturist, who became a member of the London Sketch Club in 1914 and illustrated a number of English books and magazines, such as* Punch *and* The Graphic.

Cyril Cowell, *The Squirrelquins Bath Night* and *The Squirrelquins Bedtime Story,* both signed, inscribed as title, pencil and watercolour heightened with white, unframed, 20thC, 7 by 11in (18 by 28cm) and 6½ by 11in (16 by 28cm).
£400–600 *CSK*

Cyril Cowell, *Perrompeddy Pom, Pom, Pom!* and *Blindman's Buff,* both signed, pencil and watercolour heightened with white, unframed, 20thC, 7 by 11in (18 by 28cm) and 6½ by 11in (16 by 28cm).
£500–700 *CSK*

Charles James Folkard, *The Wise Men of Gotham, 'So they left the Eel to be drowned',* signed and inscribed as title on reverse, pen and black ink and watercolour, unframed, 10 by 7in (25 by 17cm).
£1,800–2,500 *CSK*

This illustration appeared in Mother Goose Nursery Tales, *1923, No. 6.*

Lawson Wood, *Pop riding his Bicycle with his assistant,* signed, pencil, watercolour and bodycolour, unframed, 17 by 13½in (43 by 34cm).
£1,200–1,800 *CSK*

Dorothy Marion Wheeler, *See Saw, The Picnic,* and *Making Friends,* all signed with initials 'D.M.W.', inscribed as titles, pencil and watercolour heightened with white, unframed, 20thC, 9 by 6in (22.5 by 15cm).
£550–650 *CSK*

Helen Beatrix Potter, *Studies of Newts,* and *Sticklebacks and Dogfish,* dated 'Oct.84' and 'Oct.17.84', pencil and watercolour, unframed, 7½ by 4in (19 by 10cm).
£2,200–2,900 *CSK*

These drawings were executed at Bush Hall, Hertfordshire.

Dorothy Marion Wheeler, *The Lamplighter,* inscribed as title, pencil and watercolour heightened with white, unframed, 7½ by 5in (19 by 12.5in).
£150–200 *CSK*

Helen Beatrix Potter, *Duchess in Ribby's Kitchen*, and *Duchess carrying a Bouquet of Flowers*, pencil, pen and brown ink, unframed, 5 by 8in (12.5 by 20cm), and 2 others.
£4,700–5,200 *CSK*

Dorothy Marion Wheeler, *Caught, Fairy Lullaby, Hide and Seek,* and *Fairy Secrets,* all signed with initials 'D.M.W.', inscribed as titles, pencil and watercolour heightened with white, unframed, 20thC, 9 by 6in (22.5 by 15cm).
£700–800 *CSK*

Helen Beatrix Potter, *The Mice Dance,* and *The Fiddler and the Blind Mouse,* pencil, pen and brown ink, unframed, 7 by 4½in (17.5 by 11.5cm).
£8,500–9,500 *CSK*

Helen Beatrix Potter (1866-1943)

Beatrix Potter's father, Rupert (1832-1914), was a wealthy barrister and amateur artist in his own right, who would copy illustrated magazines and books and even designed and painted plates for his children's nursery. Her brother, Walter Bertram Potter, was a talented draughtsman at an early age who, with Beatrix, perfected wildlife studies, specialising in birds and bats. His short career as an artist included exhibiting 13 works at the Royal Academy, and 14 works at the RSA, ending in 1905 when he, like Beatrix, turned to farming.

Beatrix began her artistic career as a student at South Kensington, excelling in 'Practical Geometry, Perspective, Model Drawing and Freehand Drawings', then illustrating for greeting cards and books, producing 19 books by 1913. One of the most significant book projects was *The Tale of the Pie and the Patty Pan*, 1905, with locations taken from Sawrey and Hawkshead, which she completed in collaboration with her fiancé, Norman Warne, who died before publication. In later years Beatrix turned to sheep farming in the Lake District, where she married William Heelis, a local Ambleside solicitor.

Dorothy Marion Wheeler, *Happy Song, A Fairy Tale, The Fairy Swing,* and *Fairy Flutes,* all signed with initals 'D.M.W.', inscribed as titles, pencil and watercolour heightened with white, unframed, 20thC, 7½ by 5½in (18.5 by 13.5cm).
£775–850 *CSK*

Helen Beatrix Potter, *Ribby Knitting at the Cottage Door,* numbered '45', pencil, pen and brown ink heightened with white, unframed, 5 by 8in (12.5 by 20cm).
£4,000–4,500 *CSK*

This drawing is an alternative version for The Tale of the Pie and the Patty Pan, 1905, p45. *The cottage is now the National Trust Information Office, Hawkshead.*

Helen Beatrix Potter, *Studies of Fish,* dated 'Sept. 84', and 'Sept. 20. 83' on reverse, pencil and watercolour, unframed, 7 by 4½in (17.5 by 11.5cm).
£2,000–2,500 *CSK*

A Patent Certificate of Registration dated 17th June, 1910, presented to and signed by Miss Beatrix Potter, including 3 photographs, side, front and back view of the Jemima Puddleduck doll, 13 by 8in (33 by 20cm), 4 artist's proofs by Beatrix Potter for *The Fairy Caravan*, 1929, an unfinished interior study and a group of related photographs, newspapers and letters relating to the family, Beatrix's farming career and her life as an artist.
£4,000–4,500 *CSK*

Donald McGill, '*I only started this Mornin! Guv'nor. What Time do we go on Strike 'ere?'* signed, inscribed as title on reverse, pencil and watercolour, 8 by 6in (20 by 15cm).
£450–550 *CSK*

A. E. Bestall, a proof copy of *Rupert Bear and the Baby Dragon,* including 16 watercolour illustrations and accompanying printed text in Latin, 20thC, 6 by 4½in (15 by 11.5cm).
£2,000–2,500 *CSK*

Norman Thelwell, '*Beware of the Swimming Pool'*, signed '.thelwell.', inscribed as title, pencil, pen and black ink and watercolour heightened with white, unframed, 10½ by 4½in (27 by 11.5cm).
£850–950 *CSK*

This illustration was a design for a Christmas card.

Norman Thelwell (b1923)

Norman Thelwell was born in Birkenhead on 3rd May, 1923. He studied at Liverpool College of Art and taught at Wolverhampton School of Art 1950-57. A regular contributor to *Punch* from 1952, he worked as a cartoonist for newspapers and first produced his own comic books *Angels on Horseback* in 1957. A talented commercial designer, his comic inventions found their way on to posters, book jackets, greeting cards and tea towels.

Two unframed book jacket designs for Essex Hopes' *Pen goes North* and P. G. Wodehouse's *P. S. Smith Journalist,* both inscribed as title and further extensively inscribed, largest 13 by 10in (33 by 25cm).
£550–600 *CSK*

Norman Thelwell, '*Belt Up'*, signed '.thelwell.', pencil, pen and black ink and watercolour, unframed, 11 by 14in (28 by 35.5cm).
£1,000–1,500 *CSK*

This was a book jacket design for Thelwell's Motoring Manual, *published by Methuen, 1974.*

Ronald William Fordham Searle, *Hungarian Children, Traiskirchen Transit Camp, Austria,* signed, numbered '3', inscribed as title, dated '3 November 1959', pen and brown ink, framed, 15 by 21in (38 by 53cm).
£300–500 *CSK*

Norman Thelwell, '*Chasing the Mail Coach'*, signed '.thelwell.', pencil, pen and black ink and watercolour heightened with white, unframed, 7 by 9in (17 by 23cm).
£500–600 *CSK*

This illustration was the first design for a greetings card for the General Post Office in the early 1970s.

John M. Burns, book jacket design for *Gangsters on the Coast by Moonlight,* pencil and watercolour, unframed, 15½ by 10in (39.5 by 25cm), and 5 other unframed illustrations, 20thC.
£70–90 *CSK*

Aldous Huxley, *Brave New World, London,* Chatto & Windus, first edition, 1932.
£550–600 *CSK*

Ronald William Fordham Searle, *Fessi Family,* signed, numbered '17', inscribed as title, dated '9 Nov 1959', pencil, pen and brown ink, unframed, 16 by 21in (40.5 by 53cm).
£300–500 *CSK*

Ronald Searle (b1920)

Ronald Searle was sympathetic to the plight of European refugees, having experienced wartime deprivations of his own. While incarcerated at Changi Gaol, Singapore in 1942, he managed to produce a visual record of life in the prison camp, exhibiting his powerful drawings on his return to Britain. In 1959 he was invited by the United Nations High Commissioner for Refugees to record the plight of European refugees in camps in Austria, Italy and Greece to help stir public sympathy. Forty of his drawings were published in *Refugees,* Penguin Books, 1960, with a graphic text by Kaye Webb describing the plight of his subjects. The proceeds were donated to the United Kingdom Committee of the World Refugee Year.

H. Fox, design for a book jacket cover for *The Golden Fear,* by Simon Harvester, published by Jarrolds, signed, inscribed as title, watercolour and bodycolour, unframed, 20thC, 15½ by 12in (39.5 by 31cm).
£40–60 *CSK*

A British Heritage bookmark, depicting Sir Winston Churchill.
£10–15 *MA*

Ronald William Fordham Searle, *Assyrian Refugees, Aigaleo, Athens,* signed, numbered '37', inscribed as title, dated '18 November 1959', pencil, pen and brown ink and felt tip pen, unframed, 14 by 20in (36 by 51cm).
£400–500 *CSK*

ARTISTS' MATERIALS

A Victorian pencil sharpener, with 11 adjustable sharpener heads on a turned ivory and silver mounted handle, London 1885, by Louis Dee, retailed by Clark, 20 Old Bond Street, in original case.
£470–520 *DN*

An artist's oak studio easel, with adjustable winding mechanism, late 19thC, 65in (165cm) unextended.
£250–400 *CSK*

An artist's oak studio easel, with adjustable winding mechanism above a materials shelf, late 19thC, 74in (188cm) unextended.
£1,800–2,200 *CSK*

Miller's is a price GUIDE not a price LIST.

TYPEWRITERS

A mahogany easel, with adjustable picture rest and open brush shelf, c1900, 63in (160cm) high.
£750–850 *S*

A late Victorian oak artist's studio easel, with adjustable winding mechanism above a materials shelf, 62in (157cm) unextended.
£850–950 *CSK*

A Merritt typewriter, No. 4545, with linear index mechanism, mahogany stained wood base and cover, with instruction sheet.
£400–600 *CSK*

A Babycyl typewriter, with alloy typewheel and japanned tinplate casing.
£250–350 *CSK*

A Picht typewriter, No. 14002, with sliding brail index and type wheel, in oak case with 'Herde & Wendt, Berlin' retailer's label and instructions in lid, early 20thC.
£500–700 *S*

A Eureka (Stollwerck) tinplate typewriter, in leatherette covered fitted card stationery cabinet, with instruction sheet, writing paper with Eureka logo, card cover damaged, 14in (36cm) wide.
£400–500 *CSK*

A group of papers dealing with the early typewriter industry, including 4 letters between The Standard Furniture Co. and Wyckoff, Seamans & Benedict/Remington, with autographs and signatures, American, early 20thC.
£350–450 *S*

A Morris typewriter, by The Hoggson & Pettis Manufacturing Co., New Haven, Conn., U.S.A., with sliding index mechanism over circular platen, in a steel frame, on japanned and gilt lined iron trellis base, in wood box with maker's descriptive booklet and instructions issued by the sale agent for Great Britain, H. J. Griswold, 3 Station St., Leicester.
£5,500–6,000 *CSK*

Patented in 1887, the Morris is one of the rarest of the many cheap, simple typewriters produced in the late 19thC. The index plate on this example is made of black, celluloid-like material, and the rubber type is decomposed. Two ink pots with detachable spouts are included in the box. Paul Lippman American Typewriters, a Collector's Encyclopedia, 1992 stated that only 4 examples of the Morris were known. This is not one of those 4.

A Columbia (Spiro) typewriter, No. 239, the upper case model with italic typeface and differential spacing, in wood case, damaged.
£3,000–4,000 *CSK*

A Hammond Model Two typewriter, with a two-row curved keyboard and 'piano' keys, American, c1893.
£600–650 *S*

CALCULATORS

A Gardner typewriter, with 14 keys, typesleeve and nickel plated frame, on japanned iron base with gilt scrolling.
£3,500–4,500 *CSK*

Patented in 1889, the Gardner was made in Manchester in the early 1890s, and was chiefly remarkable for its relative simplicity and small number of components. In addition to the 14 keys, there is a space key and a three-position shift key, which have to be pressed simultaneously for certain letters to be typed.

A Tachylemme ready reckoner, invented by G. L. Chambon, with percentage columns and 4 rotatable cylinders for units, tens, hundreds and thousands, in glazed wood case, with cardboard carton, 7in (17.5cm) wide.
£600–700 *CSK*

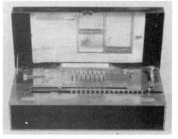

A 'The Millionaire' calculator, by Hans W. Egil, No. 1799, the brass bedplate with 8 sliding indices, 24 digital displays, function selector and operating handle, in metal case with instructions in lid, Swiss, c1910, 25½in (64cm) wide. **£1,100–1,500** *S*

A calculator, by Léon Bollée, Le Mans, the flat oxidised brass bed with 14 pairs of columns beneath a sliding carriage of 6 stacks of 10 hinged indices, with addition and subtraction levers at each side, 13½in (34.5cm) wide.
£6,000–7,000 *CSK*

Léon Bollée is credited with the invention of direct method multiplication, 1887.

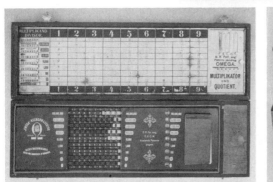

A Justin Wm. Bamberger & Co. Omega calculator, the removable panels with sliding indices, in paper covered case with stylus storage compartment, German, early 20thC, 18in (46cm) wide.
£950–1,200 *S*

A Hans W. Egil 'Madas' calculator, No. 9336, the brass bedplate with 9 sliding indices, 16 digital displays, function key and operating handle, with metal cover with instructions inside, Swiss, c1915, 24in (60cm) wide.
£550–700 *S*

A Mercedes desk-top calculator, No. 1598, with central crank, 6 sliders on angled top, on drum containing 20 hand-rotated geared rods radially disposed, on circular iron base, 6½in (16cm) diam.
£6,000–7,000 *CSK*

An adding machine, by Edward Greaves, Sheffield, the cast brass top-plate with 4 apertures for digits, on white metal dials rotated by pinned brass ratchet wheels, operated by a push-button at rear, missing, in cast iron casing, damaged, mid-19thC, 5in (13.5cm) wide.
£1,500–2,000 *CSK*

Edward Greaves is difficult to identify among the several Sheffield businesses with this name, but is probably the Edward Greaves brassfounder, listed in Directories between 1845 and 1871. He was described also at times as a steel manufacturer and maker of tuning forks, Aeolian pitch pipes and patent portable metronomes.

A Curta mechanical calculator, in a cylindrical plastic case, Model II No. 544153, by Contina Ltd., Lichtenstein, with instructions, c1969.
£200–250 *DN*

ANTIQUITIES

An Attic black figure band cup, decorated with palmettes with tendrils flanking the handles, details in added red and white, the reserved tondo centering a dot and 2 circles, the decoration on one side highly worn, circa 540 B.C., 8½in (21.5cm) diam.
£2,000–2,500   *S(NY)*

A banded alabaster jar, 1st Dynasty, 2965-2815 B.C., 5½in (14cm) diam.
£2,500–3,500   *S(NY)*

An alabaster jar, with flattened base and wide flat shoulder, 1st/2nd Dynasty, 2965-2750 B.C., 5½in (14cm) diam.
£450–550   *S(NY)*

Two Apulian Xenon group oinochoai, each with pedestal foot, high angular handle and Medusa masks moulded at the base of the spout, the body painted in added red with a laurel wreath, rays on the shoulder, late 4th Century B.C., 7 and 7½in (17.5 and 18cm) high.   **£600–700**   *S(NY)*

An Attic black figure band skyphos, with disk foot reserved on the edge and short stem, the body painted on one side with a lion striding between apopotraic eyes, and on the other with a panther between the eyes, palmettes with tendrils flanking the handles, details in added red, circa 540-530 B.C., 8in (20cm) diam.
£2,000–2,500   *S(NY)*

An Attic black figure olpe, circa early 5th Century B.C., 9in (22.5cm) high.
£1,200–1,700   *S(NY)*

A banded alabaster jar and cover, with flat base and shallow domed cover, 3rd-4th Dynasty, 2705-2520 B.C., 4in (10cm) diam.
£1,700–2,200   *S(NY)*

An Apulian red figure fish plate, painted with a grey mullet, a flatfish and a small horn shell, a spiral wave pattern on the rim, details in added white and brown wash, circa 350-325 B.C., 8½in (21cm) diam.
£4,000–5,000   *S(NY)*

Attributed by A.D. Trendall to the Perrone-Phrixos Group.

An Apulian red figure pelike, details in added white and yellow, circa 330-320 B.C., 13in (33cm) high.
£1,200–1,700   *S(NY)*

An Apulian red figure fish plate, painted with a striped bream, a dogfish and a wrasse, a spiral wave pattern on the rim, details in added white, brown, and yellow, circa 350-325 B.C., 9in (22.5cm) diam.
£3,000–3,500   *S(NY)*

An Attic black figure band cup, each side painted with a young horseman galloping to right and flanked by running youths and standing draped men, palmettes with tendrils flanking the handles, a dotted circle in the reserved tondo, details in added red, circa 540 B.C., 8in (20cm) diam.
£2,000–2,500 *S(NY)*

An Apulian red figure hydria, with ogee foot in 2° and contoured overhanging rim, early 4th Century B.C., 10in (25cm) high.
£2,000–2,500 *S(NY)*

A Paestan red figure Lebes Gamikos and cover, painted in red over the glaze with a woman seated on a tendril and holding a basket and sash, flying Eros holding a ring and sash on the reverse, a palmette flanked by scrolls under each handle, circa 340-320 B.C., with cover 7½in (19cm) high.
£950–1,200 *S(NY)*

An Attic black figure oinochoe, with torus foot, high cylindrical handle and trefoil mouth, the details in added red and white, a graffito under the foot, circa 510-550 B.C., 8½in (21cm) high.
£3,000–4,000 *S(NY)*

An Attic black figure lip cup, the tondo painted within a border of alternating black and red tongues with a spread-winged standing swan, circa 540-530 B.C., 8in (20cm) diam.
£2,500–3,000 *S(NY)*

A Mycenaean buffware jug, with broad rounded body, strap handle with single rib, and restored spout, the shoulder painted in brown over a buff slip with papyrus like vegetation, a spiral scroll band below the neck, circa 1450-1400 B.C., 11in (28cm) high.
£5,000–5,700 *S(NY)*

An Attic red figure nolan amphora, with disk foot, triple handles and echinus mouth, circa 460 B.C., 13½in (34cm) high.
£3,000–4,000 *S(NY)*

An Attic black figure trefoil oinochoe, with torus foot and high cylindrical handle, a 5 pointed star grafitto under the foot, circa early 5th Century B.C., 9in (23cm) high.
£2,000–2,700 *S(NY)*

Perhaps by the Painter of Vatican G 49.

An Etruscan red figure skyphos, both sides painted with a hippocamp swimming to left, 3 palmettes and scrolls within each handle zone, circa early 4th Century B.C., 9in (23cm) diam.
£2,000–3,000 *S(NY)*

An Apulian red figure bell krater, the details in added white and yellow, circa 360-340 B.C., 11½in (29.5cm) high.
£1,200–1,800 *S(NY)*

Attributed to the Painter of Athens, 1714.

An Attic white ground alabastron group of the negro Alabastra, with red slip on top of the disk rim, the body painted with an Ethiopian warrior, a date palm and a table on the reverse, circa 490-480 B.C., 6in (15cm) high.
£4,000–5,000 *S(NY)*

A Coptic bronze lamp, a rectangular filling hole on the back, circa 4th Century A.D., 7in (17cm) long.
£1,500–2,000 *S(NY)*

An Etruscan black figure panel amphora, with echinus foot, cylindrical handles, and flaring mouth, circa mid-6th Century B.C., 12½in (32cm) high.
£2,500–3,000 *S(NY)*

An Attic black figure neck amphora, with spreading disk foot, triple handles and echinus mouth, details in added red and white, circa early 5th Century B.C., 10in (25cm) high.
£5,000–6,000 *S(NY)*

An Etruscan black figure oinochoe, circa late 6th Century B.C., 9½in (24cm) high.
£1,500–2,000 *S(NY)*

An Etruscan red figure oinochoe, Faliscan, the convex handle with arms extending on to the cut-away spout, circa late 4th Century B.C., 12in (30cm) high.
£1,200–1,700 *S(NY)*

An Etruscan black figure panel amphora, with echinus foot, cylindrical handles, and flaring rim, one side painted with a rampant griffin, the other with a stalking panther, linked lotus buds above, rays above the foot, the details in added red, circa 525-500 B.C., 14in (36cm) high.
£7,000–8,000 *S(NY)*

Attributed to the Tolfa Group.

A miniature bronze Ichneumon coffin, the sacred mongoose standing on top of a fragmentary coffin open at one end, Late Period, 716-30 B.C., 5in (13cm).
£1,200–1,700 *S(NY)*

An Attic red figure lekythos, with black figure palmettes on the shoulder, circa mid-5th Century B.C., 12in (30cm) high.
£3,500–4,000 *S(NY)*

Attributed to the Bowdoin painter.

A bronze furniture attachment, from a bed or chair, the head of a lion crowning the corner, Egypt? circa 3rd Century B.C. or earlier, 4½in (11cm) high.
£600–800 *S(NY)*

A Syro-Phoenician copper figure of a God, standing with his clenched hands extended and formerly holding attributes, wearing a long kilt and conical headdress, the eyes recessed for inlay, circa 1400-1200 B.C., 6in (15cm) high.
£5,000–6,000 *S(NY)*

A bronze figure of the Apis bull, 26th/30th Dynasty, 664-342 B.C., 3in (7.5cm) long.
£1,300–1,700 *S(NY)*

A bronze figure of Amun-Min, holding his erect phallus in the left hand and flail in the raised right hand, wearing a broad collar, braided beard with curled tip, and the crown of Amun with sun disk and fragmentary plumes, the beard straps and long eyebrows and cosmetic lines engraved, 26th Dynasty, 664-525 B.C., 4½in (11cm) high without tenon.
£2,000–3,000 *S(NY)*

A Neo-Assyrian bronze head pendant of Pazuzu, his demonic face with bared fangs protruding from the wide mouth, and fierce bulging eyes beneath the prominent brows, a pendant loop on his bald crown, circa 800-700 B.C., 2in (4.5cm) high.
£2,000–3,000 *S(NY)*

A Greek bronze mug, Magna Graecia, with ribbed body, sharply flaring mouth, and strap handle with lower attachment terminating in the head and forepaws of a panther skin, the upper ends of the ribs with finely engraved contour, 4th Century B.C., 4in (10cm) high.
£3,000–3,500 *S(NY)*

A bronze figure of Harpocrates, the feet restored, 26th-30th Dynasty, 664-342 B.C., 4½in (11cm) high.
£1,400–1,900 *S(NY)*

A bronze anchor axe, with deep crescentic blade joined at the centre to the open shaft hole, a knob on top of the carination, circa 2200-2000 B.C., 6½in (16cm) wide.
£2,500–3,500 *S(NY)*

A bronze figure of Amun, his face with finely modelled features, 22nd-26th Dynasty, 944-525 B.C., 5in (12.5cm) high.
£1,700–2,000 *S(NY)*

Three bronze deities, 26th-30th Dynasty, 664-525 B.C., 3½, 5 and 6in (9, 13 and 15cm) high.
£1,200–1,800 *S(NY)*

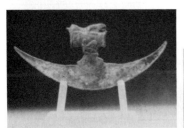

A Luristan bronze and iron axe head, with crescentic iron blade and bronze shaft hole, surmounted by a couchant feline with gaping jaws, a lion head forming part of the attachment to the blade underneath, circa 8th Century B.C., 10in (25cm) long.
£3,500–4,000 *S(NY)*

An Etruscan bronze stamnos handle, with fluted grip, the lanceolate attachments each repoussé and finely engraved with the head of a silen beneath twin volutes with palmettes, dotted ivy leaves in the border, late 5th-4th Century B.C., 5½in (14cm) high.
£1,500–2,000 *S(NY)*

A bronze figure of Herakles, Hellenistic or early Roman, circa 2nd Century B.C.-1st Century A.D., 4⅓in (11cm) high.
£2,500–3,000 *S(NY)*

An Etruscan bronze mirror, with equine handle and notched perimeter on the reflecting surface, the reverse freely engraved with the 2 Dioscuri stepping towards each other and wearing boots, tunics and Phrygian caps, a 4-pointed star in the field, circa 3rd Century B.C., 8½in (21cm) high.
£900–1,200 *S(NY)*

A bronze situla, the base in the form of an open lotus flower, Late Period, 716-30 B.C., 7in (17cm) high.
£2,500–3,000 *S(NY)*

A bronze figure of Khnum, wearing pleated Royal kilt with central tab, and striated tripartite wig surmounted by the rush-atef crown with ram's horns and flanking uraei, the god's woolly coat indicated on the forehead, Ptolemaic Period, 304-30 B.C., 5½in (14cm) high.
£2,500–3,500 *S(NY)*

A geometric bronze spectacle fibula, formed from a single wire of square section turned into a double spiral with figure eight in between, Greek or Italic, 8th Century B.C., 5½in (14cm) long.
£850–1,200 *S(NY)*

Four limestone canopic jars, each of ovoid form, the lids in the form of the heads of the Four Sons of Horus, comprising human-headed Imset, hawk-headed Quebehsenuf, baboon-headed Hapy, and jackal-headed Duamutef, the first 3 heads with black painted detail, 26th Dynasty, 664-525 B.C., 13 and 14in (33 and 36cm) high.
£7,000–8,000 *S(NY)*

A Luristan bronze horsebit, each cheek piece in the form of the addorsed forequarters of 2 walking horses with stylised ribbed manes, a rider seated side-saddle on their back, the bit with spiral terminals, circa 8th Century B.C., 4 and 5in (10 and 12.5cm) wide.
£3,500–4,500 *S(NY)*

A Luristan bronze axe head, with long curving blade and simulated thongs binding 4 prongs to the shaft hole, circa 8th Century B.C.
£400–500 *S(NY)*

Robert Hay first visited Egypt as an officer in the Royal Navy in 1824, and was so taken with the country that he returned repeatedly between 1828 and 1839. He made a number of trips down the Nile, collecting antiquities and recording monuments with a number of accomplished artists, including Frederick Catherwood and Joseph Bonomi. They made plans, sketches and watercolour drawings of many of the tombs and temples in Egypt and Nubia, which are now preserved in the British Museum. After Hay's death much of his collection was sold at auction in the Crystal Palace.

A limestone sphinx of a King, couchant and wearing a wide beard and nemes headcloth with queue, his tail curled around the right hindquarter, Late Period, 716-30 B.C., 14½in (37cm) long.
£2,200–2,700 *S(NY)*

A bronze Syrian or Levantine deity, with extended arms formerly holding attributes, crescentic ears, conical headdress and pendant loop behind, circa 1400-800 B.C., 4⅓in (11cm) high.
£300–400 *S(NY)*

A limestone servant figure of a man, seated on the ground and holding his hands over his knees, an instrument in the right hand, wearing a black centrally parted wig with head band tied behind, his skirt left white, the body painted yellow, traces of blue on the head band, 6th Dynasty, 2360-2195 B.C., 4in (10cm) high.
£2,000–3,000 *S(NY)*

A Cypriot limestone head of a Votary, his long face with smiling mouth and almond shaped eyes beneath finely arched brows, the flaps of his pointed cap turned up, 5th Century B.C., 9in (23cm) high.
£1,200–1,700 *S(NY)*

A limestone throne, with traces of red and yellow pigment, Ptolemaic Period, 304-30 B.C., 4in (10cm) high.
£1,200–1,700 *S(NY)*

A bronze pendant, Anatolia or the Caucasus, in the form of an aquatic bird, with 4 openings in the body, spatulate beak, and large globular eyes, circa 8th-7th Century B.C., 3in (7.5cm) long.
£500–600 *S(NY)*

A limestone obelisk, one side carved in sunk relief with a column of inscription: 'the one honoured by Anubis on his Mountain, the sole friend, Hem-Re', 6th Dynasty, 2360-2195 B.C., 12in (30cm) high.
£900–1,100 *S(NY)*

A limestone stele, carved in sunk relief with the owner, Kemen-Set-Meri, making an offering of a basket on stand to Osiris, 2 offering stands with vessels between them, the columns of inscription reading 'Speech of Ka..., born of Kemen-Set-Meri (Kemen beloved of Set), Foreigner', 15th Dynasty Hyksos, 1640-1530 B.C., 9 by 8in (23 by 20cm).
£1,500–1,800 *S(NY)*

A limestone funerary stele, with traces of red pigment, 12th Dynasty, 1938-1759 B.C., 23 by 12½in (58 by 32cm).
£3,000–5,000 *S(NY)*

Ten limestone artifacts, comprising 2 head rests, a table, a stool and a semi-circular stool, 2 offering tables, a small trough, a weight and a mortar, Tell el Amarna, 18th Dynasty, reign of Akhenaten, circa 1350-1336 B.C., 5 to 20in (12.5 to 51cm).
£2,000–2,500 *S(NY)*

These objects were found in the living rooms of the houses in the Eastern Village. According to the report 'Both stools and tables proved remarkably useful to the excavators at lunch time'. Of the stone table, 'the top was smooth, so smooth that one suspected people of the bad habit of sitting on it, and the underside was hollowed out so as to leave outstanding only 2 narrow ridges along the sides and a couple of crossbars; probably this was to give a smaller bearing surface and so to secure greater steadiness on a floor often none too even'.

A limestone relief fragment, carved in sunk relief with a lady, probably the goddess Hathor, the inscription translating 'the goddess Hathor, Mistress of Dendera, Lady of Heaven'; remains of blue, red and black pigment, late 18th-19th Dynasty, c1400-1190 B.C., 7in (17cm) high.
£3,000–3,500 *S(NY)*

Found near Karnak, according to an old label.

A limestone relief fragment, carved in sunk relief with a funerary procession, the man at left holding a child against his breast and leading another child with his left hand, followed by 5 or 6 men, very worn, followed by another man with a child standing before him and a man squatting down next to the child, the inscription at left reading 'the head of the fisherman...', late 18th Dynasty, circa 1332-1292 B.C., 13 by 21in (33 by 53cm).
£3,500–4,500 *S(NY)*

A limestone lintel fragment, carved in sunk relief with the owner Meru, 3 lines of inscription reading 'that he may be buried in the West, the one honoured by the Great God, ... House of God...Meru', 5th-6th Dynasty, 2520-2195 B.C., 9 by 12in (23 by 30cm).
£4,500–5,500 *S(NY)*

A limestone relief fragment, carved in sunk relief, with a column of inscription, 19th Dynasty, 1292-1190 B.C., 10in (25cm) square.
£2,000–2,500 *S(NY)*

A limestone round-topped stele, carved in sunk relief with a figure of the King raising his hands in adoration before the Lion of Leontopolis, the sacred lion striding on top of a shrine and wearing the sun disk, the god of Leontopolis striding at left and holding a was-scepter, a winged disk in the arch, the remaining inscription reading 'Living Lion'; traces of red and black pigment, late Ptolemaic Period/early Roman Period, circa 100 B.C.-100 A.D., 16in (40.5cm) high.
£2,000–2,500 *S(NY)*

A limestone relief fragment, carved in shallow relief with part of a frieze showing the sacred barque of Khonsu resting on a shrine, a shrouded statue of the king under the baldachin, censing royal figures and an emblem of Tutu on board, the head of Khonsu on the prow, his name in the panel above, 18th Dynasty, 1540-1292 B.C., 18½ by 15in (47 by 38cm).
£3,700–4,500 *S(NY)*

Representations of this type generally show 3 barques in sequence, the sacred barques of Khonsu, Amun, and Maat (the Theban Triad), each set down on a separate pedestal.

A fragmentary limestone false door, inscribed for Dwa-i-Ra, the owner striding at right and holding a baton and staff, flanked by 2 smaller figures also representing the owner, the left side showing a man called Ted-Sheri, probably a son or other relative, other sons flanking him; in 3 sections, 6th Dynasty, 2360-2195 B.C., 16½ by 24in (42 by 61cm).
£6,000–7,000 *S(NY)*

A limestone stele, carved in shallow relief with the owner, Renef-Seneb, seated and smelling lotus blossom, his son standing before him, the offering table at right, the 'bostrephedon' inscription, in 2 lines, reading: 'May the King give an offering, may come forth at the voice funerary offerings to the ka of Renef-Seneb; May the King give an offering, may come forth at the voice funerary offerings, oxen, geese, cakes, clothes to the double of Mak...', a row of finely formed vessels below the inscription, 12th Dynasty, 1938-1759 B.C., 17 by 11in (43 by 28cm).
£2,500–3,500 *S(NY)*

An indurated limestone relief fragment, carved in sunk relief with 2 Horus falcons perched on top of date palm capitals, circa 1st Century A.D., 6 by 9in (16 by 23cm) framed.
£1,200–1,700 *S(NY)*

A polychrome limestone stele of Idi, the inscription reading 'An offering which the King gives, and Anubis gives, an offering of bread and beer to the sole friend Idi', 1st Intermediate Period, 2180-1987 B.C., 14 by 12in (36 by 31cm).
£4,500–5,500 *S(NY)*

A Roman marble head of
Heracles, circa late 2nd-3rd
Century A.D., 4in (10cm) high.
£1,500–2,000 *S(NY)*

A Roman marble head of
Aphrodite, her pierced ears
ornamented with 2 gold filigree
earrings with globular pendants,
circa 1st-2nd Century A.D.,
2½in (6cm) high.
£1,500–2,500 *S(NY)*

A marble torso of a Woman or
Goddess, after a Hellensistic
prototype, the back carved
flat, antique restorations
removed, circa 1st Century B.C.,
27in (69cm) high.
£12,000–15,000 *S(NY)*

A marble head of Aphrodite, the
small mortise on the crown perhaps
for insertion of a headdress, circa
3rd/2nd Century B.C., 4in (10cm).
£5,000–6,000 *S(NY)*

A marble herm, the shaft
surmounted by a head of
Dionysus, with symmetrical
beard of voluted curls, parted
lips, and heavy grapevine wreath,
Roman Imperial, 1st Century A.D.,
33in (84cm) high.
£6,000–7,000 *S(NY)*

*Small herms were set up beside
the doors of Roman houses and
along paths in peristyle gardens.
A number have been discovered in
the gardens of Pompeii and
Herculaneum.*

A marble cinerarium, the
fragmentary cover carved
with an open flower, finial
restored, Roman Imperial, circa
200-250 A.D., 20in (51cm) high.
£2,500–3,000 *S(NY)*

A Hellenistic marble torso of
Apollo or Dionysus, inspired
by a Praxitelian original of the
4th Century B.C., circa 2nd
Century B.C., 9in (23cm) high.
£3,000–4,500 *S(NY)*

A marble cinerarium, finial
restored, the base carved flat
at a later date, Roman Imperial,
circa 2nd Century A.D., 12in
(31cm) high.
£3,500–4,000 *S(NY)*

A magnesite marble figure of
Osiris, 26th Dynasty, 664-525 B.C.,
4in (20cm) high.
£1,000–1,500 *S(NY)*

A Roman marble Corinthian capital, circa 2nd-3rd Century A.D., 16½ by 22in (42 by 56cm). **£3,500–4,500** *S(NY)*

An Etruscan terracotta votive head of a boy, circa 2nd Century B.C., 9in (23cm) high. **£900–1,100** *S(NY)*

A Roman marble Corinthian capital, boldly carved with 2 tiers of acanthus leaves beneath outer helices and small inner helices, quatrefoils on the abacus, 2nd/3rd Century A.D., 21 by 25½in (53 by 65cm). **£9,000–12,000** *S(NY)*

A Roman marble Corinthian capital, circa 2nd-3rd Century A.D., 20 by 23in (51 by 58cm). **£7,500–9,000** *S(NY)*

A terracotta figure of Aphrodite, with remains of pigment, circa 1st Century A.D., 11½in (29cm) high. **£900–1,100** *S(NY)*

A terracotta head of a Goddess, her lobed centrally parted coiffure surmounted by a polos, long tresses falling onto the shoulders, Magna Graecia, circa mid-5th Century B.C., 3½in (9cm) high. **£900–1,100** *S(NY)*

A Roman marble Corinthian capital, circa 2nd-3rd Century A.D., 18 by 21in (46 by 53cm). **£8,500–10,000** *S(NY)*

An Etruscan terracotta head of a boy, 4th Century B.C., 10in (25cm) high. **£700–800** *S(NY)*

A Bactrian terracotta mother and child, fragmentary applied necklaces and tiara, her large eyes and other details incised and with traces of reddish black pigment, circa mid-1st millennium B.C., 8in (20cm) high. **£800–1,000** *S(NY)*

A terracotta head of Herakles, wearing a diadem and the lion's skin with the paws tied in a Herakles knot beneath his chin, the surface with remains of brown wash and traces of red paint, Magna Graecia, circa early 4th Century B.C., 4in (10cm) high. **£950–1,100** *S(NY)*

A Roman terracotta campana relief, moulded in high relief with a draped woman wearing a wreath and reaching out to touch the tendrils of a plant, festooned palmettes in the border above, circa early 1st Century A.D., 7½ by 8½in (19 by 21cm).
£700–900 *S(NY)*

This fragment belongs to a group of Roman architectural reliefs which were named for the 19thC collector the Marchese Campana.

A Roman redware cylindrical flask, with twisted handles, the body moulded on each side with different erotic scenes, Asia Minor, circa 2nd Century A.D., 8½in (21cm) high.
£2,200–2,700 *S(NY)*

A black glaze terracotta pedestal, with square base, fluted stem and overhanging rim moulded in relief with an ovolo kymation, south Italy, 4th Century B.C., 4½in (11cm) high.
£350–500 *S(NY)*

Two large buffware storage jars, one with remains of a black painted 2 line inscription on the shoulder, Tell el Amarna, 18th Dynasty, period of Akhenaten, circa 1350-1336 B.C., 25½ and 26½in (65 and 67cm) high.
£2,000–2,700 *S(NY)*

An Attic pottery flask, in the form of an almond with reserved body and stippled detail, the twin handles and mouth black glazed, 4th Century B.C., 5½in (14cm) long.
£2,000–2,700 *S(NY)*

These vases were probably used to hold almond oil.

Two Cypriot buffware pitchers, together with a Cypriot redware bottle with incised geometric ornament, circa 7th Century B.C., 10in (25cm) high.
£1,200–1,700 *S(NY)*

An Iranian buffware rhyton, in the form of a couchant stag with applied pronged horns and curled tail, the pouring hole between the forelegs, the human figure on one flank and other details painted in red, Azerbaijan, circa 8th Century B.C., 10in (25cm) long.
£450–500 *S(NY)*

A Cypriot terracotta figure of a votary, circa late 6th Century B.C., 13in (33cm) high.
£1,200–1,500 *S(NY)*

Five faience vessel fragments, comprising fragments of a cylindrical jar painted with the names of Rameses II adjacent to the name of Montu the Theban war god, a large bowl painted inside with the head of Hathor and a flower, 2 bowls with lotuses, and a bowl with a leaf and another motif, 18th-19th Dynasty, 1540-1190 B.C., 2 to 4½in (5 to 11cm).
£2,000–2,700 *S(NY)*

Three Apulian black glaze mugs, 4th Century B.C., 3in (8cm) high.
£800–1,200 *S(NY)*

A granite hand, from the figure of a seated king or god, 19th-20th Dynasty, 1292-1075 B.C., 8in (20cm) long.
£2,000–2,700 *S(NY)*

A green schist crown, from a figure of the Hathor Cow, one ear and her horns remaining, the crown composed of the sun disk surmounted by ostrich plumes, 26th/30th Dynasty, 664-342 B.C., 9in (23cm) high.
£1,000–1,200 *S(NY)*

A Tarantine gilt terracotta lion, circa 4th-1st Century B.C., 3½in (9cm) long.
£400–500 *S(NY)*

A Hellenistic lead glazed skyphos, with splayed foot and ring handles surmounted by volutes, the body moulded in relief beneath the copper green glaze with 3 ovolo pine cone bands, amber yellow glaze inside, Asia Minor circa 1st Century B.C., 5½in (14cm) wide.
£1,500–2,200 *S(NY)*

A fragmentary Seljuk minai bowl, painted over the white glaze, circa early 13th Century, 7½in (19cm) diam.
£3,000–4,000 *S(NY)*

A grey serpentine or steatite bust of a woman, holding her arms to her sides and wearing a broad beaded collar and striated tripartite wig, 26th-30th Dynasty, 664-342 B.C., 3in (7.5cm) high.
£2,000–2,700 *S(NY)*

A Cartonnage coffin, in the form of a baboon seated with forepaws resting on his knees, straps crossing on his chest, the details painted in yellow on brown ground, late Ptolemaic/Roman period, circa 100 B.C.-100 A.D., 9in (23cm) high.
£350–450 *S(NY)*

An ivory or bone clapper, in the shape of a human left arm and hand, with crosshatched wristlet and incised joints on the fingers, 12th Dynasty, 1938-1789 B.C., 6½in (16cm) long.
£1,500–2,000 *S(NY)*

A fragmentary black porphyritic jar, of broad rounded form with flat everted rim and one tubular handle remaining, the matrix with white inclusions, late Predynastic Period, circa 3300-3000 B.C., 6in (15cm) diam.
£1,500–2,000 *S(NY)*

Two Seljuk lustre painted star tiles, decorated in reserve white against a brown ground, Kashan, early 13th Century, 6in (15cm) diam.
£4,000–5,000 *S(NY)*

ARTS & CRAFTS

A patinated and embossed metal wall sconce, possibly Scottish, with a circular copper panel embellished with a formalised peacock, its tail feathers set with plaques of abalone, with 2 sconces below, 20in (51cm) high.
£1,200–1,700 *P*

An oak cocktail cabinet, the top with rotating tray containing Doulton Lambeth silicon copper finish tobacco jar and ashtrays, above a drinks cupboard with sliding frieze drawer, open platform and panelled cupboards beneath, on splayed tapering supports bearing the trade plaque of Brew & Fountain, London, 58in (147cm) high. **£500–700** *DaD*

A Scottish stained beech and brass mounted cabinet, with central embossed and brass plaque in the style of Margaret MacDonald MacKintosh, the base fitted with a further hinged flap enclosing fitted interior, on square tapering supports with tapering block feet, 40in (101.5cm) wide.
£1,400–2,000 *CSK*

A pair of oak armchairs, possibly Dutch, each with solid seat and broad apron at the front, on 3 tapering supports.
£600–800 *P*

H. P. Berlage, the Dutch architect, designed chairs with 3, 4 or 5 legs.

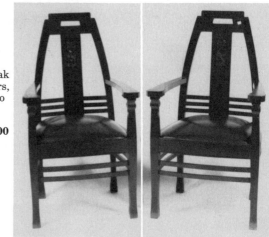

A pair of teak dining chairs, attributed to Peter Behrens.
£2,000–3,000 *SWO*

A late Victorian Arts & Crafts inlaid walnut breakfront side cabinet, with black marble top, above an inlaid panelled door, on plinth base, adapted, 57in (137cm) wide.
£1,200–1,700 *CSK*

A late Victorian Arts & Crafts blue painted cast iron hall stand, with circular mirror, 6 hooks, the base with drip pans, Kite registration mark, 72in (182.5cm) high. **£400–600** *CSK*

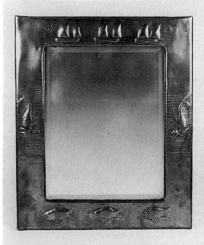

A wall mirror, the copper frame decorated with fish and yachts, 20in (51cm) high.
£200–300 *CSK*

A Donegal hand woven woollen carpet, possibly a design from the Silver Studios and retailed through Liberty & Co., woven with a formalised border of stylised leaves in shaped panels in blue, mauve and cream against a green field, 123in (312cm) square. **£1,000–1,500** *P*

A collar, finely embroidered in silks in shades of mauve and green with violets against a cream ground, framed and glazed, 13 by 19½in (32 by 48.5cm). **£100–150** *P*

An embroidered linen picture, in the style of Walter Crane, embroidered in coloured silks with a lady holding a large sunflower, framed and glazed, 17½ by 13½in (44.5 by 34cm). **£150–200** *P*

An oak and stained glass firescreen, 43in (109cm) high. **£400–500** *CSK*

A 'Cambridge' oak bookcase, possibly designed by W. J. Neatby, with broad plain top, on tapering supports, with small side shelf, decorated with a coat-of-arms, 45½in (115.5cm) high. **£500–600** *P*

A bronze casket, the lid cast in relief with the central motif of a cat, with mouse at each corner, and frieze of running cats, 8in (20cm) long. **£200–300** *P*

An Italian coloured mosaic portrait of the Renaissance Prince Gaston de Foix, in carved wood frame, 24 by 20in (62 by 51cm). **£900–1,200** *CSK*

An oak reclining chair, with adjustable ladder back, web seat, with loose cushions covered in Sanderson's William Morris Compton fabric. **£300–400** *P*

ART NOUVEAU
Furniture

A mahogany display cabinet, inlaid with light woods, copper and brass, on arched feet with rectangular pads, 70in (177.5cm). **£1,000–1,500** *P*

A French inlaid walnut and rosewood side cabinet, the inside of the doors depicting crows amongst a seascape, on splayed scrolled bracket feet, 36in (91.5cm) wide. **£1,500–2,000** *CSK*

An inlaid mahogany display cabinet, with a pair of stained glass leaded doors, on block feet, 48in (122cm) wide. **£2,000–2,500** *CSK*

A pair of oak side chairs, the design attributed to Dr. Christopher Dresser, upholstered in green velvet, on casters, with paper labels 'Miller & Beatty, House Furnishers, Grafton Street, Dublin', c1880. **£8,000–10,000** *C*

These chairs appear to date from the period when Dr. Christopher Dresser was associated with the Art Furnishers Alliance, an ambitious enterprise which was typical of Aesthetic Movement idealism. They formed part of a ten-piece suite designed for Edward Cecil Guinness, the Rt. Hon. The Earl of Iveagh.
A brilliant designer of ornaments, Dresser often made use of geometric iconography such as dots, lines and zigzags. Although the use of these decorative elements is universal, only Dresser in the 19thC would use them with the precision which is visible here on the original fabric.
Another feature demonstrating the characteristic ingenuity of Dresser is his use of recessed casters. Often these are clumsily positioned and disturb the symmetry of a piece.

A pair of Morris & Co., ebonised beech open armchairs, with spindle top rails above rush seats, on turned legs with stretchers, one chair with missing seat, and a similar corner chair. **£300–500** *CSK*

An oak desk, with inset red leather writing surface, fitted with 8 drawers and oxidised metal handles, on square section legs. **£900–1,000** *BWe*

A mahogany armchair, after a design by George Jack of the Saville Chair for Morris & Co., with scroll ends supported on slightly curved spindles, on square back supports and turned front supports, on casters. **£550–650** *P*

Morris & Co., 1861-1940

Established originally as Morris, Marshall, Faulkner & Co., this association of like-minded craftsmen advocated simplicity and good quality hand crafting in furniture construction. The main designer since its foundation, William Morris, took sole control in 1875 and the company adopted the name by which it is still known today. Much of Morris' furniture had an oriental influence.

A wing backed armchair, attributed to Morris & Co., with shaped back, stuff-over arms and seat, covered in Morris designed Peacock and Dragon woven woollen fabric in blues, green and beige, raised on turned and square mahogany supports.
£900–1,200 *P*

A walnut settle, with overall scrolling foliate tracery, above a hinged seat flanked by stork-carved arm terminals, slight damage, 52in (132cm) wide.
£700–800 *CSK*

A late Victorian oak reclining armchair, by Morris & Co., after a design by Philip Webb, the buttoned back with turned finials, above padded arms, on square section legs joined by bobbin turned stretchers.   **£670–720** *CSK*

A Morris & Co., 'Saville' armchair, designed by George Jack, on shaped supports covered in a woven woollen blue and beige fabric.
£1,000–1,500 *P*

An Edwardian hall stand, with circular mirror inset to the back and 3 tiles with stylised flower heads, over stick stand base.
£350–450 *BWe*

An oak dressing table, by Liberty & Co., with maker's label, 47½in (120cm) wide.
£600–800 *CSK*

An oak and inlaid dressing table and wardrobe, 68in (172cm) high.
£900–1,200 *P*

A mahogany fire screen, with silk embroidered panel, stamped 'Morris & Co, 449 Oxford S', with registration number '1261', 44½in (113cm) high.   **£1,000–1,500** *C*

A marquetry nest of tables, inlaid with various woods showing flowers and leaves, each supported on fluted uprights, on shaped feet with scroll supports united by a stretcher, the tallest 29in (74cm) high.
£700–900 *P*

A mahogany lady's desk, the shaped top having columned supports and drop front, with 3 panels inlaid and painted with stylised flowering trees, enclosing birch compartments with satinwood veneered drawers, small central cupboard with inlaid oval coloured panel of flowers, central drawer and undershelf with inlaid back panel, 50½in (128cm) high.
£750–900 *P*

An upright piano, labelled 'Winklemann Braunschweig, Liberty & Co., London', and numbered '8843', 58in (147cm) wide, and an oak stool, with square tapering legs joined by stretchers, labelled 'Liberty & Co, London'.
£800–1,200 *CSK*

A walnut and fruitwood 2-tier table, the removable top carved with the head of a maiden with long flowing hair and flowers on sinuous stems, on elaborate supports of sinuous plant form with carved undertier, 31in (78.5cm) high.
£700–900 *P*

An oak side table, stamped '986 Morris & Co., 449 Oxford St. W', 54in (137cm) wide.
£600–700 *P*

A mahogany and marquetry occasional table, on casters, possibly a design by Christopher Dresser, 26½in (67.5cm).
£800–900 *P*

Make the most of Millers's

Unless otherwise stated, any description which refers to 'a set' or 'a pair' includes a valuation for the entire set or the pair, even though the illustration may show only a single item.

A pair of mahogany and walnut marquetry wardrobes, possibly Austrian, with elaborate brass hinges, and drawer below, 83in (210cm) high.
£700–900 *P*

A mahogany 'Thebes' stool, by Liberty & Co., with dished slatted wood seat, on turned and ribbed supports, united by turned stretchers and spindles.
£700–900 *P*

A pair of Morris & Co., ebonised seven-tier whatnots, the design attributed to Philip Webb, on turned and square section supports, various ball finials missing, c1875, 57in (142.5cm) high.
£3,000–4,000 *C*

Glass

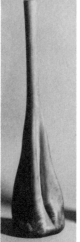

A Daum acid etched solifleur, the clear glass cased in yellow streaked with aubergine and flecked with green, with acid etched mark 'Daum Nancy', 23½in (60.5cm) high.
£450–550 *CSK*

A Daum solifleur, of ribbed cylindrical form flaring to trefoil base, the satin finished opalescent mottled yellow glass fading to indigo around the base, each side lightly etched with peacock feather motifs, etched 'Daum Nancy', 30½in (77.5cm) high.
£1,200–1,700 *CSK*

Daum Frères

The Daum brothers, Auguste (1835-1909) and Antonin (1864-1930) worked together with Emile Gallé before establishing their own glassworks in Nancy. No distinction has so far been made between their work. The firm, now operating as Cristallerie Daum, is still in business today. Although Daum Frères produced some carved and enamelled pieces, most of their Art Nouveau wares are cameo glass or acid cut and colour enamelled. Early Daum pieces tend to be enamelled.

A Daum fleur-de-lys pitcher, the clear glass with martelé effect, heightened with gilding, the underside with gilt mark 'Daum Nancy', c1895, 7½in (19cm).
£400–500 *S*

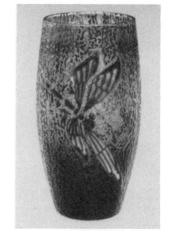

A Gallé dragonfly enamelled vase, the underside with engraved mark 'Emile Gallé', 4⅓in (11cm).
£1,500–2,000 *S*

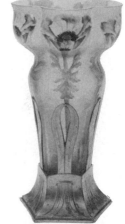

A Daum enamelled glass vase, acid etched in relief with poppies on leafy stems, painted in pink, yellow, white, green, brown and gilding, supported in a gilt bronze leaf form armature and base, signed 'Daum, Nancy' with cross of Lorraine, 10in (24.5cm) high.
£800–1,200 *P*

Loetz Decoration

The thick, solid body of Loetz iridescent wares tends to be dark, with finely controlled decoration displaying a spectrum of colours. Vessels with deep purple bodies, highlighted with silver and peacock blue iridescence, were very popular and are the most collectable today. Dark amber glass with green gold iridescence was also popular.

A Loetz glass vase, in the form of a conch shell, the amber glass body with continuous iridescent spotting, on shaped clear glass base, slight damage, 5½in (14cm).
£200–250 *P*

A Gallé cameo glass vase, overlaid with purple glass, acid etched with marsh plants against a pink ground, signed 'Gallé', 4½in (11.5cm) high.
£370–400 *P*

A Loetz vase, the deep blue glass with random bubble pattern, decorated with a band of iridescent combed trails, cased in clear glass, the base drilled, 14⅓in (37cm) high.
£450–500 *CSK*

A Loetz iridescent glass vase, decorated with meandering bands of amber orange and silver blue feathering, against a golden splashed ground, signed 'Loetz Austria', 4in (10cm) high.
£850–1,000 *P*

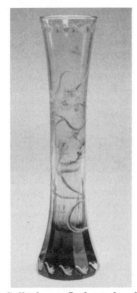

A Gallé dragonfly faceted and enamelled vase, heightened with gilding, the underside with engraved mark 'Cristallerie d'Emile Gallé Nancy Modèle et décor déposés', 11½in (29cm) high.
£2,000–2,700 *S*

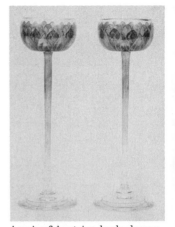

A pair of Austrian hock glasses, the bowls enamelled in blue, green and gilt with a flowerhead, 6½in (16cm) high.
£600–700 *CSK*

Metalware

A Liberty silver casket, designed by Oliver Baker, with overall pierced and scrolled decoration, gilt interior, with key, stamped maker's marks, with Birmingham hallmarks for 1900, 10in (24.5cm) long, 2879g.
£3,300–3,700 *C*

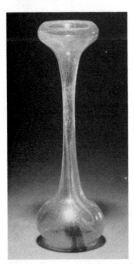

A set of 48 clear glasses, designed by Josef Hoffmann for Lobmeyer, comprising: 12 each of claret, hock, champagne, and port glasses, c1908, 4½ to 6in (11 to 15cm) high.
£900–1,200 *S*

An A. J. Couper & Sons Clutha vase, designed by Dr. Christopher Dresser, the bulbous body with tall flared cylindrical neck and inverted rim, green tinted glass with milky white striations and with foil and air bubble inclusions, 19⅛in (49cm) high.
£2,000–3,000 *C*

A Wiener Werkstätte deep green glass vase, designed by Josef Hoffmann and made by Meyr's Neffe, bearing 'WW' monogram on square base, 5in (12cm) high.
£900–1,500 *P*

An Orrefors 'Ariel' glass vase, designed and signed by Edvin Öhrström, the heavy glass of oviform shape, internally decorated with Gondoliere pattern, marked 'Orrefors', and 'Ariel Nr. 463E', 8in (20cm) high.
£1,700–2,200 *P*

A Liberty silver chalice, designed by Archibald Knox, the deep conical bowl above 4 slender interlocked stems, enclosing an onyx stone mounted on the broad circular foot, stamped maker's marks 'L&C°, R^D 370236', with Birmingham hallmarks for 1900, 9½in (24cm) high, 550g.
£9,500–12,000 *C*

A pair of Liberty silver candlesticks, the tapered fluted stems beneath flared sconces, on flange feet, each with blue and green enamelled entrelac medallions, one stem re-soldered to foot, stamped maker's marks, with indistinct Birmingham hallmarks, 6½in (16.5cm) high, 345g. **£1,700–2,200** *C*

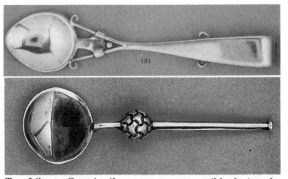

Two Liberty Cymric silver spoons, one possibly designed by Oliver Baker, with egg-shaped bowl, 7½in (19cm) long, and an enamelled silver spoon, with circular bowl, half enamelled in blue, the slender handle having a ball knop with scale pattern, 4⅛in (10.5cm) long, both marked 'L&Co.', 'Cymric', Birmingham 1901 and 1902 respectively. **£550–600** *P*

A pair of Georg Jensen twin-branch candelabra, with detachable nozzles, stamped marks on base 'Georg Jensen' and '244', 8½in (21cm) high, 2843g. **£5,200–6,000** *C*

A Liberty Cymric silver dressing table set, comprising: a hand mirror, hairbrush, clothes brush, and a comb, the surfaces embellished with knot motifs and large cabochons of turquoise matrix, some marks worn, marked 'L&Co', Birmingham 1904, mirror 11in (28.5cm) long. **£400–500** *P*

A 75-piece set of Georg Jensen 'Acorn' pattern silver flatware, designed by Johan Rohde, comprising: 8 each of dinner knives and forks, dessert knives and forks, fish knives and forks, soup spoons, dessert spoons and coffee spoons, 2 serving spoons and a butter knife, maker's marks, post-1945 and London import marks for various dates 1937-1979. **£3,000–4,000** *P*

A canteen of Georg Jensen Pyramid pattern white metal flatware, designed by Harald Nielsen, various marks, 1926. **£6,000–7,000** *S*

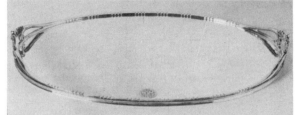

A Georg Jensen silver tray, with slightly raised rim, notched decoration arranged in groups of 3, having scrollwork handles with openwork foliate detail, monogram medallion, maker's marks 1925-32 and London import marks for 1927, 17½in (44.5cm) wide. **£2,000–2,500** *P*

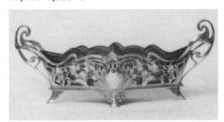

A W.M.F. comport, with blue glass liner, 18in (46cm) long. **£500–700** *ASA*

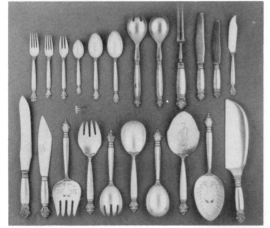

A W.M.F. Britannia metal
desk ornament, modelled as a
speedboat, having hinged front
and back canopies, stamped
maker's marks, indistinct
inscription on edge of base,
11½in (29cm) long.
£600–700 P

A 211-piece Acanthus pattern
white metal flatware service, by
Georg Jensen, each piece with
stamped maker's marks,
11,676g, and 10 various pieces
of Danish flatware.
£5,000–5,700 C

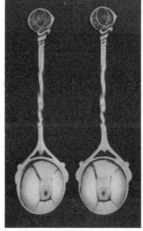

A W.M.F. pewter plaque,
6in (15cm) diam.
£100–200 ASA

A Liberty silver comport, with
lightly beaten effect and Celtic
inspired motifs, Birmingham
mark 1927, 7in (17.5cm) high.
£350–400 Mit

A set of 6 Liberty enamelled silver
coffee spoons, the twisted stems
elaborately attached, circular
green and blue enamelled tops,
marked 'L&Co', Birmingham
1910, 4in (9.50cm) long, in
original wooden fitted case.
£500–600 P

A Hukin and Heath plated oil and
vinegar set, designed by
Christopher Dresser, with
circular base, central stem with
open scrollwork panels and
T-shaped handle, flanked by
2 glass bottles of angular form
with shaped collars and handles,
on oval supports, marked and
numbered '1868', and with design
registration mark for 11th April
1878, 9½in (23.5cm) high.
£3,000–4,000 P

A W.M.F. jardinière, c1900,
9in (22.5cm) high.
£300–500 ASA

A W.M.F. easel mirror, c1900.
£600–900 ASA

A W.M.F. electroplated metal
mounted green glass decanter
and stopper, the base cast with
profiles of young maidens, with
exaggerated whiplash handle,
hinged stopper cast with berries
and flowers, marked, c1900, 16in
(41cm) high.
£800–900 C

A pair of Guild of Handicraft
electroplated dish covers, with
intertwined wirework handles,
largest 16in (40.5cm) long.
£800–1,200 C

A W.M.F. electroplated tea service, stamped in relief with bands of stylised scrolls, comprising: a teapot, hot water pot, milk jug, twin-handled sugar basin and cover and oval tray, stamped marks, hot water pot 8½in (21cm) high.
£700–900 *CSK*

A Guild of Handicraft electroplated muffin dish, designed by C. R. Ashbee, the domed cover with wirework finial set with cabochon chrysoprase, 9in (23cm) diam.
£800–900 *C*

A William Hutton & Sons 6-piece silver dressing table set, designed by Kate Harris, stamped in relief with a young woman in modest nightclothes, framed by stylised lilies, comprising: a hand mirror, 2 clothes brushes, 2 hair brushes and a tray, stamped marks, London 1901/2.
£1,200–1,700 *CSK*

An Art Nouveau style copper and brass mirror, with floral decoration, 20in (50.5cm) high.
£100–125 *SUL*

A Continental plated mirror, cast in high relief with flowers and leaves, a maiden with long flowing hair at the base, easel back, bevelled glass, stamped 'Walker & Hall, Sheffield', 19in (48cm) high.
£600–700 *P*

A W.M.F. mirror, embellished in high relief, with stamped marks, 14½in (36.5cm) high.
£900–1,200 *P*

A pair of silver overlay decanters, 12in (30.5cm) high.
£400–450 *SUL*

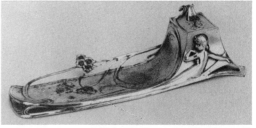

A W.M.F. silvered pewter inkwell, the shaped rectangular footed tray pierced and cast in relief with foliage and flowers and a naked maiden, rising at one end to form a square inkwell with hinged cover, stamped marks, 12in (30.5cm) long.
£200–300 *CSK*

A patinated bronze inkwell, cast from model by Oscar Späthe, in the form of a naked woman bent over a large box, a small inkwell with sliding top on the other side, signed in the bronze and dated 1914, 7in (18cm) high.
£600–700 *CSK*

A Victorian Art Nouveau silver framed dressing table clock, Birmingham 1898, 6½in (16cm) high.
£370–420 *Bea*

A patinated bronze head of a young girl wearing a blindfold, on tapering square base, 13½in (34cm) high. **£200–400** *CSK*

A Heath and Middleton silver mounted claret jug, designed by Christopher Dresser, with silver collar and lid and an ebonised rod handle, marked 'JTH/JHM', Birmingham 1893, 17in (43cm) high. **£2,200–2,700** *P*

A wrought iron and glass table lamp, by Edgar Brandt, the circular domed shade formed by an armature of shaped openwork motifs with frosted glass blown within, supported on 4 arms above a reeded stem and spreading circular base, stamped on base 'E. Brandt', 20in (50cm) high. **£2,000–3,000** *P*

Ceramics

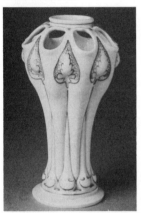

A Meissen porcelain 'Jugendstll' vase, designed by Karl Gross, with 8 oval apertures at the top and vertical lobes, painted in underglaze blue, with heart shaped leaf motifs and other linear decoration, crossed swords mark, inscribed with shape number 'W136', 8in (20cm) high. **£400–600** *P*

A Martin Brothers stoneware double face jug, in biscuit brown tones, with brown hair, loop handle and exaggerated neck and spout, signed 'R. W. Martin & Bros, London & Southall', dated '5-1900', 9in (23cm) high. **£800–1,000** *P*

A Martin Brothers jardinière, pierced and modelled in high relief with fleur-de-lys, each corner modelled with grotesque creatures, on spherical feet, with blue and brown glazes, incised signature 'R. W. Martin, Southall', slight damage, 14½in (36.5cm) high. **£2,500–3,500** *C*

A Royal Dux centrepiece, the porcelain glazed in shades of green, brown and rust, the underside with applied triangular 'Royal Dux Bohemia' mark, numbered '694', c1900, 13½in (34cm). **£800–900** *S*

A Martin Brothers stoneware grotesque jug, with dark brown glaze, each side modelled in relief, damaged, incised factory mark, dated '1-1897', 10in (25cm) high. **£250–300** *CSK*

A William de Morgan lustre dish, with sunken centre, decorated in lemon and café-au-lait tones, impressed on underside 'H. Davis', 17in (43cm) diam. **£800–1,000** *P*

A Martin Brothers stoneware vase, incised and coloured with birds in flight above iris and leaf grass, against a textured buff coloured ground, the short neck decorated with a swarm of small insects, star crack to base, incised '1-1891, R. W. Martin Bros. London & Southall', 8½in (21cm).
£200–300 *S(S)*

A William de Morgan Persian style lustre vase, painted in the Sunset and Moonlight Suite palette, with foliate panels flanked by formalised foliage and flowers in silvery and pale ruby tones against a powder blue ground, with red lustre interior to neck, signed on base 'De Morgan I&P, Fulham', 14½in (37.5cm) high.
£1,700–1,900 *P*

A William de Morgan dish, decorated in ruby lustre with 2 panthers, on a leaf scroll ground, within a line rim, the reverse with a band of C-scrolls, c1885, 8½in (21cm) diam.
£400–600 *DN*

A William de Morgan ruby lustre dish, with deep centre and broad everted rim, painted with radiating panels of serpents, alternating with panels of scales, the underside with large star motif, 10½in (26cm) diam.
£650–850 *P*

A Foley Intarsio plate, by Frederick Rhead, c1898, 12in (30cm) diam.
£400–425 *AJ*

A pair of Martin Brothers stoneware vases, incised with curving leaf forms and floral motifs in brown, against a blue ground of stylised seed pods, incised 'R. W. Martin London 10-75', numbered 'J9' and 'J10', 13in (33cm) high.
£300–500 *P*

A William de Morgan vase, the body with a brown foliate design, the neck with chevrons and zig-zag foliate motifs, restored, 27in (69cm) high.
£3,500–4,500 *S*

A William de Morgan 3-piece blue and white tile panel, depicting 2 men-of-war ships, central tile damaged, Merton Abbey mark, each tile 8in (20cm) square.
£1,000–1,500 *CSK*

A Martin Brothers grotesque jar and cover, conceived as an imaginary beast squatting on all fours, with detachable head, signed on the body and head, dated '5.85', 9in (22cm).
£5,000–6,000 *S*

A Martin Brothers stoneware model of a bird, the body in browns and greens with blue speckling on the pointed head, on circular ebonised base, signed on the base and head, 8½in (21cm).
£2,500–3,000 *P*

Moorcroft

A Moorcroft Pottery Coronation mug, made for Liberty & Co., the straight sides tapering to the top, decorated in green, grey and blue with a crown, a mace and sceptre and inscription, painted 'W.M.' to inside of base, painted inscription to base 'From Mr & Mrs Lasenby Liberty The Lee Manor, Bucks - designed by AL'(?), 4in (10cm).
£350–400 *P*

A William Moorcroft muffin dish and cover, Florian Bluebell design, on a yellow ground, marked 'Made for Liberty', c1904, 8in (20cm) diam.
£1,200–1,400 *RUM*

A William Moorcroft King VI Coronation commemorative tea set, c1937.
£3,500–4,500 *RUM*

A Moorcroft pottery commemorative mug, marking the outbreak of peace, made for Liberty & Co., decorated with a thistle, a shamrock and a rose in green, pink and blue on a buff ground, between bands in blue, decorated with the inscription 'August 4th 1914 November 11th 1918 Pro Rege Pro Patria Peace 1919', impressed 'Moorcroft Burslem' and inscribed in green 'from Lady Liberty', 4in (9.50cm).
£300–400 *P*

A William Moorcroft King George VI Coronation commemorative mug, c1937, 4in (10cm) high.
£300–400 *RUM*

A William Moorcroft Tulip design Hesperian Ware vase, made for Osler's, c1902, 12in (30cm) high.
£2,500–3,000 *RUM*

A William Moorcroft Sicilian shape chocolate pot and cover, decorated with Tulip and Poppy design, c1902, 8in (20cm) high. **£250–350** *RUM*

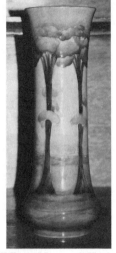

A William Moorcroft Hazledene Landscape vase, decorated in shades of green, signed 'W. Moorcroft Des', c1903, 9in (22.5cm). **£1,500–1,800** *RUM*

A William Moorcroft vase, with Cornflower design, James MacIntyre & Co. backstamp, signed in green, c1912, 9in (22.5cm) high. **£1,400–1,800** *RUM*

A William Moorcroft Sicilian shape chocolate jug and cover, Tulip design with pink background, c1902, 8in (20cm) high. **£350–450** *RUM*

A William Moorcroft Pomegranate design vase, impressed 'Burslem', signed in green, c1916, 8in (20cm) high. **£500–600** *RUM*

A William Moorcroft Toadstool design vase, c1918, 10in (25cm) high. **£1,500–2,000** *RUM*

A MacIntyre Moorcroft Florian Ware onion shaped stem vase, with Iris pattern, slip trailed in white, decorated in shades of blue, printed mark in brown, rim chipped, initialled 'W.M.Des.', inscribed in green, numbered 'M705' in blue, 9in (23cm) high. **£350–400** *HSS*

A William Moorcroft Florian Ware Honesty design vase, c1903, 8in (20cm) high. **£900–1,200** *RUM*

A William Moorcroft Spanish design vase, impressed 'Burslem', signed in green, c1915, 12in (30cm) high.
£2,000–2,500 *RUM*

A William Moorcroft Duraware water jug and cover, in Poppy design, c1902, 8in (20cm) high.
£250–350 *RUM*

A William Moorcroft vase, made for Tiffany & Co., New York, with Lustre Grape design, c1909, 10in (25cm) high.
£3,500–4,000 *RUM*

A William Moorcroft Florian Ware vase, with blue Poppies and yellow Tulips design, c1908, 10in (25cm) high.
£1,000–1,400 *RUM*

A Moorcroft Moonlit Blue design vase, tube-lined with tall trees and rolling hills, with green details against a powder blue ground, impressed 'Moorcroft, Made In England', 10in (25.5cm).
£3,500–4,500 *S*

A William Moorcroft large flambé Landscape design vase, c1926, 15in (40cm) high.
£4,500–5,000 *RUM*

A William Moorcroft Spanish design two-handled trumpet vase, impressed 'Burslem', c1915, 10in (25cm) high.
£1,800–2,200 *RUM*

A William Moorcroft Persian design vase, impressed 'Burslem', signed in green, c1916, 9in (22.5cm) high.
£1,500–2,000 *RUM*

A William Moorcroft vase, with large Cornflower design, impressed 'Burslem', signed and dated 1915, 17½in (43cm) high.
£5,000–6,000 *RUM*

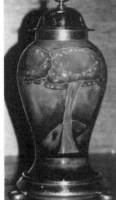

A William Moorcroft Landscape design vase, decorated with Windswept Corn in tones of pink and grey, c1935, 9in (22cm) high. **£700–900** *RUM*

A William Moorcroft Eventide vase, with Tudric mounts, c1925, 6½in (15cm) high. **£1,000–1,400** *RUM*

A William Moorcroft Florian Ware Poppy design vase, on ochre ground, c1904, 8in (20cm) high. **£2,000–2,500** *RUM*

A Moorcroft Pottery vase, the baluster body painted with a Freesia design on a cream and blue wash ground, 10½in (26cm) high. **£300–400** *Bea*

A William Moorcroft Waratah design vase, in shades of blue and orange, c1930, 8in (20cm) high. **£3,000–4,000** *RUM*

A William Moorcroft Spanish design vase, impressed 'Burslem', signed in green, c1914, 8in (20cm) high. **£1,000–1,400** *RUM*

Doulton

A Royal Doulton Prestige Study, 'Matador and Bull', by Peggy Davis, HN 2324, introduced to order in 1964, 16in (40.5cm) high.
£1,500–2,000 *P*

A Royal Doulton figure, 'The Orange Vendor', designed by C. J. Noke, 6½in (16.5cm) high.
£200–220 *Mit*

A Royal Doulton figure, entitled 'Folly', HN 1335, withdrawn 1938.
£700–800 *Bea*

A set of 12 Royal Doulton 'Lord of the Rings' figures, by Harry Sales, with a custom-made base.
£950–1,500 *P*

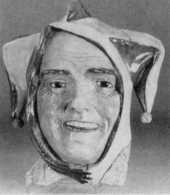

A Royal Doulton jester wall mask, the naturalistic face within a red, yellow and green hood, incised numerals '933', printed factory mark, c1930-40, 11in (28cm) high.
£250–350 *S(S)*

A Royal Doulton figural book end, modelled as the Dickens character Sairey Gamp, produced 1934-39, 3½in (9.5cm) high, mounted on a wooden base.
£400–500 *P*

A Royal Doulton figural book end, modelled as the Dickens character Toby Weller, produced 1934-39, 4in (10.5cm) high, mounted on a wooden base.
£400–600 *P*

A Royal Doulton character jug, 'The Hatless Drake'.
£900–1,200 *Bea*

A Royal Doulton jester wall mask, HN 1674, date code for 1935.
£200–300 *P*

Three Royal Doulton character jugs, comprising: 'Johnny Appleseed', D 6372, 'Cardinal', D5614, and 'Monty', D 6202, green printed factory marks, after 1936, 6in (16cm) high.
£250–300 *S(S)*

A Royal Doulton figure, 'Dunce', by C. J. Noke, HN 6, 'Potted by Doulton & Co.' on base, 1913-38, 10½in (26.5cm) high.
£2,000–2,500 *P*

A Royal Doulton character jug, 'Old King Cole', with yellow crown, printed mark in green, 5½in (14cm) high.
£600–800 *HSS*

A Royal Doulton prototype character jug, 'The Village Blacksmith', probably designed by Garry Sharpe in late 1950's, the handle in the form of a tree with anvil, wheel and horseshoe beneath, glazed in blue, brown, black and green, unmarked, hairline crack to face, 7½in (19cm) high.
£6,000–8,000 *P*

The 'Blacksmith of Williamsburg' jug, released in 1963, shows how Royal Doulton revised their approach to the blacksmith as a craftsman by making the handle, in the form of a hammer and anvil, a much stronger feature. This may explain why the company decided not to release this jug, although luckily it was not broken up but thrown out (hence the damage) and then rescued.

A Royal Doulton Shakespeare jug, decorated with figures in relief, glazed in polychrome, numbered '796' from an edition of 1,000, 10½in (27cm) high.
£250–300 *P*

A Royal Doulton Lambeth brown saltglazed stoneware owl jug, by Mark V. Marshall, moulded in low relief with eye and foliate wing outlines, slip trailed in white, decorated in brown, blue, green and white, some damage, impressed Doulton Lambeth rosette mark over 'England' over '3445ttt', incised 'M.V.M.160', 10½in (27.5cm) high.
£450–500 *HSS*

A Royal Doulton twin-handled loving cup, 'The Three Musketeers', numbered '136' from a limited edition of 600, with figures in relief, 10in (25.5cm) high.
£270–320 *P*

A Royal Doulton loving cup, designed by Charles Noke, commemorating the Coronation of George VI and Queen Elizabeth, numbered '498' of a limited edition of 2,000, printed and inscribed in green, 1937, 6½in (16cm) high.
£200–250 *HSS*

A pair of Doulton lamp bases, c1886-1914, 15in (38cm) high.
£200–250 *WAG*

A Royal Doulton pottery jug, moulded and painted with the 'Regency Coach' pattern, number 80 of limited edition of 500, slight damage, 11in (27.5cm) high.
£200–300 *Bea*

A Royal Doulton Lambeth stoneware shaving jug, decorated in the Harvest design, with silver rim, c1907, 4in (10cm) high.
£200–250 *HER*

A pair of Doulton faience vases, each boldly painted with flowers on a cream and brown ground, 14½in (37.5cm) high.
£200–250 *Bea*

A Doulton vase, c1886-1914, 16½in (42cm) high.
£150–175 *WAG*

A Royal Doulton teapot and lid, modelled as the Dickens character Old Charley, in brown, red, blue and black, issued in 1939, 7in (18cm) high.
£850–1,000 *P*

A Doulton Lambeth umbrella stand, by Mark Marshall, decorated with 'Darwin's Habits of Climbing Plants', in shades of brown and green against a deep blue ground, base chipped, numbered to interior, MVM monogram, dated '1884', 21½in (55cm) high.
£500–700 *P*

A Liberty Tudric pewter architectural timepiece, the tapering square section body with pointed pyramid top, stylised plant form motif, enamelled mauve centre and below the face, marked 'Tudric' and '0629', 7in (18cm) high.
£550–750 *P*

Miscellaneous

A Gallé marquetry tray, depicting a ruined folly surrounded by trees, the gallery with 2 handles in the form of lizards, signed, 15½in (40cm) wide.
£300–400 *CSK*

A Goldscheider terracotta lamp in the form of a bust of a maiden, with arum lilies, in shades of brown and green, impressed factory marks, 24in (61cm) high.
£1,000–1,500 *CSK*

A Benham & Froud ebonised and brass coal box, possibly designed by Christopher Dresser, with turned brass handle, elaborate hinges and strapwork, on solid feet, 19in (48cm) high, with shovel.
£300–400 *P*

A string of W.M.F. 'Ikora Crystal' iridescent glass beads, 15in (38cm) long.
£350–400 *CSK*

ART DECO
Furniture

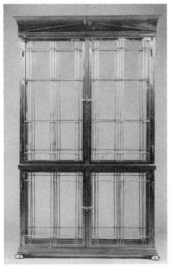

An Art Deco style steel and glass vitrine, in 2 sections, 49½in (125cm) wide.
£1,500–2,000 *CSK*

A pair of oak open armchairs, each with circular padded back above deep padded seat, on square legs.
£1,500–2,000 *CSK*

A three-piece 'cloud' suite, with a three-seater settee and 2 armchairs, the rounded sides with veneered edges, covered in cream leather and leatherette, with loose cushions.
£600–800 *P*

A pair of mahogany open armchairs, each with arched top rail and reeded back above down-scrolled arms, caned seat and square section legs, joined by stretchers.
£500–800 *CSK*

A pair of laminated birch armchairs, in the style of Alvar Aalto, each with solid seat and back flanked by downswept arms transforming to leg.
£800–900 *CSK*

A wrought iron standard lamp, stamped 'L. Katona' and twice 'Made in France', 69in (175cm) high.
£4,000–5,000 *P*

A bird's-eye walnut and rosewood vitrine, the bevelled glass door enclosing shelves and veneered and ebonised interior, on block feet, 44in (111cm) wide.
£700–900 *P*

A Heal & Son oak adjustable chair, with rounded rectangular back, slatted sides and downswept arms, on bun feet.
£200–300 *CSK*

A tan leather upholstered walnut 'cloud' suite, comprising: 2 armchairs and a settee, each with scalloped backs, the settee 65in (165cm) wide.
£1,100–1,600 *CSK*

A pair of wrought iron gates, 79in (200cm).
£1,500–2,000 *C*

A Heal & Son oak cabinet,
stamped '70', 59½in (151cm) high,
and a Heal & Son oak chest of
drawers, both designed by Sir
Ambrose Heal, c1912, 35½in
(91cm) high.
£1,800–2,200 *C*

An ebonised and gilt painted
three-piece suite, comprising: a
chaise longue, and a pair of tub
armchairs, on reeded bun feet.
£2,000–2,500 *CSK*

A Heal & Son mahogany desk,
with crossbanded leather lined
top above central frieze drawer
flanked by 8 graduated drawers
and faceted bun feet, labelled
'Heal & Son, Ltd. London, W',
42in (106.5cm).
£700–900 *CSK*

A wall mirror, the bronze frame
applied with leaping dolphins
and stylised waves, the mirror
etched and frosted on the reverse
with Neptune astride sea horses,
trampling a mermaid, 22in
(56cm) diam.
£1,000–1,200 *CSK*

Heal & Son
1810 - present

Ambrose Heal (1872-1959)
designed all the furniture for
the family firm from 1896
until the 1950s. His early
pieces have a strong affinity
with the English Arts &
Crafts movement.

Heal's preferred light coloured
woods, especially limed oak.
After WWI they began to use
weathered oak instead of
unpolished wood. Work of the
1930s was more avant garde,
and tended to combine
contemporary features with
more traditional elements.

Although their furniture is
hand-finished, modern
techniques such as screw-
fixing were used. Most pieces
are stamped or labelled.

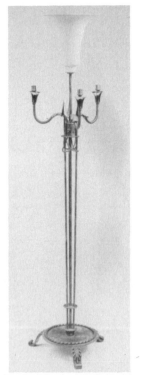

A standard lamp, attributed to
Gilbert Poillerat, in gilded
wrought iron, the circular base
supported on 3 scroll feet, the
stem formed by rods terminating
with spear points, with three-
branch lights and a central light
with trumpet-shaped shade,
70in (177cm) high.
£500–700 *P*

*This model is typical of the work
of Poillerat.*

A wrought iron overmantel mirror,
signed 'Serebours, Valencienne',
49½in (125.5cm) high.
£400–500 *P*

A wrought iron and painted metal
firescreen, the frame enclosing a
scene of Pan playing his pipes and
2 nude maidens, in a wooded
glade with sunray backdrop,
painted in shades of green and
brown, the screen resting on
2 scrolled feet, 74in (189cm) wide.
£2,500–3,500 *C*

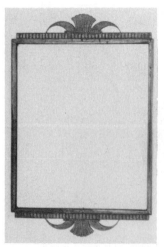

A wrought iron mirror, by Edgar
Brandt, with ribbed bands at the
top and bottom, surmounted by
stylised plant form motifs,
stamped, 18in (45cm) high.
£800–1,200 *P*

A Continental masur birch and walnut bedroom suite, comprising: a wardrobe, 75in (190.5cm) high, a double bed with sleigh footboard, 84in (213cm) long, a pair of bedside cabinets, a cheval mirror, a side cabinet, a pair of upright chairs, an armchair with amber composition spherical pulls and walnut veneered edging. **£1,500–2,000** *P*

A vellum and rosewood coffee table, the top decorated with a central octagon of vellum, with a further 8 satellite segments completing the circle, covered with glass, on 4 rosewood square supports united by a circular hoop base, with a glass top, 43½in (110.5cm) diam. **£450–650** *P*

A painted four-fold screen, by Gladys Hynes, painted in shades of brown, red, black, cream and white with kangaroos, ibix and various species of monkey, reserved against a silver painted ground, each panel within a silver frame, signed twice, 66in (167.5cm) high. **£2,000–3,000** *P*

Gladys Hynes (1888-1958), painter and sculptor, studied at London School of Art under Frank Brangwyn and later in Newlyn under Stanhope and Elizabeth Forbes.

A Heal & Son limed oak sofa table, designed by Sir Ambrose Heal, with canted rectangular twin flap top above a frieze of 2 short drawers and twin column turned tapered legs, on trestle ends, c1915, 62½in (158.5cm) extended. **£1,500–2,000** *C*

A burr walnut dining suite, comprising: an extending draw-leaf dining table with extra leaf, on supports joined by a central stretcher, 77½in (197cm) fully extended, a set of 6 dining chairs, each with canted rectangular padded back, on square tapering legs, a pedestal sideboard with 3 short and one long drawer above 2 cupboard doors on a plinth base, and a side table, with 2 short drawers on rectangular supports, 40½in (103cm) wide. **£1,500–2,000** *CSK*

A walnut and marquetry suite, inlaid with leaf borders and foliate panels, comprising: a draw-leaf dining table, 85½in (217cm) extended, a set of 8 dining chairs, including a pair of armchairs, a pedestal sideboard, a bureau, 32½in (82cm) and a display cabinet, 20in (51cm). **£1,500–2,000** *CSK*

A bird's-eye maple dining room suite, comprising a dining table, 6 dining chairs with scalloped backs above padded seats, on tapering legs, a sideboard with stepped rounded rectangular top above hinged compartment and 4 cupboard doors, on U-shaped support, on plinth base, the dining table, 72in (182.5cm) wide. **£1,500–2,000** *CSK*

A walnut 3-tier coffee table, each made as three-quarters of a circle and juxtaposed on solid supports, 20in (50.5cm) high. **£500–600** *P*

A limed oak refectory table, with ivory plaque, labelled 'Heal & Son, London, W', 78in (198cm) wide.
£3,000–3,500 *CSK*

Glass

A Czechoslovakian pressed glass blue 'mermaid' ten-piece dressing table set, c1928, tray 10½in (26.5cm) diam.
£80–100 *BKK*

A pair of glass lamps, each with a globular shade, decorated in relief with geometric panels picked out in soft colours and screwed into a black glass three-legged base, probably American, 7½in (19cm) high.
£300–400 *P*

An inlaid burr elm centre table, the radially veneered, cross-banded top above 4 tapering uprights terminating in an X-stretcher, labelled 'Waring & Gillow Ltd', 39in (99cm) wide.
£1,500–2,000 *CSK*

A Verlys shallow opalescent glass bowl, pale amber tinted, decorated in relief with fish and kingfishers, signed, 13in (33cm) diam.
£170–220 *MCA*

A green glass bowl, decorated with fish centrepiece, c1932, 8½in (21cm) diam.
£40–50 *BKK*

A Sowerby pink glass stylised vase, c1932, 6½in (16cm) high.
£20–25 *BKK*

A Sowerby amber pressed glass bowl, with holly leaf and berry design, on a black plinth, c1936, 15½in (39cm) diam.
£40–50 *BKK*

A gilded wrought iron console table and mirror, the mirror frame with hammered finish, with stylised leaf and flower cresting above rectangular black marble top, supported on a large frame decorated with central fountain design, flanked by stylised foliage and hammered and scored vertical bars, on bun feet, 77in (196cm) wide.
£3,000–4,000 *CSK*

A Whitefriars green crackleglass tazza, on a chrome plated stand, c1930, 6in (15cm) high.
£30–35 *BKK*

A Jobling green glass dancing girl figure, in a matching bowl, on a plinth, c1934, 9in (23cm) diam.
£35–45 *BKK*

Lalique

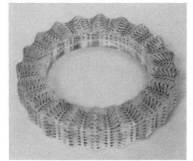

A Lalique blue stained glass ashtray, 5½in (13.5cm) diam.
£200–300 *ASA*

A frosted opalescent glass ashtray, 'Louise', in the form of a flowerhead, with black enamelled stamens and traces of blue staining, slight damage, moulded 'R. Lalique' mark, 3in (7.5cm) diam.
£250–300 *CSK*

A clear and frosted glass lemonade set, 'Jaffa', intaglio moulded with vertical serrated foliage, comprising lemonade jug, 6 beakers and circular tray, etched 'Lalique France', slight damage, the jug 9in (23cm) high.
£600–700 *CSK*

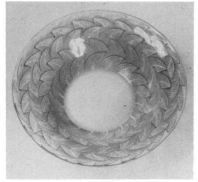

A rose tinted glass bowl, moulded with bands of overlaid pointed leaves, with etched highlights, mark 'R. Lalique, France', 12in (31cm) diam.
£300–350 *Bri*

A frosted glass car mascot, 'Pintade', modelled as a female guinea fowl, with chromed mount, on black glass base, slight damage, signed 'R. Lalique France', 5in (13cm) high.
£1,200–1,500 *P*

A blue stained opalescent glass vase, 'Ceylan', moulded with love birds, with light fitting and contemporary painted shade, etched 'R. Lalique, France', 9½in (24cm) high.
£2,200–2,700 *Bea*

A frosted glass box and cover, 'Coquilles', intaglio moulded with a radial design of stylised shells, the reserve with traces of blue staining, indistinct moulded signature, 2½in (7cm) diam.
£150–200 *CSK*

An amber glass orangeade set, 'Blidah', moulded in relief with fruit and foliage, comprising: an oviform jug, 6 large beakers and a circular tray, stencil etched 'R. Lalique', height of jug 8in (20cm) high.
£1,000–1,200 *CSK*

A clear and frosted glass decanter, 'Saint-Cyr', stencil etched 'R. Lalique', 11in (28cm) high, and 4 'Riquewhir' white wine glasses, etched and numbered, one slightly damaged, and 8 crescent dishes, intaglio moulded with stylised wheat.
£500–600 *CSK*

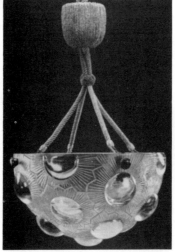

A pair of clear glass ceiling lights, 'Soleil', with brown staining and silk hanging cords, wheel cut mark 'R. Lalique France', after 1926, 12in (30.5cm) diam.
£2,000–2,500 *S*

A clear and frosted glass lemonade set, 'Hespérides', intaglio moulded with spiralling foliage, comprising: a jug, 6 beakers and a circular tray, stencil etched 'R. Lalique', slight damage, jug 8½in (21.5cm) high.
£2,300–2,700 *CSK*

A part table service, 'Vigne, Strié', of reeded design with knopped stems, moulded in relief with grapes and stained jade green, comprising: 2 carafes, 11 water glasses, 8 white wine glasses, 8 red glasses and 5 champagne cups, slight damage, etched 'R. Lalique'.
£2,500–3,000 *CSK*

A clear and frosted glass part table service, 'Borgeuil', moulded in relief with panels of triangles, comprising: a decanter and stopper, lemonade jug, 8 water glasses, 11 white wine glasses, 11 red wine glasses, 2 champagne flutes, 6 sherbert bowls and 7 plates, slight damage, stencil etched 'R. Lalique'.
£1,500–2,000 *CSK*

A clear and frosted glass drinks set, 'Chinon', the stems moulded in relief with bands of spirals, stained pink, comprising: jug, 6 water and 6 white wine glasses, stencil etched 'R. Lalique', slight damage, one white wine glass broken, the jug 7in (17cm) high.
£750–800 *CSK*

A frosted glass car mascot, 'Grenouille', modelled as a small frog in crouched position resting on a circular base, chrome mounted, signed 'R. Lalique, France', 2½in (6cm) high.
£7,000–8,000 *P*

A collection of clear glasses, heightened with black enamel, 'Unawihr' comprising: 8 water glasses, 7 champagne glasses, 8 Madeira glasses, 8 liqueur glasses and a champagne glass in the 'Saint-Nabor' pattern, each glass engraved 'R. Lalique France', and some with engraved catalogue number, 3½in to 5in (9.5 to 12cm) high.
£3,000–3,500 *S*

A polished and frosted glass vase, 'Sauterelles'.
£1,700–2,200 *P(S)*

A polished and satin glass car mascot, 'Victoire' or 'Spirit of the Wind', modelled as a siren, mounted on original Breves Galleries chrome base, moulded 'R. Lalique France', 10in (25cm) long.
£5,500–7,500 *P*

A frosted glass hanging lamp shade, 'Lierre', moulded on the underside with 8 vertical branches of ivy leaves, heightened with traces of pale brown staining, with moulded mark 'R. Lalique France', 14in (36cm) diam.
£650–850 *P*

A glass plafonnier, 'Dahlias' heightened with brown staining and hanging chains, wheel cut mark 'R. Lalique France', after 1921, 12in (30.5cm) diam.
£800–1,000 *S*

An opalescent glass vase, 'Bacchantes', moulded in high relief with a frieze of naked Bacchantes, signed on the base in block letters 'R. Lalique France', 10in (24.5cm) high.
£8,000–10,000 *P*

An opalescent glass vase, 'Terpsichore', moulded on each broad side with 2 naked maidens, linked by highly stylised folds of drapes, signed in block letters on base 'R. Lalique France', 8in (20cm) high.
£8,200–9,000 *P*

A Lalique style scent bottle and stopper, the moulded malachite glass depicting bathing nymphs in relief, flowerhead borders, the clear glass stopper cut as flowerheads, 6½in (16cm) high.
£400–600 *WW*

A blue stained globular vase, 'Ormeaux', moulded with overlapping leaves, minor damage, etched mark and number '984', 6in (15cm) high.
£350–450 *DN*

A glass pendant, 'Feuilles', in rich blue tone and moulded with leaves, signed 'R. Lalique', 2in (5.5cm) diam.
£300–400 *P*

A clear and frosted moulded glass figure, 'Suzanne', with a bronze underlight, signed and numbered '833', c1920, 9in (23cm) high.
£800–900 *HOLL*

An opalescent glass clock, 'Inseparables', the Swiss made movement with painted dial and similar decoration, 4½in (11.5cm) high.
£1,400–2,000 *AH*

Metalware

A gilt spelter table lamp, the stepped base surmounted by 2 dancers supporting a marbled glass globe shade, 20½in (52cm).
£550–650 *CSK*

A Lorenzl bronze figure, modelled as a naked Eastern seated figure, stamped 'Made in Austria' and artist's signature, on a shaped hexagonal marble base, 13½in (34.5cm) high.
£300–500 *P*

A lacquered silvered bronze group, cast from a model by Bruno Zach, of a couple dancing a pas de deux, on a grey onyx base, signed in the bronze, 17in (44cm) high. **£1,400–2,000** *CSK*

A bronze bust, 'The Age of
Innocence', cast from a model by
Alfred Drury, overall green
patination, on green marble base,
9½in (24cm) high.
£1,000–1,200 *P*

A bronze figure, on
onyx base,
signed 'Lorenzl',
11½in (29.5cm).
£350–400 *P*

A gilt spelter table lamp, in the
form of a young woman holding a
light, on an alabaster base, 20in
(51cm) high.
£400–500 *CSK*

A patinated bronze figure,
'La Cigalle', cast from a model by
E. Picault, depicting a naked young
woman, seated beneath a tree,
holding a mandolin, signed,
22½in (57cm) high.
£1,700–2,200 *CSK*

A bronze figure of a naked
woman, presumably Eve, holding
a snake, signed 'Jean Idrac' on
base, founders Thiebault Frères,
28in (71.5cm) high.
£1,500–2,000 *P*

*Jean Antoine Marie Idrac, 1849-84,
born in Toulouse, studied under
Guillaume and Falguière. He won
the Prix de Rome in 1869.*

Locate the source

*The source of each
illustration in Miller's
can be found by checking
the code letters below
each caption with the list
of contributors.*

Bronze & Ivory Figures

A pair of spelter figures,
13in (33cm) high.
£100–135 *WAG*

A bronze table lamp, cast in the
form of a gilt puma seated
beneath a black patinated tree,
15½in (39cm) high.
£200–300 *CSK*

A silver tazza, with shallow
circular bowl supported on ribbed
amber coloured composition stem,
above a foot of spreading
concentric circles, marked 'Jean
E. Puiforcat', with French control
marks and London import marks
for 1945, 8in (20.5cm) diam.
£2,300–2,700 *P*

A gilt bronze and ivory figure,
'Aphrodite with Bowl of Fruit',
cast and carved from a model by
Ferdinand Preiss, signed 'F.
Preiss' and foundry mark for
Preiss & Kassler, Berlin, on a
circular base, 9in (23cm) high.
£1,500–1,600 *P*

A gilt bronze and ivory figure, 'Juggler', cast and carved from a model by Colinet, of a naked young woman balancing ivory balls on outstretched limbs, on a black onyx base, inscribed 'Colinet', 7in (18cm) high.
£400–600 *CSK*

A bronze and ivory figure, 'The Tennis Player', by F. Preiss, on onyx base, 11in (28cm) high.
£6,600–7,000 *L&E*

A Goldscheider patinated bronze and ivory figure, cast and carved from a model by Van der Straeten, on circular marble base with artist's name, the bronze with foundry marks, 14in (35.5cm) high.
£800–1,000 *P*

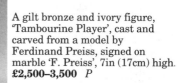

A gilt bronze and ivory figure, 'Tambourine Player', cast and carved from a model by Ferdinand Preiss, signed on marble 'F. Preiss', 7in (17cm) high.
£2,500–3,500 *P*

A bronze and ivory figure, 'Demeter', or 'Ceres', cast and carved from a model by Ferdinand Preiss, signed on bronze 'F. Preiss', on a marble base, 10½in (26.5cm) high.
£1,200–1,500 *P*

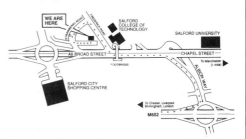

A gilt bronze and ivory figure, 'Phyrne with Mirror', cast and carved from a model by Ferdinand Preiss, signed 'F. Preiss' and foundry mark for Preiss & Kassler, Berlin, on a circular base, 9in (22cm) high.
£1,500–1,700 *P*

A patinated bronze and ivory figure, cast and carved from a model by Lorenzl, fingers damaged, signed in the bronze, 13in (33cm) high.
£800–1,000 *CSK*

Ceramics

A Beswick polychrome painted pottery wall mask, modelled as a young woman with blonde curls and a green beret, and another of a girl with pigtails, hairline crack, printed factory marks, largest 8in (20cm) high.
£250–350 *CSK*

A Goldscheider pottery figure, by Dakon, modelled as a naked fan dancer, with mauve and black floral decoration, painted factory marks, impressed '6214 140 4', on rectangular base, 13in (33cm).
£550–600 *P*

An Essevi pottery wall mask, modelled as a masked woman in red, purple, pink, yellow and blue hat, a monkey resting on her arm, painted marks dated '11-6-37'.
£600–750 *P*

A Goldscheider terracotta wall mask, modelled as a girl with black curly hair, a green scarf, holding a yellow fruit, printed 'Made in Austria', stamped '6774', 8in (20cm) high.
£250–300 *P*

A Goldscheider figure, by Lorenzl, modelled as a young woman in a clown's pink, blue and yellow costume, factory marks and 'Lorenzl', 'R' on base, 12in (30.5cm) high.
£500–600 *P*

A Goldscheider figure, 'Butterfly Dancer', with polychrome glazed decoration, printed factory marks 'Goldscheider, Wein, Made in Austria, Hand Decorated', incised '5960 516 6 19', 16in (40.5cm) high.
£1,400–1,800 *C*

A Goldscheider pottery plaque, depicting two women, one with orange hair, the other with brown, blurred factory marks and 'Made in Austria', scratched number '6663/4' and 'P', 10in (25cm) high.
£400–500 *P*

A Goldscheider pottery wall mask, modelled as a woman with curly green hair and orange lips, clasping a string of black beads, painted factory mark to base, 12½in (31.5cm) high.
£300–500 *P*

A Goldscheider pottery figural lamp, modelled as a woman, decorated in yellow, red and green floral dress, leaning against a jagged column supporting green cloth shade, marked 'Goldscheider Wien' to base, 19½in (49.5cm) high without shade.
£400–600 *P*

A Poole Studio Pottery wall plate, by Tony Morris, painted in abstract manner in bright colours with a harbour scene, impressed 'Poole Studio', signed with 'TM' monogram, 14½in (37cm) diam.
£400–500 P

A French crackle glazed pottery figure, painted in shades of grey and cream, painted mark 'Editions Kaza', on a rough base, 19½in (49cm) wide.
£700–900 CSK

A glazed pottery ceramic wall plaque, modelled in the form of a boy pulling down a branch to pick grapes, standing on an urn, minor damage, 38½in (98cm) high.
£300–400 CSK

A Lenci polychrome painted pottery dish, restored, painted factory marks, 15in (38cm) wide.
£1,200–1,700 CSK

A Knörlein pottery double wall mask, showing a mother's face with orange lips and curls, and a child's face with orange lips and brown curls, signed 'R. Knörlein' and 'RK' monogram number 'V.31'.
£330–400 P

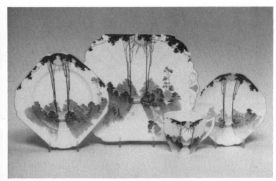

A Shelley Low Queen Anne shape tea service, each piece printed in black with a woodland scene at sunrise, picked out in yellow, within yellow line borders, comprising: 12 tea cups, saucers, and tea plates, milk jug, sugar bowl, 2 bread and butter plates, printed marks in green and pattern number '116678'.
£450–600 DN

A Gray's pottery tea set, painted in blue, yellow and green, comprising: teapot and cover, milk jug, 6 cups and saucers, 6 plates, minor damage, printed factory marks. £100–200 CSK

Clarice Cliff

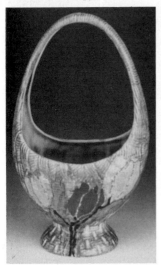

A Bizarre Gaiety flower basket in the Clouvre pattern, painted in colours on a matt blue ground, printed factory marks, 14in (36cm) high.
£300–400 CSK

A plate, centrally decorated with a black roofed cottage in a stylised wooded landscape, on an orange ground, impressed numerals, 9in (23cm) diam.
£300–400 DN

An Original Bizarre tankard coffee service for 6, with early gold mark, c1928, coffee pot 7in (17.5cm) high. **£550-650 BKK**

An Original Bizarre candlestick, c1928, 8in (20cm) high.
£250–300 BKK

An Original Bizarre baluster vase, shape number '186', c1928, 6in (15cm) high.
£350–380 BKK

A five-piece hen and chicken cruet, shape '560', c1934, 5½in (14cm) high.
£300–400 BKK

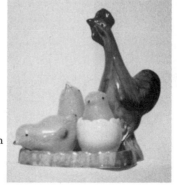

Two Bizarre plates, each centrally decorated with the Alpine pattern, within black and orange borders, printed and impressed marks, 9in (23cm) diam.
£450–550 DN

A Bizarre tureen and cover, decorated in the Blue Crocus pattern, painted in colours, printed factory marks, 9½in (24cm) diam.
£350–450 CSK

Clarice Cliff Marks and Identification

Clarice Cliff pieces are marked in a variety of different ways. They often carry impressed dates, although these may indicate the date of production rather than of design or decoration. The pattern name was often given alongside the Clarice Cliff signature. Pattern names and signatures were initially handwritten; later they were stamped and eventually were lithographed. Pieces also carry the factory name, which was printed. Marked fakes exist, but can usually be identified as such.

The pottery was produced by Wilkinson's at their Newport works in Stoke-on-Trent, and their pattern books and contemporary advertisements can be used to identify patterns. Sometimes different names were used for the different colours in which patterns appeared.

On genuine pieces the mark is usually smooth - a crackle effect may be cause for suspicion, although a few genuine pieces have appeared with such crazing.

There are some genuine Clarice Cliff reproductions, but these are clearly dated - hand painted signatures and marks were phased out from around 1931.

A Peter Pan Crocus conical shape coffee service for 4, c1930, coffee pot 7in (17.5cm) high.
£1,000–1,100 *BKK*

An Athens shape jug, decorated in Orange Roof Cottage pattern, shape number '24', c1932, 8in (20cm) high.
£200–250 *BKK*

l. A Newport Pottery Fantasque Bizarre Secrets glazed earthenware vase, the underside with printed mark, impressed pattern number '515', 1933-35, 5in (12.5cm) high.
£400–600
r. A Newport Pottery jug Café-au-lait Isis polychrome glazed earthenware jug, the underside with printed factory mark, impressed 'Isis', 1931-33, 9½in (24cm) high.
£650–850 *S*

A Lotus jug, brightly painted with the Windbells pattern, 11½in (29.5cm) high.
£550–650 *Bea*

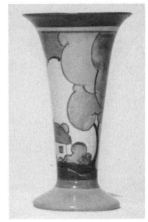

A Blue Autumn trumpet vase, shape number '270', c1932, 6in (15cm) high.
£300–350 *BKK*

A Biarritz trio, decorated in a banded/tartan pattern, c1936.
£100–120 *BKK*

A Tennis pattern and Conical shape teaset, comprising 24 pieces, printed facsimile signature, some with impressed date for 1930, teapot 5½in (14cm) high, and an extra plate with banded pattern.
£6,500–7,500 *Bea*

An Isis jug, painted with a version of the Tulip pattern, a blue and multi-coloured band above and below, 10in (25cm) high.
£450–550 *Bea*

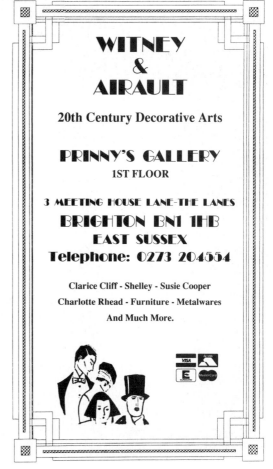

A Nasturtium pattern Humpty sugar bowl, c1934, 3in (7.5cm) high.
£85–100 *BKK*

A ribbed pottery jug, painted with the Blue Firs pattern, 7in (17.5cm) high.
£350–450 *Bea*

A Conical sugar sifter, painted with Oranges pattern, 5½in (14cm) high.
£350–400 *Bea*

A Spring Crocus pattern tea service, comprising: 11 teacups with lemon borders, 12 saucers, 12 tea plates and 2 bread and butter plates with brown centre panels, panelled milk jug and circular sugar basin, c1930.
£850–1,000 *CAG*

An Autumn Crocus beaker, c1931, 4½in (11.5cm) high.
£100–125 *BKK*

A Bizarre centrepiece, decorated in the Rhodanthe pattern, painted in colours, comprising: 4 cube candlesticks, 2 rectangular and 2 curved flower troughs, damaged, printed factory marks.
£550–650 *CSK*

A Bizarre faceted baluster shaped vase, with flared neck, decorated with a version of the Autumn pattern, on an orange ground, printed mark and moulded shape number '360', 8in (20cm) high.
£650–750 *DN*

A Conical sugar sifter, painted with the Lorna pattern, 5½in (14cm) high.
£350–400 *Bea*

A Newport Pottery Bizarre Sliced Fruit pattern vase, decorated in green, blue, brown and pink, within white orange bands, printed mark in black, shape number '204', 11in (28cm) high.
£200–300 *HSS*

A Fantasque Bizarre Newport Pottery Secrets pattern vase, of baluster form with green and yellow banded ribbed neck, printed mark in black, 8in (20cm) high.
£370–420 *HSS*

Miscellaneous

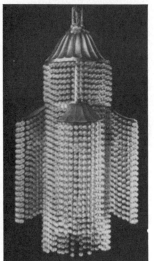

A French silvered-bronze and frosted glass chandelier, in the manner of Ruhlmann, the fluted domed circular cap supporting strings of beads above 4 fluted flanges similarly beaded, 30in (76cm) long. **£1,000–1,500** *C*

A glass necklace, with etched and cut glass panels decorated with geometric motifs, between black bars, 16in (41cm) long.
£150–200 *CSK*

A French marble clock garniture, the 7-day striking movement marked 'Paris', c1926, 18in (45.5cm) wide.
£200–250 *BKK*

The clock weighs over 50lbs!

A French diamond and blue enamel pendant, with diamond and black enamel cluster, terminating in single lapis lazuli bead drop, the blue enamel flecked with gilt to resemble the drop, the reverse with pierced and engraved foliate panel, stamped 'Lang Paris', on staple link neck chain, in fitted case.
£1,000–1,500 *CSK*

A plaster figure group, of a young girl kneeling with 2 borzoi dogs, c1928, 26in (66cm) wide.
£100–125 *BKK*

A hand woven woollen carpet, in shades of brown with a geometric pattern of overlapping shapes and lines, zig-zag motifs and crescent shapes against a beige field, 104½ by 138in (265 by 350cm).
£1,000–1,500 *P*

A dolls' house, modelled as a modernist two-storey house with a flat roof, balconies, garage and eau-de-nil painted metal windows, painted cream, 23in (59cm) high.
£120–160 *P*

A plaster figure group of a young girl, seated on a tree trunk, with a borzoi dog, signed on the base, c1928, 28½in (72.5cm)
£100–125 *BKK*

LEATHER & LUGGAGE

l. & r. A selection of ladies' handbags, of brown and black crocodile leather, some printed, others of plain leather, smaller wallets and a pair of shoes.
£300–400

c. A lady's brown crocodile leather dressing case, the interior fitted with spot-hammered silver topped flasks and mounted brushes, London 1910 and 1912, each piece monogrammed, and a brown leather writing case, Mappin & Webb Ltd. Oxford St. London W., 18 by 13in (46 by 33cm).
£600–800 *CSK*

A George III brass mounted leather post-bag, the lock plate inscribed 'Earl of Liverpool, Pitchford Hall', 12½in (30cm) wide.
£1,200–1,700 *C*

A French cricket bag, stamped 'L.V.', 32in (81cm) wide.
£80–100 *WIG*

A fitted crocodile travelling case, with blue/green mounted fittings, 19in (48cm) wide.
£600–800 *WIG*

A picnic box, The Coracle, containing cups, saucers and other fittings, c1920, 20in (51cm) wide.
£60–80 *WIG*

A Louis Vuitton trunk, with brass mounts, 40in (101.5cm) wide.
£600–800 *WIG*

An embossed and stamped leather black jack water bottle, c1700, 9in (23cm) high.
£200–250 *C(S)*

A crocodile suitcase, with silver fittings, in good original condition, 26in (66cm) wide.
£300–400 *WIG*

PAPIER MACHE

A black papier mâché lacquered tray, applied with gilded floral sprays and insects, 19thC, 31½in (80cm) wide.
£800–1,000 *WL*

A decorated papier mâché box, c1890, 7½in (19cm) square.
£40–50 *DUN*

A papier mâché pole screen, decorated with flowers, c1840, 58in (147cm) high.
£300–400 *STA*

A pair of papier mâché oval occasional tables, c1870, 29in (73.5cm) high.
£900–1,200 *Mit*

A papier mâché tray, decorated with Chinese figures, c1840, 22½in (57cm) wide.
£250–350 *STA*

TUNBRIDGE WARE

A papier mâché tray, c1840, 20in (50.5cm) wide.
£500–600 *Mit*

A Tunbridge ware ruler, 9in (23cm) long.
£25–35 *WAG*

An inkwell and stand, with stamp boxes and pen, c1870, 8in (20cm) wide.
£550–600 *WAG*

A pair of Tunbridge ware tilt-top tables, c1850, 8in (20cm) diam.
£600–650 *WAG*

A papier mâché tray, decorated with flowers, 24½in (61cm) wide.
£300–400 *STA*

TARTAN WARE

A painted Tartan ware ruler, 19thC, 8in (20cm) long.
£35–45 *WAG*

A papier mâché heart-shaped box, c1860, 3in (7.5cm) wide.
£150-200 *DUN*

A Macbeth Tartan ware string box, 4in (10cm) diam.
£175–200 *WAG*

A Prince Charlie Tartan ware glass case, with a view of The Popping Stone, Gilsland, 3in (7.5cm) high.
£80–100 *WAG*

SPORT
Snooker & Billiards

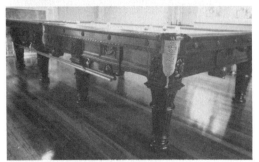

A Victorian full size billiard table, by Thurston & Son, c1860. **£16,000–18,000** *FB*

A Victorian full size billiard table, with decorative inlay, by Orme & Son, c1850.
£13,000–14,000 *FB*

A full size mahogany billiard table, by E. J. Riley, c1920.
£4,000–4,500 *FB*

A late Victorian carved oak full size billiard table, by Burroughes and Watts, the frieze carved with scrolling foliage and grotesques, on 8 acanthus carved baluster supports, baize and pockets reconditioned.
£13,500–18,000 *CSK*

A full size billiard table, by George Wright, c1890.
£5,000–5,500 *FB*

A Peruvian mahogany snooker table, on cabriole legs with claw-and-ball feet, 20thC.
£2,000–2,200 *FB*

A full size Corom table, in Brazilian mahogany, by Burroughes & Watts, c1870.
£12,000–14,000 *FB*

A full size Russian walnut billiard table, c1920.
£6,500–7,000 *FB*

A full size Brazilian mahogany billiard table, by Burroughes & Watts, c1900.
£5,000–5,500 *FB*

A full size billiard table, by
Burroughes & Watts, c1890.
£15,000–18,000 *FB*

An English solid oak snooker
table, by E. J. Riley, c1920, 84in
(213cm) long.
£2,000–2,500 *FB*

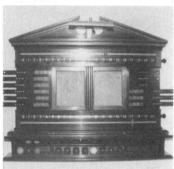

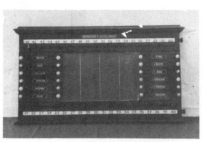

A full size mahogany life pool
scoreboard, c1890, by Burroughes
& Watts.
£1,500-1,800 *FB*

A full size flame mahogany life
pool scoreboard, with ball box,
by Burroughes & Watts.
£2,500-3,000 *FB*

A Victorian mahogany billiard
room door, with glass panel.
£850-1,000 *FB*

A full size snooker table, with
green baize playing surface,
leather bound pockets, oak framework,
on 8 heavy bulbous legs, complete
with accessories, 149½in (380cm) long.
£3,000–3,700 *WL*

A walnut billiard table, inlaid with satinwood, by
Orme & Son, 108in (274cm) long.
£7,500–8,000 *WBB*

A dual height billiard dining table,
by E. J. Riley, serpentine shaped, with
cabriole legs, 96in (243.5cm) long.
£4,000–6,000 *WBB*

A full size rosewood billiard table,
by Burroughes and Watts.
£5,500–6,000 *WBB*

A full size solid walnut billiard
table, by Burroughes and Watts,
with steel block cushions, c1870.
£20,000–25,000 *WBB*

*This table apparently once
belonged to King Edward VIII.*

An Imperial Austrian Biedermeier three-quarter
size billiard table, by Seifert & Son, made for the
Vienna International Exhibition, with 6 pockets,
baize lined on a single marble slab, on 6 tapering
legs with acanthus capitals, the whole veneered in
Hungarian ash with mahogany rounded corners
and bandings, one end inlaid in mother-of-pearl 'H.
Seifert & Sohn in Wien' on a rosewood ground, the
other end similarly inlaid and with a medallion
'Wiener Weltausstellung 1873' and another 'von
der Fortschritts Medaille', 108in (273cm) long.
£14,000–18,000 *S*

Cricket

A Doulton limited edition
W. G. Grace cricketing jug, the
handle depicting a hat, bat and
stumps, c1880, 7½in (19cm) high.
£750–800 *HER*

A Copeland parian figure of
Young England, after George
Halse, modelled as a young boy
reading a book, with a cricket bat
beside him, repaired, impressed
marks, c1870, 16in (40cm) high.
£350–400 *CSK*

A silver and painted enamel
vesta case, advertising 'The
Sportsman for Cricket News',
depicting a kangaroo batsman
with a lion as wicket keeper, the
reverse with inscription,
hallmarked Chester 1899.
£550–600 *CSK*

A commemorative printed
silk handkerchief, with a blue
border, the centre depicting 'The
Australians 1888', with the team
list below, slight wear, 16in
(40.5cm) square.
£250–300 *CSK*

Four photographs, including a
studio portrait photograph of
MacLaren as a young man,
wearing cricket whites, c1890,
published in *Archie. A Biography
of A. C. MacLaren,* by Michael
Down, 1981, framed and glazed,
10½ by 8½in (26.5 by 21.5cm), and
one of MacLaren at the wicket,
signed on the image, mounted,
c1900, 11 by 9in (28 by 22.5cm).
£200–250 *CSK*

A letter from F. E. Woolley to
Robin McConnell, dated 1st
July 1958, enclosing a signed
photograph of himself,
inscribed 'when I got my
Kent Blazer', 1906, 5½ by
3½in (14 by 9cm).
£150–200 *CSK*

A collection of postcards,
including one of George Gunn,
inscribed by John Richmond
Gunn on reverse, c1912.
£350–400 *CSK*

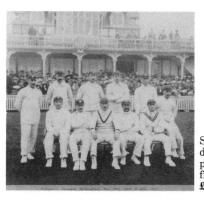

Seven team photographs,
depicting A. C. MacLaren, two
published in *Archie. A Biography,*
framed and glazed, 1894-1902.
£770–850 *CSK*

A photograph of A. C. MacLaren, W. G. Grace, K. S. Ranjitsinhji and 2 others, c1914, 3 by 5in (7.5 by 12.5cm), and another.
£120–150 *CSK*

A reproduction of an engraving of Marylebone Cricket Club, the new pavilion at Lord's, entitled 'A Century of English Test Cricketers', autographed by 100 English test players from 1948 onwards, 20 by 30in (50.5 by 76cm), framed and glazed.
£200–250 *CSK*

A front cover illustration for *Men Only*, by Edward S. Hynes, depicting Don Bradman, pencil, pen and black ink and watercolour, signed and dated 1947, 20 by 13½in (51 by 34cm), unframed.
£500–700 *CSK*

A 16 page printed souvenir brochure of Gloucestershire -v- Hampshire, at Bristol, August 4th, 6th and 7th, 1934, the title signed by W. R. Hammond and the members of both sides, inscribed, together with the printed scorecard for Gloucestershire -v- South Africa, August 10th-13th, 1935.
£375–425 *CSK*

A portrait photograph of Charles Macartney at the wicket, signed on the image, c1912, mounted on card, c1912, 11 by 7in (28 by 18cm).
£300–350 *CSK*

Tennis

A pair of bronze figures playing tennis, on marble plinths, c1940, 10in (25cm) high.
£900–1,000 *CSK*

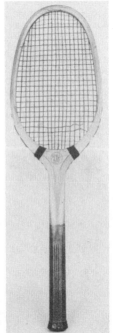

A 'Burlington' wooden handled tennis racket, with an oval shaped head, together with a contemporary canvas racket cover trimmed in leather, c1910.
£250–300 *CSK*

An album containing a collection of 37 autographs of Wimbledon tennis players of 1920, including Suzanne Lenglen, 22 accompanied with official postcard photographs, including those of A. W. Gore and William Tilden.
£150–250 *CSK*

Fishing

A wicker creel.
£20–30 *WIG*

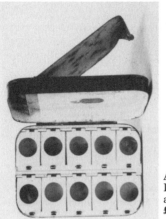

A black fly box, by Ogden of London, with sprung windows and line compartment, c1920.
£60–80 *MSh*

A silver mounted fishing plaque on a mahogany shield, 25in (64cm) high.
£600–800 *WIG*

A walking stick fishing rod, in three sections, with an ivory knob, 37in (94cm) long.
£40–80 *WIG*

A three-piece bamboo fishing rod.
£10–15 *WIG*

A folding trout net, by Ogden Smith, in a canvas case, 25in (64cm) long.
£30–40 *WIG*

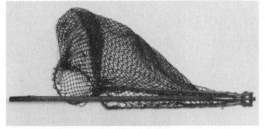

A brass folding landing net, with bamboo handle.
£30–40 *WIG*

A folding head trout net.
£10–15 *WIG*

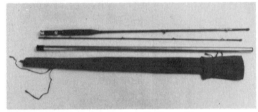

A trout fly rod, by C. Farlow & Co., with
2 spare tips, in aluminium tube and canvas case.
£40–60 *WIG*

A Hardy's split cane salmon fly
rod, with a spare tip, c1930,
144in (366cm) long.
£80–120 *MSh*

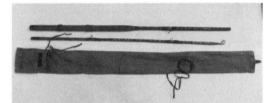

A two-piece bamboo fishing rod,
in a canvas case.
£20–30 *WIG*

A two-piece split cane salmon rod,
120in (304.5cm) long, with a
Hardy reel.
£60–80 *WIG*

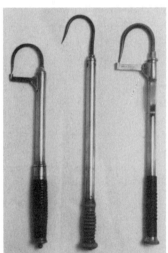

Three salmon gaffs.
£20–40 each *WIG*

A brass telescopic salmon
gaff, with a lignum vitae
handle, c1880.
£80–120 *MSh*

A 2⅛in wide brass drum
multiplying reel, with lock
mechanism and ivory handle, c1830.
£140–200 *MSh*

A leather creel, with brass lock
and embossed lid, excellent
condition, 19thC.
£1,800–2,000 *WIG*

A trout, in a glass case with a
gold border, probably by J. Cooper
& Sons, London, 23in (59cm) long.
£300–400 *WIG*

A carved wood salmon, mounted on board, inscribed
'Killed by Victor Bonney at Eden on the Deveron,
October 1926, Weight 46lbs, Length 49½ins and Girth
26½in', minor repair, 57in (144.5cm) long overall.
£1,250–1,700 *RBB*

Top: A stuffed and mounted roach, in a glass case, 1946, 15in (38cm) long.
£520–590
Bottom: A stuffed and mounted trout, in a river bed setting, in a bowfronted glazed wood case, 1927, 21in (53cm) long.
£480–520 *JH*

A stuffed and mounted pike in a river bed setting, in a bowfronted glazed wood case, 1925, 39in (99cm) long. **£800–900** *JH*

A 2½in wide brass multiplying drum reel with ivory handle, c1880.
£120–180 *MSh*

A 2in brass multiplying reel with ivory handle, c1860.
£120–180 *MSh*

A 4¾in brass salmon reel, with the star and planet mechanism and ebony handle, made by Malloch of Perth, c1890.
£220–280 *MSh*

A 2½in bell metal trout reel, by Malloch of Perth, c1930.
£30–50 *MSh*

A 4in brass sidecasting salmon fishing reel, made by Malloch of Perth, c1900. **£120–160** *MSh*

A 4in Hardy Perfect narrow drum, c1920. **£40–60** *WIG*

A 4½in brass salmon fly reel, by Enright and Son, c1900.
£90–140 *MSh*

A brass 1½in pole winch, with ivory handle, c1830.
£150–250 *MSh*

A 1¾in wide drum multiplying reel with lock mechanism and ivory handle, c1830.
£140–200 *MSh*

An Illingworth No. 3 fishing reel, in original triangular case.
£40–60 *WIG*

A 4in Hardy reel, 'The Longston', with twin handles. **£30–40** *WIG*

A 4½in alloy reel, with single handle. **£10–20** *WIG*

A 4in Hardy Perfect, with 100% finish. **£300–400** *WIG*

A 4in Moulet Français 'Décantelle' alloy reel, with twin handles. **£30–40** *WIG*

A 4in Hardy Perfect, with 80% original finish. **£200–250** *WIG*

A 3in Hardy Perfect, with ivorine handles and tension screw. **£50–80** *WIG*

Miscellaneous

A 3½in St George reel, with notched brass foot. **£40–60** *WIG*

A 3¾in Hardy reel, with agate line guard. **£25–35** *WIG*

Two boxing cartoons, by Roy Ullyett, both signed, pencil, pen and black ink, brush and blue crayon, largest 14 by 9½in (35.5 by 23.5cm), and three others. **£200–250** *CSK*

Roy Ullyett was born at Leytonstone, Essex, in 1914. He began as sports correspondent for The Star *and then as cartoonist to the* Daily Express *from 1953. His work is represented in the paper's annuals from 1956-74. He has illustrated over 20 books with sports cartoons, including '*I'm the Greatest. The Wit and Humour of Muhammed Ali*', 1975, and '*Cue for a Laugh*', 1984.*

An Ayres double croquet set, with 4 large and 4 small mallets, 8 balls, hoops, markers and other accessories, in a pine box, early 20thC, 42in (107cm) long. **£500–600** *S(S)*

A steel Olympic torch, with Olympic emblem, inscribed, 'XIVth Olympiad 1948: Olympia to London. With Thanks to the Bearer', 16in (41cm) high. **£720–770** *CSK*

A brass bound leather cartridge magazine, by J. Purdey & Sons, London, 19in (48cm) wide. **£250–300** *WIG*

ORIENTAL
Cloisonné

An enamel tray, by Namikawa Sosuke, the graduated yellow to grey ground decorated partly in musen (wireless technique), the underside decorated on a brown ground with shakudo rum, slight damage, signed in a silver wire seal 'Sosuke', Meiji period, 12in (30cm).
£5,000–6,000 *S*

A pair of cloisonné enamel vases, decorated largely in musen, on a robin's egg blue ground, with Ando Jubei mark, Meiji period, 10in (25cm).
£1,200–1,700 *S*

Furniture

A Japanese rosewood bonheur du jour, the crescent-shaped top with key pattern carved edges above a single long drawer, all raised on stem and flowerhead carved knees and cabriole legs, 45in (114cm) wide, with a matching chair with fanned back, marked on seat rail 'Arthur & Bond, Yokohama'.
£2,000–3,000 *DaD*

A moriage and musen cloisonné enamel vase, decorated in low relief, with some details in wireless technique on a blue grey ground, slight damage, Hattori Tadasaburo mark on leaf-shaped tablet, 12in (30cm).
£4,000–4,500 *S*

A Chinese cloisonné bottle vase, decorated on a turquoise ground reserved with key frets, slight damage, 16in (41cm) high.
£800–1,000 *CSK*

Locate the source
The source of each illustration in Miller's can be found by checking the code letters below each caption with the list of contributors.

A Chinese toilet box, 19thC, 18in (46cm) high when open.
£400–450 *STA*

A cloisonné enamel vase, decorated in gold wire on a black ground, slight damage, mark for Miwa Tomisaburo, Meiji period, 8in (20cm).
£8,000–9,000 *S*

A Japanese cloisonné vase with silver rims, decorated in silverware on a dark blue ground, with seal mark, 7½in (18.5cm) high. **£300–800** *CSK*

A Chinese cabinet, with black lacquer and chinoiserie decoration, 43in (109cm) wide.
£3,000–3,500 *MEA*

A Chinese cabinet, with red lacquer and chinoiserie decoration and engraved and chased brass mounts, enclosing an arrangement of 10 drawers, on a moulded stand with cabriole legs and pad feet, 41in (104cm) wide.
£2,500–3,500 *MEA*

An elmwood cabinet, in 2 sections, the upper section with panel doors mounted with a brass escutcheon and bar locking system, above a similar arrangement in the base, the apron carved with sprays of flowers and foliage, on short legs carved with scrolls, the wood of rich honey colour with a strong grain pattern, Qing Dynasty, 19thC, 92in (233.5cm) high.
£650–850 *S*

A wood and cloisonné enamel cabinet, enclosing 9 panels, Meiji period, 31in (79cm) high.
£4,000–5,000 *S*

An export lacquer cabinet, enclosing one long and 9 shorter drawers of various sizes, with engraved gilt copper mounts, the lacquer and handles of the drawers probably later, early Edo period, 17thC, 36in (91.5cm) wide.
£7,500–10,000 *S*

A wood and lacquer display cabinet, with drawers and sliding door compartments, the panels decorated in iroe hiramakie and takamakie and various inlays, the stand modelled as a bamboo frame, slight damage, Meiji period, 70in (177.5cm) high.
£2,700–3,200 *C*

A Japanese kinji ground rectangular cabinet and stand, on 4 feet with geometric bronze mounts, inlaid in ivory, mother-of-pearl, horn and coral, some pieces of inlay missing, slight damage, 64in (162.5cm) high.
£25,000–3,500 *CSK*

A lacquer cabinet, decorated on a nashiji ground, in gold and coloured takamakie, hiramakie, togidashi and mura-nashiji, with a chinoiserie stand, slight damage, 19thC, 30in (76cm) high.
£3,500–4,500 *S*

A part lacquered wood display cabinet, with some details inlaid in ivory, supported on a matching stand, some pieces lacking, 96in (243.5cm) high.
£14,500–16,000 *S*

A lacquer chest with chinoiserie decoration, late 19thC, 13½in (34cm) high.
£150–200 *STA*

A Japanese lacquer table cabinet, with bronze foliate mounts, decorated in iroe hiramakie and takamakie, slight damage, 10½in (26.5cm) high, and a lacquer table cabinet, 10in (25cm) high. **£350–450** *CSK*

A pair of Chinese Zitan wood and silver wire inlaid side cabinets, with profusely carved panelled doors depicting sea serpents, above similar doors, on square legs, 16in (41cm) wide. **£3,000–3,500** *CSK*

A hardwood desk, the top with inset central panel, with butterfly-shaped bronze lock plates, the legs joined by stretchers enclosing a cracked ice pattern shelf, Qing Dynasty, 47½in (121cm) wide. **£700–1,000** *S*

A gold lacquer shodana, with details in kirigane and powdered raden, inlaid with ivory and some horn, metal mounts and a wood stand, restored, later hinges, 22in (56cm) high. **£2,500–3,500** *S*

A rosewood side table, the panelled top with scroll ends above a pierced apron, centred on a cash embellished with endless knots, on rectangular supports joined by stretchers, Qing Dynasty, 50in (127cm). **£650–800** *S*

A lacquer chest with chinoiserie decoration, enclosing various drawers and compartments, late 19thC, 16in (41cm) high. **£300–350** *STA*

A Chinese export twin flap gateleg games and tea table, with black and polychrome lacquer, slight damage, 32in (81cm) wide. **£1,200–1,700** *C*

A Japanese two-fold ivory screen, carved with panels of lohans and figures at leisure on terraces and in interiors, the reverse with 2 ho-o among flowering trees, the pierced upper friezes with further ho-o, signed, 10in (25cm) high. **£700–900** *CSK*

A rosewood scroll table, the panelled top carved around the edges to simulate bamboo, set above an apron carved to resemble bamboo shoots extending on to the supports, Qing Dynasty, 19thC, 60in (152cm). **£1,200–1,600** *S*

A Chinese coromandel lacquer four-leaf screen, decorated with chinoiserie figures amidst a mountainous river landscape, within a foliate scrolled inner border, the outer border with vases of flowers and foliate sprigs, 18thC, each leaf 19½in (49cm) wide. **£1,500–2,000** *CSK*

Inros

A single case inro, with interior tray, the black lacquer ground carved with karakusa, with a pewter kiku-mon 'clasp' on either side, and the interior of nashiji, signed 'Tsuchida Soetsu', damaged, 17thC, 2½in (6cm).
£1,000–1,200 *S*

A gold lacquer five-case inro, some wear and losses to kirigane, signed 'Kansai ga', 19thC, 3½in (9cm).
£2,000–2,500 *S*

A four-case inro, decorated in gold, pewter and mother-of-pearl, unsigned, slight wear, 3in (8cm).
£1,400–1,700 *S*

A three-case inro, inlaid in tortoiseshell, the cord runners of silver and the interior of nashiji, unsigned, slight damage, 17thC, 2½in (6cm).
£650–850 *S*

Inro

An inro is a small Japanese compartmented medicine box worn on the belt (obi). It is usually attached by the netsuke or toggle.

A wooden two-case inro, crisply carved in relief, signed 'Teisai', 19thC, 2½in (7cm). **£600–800** *S*

A gold lacquer four-case inro, with ivory netsuke of a minogame stalking a crab which appears from inside a clam, unsigned, damaged, 19thC, 4in (10cm).
£1,000–1,200 *S*

A single case inro, with interior tray, in the form of a covered jar, bearing a kinji ground and with a band of black lacquer with hirame and strips of inlaid aogai, a branch of plum blossom in takamakie at the top, the interior is of roiro and kinji, unsigned, slight damage, 19thC, 3in (7.5cm).
£1,000–1,200 *S*

A gold lacquer four-case inro, decorated with Daikoku and Ebisu as Manzai dancers, in gold and coloured takamakie, the faces and hands inlaid with silver, the interior with nashiji, with stamped metal ojime, bearing a peacock in relief, slight wear and damage, signed 'Nikkosai', 3½in (9cm). **£1,500–2,000** *S*

A gold lacquer four-case inro, the inro and netsuke both signed 'Kajikawa saku', with red koro seal, the inro 3½in (9cm).
£2,000–2,500 *S*

A four-case inro, Koma style, the roiro ground with clouds of nashiji, decorated with a Yamabushi priest's oi and axe, resting among maple and paulownia over a stream, the design continued on the reverse, in gold and coloured takamakie with details of inlaid aogai, the interior of nashiji, damaged, unsigned, 19thC, 3½in (9cm), with wood netsuke, signed 'Tokoku'.
£1,500–2,000 *S*

A six-case inro, bearing a nashiji ground and decorated with a long winding snake in white lacquer, and flakes of aogai, the eye of mother-of-pearl and the interior of nashiji, with cloisonné enamel ojime, unsigned, 19thC, 4½in (11cm).
£1,400–2,000 *S*

A four-case inro, in gold, silver and coloured takamakie with details of e-nashiji and gold foil, the interior of nashiji, foil slightly lifting, signed 'Jukakusai Hisataka', with 'kao', 3½in (9cm).
£2,500–3,000 *S*

A four-case rock crystal or quartz inro, the clear material devoid of decoration and with external cord runners, Meiji period, unsigned, 4in (10cm).
£3,500–4,000 *S*

A gold lacquer four-case inro, in the style of Kakosai Shozan, bearing a kinji ground and decorated with 9 grazing horses in gold and coloured takamakie, the interior of nashiji, with lacquered wood manju, decorated with plum blossoms, the inro unsigned, the manju signed 'Kazan', slight damage, 19thC, the inro 3½in (9cm).
£1,500–2,000 *S*

A five-case gold lacquer inro, bearing a kinji ground and decorated with 2 edible fish and bamboo hanging on a tasselled cord, the reverse with wild flowers in gold and coloured takamakie and gold foil, the interior of nashiji, the fish originally covered with gold foil, signed 'Yasushige saku', 19thC, 4in (10cm).
£2,400–2,800 *S*

A three-case inro, formed from stitched cherry bark and decorated with a Naminari mask, baton, eboshi and 2 arrows among large leaves, in gold and red taka-makie, the mask, hat and baton inlaid in enamelled pottery, slight damage, signed 'Narisoku', 19thC, 3in (8cm). **£1,200–1,700** *S*

A four-case black lacquer inro, in the style of Shibata Zeshin, bearing a black ishime ground and decorated in relief with Futen running through the clouds carrying his sack of wind, the figure depicted in an antique style, the sack of gold and silver powder, the interior of kinji and nashiji, unsigned, 19thC, 3in (8cm).
£1,400–1,700 *S*

Ivory

An ivory tusk vase with silver rims, minor pieces missing, signed 'Masayuki', the carved and pieced wooden stand with mythical beast masks above 4 scroll supports, damaged, 19thC, 35in (89cm) high overall.
£3,500–4,500 *C*

> **Miller's is a price GUIDE not a price LIST.**

A sectional ivory group of 2 boys at play, the older boy shaking a winnowing basket containing the younger boy, slight age cracks and minor restoration, signed 'Biho', Meiji period, 6½in (16cm).
£1,700–2,000 *S*

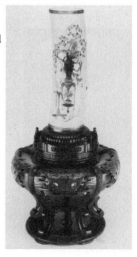

A Japanese ivory carving
of a standing bijin, minor age
cracks and damage, signed,
9½in (23.5cm) high.
£900–1,200 *CSK*

A Japanese ivory carving of
an eagle attacking a wolf,
on raised rockwork, above
3 cubs, the eyes inlaid in
mother-of-pearl and horn,
signed, 9in (23cm) high.
£1,400–1,700 *CSK*

A Japanese ivory carving
of a young warrior, signed,
small age crack, 8in
(20cm) high.
£2,500–3,000 *CSK*

A Chinese ivory figure of a female
archer, dressed in elaborate chain
mail, the details stained black, on
a wood stand, 15in (38cm) high.
£500–600 *CSK*

A Japanese ivory carving,
some age cracks, old
damages, signed
'Masanobu', 5in (13cm)
high. **£350–450** *CSK*

A Chinese red stained ivory
vase with tall ribbed neck,
age cracks, slight rubbing,
inscribed to base, 7in
(18cm) high.
£500–700 *CSK*

A Japanese ivory figure,
11in (28cm) high.
£480–520 *WIL*

An ivory tusk vase, carved in low
relief, inlaid in mother-of-pearl,
stained bone and horn, slight
damage, 19thC, 7in (17.5cm).
£800–1,000 *S*

A Chinese ivory brush pot, carved
in relief with a continuous band of
figures seated at a table playing
Go, figures mounted on an ox and
a horse below wisteria and pine
trees before a rocky landscape,
minor age cracks, 4½in (11cm).
£900–1,200 *CSK*

Jade

A Chinese reddish brown jade carving of
a recumbent horned mythical lion, its
tail flicked to one side, with celadon inclusions,
small chips, Ming Dynasty, 3in (7.5cm)
long, on a wood stand. **£400–500** *CSK*

A Chinese pale celadon jade brush washer,
modelled as an open lotus, carved to the
exterior with a shell and leafy tendrils,
5in (13cm) long, on wood stand, and a
green quartz carving of a reclining Budai,
3½in (9cm) long, on wood stand.
£400–500 *CSK*

Lacquer

A pair of Japanese black lacquer quatrefoil stands, damaged, 8in (20cm) high. **£400–500** *CSK*

A group of 7 lacquer masks, including Ko-beshimi, Asakura-jo, a young woman and a villain, the second signed 'Omi-uchi', and a Kakihan, all with some damage, 18th and 19thC, the largest 9½in (24cm) long.
£2,500–3,500 *C*

A Japanese lacquered and giltwood Noh mask of Tengu, with long nose and bushy eyebrows, the nose damaged, 8in (20cm) high.
£250–300 *CSK*

A Japanese black lacquer zushi, the 2 doors opening to reveal a giltwood throne with flame mandorla, with a Chinese soapstone seated figure of Guanyin wearing robes and holding a scroll and necklace, the details in black and red, damaged, 19thC, the zushi 18in (46cm) high. **£600–700** *CSK*

A late Ming bronze censer, with high loop handles, the body cast with taotie between vertical flanges, early 17thC, 10in (25cm) high. **£600–700** *CSK*

Metal

A late Ming gilt bronze figure of a Buddha, some areas regilt, early 17thC, 16½in (42cm) high.
£1,700–1,900 *CSK*

A Chinese bronze tripod censer, and pierced domed cover, with Buddhistic lion finial, flaring foliate handles, decorated with alternating shaped panels of lion masks and scrolling foliage, set on a raised stand decorated with coiled dragons, 21½in (54cm).
£500–600 *CSK*

A bronze koro and cover, shaped as a persimmon, with a monkey holding a persimmon branch, his coat engraved with gilt birds and leaves, Meiji period, 12in (30.5cm).
£2,200–2,700 *S*

A Japanese bronze group, modelled as a young boy with a tortoise, stamped seal mark, 8in (20cm) high.
£1,200–1,800 *CSK*

A Chinese bronze incense burner, 18thC, 18in (45.5cm) long. **£850–950** *ChC*

A parcel gilt bronze model of a rice farmer, by Miyao Esuke of Tokyo, signed with seal, Meiji period, on a gilt lacquered wood stand, 8in (20cm) high with stand.
£1,200–1,700 *S*

A parcel gilt model of a mask carver, by Miyao Esuke of Tokyo, signed with seal, the mallet replaced, on a gilt lacquered wood stand, 7in (18cm) high with stand.
£1,200–1,700 *S*

A Japanese bronze group, modelled as an eagle, perched on rockwork, looking at a coiled dragon, 22in (56cm) high.
£1,500–2,000 *CSK*

A Japanese bronze figure of a happy traveller, with gilt decoration, signed, 19thC, 9in (22.5cm) high, on a gilt decorated hardwood base.
£1,200–1,700 *HSS*

A late Ming gilt bronze model of a bearded Immortal, wearing a tabbed hat and long flowing robes, early 17thC, 10in (25cm) high.
£250–350 *CSK*

A Japanese patinated bronze model of a rabbit, early 19thC, 3½in (8.5cm) wide.
£450–500 *ChC*

A Japanese bronze group of a monkey, perched on a large persimmon, slight damage, 11½in (29cm) high.
£750–850 *CSK*

A Japanese bronze figure group, modelled as an adult terrapin with 2 babies, signed, 10in (25cm) long.
£1,700–2,000 *HSS*

A Japanese bronze model of an eagle, mid-19thC, 12in (30.5cm).
£2,250–2,500 *ChC*

A pair of Japanese green patinated bronze vases, with everted leafy necks, decorated in part silver in relief with irises, above ropes tying the stems, signed 'Seiya', 11in (28cm) high.
£750–850 *CSK*

A Chinese bronze model of a mythical beast, with long plumed tail, with a snake on its haunches, on a wood stand, old wear, 17th/18thC, 7in (17.5cm) long.
£300–400 *CSK*

A Japanese bronze teapot and cover, with loop handle applied with gilt, silver, copper and bronze insects and butterflies, signed, 4½in (11cm) high.
£700–900 *CSK*

A Japanese green patinated bronze koro, and pierced domed cover, one leg loose, one karashishi missing from base, old damage, 47in (119cm) high.
£3,500–4,500 *CSK*

A Japanese bronze spherical teapot and domed cover, modelled as a leaf, with loop handle, decorated in gilt and silver hirazogan and takazogan with quails among millet, 5in (12.5cm) high.
£700–800 *CSK*

Netsuke

An ivory netsuke of a shishi, lying with its head turned to the right and its forelegs outstretched, its mouth open and containing a loose ball, the ivory is slightly worn and bears a rich patina, unsigned, 18thC, 2in (5cm).
£700–800 *S*

An ivory netsuke of Raiden, the thunder god crawling on hands and knees, holding his geta and with his drum strapped to his back, ivory slightly worn, unsigned, 2⅜in (6cm).
£1,000–1,200 *S*

An ivory netsuke of a shishi, the lion dog standing on one hind paw, the other supported on a large smooth ball, ivory worn, unsigned, 2in (5cm).
£800–900 *S*

The model is recorded as having been carved by Okatomo, Okatori and others of the Kyoto school, working during the latter part of the 18thC.

An ivory netsuke of a woman, by Ueda Kohasai of Osaka, the ivory slightly stained, signed, one finger damaged, 19thC, 1½in (3.5cm).
£700–800 *S*

A boxwood netsuke of a sennin, wearing a large sedge hat, an oni peering through a hole in the top, 18thC, 3in (8cm) high.
£1,500–1,800 *C*

An ivory netsuke of a baby boy, by Toshimune, the ivory stained, signed on an oval tablet, Edo, late 19thC, 2in (5cm).
£750–850 *S*

Netsuke

- Netsuke are Japanese carved toggles, originally made to secure a portable medicine box (inro) or similar item, which hang from the waist on a cord. Usually made of wood or ivory, they date from about 16thC.

- There is keen competition for signed netsuke by acknowledged masters of the art, as well as for those depicting rare or novel subjects.

- Ivory is not necessarily more valuable than wood, especially since ivory netsuke were mass produced for export in the late 19thC.

- Inlaid netsuke often command a premium.

- Copies and fakes are numerous. In a genuine netsuke, the hole is designed to be invisible.

- Recent copies lack patina. The grain of genuine ivory is only visible at certain angles, whereas simulated ivory grain is always visible and very regular.

- Signatures on fakes are often moulded, not carved.

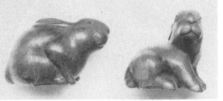

A wood netsuke of a hare, crouched on all fours, with its nose pointed forward, the eyes inlaid, signed 'Yoshinobu', 2in (5cm) wide, and another wood netsuke of a hare, signed 'Masanao', both late 18th/19thC, 1½in (3.5cm) wide.
£1,500–2,000 *C*

Like the fox, the hare is credited with an abnormal span of life and does not become white until it is five hundred years old. It is said to conceive by licking the fur of its male companions, by gazing long at the moon, or by leaping over the waves of Lake Biwa, as in the play Chijubushima.

A boxwood netsuke of a wolf with a hare, its prey caught under the wolf's paw, eyes inlaid in dark and pale horn, signed 'Tomotada', 18thC, 1½in (3.5cm) high.
£800–900 *C*

A Kurogaki wood netsuke figure of a man-faced kirin, the beast standing on its hind legs, its face bearing an angry expression, the eyes of ivory with pupils of dark and light horn, the 2-toned wood slightly worn, unsigned, 24½in (11cm). **£1,400–1,700** *S*

An ivory netsuke of a mother and child, by Kikugawa family, her robe engraved with scattered sunbursts and etched black, signed, Edo, 19thC, 1½in (3.5cm).
£650–750 *S*

A coloured ivory netsuke of a hotei, by Yusaki (Homei), stained red and with inlaid decoration, other details of mother-of-pearl, horn and metal, signed on a pearl tablet, Meiji peroid, 1½in (3.5cm).
£750–950 *S*

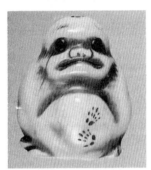

An ivory netsuke of a snowman, by Karaku of Osaka, carved in stained ivory, the eyes inlaid, 3 hand prints on the body, slightly worn and damaged, signed, 19thC, 2in (5cm).
£700–800 *S*

A coloured ivory netsuke of a ronin, by Takamura Koun, the warrior seated on a camp stool, wearing formal dress decorated with a typical formal design, partly painted and with inlaid details, signed on a red lacquer tablet, Meiji period, 1½in (3.5cm).
£1,200–1,700 *S*

A coral group netsuke of 2 coral divers, by Ryukosai Jugyoku of Edo, the fishermen carved from umimatsu, climbing and sitting on the large coral rock, their skirts with traces of green pigment, signed on a green stained ivory tablet, 19thC, 1½in (3.5cm).
£850–1,000 *S*

A wood netsuke of a rabbit, 1in (2.5cm), and another of an egg tester with an egg raised to his eye, signed 'Hidari Issan', 2½in (5.5cm) high.
£700–800 *C*

A painted ivory netsuke of Okame, by Meiun, painted and inlaid with various materials, signed on an inlaid tablet, late 19thC, 2in (4.5cm).
£750–850 *S*

The work is in the style of Homeo (Yasuaki).

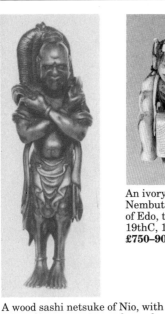

An ivory netsuke group of Oni Nembutsu and son, by Gyokusen of Edo, the ivory stained, signed, 19thC, 1½in (3.5cm).
£750–900 *S*

An ivory netsuke of Kinko on his carp, by Masatsugu of Osaka, the sennin seated on the back of the carp, reading a calligraphic scroll, the ivory slightly worn and bearing good colour, signed in an oval reserve, early 19thC, 2½in (6cm).
£750–800 *S*

A wood sashi netsuke of Nio, with grimacing expression and a rush mat strapped to his back, signed '...kawa Yutaka', 19thC, 4⅛in (10.5cm) long.
£2,000–2,500 *C*

Himotoshi

The himotoshi is the drilled hole in a netsuke or inro through which the cord passes. It is often artfully disguised as part of the carving.

A wood netsuke of a cat, seated on a circular mat, the eyes inlaid with pale translucent horn, the wood slightly worn, unsigned, early 19thC, 2in (5cm).
£1,400–1,600 *S*

A wood netsuke of a turtle, by Hideharu of Nagoya, the wood stained and the eyes inlaid, signed in a rectangular reserve, 19thC, 2in (5cm).
£1,200–1,500 *S*

A wood netsuke of a desiccated fish, lying on its side, its mouth open, the himotoshi passing through the slit stomach, and the eyes inlaid with shell, unsigned, early 19thC, 5in (12.5cm).
£650–850 *S*

A wood netsuke of a piebald puppy, by Masanao of Ise, Yamada, holding the cord of a discarded sandal in its mouth, one hind leg forming the himotoshi, the wood stained and the eye pupils inlaid, signed, 19thC, 1½in (4cm).
£650–850 *S*

An ivory netsuke of a dog, by Kyoto school, the leg forming the himotoshi, eyes inlaid, ivory slightly worn, unsigned, 19thC, 2in (5cm).
£750–900 *S*

A wood netsuke manju in the form of a ho-o bird, by Toyokazu of Tamba, carved and pierced in crisp detail, the one visible eye inlaid with pale translucent horn, signed, 19thC, 1½in (4cm).
£870–1,000 *S*

A wood netsuke of a woman, by Masanao of Ise, Yamada, the wood slightly worn, good patina, signed, 19thC, 1½in (4cm).
£800–900 *S*

A coloured ivory netsuke of a sake seller, by Tomei, with painted details, and inlaid with various materials, signed on a red lacquer tablet, Meiji period, 2in (4.5cm).
£600–700 *S*

A boxwood netsuke of a monkey, one arm forming the homotoshi, the wood lightly stained and the eyes of pale translucent horn, unsigned, late 19thC, 1½in (4cm).
£650–800 *S*

A stained ivory netsuke, carved as a snail crawling over a roof tile, signed, 2in (5cm) wide.
£400–450 *CSK*

An ivory netsuke, modelled as a figure of Ebisu holding a large sack beside him, 1½in (3.5cm) high.
£250–300 *CSK*

An ivory netsuke, carved as a frog wrapped in a lotus leaf with a snail on top, 2in (5cm) wide.
£200–300 *CSK*

Wood

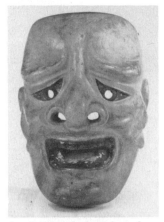

A painted and gessoed wood Noh mask, of a male head with grimacing expression and protruding tongue, old wear, 8in (20cm) long. **£300–500** *CSK*

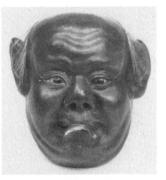

A painted and gessoed wood Noh mask, modelled as the head of an old man, with inlaid glass eyes, wear to lip, 3½in (8.5cm) long.
£75–100 *CSK*

A Chinese hardwood box and cover, in the form of archaic jade, the cover carved with a central shou symbol within stylised scrolls and pomegranate, within shaped handles, 18th/19thC, 7in (17.5cm) wide.
£450–550 *CSK*

A boxwood sceptre, the stems bound with later cord, 19thC, 19in (48cm).
£1,700–2,000 *S*

A figured carving, c1890, 19in (48cm).
£150–200 *WAG*

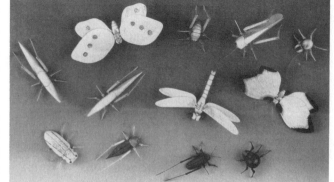

A collection of 12 Japanese wood and ivory articulated models of insects, including 2 butterflies, a dragonfly, various cicadas and 2 stag beetles, 3½ to 1½in (8.5 to 3.5cm), in a wood box.
£2,000–3,000 *CSK*

Kozuka

Two Goto school shakudo kozuka, both bearing a nanako ground, the first decorated with 2 monkeys, the other with a long-tailed bird on a flowering cherry branch, details in gold and silver, unsigned, Edo period, one 17thC, the other 18th/19thC.
£500–600 *S*

Two shibuichi kozuka, one with detail inlaid in gold, silver and copper, signed 'Togakushi Masatsune' with kao, the other inlaid in mother-of-pearl, lacquer and horn, the reverse with a silver and gold linear design, Edo period, 19thC.
£1,400–1,700 *S*

Two Nara school kozuka, the first of iron, inlaid with flowers in gold, copper, shakudo and shibuichi, signed 'Tou', with seal 'Yasuchika', the second of shibuichi, signed 'Tsuchiya Tsunechika, shidai Yasuchika, Edo period, 18th/19thC.
£650–750 *S*

The maker of the first was possibly Yasuchika I, while that of the second, Kunechika, (called Tsunechika) was the third son of Yasuchika V.

A Goto style shakudo kozuka, decorated with gold and silver on a silvered ground, within a polished shakudo frame, unsigned, Edo period, 19thC.
£750–850 *S*

Kozuka

A kozuka is a Japanese sword sheath, usually highly decorated.

Tsuba

A Kyo-Shoami tsuba, carved and pierced with a bird perched among foliate branches, details in gold nunome, unsigned, with tomobako, bearing an hakogaki by Dr. K. Torigoe, early Edo period, late 17thC, 3in (8cm).
£500–600 *S*

A Namban tsuba, of mokko form, carved with the letters 'YQH' and 'FU', the reverse with a band of karakusa within the raised rim, bearing traces of gold nunome, unsigned, with tomobako, Edo period, 17th/18thC, 2⅜in (6cm).
£450–550 *S*

Tsuba

Tsuba is the name of the guard on a Japanese sword, usually consisting of an ornamental plate.

Three Sukashi tsuba, the first of Tosa Myochin type, bearing a simple divided cross within the pipe rim, the second of similar type, the bamboo pipe rim enclosing a bamboo cross, the third of Ko-Umetada type, pierced with 2 large holes, flanking over large ryohitsu, some rust to all, unsigned, 3 to 3⅜in (8 to 8.5cm).
£600–700 *S*

A tsuba, by Umetada Tomotsugu, inlaid in hirazogan with a flowering plum tree, details in gold, silver and copper, the reverse with a similar design, the edge with a fine band of karakusa in gilt takazogan, signed, with buff coloured NBTHK paper, 3⅜in (8.5cm).   **£700–800** *S*

An iron tsuba, Nara style, carved with a running tiger beneath a rain shower, details in gold and silver, unsigned, late 18thC, 3in (7.5cm).   **£500–600** *S*

A Bushu school tsuba, by Masanori, carved and pierced with flowering cherry branches, slight details in gold, signed 'Bushu ju Masanori', with tomobako, Edo period, 19thC, 3in (7.5cm).
£300–400 *S*

Arms & Armour

A silver mounted aikuchi, blade
by Yamato Daijo Masanori,
surface scratches, 17thC, mounts
19thC, 12in (31cm).
£5,000–6,000 S

A silver and enamel mounted
aikuchi, the blade 8in (21cm),
signed 'Yoshimitsu', 19thC.
£4,200–5,000 S

A Shinshinto aikuchi, the blade
by Yoshitsugu, 7in (18cm),
mounts by Hirotaka, 19thC.
£4,000–5,000 S

An aikuchi, blade attributed to
Kotaro Moritoshi, mounts by Goto
Sei-i, both 19thC.
£7,000–9,000 S
*With Hozon Token certificate,
No. 312045, 1988, attributing the
blade to Kotaro Moritoshi.*

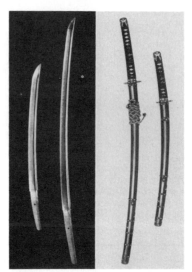

A Goto-style mounted daisho, the
dai after Tadatsuna, 18th/19thC,
sho by Kanesada, 19thC, 28in
(71cm), blade 18in (46cm).
£10,000–12,000 S

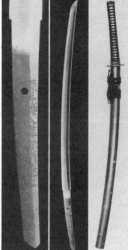

Daisho

A pair of Samurai swords, one long (dai) called the katana,
the other short (sho) called the wakisashi.

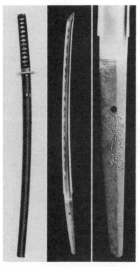

A Shinshinto katana, blade
by Moritoshi, dated '1840',
mounts 19thC, 24in (61cm).
£7,000–8,000 S

An aikuchi, the blade
16thC, the mounts 19thC.
£1,400–1,700 S

A pistol mounted as a
tanto, 19thC.
£2,600–3,000 C

An aikuchi, the blade 11in
(29cm), 19thC.
£1,300–1,700 S

A katana, the blade by Nyudo
Shoken Motooki, dated '1861', the
mounts 19thC, 26in (66cm).
£4,000–5,000 S

Tanto

A tanto is a Japanese Samurai dagger used with the tachi.

A tanto, the blade after Shinkai, 10in (25cm), 19thC.
£2,600–3,000 *S*

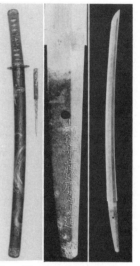

A wakisashi blade, by Wakasaka Fuyuhiro II, c1615, 20½in (52cm).
£1,000–1,500 *S*

A wakisashi blade, 18th/19thC, 20in (51cm), in shirasaya.
£1,300–1,700 *S*

A wakisashi, 17thC, the blade 18in (45cm), mounts 19thC.
£1,500–2,000 *S*

A tanto, the blade inscribed 'Yoshimitsu', 19thC, 8in (20cm).
£1,200–1,700 *S*

A wakisashi, the blade by Kazuma (no) Kami Munemichi, late 17th/early 18thC, mounts 19thC.
£6,000–7,000 *S*

A wakisashi, the blade banded with black lacquer, 16thC, 13in (33cm), mounts 19thC, signed 'Isshi hitsu'.
£1,200–1,700 *S*

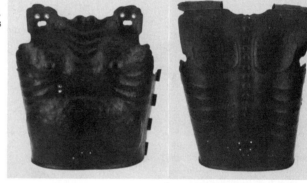

A russet iron mempo, with detachable tengu nose, the interior lacquered in red, 4-plate yodarakake, chipped, Edo period, 9in (23cm). **£1,000–1,500** *S*

A repoussé iron do, formed as a human torso, the ribs and nipples embossed, the left gyoyo with a constellation, the right lacking, the interior lined with lacquered cloth, 18th/19thC.
£6,000–7,000 *C*

A russet iron so-men, the upper part and nose section detachable, the ears riveted, horse hair moustache, the interior of upper part lined with brocade, lower part lacquered in red, with 3-plate yodarakake, chipped, one fixing to nose section lost, probably 18thC, 13in (33cm).
£2,500–3,500 *S*

A russet iron mempo, of 4-part construction with detachable nose and horse hair moustache, the teeth and interior lacquered, 5-plate yodarakake, chipped and restored, Edo period, 10in (25cm).
£1,000–1,200 *S*

SNUFF BOTTLES

A famille rose porcelain figure shaped snuff bottle, modelled as a reclining female, wearing a blue jacket and green trousers, with her head resting on one hand and one leg crossed over the other, the stopper in the form of her left foot, restored, 19thC.
£800–1,000 *S(S)*

A seal-type glass overlay snuff bottle, opaque white overlaid in brown and carved on one side with a figure on a horse and the other with geese amongst plants, Yangzhou School, c1880.
£2,200–2,700 *S(S)*

A Jasper snuff bottle, the stone of mottled green and ochre colour with red inclusions, 1750-1850.
£300–350 *S(S)*

A fine Asagi-ito-odoshi yoko-hagi okegawa-do, signed 'Myochin Muneyoshi saku', 19thC.
£7,500–9,000 *C*

A 'famille rose' moulded porcelain snuff bottle, moulded in relief with the 18 lohan in various poses on a green wave ground, minor chips, red painted four-character Qianlong seal mark, 19thC.
£300–350 *S(S)*

Miscellaneous

A painted fan, by Shiko Munakata, decorated in ink and colour on paper, depicting foliage, with a calligraphic inscription, in giltwood frame, glazed, signed 'Shiko' and seal Shiko, 15½ by 25in (39 by 64cm).
£2,500–3,500 *S*

A cinnabar lacquer snuff bottle, carved with 4 fighting dragons on a ground of waves, lacking stopper, 19thC.
£300–400 *S(S)*

A porcelain snuff bottle, covered in a speckled Robin's egg blue glaze, 19thC.
£400–450 *S(S)*

A chinese embroidered silk headband, c1900.
£30–40 *STA*

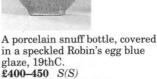

A glass snuff bottle, of deep dark yellow colour, carved on either side with fish, 19thC.
£300–350 *S(S)*

Locate the source
The source of each illustration in Miller's can be found by checking the code letters below each caption with the list of contributors.

A porcelain snuff bottle, white glazed ovoid bottle encased in a yellow glazed two-handled open basket, minor chip, 19thC.
£400–500 *S(S)*

A cinnabar lacquer snuff bottle, carved with 2 bands of fruiting melon vine on a cell pattern ground, incised Qianlong seal mark, 19thC.
£500–600 *S(S)*

A four-colour overlay glass snuff bottle, the opaque white bottle overlaid in green, yellow, blue and pink, carved with flowering plants, 19thC.
£450–500 *S(S)*

A yellow glass snuff bottle, with lemon colour metal and jade stopper, 19thC.
£200–250 *S(S)*

A cinnabar lacquer snuff bottle, carved with butterflies on lilies against a cell pattern ground, chipped, late 19thC.
£100–150 *S(S)*

A cinnabar lacquer snuff bottle, carved with 2 panels of figures in landscape within floral meander borders, incised Qianlong seal mark, 19thC.
£300–350 *S(S)*

An ivory snuff bottle, carved as a giant double gourd, a crouching child clinging to one side of it, matching stopper, chipped.
£170–220 *S(S)*

An amber snuff bottle, with pale opaque inclusions, the shoulders carved with a fierce mask and ring handles.
£400–500 *S(S)*

A glass snuff bottle, of deep dark yellow colour, carved on one side with a lion-dog amongst cloud scrolls, the other with a temple emerging from clouds and flanked by birds, 19thC.
£520–600 *S(S)*

An overlay glass snuff bottle, the white bottle overlaid in red, uncarved except the foot, chipped, 19thC.
£250–300 *S(S)*

A jasper snuff bottle, the mottled brown and yellow stone carved with blossoming lotus.
£200–300 *S(S)*

A wood snuff bottle, inlaid with metal wire with a floral design, and another decorated with mother-of-pearl, 20thC.
£100–150 *S(S)*

AFRICAN ART

A Senufo Sikasso figure, the smooth coiffure divided in 3 parts, raised square scarification on the back of the neck, incised scarification on the abdomen, rich brown patina, 13½in (34cm) high.
£9,200–11,000 *S*

This type of figure is alleged to represent Katielo, the mother goddess. It has been sculpted in the style of the bronzes of the Senufo Sikasso area.

A Dogon maternity figure, the bent legs supporting an elongated torso, hands resting on the abdomen, conical breasts, the angular shoulders beneath a cylindrical neck and a massive head with beard, arrow shaped nose and striped coiffure under a flat base, a baby in the back, weathered patina, 15in (38cm) high.
£7,500–10,000 *S*

A Dogon maternity figure, with smooth oily patina, 21½in (54cm).
£15,000–17,000 *S*

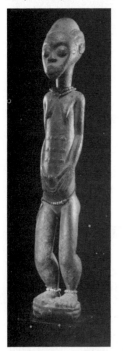

A Senufo Deble standing male figure, scarification on the cheeks and around the mouth, dark brown patina, Inagaki base, 35½in (90cm) high.
£40,000–50,000 *S*

A Baule female figure, with brown encrusted patina, 19in (48cm) high.
£14,000–29,000 *S*

The spirit spouse for whom a figure is made will indicate to the sculptor, the client, or the diviner, how the figure should be carved, and sometimes where a tree in the forest should be used.
Only 2 similar figures of such quality and with the same scarifications on the upper torso are known and presently kept in the Metropolitan Museum, New York.

A Dogon figure, the square base supporting the angular body with a raised arm, the elongated neck supporting a diminutive head with triangular nose, weathered patina, 10½in (27cm) high.
£12,000–15,000 *S*

A Mossi figure, red rich patina, 26in (66cm) high.
£4,000–5,000 *S*

An Archaic Dan Kran mask, with brown patina, back with an old label from Express Transport reading 'Preteur Tristan Tzara, Masque Dan, BeBo576', 9in (22cm) high.
£7,500–10,000 *S*

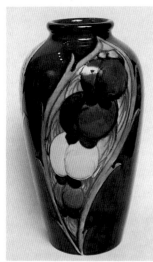

A Moorcroft Wisteria Peacock Feather design vase, c1928, 12in (31cm) high.
£1,100–1,300 *LIO*

A Moorcroft MacIntyre Alhambra pattern vase, c1903, 11in (28cm) high.
£900–1,000 *LIO*

A Moorcroft Pansy vase, c1914, 10in (25cm) high.
£1,300–1,600 *LIO*

A Moorcroft MacIntyre Florian Ware pedestal vase, c1900, 12in (31cm) high.
£1,400–1,800 *LIO*

A Moorcroft Spring Flower vase, c1949, 12⅝in (32cm) high.
£650–750 *LIO*

A Moorcroft MacIntyre Barraware design octagonal bowl, c1903, 6in (15cm) diam.
£450–550 *LIO*

A Moorcroft MacIntyre Florian Ware vase, c1900, 8in (20cm) high.
£850–950 *LIO*

A Moorcroft Waving Corn pattern bowl, c1930, 8in (20cm) diam. **£400–500** *LIO*

A Moorcroft MacIntyre Tulip vase, c1905, 10in (25cm) high.
£1,500–2,000 *LIO*

A Moorcroft MacIntyre 18thC design trio, c1905.
£300–400 *LIO*

l. A Moorcroft MacIntyre Wisteria pattern jardinière, c1912, 8in (20cm) high.
£2,000–2,500 *LIO*

A Clarice Cliff Bizarre Stamford shape Gibralter pattern teapot, milk jug and sugar bowl, chip to cover, printed factory marks.
£1,800–2,000 *CSK*

A Clarice Cliff 'teepee' teapot, designed in 1951 by Betty Sylvester, 7½in (19cm) high.
£700–800 *HEW*

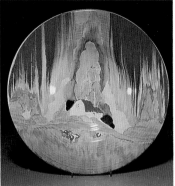

A Clarice Cliff wall plate, decorated in Forest Glen pattern, printed factory marks, 18in (46cm) diam.
£1,400–1,600 *CSK*

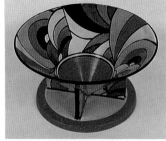

A Clarice Cliff footed Conical bowl in the Swirl design, shape 382, 9in (23cm) diam.
£2,000–2,200 *HEW*

A Clarice Cliff Conical coffee set, in Orange Trees and House pattern, pot 7in (17.5cm) high.
£1,800–1,900 *HEW*

A Clarice Cliff Appliqué Bizarre Conical coffee set, in the Avignon pattern, printed and painted marks, pot 7in (17.5cm) high.
£4,000–4,500 *CSK*

A Clarice Cliff Bizarre umbrella stand, decorated with Sliced Fruit pattern, printed factory marks, 27½in (69.5cm) high.
£2,000–2,500 *CSK*

A Clarice Cliff Bizarre Dover jardinière, in the Summerhouse pattern, 8in (20cm) diam.
£1,100–1,300 *CSK*

A Clarice Cliff ribbed charger, decorated in Clovelly pattern, printed factory marks, 18in (46cm) diam.
£1,000–1,200 *CSK*

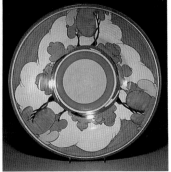

Two Clarice Cliff Bizarre table decorations, 'Age of Jazz', printed factory marks, largest 7½in (19cm) high.
£3,800–4,800 each *CSK*

A Clarice Cliff Daffodil shape Alton design jug, c1930.
£500–550 *HEW*

A Clarice Cliff Fantasque Bizarre ribbed wall charger, decorated in the Blue Autumn pattern, printed factory marks, 18in (46cm) diam.
£2,000–2,500 *CSK*

A Clarice Cliff Bizarre Athens shape jug, decorated in Geometric pattern, early mark, 9in (23cm) high. **£275–300** *WTA*

A Clarice Cliff biscuit barrel, decorated in early Geometric pattern, 5½in (14cm) high. **£400–420** *HEW*

A Clarice Cliff Fantasque Bizarre Stamford shape tea set, in the Red Roofs pattern, restored, printed factory marks, teapot 4½in (11.5cm) high. **£3,000–3,500** *CSK*

A Clarice Cliff Bizarre Goldstone pattern jug, shape number 564, 7in (17.5cm) high. **£175–200** *WTA*

Three Clarice Cliff Bizarre Lotus shape jugs, Newport Pottery, c1931, 11in (28cm), **£1,000–1,500 each**, and *r*. a Clarice Cliff Fantasque Blue W pattern Lotus shape jug for Wilkinson Ltd., c1930, 11in (28cm) high. **£2,500–2,700** *S*

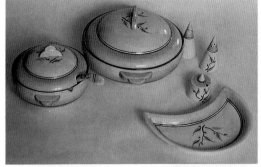

l. A Clarice Cliff 12 place setting dinner service. **£1,000–1,500** *ASA*

A Clarice Cliff Inspiration Bizarre ribbed charger, printed and painted factory marks, 17in (43cm) diam. **£1,500–1,700** *CSK*

A Clarice Cliff Lotus shape jug, in Sunray design, 12in (30.5cm) high. **£2,000–2,300** *HEW*

Two Clarice Cliff Inspiration Bizarre Persian pattern vases, painted factory marks, *l*. **£2,800–3,000** *r*. **£2,000–2,200** *CSK*

A Clarice Cliff Bizarre old Newport shape bowl, in Green Capri pattern. **£225–250** *WTA*

A Burleigh ceramic wall mask of a Red Indian, 6in (15cm) high. **£120–140** *WTA*

A Clarice Cliff Bizarre early Geometric pattern vase, shape number 264, marked, 8in (20cm) high. **£250–270** *WTA*

A Clarice Cliff Greek shape jug, decorated in Canterbury Bells pattern, 9in (23cm) high. **£300–350** *WTA*

A Wadeheath painted jug, 11in (28cm) high. **£65–75** *WTA*

A Minton tube line decorated jardinière, c1890, 10in (25cm) diam. **£250–350** *ASA*

A Clarice Cliff Bizarre early Geometric pattern Perth jug, marked, 5in (13cm) high. **£225–250** *WTA*

A Gustavsberg pottery dish, overlaid with silver, Swedish, c1930, 8in (20cm) diam. **£150–200** *ASA*

A Charlotte Rhead double-handled vase, decorated in Persian Rose pattern, 8in (20cm) high. **£120–140** *WTA*

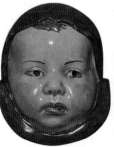

An Arthur Woods ceramic wall mask, 5½in (14cm) high. **£80–100** *WTA*

A Carlton Ware two-person tea set. **£200–225** *WTA*

A Burleigh early Geometric jug, 10in (25cm) high. **£80–100** *WTA*

A Clarice Cliff ceramic wall mask, 6in (15cm) high. **£350–400** *WTA*

A Shelley Regency shape two-person tea set. **£180–200** *WTA*

A porcelain bowl, by Dame Lucie Rie, the interior in manganese inlaid with vertical sgraffito, the exterior with unglazed band of sgraffito, impressed 'LR' seal, c1960, 8½in (20cm) diam.
£2,500–3,000 *C*

A stoneware bowl, by Dame Lucie Rie, the well with green mottled band, impressed 'LR' seal, c1960, 13in (33cm).
£2,000–3,000 *C*

A porcelain sgraffito bowl, by Dame Lucie Rie, the well with inlaid pink cross hatching, restored, impressed 'LR' mark, c1978, 10in (25cm) diam.
£2,000–3,000 *C*

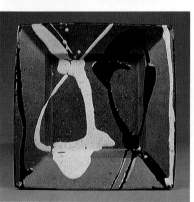

A stoneware press moulded square dish, by Shoji Hamada, decorated with tenmoku and ash rice-husk pours, the reverse with tenmoku glaze, c1956, 12in (30.5cm) square. **£6,000–7,000** *C*

A 'knitted' stoneware sgraffito bowl, by Dame Lucie Rie, impressed 'LR' seal, c1978, 10½in (27cm) diam.
£2,500–3,500 *C*

A stoneware bottle, by Dame Lucie Rie, the rim incised with radiating lines, impressed 'LR' seal, c1967, 16in (40cm) high.
£6,000–8,000 *C*

A St. Ives ying qing porcelain bottle by Bernard Leach, impressed 'BL' and seal, c1960, 9in (23cm) high.
£1,300–1,600 *C*

A stoneware composite vase, by Hans Coper, covered in a matt black glaze, impressed 'HC' seal, c1970, 8in (20cm).
£3,500–4,500 *C*

l. A stoneware goblet vase, by Hans Coper, with interior funnel, impressed 'HC' seal, 5½in (14cm) high.
£4,500–5,000 *C*

A 'Counterpoint' vase, by Elizabeth Fritsch, 1989, 11½in (29.5cm).
£3,000–4,000 *C*

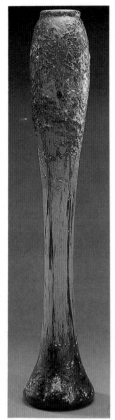

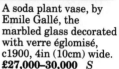

An enamelled smoked glass two-handled vase, by Emile Gallé, with stylised landscape in Japanese taste, enamelled mark to underside, c1880, 7in (17.5cm) high.
£19,500–20,000 *S*

A soda plant vase, by Emile Gallé, the marbled glass decorated with verre églomisé, c1900, 4in (10cm) wide.
£27,000–30,000 *S*

An impressionistic Mimosa Blossom vase, by Schneider, wheel cut mark with an engraved urn, c1915, 30½in (77.5cm) high.
£12,000–13,000 *S*

A cameo glass lamp, by Emile Gallé, decorated with cherry blossom and humming birds, c1900, 10in (25cm) high.
£18,000–20,000 *S*

An Austrian copper overlaid glass vase, c1900, 13in (33cm) high.
£700–1,000 *ASA*

A Lalique satin smoked glass vase, Bacchantes, damaged, wheel cut mark, 9½in (24cm) high.
£3,800–4,200 *CSK*

A painted steel and plastic lamp, by Martine Bedin for Memphis, with label, 1981, 12in (30cm).
£300–500 *S*

A set of 4 Stuart enamelled crystal sundae dishes, c1920, 4in (10cm) high.
£100–150 *ASA*

A Loetz glass dish, with pedestal base, 10in (25cm) diam.
£500–700 *ASA*

A Daum table lamp, acid-etched with fruiting vines, with applied and carved snails, signed, 19in (48cm) high. **£40,000–45,000** *C*

An acid-etched and carved cameo bowl, by Emile Gallé, marked and stamped, 9in (23cm) high. **£4,500–5,000** *C*

A Lalique Source de la Fontaine frosted glass sculpture, Telphuse, on a later wood base, minor damage, 18½in (47cm) high. **£5,000–6,000** *CSK*

A decorated glass lamp, marked 'Daum Nancy', c1900, 14in (36cm) high. **£10,500–11,500** *S*

A decorated, etched and enamelled glass vase, marked 'Daum Nancy', c1900, 16in (40cm) high. **£6,000–6,500** *S*

A carved cameo glass peony lamp, by Emile Gallé, engraved mark, c1900, 12in (30cm) high. **£4,500–5,000** *S*

A pair of Austrian wrought iron and brass candlesticks, c1890, 16½in (42cm) high. **£300–400** *ASA*

A cameo glass Clematis vase, by Emile Gallé, marked, c1900, 16in (40.5cm) high. **£5,500–6,000** *S*

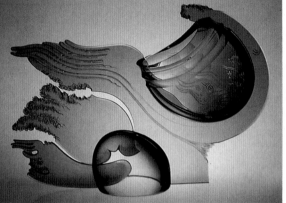

A blown and cut glass sculpture, by Ray Flavell, entitled Eye of the Storm, with engraved and sandblasted decoration, signed, 1993, 14in (36cm) high. **£4,000–4,500** *C*

A cameo glass vase, by Emile Gallé, 8in (20cm) high. **£700–900** *ASA*

A carved cameo glass Wistaria vase, against a martelé ground, with engraved mark 'Daum Nancy', c1900, 10in (25cm) high. **£9,500–10,000** *S*

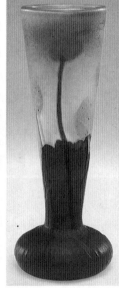

A deeply carved cameo glass vase, L'onion, marked, dated 1900, 13in (33cm) high. **£23,500–25,000** *S*

An etched and textured glass geometric lamp, chromium plated metal mounts, marked 'Daum Nancy, France', c1920. **£9,500–10,000** *S*

An Arts & Crafts leaded glass table lamp, 23in (59cm) high.
£1,000–1,500 *ASA*

A satin finished glass vase, Borromée, by Lalique, decorated with peacocks, etched in script, 9in (23cm) high.
£16,000–16,500 *C*

A Tiffany Studios leaded glass and bronze Poppy table lamp, shade stamped and numbered '1531', base stamped '443', 26½in (67.5cm) high.
£16,500–18,000 *C*

An opalescent glass vase, by Lalique, Formose, rim ground slightly, moulded mark, 7in (18cm) high.
£4,800–5,200 *CSK*

A Lalique hand mirror, Narcisse Couché, etched mark, 12in (30cm) long.
£1,000–1,200 *CSK*

A glass vase, by Schneider, decorated with internal bubbling and applied trails, etched mark, c1930, 13in (33cm) high.
£3,800–4,200 *S*

A Clutha vase, by A. J. Couper & Sons, designed by Christopher Dresser, c1880, 18⅜in (47.5cm) high. £9,000–9,500 *C*

A pâte de verre and wrought iron mask lamp, by Gabriel Argy-Rousseau, marked, c1920, 5½in (14cm) high.
£6,500–7,000 *S*

Two Le Verre Français cameo bowls, each decorated with a band of fruit, incised factory marks, 10in (25cm) high.
£1,500–2,000 *CSK*

A clean-lined cast brass table lamp on a tripod base, fitted with a fluted finely acid-etched glass shade, c1895. £650–750 *TOL*

A mould-blown carved and acid-etched triple overlay Calla Lily vase, by Emile Gallé, signed, 14½in (37cm) high.
£50,000–55,000 *C*

A French bronze bust, entitled 'Mignon', cast from a model by Emmanuele Villanis, inscribed and dated '1896', 22½in (57cm) high. **£1,800–2,200** *C*

A brass and copper champagne bucket, 8in (20cm) high. **£200–300** *ASA*

Two French bronzes, each cast from a model by Emmanuele Villanis, *l.* inscribed 'Cendrillon', signed, c1895, 12in (30.5cm) high, *r.* inscribed 'Dalila', signed, c1890, 12½in (32cm) high. **£1,500–2,000 each** *C*

A Goldscheider terracotta bust of Huckleberry Finn, c1900, 21in (53cm) high. **£500–800** *ASA*

A Puiforcat white metal bowl and cover, on a circular foot, with jade ring finial, stamped 'Jean E Puiforcat' and French marks, 9½in (24cm) high, with original grey cotton satin bag. **£26,000–30,000** *C*

A silver and enamel pot and cover, by Thomas Latham & Ernest Morton and Laurent, maker's mark, Birmingham 1901, 3½in (9cm). **£1,000–1,200** *S*

A French gilt bronze figure of an actress, cast from a model by Agathon Léonard, entitled La Costume, signed and impressed, late 19thC. 21in (52.5cm) high. **£5,000–6,000** *C*

A French parcel gilt bronze group, entitled Le Rêve et Gloire au Travail, signed 'Math Moreau', 20thC, 42in (106.5cm) high. **£4,000–6,000** *C*

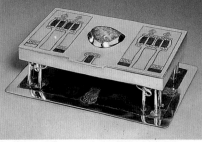

A silver and enamel cigarette box, by W. H. Haseler & Co., designed for Liberty & Co., minor loss to enamel, stamped maker's marks 'WHH', Birmingham 1904, 8in (20cm) wide. **£14,000–15,000** *C*

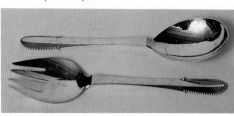

A pair of large silver servers, by Georg Jensen, c1930. **£300–500** *ASA*

A silvered bronze bust, by Merigh Bearing, with foundry seal, 11in (28cm) high. **£500–800** *ASA*

A French gilt bronze figural lamp, by Emmanuelle Villanis, fitted for electricity, signed, 31in (79cm) high.
£3,500–4,500 *C*

A Puirforcat white metal and parcel gilt soup tureen, on circular tray, stamped 'Puirforcat, Paris', with French marks, the bowl 11in (28cm) diam, the tray 15in (38cm diam, 4,972g.
£8,000–10,000 *C*

A Hagenauer electroplate group, modelled as a jazz band, each piece stamped 'wHw, Made in Austria', 11½in (28.5cm) high.
£4,000–5,000 *CSK*

An Art Nouveau gilt bronze figure, by Louis-Convers, signed in the bronze, 12½in (31.5cm) high.
£1,300–1,600 *CSK*

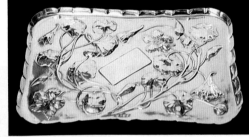

An Art Nouveau silver tray, c1900, 11in (28cm) wide.
£200–300 *ASA*

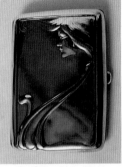

A silver cigarette case, by William Hutton.
£200–300 *ASA*

A French parcel gilt bronze bust, by Eugène Laurent, signed and stamped, 22in (56cm) high.
£4,000–6,000 *C*

An Art Nouveau silver dressing table set, c1900.
£200–300 *ASA*

An green Art Nouveau terracotta figure, La Perla, by Rossi, 36in (92cm) high.
£1,500–2,000 *ASA*

A seven-piece brass and marble desk set, by Josef Hoffmann, comprising: a box with hinged cover, inkwell with hinged cover, candlestick, cylindrical beaker, 2 pen trays and a paperweight, c1908. **£4,000–6,000** *S*

A bronze and ivory figure, 'Vanity', by F. Preiss, 9in (22.5cm) high. **£3,500–4,500** *ASA*

A cold painted bronze and ivory figure, 'Dancer of Palmyra', cast and carved by D. H. Chiparus, 17in (43cm) high. **£5,000–5,500** *CSK*

A cold painted bronze and ivory figure, 'Danseuse au Bandeau', cast and carved by Paul Philippe, 26in (66cm) high. **£9,000–9,500** *CSK*

A cold painted bronze and ivory figure, 'Hindu Dancer', by Chiparus. **£6,800–7,200** *CSK*

A cold painted bronze and ivory figure, 'The Nimble Dancer', by D. H. Chiparus, on onyx base, c1920, 18½in (47cm). **£8,000–9,000** *S*

A cold painted and patinated bronze and ivory figure, 'Danseuse sur Pointe', by J. Descomps, 27½in (70cm) high. **£8,000–9,000** *C*

A pink and grey tinted gilt bronze and ivory figure, 'Spring Awakening', by F. Preiss, signed, on a stepped black onyx column. **£9,000–10,000** *CSK*

A bronze figure, by Marquet, 'Dagger Dancer', 19in (48cm) high. **£1,500–1,800** *ASA*

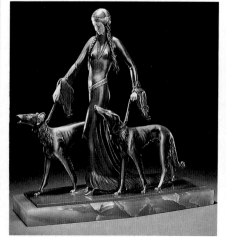

A bronze and ivory figure, 'Innocence', by D. H. Chiparus, 9½in (23.5cm) high. **£3,000–4,000** *ASA*

A bronze and ivory figure, 'Little Sad One', by D. H. Chiparus, c1920. **£4,000–5,000** *ASA*

A bronze and ivory sculpture, 'The Aristrocrats', cast and carved from a model by Professor Otto Poertzel, mounted on a shaped onyx base, 16in (40cm) high. **£10,500–12,500** *C*

A patinated gilt bronze and ivory figure, 'Dancer with Ring', by D. H. Chiparus. **£9,000–10,000** *CSK*

A cold painted bronze, ivory and marble figure, 'Theban Dancer', by Claire J. R. Colinet, marked, c1930, 10½in (26.5cm).
£9,000–10,000 *S*

A cold painted bronze, ivory and onyx figure, 'The Flute Player', by Ferdinand Preiss, c1930, 19in (48cm).
£5,500–6,500 *S*

A cold painted bronze, ivory and marble figure, 'Dancer in Hooped Skirt', by Paul Philippe, marked, c1930, 16in (41cm).
£4,500–6,000 *S*

An Arts and Crafts turquoise and silver necklace, c1900.
£300–400 *ASA*

A cold painted gilt bronze and ivory group, 'Les Amis de Toujours', cast and carved by D. H. Chiparus, on shaped brown onyx base, 14in (35cm) high.
£7,500–8,500 *CSK*

A cold painted silvered and gilt bronze and ivory figure, 'Mandolin Player', by F. Preiss, base inscribed.
£6,000–7,000 *CSK*

A lightly hammered pewter and enamel Tudric clock, by Archibald Knox for Liberty & Co., underside stamped, c1903, 5½in (14cm) high.
£3,000–3,500 *S*

A silvered bronze and ivory figure, 'Torch Dancer', cast and carved by Ferdinand Preiss, signed, torches replaced, on a faceted onyx base, 17in (43cm) high.
£5,500–6,500 *CSK*

A French Art Nouveau silver pendant, set with moonstones and sapphires.
£400–600 *ASA*

A patinated bronze and ivory figure, 'Simplicity', by D. H. Chiparus, 13in (33cm) high.
£4,200–4,800 *CSK*

r. An Art Nouveau mantel clock, inlaid with mother-of-pearl and satinwood stringing, 10in (25cm) high.
£200–300 *RID*

An ebonised oak ladder back chair, designed by Charles Rennie Mackintosh, re-upholstered, 1903.
£17,500–20,500 *C*

A wicker bed with canopy, and bedside table, c1934, bed 93in (236cm) long, bedside table 22in (56cm) high.
£5,500–8,500 *S*

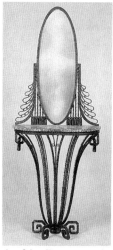

A pair of Art Deco wrought iron and marble mirrored consoles, attributed to Edouard Schenk, 85in (216cm) high.
£5,500–8,500 *C*

An Italian lacquered wood and laminated plastic table, Flamingo, by Michele de Lucchi for Memphis, 1984.
£700–900 *S*

An ebonised and giltwood vitrine, by Dagobert Peche, c1914, 32½in (82cm).
£5,000–7,000 *C*

A walnut canopied sideboard, 97in (245cm) high.
£1,500–2,000 *C*

An oak settle, designed by Sir Edwin Lutyens, for The Drum Inn, Cockington, Torquay, 1934, 59in (149cm) high.
£4,000–6,000 *C*

A centre table, designed by Pierro Fornasetti, 21in (53cm) high.
£5,000–5,500 *C*

A Wiener Werkstätte giltwood mirror, designed by Dagobert Peche, 18 by 19in (46 by 48cm).
£5,000–7,000 *C*

A pigmented veneer inlaid figured ash extending dining table, by Nick Allen, 1986, 118in (301cm) wide.
£2,000–3,000 *C*

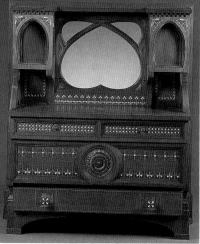

An oak chest of drawers, with shaped mirror, flanked on either side by a vitrine, designed by Carlo Bugatti, inlaid with various woods, 62in (156cm) high.
£23,500–25,000 *C*

A pair of carved oak open armchairs, the design attributed to Dr. Christopher Dresser, with padded back, arms and seat, c1880.
£20,000–25,000 *C*

A mirror polished stainless steel chair, Little Heavy, by Ron Arad, with concave back and seat, 1989.
£4,000–6,000 *C*

A reversible four-leaf screen, by Fornasetti, printed in colours as a bookcase filled with objects between books, the reverse with antique musical instruments, on casters, each leaf 51in (130cm) high. **£4,000–5,000** *C*

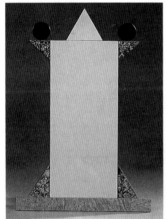

A mirror, Diva, with laminated plastic, by Ettore Sottsass for Memphis, 1984, 42½in (108cm).
£500–800 *S*

A Gothic oak library table, c1880, 43in (109cm) diam.
£500–700 *S*

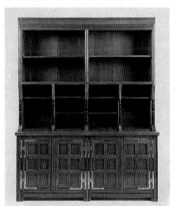

A walnut and ebonised bookcase, by Marsh & Jones, the design attributed to Charles Bevan, c1880, 97in (246cm) high.
£5,000–6,000 *C*

A set of 6 inlaid chairs, by Liberty & Co., c1900.
£2,000–2,500 *ASA*

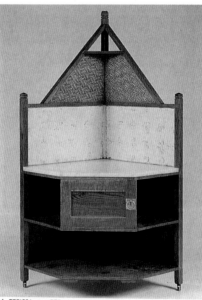

A William Watt pine corner washstand, designed by E. W. Godwin, the triangular pediment inset with raffia panels, the canted base with marble top, with electroplated lock plate and loop handle, on casters, 59in (151cm) high.
£17,500–21,000 *C*

A set of 6 oak side chairs, designed by George Edmund Street, each with a curved and chamfered back carved with Tudor Rose decoration, on turned legs with H-shaped stretchers.
£3,000–5,000 *C*

A Japanese brown silk damask kosode, woven with saya patterns, lined with crimson silk, with padded hem, late 19thC. **£4,000–4,500** *CSK*

An Oriental embroidered shawl. **£180–220** *HCH*

A taffeta dress, c1830. **£150–200** *HCH*

A fan, the mother-of-pearl stick carved and pierced with figures and painted with fruit, with ivory guardsticks, repaired, c1730, 11½in (29cm). **£1,800–2,200** *CSK*

A north European fan, painted with Harlequin, Pierrot and Punchinello, c1760, 10½in (27cm). **£3,500–4,000** *CSK*

A fan, with carved and pierced ivory sticks, in contemporary box, Flemish or English, c1750. **£2,500–3,500** *CSK*

A tailcoat and waistcoat, in MacIntyre and Glenorchy tartan, with kilt and plaid of Hunting Cumming, and a blue bonnet, 1822. **£3,600–4,000** *CSK*

A beaded evening dress, c1920. **£230–250** *HCH*

A woolwork tapestry waistcoat, 18thC. **£100–150** *HCH*

A Brussels Biblical tapestry panel, after Bernard van Orley, lacking border, repaired, mid-16thC, 48 by 36in (122 by 91.5cm).
£4,500–5,500 *S*

A Brussels tapestry of children playing, after Peter van Aelst, c1700, 102 by 108in (259 by 274cm).
£42,000–45,000 *S*

A Brussels mythological tapestry, from the Story of Ulysses, with Brussels town mark and unidentified weaver's mark, extensively repaired, late 16thC, 84 by 44in (213 by 111.5cm).
£19,000–22,000 *S*

A Louis XVI Aubusson tapestry sofa back, with narrow floral border, in gilt frame, c1780, 19 by 49in (48 by 124.5cm).
£2,500–3,000 *S*

A late Louis XV Aubusson tapestry sofa back, with later silk spandrels, in a gilt frame, c1770, 24 by 61in (61 by 155cm).
£2,000–2,500 *S*

A Flemish large leaved verdure tapestry, Enghien or Grammont, with associated contemporary border, extensive repairs, late 16thC, 93 by 89in (236 by 226cm).
£12,000–15,000 *S*

An Italian silk and metal thread tapestry reduction, San Michele, Rome, by Filippo Cettomai, woven with the Sacrifice of Isaac, with gold galon fringe, signed, c1780, 34in (86cm) square.
£1,000–2,000 *S*

A Brussels mythological tapestry of Europa and the Bull, probably reduced, border cut and joined, late 17thC, 123 by 89in (312.5 by 226cm).
£8,500–9,500 *S*

A pair of Louis XIV Aubusson entre fenêtre tapestries, one woven with Susannah and the Elders and the other with a reclining female figure, both 132in by 49in (335 by 124cm).
£6,000–7,000 *S*

A Brussels mythological tapestry, attributed to Jakob van der Borght, woven with Apollo and the Muses, late 17thC, 137 by 156in (247 by 395cm). **£21,000–25,000** *S*

A Brussels classical tapestry, attributed to Daniel Eggermans the Elder, with Brussels town mark and indistinct weaver's mark, worn and faded, c1630, 144 by 168in (336 by 440cm). **£7,800–8,200** *S*

A Flemish floral medallion tapestry antependium, Enghien or Brussels, attributed to Nicholas Hellinck, some minor repairs, c1560-70, 69 by 122in (175 by 400cm). **£16,500–18,500** *S*

An Aubusson verdure landscape tapestry, repaired, early 18thC, 104in (265cm) square. **£8,000–10,000** *S*

A Brussels tapestry of children playing, after Peter van Aelst, c1700, 102 by 104in (259 by 264cm). **£40,000–44,000** *S*

A Paris tapestry fragment, attributed to the atelier of Philippe de Maecht, c1610, 106 by 48in (269 by 122cm). **£2,500–3,000** *S*

A Louis XIII Paris entre fenêtre tapestry, c1630, 132 by 71in (335 by 180cm). **£11,000–13,000** *S*

A Flemish verdure landscape tapestry panel, repaired, early 18thC, 102 by 87in (259 by 221cm). **£3,500–5,500** *S*

A pair of Brussels tapestry border panels, late 17thC, 62 by 24in (157 by 61cm). **£5,500–6,500** *S*

A Flemish verdure landscape tapestry, Lille or Oudenarde, the border cut and joined, c1740, 99 by 204in (250 by 538cm). **£17,500–19,500** *S*

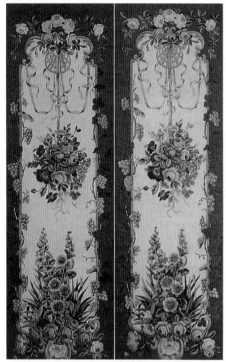

A pair of Aubusson entre fenêtres, mounted and stretched, each 156 by 48in (396 by 122cm).
£6,500–7,500 *C*

A George III period needlework darning sampler, by Frances Brooks, 1800, 16in (41cm) square, framed and glazed.
£650–850 *MCA*

l. A George II petit point needlework panel, with inscription, dated 'April 1783', restored, in a later mahogany frame.
£1,400–1,600 *C*

A woolwork picture, worked in tent stitch with a rural scene, late 19thC, 22 by 27½in (56 by 70cm).
£2,000–2,500 *S(S)*

A tapestry portrait of King George III, perhaps after Benjamin West, wearing the sash and badge of the Order of the Garter, some moth damage, c1770, 16in (41cm) high, in gilt frame.
£1,800–2,200 *S*

A French Chancellery tapestry panel, with Continental coats-of-arms and inscription, c1800, 48 by 49in (122 by 124.9cm).
£6,000–8,000 *CNY*

An English needlework card case, worked in coloured silks in petit point, lined in salmon coloured velvet, clasp incomplete, 17thC, 4½ by 3in (11 by 7.5cm).
£900–1,000 *CSK*

Three needlework cushions, with silk fringes, the largest 22 by 23in (56 by 58cm).
£4,200–4,600 *S*

A set of 3 French needlework cushions, early 19thC, 16 by 14in (41 by 36cm).
£1,100–1,500 *S*

A needlework cushion, worked with polychrome flowers and leaves, with a braided fringe, restored, 21 by 23in (53 by 59cm). **£1,500–2,000** *S*

A set of 3 Aubusson tapestry covered cushions, with braided borders, 19thC, comprising: a pair, one with a pheasant, the other with a parrot, 26 by 20in (66 by 50cm), and a smaller one with turtledoves. **£4,500–5,000** *S*

A French needlework cushion, worked with an urn of flowers, braided tassel fringe, early 18thC, 21 by 23in (54 by 58cm). **£900–1,200** *S*

Two French needlework cushions, each with braided tassel fringe, 18thC, 18 by 16in (46 by 41cm). **£2,300–2,600** *S*

Two French needlework cushions, each worked in gros and petit point, with braided silk fringes, some repairs, the larger 19½ by 23½in (50 by 60cm). **£1,300–1,600** *S*

A French needlework cushion, with a silk fringe, repaired, early 18thC, 18in (46cm) square. **£1,300–1,500** *S*

A Brussels border fragment, made up into a cushion, worked with an architectural capital, braided tassel fringe, late 17thC, 24 by 18½in (61 by 47cm). **£550–750** *S*

A needlework cushion, worked with flowers on a lobed yellow ground, early 19thC, 30 by 19in (76 by 48cm). **£1,500–1,600** *S*

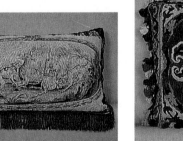

A Louis XVI Aubusson tapestry cushion, woven with an oval medallion of a stag at bay, gold galon fringe, some wear, late 18thC, 20 by 33in (50 by 84cm). **£900–1,200** *S*

A French needlework cushion, with braided tassel fringe, early 18thC, 21½ by 23in (54 by 58cm). **£1,000–1,200** *S*

A French armorial needlework cushion, worked in gros and petit point, with braided silk fringe, early 19thC, 18in (47cm) square. **£1,800–2,000** *S*

A Merton Abbey altar rail kneeler, designed by
William Morris, 257½ by 11½in (654 by 30cm).
£2,000–2,500 *C*

An embroidered panel, in wool
and silk polychrome petit point,
mid-18thC, 36 by 89½in (92 by
227cm). **£5,500–6,500** *S*

A Donegal carpet, designed
by Gavin Morton and G. K.
Robertson, c1900, 151 by 141in
(408 by 359cm).
£9,000–12,000 *C*

A French Art Deco Savonnerie
carpet, c1930, 119 by 77in
(302 by 195.5cm).
£6,500–7,500 *S(NY)*

A French Art Deco Savonnerie
carpet, c1930, 107 by 70in
(271.5 by 177.5cm).
£6,500–7,500 *S(NY)*

An embroidered silk on linen
portière, Pigeon, by Morris &
Co., designed by J. Henry
Dearle, 117 by 62½in
(297 by 159cm).
£13,500–16,500 *C*

A Donegal carpet, designed
by C. F. A Voysey, damaged,
236 by 178in (650 by 432cm).
£2,500–3,500 *C*

A French Art Deco Savonnerie
carpet, c1930, 164 by 105in
(416 by 267cm).
£7,000–10,000 *S(NY)*

A Donegal Arts and Crafts carpet,
reduced in length, restored, c1898,
238 by 174in (606 by 452cm).
£17,500–20,000 *C*

A Chinese antique carpet,
137 by 111in (348 by 282cm).
£3,500–4,500 *CSK*

A Soumac rug, east Caucasus,
some damage, late 19thC,
83 by 62in (210.5 by 157cm).
£5,000–7,000 *S(NY)*

A Ukrainian rug, cut and
pieced together, mid-19thC,
97 by 70in (246 by 178cm).
£8,000–10,000 *S(NY)*

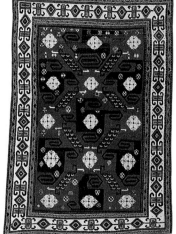

A Kazak pinwheel rug, south
west Caucasus, repaired, c1875,
100 by 70in (254 by 177.5cm).
£20,000–25,000 *S(NY)*

A Karagashli rug, north
east Caucasus, restored,
late 19thC, 63 by 40in
(160 by 101.5cm).
£6,000–8,000 *S(NY)*

A Star Kazak rug, south west Caucasus,
damaged and restored, late 19thC,
75 by 50in (190.5 by 127cm).
£46,000–50,000 *S(NY)*

A Gabbeh rug, south Persia,
early 20thC, 89 by 60in
(226 by 152cm).
£5,500–6,500 *S(NY)*

A Russian needlepoint carpet, minor restorations
throughout, c1830, 144 by 119in (366 by 302cm).
£22,000–25,000 *S(NY)*

A European
needlework carpet,
mid-19thC, 167 by
77in (425 by 196cm).
£5,500–6,500 *C*

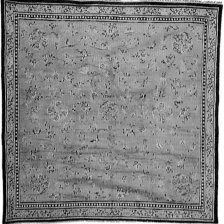

A Ninghsia carpet, west China, repiled and rewoven areas, mid-19thC, 129 by 131in (328 by 333cm).
£18,000–22,000 *S(NY)*

A Ladik prayer rug, central Anatolia, repaired, c1800, 73 by 44in (185 by 111.5cm).
£8,000–10,000 *S(NY)*

A Karachopt Kazak rug, south west Caucasus, some damage, c1900, 112 by 64in (284 by 163cm).
£8,000–10,000 *S(NY)*

A Kazak rug, south west Caucasus, some damage, c1900, 106 by 42in (269 by 106.5cm).
£4,000–6,000 *S(NY)*

A Herez carpet, north west Persia, c1900, some damage, 228 by 142in (584 by 361cm).
£15,000–20,000 *S(NY)*

A Charles X Aubusson carpet, backed, slight damage, repaired, 115 by 101in (292 by 256.5cm). **£46,000–50,000** *C*

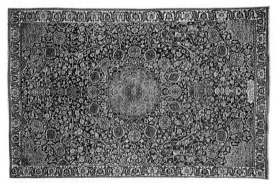

A Khorossan carpet, north east Persia, re-piled areas, outer borders missing, repaired, late 19thC, 140 by 156in (610 by 396cm).
£12,000–14,000 *S(NY)*

A Charles X Aubusson carpet, restored throughout, c1820, 154 by 151in (381 by 373cm).
£15,000–17,000 *S(NY)*

A Senufo mask, the elaborate coiffure divided into 8 incised parts and surmounted by a stylised head of a bird, raised scarifications on the forehead and the cheeks, holes around the edges for attachment, brown patina, 13in (33cm) high.
£7,000–8,000 *S*

A Dan bird Dan mask, the round face with a bird beak-shaped mouth, triangular nose, pierced slanted eyes beneath a domed forehead, semi-circular ears, 3 scarifications around the face, holes around the edges for attachment, black patina, 13in (33cm) high.
£9,000–11,000 *S*

This example of bird mask could be considered to be an archetype because of its perfect rhythm and the echoes of the general lines between the ears and coiffure.

An Idoma mask, the face with incised beard, pierced mouth, triangular nose, pierced coffee bean eyes and flared ears, smooth coiffure, raised scarifications on the temples and top of the nose, holes around the edge for attachment, black patina, 9in (23cm) high.
£7,000–10,000 *S*

An Ibo figure, with remains of yellow and white pigment, brown weathered patina, 24½in (63cm) high.
£2,500–3,500 *S*

A Lobi-Gurunsi figure, brown encrusted patina, 31in (78cm) high. **£6,500–9,000** *S*

An Ibibio mask, the face with flattened mouth, tubular eyes and high forehead, raised scarifications on the temples and the forehead, metal inset on the upper lip, holes around the edge for attachment, black encrusted patina, 12in (30cm) high.
£7,000–8,000 *S*

An Ibo headdress, with remains of white and black pigment, brown patina, 13in (33cm) high.
£4,000–5,500 *S*

A Dan Guerze mask, with holes around the edges for attachment, black encrusted patina, 10in (25cm) high.
£6,000–10,000 *S*

A Lobi-Turka figure, the elongated head with incised mouth and eyes, brown encrusted patina, 10in (25cm) high.
£2,000–3,000 *S*

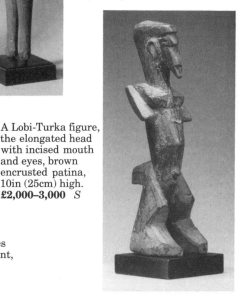

A Wurkun figure, of stylised form, the openwork body with male and female genitals, copper inset eyes, crested coiffure, fibre rope around the neck, black encrusted patina, 37½in (95cm) high.
£45,000–60,000 *S*

This figure has some interesting features which give it a magical or highly symbolic meaning: the different orientation of the ears, (one turned to the front, as normal, but the other one is turned toward the earth); the male and female genitalia represented one above the other, and 2 small protrusions on the back.
The use of this figure is not really clear, but traces of wear on the arms suggest that the piece was possibly planted in the ground near the head of a dead person, taking his vital strength.

A Kongo Dondo female figure, with hole for fettish material at the front, rich dark brown patina, 10in (25cm) high. **£5,200–6,500** *S*

An Agni figure, with remains of white and blue pigment, black patina, 14½in (37cm) high.
£3,500–4,500 *S*

A Lwalwa mask, with pierced slit eyes under a smooth forehead, holes around the edges for attachment, remains of white pigment, red patina, 16in (41cm) high.
£6,000–8,000 *S*

A Tiv male figure, the base supporting a stool, the figure seated with bent legs, light brown weathered patina, 29in (74cm) high.
£15,000–20,000 *S*

The exaggerated genitals are a connotation of power and authority.

A Keaka paternity figure, the enlarged feet supporting bent legs, the elongated torso framed by the set apart arms, the round head with beard, open mouth showing teeth, stylised coffee-bean eyes, all beneath a pair of horns, the baby in the back of the figure shaped as a stylised turtle, deeply encrusted patina, 39in (99cm) high.
£50,000–60,000 *S*

Paternity figures are rare in African Art, nevertheless, it seems that a few figures of this theme can be found in the Keaka tribe, but only one has a turtle in the back instead of a baby. The turtle, in African and classical mythology, is related to the idea of immortality (the animal hibernates every winter and reawakes every spring). The present example is also exceptional by its size.

The style of this headdress can be related to the Southern Yaka tribes near the Tchokwe.

A Yaka headdress, the base supported by the figure of a leopard eating another animal and copper nails inset in the face, light brown patina, 7½in (19cm) high.
£8,000–10,000 *S*

A Yaka headrest, the base supporting the figure of a bird with a long beak eating a fish, light brown patina, 6in (15cm) high.
£7,500–8,500 *S*

A Songye fetish figure, with remains of a yellow pigment, light brown patina, 9in (23cm) high. **£1,800–2,500** *S*

A Yaka-Zombo amulet, the 2 copulating figures with hands on their abdomen and enlarged bead heads, brown shiny patina, 8½in (21cm) high. **£8,000–10,000** *S*

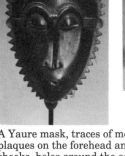

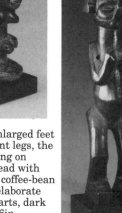

A Luba female figure, with rich dark brown patina, 3½in (9cm) high. **£1,000–1,500** *S*

A Yaure mask, traces of metal plaques on the forehead and the cheeks, holes around the edges for attachment, black patina, 17in (43cm) high.
£18,000–25,000 *S*

A Kuba cup, with overall incised geometric decoration and the handle in the form of 2 hands, rich brown patina, 8in (20cm) high.
£4,000–5,500 *S*

A Yaka figure, with enlarged feet supporting slightly bent legs, the arms with hands resting on elongated torso, the head with trumpet-shaped nose, coffee-bean eyes and flared ears, elaborate coiffure divided in 3 parts, dark brown shiny patina, 16in (41cm) high.
£5,200–6,500 *S*

A Luba figure, with rich red patina, 24in (61cm) high.
£10,000–12,000 *S*

A Songye male magical community figure, with coffee-bean eyes inset with a copper nail and a cowrie shell, a smooth forehead and a horn showing inside the mouth, snakeskin necklace, brown patina, 40in (102cm) high.
£48,000–52,000 *S*

An Azande figure, with a metal
ring around the neck, strings of
beads around the waist, encrusted
patina, 6in (15cm) high.
£5,000–6,000 *S*

A Lega figure, the coiffure
composed of vegetable plaits, with
remains of white pigment on the
face, light brown patina, 12in
(31cm) high.
£8,000–10,000 *S*

A Sikasingo figure, with large
coffee-bean eyes, under a
flattened coiffure, brown patina,
15in (38cm) high.
£11,000–13,000 *S*

An East African figure, the
annulated base supporting the
monkey figure with bent legs, the
arms with hands holding a cup
against the torso, rich brown
patina, 19in (48cm) high.
£12,000–16,000 *S*

An Hemba ancestor figure,
dark brown patina, 20in
(50cm) high.
£23,000–27,000 *S*

*Amongst the Hemba, the ancestor
was venerated by its clan, the cult
of the ancient dominating the
values of the society. The figure
expresses the dependence of the
world of the living on that of the
dead and is thus a funerary and
religious symbol and indicates the
ownership of land and the
possession of social authority, both
of which are based on the
organisation of clans and
lineages. Even the wood out of
which many of these figures are
carved possesses a religious
significance.*

An Ibibio mask, the head with
pointed chin, open mouth showing
teeth, pierced round nose, pierced
almond shaped eyes, high
forehead with pointed coiffure,
raised scarifications on the
forehead, remains of white and
black pigment, holes around the
edge for attachment, black patina,
14in (36cm) high.
£24,000–27,000 *S*

A Luba-Kasai War Fetish figure,
the cylindrical torso with hands
resting on the abdomen, the
elongated neck supporting the
oval face with crescent-shaped
mouth, triangular nose, coffee-
bean eyes under an elaborate
incised coiffure, scarification on
the torso, the chin and the
forehead, rich brown patina,
10½in (27cm) high.
£7,500–9,000 *S*

FANS

An ivory brisé fan, painted and lacquered with Juno and other goddesses feasting, the Goddess of Discord presenting the Golden Apple to the finest of the goddesses, the verso with lovers and putti beside a large fountain, damaged, early 18thC, 8½in (21cm).
£1,700–2,000 *CSK*

A pierced gilt fan, with mother-of-pearl sticks carved with figures and backed with mother-of-pearl, slight wear, Dutch or Flemish, c1760, 10½in (26cm), in glazed fan-shaped case.
£1,200–1,700 *CSK*

A black lace fan, mounted over ivory satin, with mother-of-pearl sticks, the guardsticks applied with carved mother-of-pearl putti, slight damage, c1870, 10½in (26.5cm), in a box.
£400–500 *CSK*

A Canton ivory brisé fan, finely carved and pierced with figures, pagodas and beasts, the central escutcheon with monogram and crest above, repaired, c1790, 10in (25cm).
£1,000–1,200 *CSK*

A Chinese fan, the leaf with a hand-coloured map of China, the verso with a Gazeteer, listing the 23 provinces and their governors, with bamboo sticks, in embroidered fan case, leaf worn, mid-19thC, 12in (30.5cm).
£700–800 *CSK*

A handscreen printed with The Winter Evening's Recreations in the Ladies Screen', published by Jones Leycock's Toyshop, 25 Ludgate Street, St. Paul's, with a wooden handle, some wear, probably mid-18thC.
£1,800–2,200 *C(S)*

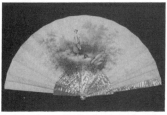

A fan, the satin leaf painted with a milkmaid, signed 'F. Houghton', with mother-of-pearl sticks, partly painted with the continuation of the landscape, c1885, 11½in (29cm), in a box.
£400–500 *CSK*

An ombrelle éventail, the mount of pink silk with an overlay of lace, opening in the form of a half umbrella shaped scallop shell, the handle of bone carved with a tassel, the metal slide stamped 'Bollack Frès, Brevet SGDG', c1858, 18in (46cm).
£600–700 *CSK*

A painted fan, the ivory sticks finely carved and painted with figures and landscape vignettes, the handle carved with acanthus, damaged, c1740, 11in (28cm).
£400–450 *CSK*

A printed fan, the leaf a hand-coloured engraving of 3 monarchs with figures mourning Frederic II, with bone sticks, damaged, c1775, 10in (25cm).
£500–1,000 *CSK*

A fan, made in Canton for the European market, the leaf painted with the ascent by balloon of Mm. Charles et Robert above Nesles, the verso with Hongs at Canton, the mother-of-pearl sticks carved with Chinese figures, pierced and gilt, damage and repairs, c1785, 11in (28cm).
£3,500–4,500 *CSK*

The ascent took place in 1783, but it probably took about a year for prints of it to arrive in Canton.

A Brussels lace fan, the leaf worked with the return of the hero, within floral borders, attached to the sticks by 4 rows of loops at the back, the ivory sticks carved and pierced, with backing guardsticks acting as stretchers, damaged, c1730, 11in (28cm), in a contemporary fan box.
£5,000–5,500 *CSK*

An Italian fan, the chicken skin leaf painted with the sale of putti within Pompeiian decoration, the verso signed in red 'Camillo Buti, Rome 1791', the ivory Chinese sticks pierced, the guardsticks carved with Chinese scenes, slight damage, 10in (25cm).
£1,200–1,700 *CSK*

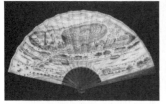

A souvenir fan, from l'Exposition Universelle de 1867 - Paris, vue prise du Tracadero, a hand-coloured lithograph with figures, omnibuses and boats by Alp Guilletat, 48 Rue de Paris, Belleville and printed by Treuillot, with wooden sticks, slight damage, 10in (25cm).
£300–500 *CSK*

A fan, the silk leaf finely painted with a scene of Cleopatra and her attendants, signed 'F. Houghton', within a frame of Brussels lace, the smokey mother-of-pearl sticks pierced and gilt, damaged, c1880, 11½in (29cm).
£1,000–1,200 *CSK*

A German printed fan, the leaf a hand-coloured engraving of 3 vignettes, 2 inscribed 'Der gute Mann, Das gute Weib', the reserves with bunches of flowers, by F. Sussenberger and R. Sommer..c?, with bone sticks, damaged, c1780, 11in (28cm).
£500–700 *CSK*

A fan, the cannepin leaf signed 'E. Ruvaux', the mother-of-pearl sticks carved with kingfishers and bullrushes and painted, c1870, 11in (28cm).
£400–500 *CSK*

A 1794 almanac fan, the leaf with a hand-coloured etching and sprigs of flowers, with Duty stamp, wooden sticks, 11in (28cm).
£550–700 *CSK*

A Brussels lace fan, with tortoiseshell sticks, the upper guardstick with gilt metal monogram 'E.S.', set with rose diamonds, c1890, 14in (36cm).
£400–600 *CSK*

A fan, the silk leaf finely painted with a scene of Cleopatra and her attendants... *[see main column]*

A fan, the leaf painted with Vesuvious erupting by night on 8th August 1779, with manuscript inscription, and 2 smaller vignettes of Vesuvious by day and the Port of Galigoli, with ivory carved and pierced sticks, 1779, 11in (28cm), in damaged fan-shaped case.
£800–1,200 *CSK*

A fan, the leaf painted with a lady and Cupid with a gazebo beyond, signed 'Loys', the scalloped border edged with sequins, the mother-of-pearl sticks gilt, c1890, 9in (22.5cm), in Duvelleroy London box.
£720–800 *CSK*

This fan was said to have been left by Queen Mary at Airlie Castle in September 1921.

A fan, the leaf painted with the Vintage, with wine cellars beyond, the verso with a woman with a basket, the ivory sticks carved and pierced with figures and painted with chinoiserie, damaged, c1750, 11in (28cm).
£500–800 *CSK*

SEWING
Sewing Machines

An Improved Taylor's sewing machine, with friction drive, oval stitchplate, and figure-of-eight base, slight damage.
£350–550 *CSK*

An American hand sewing machine, with pictorial transfer and wood plinth with patent dates to 1874 on brass plaque.
£400–500 *CSK*

The Mary of Guise gilt metal miniature spinning wheel, with red, green and gilt japanned pine base with chinoiserie scenes, within a gilt metal border, the gilt metal wheel and winder mounted with red and blue semi-precious stones, in a later white painted and chased display cabinet, fitted with 2 doors, enclosing a red velvet-lined base, and inscribed to the underside 'Edinburgh Museum of Science and Arts, 118.62 loan', the case 22½in (56.5cm) wide.
£3,500–5,000 *C(S)*

A Continental scale model of a spinning wheel, the 8-spoked wheel supported upon turned spindles, with baluster-turned legs and stretchers, bun feet, 31½in (80cm) high.
£300–400 *P*

A Scottish ivory mounted mahogany and walnut spinning wheel, on turned tapering tripod support, 18thC. **£300–400** *C(S)*

Spinning Wheels

A spinning wheel, with turned yew spindle and ash wheel, pedal and stretcher, bone inlaid plaque with initials and dated '1799' to the pilaster support, late 18thC.
£200–250 *WW*

Miscellaneous

A Dutch needlework casket, worked in coloured wools and silks in petit point, the animals among stylised flowers and trees against a black ground worked in gros point, lined in pink damask, c1800, 14in (36cm) wide.
£550–1,000 *CSK*

A parquetry sewing box, the lid, front and sides inlaid with portraits of steam and sailing ships, the interior fitted with a pincushion and accessory compartments, mid-19thC, 13in (33cm) wide. **£1,000–1,200** *S*

TEXTILES

The earliest needlework originated from the necessity to make clothing and shelter. Today those interested in collecting and studying needlework are fortunate that many of our museums and stately homes have wonderful collections of infinite variety. One visit to the Victoria and Albert Museum will immediately demonstrate the significance that the needle and thread, in all its forms, has had throughout history on the daily lives of our forebears, whether used for domestic, religious or other purposes.

For the collector interested in textiles the possibilities for sources are limitless. Forming a collection can be most rewarding, whether concentrating on one particular area of textiles or selecting pieces that appeal from a broader base.

Whatever the particular interest there are some basic principles that should be borne in mind. Condition of the item, freshness of colour and originality of design are all important factors. Ultra violet light accounts for around 45% of damage by fading, and the brilliance of the light and the heat generated by it leads to deterioration and weakening of the fabric.

Three terms which are often used incorrectly when describing textiles are:
Needlework, which is carried out with a needle and thread.
Weaving, which is worked on a loom with many threads simultaneously.
Tapestry Weaving, which is the term chiefly used for pictorial hangings and worked on a loom. The term tapestry is often incorrectly applied to 17thC canvas embroidery.

The prices achieved for important hangings, costumes and textiles can, at times, be prohibitive. For example, a young girl's bodice of fine linen, c1610, sold at Christie's South Kensington recently for £50,000, and the Duc d'Antin Don Quixote tapestries woven at La Manufacture Royale des Gobelins, between 1717 and 1780 achieved £700,000 at Christie's.

However, needlework in general is still relatively undervalued in relation to many other of the decorative arts. This particularly applies to much of the 17thC domestic furnishings such as bed valances, pillow covers and pictures worked in petit point, and those delightful raised work examples which do come on the market from time to time.

It is, of course, important that many of the major pieces and those of historical significance should be acquired by public collections, as these provide a wonderful reference study for the enthusiast, student and collector. One such study centre is situated at Hampton Court Palace where the Embroiderers Guild houses its international collection. Perhaps lesser known is the teaching collection formed by Rachel B. Kay-Shuttleworth at Gawthorpe Hall, Padiham, Burnley, Lancashire.

A needlework portrait, embroidered in coloured silks, c1660. PC

Conservation

Caring for a textile is important to prevent any future damage occurring, particularly, if it is to be placed on show. Some practical work can be undertaken providing great care is exercised. This is particularly applicable to framed needleworks, e.g. samplers, silk and wool-work pictures. Many of these items have, over the years, suffered from moth and damp; the mould growth rotting the fabric and causing staining and deterioration.

It is vital that such pieces are removed from ill-fitting frames, and where the paper backing has been torn, as this allows dust and insects to filter through. Fabrics should never be washed without extensive tests for fear of shrinkage to the ground fabric and fugitive colour bleeding in the vegetable dyes. Old wood backings and nails, which with age darken and discolour the fabric, should be carefully removed and dust cleaned from the fabric. This is achieved by placing the sampler under a fine and well secured net and gently vacuuming with a hand held cleaner, taking care not to come into contact with the actual sampler. Acid free board and unbleached, pre-shrunk cotton calico should then be used as a mount. When dealing with moths, any eggs or larvae should be gently removed and paradichloro-benzene crystals may be used, which should not come into direct contact with the fabric but should be wrapped in acid-free paper and placed in an acid-free box for treatment.

Specialist films of clear UV filter can reduce ultra violet brilliance when fitted to flat glass and museum conservation glass is now available from specialist suppliers. For those who do not wish to attempt such work themselves, there are a number of good textile conservationists. A list of their names may be obtained for a small fee from:
The Conversation Unit, Museums and Galleries Commission, 16 Queen Anne's Gate, London SW1H 9AA. Telephone 071 233 3686.

Samplers

Amongst collectors and needleworkers alike, there is still great interest in those decorative embroideries, often worked by children, known as samplers.

The word sampler comes from the Latin word 'examplar', literally meaning example or model. From contemporary records we know that samplers existed in Europe from the early 16thC, although the earliest known survivor is one dated 1598 by Jane Bostocke and forms part of the collection at the Victoria and Albert Museum, London.

Originally samplers were worked to provide a portable record of stitches and patterns in an age when printed patterns either did not exist or were very rare. These early samplers were generally worked by adults and used as a practical tool of both professional and amateur needleworkers. They were frequently worked on long strips of bleached or unbleached linen, the shape being determined by the width of the cloth, the selvage often placed at the top and bottom of the sampler and the sides neatly hemmed. From samplers thought to date from the 16thC we can see that they display the types of stitches and patterns characteristic of contemporary costume and household textiles.

The first printed pattern book was published in Augsburg in 1523, and from this date onwards printed patterns appeared with increasing regularity. In England the first printed patterns for textiles appeared in 1587, and so from the end of the 16thC we can see a change not only in the function of samplers but also in their form. Samplers of the 17thC in general retained their long narrow shape, wide variety of stitches and numerous patterns and motifs suggesting that they were still used for reference. The surprisingly good condition in which we find some of the survivors of the 17thC suggests that like their predecessors these samplers were also kept rolled away when not in use.

A sampler, by Mary Howes, worked in brightly coloured silks, 1821. PC

The meticulously repeated rows of border patterns and the increasing inclusion of alphabets suggests that samplers were becoming used as teaching exercises and were worked by children. Many of these 17thC survivors show a high degree of technical skill, and their justifiably proud creators often included their own names, age and even the name of their teacher.

As we progress into the 18thC we start to see new developments. The length of samplers shortens and the shape becomes squarer. This, together with the introduction of border patterns surrounding the sampler, suggests that they were worked with the intention of being displayed rather than rolled away. It also appears that a broadening of their educational role was taking place.

A sampler, worked by Charlotte Harris, aged 10, depic ting Adam and Eve, the Tree of Life, and a Royal palace, 1835. PC

During the 18th and 19thC at least one sampler would have been worked by the majority of young girls during the course of their education. Examples range from those worked in orphanages and charity schools where their purpose was aimed at providing the necessary skills to enter domestic service, to those worked by the middle classes, whose aim was to brush up on their embroidery skills, provide a suitable leisure occupation, and to show the degree of accomplishment achieved whilst at school.

One common theme evident in many 18thC samplers is that of a religious or moral nature. Biblical passages, psalms and hymns, along with representation of Adam and Eve, the Tree of Life, and later Solomon's Temple are all common subject matter. Towards the end of the 18thC one sees the emergence of map samplers, these were often worked to a commercially produced pattern printed on satin or silk and frequently sold with the coloured threads with which to work them.

The fashion for map samplers comes largely from the education of the wealthy and middle classes, often being worked as a final leaving task at well-to-do finishing establishments. As we move into the 19thC, naturalistic subjects become increasingly popular, no doubt influenced by the fashion for silkwork pictures and the widespread availability of printed patterns. Birds, trees, animals, houses and people are all popular subjects as well as the ubiquitous alphabets and numerals.

The move away from the original function of samplers along with changes in their subject matter coincides with a decline in the variety of stitches to be found on all but the most complicated examples. Cross stitch becomes the most prevalant stitch found on samplers made in the 19thC, so much so that it even came to be referred to as 'sampler stitch'.

During the middle years of the 19thC the popularity of Berlin woolwork inevitably influenced the form and content of samplers. Motifs derived from Berlin woolwork patterns appear on contemporary samplers, and many mid-19thC samplers are worked in brightly coloured wool on canvas backing.

In the last years of the 19thC we see the emergence of a new form of plain sewing sampler. This was a type of work produced by schoolgirls intended to teach them basic sewing skills, particularly those required for dressmaking and repairing household textiles. These finely worked samplers were generally produced by older girls, sometimes by trainee teachers taught at the many ladies' colleges that sprang up throughout Britain at the end of the 19thC.

With the outbreak of the WWI, came mass production of clothes and household textiles, and the availability of the sewing machine sparked a general decline in the importance of needlework as part of the education of young ladies, and with this a decline in the working of samplers.

It is the decorative sampler which is the most familiar and possibly the most appealing. There is, however, much more to this type than its visual impact and naïve charm which we find so attractive today. Butterflies the size of houses, flowers the size of trees, all bring broad smiles to the face and delight the eye. To stop at this stage of appreciation would be to miss so much. Looking at samplers is rather like reading a book - many clues are there if we know where to look, and take time to interpret what we see. By researching the names, dates and places inscribed upon them, we are provided with a fascinating insight into the lives of the young needleworkers, and a glimpse into the social history of the time. It is this human element which is so intriguing.

Joy Jarrett

Embroidery

An embroidered picture, finely worked in shades of cream and brown wools, depicting a lion walking with palm trees behind, framed, early 19thC, 21½ by 29½in (54 by 75cm).
£3,000–3,500 *CSK*

An embroidered picture, unfinished, worked in coloured silks and raised work, the pen and ink design with Hercules and the lion surrounded by Music, Beauty, an elephant and a horse, a castle, a fountain and plants, within a border of flowers and animals, c1660, 15 by 21in (38 by 53cm), framed and glazed.
£1,600–2,000 *CSK*

A Cyclades panel, composed of various lengths of embroidery including one of linen worked with green silk dancing women and leafy columns, the panels of embroidery 18thC, made up in the 19thC, 76 by 28in (193 by 71cm).
£450–650 *CSK*

A piece of Spanish devotional silk embroidery, on ivory silk, the reverse covered with contemporary crimson silk damask, bound with gilt braid, the glass replaced, late 17thC, 9½ by 8in (23.5 by 20cm).
£300–400 *P*

A fine embroidered picture worked in coloured silks, hung from a tasselled ribbon, within a border of heads of corn and flowers including roses and convolvulus, late 18thC, 17½ by 15½in (44 by 39cm), framed and glazed.
£200–300 *CSK*

An Ottoman panel, composed of 2 lengths of handwoven natural linen, embroidered on 3 sides with a border of vine leaves and palmettes, the field worked with ogival palmettes among undulating fruiting vines, cut down from a larger hanging, 44 by 77in (111.5 by 195.5cm). **£1,200–1,700** *CSK*

An American embroidered letter or comb case, composed of 6 pockets of dark blue wool and green velvet, each worked in coloured wools, the top panel embroidered in silks 'J. & Ann Anderton 6 of Oct', with red silk binding, backed with glazed printed cotton, c1820, 27in (69cm). **£500–600** *CSK*

A German border of green wool, embroidered in coloured wools, c1700, 8 by 116in (20 by 294.5cm). **£800–900** *CSK*

Lace

A Flemish border of small scale bobbin lace, worked with blocks of a stylised plant motifs in bobbin made tapes, early 17thC, 60 by 2in (152 by 5cm). **£200–250** *CSK*

A length of bobbin lace, worked with urns of flowers above an S-scroll border, possibly Danish, early 17thC, 15 by 3in (38 by 7.5cm), and another Flemish border composed of floral scallops, early 17thC, 40 by 4in (101.5 by 10cm). **£250–300** *CSK*

A flounce of reticella, worked with a double gallery of diamonds, edged with vandyked bobbin lace, c1600, 60 by 6in (152 by 15cm). **£200–250** *CSK*

A Flemish border of bobbin lace, worked with scallops of stylised flowering sprays, c1620, 34 by 2in (86 by 5cm), with attached looped edge. **£150–200** *CSK*

A border of fine drawn thread work lace, worked with wheel detail, probably Spanish, 17thC, 38 by 4in (96.5 by 10cm). **£200–250** *CSK*

A length of needle lace, early 17thC, 20 by 3in (51 by 8cm). **£150–200** *CSK*

Caring for Lace

- Early lace was usually made from linen, a robust fibre, so pieces can be framed and wall hung.
- Never display lace using pins - rust stains are very difficult to remove.
- Store lace between sheets of acid free tissue paper.

A flounce of Buratto lace, worked with stylised angular flowering shrubs between borders of small floral devices, 17thC, 9 by 40in (22.5 by 101.5cm). **£300–500** *CSK*

A border of densely worked bobbin lace, made of narrow woven tapes, with a vermicular floral design, possibly Hungarian, 17thC, 80 by 6in (203 by 15cm). **£400–450** *CSK*

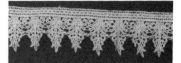

A border of fine bobbin lace, worked with pointed scallops of sheaves of curling plaited bands, c1615, 50 by 3in (127 by 7.5cm). **£420–500** *CSK*

A collection of Venetian raised needle lace, including 2 lengths worked with pomegranates and scrolling foliage, early 17thC, 26 by 4in (66 by 10cm). **£400–500** *CSK*

A border of early 17thC style free flowing needle lace, worked with a narrow gallery pierced by scrolling foliage, late 19thC, 32 by 6in (81 by 15cm). **£150–200** *CSK*

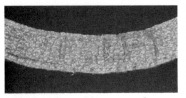

A bertha of metal lace, wound on a yellow silk foundation thread, worked with a border of fans on either side, with quatrefoil devices worked with wheatears, backed with salmon pink silk, 17thC, 50 by 3in (127 by7.5cm).
£200–400 *CSK*

This is a rare piece from a 17thC dress. It is shaped by soft gathers in the backing silk, the original yellow floss silk stitches are still present.

A flounce of tape lace, finely worked with formal floral urns and swagging, with elaborate bobbin lace fillings and circular mesh ground, c1800, 11 by 104in (28 by 264cm).
£370–420 *CSK*

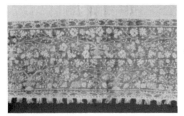

A Buratto valence, worked with 2 interlocking rows of spreading flower vases, c1800, 7 by 68in (17.5 by 172.5cm).
£300–400 *CSK*

A flounce of Argentan needle lace, with urns of flowers alternating with palm trees mounted on rocaille bases with spider web fillings, c1720, 23 by 120in (59 by 304.5cm).
£3,000–4,000 *C*

A length of Punto in Aria needle lace, with formally scrolling flowering vines and cornucopiae, early 17thC, 12 by 14in (30.5 by 35.5cm).
£250–300 *CSK*

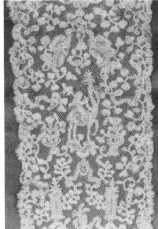

A pair of lappets and matching cap back of Brussels bobbin lace, the lappets worked with Hermes carousing with a knight in armour, the square ends worked with a drum and hunting horns, the cap worked with fountains and barrels, c1695, the lappets 19 by 3in (48 by 7.5cm), the cap 12in (30.5cm) wide.
£5,000–5,500 *CSK*

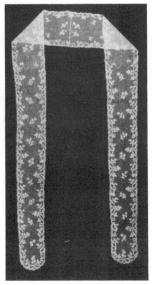

A border of raised Venetian needle lace, worked with a repeating pattern of formal flowers, with a raised cordonnet, early 17thC, 40 by 3in (101.5 by 7.5cm).
£300–350 *CSK*

A length of Punto in Aria lace, with an undulating ribbon and fleurs-de-lys terminals, early 17thC, 80 by 4in (203 by 10cm).
£550–600 *CSK*

A set of Continental bed coverings, comprising a buff coloured coverlet and 3 shams finely worked in bobbin, filet and needle lace, 3 sides with vandyked edges with tassels, 19thC, 78 by 96in (198 by 243.5cm).
£1,000–1,200 *CSK*

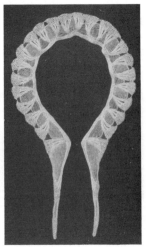

A collar of fine needle lace, worked with an Art Nouveau design and long tapering swallow tail collar points, c1910. **£700–800** *CSK*

A pair of Valenciennes bobbin lace lappets, worked with small scattered sprigs, late 18thC, 60 by 3in (152 by 7.5cm).
£150–200 *CSK*

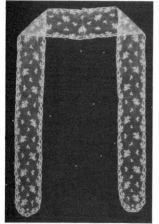

A pair of Lille bobbin lace lappets, worked with a border of leaves and flowers, the field scattered with floral sprigs, late 18thC, 60 by 3in (152 by 7.5cm), and a small Lille bobbin lace fragment.
£150–200 *CSK*

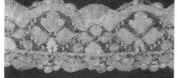

A length of white metal bobbin lace, with a double scalloped edge and trefoil designs, part of a dress robing, 18thC.
£200–300 *CSK*

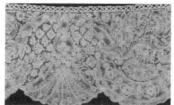

A flounce of Brussels style bobbin lace, worked with urns of flowers with large fern-like leaves with curled fern buds at the base, probably East Devon, c1800, 6 by 140in (15 by 406cm).
£500–550 *CSK*

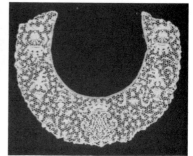

A collar formed from French needle lace, worked with a monogram 'MM' (?), with cupids and interlocked hearts with hands interlocked beneath, the lace early 18thC, the collar made in 19thC.
£1,200–1,700 *CSK*

The Victoria and Albert Museum holds another collar of this lace, with a note stating that the crest is that of Maria Theresa of Austria. The museum's collar Accession No is T.30-1949 and forms part of the Lady Ludlow Bequest.

A Brussels cutwork tablecloth, worked with a looped cut work ribbon border, the field sprigged with flowers, the ground composed of embroidered linen spots, linked by knotted threads, c1860, 66in (167.5cm) square.
£1,200–1,700 *CSK*

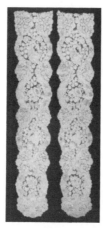

A flounce of Brussels Point de Gaze lace, worked with roses, c1860, 18 by 237in (46 by 602cm). **£1,000–1,400** *CSK*

A pair of Brussels bobbin lace lappets, worked with 'Bizarre' ovals and flowers, c1740, 4 by 22in (10 by 56cm).
£550–600 *CSK*

Needlework

An English needlework picture, worked in coloured silks and silver metal threads in tent stitch, against a silver metal ground, mid-17thC, 14 by 10in (36 by 25cm), framed and glazed.
£1,000–1,200 *CSK*

A needlework picture, worked in coloured silks and metal threads in tent stitch, c1700, 14½ by 6⅜in (36.5 by 16cm), framed and glazed.
£1,200–1,700 *CSK*

Six shaped needlework chair pieces, worked in coloured wools and silk thread highlights in petit and gros point, the chair back with an urn filled with crimson flowers within a foliate cartouche and blue border, early 19thC, 20½ by 33in (52 by 84cm).
£500–600 *CSK*

A needlework seat cover, with coloured wools and silk threads in petit point, c1700, 24 by 21in (61 by 53cm).
£300–400 *CSK*

Tapestries

A George III needlework picture, 12 by 16in (30.5 by 41cm).
£400–500 *AG*

A needlework portière, worked in brightly coloured wools against a black ground, with tasselled fringe, c1860, 74 by 125in (188 by 317.5cm).
£500–800 *CSK*

A Flemish parkland tapestry, c1600, 122½ by 125½in (310 by 318cm).
£14,000–16,000 *S(NY)*

A Flemish parkland tapestry fragment, within a beaded border, early 17thC, 61 by 60in (155 by 152cm).
£2,000–3,000 *S(NY)*

A Flemish Biblical tapestry panel, depicting the anointing of David, 17thC, 94 by 74in (239 by 188cm).
£2,000–2,500 *S(NY)*

A large French tapestry panel, woven with an assembly of Greek gods, including Jupiter enthroned with Juno at his feet, with Solomonic columns behind, c1700, 106 by 73in (269 by 185cm).
£3,500–4,000 *CSK*

Originally part of a larger tapestry, 'Diana Imploring Jupiter for the Gift of Chastity', one of the series of 'L'Histoire de Diane', designed by Toussaint Dubreuil of the School of Fontainebleau, at the end of the 16thC.

A Continental armorial tapestry, the centre with a coat-of-arms (replaced) and scrolling strapwork cartouche, on a stylised mille fleur ground surrounded by addorsed dolphins, on a field alternating with sections of rose and blue ground, woven with scrolling cornucopiae, the whole within a border of scrolling foliage interspersed with urns and also alternating with colour, late 16thC, 104½ by 111in (265 by 282cm). **£11,000–13,000** *S(NY)*

A Flemish parkland tapestry fragment, c1600, 92 by 40in (234 by 102cm). **£4,000–5,000** *S(NY)*

A Brussels historical tapestry panel, depicting a couple beneath a red cloak, 17thC, 116 by 75in (295 by 191cm).
£6,000–6,500 *S(NY)*

A Flemish historical tapestry panel, depicting an emperor, probably Alexander, on a pacing white horse, with a partial border on the left side, 17thC, 79 by 80in (201 by 203cm).
£7,200–8,000 *S(NY)*

A Flemish verdure tapestry fragment, 18thC, 58 by 52in (146 by 132cm).
£2,500–3,500 *S(NY)*

A Franco-Flemish verdure tapestry, c1700, 111 by 72in (282 by 183cm).
£3,000–4,000 *S(NY)*

A Flemish parkland tapestry, c1600, 123 by 124⅛in (312.5 by 316cm).
£12,500–14,000 *S(NY)*

A pair of Aubusson tapestry hangings, with red borders, with a sub pattern of darker red scrolling, late 19thC, 156 by 53in (396 by 134.5cm).
£7,000–8,000 *CSK*

A Flemish tapestry panel, repaired, 17thC, 84 by 44in (213 by 111.5cm).
£1,200–1,700 *CSK*

Two Aubusson tapestries, woven with 2 versions of Joseph's Dream, both with night skies, within a border of flowers, acanthus leaves and busts, each signed 'Mr dAub', one also signed 'Ane Grel', repaired, with 18thC lining, late 17thC, largest 102 by 64in (259 by 162.5cm).
£10,000–12,000 *CSK*

There are 3 other known tapestries of this subject also signed Grellet, with different borders. 'Ane.' probably refers to the elder of a large tapestry weaving family, as Antoine Grellet was 18thC.

Locate the source

The source of each illustration in Miller's can be found by checking the code letters below each caption with the list of contributors.

A Franco-Flemish verdure tapestry, early 18thC, 108 by 151in (274 by 384cm).
£7,000–8,000 *S(NY)*

A Flemish hunting tapestry panel, c1600, 102½ by 117½in (260 by 298cm).
£6,000–7,000 *S(NY)*

A Brussels tapestry, worked in green, red, blue, yellow and gold within a narrow entwined ribbon and flowerhead border, cut down, 17thC, border possibly later, 84 by 101in (214 by 257cm).
£6,700–7,200 *HSS*

A Flemish historical tapestry, depicting a barely draped and throned figure of a youth, possibly David, within an associated trelliswork border entwined with fruiting vines interspersed with flower-filled baskets, masks and allegorical figures, c1600, 137 by 118in (348 by 300cm).
£8,000–9,000 *S(NY)*

A Flemish verdure tapestry, c1600, 130 by 132½in (330 by 335cm).
£7,500–8,500 *S(NY)*

A Flemish tapestry panel, with a classical caryatid figure armed with a bow and arrow, repaired, 17thC, 88 by 26in (223.5 by 66cm).
£1,000–1,200 *CSK*

A Franco-Flemish verdure tapestry, early 18thC, 122 by 127in (310 by 323cm).
£11,500–13,000 *S(NY)*

A Mortlake mythological tapestry, depicting Vulcan's forge, and a sculpture of Zeus within guilloche chain border, late 17thC, 92 by 86in (234 by 218cm).
£4,000–5,000 *S(NY)*

A Franco-Flemish verdure tapestry fragment, 18thC, 78½ by 45in (199 by 114cm).
£2,000–2,500 *S(NY)*

A Flemish hunting tapestry fragment, 17thC, 48 by 63in (122 by 160cm).
£1,500–2,000 *S(NY)*

A Continental tapestry, woven in 17thC verdure style, with a bird standing by a lake with an aquaduct and buildings behind, in a wooded landscape and flowers in the foreground, within a floral border, c1900, 38 by 55in (96.5 by 139.5cm).
£1,500–2,000 *CSK*

A verdure tapestry, woven in many colours, repaired, probably Flemish, repaired, c1700, bound with later blue wool border, 80 by 70in (203 by 177.5cm).
£4,000–5,000 *CSK*

A Flemish verdure tapestry, late 17thC, 100 by 83in (254 by 211cm).
£10,000–12,000 *S(NY)*

An Aubusson verdure tapestry
panel, c1700, 97 by 41in
(246 by 104cm).
£3,500–4,000 *S(NY)*

A Flemish mythological tapestry,
depicting Orpheus and Eurydice,
18thC, 102 by 87in (259 by 221cm).
£6,000–6,500 *S(NY)*

An Aubusson verdure tapestry
fragment, 18thC, 59 by 44in
(150 by 111cm).
£3,000–3,500 *S(NY)*

An Aubusson Biblical tapestry,
depicting the meeting of Esther
and Ahasuerus, 17thC, 102 by
99in (259 by 252cm).
£3,000–3,700 *S(NY)*

A Flemish verdure tapestry,
18thC, 105½ by 148in
(268 by 376cm).
£6,500–7,000 *S(NY)*

A pair of Aubusson tapestry
hangings, woven with a basket of
flowers including chrysanthemums
and hydrangeas hung from a
large blue tied ribbon, against a
cream ground, the base with rich
leaves and flowers, within a pale
green border, late 19thC, 128 by
42in (325 by 106.5cm).
£4,000–4,500 *CSK*

A Flemish historical tapestry,
centred by 2 men crowning an
emperor, with soldiers, within
an elaborate border incorporating
Zeus, Mercury and Diana,
interspersed with birds in the
clouds above, allegorical figures
in the corners, the sides with
animals, and Neptune in his
chariot flanked by boating parties,
120 by 128in (305 by 325cm).
£10,000–12,000 *S(NY)*

A Flemish verdure tapestry,
early 18thC, 120 by 161in
(305 by 410cm).
£9,000–11,000 *S(NY)*

A Franco-Flemish verdure
tapestry fragment, 18thC,
86 by 44in (218 by 111cm).
£1,500–2,000 *S(NY)*

Samplers

A sampler, by Annabel Jarvis, worked in coloured silks in various stitches with roses and other flowers and a young woman holding a bird, a frog and a stag behind, dated '1697', 11 by 8½in (28 by 21cm), framed and glazed.
£2,700–3,200 *CSK*

A sampler, by Ann Marson, worked in coloured silks in various stitches, with a verse 'Let Virtue Be The Name', with geometric borders, dated '1749' 12 by 8½in (30.5 by 21cm), framed and glazed.
£1,600–2,000 *CSK*

A sampler, by Rebecca Keeves, worked in coloured silks, dated '1792',12 by 13½in (30.5 by 34cm), framed and glazed.
£450–500 *CSK*

A sampler, by Harriet Sharp, worked in coloured silks with a verse 'On Youth' with flowering trees below and a pair of collared animals, within a stylised floral border, dated '1819', 15½ by 11in (39 by 28cm), framed and glazed.
£180–220 *CSK*

A label on the back reads 'From the Yorkshire School of Art Needlework, Margaret Stretton, 211, Glossop Road, Sheffield'.

A sampler by Mary Pardoe Wilson, worked in coloured silks with 4 verses interrupted by a band of flowering plants and a pair of rabbits and lions, within a stylised floral border, 1837, 20 by 12in (50.5 by 30.5cm), framed and glazed.
£580–620 *CSK*

A needlework sampler, by Eleanor Farmer, worked with a manor house before a paddock with horses, flanked by trees, inside a looped floral border, late 18thC, 16 by 11½in (41 by 29cm).
£400–600 *S(S)*

A sampler, by Ann W... Age 13, worked in coloured silks with alphabets and numerals and a verse flanked by 2 urns, with naturalistic flowers and a singing longtailed bird, early 18thC, 18 by 8in (46 by 20cm), framed and glazed.
£450–650 *CSK*

A sampler, by Sarah Skey, worked in shades of cream and brown silks, with a verse 'Brothers', early 19thC, 15½ by 12½in (39 by 32cm), framed and glazed.
£300-400 *CSK*

An inscribed label on the reverse reads: 'This sampler was presented to Dr. Reid in April 1926 by Ms. Philips of Bednall - It belonged to her Great, Great, Great Grandmother'.

A sampler, by Sarah Willson, dated '1837', worked in coloured silks with a central verse 'This is the God', 20½in (52cm) square, framed and glazed.
£700–800 *CSK*

A sampler, by Charlott Easelsder, dated '1839', worked in coloured silks with spot motifs including a house, Adam and Eve flanking the apple tree, a saddled horse with rider, a young woman and her dog, 15 by 13in (38 by 33cm).
£800–900 *CSK*

A sampler, by Selina Gilkes, dated '1839', finely worked in coloured silks with a verse 'Surrounded by the Works of God...', flanked by pink flowering stems and below, a pair of flower-filled urns and flying birds, within a stylised floral border, 13½ by 11in (34 by 28cm), framed and glazed.
£600–700 *CSK*

A sampler, by Mary Howes, dated '1821', worked in coloured silks with a verse 'How blest are they'..., 12 by 12½in (30 by 31cm), framed and glazed.
£1,500–2,000 *CSK*

A sampler, worked in coloured silks, with spot motifs, borders of Tudor roses and sprays of flowers, a frieze of boxers, another of artichokes and another of acorns, slightly stained, with initials 'ER' and 'IT' and dated '1723', 34 by 8½in (86 by 21.5cm).
£1,700–2,200 *C(S)*

A sampler, by Saley England, Aged 10, dated '1820', worked in coloured silks with 'My child if sinners intice thee consent thou not', 13in (33cm) square, mounted.
£350–400 *CSK*

A sampler, by Elizabeth Fry, dated '1831', worked in coloured silks with a verse, spot motifs including trumpeting angels, birds and stags, within a stylised floral border, 15½ by 12in (39 by 31cm), framed and glazed. **£600–700** *CSK*

Some Collections to Visit

City of Bristol Museum and Art Gallery, Georgian House, Great George Street, Bristol.

Fitz William Museum, Cambridge, Trumpington Street, Cambridge, CB2 1RB.

The Manx Museum and National Trust, Douglas, Isle of Man, 1MI 3LY.

Hove Museum and Art Gallery, 19 New Church Road, Hove, East Sussex.

Llandrindod Wells Museum, Temple Street, Llandrindod Wells, Powys, BN3 4AB.

Platt Hall (Gallery of English Costume), Rusholme, Manchester.

Montacute House, Montacute, Somerset, TA15 6XP.

Nottingham Museum of Costume and Textiles, 51 Castlegate, Nottingham, NG1 6AF.

Old House Museum, Cunningham Place, Bakewell, Derbyshire,

Rufford Old Hall, Liverpool Road, Rufford, Lancashire, L43 1FG.

Priest House, West Hoathly, Nr. East Grinstead, West Sussex, RH19 4PP.

Strangers Hall Museum, Charing Cross, Norwich, Norfolk, NR2 4AL.

Victoria and Albert Museum, Cromwell Road, South Kensington,, SW7 2RL.

Wells Museum, 8 Cathedral Green, Wells, Somerset, BA5 1RE.

Whitby Museum, Panner Park, Whitby, North Yorkshire, YO21 1RE.

Whitworth Art Gallery, University of Manchester, Oxford Road, Manchester, M156 6ER.

Lady Lever Art Gallery, Liverpool.

• It is always advisable to make sure that a collection is available for viewing before travelling long distances.

A sampler, by Jacobeane Mcpherson, worked in coloured silks with a grand house and a gentleman standing on the steps in front, surrounded by spot motifs including 6 rabbits and flying birds, and 2 bands of roses and carnations above, within a stylised floral border, 18thC, 12½in (31cm) square, framed and glazed.
£1,500–2,000 *CSK*

A sampler, by Charlotte Jones, worked in coloured silks with 2 verses and spot motifs of flower filled urns, and pairs of birds, dated '1777', 16 by 12in (41 by 30.5cm), framed and glazed.
£250–300 *CSK*

A petit point sampler, depicting the alphabet, numbers and various patterns with attached silvered oval plaque inscribed 'The first prize given at Miss Renous School Mid Summer 1810', 8 by 8½in (20 by 21cm), in an ebonised frame.
£350–400 *DA*

Susani

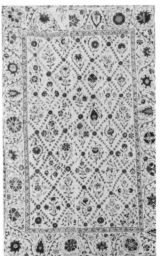

A sampler by Elizabeth Gardner, finely worked in coloured silks with 2 verses and spot motifs including a young girl with a dog, a duck and a turkey, flowering trees and other birds, within a stylised floral border, 1850, 12 by 16½in (30.5 by 42cm), framed and glazed.
£600–650 *CSK*

Susani

According to legend, embroidered susanis (the word means stitch or needle in Persian), were laboriously stitched by young girls before they were married. They were used as a covering for the bridal bed and ripped in half when the bride lost her virginity!

A Bokhara susani, composed of 6 panels of unbleached cotton, embroidered with a border of elegant trailing leaves and palmettes in pale green, orange, pink and cream silks, the field with a diamond leaf lattice enclosing flowering sprays, mid-19thC, 92 by 64in (233.5 by 162.5cm).
£780–900 *CSK*

A Bokhana susani, displaying a colourful variety of large flowers to the wide border and central field, stripes and tendrils between, worked in chain stitch on a dark brown twill weave ground, Uzbekistan, 19thC, 65 by 89in (165 by 226cm).
£600–800 *P*

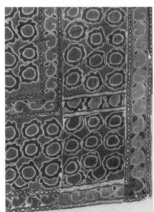

A susani, embroidered with irregularly shaped magenta flowers, outlined in lime green, divided into border and field by a narrow band of monochrome leaves, possibly Tajikistan, late 19thC.
£450–550 *CSK*

A susani, the border of couched silk embroidered quartered roundels and palmettes, the field with central stella medallion in a field sprigged with flowering shrubs, mid-19thC, 117 by 70in (297 by 177.5cm).
£1,800–2,000 *CSK*

A Bokhari susani, composed of 4 panels of unbleached cotton, embroidered with a border of deep pink and orange rosettes and palmettes, interspersed with dark green serrated leaf stripes, the field with a diamond leaf lattice filled with irises and other flowers, mid-19thC, 64 by 43in (162.5 by 109cm).
£1,700–2,000 *CSK*

A Continental cap of ivory silk, composed of 6 panels divided by gilt metal braid, with 3 embroidered scenes of a widow at a tomb, a dalmation and a bridge or mausoleum over a river, worked in coloured silks in tiny knot stitch, each scene duplicated, with gilt metal fringing and button top decoration, possibly with mourning associations, c1780.
£250–400 *CSK*

A fine white cotton baby's bonnet, with a long panel of Hollie point, the crown worked with the words 'From an English Friend, IR', with birds and flowers, 18thC.
£400–500 *CSK*

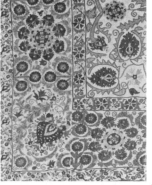

A Bokhara susani, consisting of 5 panels of undyed linen, closely embroidered, the foliage in 2 shades of green, lined, Uzbekistan, 19thC, 61 by 93in (155 by 236cm).
£1,700–2,000 *P*

A green satin embroidered jacket, formerly owned by the late racing tipster, Prince Monolulu.
£500–600 *AAV*

A grey silk dress, trimmed with green satin cuffs, with green bows at the centre back, the skirt with green silk puffs trimmed with black lace, c1876, with matching bonnet, and a dress of brown velvet and grey ribbed silk, c1890. **£700–800** *CSK*

Costume

A pair of child's stays or corset, of ivory silk, finely stitched in silk and bound in silk, boned and lined with silk, c1770, and another.
£1,500–2,000 *CSK*

These were reputedly the property of Miss Anna Maria Dacres, later Mrs Adams, dresser and later wet nurse to the daughters of George III. These corsets are so finely made that it seems most probable they were made for one of the Princesses. The unfinished corset is inscribed four times 'PE'.

A sack-backed open robe and petticoat of pink silk brocaded with sprays of orange and pink flowers and trimmed with a flybraid, the bodice slightly altered, slight damage, c1758.
£8,200–9,000 *C(S)*

By repute this robe was worn by Miss Threipland at a Ball given by Bonnie Prince Charlie in 1745.

A mushroom coloured silk taffeta dress, with old gold satin design of exotic small flowers, the skirt elaborately pleated, the label possibly for W. Tarn, c1876.
£700–800 *CSK*

l. An embroidered silk evening gown, applied with large pearl and crystal beads, the organza overskirt embroidered overall with tiny spots, the ivory waistband stamped in green 'Doucet, 21 Rue de la Paix, Paris', and numbered to the reverse '69180', c1911.
£450–700

c. A French ivory satin and brocaded velvet evening coat, with appliquéd diamond shaped panel embroidered in silver with crystal fringing, the satin woven with a large scale design of irises and maidenhair ferns, lined in pale lilac satin, woven ivory and grey label, numbered '25881', c1912.
£700–900

r. A striped ivory satin and silk gauze gown, the bodice inset with chemical lace in imitation of Venetian needlepoint, slight stain to sash, the waistband stamped in green 'Doucet, 21 Rue de la Paix, Paris', c1911.
£400–600 *S*

Jacques Doucet inherited the family lingerie business which he transformed into a top couture establishment. He dressed the top society of Paris and some of the leading and most glamorous actresses of the day, including Sarah Bernhardt and Rejane. He recognised Poiret's talent for design and trained him to sketch his ideas, cut and drape fabrics. He was also renowned for his knowledge of art, and amassed an impressive collection of 18thC paintings which he sold in 1912 in order to concentrate on 20thC artists, including Modigliani, Picasso and Miró.

A dress of checked muslin, printed with brown stars, the skirt with 2 printed deep flounces, mid-19thC.
£350–400 *CSK*

A midnight blue panne velvet tunic, stencilled with gothic beasts, with long slit medieval style sleeves, unsigned, by Gallenga, c1910.
£1,400–1,700 *CSK*

A yellow silk long sleeved jacket, embroidered with flowering shrubs, irises and roses, lined with green cotton, embroidery 18thC, jacket 19thC.
£500–600 *CSK*

An ivory satin evening dress, with cut-away midriff trimmed with silver braid, paste and simulated pearls, labelled in side-seam 'Balenciaga, 10 avenue Georges V, Paris', c1960.
£400–600 *CSK*

A Chinese red silk informal robe, embroidered in coloured silks with sprigs of blossom and butterflies, the sleeve bands of ivory silk, the borders of black silk, with same motifs as on robe, 19thC.
£750–800 *CSK*

A lilac tweed suit, bound and faced in lilac jersey, with 4 appliquéd pockets, lilac jersey bound gilt buttons, a straight skirt and matching long sleeved blouse, jacket labelled 'Chanel', the reverse with canvas tag stamped '10822', c1960.
£300–400 *CSK*

A dress of yellow challis, printed with sprays of red and yellow flowers, with Bishop sleeves, pleated at the shoulder and neck, slight damage, c1835.
£800–900 *CSK*

An afternoon dress, possibly a wedding dress, of white silk with plastron of maroon satin, the cuffs and trained skirt piped in maroon, labelled 'W. Tarn & Co. 163-173 Newington Causeway and 5-17 New Kent Rd.', c1876.
£600–700 *CSK*

A Taoist priest's red silk robe, embroidered in coloured silks and gilt threads, the back with an asymmetrical representation of the pantheon of the heavens, with the Jade Emperor seated and surrounded by other figures, the borders filled with demi-gods and others, also with the 12 Imperial symbols of authority within roundels, lined in ivory silk, probably re-lined, slight damage, c1750.
£29,000–33,000 *CSK*

A Chinese blue silk dragon robe, embroidered in coloured silks with 9 dragons in gilt threads chasing flaming pearls among clouds, Buddhist and Taoist emblems, also pomegranates and blossom in Peking knot stitch, above a sea-wave border with peonies, with horseshoe cuffs, lined with natural cotton and trimmed with fur, c1800.
£1,700–2,200 *CSK*

A Chinese blue summer weave gauze dragon robe, embroidered in metal threads with 9 dragons chasing flaming pearls among clouds and Taoist emblems, above a sea-wave border, with horseshoe cuffs, late 19thC.
£1,000–1,200 *CSK*

A Chinese dark brown silk formal robe, damask woven with cloud patterns, embroidered in brightly coloured silks with dragons chasing flaming pearls over a sea-wave border, the horseshoe cuffs, hip and skirt decoration of the same, lined in pale grey silk, late 19thC. **£1,700–2,000** *CSK*

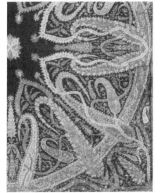

A rumal shawl, c1845, 80 by 74in (203 by 188cm).
£1,500–2,000 *CSK*

A pair of pale green rubber swimming shoes, the uppers with cut-outs and cream trim, the sides with a silver wing design, with ankle strap, 'Phillips Silver Wing, Made in England', fitted with shoe trees, c1920.
£1,200–1,700 *CSK*

A Paisley shawl, with a swagged border, the corners woven with the initials 'RG', 1863-5, 64 by 128in (162.5 by 324.5cm).
£300–500 *CSK*

A Canton scarlet silk shawl, embroidered in white with peonies and leaves, cars, trains and motorcycles, with a knotted fringe, 60in (152cm) square.
£900–1,200 *CSK*

An ivory wool 'moon' shawl, woven with dense pink medallions and blue and green flowers, the field with boteh against a ground of hooked vines, joined, early 19thC, 62 by 66in (157 by 167.5cm).
£4,500–5,000 *CSK*

A pair of black satin lady's boots, embroidered in coloured silks with a peacock on the toe and trailing flower sprigs with corn, 2½in (6cm) heel, the top faced in silk and stamped 'Méliès', c1880.
£1,200–1,700 *CSK*

A pair of brown silk lady's shoes, decorated with pink ribbonwork and chain stitch in pink silk, the rounded toe with a bow, pink silk binding and matching pink leather covered 1½in (4cm) heels, both shoes labelled 'Parry Shoemaker, 1 Little Argyll Street', c1795. **£900–1,200** *CSK*

A pair of linen pockets, false-quilted in yellow silk with feathers, stylised roses against a vermicelli design, bound with yellow silk, early 18thC. **£500–800** *CSK*

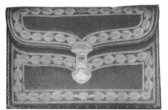

A red morocco wallet, embroidered in gold thread, with a gilt clasp, containing a pair baby's mittens and cuffs, with a note saying 'Baby's glove and cuffs, James VI', all early 18thC, with a pencil drawing. **£730–800** *C(S)*

A needlework purse, worked in green silk and gold thread in eye stitch with the initials 'P.C.S.' and hearts, c1700. **£600–900** *C(S)*

A silk purse of ivory satin, commemorating the recovery of George III, printed with a stipple engraving of a medallion of the King, April 23 1789, suspended from a ribbon bow and flanked by a palm frond and myrtle, the reverse printed with the same design, marked 'I. Bull & Co.' **£250–350** *CSK*

On April 23rd 1789 there was a public Thanksgiving service held at St Paul's Cathedral, which was attended by George III himself.

Three crimson velvet gaming purses, embroidered with various designs in silver metal threads, and 2 others, all 17thC. **£350–400** *CSK*

A purse, with brown ground, woven in coloured silks, depicting a stag hunt, 4 by 6in (10 by 15cm), and another of ivory silk embroidered in coloured silks with carnations and irises, 5 by 6in (12.5 by 15cm), late 17thC. **£200–250** *CSK*

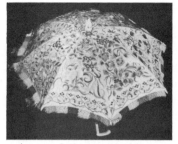

A parasol, the ivory handle densely carved with flowers and phoenix, with a carved ivory finial of Liuhai, the god of Good Fortune, pale blue silk shade embroidered with flowers, with mother-of-pearl spoke ends, Canton, c1880. **£450–550** *CSK*

A needlework purse, embroidered in blue and purple against a yellow ground, with Tudor roses and thistles and fleurs-de-lys, crowns and crossed swords, and initials 'J.R.VIII' for the Old Pretender, early 18thC. **£1,000–1,500** *C(S)*

RUGS & CARPETS

An Agra antique carpet of a Yomut design, the shaded blackcurrant field with 5 columns of 7 Tauk Nuska guls divided by cruciform shapes, surrounded by ivory meandering hooked vine and serrated and hooked lozenges between lapped and zig-zag stripes, minor moth damage, 84 by 75in (213 by 191cm).
£500–700 *CSK*

An Akstafa runner, the royal blue field with a variety of motifs, in an ivory border of polychrome hooked panels between skittle pattern stripes, 129 by 42in (328 by 107cm).
£700–1,000 *CSK*

An Agra antique carpet, the burgundy field with an overall design, areas of wear and colour run, 192 by 141in (487 by 357cm).
£6,500–8,000 *C*

Rug or Carpet?

In Britain and Continental Europe, the distinction between rugs and carpets is based on size. A piece small enough to hang on a wall, or up to approximately 72in (182cm) long, is usually referred to as a rug. Anything longer is a carpet.

However, in practice the terms are more or less interchangeable. In the United States all rugs and carpets are known as rugs.

A Bijar antique runner, the indigo field with stylised design, turtle palmette border and outer blue flowerhead vine stripe, cut, slight wear, dated at one end, 153 by 43in (388.5 by 109cm).
£900–1,200 *CSK*

A Bijar antique rug, the shaded light blue field with a bold design in a yellow meandering flowerhead border between similar brown stripes, repaired, 111 by 57in (282 by 144.5cm).
£1,500–2,500 *CSK*

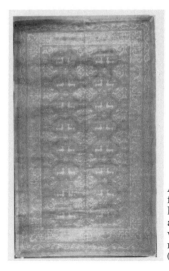

A Hamadan kelleh, with blue flowerhead vine border between boteh vine and S motif stripes, 145 by 61in (368 by 155cm).
£400–600 *CSK*

A Donegal carpet, the steel blue field with overall diagonal floral lattice design, floral vine and animal border between wide vine, floral and plain stripes, minor repair, 189 by 114in (479 by 289cm). **£1,600–2,000** *CSK*

A Heriz carpet, the ivory field decorated with an all-over pattern in copper red, blue and turquoise within a broad indigo meander border with large palmettes and floral motifs, 118 by 85in (300 by 216cm). **£500–600** *P*

A Heriz carpet, the shaded rust shaped field with 3 large hooked indigo medallions, 170 by 130in (431 by 330cm).
£1,500–2,000 *CSK*

A fine Heriz carpet, the shaded brick red field with angular vines and floral motifs, minor repair, 119 by 95in (302 by 241cm).
£900–1,200 *CSK*

A Heriz carpet, the ivory field with pistachio green, rust, yellow and blue surrounded by indigo stylised turtle palmette border, between yellow floral stripes, 125 by 92in (317 by 234cm).
£700–900 *CSK*

An Isfahan rug, the royal blue field with a variety of flowering trees, a pale grey border, and light blue arabesque vine stripes, 67 by 41in (170 by 104cm).
£800–900 *CSK*

A Karabagh antique runner, the indigo field with a variety of flowerheads, the border with outer indigo and black angular floral stripe, worn, 106 by 47in (268 by 119cm).
£5,000–6,000 *C*

A Karabagh rug, the brick red plain field with central shaped floral medallion, surrounded by stylised ivory floral frame border, floral skirt at each end, slight wear, 84 by 55in (213 by 140cm).
£400–500 *CSK*

A pair of Kashan rugs, the ivory field with overall meandering vines in various colours, 78 by 52in (198 by 132cm).
£1,400–1,700 *CSK*

AnKazak antique rug, with a brick red field and indigo medallions, minor wear, 94 by 65in (238 by 165cm).
£700–900 *CSK*

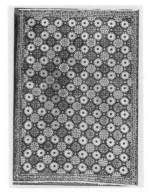

A Kashan carpet, the field with overall lattice containing stylised flowerheads in various colours, surrounded by narrow ivory meandering flowerhead vine border between blue floral stripes, 125 by 92in (317 by 234cm).
£700–1,000 *CSK*

A Kashmir needlework rug, with all-over naturalistic floral design predominantly in tones of red, pink, blue and green on a beige ground, pale blue ground figured and bordered, 66 by 43in (167.5 by 109cm).
£450–550 *MCA*

A Kuba antique runner, with light blue field, broad ivory border, shaded brick red flowerhead and skittle pattern stripes, repaired, 123 by 35in (312.5 by 89cm).
£4,500–5,000 *C*

A Keiseri silk rug, the aqua-blue field with floral vines and medallions, with pendants in various colours, 99 by 64in (251.5 by 162.5cm).
£700–1,000 *CSK*

A Mudjur antique prayer rug, the shaded dusty red field with shaded green mihrab arch, in a yellow flowerhead and floral panel border between light blue and brown flowerhead stripes, slight wear, repaired, 68 by 46in (173 by 116cm).
£400–500 *CSK*

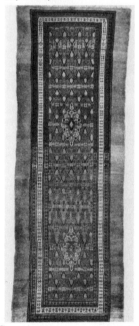

A Serapi antique runner, with stylised floral lattice pattern in shades of blue, yellow, pistachio green, and ivory, on a shaded camel field, 110 by 38in (279 by 96cm).
£600–700 *CSK*

An antique Shiraz rug, the indigo field with overall diagonal rows of stylised boteh in pistachio green, camel, ivory, yellow, blue and brick red, short kelim at each end, overall wear, 83 by 69in (211 by 175cm).
£400–600 *CSK*

A Qum silk rug, on salmon pink field with pendants and olive green spandrels, in shaded indigo turtle palmette border, between floral stripes, 83 by 55in (211 by 140cm).
£1,000–1,200 *CSK*

A Serab carpet, 124 by 89in (315 by 226cm). **£400–600** *CSK*

A Tabriz carpet, the indigo field with palmettes and leafy vines in various colours, around cusped tan medallion containing similar motifs, ivory floral spandrels surrounded by brick red palmette and flowerhead vine border, between ivory palmette and leafy vine stripes, 148 by 108in (376 by 274cm).
£1,500–2,000 *CSK*

A Shirvan prayer rug, the indigo plant trellis mihrab with an ivory prayer arch and star border, north east Caucasus, repaired, 54 by 35in (138 by 89cm).
£1,400–1,700 *S(S)*

A Shiraz antique rug, with a variety of stylised flowerheads, animal and human figures, on a shaded indigo field, 96 by 61in (244 by 155cm).
£500–800 *CSK*

A Soumak rug, in indigo, brick red and pale gold, late 19thC, 82 by 41in (208 by 104cm).
£900–1,000 *WW*

A pair of Tabriz rugs, with ivory field and overall multi-coloured angular vines, indigo stylised panelled flowerhead border, between floral and vine stripes, signed at one end, each 81 by 57in (206 by 145cm).
£900–1,200 *CSK*

PINE
Bookcases

A George III style pine bookcase, with foliate carved swans' neck pediment above a pair of glazed doors, and a pair of cupboard doors, on plinth base, 53in (134.5cm). **£1,500–2,000** *CSK*

A breakfront secrétaire pine bookcase, the fall front drawer applied with moulding and enclosing a fitted interior, on plinth base, damaged, early 19thC, 99in (251.5cm). **£4,500–5,500** *CSK*

A pine glazed bookcase, c1880, 52in (132cm). **£700–800** *OCP*

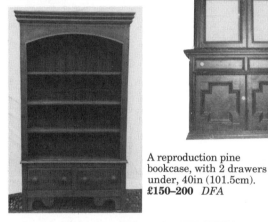

A reproduction pine bookcase, with 2 drawers under, 40in (101.5cm). **£150–200** *DFA*

A painted pine glazed bookcase, with china handles, 19thC, 52in (132cm). **£900–1,000** *OCP*

An Irish pine glazed bookcase, with china knobs, c1840, 37in (94cm). **£450–550** *DMe*

Boxes and Chests

An Irish waxed pine blanket box, c1880, 18½in (47cm). **£70–90** *DFA*

An Irish waxed pine blanket box, c1900, 27in (69cm). **£60–80** *DFA*

A pine box for explosives, marked
'Nobel's Explosives Co., Dublin',
restored, c1920.
£40–50 *DFA*

A pine sea chest, c1860, 35in (89cm).
£100–120 *AL*

A pine cutlery box and a
condiment box, Dublin, c1900,
14in (36cm) long.
£30–35 each *DFA*

A European pine chest, with
domed top, c1930.
£130–150 *OCP*

A pine salt box, c1930,
13in (33cm).
£30–40 *OCP*

A pine cupboard with egg racks,
mid-19thC, 20in (51cm) high.
£70–90 *FP*

A European painted
pine chest, with
original paintwork,
19thC, 49in (124.5cm).
£400–500 *OCP*

A European painted
pine chest, 19thC,
52½in (133cm).
£300–400 *OCP*

An Austrian decorated pine
panelled chest, the front painted
with flowerheads within arches,
trailing foliage and geometric
flowers, dated '1687', the panelled
hinged lid with a dentil moulded
edge, above 5 panels and shaped
aprons on bracket feet, c1700,
73in (185cm).
£5,000–6,000 *CSK*

A pine mule chest,
with 2 drawers,
replacement knobs
and feet, c1850,
44in (111.5cm).
£300–400 *AL*

Chests of Drawers

A pine box, with hinged lid and
candle box, c1880, 32in (81cm).
£155–175 *AL*

A chest of drawers, with dummy drawer at
base, back replaced, c1860, 33in (84cm).
£135–145 *AL*

A pine chest of drawers, c1840, 42in (106.5cm).
£365–465 *AL*

A pine chest of drawers, c1830, 52in (132cm).
£600–630 *AL*

A pine chest of drawers, c1845, 34in (86cm).
£250–350 *DMe*

A pine chest of drawers, with bracket feet, c1880, 34in (86cm) wide.
£500–535 *AL*

A painted pine chest of drawers, c1880, 41in (104cm) high.
£500–600 *AL*

A blue painted pine chest of drawers, with pottery knobs, c1870, 39in (99cm).
£400–465 *AL*

A pine filing cabinet, c1890, 48in (122cm) high.
£225–235 *AL*

A nest of drawers, c1870, 78in (198cm) high. **£650–750** *UP*

A flight of pine standing drawers, c1870, 44in (111.5cm).
£1,250–1,350 *AL*

A flight of pine drawers, c1880, 25in (64cm) high.
£240–280 *AL*

Chairs

A Scottish pine chest of drawers, c1890, 47in (119cm) wide.
£645–665 *AL*

A pine captain's chair, with beech and elm seat, partly stripped, late 19thC. **£80–90** *DFA*

An Irish pine high chair, early 20thC, 19in (48cm) wide.
£100–130 *DFA*

A small flight of pine drawers, with replacement knobs, 13in (33cm) wide.
£175–195 *AL*

An Irish pine settle bed, Co. Clare, c1850. **£300–350** *HON*

A pine bow-shaped settle, 19thC, 62in (157cm) wide. **£500–600** *OCP*

Cupboards

A George II style pine corner cupboard, with foliate cornice above 2 pairs of panelled cupboard doors, with egg-and-dart moulding, on plinth base, 43in (109cm).
£1,300–1,700 *CSK*

A Irish bowfronted painted pine corner cupboard, with glazed doors, c1840, 76in (193cm) high.
£1,200–1,350 *DFA*

An Irish pine corner cupboard, with astragal glazed doors, 3 drawers over 2 doors to base, early 19thC, 42in (106.5cm).
£1,400–1,800 *TPC*

A Michelangelo. Only in Florence.

A Van der Tol. Only in Almere.

We carry one of the world's finest collections of antique pine furniture.

Available in unstripped, stripped and finished & painted versions. Plus pine

reproductions and decorative items. We offer quality, quantity & profit and

full packing service. Please visit our 65.000 sq.ft. warehouse

in Almere and enjoy the personal and friendly service.

Jacques van der Tol
unique antique pine furniture

A pine linen press, with stencilled decoration, c1880, 48in (122cm).
£600–800 *DFA*

A Georgian pine glazed cabinet, with swans' neck pediment, with a pair of astragal glazed doors with oval centres, fitted shelves to interior, the sides having moulded decoration, with fitted drawer below, on bracket feet, 57in (144.5cm).
£1,500–2,000 *RBB*

An Irish pine wardrobe, c1790, 54in (137cm).
£1,000–1,100 *UP*

A tin lined proving cupboard, with replacement feet, c1870, 43½in (110cm).
£450–525 *AL*

A painted pine corner cupboard, 20thC, 19in (48cm) .
£65–75 *OCP*

A pine huffer, or warming cupboard, with a tin lining, c1850, 43½in (110cm). **£500–535** *AL*

A European pine corner cupboard, 19thC, 52in (132cm) high.
£300–400 *OCP*

A Swiss pine and walnut side cabinet, with upper cupboard enclosed by a geometrically moulded panelled door, raised on shaped bracket supports with an open shelf between, the lower section with canted angles and central raised panelled cupboard door, on moulded plinth, restored, 28in (71cm) wide.
£2,300–2,600 *CSK*

A pine press cupboard, c1860,
44in (111.5cm).
£850–950 *UP*

A painted pine linen press, with
5 drawers, c1840, 63in (160cm).
£800–900 *OCP*

A pine wardrobe, with
2 painted panelled doors,
c1900, 48in (122cm).
£300–400 *OCP*

A pine compactum, with
carved pine and gesso
decoration, 19thC,
60in (152cm).
£1,000–1,500 *TPC*

A pine cupboard, with one drawer
above 2 panelled doors, galleried
top, c1880, 36in (91.5cm).
£600–650 *AL*

A 4 door cupboard, with
replacement side and plinth,
85½in (216cm).
£350–400 *AL*

A Welsh pine press
cupboard, 18thC,
54in (137cm).
£900–1,200 *TPC*

A pine pot cupboard,
c1870, 15in (38cm).
£175–185 *AL*

A painted pine cupboard,
with Adam style gesso
decoration, 18thC,
52in (132cm).
£1,400–1,500 *OCP*

*This cupboard was
originally set into a wall
of a house built in 1777.*

An Irish pine cupboard, with 2 drawers inside, and 2 further drawers below, the panels decorated with carving, restored, with later additions, c1890, 48in (122cm).
£500–600 *DFA*

A painted pine cupboard, 58in (147cm) wide.
£500–600 *OCP*

Originally a deep bed cupboard, bed now missing.

A Georgian style pine kitchen cupboard, 50in (127cm).
£800–1,000 *DFA*

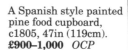

A pine breakfront housekeeper's cupboard, with 4 blind panel doors to top, the base with central panel door and 7 drawers, on bracket feet, 84in (213cm).
£1,200–1,800 *TPC*

A pine wall cupboard, 14½in (37cm) wide.
£30–50 *DFA*

A Spanish style painted pine food cupboard, c1805, 47in (119cm).
£900–1,000 *OCP*

A Gothic style pine chiffonier, c1850, 31in (79cm).
£300–350 *DMe*

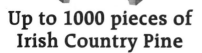

Desks

A pine partners' desk, c1880, 60in (152cm).
£1,000–1,250 *UP*

Dressers

An Irish pine desk, with
2 cupboard doors, c1850,
23½in (60cm) wide.
£170–220 *DMe*

An Irish pine pot board dresser,
with scratch carved breakfront
cornice, c1790, 60in (152cm).
£1,200–1,500 *OCP*

A pine dresser, with later
paintwork, c1870, 56in (142cm).
£400–500 *OCP*

An Irish pitch pine folding school
desk, c1920, 24in (61cm).
£25–30 *DFA*

A pine dresser base, with
sycamore top, early 19thC,
62in (157cm).
£500–600 *FP*

A two-piece pine dresser,
c1800, 84in (213cm).
£2,000–2,500 *AL*

An Irish pine dresser, with
moulded cornice, 3 drawers,
c1820, 59in (149.5cm).
£800–900 *OCP*

An Irish dresser, c1860,
44in (111.5cm).
£1,000–1,250 *UP*

An Irish stripped pine
dresser, with added
pillars, c1880,
50in (127cm).
£350–400 *DFA*

An Irish fiddle front dresser, c1850, 51in (129.5cm).
£1,250–1,350 *UP*

A pine dresser, with shoe feet, c1880, 50in (127cm).
£500–600 *OCP*

An Irish double chicken coop pine dresser, 19thC, 58in (147cm).
£600–800 *OCP*

A pine dresser, with open delft rack, shaped sides, dentil and carved pine cornice and frieze, on bracket feet, 19thC, 108in (274cm).
£1,500–2,000 *TPC*

A one-piece pine dresser, c1880, 37in (94cm) wide.
£650–700 *AL*

An Irish chicken coop dresser, 19thC, 56in (142cm).
£500–700 *OCP*

Miller's is a price GUIDE not a price LIST.

A Scottish pine dresser, c1860, 78in (198cm).
£1,200–1,400 *AL*

An open base pine dresser, with potboard.   **£900–940** *AL*

An Irish plate rack dresser, Dublin, c1880, 54in (137cm).
£400–500 *DFA*

An Irish pine dresser, c1850, 50in (127cm).
£850–950 *UP*

A two-piece dresser, with new back, c1870, 51in (129.5cm).
£660–750 *AL*

Fire Surrounds

A pine fire surround with dentil moulding under mantel shelf, supported on 2 large turned and fluted columns, 19thC, 60in (152cm).
£400–600 *TPC*

A George III carved pine fire surround, the swag carved frieze centred by a tablet carved with an urn and flower swags, the jambs with pendant flowers, c1780, 75in (190.5cm).
£2,500–3,500 *S*

A carved pine fire surround, early 19thC, 48in (122cm).
£300–500 *TPC*

A George III, Robert Adam style, pine fire surround, the frieze with raised carved pine classical decoration of urns, swags, paterae, flambé and quiver motifs, above carved sides with pendant harebells, 77in (195.5cm).
£1,500–1,700 *B*

Racks and Shelves

A pine Liberty shelf, c1880, 12in (31cm) wide.
£90–100 *AL*

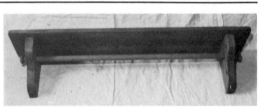

A pine towel rail, 20thC, 38in (96.5cm) long. **£30–45** *DFA*

A pine plate rack, c1870, 19in (48cm) wide.
£60–80 *AL*

A set of pine hanging shelves, with spice drawers, 38½in (98cm).
£80–90 *OCP*

A pine bottle rack, altered to take wine bottles, partly 19thC, 45in (114cm).
£400–500 *OCP*

A pine shoe rack.
£85–110 *FP*

A pine bookcase, c1880, 50in (127cm).
£100–125 *AL*

Stools & Benches

A pine bench, 19thC,
53in (134.5cm) long.
£25–35 *DFA*

A pine bench, c1900, 70in
(177.5cm) long.
£70–80 *DFA*

Tables

An Irish waxed pine side table,
with 2 drawers and turned legs,
c1880, 39½in (100cm).
£80–100 *DFA*

In the Pine section when
there is only one
measurement it refers to
the width of the piece,
unless otherwise stated.

A pine stool, c1910,
11in (28cm) diam.
£25–30 *DFA*

An Irish pine stool, restored,
c1910, 24in (61cm).
£20–25 *DFA*

An Irish pine
table, with
turned legs,
restored, c1900,
25½in (65cm).
£45–65 *DFA*

A pine sofa table, with 4 drawers, considerable
alterations, restored, 83in (210.5cm) long.
£250–300 *DFA*

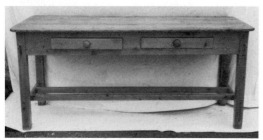

A pine serving or side table, with 2 drawers
above double stretchers, c1860, 67in (170cm).
£250–350 *DFA*

An Irish late Georgian or Regency pine table, in good condition, 52½in (133cm) diam.
£1,000–1,250 *DFA*

A Victorian carved pine console table, with marble top, 48in (122cm) wide.
£900–1,000 *OCP*

Washstands

A pine washstand, with turned legs, 19thC.
£175–200 *FP*

An Irish waxed pine washstand, with undershelf, c1870, 30in (76cm).
£60–70 *DFA*

A pine table, late 19thC, 21in (53cm) wide.
£50–65 *DFA*

A pine washstand, with drawer, c1845, 37in (94cm).
£120–200 *DMe*

A pine washstand, with marble top, c1870, 37in (94cm).
£250–300 *AL*

A pine bedside table, with a towel rail, c1880, 21in (53cm).
£70–85 *DFA*

A pine washstand, with basin hole, c1900, 22in (56cm).
£30–50 *DFA*

A pine washstand, with fretwork gallery and turned legs, c1860.
£130–150 *SA*

Miscellaneous

A child's painted pine settle, with original paintwork, c1860, 36½in (93cm) high.
£600–700 *OCP*

An Georgian Irish pine cradle, c1800, 17in (43cm).
£50–80 *DFA*

A set of pine hanging spice drawers, 19thC, 8in (20cm).
£50–60 *OCP*

A pine butter churn, c1940, 16½in (42cm) diam.
£50–60 *OCP*

A pine butcher's block, on original table base, 20thC, 61in (155cm).
£250–300 *DFA*

A carved and painted pine bird, 19thC, 14in (36cm).
£1,100–1,250 *ChC*

A pine candle holder, c1900, 32in (81cm) high.
£30–40 *OCP*

A pine food safe, c1880, 38in (96.5cm) wide.
£300–400 *OCP*

A pine fire screen, c1900, 29in (74cm) wide.
£70–80 *OCP*

A pair of pine pillars, c1800, 87in (221cm) high. **£500–600** *DFA*

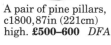

A painted pine child's cot, with original red paint, 38in (96.5cm) wide.
£300–350 *OCP*

An Irish pine pestle, late 19thC, 15½in (39cm). **£18–20** *DFA*

A pine fire screen, c1900, 29in (74cm) wide. **£70–80** *OCP*

A pine folding towel rail, 52in (132cm) wide extended. **£85–95** *OCA*

A pitch pine pillar, 19thC, 51in (129.5cm) high. **£100–130** *DFA*

A late Victorian panelled saddle horse, the gabled top with a pair of hinged flaps and a detachable covered pole with branches, marked 'Musgrave & Co. Belfast', one end mounted with pivoted iron carrying handles, the other raised on casters, 56in (142cm) long. **£800–1,000** *S(S)*

An Irish pine washing dolly, 19thC, 36½in (93cm) high. **£30–45** *DFA*

Stripped Pine

Pine is a soft, straight grained wood that ranges in colour from yellow to nearly white. It is often used to make the carcass of a piece of furniture which is then veneered. It has also been used extensively to make household furniture which was then almost always painted.

People who strip pine commercially normally strip the furniture in a tank of caustic soda and then hose it down. This can sometimes leave the pine looking a little 'acid' in colour, but it is possible to rectify this by waxing the furniture with a slightly darker coloured wax. Apply the wax evenly all over the surface, and polish off when the desired colour is attained, after which neutral wax can be used.

A pair of Edwardian pine butter pats, 9in (22.5cm) long.
£8–10 *DFA*

A pine cart, with later wheels, c1900, 29½in (75cm).
£70–80 *DFA*

A pine flour bin, c1850, 27in (69cm).
£120–180 *DMe*

A pine dog kennel, c1880, 25½in (65cm) wide.
£80–120 *DFA*

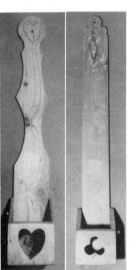

Two pine candle holders, c1880, 30 and 34in (76 and 86cm) high.
£30–40 each *OCP*

Two sets of painted pine hanging spice drawers, 19thC, 6in (15cm).
£40–50 each *OCP*

A pair of Irish pine butter bowls, 19thC, 17 and 13½in (43 and 34cm) diam.
£45–55 *DFA*

ARMS & ARMOUR
Armour

A cuirassier's helmet, good colour and patina, restored, early 17thC.
£2,100–2,700 *WAL*

A cabasset, formed in one piece, with pear stalk finial to crown, slight damage, c1600.
£140–170 *WAL*

An Indian mail and lamellar shirt, the back with 3 vertical rows of lamellae, 17thC, weight 9½ kilos.
£1,000–1,200 *WAL*

This is one of a group of shirts taken at the Siege of Adoni in 1689 when the Adilshahi Dynasty fell to Aurungzebe, then retained at Bijapur.

A pair of German Imperial iron and brass pickelhaube, with gilt crests.
£1,700–2,000 *CoH*

A cabasset, formed in one piece, with pear stalk finial to crown, some damage, c1600.
£170–220 *WAL*

A German bulletproof cuirassier breastplate, stamped with crowned 'FW' of Frederick Wilhelm, regimental number 'A15' and maker's name 'Hartkopf', original hessian lining with large internal pouch, some damage, 19thC.
£350–400 *WAL*

An Indian mail and lamellar shirt, 3 vertical rows of lamellae to back, spine plates each with shaped bottom edge, slight rust, 17thC, weight 12½ kilos.
£650–700 *WAL*

A three-quarter suit of armour, with unusual coronet helmet, mainly 19thC.
£1,500–1,800 *WIG*

A mail shirt, made from rivetted links of graduated sizes, slight rust, 16th or 17thC, weight 6½ kilos.
£440–480 *WAL*

Care of Armour

- Treat rust with equal quantities of turpentine and paraffin, and a little methylated spirit.
- Polish armour with balls of newspaper and protect it with wax.

A cabasset, formed in one piece with pear stalk finial, brass rivet heads, struck with armourer's mark, slight damage, c1600.
£140–170 *WAL*

A cabasset, formed in one piece, with pear stalk finial, brass rivet heads, struck with armourer's mark, roped border, contemporary repair, c1600.
£170–200 *WAL*

A cabasset, formed in one piece, with brass rivet heads, small crack to finial, c1600.
£170–200 *WAL*

A composite cuirassier's armour of bright steel, studded with rivets, with turned edges, comprising: close helmet with fluted ovoidal 2-piece skull, single neckplate front and rear, gorget of 2 plates, pauldrons and full arm defences including fingered gauntlets, cuirass, and knee length tassets and skirt of upward lapping lames, on wooden dummy with later greaves and sabatons, probably German, early 17thC. **£7,000–8,000** *C(S)*

A suit of pikeman's armour, the pot helmet with steel rivets, gorget, 2 armourer's marks at neck, thigh guards decorated with steel rivets. **£3,000–4,000** *L*

A Netherlands or Flemish cavalry trooper's pot helmet, the skull made from a single piece of metal decorated with 6 ridges and topped with suspension loop, the peak with articulated noseguard, hinged cheek pieces and fully articulated lobster tail style neckguard of 4 lames, some minor damage, mid-17thC. **£800–900** *ASB*

An Indo-Persian kula khud, the deep skull carved and chiselled with flowers, foliage and small oval beamquets bearing Kufic inscriptions, possibly verses from the Koran, with adjustable nasal bar and single plume holder, large square section spike to top and fine chainmail flap to the brim decorated with jagged edges, slight damage, 19thC. **£500–600** *ASB*

An officer's dark green peaked forage cap, probably 6th Jat Light Infantry, black oak leaf lace headband, gilt embroidered peak and piping, black braided top ornament and oak leaf lace headband bearing gilt '6' surmounted by strung bugle, leather and silk lining, damaged. **£300–350** *WAL*

An other ranks' white metal helmet of the 6th Dragoon Guards, brass mounts, leather backed chin chain and rosettes, brass and white metal helmet plate, white hair plume with small rosette, leather lining, restored and polished bright. **£600–700** *WAL*

Headdress

A German Imperial gilt helmet plate, with star of the Black Eagle, possibly from a Guard's officer's dress helmet, together with various other regimental badges and insignia, including some Third Reich items. **£170–200** *DN*

An officer's astrakhan busby of the Wiltshire Rifle Volunteers, black cord trim and boss bearing blackened white metal badge with polished highlights, bugle badge below, black hair over blue feather plume in blackened white metal socket, leather chin strap, set of cap lines and acorns. **£200–270** *WAL*

An officer's helmet of the Royal Horse Guards, gilt mounts, velvet backed chin chain and rosettes, gilt and silver plated helmet plate with enamelled centre, scarlet hair plume with large rosette, leather lining, reconditioned.
£1,200–1,700 *WAL*

A Victorian officer's black patent leather lance cap of the 9th Lancers, blue cloth side to patent leather top, gilt ornamental band to waist, metal rosette and button, beaded link chin chain and lions' head ear bosses, top mounts, gilt and silver plated helmet plate with battle honours to Afghanistan, slight damage, restored.
£1,200–1,700 *WAL*

A Victorian other ranks' lance cap of the 12th Lancers, with black patent leather skull, peak and top, crimson cloth sides, yellow and blue lace headband and wool rosette with button, brass mounts, plate with battle honours 'Penninsula', 'Waterloo' and 'Sevastopol', correct leather backed chin chain, leather and linen lining, showing wear.
£500–600 *WAL*

A Victorian other ranks' shako of the South Middlesex Rifle Volunteers, with black patent leather peak, lace bands top and bottom, blackened Maltese Cross helmet plate, leather backed blackened chin chain and rosettes, leather lining, in a tin case, slight damage.
£150–200 *WAL*

A miniature other ranks' brass helmet of the 5th Dragoon Guards, with brass mounts, bi-metal helmet plate, leather backed chin scales and ear rosettes, white over red hair plume with rosette, leather lining, 10in (25cm) high.
£300–350 *WAL*

A WWII general officer's No. 1 blue peaked cap, with scarlet headband, embroidered peak and badge, leather chin strap.
£80–90 *WAL*

> **Miller's is a price GUIDE not a price LIST.**

A Victorian officer's bell topped shako of the 12th Regiment, the black felt skull with brass mounted patent leather peak and top, gilded brass plate with silver centre incorporating castle above 'XII' within garter bearing motto 'MONTIS INSIGNIA CALPE' with battle honours for Minden, Seringapatam, Gibralter and India, cream ball with gilded support, retaining chin chain, some damage, with applied label 'Oliphant's, Cockspur St., London'.
£4,000–5,000 *S(S)*

A Victorian other ranks' helmet of the 3rd Devon Light Horse, the black pressed felt skull with integral front and rear peaks, white metal helmet plate bearing the number '3' within Devon Light Horse garter surrounded by oak leaf wreath and surmounted by a crown, white metal mounts with red and white horse hair plume, retaining lining, damaged, c1855.
£1,500–2,000 *S(S)*

An officer's helmet of the
North Shropshire Yeomanry,
damaged, c1840.
£1,500–2,000 *C*

An officer's cloth helmet of the
3rd Glamorgan Rifle Corps, with
silvered metal spike and garter
badge, in tin box, and a blue
side cap.
£700–750 *C(S)*

A Victorian officer's blue cloth
helmet of the 2nd Volunteer
Battalion The Derbyshire
Regiment, by Hobson & Sons,
silver plated helmet plate and
mounts, leather and silk lining
inscribed 'C.J. White', with chin
chain, one hook broken, in
japanned case, together with
peaked pillbox hat.
£800–900 *S(S)*

An Imperial German 1899 pattern
Artilleryman's pickelhaube as
worn by the 46th Artillery Regt.,
brass helmet plate with battle
honours, 'Peninsular', 'Waterloo',
'Gohrde', leather backed brass
chin scales, brass mounts, both
cockades, inside of neck guard
stamped '1901' with stamp of the
Battery '4te B' and maker 'Müller
Offenbach A.M.', damaged.
£400–450 *WAL*

An Imperial German Prussian
1897 pattern Hussar non-
commissioned officer's sealskin
busby as worn by the 15th Hussar
Regiment, battle honour scrolls
'Peninsular', 'Waterloo', 'El
Bodon', 'Barossa', leather backed
brass chin scales with traces of
gilding, state cockade, yellow bag,
cap lines, silk lining and leather
sweat band, restored.
£600–700 *WAL*

A French fireman's helmet,
inscribed 'Sapeurs Pompiers
de Paris', mid-19thC.
£200–250 *L&E*

Uniform

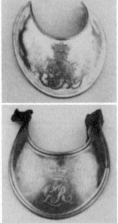

An officer's gilt gorget, engraved
with 'GR' cypher beneath a crown
and flanked by laurel sprays,
4in (10cm) and another engraved
with 'GR' beneath a crown, with
blue silk rosette ribbon, 4½in (11cm).
£180–250 *DN*

An other ranks' full dress dark
green tunic of the Loyal Suffolk
Hussars, scarlet collar, yellow
cord trim including 6 loops with
netted bosses and brass ball
buttons to chest, Austrian knots
to cuffs and skirts, white metal
collar badges, and a pair of
matching overalls with double
yellow stripe.
£50–90 *WAL*

A Russian Preobrazhensky
Guard shoulder-belt pouch, by
R. Klinger, the plain silver plated
pouch cover with rope design
surround and an enamelled
St. Andrew star affixed centre,
with red leather pouch with side
attachments and overlaid
strap, c1880.
£750–1,000 *S(G)*

Uniform

Relatively few early 19thC uniforms survive, for as well as receiving an exceptional amount of hard wear, they are particularly susceptible to moths.

Old uniforms should be carefully checked for holes and worn fabric, but a certain amount of wear is inevitable. Buttons are usually original, but contemporary replacements are acceptable.

An officer's undress sporran of a Voluntary Battalion The Gordon Highlanders, engraved white metal cantle and badge, white goat hair, 2 long black tassels, in engraved white metal sockets.
£220–270 *WAL*

A Hussar Captain's full blue dress tunic, with gilt lace, gimp and braid trim, including 6 loops with olivets and purl buttons to chest, Austrian knots braided for Captain to cuffs, shoulder cords, showing signs of wear.
£400–500 *WAL*

An other ranks' full dress scarlet tunic of the 19th County of London Battalion, green facings, scarlet shoulder straps with white edging bearing brass T/19/County of London titles, universal buttons, tailor's label inside with name 'Pte 1584 Beale, S' and '19 C... R..', a silver RMLI sweetheart badge HM 1902, and 3 other badges, some damage.
£70–90 *WAL*

An officer's scarlet coatee, of the St. George's Battalion Manchester Volunteers, blue facings, 2 lines of 10 buttons to chest, single narrow loop and button to collar and 4 similar with buttons to cuffs, c1805.
£700–800 *WAL*

A US Aero Service sergeant's tunic and breeches, for Sgt. Richard Schmidt, with pilot's shoulder badge, 3 year service chevrons, collar insignia and buttons, with photograph of Sgt Schmidt.
£150–200 *CSK*

A Lieutenant Colonel's Highlanders tunic from the Duke of Atholl's private army, with silver mounted cross belt and sporran, 19thC.
£450–550 *BWA*

A W.R. IV colonel's coatee of the 27th Foot, scarlet with buff facings, bullion lace to cuffs, collar and tails, with bullion embroidered regimental skirt badges, gilt buttons, padded bullion epaulettes bearing rank badges and W.R., moth damage.
£1,500–2,000 *S(S)*

A US Aero Service corporal's tunic and breaches, for Ptz Louis G Blaken of the Aviation Section Regiment of US Army Signal Corps, with badges of rank and 2 year service chevrons, a pocket book cover, photocopy of medal citation, photograph and service history.
£450–650 *CSK*

Truncheons

A Victorian truncheon, inscribed
'Ludgershall', original paint,
18½in (47cm) long.
£100–150 *RdeR*

A William IV truncheon, Parish
of Walcot, 15in (38cm) long.
£150–200 *RdeR*

Daggers & Knives

A Bowie knife, by Henry C. Booth
& Co., straight single edged blade,
68in (172cm), some pitting,
engraved nickel crosspiece and
pommel, ivory grips, oval nickel
escutcheon, in its leather sheath
with gilded embossed foliate
decoration and nickel mounts,
damaged. **£500–700** *S(S)*

*This knife was reputedly given
to the vendor's grandfather as a
token of appreciation for helping
one of Chief Sitting Bull's Indians
back to Aston Hippodrome where
Buffalo Bill Cody's Wild West
Show took place.*

A Wilkinson 1st Pattern F. S.
fighting knife, straight double
edged blade, 6½in (16cm), marked
with maker's trade mark and the
'F-S Fighting Knife' at forte,
reversed cross piece, plated
chequered grip defective, in its
leather sheath with plated chape.
£150–250 *S(S)*

An NSK K Senior Official's dagger
Gebruder Heller, straight double
edged blade, 8½in (21cm), nickel
crosspiece and pommel, polished
hardwood grip, in its black painted
sheath with its nickel plated
mounts and suspension chains.
£2,000–2,500 *S(S)*

A Wilkinson 2nd
Pattern F.S. fighting
knife, straight double
edged blade 7in
(17.5cm), marked with
Wilkinson trademark
and 'F-S Fighting
knife' at forte, straight
oval cross piece,
chequered brass grip,
in its leather sheath
with brass chape.
£120–170 *S(S)*

A Wilkinson 1st
Pattern F. S. fighting
knife, straight double
edged blade, 6½in
(16cm), marked with
Wilkinson trademark
and 'F-S Fighting
Knife' at forte,
reversed cross piece,
chequered plated grip,
in its leather sheath,
tongue repaired.
£300–400 *S(S)*

A fighting knife of F. S. form, straight double edged blade, 7in (17.5cm), oval 1in crosspiece, plated chequered grip, in its leather sheath with plated chape, with 2 stitched on tabs.
£170–250 *S(S)*

A Wilkinson 1st Pattern F. S. fighting knife, straight double edged blade, 7in (17.5cm), marked with Wilkinson trademark, and 'F-S Fighting Knife' at forte, reversed crosspiece, plated chequered hilt, damaged, in its leather sheath with plated chape, tongue modified to suit wide belt.
£200–300 *S(S)*

A Victorian 3rd Battalion Seaforth Highlanders dirk, by Goodall & Graham, straight single edged blade, 12in (31cm) with scalloped back and etched with crowned 'V.R.' cypher, thistles, foliate scrolls and regimental inscription, embossed brass mounts with dark hardwood grip carved with cross swords, feather bonnet and basket weave, faceted stone to pommel, in its matching leather covered sheath with companion knife and fork, damaged.
£800–900 *S(S)*

A silver mounted Argyll & Sutherland Highlanders officer's full dress dirk, by S. J. Pilling, 31 Gerrard Street, Soho, London, with ebonised wooden grip carved with Celtic basket weave pattern and decorated with small silver headed nails, foil lined paste cairngorm to pommel, straight single edged blade with twin fullers and notched back, etched overall with regimental badges, thistles and foliage, in its original black leather sheath, complete with bi-knife and fork, the sheath mounts finely chased with the regimental badges amidst Celtic monster motifs, the locket bearing previous owner's initials 'A. W.', minor rust, c1900, blade 12in (31cm).
£1,000-1,300 *ASB*

Pistols

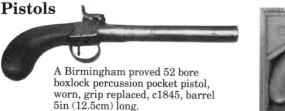

A Birmingham proved 52 bore boxlock percussion pocket pistol, worn, grip replaced, c1845, barrel 5in (12.5cm) long.
£120–150 *ASB*

A 25 bore turn-off barrel boxlock percussion pocket pistol, with octagonal barrel and chequered walnut bag shaped grip, well refinished, c1860, barrel 4in (10cm) long.
£120–150 *ASB*

A boxlock flintlock pistol, turn-off cannon barrel, the lock signed 'Archer, London', the slab sided bolt with inlaid silver wire, 7½in (19cm) overall.
£200–250 *DN*

A pair of 38 bore percussion duelling pistols, with 10in (25cm) octagonal barrels, Joseph Manton patent tablets to breeches, half stocked with engraved steel furniture, damaged, in a fitted mahogany case.
£1,000–1,200 *S(S)*

A Queen Anne silver mounted flintlock pistol with turn-off cannon barrel, the breech inscribed 'London' and signed beneath the pan 'James Freeman', the butt with silver cap, applied silver scrolls and escutcheon plate with incised badge, the lock defective and cock replaced, 11½in (29cm) overall.
£800–1,000 *DN*

A double barrelled flintlock pistol, with London proof, signed on the top barrel 'Wilson, London', swivel removed, platinum touch holes, gold line at breech, the stepped locks with sliding bolt safety catches, damp-proof pans, swan-neck cocks, plates signed 'Wilson', butt with cross-hatching, silver escutcheon plate, engraved trigger guard, c1810, 12in (30.5cm).
£700–900 *DN*

An overcoat flintlock pistol, the circular barrel with Birmingham proof, signed London, stepped lock signed 'Hamilton', swan neck cock, brass furniture comprising: ramrod pipe, trigger guard with pineapple finial, horn tipped ramrod, with jag, 9in (23.5cm) long overall.
£250–350 *DN*

Proof Marks

Most English firearms from the 18thC onwards bear the viewing mark of the checker, and the proof mark on the barrel, guaranteeing that it was safe to fire at the time of examination.

Most European countries followed a similar system. Many pistols imported into England during the 19thC bear the Belgian Liège proof mark. Some Continental guns can be found with English proof marks.

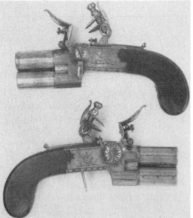

A pair of 54 bore double barrelled flintlock tap action pocket pistols, by EGG, with barrel key.
£3,400–4,000 *S(S)*

A French flintlock pistol, full stock with steel furniture, comprising: muzzle band side plate struck 'L.F.' and butt cap, steel ramrod, the steel barrel indistinctly signed, the lock with brass pan and ring neck cock signed 'Maubuge, Man of Na', 9in (23.5cm) overall.
£300–350 *DN*

A pair of Turkish silver mounted flintlock pistols, barrels with 3 flat ribs 17in (43cm), locks with swan neck cocks and frizzen springs with small rollers, fully stocked, domed butt caps with crescent and star decoration, side plates with scrolling foliage, with silver simulated ramrods, 19thC.
£2,500–3,000 *S(S)*

Top: A Continental flintlock pistol, with embossed silver pommel, 18thC, 19in (48cm) long.
£450–500
Centre: A flintlock pistol, with Miquelet lock, brass pommel, 18thC, 14in (36cm) long.
£360–420
Bottom: A pair of flintlock pistols, with bayonet attachments, 12½in (32cm) long.
£300–350 *WL*

A silver mounted flintlock pistol, by Westley Richards, 16in (41cm) long.
£500–600 *WIG*

A pair of double barrel percussion pistols converted from flintlock, the faceted barrels signed in gold 'D. Egg, London', the bolt safety catches signed in script 'D. Egg', fitted with divided belthook, c1800, conversion c1820, 12in (30cm) overall.
£1,400–1,700 *DN*

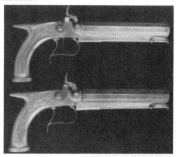

A military percussion pistol with detachable butt, the steel barrel with faceted breach and stamped '1855', sighted, with muzzle sight protector, plain lockplate engraved 'Sohl. V.C.S.', pivoted metal nipple protector, full stock plain steel trigger guard with spur, plain wooden butt, with locking spring catch, bar with sliding ring and turned armed spring catch, 28in (71cm) overall.
£600–700 *DN*

A 30 bore percussion belt pistol, retailed by Connell, 83 Cheapside, London, some pitting, leather cracked, c1850, 5in (12.5cm) long overall.
£800–900 *ASB*

A pair of 38 bore percussion side hammer box lock belt pistols, octagonal barrels 6in (15cm), with swivel rammers, nickel frame engraved with panels of thistles and 'A. Henry Edinburgh', plain hammers, spurred trigger guards, steel belt hooks, damaged.
£700–1,000 *S(S)*

Powder Flasks

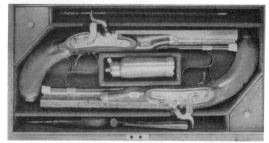

A pair of horn powder flasks, with brass mounts, 13½in (34cm) long.
£100–150 *WIG*

A pair of 20 bore percussion target pistols, by Hollis, octagonal barrel 9in (22.5cm), contained in their made-up mahogany case with copper three-way flask, steel pincer mould and turnscrew. **£1,200–1,700** *S(S)*

A powder horn, with engraved brass cap and plate with spring operated cut off and brass charger, side mounted with belt hook and loop, 10in (25.5cm).
£350–450 *DN*

A musketeer's powder flask, the wooden body with remains of velvet covering, the edges with iron binding and the front with pierced metal plate, metal charger with base spring operated cut off, 4 side suspension loops, lacking belt hook, 11in (27.5cm) long.
£450–550 *DN*

A doughnut powder flask, the wooden 5in (12.5cm) diameter body decorated overall with inlaid discs, some with incised line decoration, horn charger and 2 side mounted suspension loops.
£650–750 *DN*

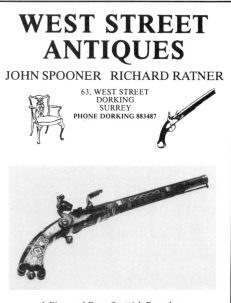

Shotguns

A Holland and Holland patent
ejector double barrelled 12 bore
shotgun, No. 20989, and a leather
covered fitted case.
£1,000–1,500 *HOLL*

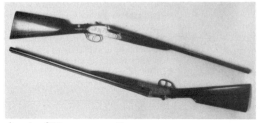

A pair of 12 gauge sporting
shotguns, with 25in (64cm)
barrels, figured walnut stocks,
and detachable locks, stamped
'John Powell'.
£2,000–2,500 *WIG*

A 12 gauge sporting shotgun, by
J. Purdey & Sons, London, with
28in (71cm) barrels.
£1,800–2,200 *WIG*

Revolvers

A 54 bore Adams Patent 5 shot double action
percussion revolver, retailed by Dickson & Son,
No. 14481 R, octagonal 6in (15cm) barrel, border
engraved frame with side mounted rammer and
sliding cylinder bolt, chequered walnut grip,
retaining much original blue finish, some rust,
rammer loose, in a fitted oak case.
£800–1,200 *S(S)*

A 54 bore 6 shot single action
transitional percussion revolver,
by Thomas Baker, No. 434,
octagonal 6in (15cm) barrel, plain
cylinder sliding on access to
provide gas seal, rounded foliate
engraved frame, long spur
hammer, chequered walnut grip
with engraved steel butt trap.
£520–600 *S(S)*

Rifles

A .500 hammer rifle, by Stephen
Grant, No. 4873, with 28in (71cm)
damascus barrels, Henrys patent
rifling, machined rib with leaf
sight to 200, frame, backlocks,
underlever and bolted hammers
with close scroll engraving,
retaining traces of hardening
colour, 14½in (37cm) figured stock
with pistol grip, cheekpiece and
steel butt plate, in its brass bound
oak and leather case.
£1,500–2,000 *S(S)*

A German wheel lock rifle, the
heavy octagonal barrel with
7 groove rifling, brass front sight
and folding leaf near sight, signed
at the breech 'Georg Zeffel in
Wiesenthal', marked on the tang
with the number 'XII', the lock
engraved with classical rural
scene, the dog head pierced and
engraved with monsters, full
walnut stock with inlaid plaques
of horn, of deer, a lion, a hare
coursing scene and decorative
panels and a small plaque with
initials 'B.E.', the butt with trap
and sliding cover decorated with
incised hunting scene, contoured
steel trigger guard with hair
trigger, horn tipped wooden
ramrod, horn bolt plate and steel
ball, together with a combined
spanner key and powder measure,
17thC. **£3,500–5,500** *DN*

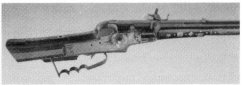

A German wheel lock rifle, c1600,
together with simple spanner,
lock defective.
£1,700–2,000 *S(S)*

Swords

A Georgian 1796 heavy cavalry officer's un-dress sword, straight single edged 34in (86cm) blade with hatchet tip, etched with crown, 'G.R.' and military trophies, with approximately 70% original blueing, engraving on backstrap 'Runkel Sohlingen', long blade section with much original polish, honeysuckle pierced guard, silver wire bound leather covered grip, in its steel scabbard, with maker's engraved label of 'D. Egg Hay Market London', good condition.
£1,000–1,500   *WAL*

A Scottish regulation basket-hilted military backsword, with spirally fluted leather-covered grip, c1770-80, 30in (76cm) blade.
£900–1,300   *C(S)*

An Irish hunting sword, curved single edged 25in (64cm) blade, with broad and narrow fullers and clipped back retaining much blued and gilt decoration in the form of Hibernia, flowers, harp etc., silver coloured metal hilt with shell guard and reeded hardwood grip, late 18thC.
£500–700   *S(S)*

A mortuary sword, the 33in (84cm) double edged blade with single fullers at forte, inscribed 'Inte Dominie', the hilt with basket and bars chiselled overall with feather-like pattern, the pommel en suite, short langets, wire bound grip.
£1,400–1,700   *S(S)*

A Scottish regulation basket-hilted military backsword, with tapering single edged blade with single fuller along the back edge on each side, iron hilt composed of flat iron bars incorporating pierced panels, and tall conical pommel slight damage, c1770-80, 30in (76cm) blade.
£470–520   *C(S)*

A Scottish officer's military broadsword, tapering straight double edged 32in (81cm) blade, struck at forte with Royal Arms mark on both sides, and 4 King's head marks and 'Andrea Farara', steel basket guard, chiselled with floral and foliate panels, and rein oval panel, red cloth faced wash leather liner, pommel tassel, the base of guard with scrolled lug, in its leather scabbard with steel locket and chape with pierced criss-cross pattern, good condition, 18thC.
£1,800–2,200 *WAL*

A French Model 1816 Heavy Cavalry Trooper's sabre, made at Klingenthal, with a 3 bar brass hilt and straight single edged blade with twin fullers and spear point, in its steel scabbard, the grip binding missing, dated '1831', blade 38in (96.5cm) long.
£300–400 *ASB*

A Scottish basket-hilted broadsword, with tapering blade of flattened diagonal section, the hilt composed of bars of near circular section incorporating shaped panels pierced with hearts and circular holes, repaired, bun-shaped pommel, and ribbed wooden grip, split, with iron-mounted leather scabbard, incomplete, early 19thC, blade 31½in (80cm) long.
£720–800 *C(S)*

An Elizabeth II Life Guards officer's state sword, 36in (91.5cm) blade, by Wilkinson Sword, No. 88218, etched with crown, Regimental badge, royal cypher, battle honours to 'St Quentin Canal', and foliage plated hilt with leather liner, mounted by brass crowned 'L.G.' and studs, wire bound fishskin covered grip, leather dress knot, in its leather covered field service scabbard, with Sam Browne frog and straps.
£500–550 *WAL*

An Edward VII officer's dress mameluke sabre of the 11th (Prince Albert's Own) Hussars, curved blade 31in (79cm), by Henry Wilkinson, Pall Mall, No. 40217, retaining most original polish, etched with crown, Royal cypher, battle honours to 'Sevastopol', regimental badge and foliage, also officer's initials 'F.G.A.A.', gilt hilt, silver sphinx and Egypt battle honour, ivory grip secured by 2 rosettes, in its plated scabbard with 3 ornate foliate decorated.
£1,200–1,700 *WAL*

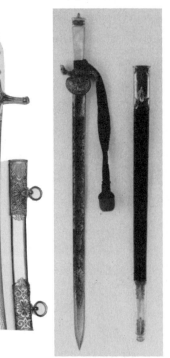

A British Highland Regiment's Staff Sergeant's basket-hilted broadsword, with red guard liner and 1897 pattern blade, in its nickel plated scabbard, crisp, a 'sleeper', dated '1904', blade 33in (84cm) long.
£350–450 *ASB*

A presentation 1827 pattern naval officer's sword, the 29in (73.5cm) pipe-back blade gilded and etched overall with scrolling foliage and naval motifs, maker's name 'Rundell Bridge & Co. 32 Ludgate Hill, London', the silver-gilt hilt with London assay marks for 1842, folding side shell, high relief scrolling foliage and cartouche with fouled anchor, lions' head pommel, wire bound sharkskin grip, the blue leather scabbard with silver gilt furniture decorated with engraved scrolling foliage and high relief naval trophies, the locket inscribed, in a velvet lined, glazed display case, together with a glazed portrait of Arthur Cumming.
£6,000–7,000 *S(S)*

An German Imperial hunting sword, straight single edged 23in (59cm) blade, with damascus finish and etched with trophies of arms, mythological figures, foliate scrolls etc., retaining much blued and gilt finish, cast shell guard with stag's head crossed rifle, sword and hunting horn, cross piece chiselled with boar's head and reversed hound head quillons, mother-of-pearl grips, hilt retaining much gilt decoration, in its matching engraved brass mounted leather sheath, with a dress knot.
£1,000–1,500 *S(S)*

Miscellaneous

A pair of iron cannons, on earlier painted carriages, early 19thC, 24in (61cm) long.
£600–800 *WIG*

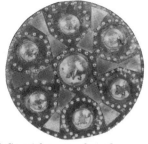

A Scottish targe of wood covered with leather, some wear and damage, 19thC, and another, largest 15in (38cm) diam.
£900–1,200 *C(S)*

A Victorian side drum of the 2nd Battalion Scots Guards, battle honours to Crimea, brass body with painted Royal arms and battle honours by Henry Potter, 30 Charing Cross, with War Department sale mark, painted wooden rims, cord tensioners, 2 straps, one stamped '2 SG 10', 15in (38cm) high.
£500–600 *WAL*

An oak gun cabinet for 3 guns, by the Army & Navy Stores, London, with brass fittings, 53in (134.5cm) wide.
£250–350 *WIG*

A brass bound mahogany gun case, mounted on a mahogany stand with ring handles, c1830, 33in (83.5cm) long.
£250–350 *WIG*

A brass bound leather gun case, by David Frazer, c1860, 32in (81cm) long.
£200–300 *WIG*

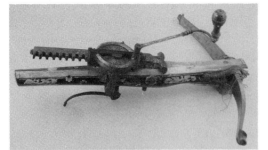

A German crossbow and cranequin, with plain steel bow, the tiller inlaid overall with panels and plaques of horn with incised scrolled decoration of flowers, birds and animals, folding peep-sight, bone nut and iron release lever together with its steel cranequin with winding handle, the ratchet assembly with pierced plate decorated with Roman gods and signs of the Zodiac on the reverse, retaining its original cord binding, 24½in (62cm) long.
£8,000–9,000 *DN*

A Bavarian bronze cannon barrel, bearing the arms of Bavaria under a helmet surmounted by 3 ostrich plumes, and on the chase with a scroll inscribed 'Vici Victurus Vivo' above the double monogram 'CAD', stylised dolphin lifting handles plain trunnions, and spool-shaped cascabel, 1726-44, 23in (59cm) barrel.
£2,000–2,500 *C*

The monogram presumably stands for 'Carolus Albertus Dux'. Charles Albert was Duke of Bavaria 1726-44.

A pair of Bavarian bronze cannon barrels, with the crowned arms of Bavaria, supported by a griffin and a lion above a scroll engraved 'Ao. 1696', stylised dolphin lifting handles, and plain trunnions, 27in (69cm) barrels.
£3,500–5,500 *C*

Medals & Orders

The Most Ancient and Noble Order of the Thistle star, by Garrard, London, silver, gold and enamel, reverse engraved 'R & S Garrard & Co.', maker's mark 'WN' stamped on back of star on backplate, with gold pin, slight enamel damage.
£2,600–3,000 *SPI*

An Order of the Lion of Zähringen, Baden, Germany, Commander's badge, gold, crystal and enamel, 2in (5cm) wide, with neck riband.
£700–900 *SPI*

A Naval Long Service group of medals, mounted for wearing.
£350-500 *S(S)*

> **Miller's is a price GUIDE not a price LIST.**

An Order of Theresa, Germany, Bavaria, by Edward Quellhorst, Berlin, badge 3in (7cm) wide, including crown, gold and enamel, back of crown stamped 'EQ'.
£1,000–1,500 *SPI*

A Naval General Service medal, 1793, Peter Parker, 1 clasp, Trafalgar, 1613.
£800–1,000 *S(S)*

A Waterloo Medal, Hanover, 1815, Soldat Wilhelm Rossing, Landwehr Bataillon Bentheim, steel clip and ring suspension, with booklet 'Das Bentheimer Landwehrbattaillon' by Dietrich Veddeler, and roll of the Battalion and photocopy from roll of other papers.
£200–250 *SPI*

A Sea Gallantry Medal (Foreign Services), V.R., small gold 1858 issue, H. Paul Langlois, February 20, 1877.
£1,800–2,200 *SPI*

An Indian Mutiny award, Sergeant J. F. Owens, 75th Foot, inscribed, marked Birmingham 1893, surmounted by an Imperial Crown, and riband buckle device engraved 'Forlorn Hope'.
£180–220 *S(S)*

A Campaign Cross 1816, Portugal, English pattern gold cross for 5 years service, hallmarks for London 1820, with straight bar swivel suspension, and silver gilt slip bar on riband, minor pitting.
£700–900 *SPI*

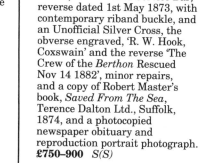

A pair of Lifesaving medals, for Coxswain Robert Hook, Lowestoft Lifeboat Station, Royal National Institution for the Preservation of Life from Shipwreck, Silver Medal, with Second Service Bar, reverse dated 1st May 1873, with contemporary riband buckle, and an Unofficial Silver Cross, the obverse engraved, 'R. W. Hook, Coxswain' and the reverse 'The Crew of the *Berthon* Rescued Nov 14 1882', minor repairs, and a copy of Robert Master's book, *Saved From The Sea*, Terence Dalton Ltd., Suffolk, 1874, and a photocopied newspaper obituary and reproduction portrait photograph.
£750–900 *S(S)*

l. A Carnegie Medal, Norway, silver, bust of Carnegie facing right, inscribed 'Konsul Damn Huun 17.11.1935', edge numbered '9256' 2½in (6.5cm) wide.
£350-450 *SPI*

r. A South Holland Life Saving Medal, Netherlands, silver, the reverse inscribed 'E. Christophersen 27 December 1859', 2in (5.5cm) wide.
£250-300 *SPI*

An Order of the Precious Golden Grain, China, First Class set of insignia, silver, silver gilt and enamel, minor damage, badge 3in (7.8cm) wide, star 4in (10cm) wide, with rosette and full sash riband, in embroidered case of issue.
£1,400–1,700 *SPI*

JEWELLERY
Bracelets

A vulcanite bracelet, with raised
fruit carving, c1865.
£15–20 *PHay*

A gold hinged bangle, modelled as
a strap and buckle, with turquoise
line decoration, 19thC.
£450–550 *CSK*

A bog oak bracelet.
£35–40 *PHay*

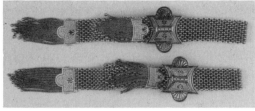

An antique gold woven mesh bracelet, the
openwork scroll and leaf clasp set with a
miniature of the doves of Pliny.
£650–750 *CSK*

An expanding horn bracelet, with
inset painted medallion, c1860.
£40–50 *PHay*

A Victorian silver domed circular panel bracelet.
£200–300 *CSK*

A pair of gold mesh bracelets, each with foliate
engraved half pearl and black enamel panel,
tassel fringe slide adjustment and tassel
fringe terminal, 19thC.
£1,200–1,500 *CSK*

Four Whitby jet expanding bracelets
£30–50 each *PHay*

A French jet bracelet, set with
glass stones, with gilt clasp,
7in (17.5cm).
£25–35 *PHay*

Brooches and Pendants

A gold hinged locket, with
diamond half pearl and turquoise
7 stone line applied motif, with
fluted shoulders and wire and
beadwork band decoration, 19thC.
£500–700 *CSK*

A Whitby jet 'blue skin' pendant,
c1860, 6cm long.
£80–120 *PHay*

A horn pendant, with hand
painted medallion, c1860,
5cm long. **£40–50** *PHay*

Whitby Jet

There are 2 types of jet:
'Blue skin' which is found very
deep in the ground.
'Yellow skin' which is found
nearer the surface, and is,
therefore, not such good quality.

A gold and silver mounted diamond floral spray brooch, 19thC. **£900–1,200** *CSK*

A Whitby jet pendant, c1860, 6cm long.
£75–100 *PHay*

A Whitby jet leaf design brooch, 6.5cm wide.
£50–80 *PHay*

A plique à jour enamel brooch, modelled as a flying bird, with white paste decoration and red paste eye.
£300–400 *CSK*

A Victorian gold quatrefoil locket-back brooch, with central half pearl and blue enamel star applied motif, with wire and beadwork decoration.
£300–350 *CSK*

A diamond and pearl flowerhead spray brooch with diamond solitaire decoration.
£600–700 *CSK*

A rose diamond and cultured pearl cluster arrow brooch. **£400–500** *CSK*

A collection of French jet brooches, 3 to 6cm wide.
£10–15 each *PHay*

A collection of bog oak brooches, c1860, 2.5 to 6.5cm wide. **£25–40 each** *PHay*

A bog oak brooch, with Gallic inscription in gold and shamrock decoration, c1860, 3.5cm diam.
£40–60 *PHay*

An antique gold and gem flower brooch, the partially opened head with turquoise half pearl and gem decoration.
£300–400 *CSK*

A gold and foiled garnet flowerhead style brooch, with lozenge-shaped drop, the locket reverse with damaged inscription.
£250–300 *CSK*

A Victorian silver gilt and cabochon garnet 5 stone Huntingdon brooch, the reverse signed 'Waterhouse & Company, Dublin'.
£300–400 *CSK*

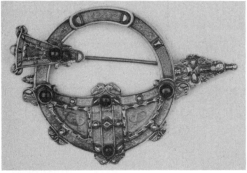

A gold locket brooch, with enamel and half pearl single stone central star motif, and a pair of matching earrings, 19thC.
£500–600 *CSK*

A collection of Whitby jet brooches, c1860, 4 to 5cm wide.
£50–100 each *PHay*

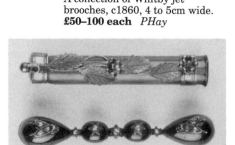

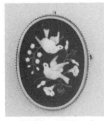

An Italian pietra dura brooch/pendant, inlaid with 2 doves amidst lily-of-the-valley and convolvulus, in a gold beaded mount, glazed back, 4cm.
£400–500 *DN*

A gilt Etruscan style pendant, with central circular cloisonné panel and graduated tassel fringe, 19thC.
£200–300 *CSK*

A cabochon garnet 4 stone bar brooch, with rose diamond cluster applied with flies and rose diamond points, and a glass posy holder brooch, with engraved foliate mount.
£500–600 *CSK*

Three Whitby jet brooches, c1860, 2.5cm diam.
£25–40 each *PHay*

A vulcanite brooch, c1850, 5cm wide.
£15–20 *PHay*

An Irish pine corner cupboard, with glazed doors to upper half and linen fold panels to base, c1820, 55in (140cm) wide.
£850–950 *DMe*

A pine bureau, the sloping front enclosing a fitted interior, above 2 short and 2 long drawers, 19thC, 42in (107cm) wide.
£600–800 *TPC*

A pine cupboard with galleried top and 2 doors, with new brass door knobs.
£500–565 *AL*

A panelled pine clerks' desk, the sloping top lifting to reveal fitted interior, 19thC, 52in (132cm) wide. **£700–900** *TPC*

A pine cupboard, with 2 cupboard doors and rope-twist columns to top, 2 drawers and cupboards to base, early 19thC, 52in (132cm) wide. **£900–1,400** *TPC*

A pine bookcase, with glazed doors to upper half, 19thC, 42in (107cm) wide.
£500–700 *TPC*

A pine chiffonier, with carved back, single drawer and 2 cupboards below, c1860, 41in (104cm) wide.
£380–420 *DMe*

An Irish pine bookcase, the upper half with glazed doors, c1830, 39in (99cm) wide.
£650–750 *DMe*

A low standing pine corner cupboard, c1850, 25in (64cm) wide. **£150–250** *AL*

A pine cupboard, with raised and fielded doors, 2 drawers with brass handles, early 19thC, 50in (127cm) wide.
£800–900 *TPC*

An Irish pine food cupboard, 4 doors with carved panels, c1810, 49in (124.5cm) wide.
£1,200–1,350 *DMe*

A pine linen press, with brass handles, 19thC, 42in (106.5cm) wide.
£700–900 *TPC*

An Irish pine food cupboard, with adjustable shelves and carved panelled doors, c1820, 51in (129.5cm) wide.
£750–850 *DMe*

A pine corner cupboard, with 2 half arched double panel doors over a single door, early 18thC, 40in (101.5cm) wide.
£1,500–2,000 *TPC*

A Georgian shell and barrel back pine corner cupboard, with dentil and reeded mouldings, 40in (101.5cm) wide.
£1,500–1,800 *TPC*

A 4 door pine cupboard, with rope twist columns, early 19thC, 48in (122cm) wide.
£800–1,000 *TPC*

A panelled pine cupboard, 19thC, 72in (182.5cm) wide.
£500–600 *TPC*

An Irish painted pine cupboard, c1875, 64in (162.5cm) wide.
£900–1,200 *DFA*

A pine dresser, with pierced fretted frieze, early 19thC, 60in (152cm) wide.
£900–1,200 *TPC*

A late Victorian gesso decorated dressing chest, with shoe hole, 36in (91.5cm) wide.
£400–500 *TPC*

An Irish pine dresser, with reeded and fluted mouldings, 18thC, 58in (147cm) wide.
£1,200–1,500 *TPC*

A pine Wellington chest, 19thC, 26in (66cm) wide.
£500–600 *TPC*

An Irish pine dresser, with 5 drawers, 2 side cupboards, and 6 cupboards below, c1830, 117in (297cm) wide.
£2,800–3,200 *DMe*

A miniature pine hanging kitchen rack, c1900, 19in (48cm) wide.
£150–185 *MofC*

An Irish pine dresser, with carved frieze, 3 drawers and 2 cupboards, c1845, 60in (152cm) wide.
£750–800 *DMe*

A painted Irish pine dresser, with china handle, original grained paint finish, c1840, 61in (155cm) wide.
£750–850 *DMe*

An Irish pine dresser, with carved frieze, 3 drawers and 2 cupboards, c1830, 66in (167.5cm) wide.
£850–950 *DMe*

A late Victorian gesso decorated pine chest, with 2 short and 2 long drawers, 36in (92cm) wide. **£300–400** *TPC*

A pine Wellington chest, the graduated drawers with brass military handles, 19thC, 26in (66cm) wide. **£400–500** *TPC*

A pine mule chest, with single drawer and side carrying handles, 19thC, 36in (92cm) wide. **£250–300** *TPC*

A pine chest, with 2 short and 3 long drawers, all with applied carved wood mouldings, 19thC, 42in (107cm) wide. **£400–500** *TPC*

A pine fielded panelled mule chest, with single long drawer, 42in (107cm) wide. **£400–500** *TPC*

A pine chest, with 4 graduated long drawers, on shaped bracket feet, 42in (107cm) wide. **£350–450** *TPC*

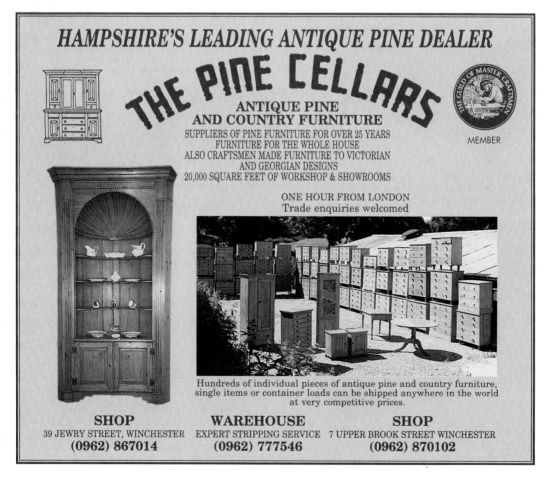

A pine drop leaf country table, c1830, 35½in (90.5cm) wide extended. **£260–320** *DMe*

A serpentine pine sideboard, with 2 drawers over 2 shaped arched panelled doors, 19thC, 48in (122cm) wide. **£300–600** *TPC*

A pine cricket table, with turned legs, 19thC, 26in (66cm) diam. **£150–250** *TPC*

A pine dresser, the top with glazed doors, 4 drawers and doors below, on bracket feet, 19thC, 72in (182.5cm) wide. **£800–1,000** *TPC*

An Irish pine dresser, the open rack with plate bars, 19thC, 54in (137cm) wide. **£900–1,200** *TPC*

A pine chest, with 2 drawers and brass handles, on bracket feet, 19thC, 42in (106.5cm) wide. **£300–350** *TPC*

A pine sideboard, with 7 drawers, and central cupboard, 18thC, 78in (198cm) wide. **£700–900** *TPC*

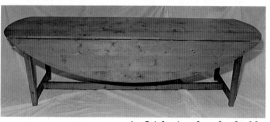

An Irish pine drop leaf table, c1840, 102in (259cm) wide. **£600–750** *TPC*

A pine sideboard, with 4 drawers over 2 plank doors, early 19thC, 40in (101.5cm) wide. **£300–500** *TPC*

A late Victorian pine compactum, with swans' neck pediment, 60in (152cm) wide.
£600–800 *TPC*

A pine highback panel box settle, with lifting seat, arms on turned supports, standing on bracket feet, early 19thC, 60in (152cm) wide.
£400–600 *TPC*

A pine gesso decorated wardrobe, with mirror and single deep drawer below, 19thC, 36in (92cm) wide.
£400–500 *TPC*

A pitch pine bench, c1900, 20in (51cm) long.
£35–40 *AHL*

l. A pine chiffonier, the arched panel doors with carved moulding, 19thC, 42in (107cm).
£600–700 *TPC*

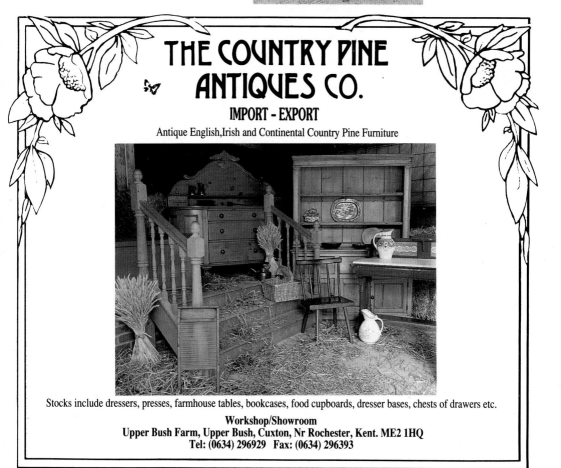

A pine washstand, with gallery back and turned legs, 19thC, 30in (76in) wide.
£200–250 *TPC*

A pine wardrobe, with fielded panels, 2 doors over one long drawer, 18thC, 58in (147cm) wide.
£800–900 *TPC*

A pair of painted pine candlesticks, c1880, 25in (63.5cm) high.
£200–225 *MofC*

A pine wardrobe, with architectural pediment and urn finials, c1860, 45in (114cm) wide.
£550–600 *AL*

A pine compactum, with mirror and gesso decoration, 19thC, 72in (182.5cm).
£750–850 *TPC*

An Arts and Crafts pine cabinet, the fall front with copper hinges, 38in (96.5cm).
£200–250 *TPC*

A pine bridge table, on brass casters, 19thC, 34in (86cm) square.
£250–300 *TPC*

An Irish pine table, with double stretcher and turned legs, c1840, 132in (310cm) long.
£1,000–1,200 *DMe*

A Dutch brass chandelier, with central baluster stem and 12 scroll branches in 2 tiers, c1680, 26in (66cm) high. **£3,000–4,000** *S*

A pair of French gilt bronze candelabra, each in the form of a naked child, re-gilt and fitted for electricity, c1860, 37in (94cm) high. **£3,500–4,000** *S*

A pair of mahogany and brass candlesticks, each with rococo cast drip pan and nozzle, fluted stem and circular base, early 19thC, 14in (36cm) high. **£1,000-1,200** *S*

A pair of French gilt bronze wall lights, each with 3 rope-twist candle arms, fitted for electricity, c1890, 67in (170cm) high. **£35,000–38,000** *S*

A pair of French bronze torchères, in the form of Oriental slaves, signed 'A. Toussant 1850' and inscribed 'F. Barbedienne Fondeurs', 40in (102cm) high. **£11,000–15,000** *S*

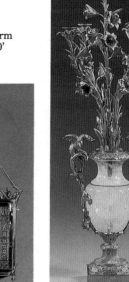

A pair of French gilt bronze wall lights, in Louis XV style, with 3 acanthus cast arms, oak leaves and acorns, fitted for electricity, c1860, 30in (76cm) high. **£5,500–6,500** *S*

A French gilt bronze hall lantern, with curved and tapering glazed panels, c1885, 49in (125cm) high. **£4,000–5,000** *S*

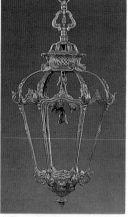

A pair of French gilt bronze wall lights, with 3 candle arms, drilled for electricity, c1880, 25in (64cm) high. **£10,000–12,000** *S*

An English brass hall lantern, with coloured and clear glass panels, c1880, 36in (92cm) high. **£3,500–4,000** *S*

A pair of French Louis Philippe rock crystal and gilt bronze candelabra, c1850, 47in (119cm) high. **£13,000–15,000** *S*

r. A Rajahstan red and green stained ivory chess set, heightened in gilt, the kings and queens in the form of elephants transporting figures in howdahs, early 19thC, kings 5½in (14cm) high.
£10,000–11,000 *CSK*

l. An Indian natural and orange stained ivory chess set, modelled in the form of Sikhs versus Muslims, 19thC, varying sizes.
£2,000–2,500 *CSK*

r. A polychrome carved wood figural chess set, with suffragettes opposing the law, the bishops as judges, the rooks as burning houses opposing cells, the pawns as policemen, pawns 3in (7.5cm) high, in original cardboard box with label.
£750-950 *CSK*

l. An Indian ivory and green stained chess set, the king, queen, bishop and pawns with carved heads, on ring turned and lobed baluster stands, the rooks of turreted form, 19thC, kings 4⅓in (11cm) high.
£2,000–2,500 *CSK*

r. An English ivory and red stained chess set, the ring turned pieces profusely carved with beaded and leaf ornament of Hastilow style turned on an ornamental lathe, the knights with plumed helmets, the rooks of turreted form, king 5½in (14cm) high, with conforming draft set and diabolos.
£7,000–8,000 *CSK*

l. A Chinese ivory and red stained figural chess set, elaborately carved, the oval plinths with trailing vines and flowers, 19thC, king 5in (12.5cm) and pawn 2in (5cm) high.
£900–1,000 *CSK*

r. An English ivory and red stained chess set, in the Staunton style, king 4⅓in (11cm) and pawn 2in (5cm) high.
£2,000–2,500 *CSK*

A bisque headed child doll, with blue lashed sleeping eyes, jointed wood and composition body, impressed 'K*R Halbig 76', in original box, 30in (76cm) high. **£900–1,200** *CSK*

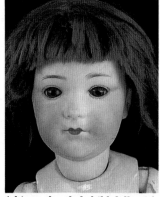

A bisque headed child doll, with jointed wood and composition body, impressed 'Armand Marseille 400AOM', 15in (38cm) high, and a Norah Wellings cloth doll. **£1,600–2,000** *CSK*

A painted wooden dolls' house, 3 stories and 5 bays, opening in 3 sections to reveal 5 rooms, with removable roof, slight damage, Christian Hacker, c1880, 27in (69cm) wide. **£2,500–3,000** *CSK*

A wax on composition 'pumpkin head' shoulder plate fashion doll, with stuffed body, slight damage, c1880, 23½in (60cm) high. **£400–600** *DN*

A poured wax child doll, with inset eyes and hair, cloth body, wax limbs and robe, with label on body 'Pierotti with Hamleys Regent Street', 16in (40.5cm). **£350–400**
A poured wax headed doll modelled as a baby, early 19thC, 6in (15cm) high, and a bed, bedding and clothing. **£350–450** *CSK*

A pressed bisque doll, with 8 ball jointed wood and composition body, impressed 'DEPOSE E.12.J.', blue stamp on back 'JUMEAU Médaille D'Or PARIS', in original box, 26in (66cm) high. **£7,000–9,000** *S*

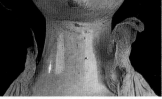

A turned and carved painted wooden doll, with flesh painted body, remains of original shift, petticoat and 2 jackets, c1770, missing fingers and legs, 11in (28cm) high. **£4,000–4,500** *CSK*

A German bisque headed girl doll, on jointed composition body, Kämmer & Reinhardt/ Simon & Halbig, 25in (63.5cm) high. **£600–700** *DN*

A dolls' walnut rocking cradle, with hood, late 19thC, 14½in (37cm) wide. **£65–75** *PCh*

A Jumeau walking/talking moulded bisque doll, with composition and wood body and straight legs, when walked her head turns from side to side and she says 'Mama', impressed '8' and stamped with a blue 'M', 22⅜in (57cm) high. **£1,000–1,500** *S*

A papier mâché headed doll, with painted features, hair in a bun, kid body, in cotton frock and straw bonnet, Sonneberg, c1830, 10in (25cm) high.
£500–700 *CSK*

A Jules Steiner bisque headed doll, with key wind stop/start movement, calls 'Mama', incised '6 Déposé', in original box, 17in (43cm) high. **£2,000–2,500** *S*

l. A poured wax headed child doll, the stuffed body with wax limbs, probably by Pierotti, 24in (61cm) high.
£850–950
A painted wooden Noah's Ark and animals, with hinged side opening, inscribed and dated May 1829, 11½in (29cm) wide.
£950–1,200 *CSK*

A German shoulder bisque doll, with cloth body, seated in a sedan chair, late 19thC, doll 8in (20cm), chair 13in (33cm) high.
£2,000–2,500 *S*

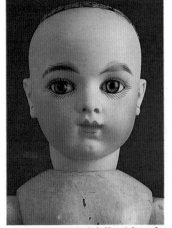

A bisque headed doll, with cork pate, jointed wood and papier mâché body, impressed 'BRU Jne 6' and stamped on the body, slight damage, 15in (38cm) high.
£5,500–6,500 *CSK*

An S.F.B.J. doll, with paperweight eyes, original dress, Paris, c1900, 14in (35.5cm) high.
£400–500 *OCS*

A bisque headed doll, with jointed wood and composition body, impressed 'K*R, SIMON & HALBIG 117 34', slight damage, the head 3in (7.5cm) high.
£2,000–2,200 *CSK*

A Chad Valley standing golden plush covered teddy bear, Hubert, with deep orange and black glass eyes, stitched nose, mouth and claws, swivel head, jointed shaped limbs, squeaker and label, c1925, 19in (48cm) high. **£700–800**

A Steiff seated golden plush covered bear, with boot button eyes, stitched nose, mouth and claws, swivel head, elongated jointed shaped limbs, button in ear, c1905, 10in (25cm) high. **£750–850** *CSK*

A Black Forest carved wooden figure of a standing bear, with glass eyes, open mouth and naturalistically stained, early 20thC, 33in (84cm) high. **£650–800** *CSK*

A Steiff golden plush covered teddy bear, with black button eyes, stitched nose, mouth and claws, swivel head, hump and blank button in ear, c1905, 30in (76cm) high. **£6,500–7,500** *CSK*

l. A signed oil on canvas, Favourite Toys, by Ray Campbell, framed, 18 by 24in (46 by 61cm). **£2,000–3,000** *CSK*

r. Two Steiff bears on wheels: c1900, 24in (61cm) high. **£1,000–1,500** and c1920, 14½in (37cm) long. **£400–500** *CSK*

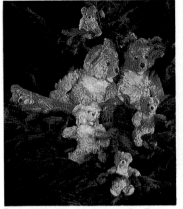

Seven Steiff teddy bears, the Zotty Family, comprising: Susan, Bruno, Thomas, Tommy, Bobby, Bertha and Floppy, slight damage, 7 to 21in (17.5 to 53cm) high.
£600–700 *CSK*

A Rivergate Bears Ltd., limited edition one of one gold brown, plush covered teddy bears, Mother and Child, with Certificate of Ownership, signed framed and glazed, 14 and 24in (35.5 and 61cm) high.
£900–1,100 *CSK*

A Steiff pale golden plush covered teddy bear, with black boot button eyes, stitched nose, mouth and claws, hump and button in ear, c1905, 16in (41cm) high.
£4,000–4,500 *CSK*

A Steiff Puss-in-Boots, with white mohair, yellow glass eyes, button in ear, wearing original costume, golden sash printed 'Steiff', c1912, 17in (43cm) high.
£1,600–2,000 *CSK*

An oil on canvas, Ted's Top, by Ray Campbell, signed and framed, 18 by 12in (46 by 30.5cm).
£1,250–1,350 *CSK*

l. A Steiff gold plush covered teddy bear, c1910, 12in (31cm) high, with a photograph of the original owner.
£800–1,000
r. An early German plush covered teddy bear, repaired, 28in (66cm high), with a print.
£1,500–2,000 *CSK*

A Merrythought limited edition one of one teddy bear, James, modelled on James Christie, c1766, in contemporary dress, with wooden podium, gavel, inkwell and quill, with label, 1993, 16in (41cm) high.
£400–600 *CSK*

A Steiff golden curly plush covered teddy bear, with growler, slight damage, c1910, 30in (76cm) high.
£2,300–3,300
Two small Steiff honey golden plush covered teddy bears, Inseparable Friends, c1908, 8 and 12in (20 and 31cm) high.
£2,000–2,500 *CSK*

A Steiff cinnamon plush covered centre seam teddy bear, blank button in ear, moth damaged, c1904, 20in (51cm) high.
£5,250–5,750 *CSK*

An automaton of a gentleman smoking a cheroot, with articulated lower jaw and eyelids, in original clothes, Gustave Vichy, c1870, 31in (78cm) high.
£8,000–8,500 *S*

l. A musical automaton of a Creole dancer, by Roullet et Decamps, with bisque head, 28in (72cm) high.
£9,500–10,000
r. A smoking monkey automaton, by Gustave Vichy, with papier mâché head, c1870, 26in (66cm) high.
£4,500–5,000 *S*

A musical automaton of a banjo player, by Gustave Vichy, c1900, 27½in (70cm) high.
£8,500–9,000 *S*

A musical automaton of a zither player, by Roullet et Decamps, c1890, 18in (45cm) high. **£3,500–4,000** *S*

A picture automaton, with paper label on reverse 'Hoyt Life Picture', c1880, 29 by 22in (74 by 56cm).
£4,800–5,200 *S*

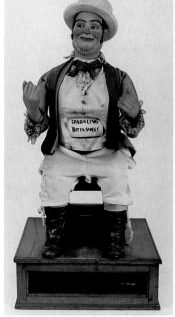

A John Bull automaton, advertising 'Bitta-Sweet', c1900.
£1,500–1,750 *LT*

A musical automaton of a tambourine player, by Roullet et Decamps, c1900, 21in (53cm) high.
£3,000–3,500 *S*

A musical automaton of a clown banjo player, by Gustave Vichy, c1890, 23in (58cm) high.
£7,800–8,200 *S*

A musical automaton of a tambourine player, by Leopold Lambert, with bisque head stamped 'Déposé Tête Jumeau', c1890, 21in (53cm) high.
£5,500–6,000 *S*

A Hornby Lord Nelson clockwork engine and tender, c1920-30, 16in (40.5cm) long. **£250–300** *HAL*

A scale model of Bristol Bulldog II, serial No. K1081, with wooden airframe, working control surfaces, flying and control wires, detailed cockpit with pilot's seat, windscreen, flying and engine controls, 33½in (85cm) wingspan. **£950–1,000** *CSK*

A Bassett Lowke London to Nottingham 2-6-4 electric tank engine, c1930-50, 12in (31cm) long. **£1,000–1,200** *HAL*

A scale model of a Moraine Saulnier 225 No. 38 aeroplane, with covered wooden airframe, slight damage, 47in (119cm) wingspan. **£2,000–2,500** *CSK*

A model of Bluebird, No. 1400, by W. Britain, made to celebrate the land speed record, c1930, 7in (17.5cm) long, in original box. **£150–165** *HAL*

A partially planked brass pinned boxwood model of an Admiral's barge, with carved oarsmen, helmsman and passenger, mid-18thC, 22in (56cm) long, on a stand. **£22,500–23,000** *CSK*

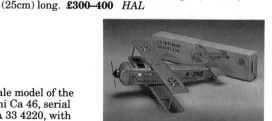

A Hornby Metropolitan clockwork engine, c1930s, 10in (25cm) long. **£300–400** *HAL*

A one third scale flying model of a Sopwith Camel, serial No. F 6314, with code letter 'B', with working control surfaces, 112in (284.5cm) wingspan. **£3,500–4,000** *CSK*

l. A scale model of the Caproni Ca 46, serial No. CA 33 4220, with fabric covered wooden airframe, finished in Italian Air Force camouflage and markings, 91in (231cm) wingspan. **£2,500–3,000** *CSK*

A Crawford's lithographed 'A-One' biscuit tin, with movable propeller, British flag on top wing, c1928, 16in (41cm) long, with original box. **£2,500–3,000** *CNY*

A horse-drawn open air trolley car, constructed of reed paper on wood, with lithographed signs, a driver, and swivelling seats, some fading, c1895, 28in (71cm) long.
£2,000–2,500 *CNY*

A Dent cast iron Mack caged delivery truck, with opening doors, c1925, 15½in (39cm) wide.
£6,800–7,200 *CNY*

A Müller & Kadeder painted tinplate biplane, on a tripod, with pilot and rear engine, lacking motor, c1912, 7in (17.5cm) long.
£1,300–1,500 *CNY*

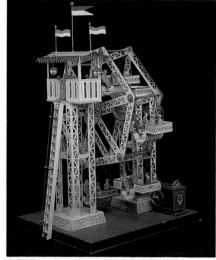

A Doll et Cie painted tinplate Russian carousel, with 2 open lattice towers supporting hexagonal wheel and 6 gondolas, 24 composition figures, hand crank and pulley mechanism also driving musical box mechanism, damaged, c1920, 13½in (34cm) wide. **£5,500–6,500** *CSK*

A Marx lithographed tinplate mechanical Harold Lloyd walker, he shuffles along, swinging his cane as his facial expression changes, slight damage, c1930, 11in (28cm). **£1,300–1,500** *CNY*

A Kenton cast iron horse-drawn overland circus calliope wagon, with 2 riders and a driver, c1940, 14½in (37cm) long.
£700–800 *CNY*

A Schuco tinplate mechanical Packard Convertible coupé, with turning front wheels, rubber tyres and detachable remote control, boxed, c1956, 11in (28cm) long.
£600–700 *CNY*

An Ives miniature elevated railway, consisting of tinplate lithographed engine, tender, passengers rail cars and track, damaged, c1906, 21in (53cm) long.
£2,000–2,200 *CNY*

A Fallows tinplate and cast iron black horse push toy, cast iron wheels 7in (17.5cm) diam, with leather reins, restored, 30in (76cm) long.
£1,500–2,000 *CNY*

An Ives mechanical toy, Old Mammy washing clothes, she turns her head and bends at the waist, c1890, 11in (28cm) high.
£9,200–10,000 *CNY*

An Althof-Bergmann stencilled tinplate twin horse-drawn omnibus, the horses on wheels, restored, c1880, 16½in (42cm) long.
£9,500–10,000 *CNY*

A Hubley cast iron horse-drawn landau with coachman, c1900, 17in (43cm) long overall.
£300–350 *CNY*

A Bliss lithographed paper-on-wood Rough and Ready No. 2 Hook and Ladder horse-drawn fire engine, rear fireman missing, c1895, 30in (76cm) long.
£2,500–3,000 *CNY*

Two lithographed wind-up tinplate walking toys, by Marx, Amos and Andy, c1932, 11½in (29cm) high.
£850–900 *CNY*

A Hubley cast iron horse-drawn Royal circus cage, with 2 lions, c1915, paint worn, 16in (41cm) long.
£1,500–2,000 *CNY*

An Ives cast iron and wood firehouse, with twin horse-drawn cast iron pumper, paint worn, c1890, 15in (38cm) high.
£3,250–3,750 *CNY*

A reed paper-on-wood lithographed Cinderella's horse-drawn coach, c1900, 26in (66cm) long overall.
£2,000–2,500 *CNY*

A carved and painted wooden rocking horse, with remains of a saddle, brass harness studs, rockers overpainted, mid-19thC, 82in (208cm) long.
£1,500–2,000 *CSK*

A German tinplate boat, Kasuga, c1912,
12in (30.5cm) long. **£800–900** *HAL*

A German chocolate tin money box, c1905,
10½in (26.5cm) high.
£200–250 *HAL*

A Günthermann tinplate coupé, c1920,
17in (43cm) long. **£1,300–1,400** *HAL*

A German tinplate R100 airship, c1920,
16½in (42cm) long. **£400–500** *HAL*

A money box in the form of a footballer,
c1895, 10in (25cm) long.
£300–350 *HAL*

A George V commemorative money
box, c1910, 5½in (14cm) wide).
£60–70 *HAL*

A Japanese tinplate
aeroplane, c1930, 6in
(15cm) wingspan.
£150–200 *HAL*

A Dreadnought Bank money box,
c1914, 7in (17.5cm) high.
£100–120 *HAL*

A Volunteer Bank money box,
c1890, 6in (15cm) high.
£250–300 *HAL*

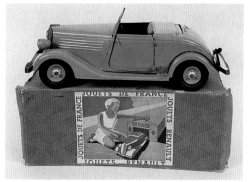

A tinplate 'Jouets de France' Renault, c1930,
13in (33cm) long, with original box.
£400–500 *HAL*

A pair of Bing tinplate fire engines, c1910,
6in (15cm) long.
£650–700 *HAL*

A Burnett tinplate car, c1920,
7in (17.5cm) long.
£200–300 *HAL*

A Japanese tinplate highway patrol
motorcyclist, c1960, 12in (30.5cm)
long, boxed. **£250–300** *HAL*

A money box, with a clown holding
a hoopla ring, c1897, 8½in (21.5cm)
long. **£250–300** *HAL*

A tinplate 'Excelsior'
steam engine, by Ernest
Plank, c1904.
£400–500 *HAL*

A Lehmann Naughty Boy
tinplate toy, 5in (12.5cm) long.
£400–500 *HAL*

A German Dux Astroman tinplate robot,
c1950, 11½in (29.5cm) high, boxed.
£300–350 *HAL*

An American money box, in the form of 2 frogs,
c1882, 8in (20cm) long.
£400–450 *HAL*

An American money box, in the form of a Red
Indian pointing a gun at a bear, 1883, 9½in
(24cm) long.
£600–650 *HAL*

A German tinplate horse-drawn tramway, c1905,
13in (33cm) long.
£500–600 *HAL*

A Victorian C.B., C.M.G. Group, awarded to Major-General A. F. Hart-Synnot, East Surrey Regiment, very minor damage to Osmania badge. **£4,200–4,800** *S(S)*

A C.M.G., D.S.O. and Bar Group, awarded to Brigadier-General A. H. S. Hart-Synnot, all mounted court style, the Japanese and French Orders chipped. **£3,200–3,600** *S(S)*

The Royal Guelphic Order, (K.C.H.), Military Division, Knight Commander's breast star, by Salter, Widdowson & Tate, 73 Strand, London, in silver, engraved, with gold pin, boxed, slight damage. **£1,000–1,200** *S(S)*

A 5 shot .32 rimfire Tranter's patent double action revolver, No. 9056, barrel 3¾in, Birmingham proved, engraved, one-piece chequered walnut butt. **£850–1,000** *WAL*

A Russian Imperial Guard's shako, (Preobrashensky Regiment), with chinscales, cockade and silver bullion plume, engraved, c1880, together with gilded brass cuirass with turned edges, a pair of bullion epaulettes and a pair of shoulder boards. **£250–300** *S(S)*

A Military Order of St. Ferdinand, by Medina of Barcelona and Madrid, 4th class breast star, in silver, with gilt, enamel and mother-of-pearl centre, slight damage, late 19thC. **£350–400** *S(S)*

A set of Dress miniatures, for Rear-Admiral the Hon. H. Carr Glyn, Naval Officer in charge during the Special Operations on the Lower Danube, 1854, mounted for wearing. **£500–600** *S(S)*

A post-1902 gilt helmet of the Gentlemen-at-Arms, Lt. Col. H. N. Schofield, V.C., with gilt acanthus ornamentation, helmet plate with Royal Arms and Garter on a silver plated cut star. **£3,500–4,500** *WAL*

A Victorian officer's blue cloth shabraque of the 9th (Queen's Royal) Lancers, double gilt lace border, fore quarters embroidered with Guelphic crown over regimental badge, rear quarters with Guelphic crowned VR cypher, in its flat tin case, slight damage. **£800–1,000** *WAL*

A Lieutenant Colonel's full dress uniform of the 11th (Prince Albert's Own) Hussars, comprising: fur busby, with nameplate 'F.G.A. Arkwright Esq, 11th Hussars', blue tunic, crimson wool pantaloons, gilt regimental lace girdle, and a pair of Hussar boots. **£2,200–2,800** *WAL*

A breast badge, Order of Sukhe Bator, Mongolia, in gold, silver and enamel, with platinum centre, screwback fitment. **£600–800** *S(S)*

General Picton's silver medal for The Defence of Gibraltar, 1783, unnamed as issued, slight damage, 6cm diam. **£550–600** *S(S)*

A Victorian Officer's full dress scarlet tunic and silver plated cuirass of the First Life Guards, slight damage. **£2,000–2,500** *WAL*

A silver livery badge, Saxe-Coburg-Gotha, Carl Eduard, by Forsyth of Edinburgh, 1909, with reverse hook and leather straps for fixing to upper arm of servant's livery. **£500–600** *S(S)*

A painted iron Armada chest, with ten lever lock, open lid supported by hinged wrought arm, with carrying handles, probably 17thC, 33in (84cm). **£1,600–2,000** *WAL*

An officer's brass (originally gilt) 1834 pattern helmet of the 7th (the Princess Royal's) Dragoon Guards, and alternative black bearskin crest, some wear. **£2,500–3,000** *WAL*

A gold and enamel memoriam ring, engraved inside 'Capn. James Newman Newman, Lost off the Haak in the Hero, 74, 24 Decr. 1811, Aged 46', in leather box inscribed 'J. Brace, 1820'. **£500–600** *S(S)*

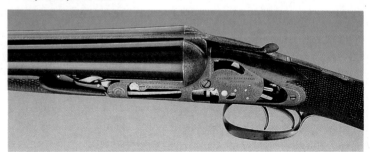

A Charles Lancaster 12 bore cutaway demonstration backlock ejector gun, No. 5461, 30in damascus barrels, scroll engraved frame, 14in well figured stock, black powder proof, built in 1884. **£2,600–3,000** *S(S)*

A gold mounted floral carved ivory panel parure, comprising: a necklace, a brooch, a pair of earrings and a bracelet, in a fitted case, damaged. **£3,500–4,000** *CSK*

A diamond set openwork pendant, with central diamond cluster and single diamond stone loop, with neck chain. **£2,000–3,000** *CSK*

A brooch, modelled as a bird feeding her fledglings in the nest, worked in textured diamond, marquise diamond, drop cut diamond, ruby and marquise ruby. **£4,000–5,000** *CSK*

A gold mounted mourning locket, with decorated glazed panel of applied hair, early 19thC. **£850–1,000** *CSK*

A Victorian gold and enamelled festoon necklace, brooch and a pair of double drop earrings, the oval turquoise centres set with pearl and rose cut diamond clusters, minor damage, c1870. **£2,000–2,500** *DN*

A brooch modelled as a kingfisher, with black opal body, calibré emerald head and diamond and marquise diamond decoration, slight damage. **£4,200–6,200** *CSK*

A silver, cabochon garnet and facetted rock crystal Scottish plaid brooch, a copy of the Lochbuie brooch, 19thC. **£300–400** *CSK*

l. A Victorian gold looped scroll brooch, with pendant, set with turquoises. **£200–250**
c. A Victorian shell cameo brooch, the frame with linked rings. **£100–150**
r. A Victorian gold quatrefoil scroll brooch, set with 3 amethysts. **£200–250** *MSW*

A miniature, attributed to Georg Engelhardt, depicting a lady's eye with a lock of hair, set in a gold beaded and inscribed brooch mount, with glazed hair back, early 19thC. **£800–900** *DN*

A gold hinged bangle, with micro-mosaic of classical ruins, the serpent border with chased scalework decoration, in a fitted case. **£2,800–3,200** *CSK*

A Swiss gold oval brooch with enamelled 18thC style miniature, a pair of pendant earrings, and a bracelet, restored, c1870. **£2,500–3,500** *DN*

A shell cameo, depicting an allegorical scene, in gold brooch mount, with scroll decoration, 19thC. **£750–850** *CSK*

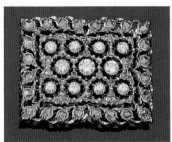

A diamond brooch, pierced in a floral and foliate design, set throughout with circular-cut and rose diamonds, by Buccellati.
£3,000–3,500 *S*

A ruby and diamond brooch, designed as a spray of leaves, set with pear-shaped rubies and eight-cut diamonds.
£600–800 *S*

A diamond set 18ct gold cluster ring, the old cut brilliant centre stone of approx. 1.2cts, surrounded by 10 small brilliants, on unmarked reeded shank.
£2,000–2,500 *MJB*

A ruby and diamond double clip brooch, set with calibre-cut rubies, brilliant cut diamonds and baguette diamonds. **£7,000–8,000** *Bon*

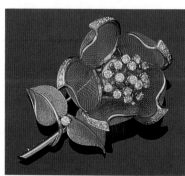

A diamond brooch, designed as a rose, the articulated petals bordered with eight-cut stones, the pistils claw set with brilliant-cut diamonds, 1950s.
£2,000–2,500 *S*

A gold and shell brooch, the oval shell cameo with the profile of the nymph Arethusa mounted within a border of gold twisted ribbon, signed 'T. Saulini F', c1870.
£2,000–2,500 *S*

A diamond floral spray brooch, the flowerhead and leaves set with brilliant-cut stones, the stem set with a line of baguette-cut diamonds.
£3,500–4,000 *Bon*

A lapis lazuli, emerald and diamond hinged bangle/pendant, set with lapis lazuli panels and bordered with circular-cut emeralds and diamonds.
£3,500–4,000 *S*

A diamond brooch, of stylized heart-shaped design, set throughout with eight and circular-cut stones, supporting a larger brilliant-cut diamond drop, c1900. **£1,500–2,000** *S*

l. A pair of Florentine mosaic brooches, one depicting butterflies the other a spray of flowers, mid-19thC.
£650–750 *S*

An Art Deco ruby, synthetic ruby and diamond brooch, set in a chequerboard design.
£1,500–2,000 *Bon*

A gold and silver-mounted diamond triple row crescent brooch, with rose diamond points. **£1,100–1,500** *CSK*

A Whitby jet brooch, with raised carving of a rose, 2.5cm high. **£80–100** *PHay*

Three horn brooches, c1860, 4cm wide. **£6–10** *PHay*

A Whitby jet brooch, with unusual design, 3½in (9cm) high. **£80–100** *PHay*

It is important that brooches have their original back fittings, as repacements affect their value.

A gold butterfly brooch, the pierced wings and body set with 10 rubies, 3 sapphires, 3 graduated opals and 14 rose cut diamonds, with safety chain, 2 stones missing. **£1,000–1,500** *HSS*

An 18ct gold, diamond and sapphire triple cluster flowerhead spray brooch. **£600–700** *CSK*

A Whitby jet carved brooch, c1860, 5cm long. **£50–60** *PHay*

A Whitby jet pendant, 2in (5cm). **£80–100** *PHay*

A Whitby jet brooch, c1860, 3in (7.5cm) wide. **£90–120** *PHay*

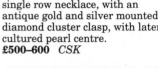

A cultured pearl uniform bead single row necklace, with an antique gold and silver mounted diamond cluster clasp, with later cultured pearl centre.
£500–600 *CSK*

Two Whitby jet necklaces, c1860, 28in (71cm) long.
£75–100 each *PHay*

A Victorian gold locket back-brooch, with central solitaire diamond and quatrefoil palmette decoration, and a pair of matching diamond single stone drop earrings.
£1,300–1,700 *CSK*

A Whitby jet collar, c1865.
£80–150 *PHay*

Necklaces

An Edwardian half-pearl flowerhead and leaf cluster triple panel necklace, with a Prince of Wales link back chain.
£500–600 *CSK*

A Bohemian garnet cluster and drop necklace, and 3 pieces of Bohemian garnet jewellery, damaged. **£300–400** *CSK*

A citrine necklace.
£550–650 *CSK*

An Edwardian amethyst and half-pearl floral cluster pendant, with central pearl drop, with neck chain, in a fitted case. **£400–500** *CSK*

A vulcanite necklace, c1860.
£50–75 *PHay*

A diamond and rose diamond openwork pendant, the flowerhead cluster centre with laurel leaf border and ribbon-bow surmount, with a belcher link neck chain.
£900–1,200 *CSK*

EPHEMERA
Advertising

Two Huntley & Palmers miniature diaries, 1886 and 1892, VG-EX. **£40–60** *VS*

An advertising booklet for Colmans, *Mr Pickwick on the Ice*, VG. **£15–20** *VS*

An advertisment for Golden Shred Marmalade, depicting a young boy playing golf with oranges, VG. **£50–60** *VS*

A collection of 10 advertisements, including Erasmic Soap, FR-VG. **£50–70** *VS*

An advertisement for Danysz Virus rat killer, by J. Hassall, VG. **£25–35** *VS*

A Midland Railway advertisement, The Best Route for Comfortable Travel. **£60–70** *VS*

A collection of 253 advertisements, including poster types, insert cards and reward cards, and a collection of postcard size advertising insert cards. **£850–950** *CSK*

A collection of 143 theatrical poster type advertising posters. **£800–900** *CSK*

EX	Excellent
VG	Very Good
G	Good
FR	Fair
P	Poor

Comics & Magazines

Chester Gould, *The Girlfriends*, daily strip, pen and ink on illustration board, July 11, 1931. **£200–250** *CNY*

Al Taliaferro, daily strip from *Donald Duck*, July 11, 1941, pen and ink on illustration board. **£650–700** *CNY*
© 1941 Walt Disney Productions

Chester Gould, *Dick Tracy*, daily strip, pen and ink on illustration board, June 16, 1943.
£200–250 *CNY*

Walt Kelly, *Pogo*, daily strip, pen and ink on illustration board, December 20, 1956.
£800–900 *CNY*

Charles Schulz, *Peanuts*, daily strip featuring Charlie Brown, pen and ink on illustration board, August 24, 1979.
£1,000–1,400 *CNY*

Basil Wolverton, comic book page from *Powerhouse Pepper*, pen and ink on illustration board.
£520–600 *CNY*

Chester Gould, *Dick Tracy*, daily strip, pen and ink on illustration board, February 25, 1943. **£260–300** *CNY*

Chester Gould, *Dick Tracy*, daily strip, pen and ink on illustration board, September 14, 1949.
£300–350 *CNY*

Dan Decarlo, comic book cover to *Archie* No. 328, pen and ink on illustration board, date unknown.
£75–100 *CNY*

Don Rosa, 26 page story plus cover from *Uncle Scrooge Comics*, Cash Flow, pen and ink on illustration board, c1980.
£5,500–6,000 *CNY*
© *Walt Disney Productions*

Burne Hogarth, *Tarzan*, a Sunday page No. 902, from the Edgar Rice Burrough's classic featuring Tarzan stalked by a deadly octopus on the sea bottom, pen and ink on illustration board, June 20, 1948.
£1,100–1,500 *CNY*

George McManus, *Bringing Up Father*, 3 daily strips featuring Maggie and Jiggs, pen and ink on illustration board, January 22, 1940, October 10, 1944, and October 10, 1945.
£750–800 *CNY*

Film & Theatre

A head and shoulders photograph of Alastair Sim, by Howard Castle, signed, 10 by 8in (25 by 20cm), VG.
£65–75 *VS*

A head and shoulders photograph of Michael Landon, signed and inscribed, 10 by 8in (25 by 20cm), VG.
£35–55 *VS*

A sepia photograph of Marie Dressler, signed, 8½ by 6in (21 by 15cm), VG.
£100–130 *VS*

A photograph of Jean Arthur, signed in later years, 10 by 8in (25 by 20cm), VG.
£70–90 *VS*

A signed photograph of Kay Kendall, 9½ by 7½in (49 by 19cm), G.
£35–45 *VS*

A sepia photograph of Clara Bow, signed and inscribed, overall spotting to image, 9½ by 7½in (24 by 19cm), G.
£150–170 *VS*

A photograph of Susan Hayward, signed and inscribed, 10 by 7½in (25 by 19cm), VG.
£170–200 *VS*

A full length photograph of Betty
Grable, from Three for the Show,
signed, 10 by 8in (25 by 20cm), G.
£60–70 *VS*

A sepia photograph of Lionel
Barrymore, signed, 10 by 8in
(25 by 20cm), VG.
£80–90 *VS*

A sepia photograph of Walter
Huston, smoking a cigarette,
signed, 10 by 8in (25 by 20cm), VG.
£50–70 *VS*

A half length photograph of Mary
Astor, signed and inscribed to
'Picture Show Readers', 9½ by 7½in
(24 by 19cm), VG.
£40–50 *VS*

A photograph of Ronald Reagan,
signed, 10 by 8in (25 by 20cm), VG.
£80–120 *VS*

A photograph of Walter Brennan,
signed and inscribed in white ink,
10 by 8in (25 by 20cm), VG.
£55–75 *VS*

A modern reproduction of Audrey
Hepburn, signed in later years,
10 by 8in (25 by 20cm), EX.
£180–200 *VS*

A photograph of Leslie Howard
and Olivia de Havilland, from
Gone With The Wind,
Picturegoer, VG.
£25–35 *VS*

A modern reproduction of a
photograph of Elsa Lanchester,
signed and inscribed in later
years, 10 by 8in (25 by 20cm), EX.
£90–120 *VS*

A colour photograph of Warren
Beatty, signed, 10 by 8in (25 by
20in), EX.
£55–65 *VS*

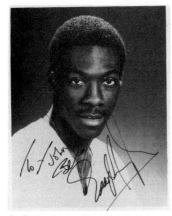

A photograph of Eddie Murphy, signed and inscribed, 10 by 8in (25 by 20cm), EX. **£30–40** *VS*

A colour photograph of Demi Moore and Chevy Chase, signed by both, 10 by 8in (25 by 20cm), VG. **£60–70** *VS*

A colour photograph of Madonna, signed, 10 by 8in (25 by 20cm), EX. **£80–120** *VS*

Tobacco Related Ephemera

Two cigarette packets, 'La Florisca', by J. Bridge & Sons, and 'Gold Flake', G. **£40–60** *VS*

A photograph of Laurel and Hardy, by Ross, VG. **£20–30** *VS*

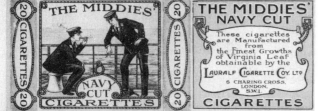

A collection of cigarette packets, mainly 20's, of mixed manufacturers, including 'The Middies' Navy Cut', G-VG. **£110–130** *VS*

EX	Excellent
VG	Very Good
G	Good
FR	Fair
P	Poor

A cigarette packet, 'Scout', by Lambert & Butler, with a Boer War scene, VG. **£170–200** *VS*

A 'G.W.R.' cigarette packet, Lambert & Butler, issued only at Paddington Station, VG. **£150–160** *VS*

A cigarette packet, 'The Scout' by Lambert & Butler, featuring a portrait of Robert Baden Powell, slight crease, G. **£200–240** *VS*

A cigarette packet, 'Merrie Maide', by D. & J. MacDonald, Glasgow, G. **£110–130** *VS*

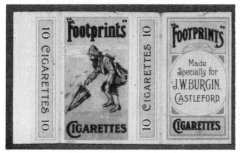

A cigarette packet, 'Footprints', by J. W. Burgin, Castleford, depicting Robinson Crusoe, G. **£200–250** *VS*

A cigarette packet, 'Kits', by
Williams, showing 2 kittens, VG.
£40–60 *VS*

A cigarette packet, 'Lucky Dream',
by the Lucky Dream Tobacco Co.,
depicting a man in a chair with
3 angels, with cigarettes on
the table, G. **£55–75** *VS*

A 'Twopenny Tube' cigarette
packet, by Franklyn Davey, VG.
£70–90 *VS*

A cigarette packet, 'Crusader',
by Adkin & Sons, London, with
Richard the Lionheart, VG.
£40–60 *VS*

A cigarette packet, 'Ocean Prince',
by Adkin & Sons, VG.
£160–200 *VS*

A Bewlay advertisement card,
by Frank Reynolds, for Flor de
Dindigul Cigars, VG.
£40–50 *VS*

> Miller's is a price GUIDE
> not a price LIST.

A cigarette packet, 'Teddy Bear',
by Thomas Bear & Sons, VG.
£60–80 *VS*

Valentines

A handmade puzzle purse
valentine, decorated with a
red heart in watercolour, pen
and ink, with a verse around
the border and inside, c1790,
4in (10cm) square folded, and
3 other greetings cards.
£700–800 *CSK*

A home-made hand coloured cut-
out paper doll valentine, with a
folded letter on a ribbon around
its neck, with a poem, and a letter
from the sender, postmarked
1813, 5in (12.5cm) high.
£350–400 *CSK*

A Bewlay advertisement card,
by Frank Reynolds, for Flor de
Dindigul Cigars, G.
£40–50 *VS*

A flower cage valentine card, stamp marked 'Dobbs Patent', with an embossed border, printed verse, lifting to reveal a cupid playing the 'cello, c1820, 8 by 9½in (20 by 24cm). **£250–300** *CSK*

A flower cage valentine card, stamp marked 'G. Kershaw', with an embossed border, hand coloured floral centre with a colourful bird lifting to reveal a man bending to kiss a lady's hand, c1835, 9 by 7½in (22.5 by 19cm).
£250–300 *CSK*

Two embossed and pierced paper lace valentines, stamp marked 'Dobbs & Kidd & Dobbs', with hand written messages, c1850, 5in (12.5cm), and 2 others, stamp marked 'Dobbs Kidd & Co.'.
£60–90 *CSK*

A three-dimensional pop-up valentine card, the light shines through the gold starred paper cut into the backdrop, with printed message, c1900, 9½in (24cm) high.
£200–250 *CSK*

Valentines

Sweethearts have been exchanging trinkets on Valentine's Day for centuries, and cards for more than 200 years.

It is thought that the tradition came to Britain with the Romans. The pagan feast of Lupercalia was on the 14th of February, when boys drew lots for girls.

The Church later named the day after St. Valentine, a Roman who was martyred on that date in 270 A.D., for trying to save Christians. His last act was said to have been a letter to his love.

Many of the cards bought in the 1920s and '30s were individually created and cut out to form paper cages, which when lifted up revealed romatic inscriptions.

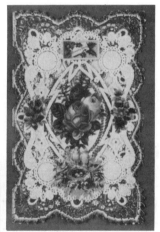

Three Victorian embossed and pierced paper lace valentine cards, with verses, 7 by 4in (17.5 by 10cm).
£140–200 *CSK*

A hand coloured lithographed valentine card, signed 'AIM', with a cupid kissing a lady, and a message, 10 by 8in (25 by 20cm).
£125–175 *CSK*

A three-dimensional chromo-lithographic pop-up card, with message, late 19thC, 7in (17.5cm) high.
£100–140 *CSK*

A heart-shaped chromolitho-graphic valentine card, by Raphael Tuck & Sons Ltd., c1900, 6in (15cm) high, and 4 others, including one by Ernest Lister.
£90–120 *CSK*

DOLLS
Wooden

A primitive painted wooden doll, with turned one-piece head and body, black painted hair, rust red eyes, mouth and cheek spots, black leather arms and pivot hinged legs, damaged, 19thC, 15½in (40cm).
£100–140 *Bea*

A turned wooden doll, with painted head, red mouth and rouged cheeks, inserted blue glass eyes with fine line eyebrows, blonde nailed-on wig, tapering torso to waist, kid lower arms, original yellow satin bodice and net skirt, in shell encrusted case with glazed arched side windows, front and chimney, c1800, 30in (76cm) high.
£2,000–3,000 *S*

A George III painted wooden doll, with red painted lips and rouged cheeks, inserted pale blue glass eyes and dotted lashes and brows, nailed blonde wig, blue kid arms, squared hips and straight legs ending in block feet, in original pink flowered sprigged cream cotton dress, c1810, 14in (36cm).
£1,200–1,800 *S*

Wax

A carved stump doll, with slashed straight back and blue painted dress, c1600, 7in (17cm) high.
£600–700 *CSK*

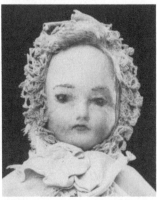

A poured wax fairy, with plaited blonde hair, wax arms and legs, metal-thread decorated white net dress, the glazed case with papered floor, glass cracked, c1830, 13in (33cm) wide.
£300–500 *S*

A Montanari waxed muslin rag baby, the face mask painted and covered with a thin layer of muslin, the cloth head enclosed in the original cream lace-edged hooded cape with a tuft of real hair on the crown, the cloth body with kid forearms, wearing original long cream cotton dress applied with pale pink satin rosettes, c1850, 12in (30cm).
£500–700 *S*

A Pierotti poured wax headed baby doll, with blue eyes, blonde inset mohair, stuffed body and wax limbs, dressed in original lace trimmed frock, bonnet, pink wool cape, socks and slippers, damaged, 19½in (49cm) high, in original wooden box, together with additional lace trimmed gown.
£1,700–2,000 *CSK*

A waxed papier mâché pumpkin head doll, with inserted black glass eyes, waxed blonde hairstyle with a beige silk bow and a pearl, blue bead earrings, cloth covered body with wooden lower limbs, wearing original pale pink net and lace dress with beige silk ribbon, c1860, 24in (61cm).
£300–400 *S*

Bisque

A Victorian wax headed doll, with glass eyes and wax limbs, wearing a purple dress edged with black velvet and lacework, 19in (48cm).
£650–750 *RBB*

A German bisque headed should plate doll, with fixed blue eyes, open mouth with 4 teeth, mohair wig, bisque arms on kid gusset body, wearing contemporary crimson wool skirt, lace trimmed blouse and underclothes, one finger chipped, late 19thC, 15in (38cm).
£200–300 *DN*

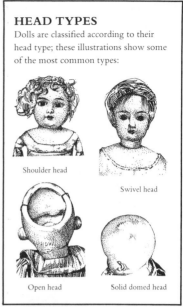

A wax on composition doll, the shoulder plate head with fixed blue eyes, long blonde mohair wig worn in a snood, wax lower limbs, cloth body, wearing contemporary blue serge and black braided jacket and skirt, leather shoes, fob watch and necklace, one leg broken, late 19thC, 19½in (49cm).
£400–450 *DN*

A French swivel head bisque fashion doll, with fixed blue paperweight eyes, blonde wig over cork pate and gusseted kid body, wearing original costume, c1880, 17in (43cm).
£1,200–1,700 *S(S)*

A French swivel head pressed bisque doll, with fixed blue glass eyes, finely painted lashes and brows, pierced ears, blonde plait over cork pate and gusseted kid body with bisque forearms, in original pink flowered silk taffeta dress and olive green silk top, damaged, c1870, 17in (43cm).
£900–1,200 *S*

A German bisque headed doll, with sleeping blue eyes, open mouth with 6 teeth, pierced ears, later blonde wig, marked '325/1A', on a composition ball jointed body, with fawn dress and broderie anglaise smock, 25in (63cm).
£250–350 *DN*

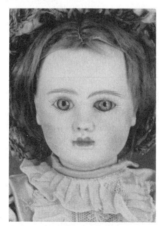

A Jules Steiner bisque doll, with fixed blue glass eyes, blonde wig and composition body, with jointed arms and straight legs, hairline crack to temple, impressed 'Fie A.7',c1887, 14in (36cm).
£700–900 *S(S)*

A bisque doll, with fixed blue glass eyes, ball jointed wood and composition body, wearing original costume, silk dress damaged, impressed '224', possibly Bahr & Proschild, German, c1880, 12in (31cm).
£750–800 *S(S)*

A German bisque doll, with fixed paperweight eyes, jointed wood and composition body, wearing original dress and bonnet, number indistinct, c1910, 19½in (50cm).
£400–600 *S(S)*

A bisque shoulder plate doll, with fixed blue eyes, moulded mouth, mohair wig, bisque lower arms, on kid gusset limbed body, damaged, late 19thC, 16½in (42cm).
£200–300 *DN*

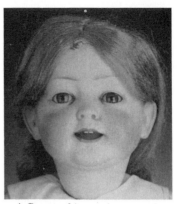

A German bisque character doll, with moulded teeth, weighted blue eyes, curved limb composition body, crack on head, impressed '170 9', c1910, 16in (41cm).
£300–400 *S(S)*

A bisque headed doll by Bruno Schmidt, 'Monica', with brown eyes and open mouth showing 4 teeth, jointed composition body, dressed in red coat and hat, embroidered cotton dress and undergarments, leather boots, head cracked, 24in (61cm), with folding steamer chair, fur rug on baize background, domed top portmanteau containing a collection of clothing.
£1,100–1,700 *CAG*

A bisque headed doll, with fixed brown eyes, open mouth, moulded upper teeth, pierced ears and composition ball jointed body, wearing embroidered lace net dress, impressed '1907 R/A DEP II', 16in (41cm) high.
£200–300 *HCH*

l. & r. A pair of all bisque dolls, with brown eyes, blonde mohair wigs, moulded and painted shoes and socks, in original regional costumes, 4in (10cm) high.
£400–500
c. A pair of bisque headed dolls' house dolls, with blue sleeping eyes, blonde mohair wigs, composition straight limbed bodies with moulded shoes and socks, the boy in plum velvet jacket, the girl in cream silk frock, impressed 'O', 5½in (14cm) high.
£500–600 *CSK*

S.F.B.J.

A moulded bisque walking/talking doll, with weighted black glass eyes, pierced ears, dark wig and jointed arms, straight walking legs, wearing peach silk jacket and white broderie anglaise dress, restored, impressed 'x 7', c1910, 20in (51cm).
£700–900 *S*

A bisque character doll, with closed pouty mouth, weighted blue glass eyes, fair real hair wig and jointed composition toddler body, wearing orange knitted dress and straw bonnet, impressed '252 -4-', damaged, c1910, 12½in (32cm).
£1,700–2,200 *S*

Heubach

A bisque headed character doll, with blue intaglio eyes, moulded and painted hair and musical hand-operated bellows turning head, damaged, impressed with Heubach sunburst '7 04', 10½in (26cm) high.
£400–600 *CSK*

A Heubach Kopplesdorf bisque character doll, wearing original clothes, c1926, 15in (38cm) high.
£200–225 *WAG*

> **Miller's is a price GUIDE not a price LIST.**

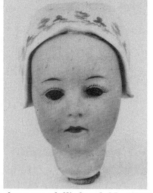

A character doll's head, No. 79 75, with brown sleeping eyes, moulded Dutch bonnet, decorated with flowers and pierced for a ribbon, chipped, impressed with sunburst and '1', 3½in (9cm) high.
£1,200–1,700 *CSK*

Jumeau

A bisque headed doll, with fixed blue eyes, painted brown lashes, closed mouth, pierced ears, original blonde mohair wig, composition ball jointed body, wearing a black lace dress with black silk underclothes, stockings, a black lace hat with beaded trimming, marked 'Tête Jumeau, Bte, S.G.D.G. 9', 20½in (52cm).
£3,000–3,500 *DN*

A bisque headed character baby doll, with painted intaglio features, moulded hair, on composition limbed body, marked '77/43', 13in (33cm).
£500–600 *DN*

A two-faced bisque doll, both faces with open/closed mouths and simulated teeth and tongue, one with fixed blue glass paperweight eyes and finely painted eyebrows, the other with slanted fixed blue glass eyes in a crying expression and moulded glass tear on nose, fair mohair wig, the heads swivelling in a cardboard cowl, the jointed wood and composition body containing a pull string and 'Mama' voice box, oval paper label on back 'Bébé Jumeau Diplome d'Honneur', wearing white broderie anglaise dress and cape, slight damage, 1890, 18in (46cm).
£4,200–5,000 *S*

J.D. Kestner

A bisque doll, with gusset jointed kid body, No. 148, with crown and ribbon stamp on back, c1896.
£600–650 *WAG*

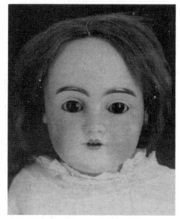

A shoulder bisque doll, with weighted brown eyes, auburn wig over plaster pate and kid body, wearing original costume, damaged, impressed 'DEP 154', 22½in (58cm).
£400–600 *S(S)*

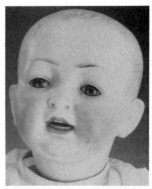

A bisque character doll, with moulded teeth, weighted blue eyes, brush stroke domed head and curved limb composition body, impressed '151', 1897, 13½in (34cm).
£600–700 *S(S)*

Kämmer & Reinhardt

A Kämmer & Reinhardt/Simon & Halbig bisque character doll, with blue glass eyes, fair mohair wig and jointed wood and composition body, wearing cream lacy dress, damaged, impressed '117 30', c1911, 12in (30cm).
£2,000–3,000 *S*

A bisque headed character baby doll, with brown wig, jointed composition body, wearing original clothing and black lace trimmed coat and bonnet, 15in (38cm).
£400–500 *L&E*

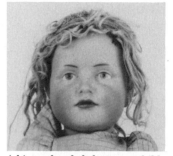

A bisque headed character child doll, with closed mouth, painted blue eyes, blonde wig, jointed body, wearing a pink cotton frock, No. 114 46, some damage, 17½in (44cm) high.
£3,000–3,500 *CSK*

Simon & Halbig

An Oriental bisque doll, with open mouth, weighted brown eyes and ball jointed wood and composition body, wearing cotton kimono, impressed 'SH 1199 DEP 7½', c1898, 18in (46cm).
£1,000–1,400 *S(S)*

A bisque character doll of 'Uncle Sam', with moulded face, white wispy beard, fixed brown glass eyes, red age lines, protruding ears and white wool wig, jointed wood and composition body, wearing original red jacket and navy trousers, the American flag pinned to his jacket, impressed 'S 1', attributed to Simon and Halbig, c1910, 13in (33cm).
£2,000–3,000 *S*

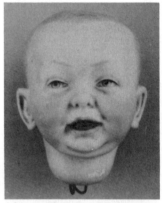

A bisque character head, with intaglio and painted features, marked 'K * R 100 36', 4½in (11.5cm). **£200–250** *DN*

A bisque headed doll, with brown wig, jointed body with flapper knees and diagonal ball joints at thighs, wearing contemporary plum velvet frock, underclothes and original shoes, No. 1078 7, head 5in (12.5cm) high.
£420–500 *CSK*

A bisque headed doll, with blue sleeping eyes, open mouth, moulded upper teeth, pierced ears, ball jointed composition body, wearing pink dress and bonnet, impressed 'K * R 50', 18½in (47cm).
£200–250 *HCH*

A Roullet et Decamps bisque walking doll, the Simon & Halbig head impressed '1078 Halbig S & H 11½', with open mouth and moulded upper teeth, flirting blue glass eyes, auburn mohair wig and wood and composition body with jointed arms and straight legs, the body containing the RD-pierced key causing her legs to walk while her head flops from side to side as if taking the first steps, while her eyes 'flirt', wearing original blue patterned dress with black satin buttons and sash and original black satin bonnet with velvet Alice band applied with pearls, together with other clothing, c1892, 24½in (62cm).
£1,000–1,500 *S*

Armand Marseille

An Armand Marseille doll, wearing original clothes, c1890, 18in (46cm) high.
£300–400 *WAG*

An Armand Marseilles bisque headed doll, with sleeping brown eyes, open mouth with 4 teeth, composition ball jointed body, damaged, No. 390, 25½in (65cm) high.
£300–350 *DN*

l. An Armand Marseille Oriental character baby doll, the bisque head with sleeping brown eyes, composition bent limbed body, wearing Chinese silk brocade and embroidered jacket and trousers, marked 'AM 353/4K', 15in (38cm).
£500–600
r. A German bisque headed 'whistling' boy doll, with intaglio features, blue eyes with highlights on eyelid line, moulded brown hair, puckered mouth, cloth body with moulded composition hands, wearing contemporary green velvet knickerbockers, waistcoat and striped shirt, whistle mechanism inoperative, marked '3 Germany/S7/P' in a canted square/74, possibly Gebruder Heubach, c1914, 12in (30cm).
£350–450 *DN*

An Armand Marseille doll, No. 390, c1909, 24in (61cm) high.
£200–300 *WAG*

An Armand Marseille doll, c1915, 24in (61cm) high.
£325–375 *OCS*

A bisque character doll, with weighted brown eyes, blonde wig and curved limb composition body, wearing knitted costume, impressed '700 7/0', c1920, 8½in (21cm).
£700–900 *S(S)*

An Armand Marseille doll, with flirty eyes, c1930, 25in (63.5cm) high.
£260–300 *OCS*

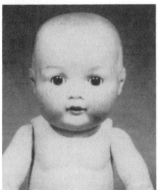

An Armand Marseille bisque headed character baby doll, with sleeping brown eyes, open mouth with 2 teeth, moulded hair, composition limbed body, No. 518, marked 'AM 518/3/2K', 15in (38cm).
£250–300 *DN*

An Armand Marseille 'My Dream Baby', with sleeping eyes, 10in (25cm) high. **£250–300**
A wrought iron dolls' bed, 17in (43cm) long.
£125–150 *WAG*

An Armand Marseilles doll, with kid body, c1890, 14in (36cm) high.
£200–225 *OCS*

Miscellaneous

A Schoenau & Hoffmeister bisque headed doll, with sleeping eyes, open mouth with 2 teeth, brown mohair wig, composition bent limbed body, wearing red silk polka dot dress with lace collar and underclothes, damaged, marked 'No. 3½', 15½in (39cm).
£400–500 *DN*

A painted cloth headed character boy doll, of Käthe Kruse type, with moulded features, the body with separately sewn thumbs, wearing an embroidered shirt, underclothes and shorts with braces, seated in a deck chair, stencil and pencil mark on foot '96106/1889'.
£450–550 *DN*

A rare matryushka or painted wooden nest doll, comprising: 20 hollow turned white wood dolls, painted in polychrome colours and depicting the legend of a very poor Siberian fisherman who catches a gold fairy fish, inscribed in Russian script on the underside of the outer case and dated '1913', in original box, with paper price on lid, together with a typed sheet explaining the legend, top half of smallest doll missing, largest doll 14in (36cm) high.
£5,000–6,000 *S*

The accompanying typed sheet also states that this nest of dolls was made and painted by Russian peasant art students, under the supervision of the Royal Russian Fine Art Society of Lady Artists and exhibited at the Royal Exhibition of Russian Peasants' Art Work, Olympia, England.

A wooden doll's house, covered in brick paper, with 4 bays and 3 floors, opening at the front to reveal 9 rooms, staircase, landings, fireplaces and original papers, G. & J. Lines Ltd., c1910.
£5,500–6,500 *CSK*

A Chad Valley black faced cloth doll, c1940, 14in (36cm) high.
£40–50 *OCS*

A composition doll, dressed as an African, c1930, 14½in (37cm) high.
£85–100 *OCS*

A Schoenau & Hoffmeister doll, c1910, 14in (36cm) high.
£340–380 *OCS*

Three bisque headed dolls, all with sleeping eyes and wigs,
l. An Armand Marseille doll, No. 390, 18½in (47cm), in glazed case.
£900–1,100
c. A Kestner doll, No. 192 4, 15in (38cm).
£1,700–2,000
r. An Armand Marseille doll, No. 390 A7M, in original box, 22in (56cm).
£400–500 *CSK*

A Jules Nicholas Steiner bisque headed bébé, with closed mouth, blue yeux fibres, pierced ears, skin wig and jointed wood and papier mâché body, dressed in white, damaged, 12in (31cm) high.
£1,700–2,000 *CSK*

TEDDY BEARS

An early German straw filled teddy bear, with wooden boot button eyes and hump, 16in (40cm) high.
£200–250 *WAG*

A Steiff blonde mohair plush covered teddy bear, with boot button eyes, felt pads, tag in ear, damaged, early 20thC, 18½in (47cm).
£2,500–3,000 *DN*

A Steiff beige plush teddy bear, with button removed, black stitched snout, black shoe button eyes, press side squeaker, wearing blue check dress, showing wear, 12in (30cm), a tabby cat on wheels with button removed, yellow glass eyes, pink lined ears, long tail, standing on 4 metal wheels joined by metal bars, 10in (25cm) high, and 2 photographs showing a little girl with the bear and cat.
£3,200–4,000 *S*

A German straw filled teddy bear, with wooden button eyes, tilt growler, c1910.
£250–300 *WAG*

An Edwardian Steiff mechanical bear, with button in the ear, boot button eyes, hand stitched nose and embroidered claws, distressed, 12in (30cm) high.
£600–700 *Mit*

A Gebruder Herman teddy bear, 'Horst', with squeaker, c1960, 12in (30cm) high.
£90–100 *WAG*

TOYS

Toys are an area of keen interest to young and old collectors alike. With a vast array of items to choose from and prices ranging from a few pounds to thousands, toys are one area of collecting that virtually offers something for everyone. Only a few homemade toys exist prior to the Industrial Revolution, so the period for toy collectors really commences with Queen Victoria's reign and continues to the present day. Tin toys were produced around the 1840s but the majority of toys at this time were still made of wood, with tin toys phasing out wooden products as the 19thC progressed. Catalogues from German toy wholesalers prior to 1860 show a far wider variety of toys in production than most realise. Other European countries made wooden toys and Russian examples are not uncommon.

In Germany, toy production began with the creation of small wooden toys displaying distinct primitive charm, called Erzgebirge, the name of the region where they were made. These cottage industry toys managed to survive the tinplate period and many wood penny toys were still produced up to WWII. Later, a vast array of finely detailed, delicately painted, horse-drawn carriages were produced. These attractive toys from

Lutz, Märklin, Staudt and others reflected daily life in the early 1800s. Simple cheap pails and baths for the dolls' house, to elaborate carousels, working dioramas and a host of others were produced, with boats and ships the zenith of the toymaker's art. Of course, the steam engine and the railway locomotive were perhaps the main focus, especially of firms such as Bing and Märklin towards the end of the century. At the same time well known names such as Schoenner, Plonk and Carette added their own production which supplied an even more affluent market.

The German company Günthermann produced a large variety of hand painted, amusing novelty toys such as clowns, acrobats and animals which delighted children and parents alike. The firm of Lehmann, with its early use of tin painting,

realised the importance of mass production, and rapidly became the market leader with a line of toys that were popular until WWII. Toy production in Germany was now a huge industry with toys shipped to all corners of the globe.

In the United States, cottage industry toy production actually predated the early German toy industry. Virtually all the toys were made for the domestic market and, as a result, are today almost impossible to find in Europe. However, there are no rules in the toy business, and surprises are what make collecting a fascinating area.

Toy production in the United Kingdom began with William Britains' toy soldiers which were doing battle all-over the world by the end of the 19thC. Britains' earliest productions were a limited line of novelty toys based on French counterparts, superbly detailed and clothed cyclists, figures and a few lead novelty figures. The market possibilities of soldier production gives the collector today a field that has more followers than most.

Unlike the Germans, however, British manufacturers seemed unable to grasp the opportunity to exploit the international market. Frank Hornby was a notable exception with his construction toy, Meccano.

To find any but the simplest pre-1900 tinplate Victorian toy, as they are loosely called, is a challenge. They were generally of a very fragile nature which accounts partly for the fact that locomotives and steam engines seem to be the main survivors. Of course, it is overall scarcity that accounts for some high prices.

Scarcity of items from the late 1800s is not a problem since mass production techniques were well underway thus ensuring large quantities of toys survived. Mass produced toys developed in response to the combination of growing demand and the availablity of new technology. With import levels increasing and people now having more money to spend on toys, there was pressure to supply a ready market with good quality toys.

With the invention of tin lithography even greater production levels could be achieved. Each toy could be quickly decorated and assembled using a tab and slot construction, without the need for laborious soldering and hand painting, which was still necessary for the opulent toy automobiles and fine locomotives of the best quality.

Tinplate toys are truly a reflection of their times, particularly with the rapid change in transport due to the advent of the motor car, and horse-drawn favourites were quickly replaced with toy cars. Even more unbelievable to children must have been the aeroplanes and airships that took to the skies. As pieces of history in themselves, tinplate toys captivated the excitement of the early years of the century, and for the most part are the only tangible reminders remaining. Many good examples are available to collectors.

The tinplate period gives the collector some of the most handsome examples from the German toy industry including luxury liners and large Dreadnoughts, superb limousines and locomotives. Many of the latter were commissioned by Bassett-Lowke of Northampton, who worked in close co-operation with Bing and other German makers. By far the largest number of toys to survive from this time are those which were produced in the largest quantities. Penny toys of every conceivable subject, usually finely lithographed, are a great favourite with collectors. Prices for these items range from £20 up to several hundreds of pounds. There are lots of cheaper locomotives and rolling stock, but not as many novelty toys as one would hope.

Between the Wars

After WWI, Germany continued to export its toys around the world. However, due to the bitterness felt after the war, toy sales decreased. Some home producers, now seeing a gap in the market, seized an opportunity to move in. It was at this time the British toy industry gained momentum by producing toys to rival German counterparts.

Early products of Burnett and Wells with their attractive lithographed vehicles captured a share of the market. Some of the

promotional products for the various biscuit manufacturers in the form of vehicles complement this group. It was left to Frank Hornby to really exploit the toy train market, and his train production in the 1920s and '30s virtually took over the market. Of course, he had already achieved great success with Meccano which continued its popularity.

Trains prior to WWI tended to be more favoured in the larger gauges of I, II, III and IV, with O gauge becoming popular towards the end of that period. Live steam and clockwork trains were the principal products up to 1914, with some electric trains also being produced. Hornby concentrated on O gauge, and this soon became standard for all toy train manufacturers. However, the OO gauge trains introduced just before the war quickly took over the O gauge market after the war. Hornby again was the main producer in the UK, with Märklin the principal producer for the German market.

This period still saw many imports from Germany's older manufacturers. Transport toys such as cars, motorcycles and aeroplanes, were as popular as ever. Shuco in Germany, and Minic in England, provided smaller, quality toys, many of which can still be found today at reasonable prices. Lehmann produced novelties, supplemented by a few automobiles, but the popularity of the novelty amusing toy was now unfortunately on the decline.

Toy soldier production was on the increase with a wide range of military equipment from Britains. German products from Lineol and Elastolin added to the armies available to the young soldier. Britains' lead animals, both farm and zoo, were also very popular. These items can still be found for a few pounds today. Diecast and moulded toys which started production in the 1920s were also growing in popularity.

The UK was the main producer of diecast toys supplying an ever-growing demand. Frank Hornby became the market leader with his models known today as Dinky toys. Other makers such as Taylor and Barrett and Johillco added to the variety of diecast toys available. The selection of toys was also complemented by US imports of Tootsie toys. These pre-war toys are much sought after and can be expensive. After the war, the firms of Matchbox, Dinky, Corgi and others produced a tremendous range to satisfy children and collectors. This is certainly one of the strongest areas of collecting today. Rare examples do bring eyebrow-raising prices if in mint condition, but for every such example there are hundreds to be bought for just a few pounds.

Post-War Toys

World War II brought great changes to the toy market. The German manufacturers of tinplate toys, their industry decimated by the war, managed to continue after the restructuring of their economy, however this revival was to take an even more severe knock with the advent of mass produced plastic toys.

Even before competition from the plastics industry arose, Germany had to take on the now mighty Japanese toy industry which seemed to exploit the gap left in the market for novelty toys. A great variety of these items were made from the 1950s to the 1970s, including clockwork and battery-operated toys, along with masses of toy cars and planes.

Realising the potential of the space age craze, the Japanese produced a fantastic range of robots and space related vehicles, giving today's collectors great scope of items at reasonable prices. Of course, this area is an established market now, with some of the rarer pieces commanding prices on a par with early toys. More and more plastic replaced tinplate, and much of this early plastic material is becoming acceptable and collectable itself. Many older collectors and dealers find it remarkable that Action Man is now so popular. The answer is, of course, that nostalgia is one of the biggest factors in collecting.

Mechanical Banks

Mechanical banks were conceived as amusing and fascinating devices to entice children to save their pennies. Most banks resemble circus characters or animals. Prices start at

a few pounds for tin and pottery banks with much higher values placed on original cast iron banks. The main bulk of mechanical banks were made in the US between 1869 and 1935, with only a few produced in the UK. Today over 95% of banks found are, in fact, reproductions made over the past twenty years in Taiwan, so be wary if you are paying a high price for what you think is an original mechanical bank. It is always wise to seek specialist advice before purchasing.

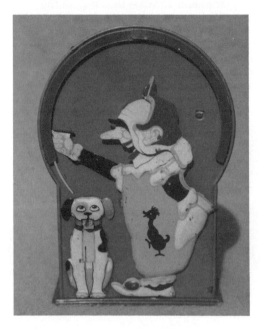

To find an old toy made before 1970 may at times appear difficult, especially at flea markets. Collectors do, however, have a tremendous choice, but may have to look to specialist dealers and salerooms for a particular item. Although some collectors will keep various toys from several periods, most have a special preference, and follow a theme. It is, therefore, unusual for a collector of diecast models to collect tin toys, or a train collector to look for space toys.

There are some problems with fakes particularly in tinplate toys. Many collectors think some of the modern tinplate products of China are older than they are, but lithographed tinplate is not practical to fake. The modern Chinese toys are collectable in their own right.

Always collect what you like without worrying about fashion, or the investment potential, and stick to prices that you can afford. The market for the most expensive toys may have been squeezed somewhat due to the recession, but generally prices at this end of the market have held steady. The same can be said for most toy areas, with perhaps a slight levelling out of prices overall, making today a good time to enter field of toy collecting.

John Haley

TOYS
Automata

A musical automaton, 15in
(38cm) high.
£500–550 *SUL*

A Gustave Vichy musical
automaton of a fruit seller, with
leather covered head, papier
mâché hands, the key wound
stop-start musical movement
playing 2 airs and contained in
the body, in original puce satin
breeches with gold satin turn ups,
pink satin coat with pierced gilt
metal buttons and edged in lace,
under glass dome, damaged,
French, c1870, 25in (64cm) high.
£15,000–20,000 *S*

A French bisque headed
automaton modelled as a lady
swimming, with blue yeux fibres,
pierced ears, skin wig, jointed
wooden body with clockwork
movement and pink silk suit,
movement patented by Martin,
crack to face, c1880, 18in (46cm).
£700–900 *CSK*

A Renou musical automaton of a
circus performer balancing a chair
on his nose, the papier mâché
head with painted features, curly
grey wig and wired body, wearing
original costume, the key wind
stop-start musical movement
within a square base, when
activated the body sways
causing the chair to swivel, face
rubbed, French, c1900, 16in
(41cm) overall.
£1,700–2,200 *S(S)*

A Jean Phalibois musical monkey
dice throwing conjuror, the papier
mâché head with articulated
lower jaw and eyes, in original
elaborate robe of black velvet and
gold satin with metal edging and
lace collar, red and gold satin
pointed hat, under a glass dome,
the base containing key wound
stop-starter, tune change and
pull-string movement playing
2 airs, 26½in (67cm) high
without dome. **£6,000–7,000** *S*

A Decamps musical automaton of
a sleeping doll, with open mouth
and teeth, articulated blue glass
eyes and pierced ears, blonde
mohair wig, lying on a scrolled
brass bed, holding an all bisque
baby in her bisque arms, the base
of the bed containing the key
wound stop-start musical
movement causing the doll to sit
up, open her eyes and lift the baby
while bending her head, then
lying back still raising the baby
up and down, both in lacy blue
and white dresses with matching
bedding, crack to baby's face,
some restoration to bed, doll's
head impressed '1079 Halbig
S & H 1½', French, c1900, 14in
(36cm) long. **£1,100–1,500** *S*

A Jean Phalibois musical
automaton of a monkey
violinist, the papier mâché
head with articulated
upper lip and eyes, wearing
the original cream satin
outfit with green and blue
satin and gold paper
edging, olive velvet hat,
the base containing the
key wind and pull string
musical movement playing
2 airs and with tune
change and stop-start
knobs, French, c1880,
26½in (67cm) high
to top of glass dome.
£7,000–8,000 *S*

A musical automaton of
3 bisque jesters, the revolving
platform on a velvet
covered base applied with
mauve sequinned butterfly
and containing the key wind
stop-start musical mechanism
causing the platform
to rotate, probably German,
c1910, 9in (23cm) wide.
£1,200–1,700 *S*

Money Banks

A 'Chief Big Moon' money bank, American, c1899, 10in (25cm) long. **£700–800** *HAL*

Games

A Victorian amboyna games compendium, the glazed ebony bordered hinged top enclosing chess pieces, a tray for cribbage and draughts and further trays including: counters, scorers, dice throwers and small model horses,14in (36cm) wide. **£1,200–1,700** *DN*

A lead cockatoo money bank, c1920, 4½in (11cm) high. **£50–60** *HAL*

A German iron money bank, early 19thC, 4in (10cm) high. **£15–20** *HAL*

A chromolithographic paper on card clockwork fishing game, 'Jeu de la Pêche', with revolving pond under a bridge with houses, by L'Ombro-Cinema,c1910, in original box. **£300–400** *CSK*

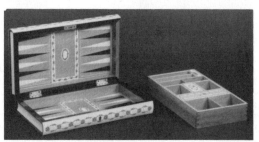

An Anglo-Indian engraved ivory and buffalo horn games box, designed as a folding book, with chessboard top, sandalwood lining with backgammon board, inset tray with boxes and covers containing cribbage board, carved ivory and ebony chess set and draughts, 19thC, box 18 by 4½in (46 by 11cm). **£3,500–4,000** *GH*

A German games box, the domed cover with a lacquered printed découpage scene depicting Mercury and a sleeping traveller, the silk and braid lined divided interior containing 4 small boxes decorated with Clubs, Hearts, Spades and Diamonds, and figures taking tea and cavorting, and a quantity of ivory counters, c1770, 7½ by 6in (19 by 15cm). **£500–600** *DN*

Rocking Horses

A carved wooden rocking horse, with original paint, c1880, 50in (127cm) long.
£800–1,000 *DFA*

A carved wooden rocking horse, with glass eyes, brass handle and swing stand on turned posts, 60in (152cm) long.
£700–1,000 *CSK*

A carved and painted wooden rocking horse, on safety trestle stand with turned posts, damaged, 59in (149.5cm) long.
£400–600 *CSK*

A Victorian grey painted rocking horse, with leather saddle, on a deal base, stamped '953', 'patented January 29th 1880', 48in (122cm) long.
£900–1,200 *C(S)*

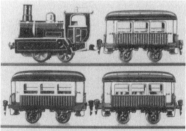

A carved and painted wooden rocking horse, with head turned to the left, neck muscles, glass eyes, remains of bridle and swing stand with turned posts, 42in (106.5cm) long.
£720–800 *CSK*

Trains

A Bassett-Lowke electric lithographed LMS three-car Euston to Watford set, slight damage, and a LMS brake end coach, c1935.
£1,800–2,200 *CSK*

A Bassett-Lowke O gauge 4-4-0 locomotive and tender, the 'Duke of York', finished in LMS maroon and black livery, clockwork driven, slight damage, c1927, boxed.
£120–170 *CSK*

A Märklin gauge III painted tinplate bogie LNWR dining car, with hinged clerestory roof, detailed interior, glass windows, opening doors and hinged corridor fall plates, slight damage, c1904, 18in (46cm) long, and a seated plaster passenger.
£3,500–4,000 *CSK*

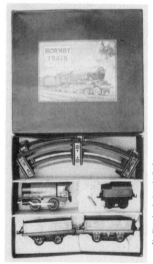

A Hornby 0 gauge M1 goods set, comprising 0-4-0 tank engine and tender, in red and black, No. 3435, and 2 LMS open goods wagons, in grey and dark brown, with a small quantity of track, slight damage, in original box.
£40–70 *WAL*

A Märklin clockwork painted tinplate 0-4-0 rack locomotive, finished in dark green, vermilion and silver, c1900, and 2 painted tinplate four-wheeled green and cream clerestory rack railway coaches with verandah ends and detailed interiors, and another similar, finished in blue and cream, c1926.
£4,500–5,500 *CSK*

Tinplate

A Bueschel lithographed tinplate key wind 'George Washington Bridge', with a Greyhound bus crossing, c1936, 25in (64cm) long. **£1,000–1,500** *CNY*

Two German clockwork lithographed tinplate walking peacocks, their tails with fanning action, probably by Eberl, 6½in (16cm) high. **£200–300 each** *CSK*

A German clockwork lithographed tinplate camouflaged anti-aircraft gun mounted on a lorry, with open crew cab, possibly by Günthermann, late 1930s, 13in (33cm) long. **£500–600** *CSK*

A lithographed tinplate wind-up 'U.S. Mail' electric type delivery truck, by Gilbert, with driver, opening rear door, and red spoked wheels, c1916, 8in (20cm) long. **£350–450** *CNY*

A Lehmann 'Naughty Boy' tinplate clockwork novelty motor toy, No. 495, patent date to May 1903, in original box. **£800–1,000** *S(S)*

A Chad Valley tinplate Carr's biscuit tin, in the form of a London Transport double decker bus, with full lithographed detail, removable roof, on 4 working wheels, 10½in (26cm) long. **£400–500** *Bea*

A Lineol tinplate clockwork camouflage painted military transport lorry, with opening driver's door, drop sides to load bed, door replaced, c1933, 12in (30.5cm) long. **£400–500** *CSK*

Ernst Paul Lehmann

E.P. Lehmann was a visionary toy maker, who began producing a series of tinplate toys in Brandenburg, Germany, in 1881. Lehmann toys are recognisable by their rare combination of ingenious movement and light-hearted pastiche of real life.

Many Lehmann toys have printed patent dates, which are useful in identifying the earliest possible date of manufacture.

A Hull & Stafford tinplate horse drawn two-wheeled gig, the blue cart with painted red and cream interior, with a fully dressed china doll, c1885, 12in (30.5cm) long. **£900–1,200** *CNY*

A lithographed tinplate clockwork organ grinder, with Mickey Mouse cranking the organ, his head moving back and forth as Minnie Mouse dances on top, printed 'Made in Germany', probably made by Distler, Mickey's tail missing, arm repaired, c1931, 8in (20cm) high, in original box. **£18,500–19,500** *CSK*

A Lehmann clockwork lithographed tinplate 'Ikarus' monoplane, EPL No. 653, finished in red and yellow, with pilot, damaged. **£450–550** *CSK*

A Masudaya lithographed battery operated tinplate Target Robot, slight damage, c1960,15in (38cm) high.
£1,000–1,500 *CSK*

A Märklin tinplate toy oven, the front decoratively embossed, with blued steel and silver finish, with 2 small and one larger nickel plated cast iron hinged door, spirit burning, cast legs, with 5 burners and pots including kettle, bain marie, and 2 covered cooking pots, short chimney, 12½in (32cm) wide.
£4,500–5,000 *S*

This stove is illustrated on page 178 of Herve's Märklin 1895-1914, and appeared in the Märklin 1909 catalogue as reference 9694.

A Märklin painted tinplate clockwork assembled 'Auto 1101c/09' constructor car chassis, and 'Auto 1103St Stream Line Body' constructor set, finished in green with blue wings and roof and green body, with original instructions, colour leaflet and boxes, c1934.
£1,000–1,500 *CSK*

A Schuco felt covered tinplate clockwork 940 Charlie Chaplin toy, dressed in grey trousers, black jacket and red tie, with a cane in his hand, slight damage, c1920, 6½in (16.5cm) high.
£600–700 *CSK*

A Marx tinplate key wind 'Amos 'n' Andy Fresh Air Taxicab', lithographed in orange and black, a dog in the front seat, c1931, 8in (20cm) long, with plexi cased box.
£700–900 *CNY*

A Märklin tinplate toy, c1880, 7½in (19cm) wide.
£450–480 *HAL*

A Tippco painted and lithographed tinplate battery operated orange and cream Mercedes 220S, with cable remote control, slight damage, 12in (30.5cm) long.
£420–500 *CSK*

A Tippco tinplate police motor-cycle, c1950, 11in (28cm) wide. **£250–300** *HAL*

A Wells lithographed clockwork tinplate second version style No. 6 'Motor BP Spirit' delivery lorry, No. 4972, with driver, c1931, 6in (15cm) long. **£550–600** *CSK*

A Tippco painted and lithographed tinplate battery operated blue 1123M Mercedes 220S Convertible, slight damage, 12in (30.5cm) long. **£850–1,000** *CSK*

A German painted tinplate pulley-driven hot air balloon, with 2 lithographed balloonists seated in the basket, with finial flag, finished in white, cream, green, blue and pink, paint flaking, 9in (23cm) high. **£500–600** *CSK*

A German painted tinplate steam jet powered windmill, finished in cream, brown, green and red, 7½in (19cm) high. **£200–300** *CSK*

A tinplate bi-plane, 19in (48cm) long. **£250–300** *HAL*

A Wells tinplate ambulance, c1925, 6½in (16.5cm) long. **£200–250** *HAL*

A lithographed tinplate key wind 'Lincoln Tunnel', c1935, 24in (61cm) long, in a plexiglass case. **£200–300** *CNY*

A heavy tinplate horse-drawn hansom cab, the black and red cab with coachman's seat, the horse with movable legs, 15½in (39cm) long. **£200–230** *CNY*

Miscellaneous

A Hubley cast iron horse-drawn 'Surrey', painted in green and red, with driver and team of horses, c1900, 12in (30.5cm) long. **£200-300** *CNY*

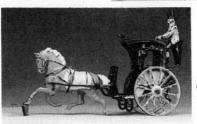

A Wilkins cast iron horse-drawn lady's phaeton, coloured red and yellow, with a lady in a blue dress, c1900, 17in (43cm) long. **£2,000–3,000** *CNY*

A Pratt & Letchworth cast iron horse-drawn black and yellow hansom cab, pulled by a tan trotting horse, with driver in a top hat, horse's wheel missing, c1895. **£650–750** *CNY*

An Ives cast iron horse-drawn orange and black ladder wagon, with 2 firemen, buckets missing, c1890, 26in (66cm) long.
£650–750 *CNY*

A Hubley cast iron red fire truck, with 2 wooden ladders, 2 drivers, and a gold eagle embossed at the sides, c1920, 15½in (39.5cm) long.
£300–400 *CNY*

A cast iron red painted 'Friendship 1774' fire pumper, with rubber hose, 16in (40.5cm) long.
£700–800 *CNY*

An Ives painted cast iron horse-drawn black and red hook and ladder wagon, No. 45, with 2 drivers, ladders and pails, c1885, 28in (71cm) long.
£1,200–1,700 *CNY*

A cast iron brown racing shell with 8 action rowers, on 4 wheels, one oar replaced, c1895, 14½in (37cm) long.
£2,200–2,800 *CNY*

A Britains Royal Horse Artillery set, No. 39, in original box.
£350–400 *WAL*

A Britains United States Marine Corps Colour Guard set, No. 2101, in original box.
£270–300 *WAL*

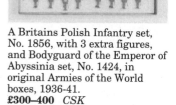

A Britains Polish Infantry set, No. 1856, with 3 extra figures, and Bodyguard of the Emperor of Abyssinia set, No. 1424, in original Armies of the World boxes, 1936-41.
£300–400 *CSK*

A Britains Coronation Display set, No. 1477, 1937, in original wooden box, with damaged cardboard lid.
£800–900 *WAL*

A Heyde Turkish caravan comprising 64 pieces.
£2,000–3,000 *CSK*

A collection of Britains and other garden series items, some damage, box damaged.
£800–900 *S(S)*

A goup of 31 Black Forest painted, composition and carved wooden figures and farm animals.
£250–300 *Bea*

A Britains model zoo, and a desert scene with Arabs, camels and palm trees, approx 100 pieces. **£150–200** *DN*

A German painted wood Noah's Ark, containing 5 figures and 84 various animals, damaged, mid-19thC, ark 21in (53cm) long. **£600–800** *S*

A Schoenhut painted wood 'Humpty-Dumpty Circus', No. 2036, c1925, 30in (76cm) long. **£2,500–3,500** *CNY*

A German hand painted wooden Noah's Ark, with hand carved animals under a hinged roof, small repairs to some figures, c1895, 15in (38cm) long.
£700–900 *CNY*

A German painted wooden Noah's Ark, with 7 figures of Noah and his family and approximately 176 pairs of animals, birds and insects, mid-19thC, ark 29in (74cm) long.
£4,200–5,000 *S(S)*

A German painted wooden Noah's Ark, with 3 pairs of people, 36 pairs and 5 single animals, 19thC, slight damage, 21in (53cm) long. **£350–550** *S*

A Dinky Toys green Lincoln Première, c1950, 4in (10cm) long. **£70–100** *HAL*

A French Dinky Char Amx bridge layer, c1965, box 6in (15cm) long. **£100–150** *HAL*

A French Dinky Supertoys Berliet tank transporter, c1955, box 12½in (31cm) long. **£80–120** *HAL*

A Dinky Toys blue Ford Consul Corsair, c1960, in mint condition, with box, 4½in (11cm) long. **£50–55** *HAL*

A French Dinky Toys fire engine, c1950, box 5in (12.5cm) long. **£100–140** *HAL*

A Dinky Supertoys Mighty Antar low loader with propeller, c1955, 12½in (31cm) long. **£150–200** *HAL*

Two Dinky Supertoys Fire Station Kits, Nos. 954 and 957, in original boxes. **£550–650** *S(S)*

A Dinky yellow and black Volkswagen Swiss Post PTT car, No. 262, in original box. **£200–300** *CSK*

A Dinky Toys Foden Flat Truck with chains, No. 505, green with 1st type cab, slight damage, in original box. **£850–950** *S(S)*

A pair of Japanese clockwork celluloid skiers, in original grey box with printed label 'Made in Occupied Japan', c1940, and a Kuramochi Japanese clockwork celluloid 'Service Boy', in original box, c1930. **£250–300** *CSK*

An Austin A35 pedal car, c1950. **£250–350** *Mit*

A French Dinky Toys Berliet container lorry, c1950, box 5in (12.5cm) long. **£70–100** *HAL*

A Beatles four-string plastic toy guitar, made by Selcol, 2 strings missing, with instruction book. **£80–100** *WAL*

A set of 4 Japanese composition Beatles nodding figures, dressed in light blue suits, standing on gold bases with printed signatures, c1964, 8in (20cm) high. **£250–300** *CNY*

A collection of 16 Fipps novelty hedgehogs, from the 1957 Cologne Garden Festival. **£250–350** *CSK*

These Hedgehogs are based on the popular German comic character created by Ferdinand Diehl. 'Mecki's' were made exclusively by Steiff, who were granted the licensing rights from 1951. These Fipps hedgehogs are possibly unlicenced copies.

A painted wood carousel ride, carved as a swan, on a tapering base, with brass handles, repainted, 51½in (131cm) high. **£1,200–1,700** *CSK*

A Schoenhut boxed painted wooden 'Humpty Dumpty Circus', c1915, in original box. **£1,200–1,700** *CNY*

A basketwork pushchair, c1910, 15in (38cm) wide. **£30–40** *DFA*

Three Pelham Hanna-Barbera puppets, in original yellow full card character boxes, with Screen Gems Inc. label, c1963. **£200–250** *CSK*

A Meccano blue and gold outfit, No. 8, strung in original two-tier box, some parts in original wrapping, 2 instruction books, motor leaflet, guarantee dated 8.8.39, 1939. **£850–950** *CSK*

Locate the source

The source of each illustration in Miller's can be found by checking the code letters below each caption with the list of contributors.

A fairground water ride vessel, in the shape of a swan, with large removable wings and 2 bench seats, damaged and repainted, 80in (203cm) long. **£1,700–2,200** *CSK*

A Reed printed wood ferris wheel, powered by hand, replacements, c1925, wheel 15in (38cm) diam. **£350–400** *CNY*

KITCHENALIA

A green glass sugar crusher, and 11 other clear glass crushers.
£250–275 *P*

A metal potato ricer, c1920, 11½in (29cm) long.
£10–12 *AL*

A cylindrical pot, containing olive spoons, whisks and other utensils.
£300–320 *P*

A Tiffany & Co., nutmeg grater, marked 'Sterling', 1½in (4cm) long.
£325–350 *P*

A copper wash dolly, with wooden handle, c1900, 17in (43cm) high.
£12–16 *AL*

A Swiss copper crêpe pan, with silver coloured metal lining, 11in (28cm) diam.
£300–350 *P*

A copper bowl, raised on a ring foot, 15½in (39cm) diam.
£260–280 *P*

A pair of electroplated domed dish covers, with interlaced Art Nouveau style handles, 11in (28.5cm) long.
£400–420 *P*

An electroplated muffin dish, 7½in (19cm) diam., and a silver coloured metal table top flambé dish, 11in (28cm) high.
£80–100 *P*

A tin fish kettle, c1890, 15in (38cm) long.
£30–35 *AL*

A copper long-handled frying pan, 14in (35cm) diam.
£375–400 *P*

A tin dustpan, c1890, 13½in
(34cm) long.
£10–15 *AL*

A tin double saucepan, with
wooden handle, and porcelain
container, c1880, 8in (20cm) high.
£35–40 *AL*

A tin oven, c1930, 13in
(33cm) square.
£25–35 *AL*

Three tin graters, c1900-20,
8 to 9in (20 to 23cm) long.
£3–7 each *AL*

A collection of tin pastry cutters,
contained in tin outer cases:
l. c1900, largest 4½in (11cm) diam.
£10–12
r. c1810, largest 7in (17.5cm) wide.
£25–30 *AL*

An icing set, complete with
nozzles and turntable, c1930,
8in (20cm) diam.
£7–8 each *AL*

A Coalport potato flask,
with hand painted sprig
design in red and green
enamels, hairline
crack, 9in (22cm) high.
£280–300 *P*

Kitchenalia

Kitchenalia collections are
growing in popularity, and
prices of items can vary
enormously particularly if
they have been owned or used
by a famous person or cook.
This was certainly the case
when buyers who attended the
Elizabeth David auction, held
at Phillips in London earlier
this year, were determined not
to return home empty handed.

A tin preserving pan,
with jars and
thermometer, c1890,
13in (33cm) high.
£25–30 *AL*

A copper food cover, c1920,
11in (28cm) long.
£20–25 *AL*

A wood and tin washboard,
c1900, 23in (59cm) long.
£12–14 *AL*

A ceramic Queen's Pudding
basin, with tin lid, c1890, 5½in
(14cm) diam.
£25–30 *AL*

BARBRA STREISAND

An Art Deco black lacquer baby grand piano, by Krakauer, serial No. 08085133, with U-shaped legs, 56in (142cm) wide, and a matching upholstered bench, 34in (86cm) wide.
£5,000–5,500 *CNY*

A Cent-a-Pack slot machine, featuring 6 different cigarette packs on the display wheel, 12in (30.5cm) high.
£275–300 *CNY*

A bronze sculpture, entitled 'Colus and Phoebe', signed 'K. Arpel 4/20', on a base, 7½in (19cm) high.
£1,500–2,000 *CNY*

A Royal Doulton demi tasse service, with green stylised floral decoration and gilt trim, comprising: a coffee pot with cover, 6 cups, 6 saucers, a sugar bowl and a creamer.
£1,000–1,500 *CNY*

An enamelled metal Coca-Cola advertising sign, 38in (96cm) diam., and an electric 7-Up advertising sign, 10in (25cm) high.
£300–350 *CNY*

A Victorian walnut davenport, with 4 side drawers, on bun feet and porcelain casters, 23in (58.5cm) wide.
£5,000–5,500 *CNY*

This was the first antique purchased by Barbra Streisand.

A patinated metal and glass figural lamp, cast from a model by F. Flora, the nude maiden in billowing drapery, signed, with a yellow and rust iridescent glass shade, 29in (73cm) high.
£3,500–4,000 *CNY*

A Hower Loughlin china plate, celebrating the 1939 World's Fair, inscribed on reverse '1 150th Anniversary Inauguration of George Washington as First President of the United States 1789-1939', with a wooden stand.
£3,000–3,500 *CNY*

Barbra Streisand

In 1994 Barbra Streisand announced that she wanted to sell some of her collections and possessions, so that others could appreciate them.

There followed a large sale at Christie's New York, where the pieces on these two pages were sold.

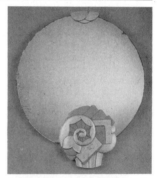

An Art Deco French giltwood mirror, with stylised foliate mount, 23½in (60cm) wide.
£550–600 *CNY*

A Favrile Tel El Amarna glass and gilt bronze vase, in rich iridescent blue glass, with gold and blue interlaced bands on the neck, on a gilt bronze domed foot, stamped 'Tiffany Studios New York', 7in (18cm) high.
£2,500–3,000 *CNY*

A gilt bronze table lamp, consisting of 12 iridescent reproduction shades supported by 12 curving stems on a layered lily pond base, the base stamped 'Tiffany Studios New York 382', 21in (53.5cm) high.
£6,000–6,500 *CNY*

A jewelled dogwood leaded glass and bronze table lamp, the shade with pink blossoms, green leaves and a clear sky-blue ground, stamped 'Tiffany Studios New York 1573-1', 20in (51cm) high.
£32,000–35,000 *CNY*

A giltwood and metal clock, by Hans Ofner, with gilded border and glass front, stylised Arabic numerals heightened with black enamel, c1909, 16in (40.5cm) square.
£6,000–6,500 *CNY*

A carved mahogany, oak and marquetry sideboard, marked 'L. Majorelle Nancy', 80½in (204cm) high.
£10,000–11,000 *CNY*

A George III mahogany line inlaid serpentine-shaped sideboard, with 3 central frieze drawers flanked by deep drawers, on square tapered legs with spade feet, 85in (216cm) wide.
£6,500–7,000 *CNY*

An enamelled glass vase, 'Soustons', by René Lalique, the edges heightened with black enamel, acid stamped, inscribed 'France', 9in (23cm) high.
£15,000–16,000 *CNY*

An etched and enamelled glass and wrought iron table lamp, the glass by Daum, the metalwork by Roge, cameo signature, 25½in (65cm) high.
£22,000–23,000 *CNY*

A gilt bronze figure, entitled 'Le Secret', cast from a model by Pierre Fix-Masseau, inscribed, impressed with the Siot-Decauville foundry seal, stamped 'N540', early 20thC, 11in (28cm) high.
£5,500–6,000 *CNY*

An overlaid and etched glass vase, by Emile Gallé, with everted rim, frosted yellow ground overlaid in red and etched to depict fuchsia blossoms and foliage, cameo signature, 8in (20cm) high.
£4,500–5,000 *CNY*

FOCUS ON AMERICA

Furniture

A 'correction' has brought sanity back to the American furniture market. Prices are back to the levels of the mid-1980s, before this many-tiered market soared to dizzying heights.

It is hard to generalise because prices are not yet firm, and collectors are very selective, but prices seem to be on an upswing and fine pieces in good condition, fresh to the market, have been making record prices. For example, at Sotheby's New York sale in January, of the late Bertram K. and Nina Fletcher Little's widely published collection of New England antiquities, a carved oak and pine lift-top blanket chest with one drawer made in North Hampton, Massachusetts 1712-22, sold for £236,000. This was a record for any blanket chest and three times what similar chests had sold for previously. It has the name of the owner 'Esther Lyman' carved on the top rail and flat scroll and leaf carving on the stiles with panels characteristic of so-called Hadley chests from the Connecticut River Valley.

In the present climate the price difference between the good and the best, fancy and simple forms has widened significantly and if a piece is not in perfect condition the difference is even more dramatic. For example, a well proportioned Philadelphia camelback sofa, without peaks and with straight tapered legs sold for £21,000 at Christie's New York in October. The legs were slightly cut down but the back had its original linen upholstery. Another very fine Philadelphia small serpentine camelback sofa, with peaks, sold at Sotheby's in January for £200,000. Certain forms, namely looking glasses, Massachusetts block front chests of drawers, and pristine candlestands have brought stronger prices.

There are fewer collectors of Classical American furniture made 1815-1840 even though recent museum exhibitions have widened the audience and a supply of good examples has pushed prices higher. One collector bought most of a private collection offered at Christie's in January paying a premium for any piece with a firm attribution to Duncan Phyfe or Charles Honore Lannuier. An upholstered armchair with arched back and scrolled arms by Phyfe sold for £67,000. A parcel gilt commode with a marble top in the French Directoire style based on a design by Pierre de la Mesangere stamped 'H. Lannuier' went for £42,000 and a set of curule back mahogany chairs with paw feet, also attributed to Lannuier, fetched £38,500.

The market for Arts and Crafts furniture which had experienced a dramatic drop in prices and then a quiet period from 1990 to early 1993 continues to show signs of recovery and good material is available once again. Generally prices have risen to within 20% of their peak but some prices paid in the mid-1980s will remain aberrations. Take for instance, a round cross stretcher dining table. Today such tables sell for £6,500 to £10,000 against a previous record of £30,000 for such a table. Morris Spindle chairs which peaked at £13,500 now fetch £6,500 to £8,000. Chairs are down in price partly because seating furniture has been reproduced successfully.

Early forms by Gustav Stickley are in demand. They represent the ultimate expression of the Arts and Crafts philosophy and the highest quality.

While many people furnish with Arts and Crafts furniture, the market for Frank Lloyd Wright's designs is a small one, with museums competing with a few American and Japanese collectors.

There seem to be buyers for every style of American furniture and with prices generally well below the highs of the late 1980s, well-educated collectors are buying with enthusiasm.

Silver

When an early piece of American silver comes up for sale it causes excitement because of its scarcity. American silver is offered at the major New York auctions twice a year, in January and June, but occasionally a fine piece turns up elsewhere. Some fine 18thC silver bought by New Hampshire collector, Eddy G. Nicholson, in the competitive 1980s was re-offered at Christie's in January and demonstrated that prices are still moving upward.

A Tiffany six-piece silver tea and coffee service, all monogrammed, lacking burner, c1920, 133oz.
£5,000–6,000 *SK(B)*

Collectors are fussy about condition. A buffed surface, modern engraving, erased monograms, or indistinct marks can prevent a piece from selling, but those with good colour and family history bring a premium.

Common forms such as baluster-shaped cans, porringers with keyhole handles and Federal sugar vases have to be pristine to sell but their prices have changed little in the last decade. Fine examples can bring around £1,350, but many sell for much less, allowing new collectors to build a representative collection of standard forms for a reasonable expenditure although they face fierce competition for masterpieces.

Nineteenth century silver is more plentiful than Colonial silver and the market has softened a bit for pieces of mixed metal in the Japanese style. 'Aesthetic movement silver went through its discovery phase from 1887 through 1990 when the market had real zest across the board, as always happens in the early phase of the collecting cycle,' suggests Jeanne Sloane of Christie's.

While there is sagging interest in the middle level of this market, the upper end continues to be strong. A small mixed metal pitcher, 6¾in high, made by Tiffany & Co., and designed by William C. Moore for the Paris Exposition in 1878, sold for £34,500 at Christie's sale of the collection of Charles H. Carpenter Jr., who wrote books on both Tiffany and Gorham, the two leading 19thC American silversmiths. From the same collection a six-piece silver tea and coffee service, with tray and waiter, designed by Louis Comfort Tiffany, sold for £68,000. A silver and silver gilt Tiffany & Co., dessert service, comprising 151 pieces of flatware, in the Aesthetic style, decorated with blackberry vines sold for £32,500. An Art Nouveau Gorham Martele silver flagon fetched £64,000.

American Indian Art

American Indian artefacts are receiving greater attention from both collectors and historians. The Heye Foundation in New York has become the National Museum of the American Indian and will occupy a new museum on The Mall in Washington D.C. with Native Americans serving as director and curator. A glossy magazine called *American Indian Arts* is available, and there are American Indian shows and sales.

The market in American Indian art is strong even though certain sacred works are not sold any more. Some Kachinas, medicine bundles, masks, and other objects considered religious have been reclaimed by tribal leaders, but current laws pertain only to objects owned by institutions receiving Federal funding, not to private collectors or dealers.

The Endangered Species Act restricts the sale of anything made from animals near extinction. For example, selling eagle feathers is a Federal offence in the USA, but eagle feathers can be bought and sold abroad.

These issues have not dissuaded collectors or dealers from acquiring Indian art and desirable objects are getting increasingly difficult to find and are immediately saleable at high prices when they do turn up. Even middle range material is hard to find, but it must be priced right to sell.

Most Indian art seems to go to auction. Sotheby's has dominated the field holding sales in New York in November and May. Up until last year Christie's sold American Indian material in London but its sale in New York in May was very successful. Skinner's in Bolton, Massachusetts and Butterfield's in San Francisco hold sales in

A *Kwakiutl wooden model totem pole, mounted on a low tapering base, surmounted by a large hawk, with black red and green painted details, signed on the back 'Charlie James', 16½in (42cm) high.* **$2,550–3,250** *S(NY)*

January and June and in between these major sales dealers and collectors travel to smaller sales anywhere where American Indian items are advertised.

The most important gathering is the Indian Market in Santa Fe, New Mexico. Every August half a dozen auctions and as many shows are held in a ten day period and thousands of objects change hands.

Prices for Northwest Coast material remain firm. At Skinner's in November a 19thC Haida face mask sold for £20,000 and a Haida 'ship pipe' made of carved and incised golden-brown wood inset with ivory figures fetched £8,000. At Butterfield's in December a very rare, early, painted spruce root hat, in fine condition and of great beauty fetched £75,000.

Plains Indian material is hot. Beadwork of high quality sells quickly but fakes abound. Props from movies have been passed off as genuine: beads and leather have been artificially aged so the novice has to look carefully and it is best to trust only experienced dealers.

Pueblo ceramics and weavings are eagerly sought. A fine, large lopsided Acoma pot will sell for more than £6,500. At a recent sale on Long Island an Acoma jar fetched more than £8,000. A Navajo wearing blanket, of homespun and commercial wool in a Third Phase chief's pattern sold for £12,500 at Skinner's during a snowstorm in January. Older and finer blankets have sold for six-figure prices.

American Indian baskets have no equal and there has been no recession at all in the market for high quality baskets. At Skinner's in November, a basket woven by the Chumash people on the southern coast of California sold for £20,500 and a Tubatulabl polychrome coiled bowl, also from California, finely stitched in black and red over a bundled willow foundation, in a pattern of sixty-one skirted figures went for £14,000.

Lita Solis-Cohen

FOCUS ON AMERICA
Furniture

A cannonball decorated bedstead, sponge painted with patterns of red dots on a yellow-gold ground, with rope mattress support, red painted curly maple side rails, probably eastern Connecticut, c1840, 54in (137cm).
£3,000–4,000 *S(NY)*

A decorated bedstead, grain painted black over ochre to simulate rosewood, Pennsylvania or Ohio, mid-19thC, 77in (195.5cm) wide.
£5,000–6,000 *S(NY)*

A Federal eagle-carved mahogany and giltwood sabre leg armchair, the panelled crest carved with water reeds above an acanthus and flowerhead carved back rail, the arm supports in the form of squatting eagles, the acanthus carved seat rail enclosing a removable slip-in seat, on acanthus carved and moulded down curving legs ending in brass animal paw feet, probably Philadelphia, c1805.
£13,500–15,000 *S(NY)*

A Queen Anne carved cherrywood secretaire bookcase, in 3 parts, restored, c1760, 37in (94cm).
£10,000–15,000 *S(NY)*

An Empire mahogany secrétaire bookcase, the upper glazed doors over 2 small drawers, with drop front writing surface, on bracket feet, damaged, 40in (101.5cm) wide.
£600–1,000 *EL*

A Federal carved mahogany armchair, the serpentine seat rail with slip-in seat, on moulded square tapering legs, repaired, probably Maryland, c1795.
£2,500–3,500 *S(NY)*

An Empire flame mahogany veneered secrétaire bookcase, with projecting cornice above glazed doors, the base with pull-out drop front with writing drawer, above 2 graduated drawers flanked by free standing S-columns, with incurved feet, 45in (114cm) wide.
£700–1,000 *SLN*

A Chippendale carved mahogany corner chair, with an acanthus carved angular cabriole front leg ending in a claw-and-ball foot, the 3 tapered legs behind joined by a turned X-form stretcher, ending in vase form feet, alterations, Boston-Salem, Massachusetts, c1760.
£10,500–12,000 *S(NY)*

A walnut armchair, the front leg stamped 'George Hunzinger, NY, patent March 30, 1869'.
£1,500–2,000 *SK(B)*

A wicker rocking armchair, by Heywood Brothers, late 19thC.
£300–400 *DMT*

A set of 6 paint decorated Windsor side chairs, with red and green floral decoration on a black ground, heightened with yellow foliage and piping, probably Pennsylvania, c1820.
£10,000–11,000 *S(NY)*

A wicker Arran chair, by Wakefield Co., c1880.
£400–600 *DMT*

An American walnut bureau, damaged, 39in (99cm) wide.
£200–300 *EL*

A set of 6 Empire mahogany dining chairs, with drop-in seats, on sabre legs, one seat missing, and an armchair.
£1,200–1,800 *EL*

A wicker rocking chair, by Wakefield Co., c1885.
£280–350 *DMT*

A Gothic revival polychrome and gilt oak bedroom suite, by Hellenbrand Industries, Batesville, Indiana, comprising a dressing table with mirror, 51½in (130cm) wide, a curule stool, and a chest of drawers, 40½in (102cm) wide.
£250–500 each *SLN*

A Sheraton mahogany chest of drawers, with shaped apron and turned legs, late 18thC, 41½in (105cm) wide.
£600–1,000 *EL*

A Federal inlaid mahogany bow-front chest of drawers, repaired, Philadelphia or middle Atlantic states, c1810, 42in (106.5cm).
£3,000–4,000 *S(NY)*

A corner cupboard, with chinoiserie decorated panelled doors, early 20thC, 73in (185cm) high.
£1,000–2,000 *EL*

A paint decorated 2 drawer dower chest, the moulded top opening to a deep well with till, the case with waisted lower section fitted with 2 small drawers, raised on circular turned tapering legs, the whole grain painted in orange and yellow, the front with simulated owl's eyes and the sides with stylised tulip motifs, Pennsylvania, slight wear and losses to paint, c1830, 46in (116.5cm).
£8,000–10,000 *S(NY)*

A pine blanket chest, the top with outset corners, opening to a well with till, the grain painted front panel with 2 convex pilasters above a dentil carved shaped skirt continuing to bracket feet, painted and decorated in brown and ochre on a cream ground, c1830, 45in (114cm).
£1,500–2,000 *S(NY)*

A Federal curly maple corner cupboard, in 2 parts, probably New York of Pennsylvania, c1820, 45in (114cm).
£7,000–9,000 *S(NY)*

A cherrywood corner cupboard, the clock with wooden works and white painted dial, arched long door below, the whole on a moulded base, Pennsylvania or New Jersey, early 19thC.
£1,500–2,500 *S(NY)*

A Federal cherrywood corner cupboard, Pennsylvania, early 19thC, 55in (139.5cm).
£3,000–4,000 *S(NY)*

A Chippendale mahogany drop front desk, with fitted interior, on ogee bracket feet, c1800, 38in (96.5cm) wide. **£700–1,000** *SLN*

A Chippendale carved walnut block front desk, with fall front, the fitted interior with mock document drawers comprising a removable box with secret drawers behind, 4 graduated drawers below, on bracket feet, Boston, Massachusetts, c1765, 40in (101.5cm).
£5,500–6,500 *S(NY)*

A Hepplewhite mahogany desk, with upper slant front section above a drawer, the lower section with drawer above a writing slide, on straight legs with stretcher, 34in (86cm) wide.
£1,000–1,500 *SLN*

A Federal inlaid mahogany tambour writing desk, the lower section with hinged baize lined writing flap, above 2 long drawers, on square tapering legs with brass spade feet, New England, branded 'JS' on lower backboard, repaired, bottom drawer replaced, c1810, 37½in (95.5cm).
£2,000–3,000 *S(NY)*

A Chippendale birchwood drop front desk, with fitted interior, feet reduced, repaired, New England, c1760, 36in (91.5cm).
£2,000–3,000 *S(NY)*

A carved and gilded pine cornucopia mirror, probably New England, early 19thC, 28in (71cm) wide.
£13,500–15,000 *S(NY)*

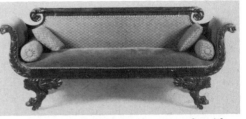

A bonnet top cherrywood courting mirror, with New England frame and an imported Continental églomisé mirror, c1795, 13in (33cm).
£13,000–15,000 *S(NY)*

A Federal inlaid mahogany and giltwood wall mirror, minor repairs, 19thC, 28½in (72cm).
£1,500–2,200 *S(NY)*

A carved mahogany sofa, with upholstered seat on acanthus carved cabriole legs, ending in animal paw feet, on casters, New York, c1825, 90½in (229cm).
£1,500–2,500 *S(NY)*

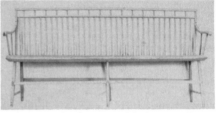

An American 'chicken-coop' Windsor painted settee, in need of restoration, early 19thC, 77in (195.5cm) long.
£2,500–3,000 *EL*

A Federal carved mahogany cane seat sofa, attributed to Duncan Phyfe, New York, repaired, c1805, 72in (182.5cm) long.
£35,000–45,000 *S(NY)*

A set of carved pine shelves, with arched back, scalloped sides and X-form stretchers, on shaped feet, Pennsylvania, early 19thC, 47in (119cm).
£1,000–1,500 *S(NY)*

A carved mahogany dolphin leg sofa, probably Philadelphia, lacking one brass caster, repaired, c1820, 82in (208cm).
£2,200–2,700 *S(NY)*

A pair of painted pine Windsor stools, each with upholstered seat in petit point with olive fringe border and brass tacks, on bamboo turned tapering splayed legs joined by stretchers, painted yellow with brown highlights, minor loss to paint, 13in (33cm) diam.
£12,000–13,000 *S(NY)*

An Empire mahogany sideboard, with 3 drawers and 4 cupboard doors below, on turned feet, 73in (185cm) wide.
£700–1,000 *SLN*

A set of painted pine shelves, with curved ends, bootjack feet, traces of red paint, Pennsylvania, early 19thC, 37½in (95cm) wide.
£1,200–1,700 *S(NY)*

An Empire flame mahogany veneered sideboard, the splashback with pineapple finials above 2 drawers, over 3 doors flanked by acanthus carved columns, on hairy paw feet, c1835, 55in (139.5cm) wide.
£1,000–1,500 *SLN*

A rococo revival rosewood settee, attributed to J & J W Meeks, New York, c1860, 64in (162.5cm) wide.
£3,000–3,500 *SK(B)*

A pair of Federal mahogany curule base stools, each repaired, probably New York, c1820.
£2,000–2,700 *S(NY)*

One stool appears to have its original stuffing.

A Federal mahogany basin stand, with single drawer and carrying handles, on ring turned legs ending in ball feet, probably New York, c1820, 17in (43cm) wide.
£1,200–1,700 *S(NY)*

A Federal mahogany basin stand, Boston, Massachusetts, repaired, c1820, 20½in (52cm).
£1,500–2,000 *S(NY)*

A mahogany serpentine front sideboard, the top with inlaid edge, the central drawer above 2 doors, flanked by 3 drawers on the left and a wine drawer on the right, on square chamfered tapered legs with line inlay, with brass fittings, damaged, New York, late 18thC, 75½in (191cm) wide.
£2,500–3,500 *EL*

An Empire style swivel top mahogany card table, 34in (86cm) wide. **£500–1,000** *SLN*

An Empire mahogany and veneered 3 drawer drop-leaf sewing stand, with 2 leaves, slightly damaged, 38in (96.5cm) wide extended.
£800–1,000 *EL*

A Hepplewhite mahogany and veneered D-end card table, with inlaid top edge, apron and legs, restored, 36in (91.5cm) wide.
£600–1,000 *EL*

A Federal mahogany drop leaf dining table, on reeded tapering legs ending in peg feet, New England, c1810, 40in (101.5cm) wide extended.
£1,500–2,500 *S(NY)*

A William and Mary maple and birchwood gateleg table, with drawer, replacements, New England, c1740, 56½in (143cm) wide extended.
£3,500–4,500 *S(NY)*

A Hepplewhite inlaid mahogany card table, with hinged top, 35in (89cm) wide.
£1,000–1,300 *SLN*

A paint decorated pine tilt-top games table, the top inlaid and painted brown, red and black the stand painted and textured green and black to simulate a branch, probably New York, c1850, 22in (56cm) wide.
£5,000–6,000 *S(NY)*

A gilt metal mounted mahogany card table, with swivel top and bird's-eye maple inlay, on reeded legs ending in brass foliate caps and casters, repaired, Boston, Massachusetts, c1820, 36in (92cm) wide.
£6,000–7,000 *S(NY)*

A pine side table, the top sponge painted in tones of green and yellow, the base painted yellow with black pinstriping, New England, early 19thC, 17in wide.
£7,500–9,000 *S(NY)*

A mahogany Pembroke table, with shaped top and cross stretcher base, damaged, 18thC, 36in (91.5cm) wide extended.
£300–500 *EL*

A pair of painted and stencilled pine window cornice boards, with a dark green ground, probably New England, c1835, 42in (106.5cm) long.
£1,500–2,000 *S(NY)*

A Federal painted and stencilled pine window cornice board, gilt stencilled against an olive green ground, now mounted with new brackets, New England, mid-19thC, 45in (114cm) long. **£1,700–2,500** *S(NY)*

A pair of Federal carved mahogany terrestrial and celestial table globes, by J. Wilson and Sons, Albany, New York, each in a mahogany stand with brass meridian and ribbed melon form baluster, continuing to leaf carved tripod legs ending in paw feet, c1830, 24in (61cm) high.
£23,000–27,000 *S(NY)*

The spheres inscribed 'The American Nine Inch TERRESTRIAL GLOBE Exhibiting with the greatest possible Accuracy, the POSITIONS of the PRINCIPAL known PLACES of the EARTH; with New Discoveries & Political Alterations 'down to the present.' PER...1829 BY J. Wilson & Sons, Albany.; and 'An American Celestial Globe Containing the Positions of all the Starts from the 1st to the 6th Magnitudes - Manufactured by J. Wilson & Co., Albany 1830'.

A carved pine coat stand, with painted brownish-green and gilt highlights, the ring turned stand fitted with turned Windsor style arms, gilt painted ball finial, animal paw feet with gilded acanthus leaf carving, New York State, mid-19thC, 64½in (163cm) high.
£850–1,000 *S(NY)*

An ormolu mounted mahogany sideboard, the marble top above a frieze with 3 drawers, with 4 tapered ormolu mounted columns below, the plinth base on acanthus carved animal paw feet, lacks backboard, New York, c1810, 72½in (182.5cm) wide.
£3,000–5,000 *S(NY)*

A wicker two-tier side table, by Heywood Bros., with stained beech top and shelf, late 19thC.
£300–400 *DMT*

Ceramics

A glazed redware model of a standing dog, attributed to John Bell, Pennsylvania, with manganese decoration on an orange ground, mid-19thC, 8½in (21cm) long.
£18,000–19,000 *S(NY)*

A slip decorated glazed redware oval pie plate, with crimped edge, the interior decorated in green, yellow and brown on a rust ground, Pennsylvania, minor damage, 19thC, 11in (28cm).
£4,000–4,500 *S(NY)*

A sgraffito decorated redware pie plate, attributed to Johannes Neesz, Tyler's Port, Montgomery County, Pennsylvania, glazed in green, blue and red on a yellow ground, 2 minor flakes, c1800, 10½in (26.5cm) diam.
£16,000–17,000 *S(NY)*

Two Mexican tin glazed earthenware plates, each painted blue and white, with figural motifs, 8½ (21cm) diam.
£350–400 *SK(B)*

Two slip decorated glazed redware pie plates, one inscribed 'ABC' in yellow slip, one with a trailed crosshatched design, old damage, one restored, mid-19thC, 9in (23cm) diam.
£950–1,200 *S(NY)*

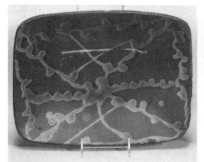

A glazed redware monkey and dog, attributed to the Bell Pottery, Strasburg, Virginia, mottled in green and yellow, damaged, mid-19thC, 9½in (24cm) long.
£15,500–16,500 *S(NY)*

A slip decorated redware loaf dish, with crimped edge, decorated in shades of green and yellow on an orange/red ground, Pennsylvania, 19thC, 10½in (26.5cm) wide.
£4,500–5,000 *S(NY)*

A cobalt blue salt glazed stoneware crock, with applied eared handles, decorated with a bird perched on a leaf, stamped 'Fulper Bros. Flemington N.J.4.', damaged, 19thC, 11½in (29.5cm) diam.
£300–400 *S(NY)*

A cobalt blue salt glazed stoneware pot, with moulded lip and tooled ring, decorated both sides with sprays of cobalt blue flowers, mounted as a lamp, late 19thC, 11in (28cm) high.
£250–300 *S(NY)*

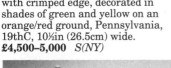

A group of 10 glazed redware items, New Hampshire and New England, some damage, 4 to 10½in (10 to 26.5cm) high. **£1,000–1,200** *S(NY)*

Two glazed redware platters,
decorated with yellow slip,
l. 14½in (36.5cm) long, and *r.* with
rim chips, 13in (33cm) diam.
£700–800 *S(NY)*

Two cobalt blue salt glazed stoneware
pitchers, one decorated with loosely painted
blue flowers, and impressed on the front 'W. H.
Lehew & Co., Strasburg, VA', the other with
cobalt blue pansies, slight damage, Virginia
and Pennsylvania, late 19thC, 10½ and 12in
(26.5 and 30.5cm) high. **£1,400–1,800** *S(NY)*

A slip decorated glazed redware
plate, with notched rim,
Pennsylvania, mid-19thC,
10½in (26.5cm).
£550–750 *S(NY)*

A group of 13 green glazed kitchen articles,
each decorated with salamander spots and
speckles, possibly New Hampshire or Maine,
some damage, 19thC, 3 to 10in (7.5 to 25cm) high.
£1,400–1,800 *S(NY)*

A cobalt blue salt glazed
stoneware crock, with stencilled
decoration, mounted as a lamp,
damaged, stamped 'Hamilton &
Jones, Star Pottery, Greensboro,
PA, late 19thC, 12in (31cm) high.
£350–450 *S(NY)*

Clocks

A Federal mahogany dwarf
clock, with brass urn finials,
the white painted dial with
red, white and blue shield
spandrels, inscribed
'Warranted by Joshua
Wilder, Hingham', c1805,
11½in (29cm).
£19,500–22,500 *S(NY)*

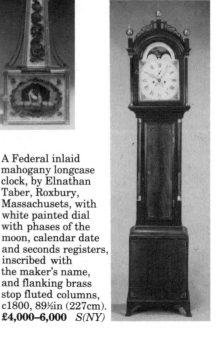

A Chippendale ebonised and
ormolu mounted mahogany
bracket clock, with engraved and
silvered dial, strike/silent
indicator and calendar date
mechanism bed, inscribed
'Effingham Embree, New York',
the reverse with hinged glazed
door exposing a brass plate, red
silk backing behind, the case front
with canted corners and mounts
in the form of a term figure with
trailing flowers and leaves, on
brass ogee bracket feet, in
imported English case, c1785,
13½in (34cm) high.
£14,000–16,000 *S(NY)*

A Chippendale walnut
longcase clock, the
engraved brass dial
with calendar date
mechanism, inscribed
'Aaron Lane, ELIZTH
Town', New Jersey,
c1780, 93½in
(237cm) high.
£5,500–7,500 *S(NY)*

A Federal inlaid
mahogany longcase
clock, by Elnathan
Taber, Roxbury,
Massachusets, with
white painted dial
with phases of the
moon, calendar date
and seconds registers,
inscribed with
the maker's name,
and flanking brass
stop fluted columns,
c1800, 89½in (227cm).
£4,000–6,000 *S(NY)*

The works of this clock were meticulously cleaned in 1986 by Wyatt Bennett of Old Greenwich, Connecticut.

A Chippendale mahogany bracket clock, the arched hood fitted with a brass handle above an arched glazed hinged door, opening to a white painted dial with strike/silent mechanism and seconds register, inscribed 'T. Lindhorst, Philada.', the moulded base on brass ogee bracket feet, in imported English case, restored, c1795, 10in (25cm). **£2,500–3,000** *S(NY)*

A carved and whale ivory inlaid mahogany watch hutch, in the form of a Chippendale longcase clock, some losses and repairs to whale ivory, probably New England, 19thC, 14½in (37cm) high. **£2,500–3,500** *S(NY)*

A Federal ormolu mounted figured mahogany lighthouse clock, by Simon Willard, Roxbury, Massachusetts, the original blown clear glass dome with a flattened ball finial with applied swirled decoration, 8-day movement, white enamel dial inscribed 'Simon Willard's Patent', with flower decorated ormolu surround and surmounted by a bell, an anthemion chased ball finial, the tapering cylindrical case below fitted with chased ormolu surround and mounted with an applied ormolu mount in the form of a crossed torch and quiver, the octagonal base below applied with ormolu leaves and acorns, the moulded base on brass hairy paw feet, c1825, 25in (64cm) high. **£134,000–138,000** *S(NY)*

The Lighthouse Clock

The lighthouse clock was an an invention of Simon Willard and is a type often referred to as an Eddystone lighthouse clock, taking its name from the Eddystone lighthouse in Plymouth, England. In 1819 Simon Willard applied for and obtained a patent for an alarm clock, for which part of the original patent still exists. While the cover of the letter is missing, it would have had the signature of President James Monroe. The patent reads in part 'The whole of the clockwork is inclosed with a handsome glafs and it is wound up without taking the glafs off, which prevents the dirt from getting into it. The whole plan of the clock I claim as my invention. The pendulum is suspended upon and connected with the pivot. Simon Willard witness. William Eliot. Robert Fenwick'.

Silver

This bowl is listed in Tiffany's ledgers as a salad bowl and is the only one listed. However, it is possible that it was originally one of a pair. The entry is dated December 1880 and the manufacturing cost of one bowl was £166.

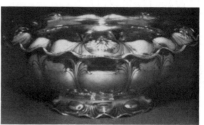

A silver and other metals salad bowl, with hammered surface, the sides engraved with water plants, repeated in silver gilt on the interior, the rim chased with overlapping lily pads applied with a brass crab and a copper and brass insects, engraved with a contemporary monogram and crest, marked on base and numbered '5638-970-660', Tiffany & Co., New York, c1880, 15in (38cm) diam. **£20,000–25,000** *S(NY)*

A bowl, Gorham Mfg. Co., Providence, R.I., Martelé, .950 Standard, marked on base and with code 'CKC', c1905, 11in (28cm) diam., 35oz 10dwts. **£1,700–2,000** *S(NY)*

An Egyptian Revival centrepiece, in the form of a Nile barge, by Gorham Mfg. Co., Providence, retailed by J.E. Caldwell, Philadelphia, marked on base and numbered '960', 20in (51cm) long, 35oz 10dwts. **£4,500–5,500** *S(NY)*

A set of 12 finger bowls and stands, with cut glass liners, in Renaissance pattern, designed by Paulding Farnham, the plates initialled 'D', the rims of the bowls engraved underneath with a name and date 'March 15th 1912', marked on bases and numbered '16181-3400', Tiffany & Co., New York, c1912, 120oz, 6in (15cm) diam.
£6,000–7,000 *S(NY)*

The engraved name 'J.R. Doremus' was the maiden name of Mrs William G. Green, whose husband was president of the New York Bank for Savings, and a major patron of the New York Eye and Ear Infirmary.

A pair of standing cups, Thomas Whartenby, Philadelphia, c1810, 5½in (14cm) high, 14oz 15dwts.
£2,500–3,500 *S(NY)*

A water pitcher, Gorham Mfg. Co., Providence, R.I., engraved with later monogram, marked on base and numbered '1340', 1886, 10in (25cm) high, 39oz.
£1,400–1,700 *S(NY)*

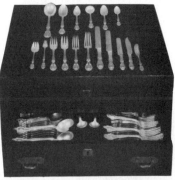

A silver St. Dunstan pattern flatware service, comprising 137- pieces, by Tiffany & Co., all with monogram, 154oz 12 dwt.
£3,500–4,500 *SLN*

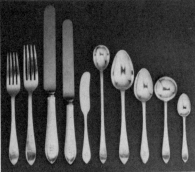

A Richelieu pattern flatware set, monogrammed, comprising 410 pieces, Tiffany & Co., New York, c1895, 442oz excluding knives, in fitted mahogany case, lined in red baize, with 'Tiffany' label.
£17,000–22,000 *S(NY)*

A Faneuil pattern flatware set, comprising 131 pieces, the majority engraved with the same monogram, Tiffany & Co., New York, 20thC, 167oz 10dwts excluding knives.
£3,500–4,500 *S(NY)*

An Old Colonial pattern flatware set, comprising 127 pieces, the backs of the terminals initialled 'T', Towle, early 20thC, 171oz excluding knives.
£3,500–4,500 *S(NY)*

A five-piece tea set, Tiffany & Co., New York, lightly chased with Indian style foliage and a die-rolled girdle of Islamic and Oriental foliate designs, marked on bases, c1870, kettle-on-stand 14in (36cm) high, 117oz, and a silver plated oval galleried tray.
£3,000–4,000 *S(NY)*

A six-piece tea and coffee set, by Tiffany & Co., New York, the bombé bodies chased with spiral flutes and the necks with running bands of acanthus, matching handles, the bases marked and monogrammed, c1885, kettle-on-stand 15in (38cm) high, 185oz.
£7,000–9,000 *S(NY)*

A seven-piece tea and coffee set, by Tiffany & Co., New York, with matching two-handled tray, marked on bases, c1920, kettle-on-stand, 12in (30cm) high, 276oz.
£9,500–12,000 *S(NY)*

Metal

A pair of Federal andirons, signed, Boston, c1810, 14½in (37cm) high.
£900–1,100 *SLN*

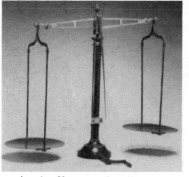

A pair of brass scales, the projecting arms supporting 2 trays, balancing on a columnar standard fitted with a crank, on a circular base, signed 'Henry Troemner, Philadelphia', early 19thC, 25½in (65cm) high.
£900–1,200 *S(NY)*

A pair of brass andirons, c1790, 18in (46cm) high.
£500–800 *SLN*

A pair of Federal brass and wrought-iron andirons, restored, probably New York, c1810, together with a brass and wrought-iron fireplace shovel and tongs, 19thC, a copper and wrought-iron bed warmer, English or Continental, 18thC.
£450–500 *S(NY)*

A pair of brass scales, signed 'Henry Troemner, Philadelphia', early 19thC, 31in (79cm) high.
£1,700–2,500 *S(NY)*

A moulded copper and sheet copper Index horse weathervane, J. Howard & Co., West Bridgewater, Massachusetts, late 19thC, now mounted on a rod in a black metal base, restored, 15½in (39cm) high.
£3,000–4,000 *S(NY)*

A bronze portrait bust of a Classical warrior, 19thC, together with 2 bronze partially nude classical figures on slate bases, and a pair of bronze figures depicting a man with a violin and a woman dancing, dressed in 18thC costume. **£1,250–1,750** *S(NY)*

Two bronze models, by Edith Baretto Parsons, 'Two Terriers', with brown patina and verdigris highlights, one signed and copyrighted, each inscribed 'Kunst Foundry, NY', 7in (17.5cm) high.
£800–1,000 *SLN*

A pair of moulded copper architectural ornaments, weathered to an all-over green verdigris, late 19thC, 42in (107cm) long.
£1,200–1,700 *S(NY)*

A Whiting sterling silver and mixed metal water jug, of hammered baluster form, with bird and floral decoration, inscribed, c1881, 8½in (21cm), 33oz.
£3,000–3,500 *SK(B)*

A moulded copper eagle weathervane, weathered to an all-over verdigris, late 19thC, 37½in (95cm) wingspan.
£2,000–2,500 *S(NY)*

A cast iron wafer iron, of scissor form, with projecting wrought iron handle, each circular mould cast on the interior with the seal of the United States, a spread-wing American eagle and shield, the eagle clutching arrows and an olive branch, 16 stars above, a banner inscribed 'E Pluribus Unum.', c1800, 29in (74cm) long.
£1,200–1,700 *S(NY)*

Tennessee was admitted to the Union on June 1, 1796 and Ohio on March 1, 1803. The 16 stars indicate the date of manufacture between these years.

A painted cast iron pug dog, c1880, 10in (25cm) long.
£300–350 *ChC*

A painted cast iron scottie dog, c1880, 10in (25cm) wide.
£300–350 *ChC*

A cast iron dog hitching post, late 19thC, now mounted on a base, 16½in (42cm) high.
£1,000–1,500 *S(NY)*

A cast iron figure of a dog, minor corrosion, late 19thC, 37in (94cm) long. **£4,000–5,000** *S(NY)*

A painted cast iron elephant, c1880, 7in (17.7cm) long.
£300–350 *ChC*

A painted sheet metal patriotic top hat, the oversized hat with upturned rim, painted in bands of blue with white stars, red and white, mounted on a black painted metal stand, damaged, early 20thC, 20in (51cm) high.
£1,700–2,200 *S(NY)*

A pair of double heart cast iron andirons, mid-19thC, 14in (36cm) high.
£1,200–1,700 *S(NY)*

A moulded cast iron running horse weathervane, the silhouetted figure with incised tail, mounted on a rod continuing to a baluster-turned pine base, some corrosion, late 19thC, 19½in (49cm) high.
£1,200–1,700 *S(NY)*

A pair of wrought and sheet iron heart andirons, New England, late 18thC, 20in (51cm) high.
£3,000–4,000 *S(NY)*

A pair of wrought iron heart andirons, New England, early 19thC, 16½in (42cm) high.
£1,700–2,200 *S(NY)*

A pewter tankard, with serpentine strap handle and moulded base, with touchmark of Samuel Hamlin, Providence, Rhode Island, early 19thC, 6in (15cm) high.
£1,500–1,700 *S(NY)*

Wood

A carved and painted pine raven, with incised eyes and feather detail, standing on cast metal legs, painted black, cracks and paint loss, New England, c1925, 27in (69cm) high.
£5,000–6,000 *S(NY)*

This figure of an oversized raven was once attached to a hunting lodge in Maine.

A carved and gilded pine Pilot House eagle, covered in original gilding, old repairs, probably New England, 19thC, 16in (41cm) wingspan.
£1,700–2,200 *S(NY)*

A carved and gilt pine eagle wall plaque, minor repairs, with painted inscription 'SEBASTOPOL, 1855', 107in (272cm) long.
£2,500–3,500 *S(NY)*

This trophy commemorates the Battle of Sebastopol, c1855.

A carved and painted wood prancer carousel horse, with leather harness, glass eyes and horsehair tail, the saddle with original red and green paint, old repairs, Looff or Dentzel, New York or Philadelphia, c1895, 62in (157cm) long.
£4,500–5,500 *S(NY)*

A carved and painted pine figure of a boxer, wearing blue shorts with orange sash and black tie shoes, late 19thC, 77in (196cm) high.
£32,000–40,000 *S(NY)*

Although the original use of this figure is unknown, it was thought to have come from a gymnasium or circus.

A carved and painted pine American eagle whirligig, decorated in bold geometric patterns in red, white, black and blue, Northwest Coast Indian, early 20thC, 21in (53cm) long.
£1,500–1,800 *S(NY)*

A carved and painted pine carousel boat side panel, painted white with details picked out in red, yellow and pink, brass handles, repairs, late 19thC, 75in (191cm) long.
£1,200–1,700 *S(NY)*

A carved and painted wood bust of a man, the cartoon-like rendering of a bald headed man with protruding eyes, sticking out his tongue, painted in flesh tones with pink shirt collar, early 20thC, 20in (51cm) high. **£1,200–1,700** *S(NY)*

A carved pine hanging wall box, with shaped backplate, carved front and sides, on a moulded base, covered in brown varnish, initialled 'CC', probably Pennsylvania, 19thC, 18½in (47cm) high.
£600–700 *S(NY)*

A carved and painted pine key trade sign, cut from a single piece of pine plank, in the form of a large house key, inscribed in black with the inscription 'YALE' and 'YALE & TOWNE MFG. CO. STAMFORD. CONN', 20thC, 42in (107cm) long.
£2,000–3,000 *S(NY)*

A carved, painted and gilded heart and hand staff, the heart carved in relief and painted red, above a blue painted ruffled cuff, used in a fraternal order, late 19thC, 64in (163cm) long.
£2,000–3,000 *S(NY)*

Textiles

A calico and cotton Log Cabin quilt, composed of blue, yellow, red, green and pink solid and printed patches arranged in the Barn Raising pattern, 88in (224cm) square.
£1,200–1,700 *S(NY)*

A pieced and appliquéd quilted cotton coverlet, worked in various printed fabrics on a natural ground in the Star of Bethlehem variation with Princess Feather quilting, New Jersey, mid-19thC, 97 by 101in (246 by 257cm). **£800–1,000** *CNY*

A needlework sampler, signed 'Emma C. Potter' Pennsylvania dated '1830', worked in blue, green, white and brown silk stitches on a linen ground, some discolouration, 18 by 15½in (46 by 39cm), framed.
£1,700–2,200 *S(NY)*

An appliquéd calico Princess Feather quilt, composed of green, pink and red printed and solid calico patches, minor fading, Cape Cod, Massachusetts, c1860, 96 by 100in (244 by 254cm). **£950–1,200** *S(NY)*

A glazed linsey-woolsey striped coverlet, consisting of 2 thicknesses linsey-woolsey, glazed top with alternating coral and gold broad stripes, heightened with herringbone quilting within broad coral linsey-woolsey borders heightened with overlapping shell quilting, the reverse a solid piece of gold linsey-woolsey, some stains and repairs, New England, late 18thC, 88 by 100in (224 by 254cm).
£850–1,200 *S(NY)*

A pieced and appliquéd calico fleur-de-lys quilt, composed of moss green and red and white printed calico patches, some fading, probably Massachusetts, c1850, 88in (224cm) square.
£1,200–1,700 *S(NY)*

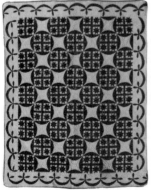

An appliquéd wool and wool felt table rug, with 2 horses, composed of red, brown, yellow, green, beige and blue fabrics, mounted on a stretcher, some wear, New England, late 19thC, 23 by 33in (56 by 84cm).
£1,500–2,500 *S(NY)*

Two pieced red and green calico quilts, The Vannort family, Chestertown, Maryland, the first with a variation of the Nine Patch and Pinwheel pattern, the second in a variation of the Variable Star pattern, minor stains and wear, 88 by 92in (224 by 234cm). **£650–900** *S(NY)*

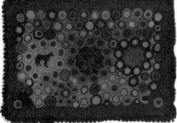

A pieced cotton Moon and Stars quilt, composed of green and brown cotton patches, all vegetable dyed, minor fading, Tennessee, c1860, 60 by 76in (152 by 193cm).
£900–1,200 *S(NY)*

A pieced and appliquéd Oak Leaf quilt, composed of brightly coloured red, slate blue, green and beige printed calico patches, minor fading, Cumberland County, Pennsylvania, c1860, 80in (203cm) square.
£900–1,200 *S(NY)*

American Indian Art

A Plains beaded hide Tipi bag, sinew sewn in yellow, green, dark blue, and translucent red and milky white against a blue ground, trimmed with pine cone and red horsehair pendants, 17in (43cm) long.
£2,000–3,000 *S(NY)*

A Great Lakes beaded cloth horse mask, probably Ojibwa, 27in (68.5cm) long.
£1,500–2,000 *S(NY)*

A pair of Northern Plains beaded and fringed hide gauntlets, in numerous colours against light blue beaded grounds, 15in (38cm) long.
£800–1,000 *S(NY)*

A Navajo pictorial weaving, 'Yei-Bichai' theme, woven in natural and aniline dyed wool against a shaded grey ground, damaged edge, 50 by 36½in (127 by 92cm).
£2,200–2,800 *SK(B)*

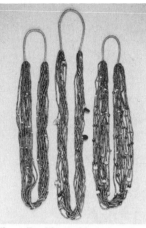

Three Pueblo necklaces, each composed of strands of rich orange coral beads, one with brass and glass trade beads, another with turquoise discs and small silver beads, the longest with brass tubular beads and 2 Mexican silver coins, 15 to 18in (38 to 45.5cm) long.
£1,700–2,200 *S(NY)*

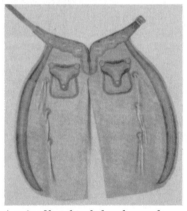

A pair of hand tooled and carved leather chaps, with stamped and pigmented leather appliqués over a suede body and engraved silver conchos and buttons, with embossed mark 'John P. Buckley, Monterey, Calif', 37in (94cm) long.
£2,200–2,600 *SK(B)*

A South western Navajo woman's blanket, of natural and aniline dyed wool, woven with a Third Phase 'nine spot' pattern in yellow and salmon-red blocks, against a violet blue, ivory and dark brown striped background, 49 by 57in (124.5 by 144.5cm).
£3,300–3,600 *SK(B)*

A Transitional Navajo blanket/rug, woven in natural dark brown, shaded ivory and aniline-dyed bright red and orange handspun wool, 77 by 55in (196 by 140cm).
£2,000–3,000 *S(NY)*

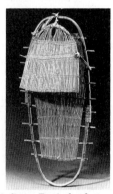

A Great Basin basketry cradleboard, probably Paiute, composed of a bent willow frame, backrest and hood, sinew bindings, cord decoration and remains of cloth, 25in (64cm) high.
£400–500 *S(NY)*

A Sioux beaded cradle, lined with floral printed cotton trade cloth, sinew sewn on canvas in yellow, dark and light blue and translucent red against a white beaded ground, the front trimmed with glass beads, beadwork and brass bells, mounted on wooden frame with decorated hide carrying straps, 42½in (108cm) high.
£3,500–4,500 *S(NY)*

A pair of Sioux quilled hide moccasins, each decorated in orange, blue, purple, green and red dyed porcupine quillwork, 9½in (24.5cm) long.
£1,700–2,200 *S(NY)*

A pair of beaded hide South western Apache moccasins, sinew stitched, hard soled, with yellow, white heart red, apple green, navy and bright blue bead decorations, south west America, 10in (25cm) long.
£450–550 *SK(B)*

A Plains polychrome, beaded and fringed hide doll, Sioux, the standing female figure in a hide dress over cotton muslin 'feed bag' body, the hide head with pigment and coloured beaded facial detail, sinew and thread sewn, damaged, 18in (46cm) high.
£1,400–1,600 *SK(B)*

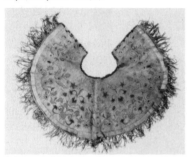

A Prairie beaded and fringed hide cape, in European style, with multi-coloured glass beads on a hide ground, the neck edged with red silk ribbon, 34in (86.5cm) long.
£2,000–3,000 *S(NY)*

A pair of Southern Plains beaded hide women's boot moccasins, probably Cheyenne, each decorated overall in rich yellow ochre mineral pigment, 21in (53cm) high.
£1,200–1,700 *S(NY)*

A Sioux quilled and fringed hide war shirt, decorated in purple, red and white against an orange dyed quillwork ground, faded, 55in (140cm) wide across arms.
£4,000–5,000 *S(NY)*

A Plains red catlinite pipe, the expanding section with wood mouthpiece, carved in shallow relief, 22in (55.5cm) long.
£400–500 *S(NY)*

An Athapaskan fringed hide jacket, possibly Slavey, decorated with red and blue wool appliquéd panels, trimmed with white and blue glass seed beads and hem tape, light blue and bright purple silk ribbon, floral printed cotton trade cloth and dark blue wool, pale red, white and purple dyed quill wrapping, 32in (82cm) long, together with a pair of fringed hide trousers with brass buttons.
£9,500–12,000 *S(NY)*

A Nootka polychrome wood forehead mask, with painted lozenge eyes below arched brows and parted coiffure, hawk's face, with hooked beak, mirrored glass inset eyes, 10in (25cm) high.
£800–1,000 *S(NY)*

An Eastern Sioux quilled hide cradle hood, decorated in yellow, green, blue, orange and red dyed porcupine quillwork, lined with printed cotton trade cloth, 21in (54cm) wide.
£2,500–3,000 *S(NY)*

A Plains ceremonial wood and stone pipe, 26in (66cm) long. **£3,500–4,000** *S(NY)*

A Plains red catlinite effigy pipehead, carved in the form of a fish, with undulating body and incised details, 8in (20cm) long.
£450–550 *S(NY)*

Toys

A Lionel Corpn. Peter Rabbit 'Chick Mobile' clockwork toy, No. 1103, track version, c1935, boxed, 8½in (21cm) long.
£750–800 *SK(B)*

A carved and painted pine monkey on a dappled grey pull-toy, New York, the monkey's head turns from side-to-side and the right arm holding the top hat up and down, c1860, 16in (40.5cm) high.
£3,500–4,500 *S(NY)*

A dog patch band, by Unique Art, 1945, boxed, 9in (22.5cm).
£500–600 *SK(B)*

A painted canvas 'knock-over' toy cat, painted in chalk pink and grey, on a wooden base, 13½in (34cm) high.
£190–220 *S(NY)*

A painted model of the clipper ship 'Flying Cloud', 44in (111.5cm) long, with display stand.
£2,500–3,000 *SLN*

Miscellaneous

A complete set of the magazine *Antiques*, 1922-92, partially bound.
£1,500–2,000 *S(NY)*

A caramel slag glass bowl, advertising 'Phenix 5', for the Phenix Nerve Beverage Company. **£150–180** *SK(B)*

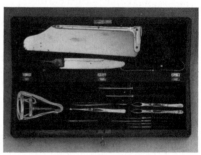

A Civil War surgeon's kit, W. F. Ford, in a velvet lined fitted brass bound mahogany case, c1860, 15½in (39cm) long. **£2,000–2,700** *S(NY)*

A diamond nine-stone circular cluster openwork brooch, with black enamel floral entwined decoration, the reverse signed 'T.B. Starr', early 20thC.
£500–550 *CSK*

An illustration advertising 'Sport Clothes', by Frank M Rines, signed within image, gouache, 1892, 9½ by 12½in (23.5 by 31.5cm).
£60–80 *SK(B)*

An enamelled two-sided trade sign for Wolf's Head Motor Oil.
£55–75 *SK(B)*

GLOSSARY

We have attempted here to define some of the terms that you will come across in this book. If there are any terms or technicalities you would like explained or you feel should be included in future, please let us know.

Aalto, Alvar (1898-1976): A Finnish Art Deco architect and furniture designer, noted for his bentwood chairs, made from the 1930s onwards.

acid engraving: Technique of decorating glass by coating it in resin, incising a design and exposing the revealed areas to hydrochloric acid fumes.

acid-gilding: 19thC technique for decorating pottery whereby the surface is etched with hydrofluoric acid and the low-relief pattern gilded.

acorn knop: Wine glass stem moulding in the shape of an upturned acorn - the cup uppermost.

Adam, Robert (1728-1792): A Scottish born architect who created a neo-classical architectural and decorative style of furniture.

Admiral jug: Toby jug depicting an admiral; originally to commemorate Lord Howe's victory over the French in 1794.

agate ware: 18thC pottery, veined or marbled to resemble the mineral agate.

air-beaded: Glass containing bubbles of air, like strings of beads.

air-twist: Helical decoration in the stem of wine glasses, developed 1740-70, in which an air bubble in the glass is drawn out and twisted to form complex spirals, e.g. lace twist, multiple spiral, spiral gauze, corkscrew multi-ply, cable, etc.

ale glass: Drinking glass with tall stem and tall narrow bowl, capacity 3-4 fluid ounces, used for strong beer, sometimes decorated with barley ears and hops, 18thC.

all-bisque doll: One with body and limbs as well as head of biscuit-fired ceramic.

American Victorian: The period between 1830-1900 that incorporates several styles of furniture; Victorian, Gothic, Victorian rococo, Victorian renaissance and Eastlake.

Amish: Followers of Jacob Amman who made up a religious sect that settled in Pennsylvania during the 1700s. They produce quilts and other primitive handcrafts that are highly prized.

Ansbach: Factory specialising in large, colourful faience ornaments from the 1730s, and porcelain tableware late 18th and 19thC.

antiquities: Generally accepted to mean objects made before AD600 in Europe, and of ancient Egyptian, Greek or Roman origin. Also used to cover the pre-Columbian era in the Americas and the products of civilisations now extinct.

architect's table: Table or desk, the top of which rises at the back to provide an angled working area.

Arita (1): Blue and white Japanese pottery imported from the mid-17thC and much imitated by European makers.

Arita (2): Japanese 18thC porcelain, typically with flower-basket pattern in blue, red and gold, also called Imari ware after the port from which it was exported.

armoire: A large French cupboard or wardrobe, usually of monumental character.

associated (1): Term used of a set of silverware in which one part is of the same design but not originally made for it - e.g. of a teapot and associated stand.

associated (2): Of weapons, any part which is not original.

Aubusson: French town producing tapestries, and tapestry-weave carpets, since 17thC although formal workshops were not established until c1743.

automata: Any moving toy or decorative object, usually powered by a clockwork mechanism.

ball-jointed doll: One with ball-jointed limbs, able to swivel in all directions, as opposed to stiff jointed.

baluster stem: Glass with a swelling stem, like an architectural baluster: 'true' if the thicker swelling is beneath, 'inverted' if above. From late 17thC.

barley-twist: Form of turning popular in late 17thC which resembles a spiral of rope.

basaltes: Black porcelain invented by Josiah Wedgwood with a polished, stone-like finish; modern reproductions are called basalt wares.

Bauhaus: Influential German artistic style which was inspired by new industrial materials, such as stainless steel, with the emphasis on cubic, unadorned shapes. The term was coined by the architect Gropius who became director of the Weimar School of Arts and Crafts in 1919, and renamed it the Bauhaus.

bébé: French dolls made by Bru and others in the latter half 19thC, modelled on actual children of 8-12 years of age.

Belleek: Very thin and iridescent parian ware, originally made at Belleek, in Ireland, late 19thC.

bisque: French term for biscuit ware, or unglazed porcelain.

Bizarre: Name of a highly-colourful range of Art Deco tableware designed by Clarice Cliff and manufactured by the Staffordshire potter, A.J. Wilkinson Ltd, in the 1930s.

bladed knop: Knop with a concave outward curve, culminating in a sharp edge.

bonheur du jour: Small French writing table of delicate proportions with a raised back comprising a cabinet or shelves.

Bow: Important London porcelain factory producing blue and white wares 1749-76, and polychrome wares 1754 onwards; early work shows Chinese influence (peony and chrysanthemum flower decorations), later work in Meissen style.

bowfront: An outwardly curving front.

bracket clock: Originally a 17thC clock which had to be set high up on a bracket because of the length of the weights; now generally applied to any small mantel or table clock.

bracket foot: A type of foot for case pieces which appears somewhat shaped as a right-angled bracket below the front edge.

Brameld: Family that acquired the Rockingham factory, Yorkshire, early 19thC; producers of the fine bone china noted for its rich enamelling and gilt decoration.

Bristol: Important porcelain factory established c1749, producing delftware, and (c1770) enamelled and gilded wares decorated with flowers and swags. Also, 17th and 18thC delftwares (bowls, figure groups, jugs) produced by several factories in the area.

Bru & Cie: Leading French doll maker 1866-99; noted for dolls in elaborate contemporary costumes.

bureau: Writing desk with either a fall, a cylinder or a tambour front.

bureau bookcase: Bureau with a glazed-fronted bookcase fitted above it.

bureau cabinet: Bureau with a solid-doored or mirrored cabinet fitted above it, often containing further fitted cupboards and drawers.

bureau de dame: Writing desk of delicate appearance and designed for use by ladies. Usually raised above slender cabriole legs and with one or two external drawers.

bureau-plat: French writing table with a flat top and drawers in the frieze.

cabriole leg: Tail curving leg subject to many designs and produced with club, pad, paw, claw-and-ball, and scroll feet.

caddy: Usually silver (but also of ceramic, wood or enamel) container for tea with a lead-lined compartment; often two compartments with a spoon and glass bowl for blending two types of leaf.

camaieu: Porcelain decoration using different tones of the one colour.

cameo glass: A sandwich of coloured glass which is then cut or etched away to create a multi-colour design in relief. An ancient technique rediscovered by Emile Gallé and popular with Art Nouveau and Art Deco glassmakers in the early 20thC.

candle slide: Small wooden slide designed to carry a candlestick.

Cardew, Michael (1901-83): English art potter, taught by Bernard Leach, and inspired by Oriental porcelain. Worked at the Winchcombe Pottery 1926-39.

Carlton House desk: A distinct type of writing desk which has a raised back with drawers which extend forward at the sides to create an 'enclosed' central writing area.

Carlton Ware: Brand name of Art Nouveau pottery made by Wiltshaw and Robinson, a Stoke-on-Trent pottery founded in 1897.

carousel figures: Horses and other animals from fairground carousels or roundabouts, usually classified as either 'jumpers' or 'standers'.

carriage clock: Originally one fitted with a device to ensure that the jolts common in the days of coach travel would not interfere with the oscillations of the balance spring. Now any small portable oblong clock of rectangular form, popular from the 19thC to the present day.

cartel clock: An 18thC French wall clock in the shape of a shield, often with a gilded bronze case and elaborately ornamented in rococo style.

cartouche: An ornate tablet or shield surrounded by scrollwork and foliage, often bearing a maker's name, inscription or coat-of-arms.

castelli: Maiolica from the Abruzzi region of Italy, noted for delicate landscapes painted by members of the Grue family.

Caughley: Shropshire factory, established c1750, producing porcelain very like that of Worcester, including early willow-pattern, often embellished by gilding.

celadon: Chinese stonewares with an opaque grey-green glaze, first made in the Sung dynasty and still made today, principally in Korea.

cellaret: Lidded container on legs designed to hold wine. The interior is often divided into sections for individual bottles.

centrepiece: Silver ornament, usually decorative rather than functional, designed to occupy the centre of a dining table.

Chaffers, Richard & Partners: Liverpool pottery manufacturer, operating around 1754-65, producing earthenwares resembling china and modelled on Worcester forms.

chaise longue: An elongated chair, the seat long enough to support the sitter's legs.

champlevé: Enamelling on copper or bronze, similar to cloisonné, in which a glass paste is applied to the hollowed-out design, fired and ground smooth.

character doll: One with a naturalistic face, especially laughing, crying, pouting, etc.

character jug: Earthenware jugs and sometimes mugs, widely made in 18th and 19thC, depicting a popular character, such as a politician, general, jockey or actor.

chesterfield: Type of large over-stuffed sofa introduced in late 19thC.

cheval mirror: Large toilet mirror in a frame with four legs, the mirror being pivoted and adjustable within the frame. Also known as a horse dressing glass and a psyche. Made c1750 onwards.

chiffonier: Generally a twin door cupboard with one or two drawers above and surmounted by shelves.

Chin dynasty: period in Chinese history AD1115-1260.

Chinese export porcelain: 16th to 18thC wares made in China specifically for export and often to European designs.

Chinese Imari: Chinese imitations of Japanese blue, red and gold painted Imari wares, made from the early 18thC.

Ch'ing dynasty: From 1644 to 1912, the period during which much decorated Chinese porcelain was exported to Europe.

chinoiserie: The fashion, prevailing in the late 18thC, for Chinese-style ornamentation on porcelain, wallpapers and fabrics, furniture and garden architecture.

chryselephantine: Originally made of gold and ivory, but now used for Art Deco statues made of ivory and another metal, typically bronze and very desirable.

Cliff, Clarice (1899-1972): Employed by A.J. Wilkinson Ltd, the pottery at Newport, Staffordshire, as artistic director in the 1930s. Designer of the colourful 'Bizarre' and 'Fantasque' ranges of mass-produced china.

clock garniture: A matching group of clock and vases or candelabra made for the mantel shelf. Often highly ornate.

cloisonné: Enamelling on metal with divisions in the design separated by lines of fine brass wire. A speciality of the Limoges region of France in the Middle Ages, and of Chinese craftsmen to the present day.

Coalport china: Porcelain manufactured at Coalbrookdale, Shropshire, from the 1790s, noted for the translucent felspathic wares produced from 1820 and the delicate colours of the figure groups.

coffer: In strict definition a coffer is a travelling trunk which is banded with metalwork and covered with leather or other material. However, the word tends to be used quite freely to describe chests of various kinds.

Colonial: An American object made during the period when the country consisted of 13 Colonies.

Commedia dell'Arte: Figures from traditional Italian theatre (Harlequin, Columbine, Scaramouche, Pantaloon) often depicted in porcelain groups in 18thC.

compound twist: In a wine glass stem, any air-twist made of multiple spirals; e.g. lace twist, gauze and multi-ply.

console table: Decorative side table with no back legs, being supported against the wall by brackets.

cordial glass: Smaller version of a wine glass, with a thick stem, heavy foot and small bowl; evolved 17thC for strong drink.

country furniture: General term for furniture made by provincial craftsmen; cottage furniture and especially that made of pine, oak, elm and the fruitwoods.

credenza: Used today to describe a type of side cabinet which is highly decorated and shaped. Originally it was an Italian sideboard used as a serving table.

crested china: Pottery decorated with colourful heraldic crests, first made by Goss but, by 1880, being produced in quantity by manufacturers throughout the UK and in Germany.

cup and cover: Carved decoration found on the bulbous turned legs of some Elizabethan furniture.

cut glass: Glass carved with revolving wheels and abrasive to create sharp-edged facets that reflect and refract light so as to sparkle and achieve a prismatic (rainbow) effect. Revived Bohemia 17thC, and common until superseded by pressed glass for utilitarian objects.

Cymric: The trade-name used by Liberty & Company for a mass produced range of silverware, inspired by Celtic art, introduced in 1899, and often incorporating enamelled pictorial plaques.

cypher: An impressed or painted mark on porcelain which gives the year of manufacture; each factory had its own set of codes; used principally mid to late 19thC.

davenport (1): Small writing desk with a sloping top and a series of real and false drawers below. Some have a writing surface which slides forward and rising compartments at the rear.

davenport (2): American term for a day bed or reclining sofa with headrest.

Davenport (3): Important factory at Longport, Staffordshire, founded 1793 by John Davenport; originally manufactured earthenware, but noted from 1820 for very fine botanical wares and Imari style decoration.

day bed: Couch with one sloped end to support the head and back whilst reclined. Either upholstered or caned. Made from 16thC until the mid-18thC. Also known in the U.S. as a davenport.

Delft: Dutch tin glazed earthenwares named after the town of Delft, the principal production centre. 16thC Delft shows Chinese influence but by 17thC the designs are based on Dutch landscapes. Similar pottery made in England from the late 16thC is usually termed 'delftware'.

Della Robbia: Florentine Renaissance sculptor who invented technique of applying vitreous glaze to terracotta; English art pottery made at Birkenhead, late 19thC, in imitation of his work.

Denby: Stoneware made by Bourne & Son, at Denby, 19thC; also known as Bourne pottery.

Derby: Important porcelain factory founded 1756, producing very fine figure groups - often called English Meissen - as well as painted wares decorated with landscapes and botanical scenes.

die-stamping: Method of mass producing a design on metal by machine which passes sheet metal between a steel die and a drop hammer. Used for forming toys as well as stamping cutlery etc.

Dresser, Christopher (1835-1904): Influential English pottery and glass designer who was inspired by Japanese art and worked for Tiffany as well as the pottery firms of Ault, Linthorpe and Pilkington.

drop-in seat: Upholstered chair seat which is supported on the seat rails but which can be lifted out independently.

Du Paquier: Porcelain from Vienna, especially chinoiserie wares produced early 18thC.

écuelle: 17thC vessel, usually of silver, but also of ceramic for serving soup. Has a shallow, circular bowl with two handles and a domed cover. It often comes complete with a stand.

eglomisé: Painting on glass, associated with clock faces: often the reverse side of the glass is covered in gold or silver leaf through which a pattern is engraved and then painted black.

electroplate: The process of using electrical current to coat a base metal or alloy with silver, invented 1830s and gradually superseding Sheffield plate.

enamel (1): In ceramics, a second coloured but translucent glaze laid over the first glaze.

enamel (2): Coloured glass, applied to metal, ceramic or glass in paste form and then fired for decorative effect.

EPNS: Electroplated nickel silver; i.e. nickel alloy covered with a layer of silver using the electroplate process.

etched glass: Technique of cutting layers of glass away, using acid, much favoured by Art Nouveau and Art Deco glassmakers. Such sculpture in high relief is known as deep etched, and layers of multi-coloured glass were often treated in this way to make cameo glass.

fairings: Mould-made figure groups in cheap porcelain, produced in great quantity in the 19th and 20thC, especially in Germany; often humorous or sentimental. So called because they were sold, or given as prizes, at fairs.

famille jaune: 'Yellow family'; Chinese porcelain vessels in which yellow is the predominant ground colour.

famille noire: 'Black family'; Chinese porcelain in which black is the predominant ground colour.

famille rose: 'Pink family'; Chinese porcelain vessels with an enamel (overglaze) of pink to purple tones.

famille verte: 'Green family'; Chinese porcelain with a green enamel (overglaze), laid over yellows, blues, purples and iron red.

Fantasque: Name of a colourful range of household china designed by Clarice Cliff and manufactured in the 1930s by the Staffordshire pottery, A.J. Wilkinson Ltd.

fauteuil: French open-armed drawing room chair.

filigree: Lacy openwork of silver or gold thread, produced in large quantities since end 19thC.

flag bottom chair: Chair made with a rush seat.

flatware: Collective name for flat pottery, such as plates, trenchers and trays, as opposed to cups, vases and bowls.

frosted glass: Glass with a surface pattern made to resemble frost patterns or snow-crystals; common on pressed glass vessels for serving cold confections.

Fulda: Factory at Hessen that produced some of Germany's best faience in the mid-18thC; in the late 18thC turned to producing Meissen-style porcelain.

fusee: 18thC clockwork invention; a cone shaped drum, linked to the spring barrel by a length of gut or chain. The shape compensates for the declining strength of the mainspring thus ensuring constant timekeeping.

Gallé, Emile (1846-1904): Father of the French Art Nouveau movement and founder of a talented circle of designers based around Nancy. Simultaneously, in the 1880s, he designed delicate furniture embellished with marquetry and began experimenting with new glass techniques. In 1889, he developed cameo glass; in 1897 'marquetry in glass', or 'marquetrie de verre'. After his death, factories continued to produce his wares, signed Gallé but marked with a star, until the 1930s.

gilding: Process of applying thin gold foil to a surface. There are two methods. Oil gilding involves the use of linseed oil and is applied directly onto the woodwork. Water gilding requires the wood to be painted with gesso.

Glasgow School: Originally the name of the Glasgow School of Art at which Charles Rennie Mackintosh studied in the 1880s, and whose new buildings he designed in the 1890s. Now used to describe the style developed by Mackintosh and his followers, a simplified linear form of Art Nouveau highly influential on Continental work of the period.

grisaille: Type of monochrome used to decorate furniture during the 18thC.

hall chair: Strongly constructed chair lacking intricate ornament and upholstery, being designed to stand in a hall to accommodate messengers and other callers in outdoor clothing. At the same time it had to be attractive enough to impress more important callers and was often carved with a crest or coat-of-arms for this purpose.

hallmark: Collective term for all the marks found on silver or gold consisting of an assay office, quality, date and maker's marks; sometimes the term is used only of the assay office mark.

handkerchief table: Table with a triangular top and a single triangular leaf. This arrangement enables it to fit into a corner when closed and form a square when opened.

hard paste: True porcelain made of china stone (petuntse) and kaolin; the formula was long known to, and kept secret by, Chinese potters but only discovered in the 1750s in England, from where it spread to the rest of Europe and the Americas.

harewood: Sycamore which has been stained a greenish colour is known as harewood. It is used mainly as an inlay wood and was known as silverwood in the 18thC.

Hirado: Japanese porcelain with figure and landscape painting in blue on a white body, often depicting boys at play, made exclusively for the Lords of Hirado, near Arita, mid-18th to mid-19thC.

hiramakie: Flat decoration in Japanese lacquerware, as opposed to carving or relief.

Hornby: manufacturers of clockwork and electric locomotives from c1910, best known today for the 'Dublo' range, introduced mid-1940s.

indianische Blumen: Indian flowers; painting on porcelain in the Oriental style, especially on mid-18thC Meissen and Höchst.

intaglio: Incised gem-stone, often set in a ring, used in antiquity and during the Renaissance as a seal. Any incised decoration; the opposite of carving in relief.

ironstone: Stoneware, patented 1813 by Charles James Mason, containing ground glassy slag, a by-product of iron smelting, for extra strength.

ivory porcelain: Development of 19thC, similar to parian but ivory coloured in biscuit form.

Jacobite: Wine glasses engraved with symbols of the Jacobites (supporters of Prince Charles Edward Stuart's claim to the English throne). Genuine examples date from 1746 to 1788. Countless later copies and forgeries exist.

Jumeau, Pierre François: Important French doll maker noted for 'Parisiennes', active 1842-99.

Kakiemon: Family of 17thC Japanese potters who produced wares decorated with flowers and figures on a white ground in distinctive colours: azure, yellow, turquoise and soft red. Widely imitated in Europe.

kashgai: Rugs woven by Iranian nomadic tribes, notable for the springy lustrous texture, and finely detailed rectilinear designs.

kelim: Flat woven rugs lacking a pile; also the flat woven fringe used to finish off the ends of a pile carpet.

kneehole desk: Writing desk with a space between the drawer pedestals for the user's legs.

knop (1): Knob, protuberance or swelling in the stem of a wine glass, of various forms which can be used as an aid to dating and provenance.

knop (2): In furniture, a swelling on an upright member.

Knox, Archibald (1864-1931): English designer of the Cymric range of silverware and Tudric pewter for Liberty's store in London, responsible for some 400 different designs.

Lalique, René (1860-1945): French designer of Art Nouveau jewellery in gold, silver and enamel, who founded his own workshop in Paris in 1885. After 1900 he turned to making figures in crystal and opalescent glass. From 1920 he emerged as the leading Art Deco glass maker, and his factory produced a huge range of designs.

lambing chair: Sturdy chair with a low seat traditionally used by shepherds at lambing time. It has tall enclosed sides for protection against draughts.

Lazy Susan: Another name for a dumb waiter.

Leach, Bernard (1887-1979): Father of English craft pottery who studied in China and Japan in order to master Oriental glazing techniques.

Lenci: Italian company manufacturing dolls with pressed felt faces in Turin in the 1920s, noted for the sideways glance of the painted eyes.

Liberty & Co.: Principal outlet for Art Nouveau designs in England. Arthur Lasenby Liberty (1843-1917) founded his furniture and drapery shop in 1875. Later he commissioned designs exclusive to his store, including Cymric silver and Tudric pewter, which gave rise to a distinctive 'Liberty style'.

linenfold: Carved decoration which resembles folded linen.

Liverpool: Important pottery production centre from the mid-18thC, noted for blue painted delftware punch bowls, and early porcelain produced by several different factories, now eagerly collected.

longcase clock: First made c1660 in England, a tall clock consisting of a case which houses the weights or pendulum and a hood housing the movement and dial. In U.S.A. also known as a tallcase clock.

lyre clock: Early 19thC American pendulum clock, its shape resembling that of a lyre.

majolica: Often used, in error, as an alternative spelling for maiolica; correctly, a richly-enamelled stoneware with high relief decoration developed by Minton, mid-19thC.

mantel clock: Clock provided with feet to stand on the mantelpiece.

Martinware: Art pottery made by the Martin brothers between 1873 and 1914, characterised by grotesque human and animal figures in stoneware.

medicine chest: Used by itinerant medics from 17thC, usually with compartments, labelled bottles, spoons and balances.

Meiji: Period in Japanese history 1868 to 1912, when the nation's art was much influenced by contact with the West, and much was made specifically for export.

mihrab: Prayer niche with a pointed arch; the motif which distinguishes a prayer rug from other types.

Mei ping: Chinese for cherry blossom, used to describe a tall vase, with high shoulders, small neck and narrow mouth, used to display flowering branches.

millefiori: Multi-coloured, or mosaic, glass, made since antiquity by fusing a number of coloured glass rods into a cane, and cutting off thin sections; much used to ornament paperweights.

Ming dynasty: Period in Chinese history from 1368 to 1644.

Minton: Pottery established by Thomas Minton, at Stoke-on-Trent, in late 18thC. Originally produced earthenwares and creamware; then, most famously, bone china. After 1850 the company produced fine copies of Renaissance maiolica and, in 1870, set up the Minton Art Pottery Studio in London as a training academy for young designers, producing fine Art Nouveau work.

Moorcroft, William (1872-1946): Staffordshire art potter, who worked for MacIntyre & Co. from 1898, and set up independently in 1913. Known for colourful vases with floral designs and his 'Florian' and 'Aurelian' wares.

Moore, Bernard: Founder of art pottery based in Longton, Staffordshire, c1900 specialising in unusual glaze effects.

Morris, William (1834-96): Regarded as the progenitor of the Art Nouveau style. The company Morris, Marshall and Faulkner (later simply Morris & Co.) was founded in 1861 to produce wallpaper, stained glass, chintz carpets and tapestries. The origins of his style can be traced to medieval Gothic, but his organic flowers and bird motifs encouraged later artists to seek inspiration for their designs in nature.

netsuke: Japanese carved toggles made to secure sagemono ('hanging things') to the obi (waist belt) from a cord; usually of ivory, lacquer, silver or wood, from the 16thC.

New Hall: Late 18thC potters' co-operative in Staffordshire making porcelain and bone china wares.

ormolu: Strictly, gilded bronze or brass but sometimes used loosely of any yellow metal. Originally used for furniture handles and mounts but, from the 18thC, for ink stands, candlesticks, clock cases, etc.

overlay: In cased glass, the top layer, usually engraved to reveal a different coloured layer beneath.

overmantel: Area above the shelf on a mantelpiece, often consisting of a mirror in an ornate frame, or some architectural feature in wood or stone

over stuffed: Descriptive of upholstered furniture where the covering extends over the frame of the seat.

ovolo: Moulding of convex quarter-circle section. Sometimes found around the edges of drawers to form a small overlap onto the carcase.

Parisienne doll: French bisque head doll with a stuffed kid leather body, made by various manufacturers 1860s to 1880s.

pate: Crown of a doll's head into which the hair is stitched, usually of cork in the better quality dolls.

pâte-sur-pâte: 19thC Sèvres porcelain technique, much copied, of applying slip decoration to the body before firing.

Pembroke table: Small table with two short drop leaves along its length. Named after the Countess of Pembroke who is said to have been the first to order one. Also once known as a breakfast table.

percussion lock: Early 19thC firearm, one of the first to be fired by the impact of a sharp-nosed hammer on the cartridge cap.

pewter: Alloy of tin and lead; the higher the tin content the higher the quality; sometimes with small quantities of antimony added to make it hard with a highly polished surface.

pier glass: Mirror designed to be fixed to the pier, or wall, between two tall window openings, often partnered by a matching pier table. Made from mid-17thC.

Pilkington: Associated with the Lancashire glass factory, this pottery produced Art Nouveau ceramics in the early 20thC, remarkable for its iridescent and colourful glazes.

Pinxton: Soft-paste porcelain imitating Derby, made in Nottingham by William Billingsley, from c1800.

plate: Old fashioned term, still occasionally used, to describe gold and silver vessels; not to be confused with 'Sheffield plate', or plated vessels generally, in which silver is fused to a base metal alloy.

pole screen: Small adjustable screen mounted on a pole and designed to stand in front of an open fire to shield a lady's face from the heat.

portrait doll: One modelled on a well known figure.

poupard: Doll without legs, often mounted on a stick; popular in 19thC.

poured wax doll: One made by pouring molten wax on to a mould.

powder flask: Device for measuring out a precise quantity of priming powder made to be suspended from a musketeer's belt or bandolier and often ornately decorated. Sporting flasks are often made of antler and carved with hunting scenes.

powder horn: Cow horn hollowed out, blocked at the wide end with a wooden plug and fitted with a measuring device at the narrow end, used by musketeers for dispensing a precise quantity of priming powder.

pressed glass: Early 19thC invention, exploited rapidly in America, whereby mechanical pressure was used to form glassware in a mould, instead of using compressed air.

puzzle jug: Delftware form made from the 17thC, with several spouts and a syphon system, none of which will pour unless the others are blocked.

Qing: Alternative spelling of Ch'ing - the dynasty that ruled China from 1644 to 1916.

quarter clock: One which strikes the quarter and half hours as well as the full hours.

Quimper faience: From the factory in Brittany, France, established late 17thC and closely modelled on Rouen wares.

rack: Tall superstructure above a dresser.

refectory table: Modern term for the long dining tables of the 17thC and later.

regulator: Clock of great accuracy, thus sometimes used for controlling or checking other time pieces.

rummer/roemer: Originally 16th/17thC German wide bowled wine glass on a thick stem, decorated with prunts, on a base of concentric glass coils, often in green glass (waldglas). Widely copied throughout Europe in many forms.

sabre leg: Elegant curving leg associated with furniture of the Regency period but first appearing near the end of the 18thC. Also known as Trafalgar leg.

St. Cloud: Factory near Paris, famous for soft-paste porcelain in the first half of the 18thC, decorated in Kakiemon style and imitation blanc-de-chine.

salon chair: General term to describe a French or French style armchair.

scent bottle: Small, portable flask of flattened pear shape, made of silver, rock crystal, porcelain or glass.

seal bottle: Wine bottles with an applied glass medallion or seal personalised with the owner's name, initials, coat-of-arms or a date. Produced from the early 17th to the mid-19thC when bottles were relatively expensive.

secrétaire bookcase: Secrétaire with a bookcase fitted above it.

SFBJ: Société de Fabrication de Bébés et Jouets; doll maker founded 1899 by merging the businesses of Jumeau, Bru and others. Products regarded as inferior to those of the original makers.

Sheraton revival: Descriptive of furniture produced in the style of Sheraton when his designs gained revived interest during the Edwardian period.

side boy: A long table made to place against a wall.

silver table: Small rectangular table designed for use in the dining room. They usually have a fretwork gallery.

Six Dynasties: Period in Chinese history AD265-589.

six-hour dial: One with only six divisions instead of twelve, often with the hours 1 - 6 in Roman numerals and 7 - 12 superimposed in Arabic numerals.

snuff box: Box made to contain snuff in silver, or any other material: early examples have an integral rasp and spoon, from 17thC.

sofa table: Type of drop leaf table which developed from the Pembroke table. It was designed to stand behind a sofa, so is long and thin with two short drop leaves at the ends and two drawers in the frieze.

softwood: One of two basic categories in which all timbers are classified. The softwoods are conifers which generally have leaves in the form of evergreen needles.

spelter: Zinc treated to look like bronze and much used as an inexpensive substitute in Art Nouveau appliqué ornament and Art Deco figures.

Steiff, Margarete: Maker of dolls and highly prized teddy bears, she first exhibited at Leipzig, 1903, but died 1909. The company she founded continued to mass produce toys, dolls and bears for export. Products can be identified by the 'Steiff' button trademark, usually in the ear.

stirrup cup: Silver cup, without handles, so-called because it was served, containing a suitable beverage, to huntsmen in the saddle, prior to their moving off. Often made in the shape of an animal's head.

Sung dynasty: Ruling Chinese dynasty from AD960-1279.

table clock: Early type of domestic clock, some say the predecessor of the watch, in which the dial is set vertically: often of drum shape.

tallboy: Chest of drawers raised upon another chest of drawers. Also known as a chest-on-chest.

T'ang dynasty: Period in Chinese history AD618-906 during which porcelain was first developed.

tazza: Wide but shallow bowl on a stem with a foot; ceramic and metal tazzas were made in antiquity and the form was revived by Venetian glassmakers in 15thC. Also made in silver from 16thC.

tea kettle: Silver, or other metal, vessel intended for boiling water at the table. Designed to sit over a spirit lamp, it sometimes had a rounded base instead of flat.

teapoy: Piece of furniture in the form of a tea caddy on legs, with a hinged lid opening to reveal caddies, mixing bowl and other tea drinking accessories.

tear: Tear-drop shaped air bubble in the stem of an early 18thC wine glass, from which the air-twist evolved.

tester: Wooden canopy over a bedstead which is supported on either two or four posts. It may extend fully over the bed and be known as a full tester, or only over the bedhead half and be known as a half tester.

tin glaze: Glassy white glaze of tin oxide; re-introduced to Europe in 14thC by Moorish potters; the characteristic glaze of delftware, faience and maiolica.

Toby jug: Originally a jug in the form of a man in a tricorn hat, first made by Ralph Wood of Burslem, mid-18thC; since produced in great quantity in many different forms.

transfer printed: Ceramic decoration technique perfected mid-18thC and used widely thereafter for mass produced wares. An engraved design is printed on to paper (the bat) using the ink consisting of glaze mixed with oil; the paper is then laid over the body of the vessel and burns off in firing, leaving an outline, usually in blue. Sometimes the outline was coloured in by hand.

trefoil: Three-cusped figure which resembles a symmetrical three-lobed leaf or flower.

tripod table: Descriptive of any table with a three-legged base but generally used to describe only small tables of this kind.

tsuba: Guard of a Japanese sword, usually consisting of an ornamented plate.

tulipwood: Yellow brown wood with reddish stripe imported from Central and South America and used as a veneer and for inlay and crossbanding. It is related to rosewood and kingwood.

Venetian glass: Fine soda glass and coloured glass blown and pinched into highly ornamented vessels of intricate form, made in Venice, and widely copied from 15thC.

verge escapement: Oldest form of escapement, found on clocks as early as AD1300 and still in use 1900. Consisting of a bar (the verge) with two flag shaped pallets that rock in and out of the teeth of the crown or escape wheel to regulate the movement.

vesta case: Ornate flat case of silver or other metal for carrying vestas, an early form of match. From mid-19thC.

vitrine: French display cabinet which is often of bombé or serpentine outline and ornately decorated with marquetry and ormolu.

waxjack: A stand for holding a coil of sealing wax, first used mid-1700s.

washstand: Stand designed to hold a basin for washing in the bedroom. Generally of two types. Either three or four uprights supporting a circular top to hold the basin and with a triangular shelf with a drawer. Or as a cupboard raised on four legs with a basin let into the top, sometimes with enclosing flaps. Also known as a basin stand.

Wedgwood: Pottery founded by Josiah Wedgwood (1730-95) at Stoke-on-Trent and noted for numerous innovations; especially creamware, basaltes, and pearlware; perhaps best known for jasperware, the blue stonewares decorated with white relief scenes from late 18thC.

Wellington chest: Distinct type of tall, narrow chest of drawers. They usually have either six or seven thin drawers one above the other and a hinged and lockable flap over one side to prevent them from opening. Made in the 19thC.

whatnot: Tall stand of four or five shelves and sometimes a drawer in addition. Some were made to stand in a corner. Used for the display of ornaments and known in Victorian times as an omnium.

WMF: Short for the Austrian Württembergische Metallwarenfabrik, one of the principal producers of Art Nouveau silver and silverplated objects, early 20thC.

yew: Hard, deep reddish brown wood used both as a veneer and solid. It is very resistant to woodworm and turns well.

Yuan dynasty: Period in Chinese history AD1280-1368 during which the art of underglaze painting was developed.

A unique blue plush covered teddy bear by Steiff, 'Elliot', with black boot button eyes, pronounced cut snout, black horizontally stitched nose, black stitched mouth and claws, swivel head, elongated jointed limbs, cream felt pads and hump, c1908, 13in (33cm) high. **£50,000-70,000** *CSK*

DIRECTORY OF SPECIALISTS

If you wish to be included in next year's directory, or if you have a change of address or telephone number, please advise Miller's Advertising Department by April 1995. Please note telephone codes have been amended in line with British Telecom's guidelines which take effect from 16th April, 1995. Finally we would advise readers to make contact by telephone before a visit, therefore avoiding a wasted journey.

ARCHITECTURAL

Cheshire
Nostalgia,
61 Shaw Heath,
Stockport.
Tel: 0161 477 7706

Devon
Ashburton Marbles,
Grate Hall,
North Street,
Ashburton.
Tel: 01364 53189

Dorset
Dorset Restoration,
Cow Drove,
Bere Regis,
Wareham.
Tel: 01929 472200

Scotland
Easy,
Unit 6, Couper Street,
Edinburgh.
Tel: 0131 554 7077

ARMS & MILITARIA

Gloucestershire
Peter Norden Antiques,
The Little House,
Sheep Street,
Stow-on-the-Wold.
Tel: 01451 830455

Lincolnshire
Garth Vincent,
The Old Manor House,
Allington,
Nr Grantham.
Tel: 01400 81358

Surrey
West Street Antiques,
63 West Street,
Dorking.
Tel: 01306 883487

West Midlands
Weller & Dufty,
141 Bromsgrove Street,
Birmingham.
Tel: 0121 692 1414

Yorkshire
Andrew Spencer
Bottomley,
The Coach House,
Thongs Bridge,
Holmfirth.
Tel: 01484 685234

BOOKS

Middlesex
John Ives,
5 Normanhurst Drive,
Twickenham.
Tel: 0181 892 6265
Reference books.

West Midlands
David Hill,
96 Commonside,
Pensnett, Brierley Hill.
Tel: 01384 70523

BOXES & TREEN

Gloucestershire
Peter Norden Antiques,
The Little House,
Sheep Street,
Stow-on-the-Wold.
Tel: 01451 830455

CARPETS

Yorkshire
Gordon Reece Gallery,
Finkle Street,
Knaresborough.
Tel: 01423 866219

CLOCKS, WATCHES & BAROMETERS

London
Newcombe & Son,
89 Maple Road,
Penge, SE20
Tel: 0181 778 0816

Old Father Time Clock
Centre,
101 Portobello Road, W11
Tel: 0181 546 6299

Pieces Of Time,
1-7 Davies Mews, W1
Tel: 0171 629 2422
Watches.

Roderick Antique Clocks,
23 Vicarage Gate, W8
Tel: 0171 937 8517

The Clock Clinic,
85 Lower Richmond Rd,
SW15.
Tel: 0181 788 1407

Berkshire
The Clock Workshop,
17 Prospect Street,
Caversham, Reading.
Tel: 01734 470741

Walker and Walker,
Halfway Manor,
Halfway, Nr. Newbury.
Tel: 01488 58693
Barometers.

Cheshire
Coppelia Antiques,
Holford Lodge,
Plumley Moor Road,
Plumley.
Tel: 01565 722197

Essex
Its About Time,
863 London Road,
Westcliff-on-Sea.
Tel: 01702 72574

Gloucestershire
Jonathan Beech,
Nurse's Cottage,
Ampney Crucis,
Nr Cirencester.
Tel: 01285 851495

Gerard Campbell,
Maple House,
Market Place,
Lechlade.
Tel: 01367 252267
Viennese Regulators

Kent
Gem Antiques,
88 High Street,
Rochester.
Tel: 01634 814129/
01622 843191

The Old Clock Shop,
63 High Street,
West Malling.
Tel: 01732 843246

Derek Robert Antiques,
25 Shipbourne Road,
Tonbridge.
Tel: 01732 358986

Lincolnshire
Pinfold Antiques,
3-5 Pinfold Lane,
Ruskington,
Tel: 01526 832057

Norfolk
Keith Lawson,
Scratby Garden Centre,
Beach Road,
Scratby,
Gt. Yarmouth.
Tel: 01493 730950

Oxfordshire
Rosemary And Time,
42 Park Street,
Thame,
Tel: 0184421 6923

North Humberside
Time And Motion,
1 Beckside,
Beverley.
Tel: 01482 881574

Shropshire
Richard Higgins,
The Old School,
Longnor, Nr. Shrewsbury
Tel: 01743 718162
*Boulle, gilding, electro
gilding, silvering,
simulated mercury,
period upholstery.*

Suffolk
Antique Clocks,
Little St. Mary's Court,
Long Melford.
Tel: 01787 880040/375931

Surrey
Brian Clisby,
86b Tilford Road,
Farnham.
Tel: 01252 716436

The Clock Shop,
64 Church Street,
Weybridge.
Tel: 01932 840407/855503

Horological Workshops,
204 Worplesdon Road,
Guildford.
Tel: 01483 576496

Sussex
Samuel Orr Fine Clocks,
36 High Street,
Hurstpierpoint.
Tel: 01273 832081

Wiltshire
P A Oxley,
The Old Rectory,
Cherhill, Nr Calne.
Tel: 01249 816227

Allan Smith Clocks,
Amity Cottage,
162 Beechcroft Road,
Upper Stratton,
Swindon.
Tel: 01793 822977

Yorkshire
Haworth Antiques,
26 Cold Bath Road,
Harrogate,
Tel: 01423 521401

Brian Loomes,
Calf Haugh Farm,
Pateley Bridge.
Tel: 01423 711163
Longcase clocks.

DECORATIVE ARTS

London

Arenski,
185 Westbourne Grove,
W11.
Tel: 0171 727 8599

Phillips,
101 New Bond St, W1.
Tel: 0171 629 6602

Rumours Decorative Arts,
10 The Mall, Upper St.,
Camden Passage,
Islington.
Tel: 01582 873561
Moorcroft.

Gt Manchester

A S Antiques,
26 Broad Street,
Pendleton,
Salford.
Tel: 0161 737 5938

Hampshire

Bona Arts Decorative Ltd.,
19 Prince's Mead
Shopping Centre,
Farnborough.
Tel: 01252 372188

Kent

Peter Hearnden,
Corn Exchange Antiques
Centre,
64 The Pantiles,
Tunbridge Wells.
Tel: 01892 539652
Charlotte Rhead

St Clere Antiques,
Sevenoaks,
(Helen & Keith Martin)
Tel: 01474 853630
Carlton Ware 1890-1989

Sussex

Witney & Airault,
Prinny's Gallery,
3 Meeting House Lane,
The Lanes,
Brighton.
Tel: 01273 204554

Wales

Paul Gibbs Antiques,
25 Castle Street,
Conwy,
Gwynedd.
Tel: 01492 593429

Yorkshire

Muir Hewitt,
Halifax Antiques Centre,
Queens Road
Mills/Gibbet Street,
Halifax.
Tel: 01422 347377
Clarice Cliff.

DESKS

Surrey

Dorking Desks,
41 West Street,
Dorking.
Tel: 01306 883327

Warwickshire

Don Spencer Antiques,
36a Market Place,
Warwick.
Tel: 01926 499857

DINING TABLES

Kent

Linden Park Antiques,
7 Union Square,
The Pantiles
Tunbridge Wells.
Tel: 01892 538615

Pantiles Spa Antiques,
4, 5, 6 Union House,
The Pantiles,
Tunbridge Wells.
Tel: 01892 541377

DOLLS

Sussex

Sue Pearson,
13½ Prince Albert Street,
Brighton.
Tel: 01273 329247

DOULTON

London

The Collector,
9 Church Street,
NW8.
Tel: 0171 706 4586

EPHEMERA

Nottinghamshire

T. Vennett-Smith,
11 Nottingham Road,
Gotham.
Tel: 01602 830541

EXHIBITIONS

London

City of London Antiques
& Fine Art Fair,
Business Design Centre,
52 Upper Street,
Islington, N1.
Tel: 0171 359 3535

Surrey

Cultural Exhibitions,
8 Meadrow,
Godalming.
Tel: 01483 422562

EXPORTERS

Devon

McBains of Exeter,
Exeter Airport,
Clyst Honiton,
Exeter.
Tel: 01392 366261

Essex

F G Bruschweiler
(Antiques) Ltd,
41-67 Lower Lambricks,
Rayleigh.
Tel: 01268 773761

Lincolnshire

MC Trading Co,
Stanhope Road,
Horncastle.
Tel: 01507 524524

Shropshire

Swainbank Antique
Exporters,
Lord Hills Estate,
Coton, Whitchurch.
Tel: 01948 880534

Suffolk

Wrentham Antiques,
40-44 High Street,
Wrentham.
Tel: 01502 75583

Sussex

Anglo AM Warehouse,
21 Beach Road,
Eastbourne.
Tel: 01323 648661

Bexhill Antique
Exporters,
56 Turkey Rd, Bexhill.
Tel: 01424 225103

British Antique
Exporters Ltd,
School Close,
Queen Elizabeth Avenue,
Burgess Hill.
Tel: 01444 245577

International Furniture
Exporters,
The Old Cement Works,
South Heighton,
Newhaven.
Tel: 01273 611251

The Old Mint House,
High Street, Pevensey.
Tel: 01323 762337

Warwickshire

Apollo Antiques,
The Saltisford,
Birmingham Road,
Warwick.
Tel: 01926 494746

West Midlands

L P Antiques,
Short Acre Street,
Walsall.
Tel/Fax 01922 746764

Martin Taylor Antiques,
140b Tettenhall Road,
Wolverhampton.
Tel: 01902 751166

FISHING

Kent

Garden House Antiques,
118 The High Street,
Tenterden.
Tel: 01580 763664

Warwickshire

James Wigington,
Tel: 01789 261418

FURNITURE

London

Adams Room Ltd.,
18-20 Ridgeway,
Wimbledon Village,
SW19
Tel: 0181 946 7047

Arenski,
185 Westbourne Grove,
W11.
Tel: 0171 727 8599

The British Antique
Furniture Restorers'
Association,
6 Whitehorse Mews,
Westminster Bridge Rd.,
London SE1
Tel: 0171 620 3761

Butchoff Antiques,
233 Westbourne Grove,
W11.
Tel: 0171 221 8174

Oola Boola Antiques,
166 Tower Bridge Road,
SE1.
Tel: 0171 403 0794

The Old Cinema,
160 Chiswick High Road,
W4. Tel: 0181 995 4166
and
157 Tower Bridge Road,
SE1
Tel: 0171 407 5371

Cambridgeshire

Simon & Penny Rumble,
The Old School,
Chittering.
Tel: 01223 861831
Oak and Country.

Cheshire

Richmond Galleries,
Watergate Building,
New Crane St,
off Sealand Road,
Chester.
Tel: 01244 317602

Cornwall

Pydar Antiques,
Peoples Palace,
Off Pydar Street,
Truro.
Tel: 01872 223516

Cumbria

Anthemion,
Cartmel,
Grange-over-Sands.
Tel: 015395 36295

Devon

McBains of Exeter,
Exeter Airport,
Clyst Honiton.
Tel: 01392 366261

Essex

F.G. Bruschweiler
(Antiques) Ltd.,
41-67 Lower Lambricks,
Rayleigh.
Tel: 01268 773761

Gloucestershire

Peter Norden Antiques,
The Little House,
Sheep Street,
Stow-on-the-Wold.
Tel: 01451 830455

Hereford & Worcs.

Lower House Fine
Antiques,
Far Moor Lane,
Winyates Green,
Redditch.
Tel: 01527 525117
Furniture and silver.

Hertfordshire

Collins Antiques,
Corner House,
Wheathamstead.
Tel: 01582 833111

Kent

Barn Full of Sofas,
Furnace Mill,
Lamberhurst.
Tel: 01892 890285

Martin Body,
Giltwood Restoration,
71 Bower Mount Road,
Maidstone.
Tel: 01622 752273

Cuthbert & Freestone,
136 High Street,
Tenterden.
Tel: 01580 766828

Garden House Antiques,
118 The High Street,
Tenterden.
Tel: 01580 763664

Linden Park Antiques,
7 Union Square,
The Pantiles,
Tunbridge Wells.
Tel: 01892 538615

John McMaster,
5 Sayers Square,
Tenterden.
Tel: 01580 762941

Pantiles Spa Antiques,
4/5/6 Union House,
The Pantiles,
Tunbridge Wells.
Tel: 01892 541377

Sparks Antiques,
4 Manor Row,
Tenterden.
Tel: 01580 766696

The Old Bakery Antiques,
St Davids Bridge,
Cranbrook.
Tel: 01580 713103
Oak and Country.

Lancashire

Preston Antique Centre,
The Mill, New Hall Lane,
Preston.
Tel: 01772 794498

Roberts Antiques,
Tel: 01253 827798

Lincolnshire

Seaview Antiques,
Stanhope Road,
Horncastle.
Tel: 01507 524524

Middlesex

Robert Phelps Ltd.,
133-135 St. Margaret's Rd,
East Twickenham.
Tel: 0181 892 1778

Northants

Paul Hopwell,
30 High Street,
West Haddon.
Tel: 01788 510636
Oak and Country.

Oxfordshire

Key Antiques,
11 Horsefair,
Chipping Norton.
Tel: 01608 643777

Rupert Hitchcock,
The Garth,
Warpsgrove,
Nr Chalgrove,
Oxford.
Tel: 01825 890241

Somerset

The Granary Galleries,
Court House,
Ash Priors,
Nr Bishop's Lydeard,
Taunton.
Tel: 01823 432402

Suffolk

Hubbard Antiques,
16 St Margaret's Green,
Ipswich.
Tel: 01473 226033

Oswald Simpson,
Hall Street,
Long Melford.
Tel: 01787 377523
Oak and Country.

Wrentham Antiques,
40-44 High Street,
Wrentham.
Tel: 01502 75583

Surrey

J Hartley Antiques Ltd,
186 High Street,
Ripley.
Tel: 01483 224318

Ripley Antiques,
67 High Street,
Ripley.
Tel: 01483 224981

Sussex

British Antique
Replicas Ltd,
School Close,
Queen Elizabeth Avenue,
Burgess Hill.
Tel: 01444 245577
Reproduction furniture.

Dycheling Antiques,
34 High Street,
Ditchling,
Hassocks.
Tel: 01273 842929
Chairs.

International Furniture
Exporters,
The Old Cement Works,
South Heighton,
Newhaven.
Tel: 01273 611251

Lakeside,
The Old Cement Works,
South Heighton,
Newhaven.
Tel: 01273 513326
Reproduction furniture

Latimer Road Antiques,
144 Latimer Road,
Eastbourne.
Tel 01323 417777

The Old Mint House,
High Street,
Pevensey,
Eastbourne.
Tel: 01323 762337

Warwickshire

Apollo Antiques,
The Saltisford,
Birmingham Road,
Warwick.
Tel: 01926 494746

Coleshill Interiors and
Antiques,
12-14 High Street,
Coleshill.
Tel: 01675 462931

Don Spencer Antiques,
36 Market Street,
Warwick.
Tel: 0926 407989/499857

West Midlands

L P Furniture (Mids) Ltd,
Short Acre Street,
Walsall
Tel: 01922 746764

Martin Taylor Antiques,
140b Tettenhall Road,
Wolverhampton.
Tel: 01902 751166

Retro Products,
174 Norton Road,
Stourbridge.
Tel: 01384 373332

Wiltshire

Chris Watts Antiques,
The Salisbury Antiques
Warehouse,
94 Wilton Road,
Salisbury.
Tel: 01722 410634

Ireland

Michelina & George
Stacpoole,
Main Street, Adare,
Co. Limerick.
Tel: 010 353 61 396409

GLASS
London

Arenski,
185 Westbourne Grove,
W11.
Tel: 0171 727 8599

Marion Langham,
Stand J30/31
Gray's Mews,
Davies Mews, W1.
Tel: 0171 629 2511
Paperweights

Avon

Somervale Antiques,
6 Radstock Road,
Midsomer Norton,
Bath.
Tel: 01761 412686

Cheshire

Sweetbriar Gallery,
Robin Hood Lane,
Helsby.
Tel: 01928 723851
Paperweights

West Midlands

David Hill,
96 Commonside,
Pensnett,
Brierley Hill.
Tel: 01384 70523
Books on glass.

GOSS & CRESTED CHINA
Hampshire

Goss and Crested China,
62 Murray Road,
Horndean.
Tel: 01705 597440

Yorkshire

The Crested China Co,
The Station House,
Driffield.
Tel: 01377 257042

JEWELLERY
Kent

Gem Antiques,
88 High Street,
Rochester.
Tel: 01634 814129/01622
843191

Somerset

Peggy Hayden,
Tel: 01935 21336
Jet jewellery.

Warwickshire

Coleshill Interiors and
Antiques,
12-14 High Street,
Coleshill.
Tel: 01675 462931

Scotland

Bow-Well Antiques,
103 West Bow,
Edinburgh.
Tel: 0131 225 3335
Scottish jewellery.

LIGHTING
London

Allegras 'Lighthouse'
Antiques,
75-77 Ridgway,
Wimbledon Village,
SW19.
Tel: 0181 946 2050

LOSS ADJUSTERS & VALUERS

London

Cunningham Hart,
59 Compton Road,
Islington, N1.
Tel 0171 354 3504

METALWARE

Gloucestershire

Peter Norden Antiques,
The Little House,
Sheep Street,
Stow-on-the-Wold.
Tel: 01451 830455

Oxfordshire

Key Antiques,
11 Horsefair,
Chipping Norton.
Tel: 01608 643777

MONEY BOXES

Yorkshire

John & Simon Haley,
89 Northgate,
Halifax.
Tel: 01422 822148

MOORCROFT

London

Rumours Decorative Arts,
10 The Mall, Upper St,
Camden Passage,
Islington, N1.
Tel: 01582 873561

Warwickshire

Lion's Den,
11 St Mary's Crescent,
Leamington Spa.
Tel: 01926 339498

MUSICAL INSTRUMENTS

Avon

Piano Export,
Bridge Road,
Kingswood,
Bristol.
Tel: 0117 968300
Pianos

Sussex

Latimer Road Antiques,
144 Latimer Road,
Eastbourne.
Tel: 01323 417777

PACKERS & SHIPPERS

London

Hedley's Humpers,
Units 3 & 4,
97 Victoria Road, NW10.
Tel: 0181 965 8733

Avon

A J Williams (Shipping),
607 Sixth Avenue,
Central Business Park,
Petherton Road,
Hengrove,
Bristol.
Tel: 0117 992166

Dorset

Alan Franklin Transport,
26 Blackmoor Road,
Ebblake Industrial Estate,
Verwood.
Tel: 01202 826539

PINE

Cheshire

Richmond Galleries,
Watergate Building,
New Crane St,
off Sealand Road,
Chester.
Tel: 01244 317602.
*Pine, country and
Spanish furniture.*

Cornwall

Pydar Pine,
People's Palace,
Truro.
Tel: 01872 223516

Gloucestershire

Camden Country Pine,
High Street,
Chipping Camden.
01386 840315

Hampshire

The Pine Cellars,
39 Jewry Street,
Winchester
Tel: 01962 777546

Humberside

Bell Antiques,
68 Harold Street,
Grimsby.
Tel: 01472 695110

Kent

Country Pine Antique Co,
The Barn,
Upper Bush Farm,
Upper Bush,
Nr Rochester.
Tel: 01634 296929

Up Country,
The Old Corn Stores,
68 St John's Road,
Tunbridge Wells.
Tel: 01892 523341/01323
487167

Lancashire

Enloc Antiques,
Birchenlee Mill,
Lenches Road,
Colne.
Tel: 01282 867101

Northants

The Country Pine Shop,
Northampton Road,
West Haddon.
Tel: 01788 510430
*Stripped antique pine,
furniture strippers
and restorers.*

Surrey

Euro-Pine,
1a/1b Beddington Lane,
Croydon.
Tel: 0181 665 5320

Sussex

Bob Hoare Pine Antiques,
Unit 0,
Phoenix Place,
North Street,
Lewes.
Tel: 01273 480557

Ann Lingard,
Ropewalk Antiques,
Ropewalk,
Rye.
Tel: 01797 223486

Graham Price Antiques
Unit 4,
Chaucer Industrial
Estate,
Dittons Road,
Polegate.
Tel: 01323 487167

Yorkshire

The Main Pine Company,
Grangewood,
The Green,
Green Hammerton,
York.
Tel: 01423 330451
*Antique and
reproductions in old pine.*

Ireland

Bygones of Ireland,
Westport Antiques
Centre,
Lodge Road,
West Port,
Co. Mayo.
Tel: 00353 98 26132

Delvin Farm Galleries,
Gormonston,
Co Meath.
Tel: 00 3531 841 2285

Honan's Antiques,
Crowe Street,
Gort,
County Galway.
Tel: 00 353 91 31407

Daniel P Meaney,
Alpine House,
Carlow Road,
Abbeyleix,
Co Laois.
Tel: 01502 31348

Old Court Pine,
Old Court,
Collon, County Louth.
Tel: 00 353 41 26270

Wales

The Pot Board,
30 King Street,
Carmarthen,
Dyfed.
Tel: 01834 871276

The Netherlands

Jacques van der Tol bv,
Antiek & Curiosa,
Antennestraat 34,
Almere Stad.
Tel: 00 31 3653 62050

PORCELAIN

London

Marion Langham,
Stand J30/31,
Gray's Mews,
Davies Mews, W1.
Tel: 0171 6292511
Belleek porcelain.

Lancashire

Robert Antiques.
Tel: 01280 703259

Northants

Peter Jackson Antiques,
3 Market Place,
Brackley.
Tel: 01280 703259
Derby porcelain.

Shropshire

Teme Valley Antiques,
1 The Bull Ring,
Ludlow.
Tel: 01584 874686

Warwickshire

Coleshill Interiors and
Antiques,
12-14 High Street,
Coleshill.
Tel: 01675 462931

Ireland

Michelina & George
Stacpoole,
Main Street,
Adare, Co. Limerick.
Tel: 010 353 61 396409

POTTERY

London

Jonathan Horne,
66b & 66c Kensington
Church St,
W8.
Tel: 0171 221 5658

Valerie Howard,
2 Campden Street,
W8.
Tel: 0171 792 9702
Mason's & Quimper.

M.S. Antiques,
40 Gordon Place,
Holland St, W8.
Tel: 0171 937 0793
Staffordshire pottery

Jacqueline Oosthuizen,
23 Cale Street,
SW3
Tel: 0171 352 6071
Staffordshire pottery

Rogers de Rin,
76 Royal Hospital Road,
SW3.
Tel: 0171 352 9007
Wemyss Ware.

Teresa Vanneck-Murray,
Vanneck House.
22 Richmond Hill,
Richmond.
Tel: 0181 940 2035
*Staffordshire pottery
and Commemorative Ware.*

Lancashire

Roy W. Bunn Antiques,
34-36 Church Street,
Barnoldswick,
Colne.
Tel: 01282 813703
Staffordshire pottery

Tyne & Wear

Ian Sharp Antiques,
23 Front Street,
Tynemouth.
Tel: 0191 296 0656
*Maling Ware and
Lustre Ware.*

Warwickshire

Janice Paull,
Beehive House,
125 Warwick Road,
Kenilworth.
Tel: 01926 55253
Mason's Ironstone.

Ireland

Michelina & George
Stacpoole,
Main Street,
Adare,
Co. Limerick.
Tel: 010 353 61 396409

Scotland

Bow-Well Antiques,
103 West Bow,
Edinburgh.
Tel: 0131 225 3335

PUBLICATIONS

London

Antiques Trade Gazette,
17 Whitcomb Street,
WC2.
Tel: 0171 930 9958

Midlands

Antiques Bulletin,
HP Publishing,
2 Hampton Court Road,
Harborne,
Birmingham.
Tel: 0121 428 2555

RESTORATION

London

B.A.F.R.A.,
6 Whitehorse Mews,
Westminster Bridge
Road, SE1.
Tel: 0171 620 3761

Peter Binnington,
B.A.F.R.A.
68 Battersea High Street,
SW11.
Tel 0171 223 9192
*Marquetry, gilding and
verre églomisé.*

Crawley Studios,
39 Wood Vale, SE23.
Tel: 0181 299 4121
*Painted furniture,
papier mâché,
tôle ware, lacquer
and gilding.*

Glen's Antiques,
Restoration,
B.A.F.R.A.,
Unit 12, Windsor Centre,
Windsor Grove,
West Norwood, SE27.
Tel: 0181 766 6789.
*Gilding and woodcarving
picture frames,
antique restoration,
specialist paint finishes,
French polishing.*

D. J. Stamford Silver
Repairs,
The Workshop,
Scope Antiques,
64/66 Willesden Lane,
NW6.
Tel: 0171 328 5833
Silver.

Avon

M & S Bradbury,
B.A.F.R.A.,
The Barn,
Hanham Lane,
Paulton.
Tel: 01761 418910.
Antique furniture.

Cheshire

A Allen Antique
Restorers,
B.A.F.R.A.,
Buxton Road,
Newtown,
Newmills.
Tel: 01663 745274.
*Boule, marquetry,
walnut, oak,
veneering, upholstery.*

Dorset

Dorset Restoration,
Cow Drove,
Bere Regis,
Wareham.
Tel: 01929 472200
Architectural.

Essex

Clive Beardall,
B.A.F.R.A.,
104b High Street,
Maldon.
Tel: 01621 857890
Period furniture.

Gloucestershire

Andrew Lelliot,
B.A.F.R.A.,
6 Tetbury Hill,
Avening,
Tetbury.
Tel: 01453 835783
*Furniture and clock
cases, included on the
Conservation Unit
Register of the Museums
and Galleries Commission.*

Hampshire

David C E Lewry,
B.A.F.R.A.,
Wychelms,
66 Gorran Avenue,
Rowner, Gosport.
Tel: 01329 286901
Furniture.

Hereford & Worcs.

Lower House Fine
Antiques,
Far Moor Lane,
Winyates Green,
Redditch.
Tel: 01527 525117
*Furniture, porcelain
and paintings.*

Malvern Studios,
B.A.F.R.A.,
56 Cowleigh Road,
Malvern.
Tel: 01684 574913
Furniture.

Phillip Slater,
B.A.F.R.A.,
93 Hewell Road,
Barnt Green,
Nr Birmingham.
Tel: 0121 445 4942
Furniture and clocks.

Bryan Wigington,
B.A.F.R.A.,
Chapel Schoolroom,
1 Heol-y-Dwr,
Hay on Wye, Hereford.
Tel: 01497 820545.
Furniture.

Hertfordshire

Charles Perry
Restorations Ltd,
B.A.F.R.A.,
Praewood Farm,
Hemel Hempstead Road,
St Albans.
Tel: 01727 853487

Kent

T M Akers,
B.A.F.R.A.,
The Forge,
39 Chancery Lane,
Beckenham.
Tel 0181 650 9179
*Longcase and bracket
clocks, cabinet making,
French polishing.*

Martin Body,
B.A.F.R.A.,
71 Bower Mount Road,
Maidstone.
Tel: 01622 752273
*Gilded furniture
and frames.*

Timothy Long
Restoration,
B.A.F.R.A.,
St John's Church,
London Road,
Dunton Green,
Sevenoaks.
Tel: 01732 743368
*Cabinet restoration,
polishing, upholstery,
brass and steel
cabinet fittings.*

Middlesex

Antique Restorations,
B.A.F.R.A.,
45 Windmill Road,
Brentford.
Tel: 0181 568 5249
*Decorative artists, carvers
and gilders.*

Norfolk

R N Larwood,
B.A.F.R.A.,
Fine Antique Restoration
& Conservation of
Furniture,
The Oaks, Station Road,
Larling,
Norwich.
Tel: 01953 717937

Oxfordshire

Alistair Frayling-Cork,
B.A.F.R.A.,
Antiques & Period
Furniture Restoration,
2 Mill Lane, Wallingford.
Tel: 01491 826221

Colin Piper Restoration,
B.A.F.R.A.,
Highfield House,
The Greens,
Leafield, Witney.
Tel: 01993 878593.
*Restoration and
conservation of fine
antique furniture, clocks
and barometers.*

Shropshire

Richard Higgins,
B.A.F.R.A.,
The Old School, Longnor,
Nr Shrewsbury.
Tel: 01743 718162
*Furniture, clock,
barometers, movements,
dials and cases, carving,
rush/cane seating.*

Somerset

M. J. Durkee,
B.A.F.R.A.,
Castle House,
Bennetts Field,
Moor Lane,
Wincanton.
Tel: 01963 33884
Antique furniture.

Staffordshire

Rockermans Leather
Lining,
Clough Street,
Hanley,
Stoke-on-Trent.
Tel: 01782 274444
*Leathering for desks
and tables.*

Sussex

J. C. Pelham,
17 Harold Mews,
St. Leonards-on-Sea.
Tel: 01424 431348
*Restoration of
glass advertisements,
picture framing.*

Wiltshire

William Cook,
B.A.F.R.A.
High Trees,
Savernake Forest,
Nr Marlborough.
Tel: 01672 513017/0171
736 4329
Furniture.

SCIENTIFIC INSTRUMENTS

Bedfordshire

Christopher Sykes,
The Old Parsonage,
Woburn,Milton Keynes.
Tel: 01525 290259

Scotland

Bow-Well Antiques,
103 West Bow,
Edinburgh.
Tel: 0131 225 3335

Michael Bennett-Levy,
Monkton House, Old
Craighall, Musselburgh,
Midlothian.
Tel: 0131 665 5753
Televisions.

SERVICES

London

Cunningham Hart,
59 Compton Road,
Islington, N12.
Tel: 0171 354 3504
*Loss adjustor, surveyors,
and valuers.*

Studio & TV Hire,
3 Ariel Way, W12.
Tel: 0181 749 3445

Hampshire

Securikey Ltd,
PO Box 18, Aldershot.
Tel: 01252 311888
Security.

Middlesex

John Ives,
5 Normanhurst Drive,
Twickenham.
Tel: 0181 892 6265
Reference books.

West Midlands

Retro Products,
174 Norton Road,
Nr Stourbridge.
Tel: 01384 373332
*Brass handles
and accessories.*

Sussex

J. C. Pelham,
17 Harold Mews,
St. Leonards-on-Sea.
Tel: 01424 431348
*Picture framing, repro
glass advertisements.*

SHIPPERS

London

Kuwahara Ltd.,
Unit 5,
Bittacy Business Centre,
Bittacy Hill, NW7.
Tel: 0181 346 7744

Hedley's Humpers,
Units 3 & 4,
97 Victoria Road, NW10.
Tel: 0181 965 8733

Avon

A. J. Williams,
607 Sixth Avenue,
Central Business Park,
Petherton Road,
Hengrove, Bristol.
Tel: 0117 9892166

Dorset

Alan Franklin Transport,
26 Blackmoor Road,
Ebblake Industrial Estate,
Verwood.
Tel: 01202 826539

SPORTS & GAMES

London

Fenwick Billiards,
The Antiques Pavilion,
175 Bermondsey Street,
SE1
Tel: 0823 660770

Berkshire

Sir William Bentley
Billiards,
Standen Manor Farm,
Hungerford.
Tel: 01488 681711

Nottinghamshire

T. Vennett-Smith,
11 Nottingham Road,
Gotham.
Tel: 01602 830541
Ephemera

TEDDY BEARS

Oxfordshire

Teddy Bears of Witney,
99 High Street,
Witney.
Tel: 01993 702616

Sussex

Sue Pearson,
13½ Prince Albert Street,
Brighton.
Tel: 01273 329247

TEXTILES

Kent

The Lace Basket,
1a East Cross,
Tenterden.
Tel: 01580 763923/763664

TOYS

Yorkshire

John & Simon Haley,
89 Northgate,
Halifax.
Tel: 01422 822148

TRIBAL ART

Yorkshire

Gordon Reece Gallery
Finkle Street,
Knaresborough,
Nr. York.
Tel: 01423 866219

WATCHES

London

Pieces of Time,
Grays in the Mews,
1-7 Davies Mews,
W1.
Tel: 071 629 2422

WINE RELATED ITEMS

Bedfordshire

Christopher Sykes,
The Old Parsonage,
Woburn,
Milton Keynes.
Tel: 01525 290259

FAIR ORGANISERS

London

City of London Antiques
& Fine Art Fair,
Business Design Centre,
52 Upper Street,
Islington, N1.
Tel: 0171 359 3535

Surrey

Cultural Exhibitions,
8 Meadrow,
Godalming.
Tel: 01483 422562

MARKETS & CENTRES

London

Atlantic Antique Centres
Ltd.,
Chenil House,
181-183 King's Road,
SW3.
Tel: 0171 351 5353

Antiquarius,
131-141 King's Road,
SW3.

Bond Street Antique
Centre,
124 New Bond Street,
W1.

Chenil Galleries,
181-183 King's Road,
SW3.
Tel: 0171 351 5353

The Mall Antiques
Arcade,
Camden Passage,
Islington,
N1.

The Old Cinema,
160 Chiswick High Road,
W4.
Tel: 0181 995 4166
and
Tower Bridge Road, SE1.
Tel: 0171 407 5371

Kent

Weald Antiques Centre,
106 High Street,
Tenterden.
Tel: 01580 762939

Lancashire

Preston Antique Centre,
The Mill,
New Hall Lane,
Preston.
Tel: 01772 794498

Lincolnshire

The Hemswell Antiques
Centre,
Caenby Corner Estate,
Hemswell Cliff,
Gainsborough.
Tel: 01427 668389

Shropshire

Bridgnorth Antique
Centre,
Old Smithfield,
Whitburn Street,
Bridgnorth.
Tel: 01746 768055

Sussex

Bexhill Antiques Centre,
Old Town,
Bexhill.
Tel: 01424 210182

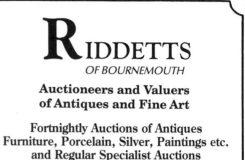

SOUTH EAST

SOUTH WEST

A U C T I O N E E R S

TRURO AUCTION CENTRE

**Calenick Street, Truro
Cornwall TR1 2SG
(0872) 260020**

Martyn Rowe
Auctioneer and Valuer

Antique Sales/Collectors Sales
Vehicle Sales, General Sales
Commercial Sales

Fax (0872) 261794

Henry Aldridge & Son Auctions

DEVIZES AUCTION ROOMS
1 Wine Street (The Old Town Hall), Devizes,
Wiltshire SN10 1AP Tel: 0380 729199

Auctioneers of Antique & General Furniture,
Specialist Sales, Collectables

Sales held every Tuesday at the Devizes Auction Centre, New Park Street,
Devizes, Wilts.
Sales commence 10am, veiwing Monday 4 pm till 7 pm
Collectables, Militaria,
Toy Sales held at regular intervals

MARTIN SPENCER-THOMAS
Auctioneers & Valuers
Bicton Street Auction Rooms, Exmouth, Devon

**Telephone
Exmouth (0395) 267403**

**REGULAR AUCTION SALES
OF ANTIQUE & GENERAL FURNITURE
& EFFECTS AT EXMOUTH**

**REGULAR SALES OF
COMMERCIAL GOODS**

**VALUATIONS FOR ALL PURPOSES TO
INCLUDE: INSURANCE, PROBATE
FAMILY DIVISION, ETC.**

**INSPECTIONS & INITIAL ADVICE
FREE OF CHARGE AND WITHOUT
OBLIGATION**

RONALD JAMES
Auctioneer and Valuer

JAMAICA INN GALLERY AND AUCTION ROOM
The Old School, Bolventor, Launceston, Cornwall. PL15 7TS
Tel & Fax: 0566 86020

*At Jamaica Inn Auction Room...
We Sell Everything.*

Antiques, China, Glass, Silver,
Jewellery, Pictures, Carpets, Rugs,
Clocks, Brass and Copper
...Every Six Weeks...

Books, Postcards, Cigarette Cards,
Toys, Dolls, Teddy Bears, Models,
Etc.
...Quarterly...

Victorian, Edwardian and Pine
Furniture, together with General
Household Items
...Once A Month...

For Further Information Contact:
**Jamaica Inn Gallery and
Auction Room**
The Old School, Bolventor,
Launceston, Cornwall PL15 7TS
Phone: 0566 86020

Michael·J·Bowman A.S.V.A.
Auctioneer and Valuer of Fine Arts and Chattels

MONTHLY SALES OF ANTIQUES
AND FINE ART AT CHUDLEIGH
COLOUR ILLUSTRATED
CATALOGUES
FREE HOME CONSULTATIONS

**6 Haccombe House, Nr. Netherton
Newton Abbot, Devon TQ12 4SJ
Tel: (0626) 872890 or (0374) 991793**

This art deco emerald
and diamond ring, the
emerald of approx. 2.5
carats, sold to an
Edinburgh telephone
bidder for £4,500 at
Chudleigh after
national advertising.

Sold for £4,500

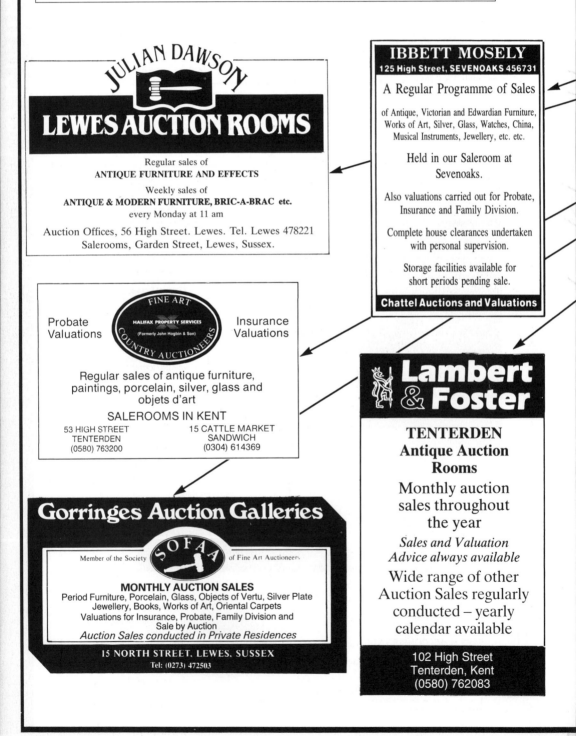

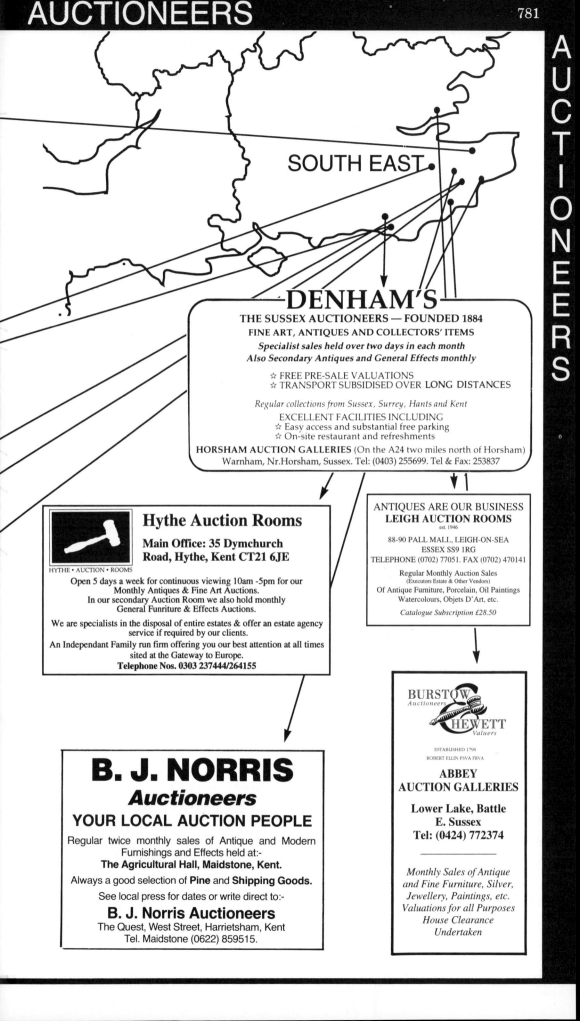

SOUTH EAST

DENHAM'S

THE SUSSEX AUCTIONEERS — FOUNDED 1884

FINE ART, ANTIQUES AND COLLECTORS' ITEMS

Specialist sales held over two days in each month
Also Secondary Antiques and General Effects monthly

☆ FREE PRE-SALE VALUATIONS
☆ TRANSPORT SUBSIDISED OVER LONG DISTANCES

Regular collections from Sussex, Surrey, Hants and Kent

EXCELLENT FACILITIES INCLUDING
☆ Easy access and substantial free parking
☆ On-site restaurant and refreshments

HORSHAM AUCTION GALLERIES (On the A24 two miles north of Horsham)
Warnham, Nr.Horsham, Sussex. Tel: (0403) 255699. Tel & Fax: 253837

Hythe Auction Rooms

Main Office: 35 Dymchurch Road, Hythe, Kent CT21 6JE

HYTHE • AUCTION • ROOMS

Open 5 days a week for continuous viewing 10am -5pm for our
Monthly Antiques & Fine Art Auctions.
In our secondary Auction Room we also hold monthly
General Furniture & Effects Auctions.

We are specialists in the disposal of entire estates & offer an estate agency
service if required by our clients.
An Independant Family run firm offering you our best attention at all times
sited at the Gateway to Europe.
Telephone Nos. 0303 237444/264155

ANTIQUES ARE OUR BUSINESS
LEIGH AUCTION ROOMS
est. 1946

88-90 PALL MALL, LEIGH-ON-SEA
ESSEX SS9 1RG
TELEPHONE (0702) 77051. FAX (0702) 470141

Regular Monthly Auction Sales
(Executors Estate & Other Vendors)
Of Antique Furniture, Porcelain, Oil Paintings
Watercolours, Objets D'Art, etc.

Catalogue Subscription £28.50

B. J. NORRIS
Auctioneers
YOUR LOCAL AUCTION PEOPLE

Regular twice monthly sales of Antique and Modern
Furnishings and Effects held at:-
The Agricultural Hall, Maidstone, Kent.

Always a good selection of **Pine** and **Shipping Goods.**

See local press for dates or write direct to:-

B. J. Norris Auctioneers
The Quest, West Street, Harrietsham, Kent
Tel. Maidstone (0622) 859515.

BURSTOW
Auctioneers
& HEWETT
Valuers

ESTABLISHED 1790
ROBERT ELLIN FSVA FRVA

**ABBEY
AUCTION GALLERIES**

**Lower Lake, Battle
E. Sussex
Tel: (0424) 772374**

*Monthly Sales of Antique
and Fine Furniture, Silver,
Jewellery, Paintings, etc.
Valuations for all Purposes
House Clearance
Undertaken*

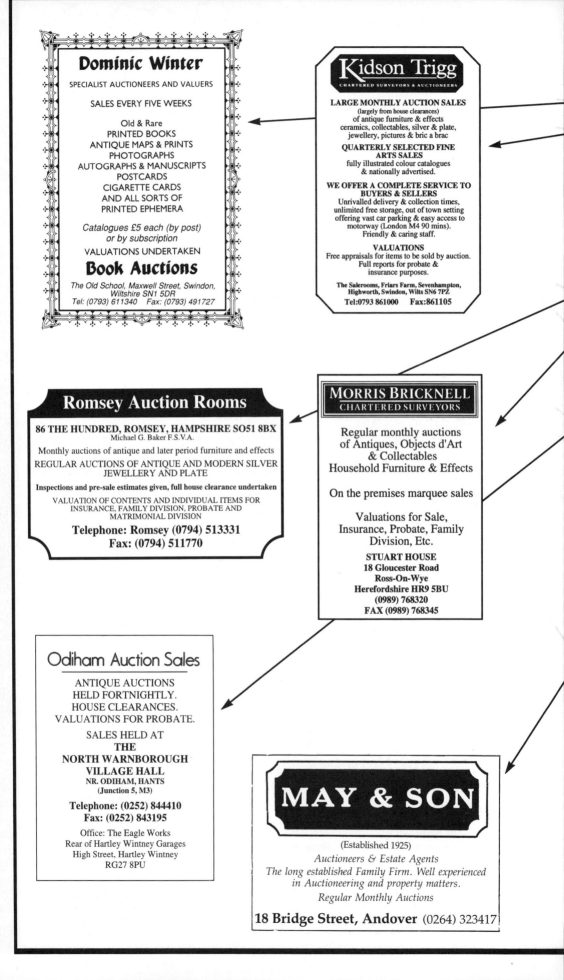

Dominic Winter

SPECIALIST AUCTIONEERS AND VALUERS

SALES EVERY FIVE WEEKS

Old & Rare
PRINTED BOOKS
ANTIQUE MAPS & PRINTS
PHOTOGRAPHS
AUTOGRAPHS & MANUSCRIPTS
POSTCARDS
CIGARETTE CARDS
AND ALL SORTS OF
PRINTED EPHEMERA

Catalogues £5 each (by post)
or by subscription

VALUATIONS UNDERTAKEN

Book Auctions

The Old School, Maxwell Street, Swindon,
Wiltshire SN1 5DR
Tel: (0793) 611340   Fax: (0793) 491727

Kidson Trigg
CHARTERED SURVEYORS & AUCTIONEERS

LARGE MONTHLY AUCTION SALES
(largely from house clearances)
of antique furniture & effects
ceramics, collectables, silver & plate,
jewellery, pictures & bric a brac

**QUARTERLY SELECTED FINE
ARTS SALES**
fully illustrated colour catalogues
& nationally advertised.

**WE OFFER A COMPLETE SERVICE TO
BUYERS & SELLERS**
Unrivalled delivery & collection times,
unlimited free storage, out of town setting
offering vast car parking & easy access to
motorway (London M4 90 mins).
Friendly & caring staff.

VALUATIONS
Free appraisals for items to be sold by auction.
Full reports for probate &
insurance purposes.

The Salerooms, Friars Farm, Sevenhampton,
Highworth, Swindon, Wilts SN6 7PZ

Tel:0793 861000   Fax:861105

Romsey Auction Rooms

86 THE HUNDRED, ROMSEY, HAMPSHIRE SO51 8BX
Michael G. Baker F.S.V.A.

Monthly auctions of antique and later period furniture and effects

REGULAR AUCTIONS OF ANTIQUE AND MODERN SILVER
JEWELLERY AND PLATE

Inspections and pre-sale estimates given, full house clearance undertaken

VALUATION OF CONTENTS AND INDIVIDUAL ITEMS FOR
INSURANCE, FAMILY DIVISION, PROBATE AND
MATRIMONIAL DIVISION

**Telephone: Romsey (0794) 513331
Fax: (0794) 511770**

MORRIS BRICKNELL
CHARTERED SURVEYORS

Regular monthly auctions
of Antiques, Objects d'Art
& Collectables
Household Furniture & Effects

On the premises marquee sales

Valuations for Sale,
Insurance, Probate, Family
Division, Etc.

**STUART HOUSE
18 Gloucester Road
Ross-On-Wye
Herefordshire HR9 5BU
(0989) 768320
FAX (0989) 768345**

Odiham Auction Sales

ANTIQUE AUCTIONS
HELD FORTNIGHTLY.
HOUSE CLEARANCES.
VALUATIONS FOR PROBATE.

SALES HELD AT
**THE
NORTH WARNBOROUGH
VILLAGE HALL**
NR. ODIHAM, HANTS
(Junction 5, M3)

**Telephone: (0252) 844410
Fax: (0252) 843195**

Office: The Eagle Works
Rear of Hartley Wintney Garages
High Street, Hartley Wintney
RG27 8PU

MAY & SON

(Established 1925)
*Auctioneers & Estate Agents
The long established Family Firm. Well experienced
in Auctioneering and property matters.
Regular Monthly Auctions*

18 Bridge Street, Andover (0264) 323417

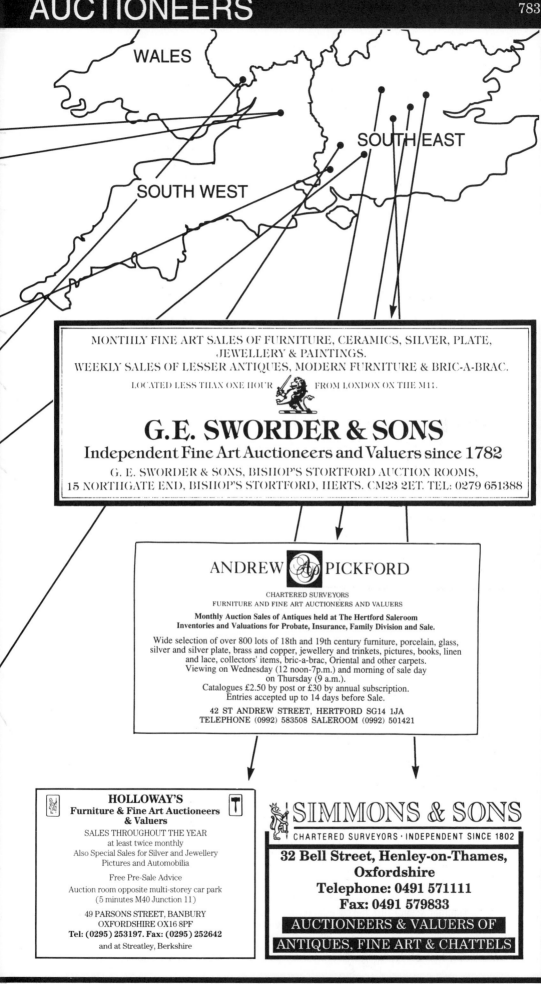

WALES

SOUTH EAST

SOUTH WEST

DOWELL LLOYD
AUCTIONEERS

—— ESTABLISHED 1944 ——

FORTNIGHTLY SALES OF ANTIQUE AND GENERAL FURNITURE

Incorporating: China, Glassware, Carpets, Pictures, Silver and Collectors Items.
Fortnightly auction of Jewellery on Tuesday with viewing on Monday

**DOWELL LLOYD AUCTION GALLERIES
118 PUTNEY BRIDGE ROAD, LONDON SW15 2NQ
TEL: 081-788 7777 FAX: 081-874 5390**

John Bellman

AUCTIONEERS

**NEW POUND BUSINESS PARK
WISBOROUGH GREEN, BILLINGSHURST
WEST SUSSEX RH14 0AY
TELEPHONE (0403) 700858**

SPECIALISED ANTIQUE AND COLLECTORS
AUCTIONS HELD MONTHLY

ANTIQUARIAN AND MODERN BOOK SALES
HELD QUARTERLY

SETTLEMENT: made 10 working days after sale

FREE PRE-SALE VALUATIONS:
offered without obligation

WRITTEN VALUATIONS: undertaken for the purposes
of Insurance, Probate or Capital Gains

ESTATES: detailed inventories and administration and
reconciliation provided

TRANSPORT: arranged by request with our
recommended carriers Gander & White

TERMS AND CONDITIONS OF BUSINESS:
available on request

For further details please contact:
RUPERT W. TOOVEY

BLACK HORSE AGENCIES
Ambrose

AUCTION ROOMS

AUCTIONEERS & VALUERS
MONTHLY AUCTION OF ANTIQUES & HIGH QUALITY
FURNITURE, GOLD, SILVER & JEWELLERY, OIL PAINTINGS,
WATERCOLOURS, PORCELAIN, GLASS & CERAMICS, CLOCKS,
WATCHES & BAROMETERS
ALL COLLECTORS ITEMS & MEMORABILIA
VALUATIONS FOR ALL PURPOSES INCLUDING INSURANCE, PROBATE

081-502 3951
FAX: 081-508 9516
MANAGER: K. LAWRENCE, LOUGHTON AUCTION ROOMS,
149 HIGH ROAD, LOUGHTON, ESSEX IG10 5LZ

PETER CHENEY
Auctioneers & Valuers

MONTHLY AUCTION SALES
ANTIQUES, FURNITURE, PICTURES, SILVER,
PORCELAIN AND COLLECTORS ITEMS
NO BUYERS PREMIUM
VALUATIONS FOR INSURANCE & PROBATE

**Western Road Auction Rooms, Western Road
Littlehampton, West Sussex BN17 5NP
Tel: (0903) 722264 & 713418**

BAYTREE AUCTIONS

Auctioneers & Valuers

Furniture * Clocks * Porcelain
Silver * Glass * Copper * Brass
Jewellery * Collector's Items
and Paintings
Quality Antique Sales
Household and Bankruptcy Clearances
Regular Fortnightly Sales
Friendly and Reliable Service
Free Advice Given

TEL: BRAINTREE
0376 328228

Unit 23, Broomhills Ind. Est.,
Braintree, Essex

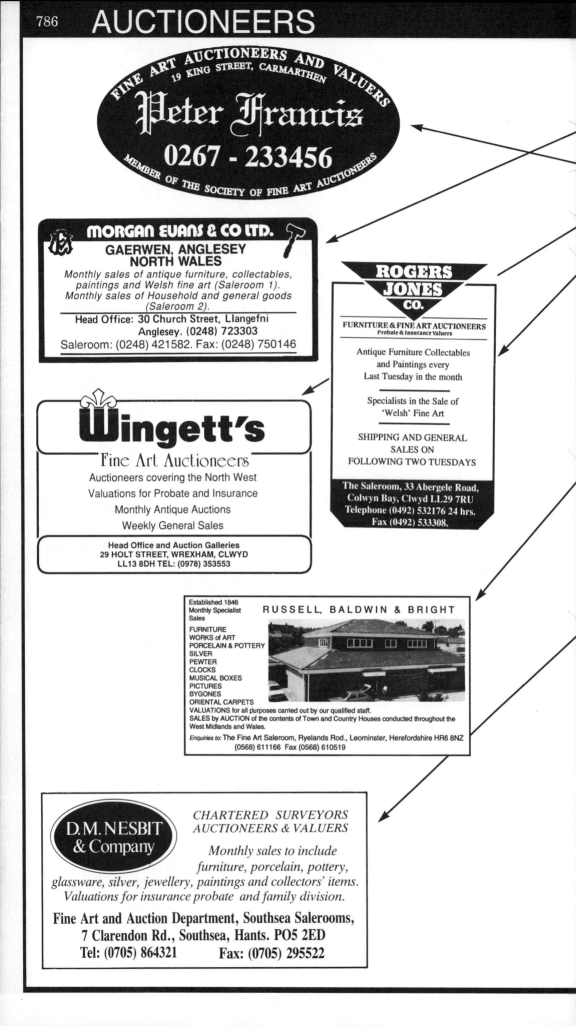

EAST MIDLANDS

WEST MIDLANDS

EAST ANGLIA

WALES

SOUTH EAST

SOUTH WEST

COOPER HIRST AUCTIONS
Chartered Surveyors Auctioneers and Valuers

★ REGULAR ANTIQUE SALES
★ HOUSEHOLD FURNITURE AND EFFECTS - Every TUESDAY at 10.00am (Viewing from 8.30am)
★ TIMBER, BUILDING MATERIALS, DIY, PLANT, MACHINERY AND VEHICLES. Every FRIDAY at 10.00am (Viewing from 8.30am)
★ BANKRUPTCY AND LIQUIDATION SALES ★
★ VALUATIONS OF ANTIQUES, FINE ART AND OTHER CHATTELS FOR ALL PURPOSES
★ HOUSE CLEARANCES, REMOVALS AND LONG/ SHORT TERM STORAGE

THE GRANARY SALEROOM VICTORIA ROAD, CHELMSFORD
Tel: 0245 260535

H HAMPTONS MARTEL MAIDES
The Old Bank, 29 High Street
St Peter Port, Guernsey
Tel (01481) 713463   Fax:(01481) 723306

Quarterly Auctions of Antique Furniture, Porcelain, Silver, Jewellery, Pictures, Clocks, Miscellanea, etc.
Fortnightly Auctions of Victorian and Later Furniture and Effects, Collectors' Items, etc.

5% BUYERS' PREMIUM. NO V.A.T.

Bourne End Auction Rooms

Station Approach, Bourne End,
Bucks SL8 5QH
Telephone No: 0628 531500
Fax No: 0494 433031

Trembath Welch
Auctioneers & Valuers
incorporating J M Welch & Son Established 1886
Chequers Lane, Great Dunmow Salerooms

Office at: The Old Town Hall
Great Dunmow
Essex CM6 1AU
Tel: 0371-873014 Fax 0371- 875936

Monthly Auction Sales: Including Victorian and Edwardian furniture, effects, collectors' items and contemporary furniture and furnishings. Held on the 3rd Wednesday, 12 noon start.
Bi-monthly Antique Auction Sales: Including period furniture, silver, china, glass, jewellery, paintings, prints, clocks etc.
Valuations conducted for Probate, Insurance and Sale
Trembath Welch a Local Firm with National Connections

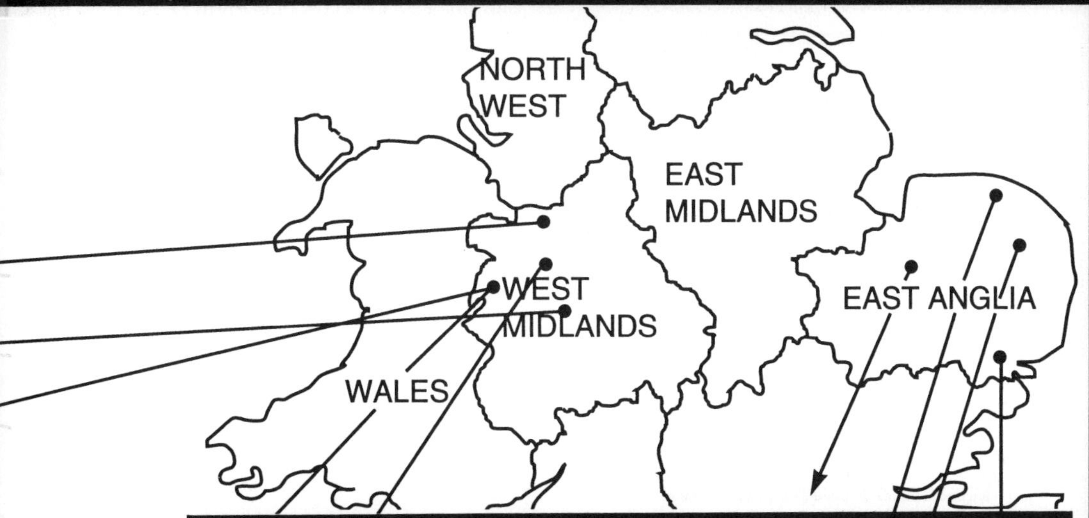

NORTH WEST
EAST MIDLANDS
WEST MIDLANDS
EAST ANGLIA
WALES

Cheffins Grain & Comins

AUCTIONEERS AND VALUERS SINCE 1825

CAMBRIDGE SALEROOM, 2 CLIFTON ROAD, CAMBRIDGE CB1 4BW
TEL: 0223 213343/358721 FAX: 0223 413396

THOS. WM. GAZE & SON

ESTABLISHED 1857

AUCTIONS

2000 LOTS EVERY FRIDAY
at the
DISS AUCTION ROOMS
including

500 LOTS. ANTIQUES and COLLECTABLES
400 LOTS. SHIPPING, BARN CLEARANCES and ARCHITECTURAL
500 LOTS. MODERN FURNITURE and EFFECTS
Specialist Sales throughout the year
Catalogues Available

AUCTION ROOMS, ROYDON ROAD, DISS, NORFOLK. TEL: (0379) 650306

AYLSHAM SALEROOMS

SALES OF
★ ANTIQUES (3-WEEKLY)
★ PICTURES (BI-MONTHLY)
★ BOOKS AND COLLECTORS SALES (BI-MONTHLY)

WEEKLY HOUSEHOLD FURNITURE ETC

AYLSHAM (0263) 733195
8 MARKET PLACE, AYLSHAM, NORFOLK NR11 6EH

Extremely fine mahogany bureau, 3'3"
Sold at Aylsham Salerooms
for £2,200

G. A. KEY

VALUATIONS FOR SALE
INSURANCE & PROBATE
PURPOSES

OLIVERS

AUCTIONEERS & VALUERS

REGULAR SALES OF ANTIQUES & WORKS OF ART

FORTNIGHTLY SALES OF VICTORIAN & LATER FURNITURE & HOUSEHOLD EFFECTS

VALUATIONS FOR INSURANCE PROBATE AND FAMILY DIVISION

OUR OWN COLLECTION SERVICE AVAILABLE FOR VENDORS

Members of the Society of Fine Art Auctioneers

The Saleroom, Burkitts Lane, Sudbury, Suffolk CO10 6HB
Telephone and Fax: (0787) 880305

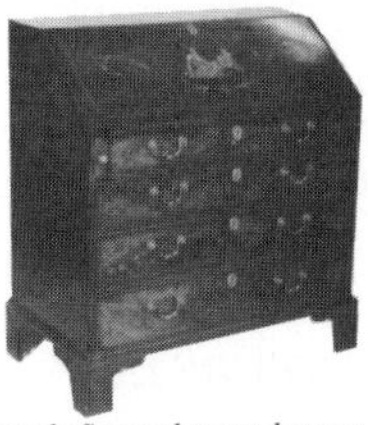

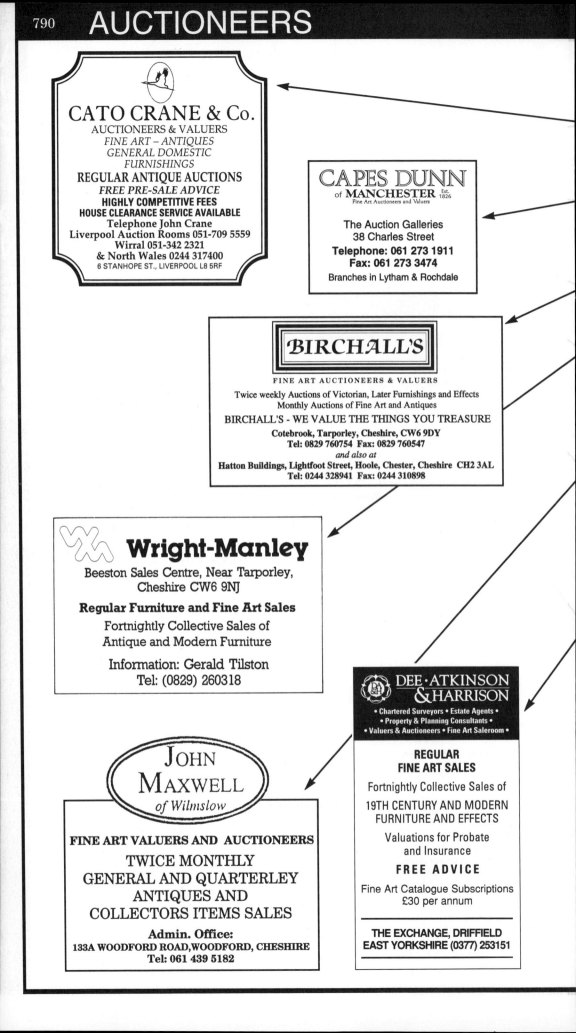

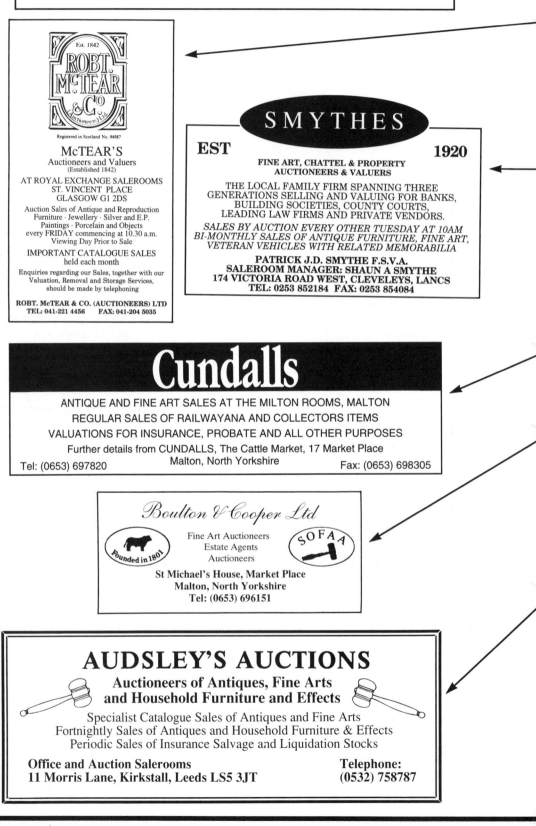

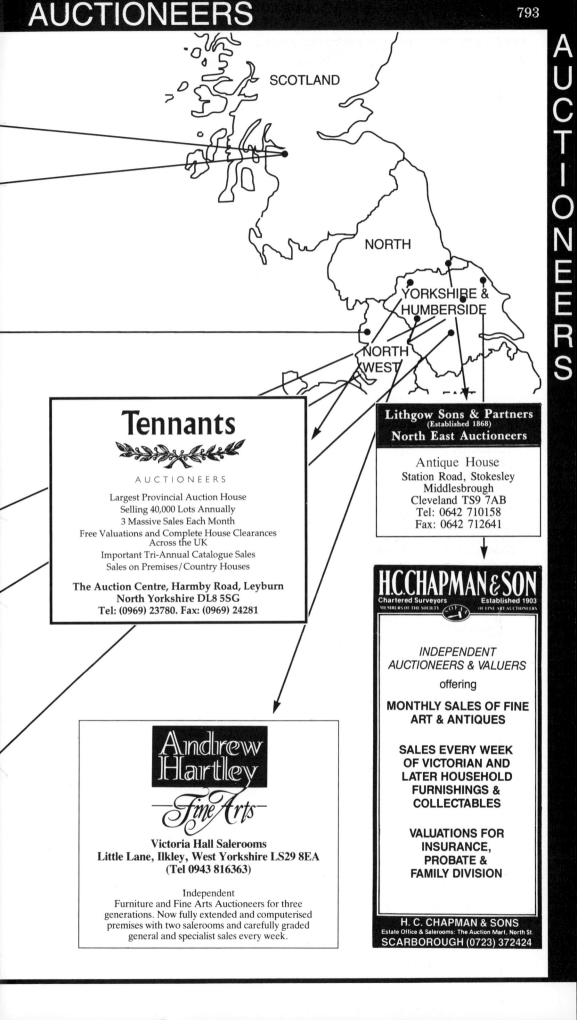

SCOTLAND

NORTH

YORKSHIRE &
HUMBERSIDE

NORTH
WEST

Tennants

AUCTIONEERS

Largest Provincial Auction House
Selling 40,000 Lots Annually
3 Massive Sales Each Month
Free Valuations and Complete House Clearances
Across the UK
Important Tri-Annual Catalogue Sales
Sales on Premises/Country Houses

**The Auction Centre, Harmby Road, Leyburn
North Yorkshire DL8 5SG
Tel: (0969) 23780. Fax: (0969) 24281**

Lithgow Sons & Partners
(Established 1868)
North East Auctioneers

Antique House
Station Road, Stokesley
Middlesbrough
Cleveland TS9 7AB
Tel: 0642 710158
Fax: 0642 712641

H.C.CHAPMAN & SON

Chartered Surveyors   Established 1903
MEMBERS OF THE SOCIETY   OF FINE ART AUCTIONEERS

*INDEPENDENT
AUCTIONEERS & VALUERS*

offering

**MONTHLY SALES OF FINE
ART & ANTIQUES**

**SALES EVERY WEEK
OF VICTORIAN AND
LATER HOUSEHOLD
FURNISHINGS &
COLLECTABLES**

**VALUATIONS FOR
INSURANCE,
PROBATE &
FAMILY DIVISION**

H. C. CHAPMAN & SONS
Estate Office & Salerooms: The Auction Mart, North St.
SCARBOROUGH (0723) 372424

Andrew Hartley
Fine Arts

**Victoria Hall Salerooms
Little Lane, Ilkley, West Yorkshire LS29 8EA
(Tel 0943 816363)**

Independent
Furniture and Fine Arts Auctioneers for three
generations. Now fully extended and computerised
premises with two salerooms and carefully graded
general and specialist sales every week.

DIRECTORY OF AUCTIONEERS

Auctioneers who hold frequent sales should contact us for inclusion in the next Edition. Entries must be received by April 1995. There is no charge for this listing. Entries will be repeated in subsequent editions unless we are requested otherwise. Please note telephone codes have been amended in line with British Telecom's guidelines which take effect from 16th April, 1995.

London

Academy Auctioneers &
Valuers, Northcote House,
Northcote Avenue,
Ealing, W5.
Tel: 0181 579 7466

Bonhams,
Montpelier Galleries,
Montpelier Street,
Knightsbridge, SW7
Tel: 0171 584 9161

Bonhams, Lots Road,
Chelsea, SW10
Tel: 0171 351 7111

Christie Manson & Woods
Ltd, 8 King Street,
St James's, SW1
Tel: 0171 839 9060

Christie's Robson Lowe,
47 Duke Street,
St James's, SW1
Tel: 0171 839 4034/5

Christie's South Kensington
Ltd, 85 Old Brompton
Road, SW7.
Tel: 0171 581 7611

Criterion Salerooms,
53 Essex Road,
Islington, N1
Tel: 0171 359 5707

Dowell Lloyd & Co,
118 Putney Bridge Road,
SW15. Tel: 0181 788 7777

Forrest & Co,
79-85 Cobbold Road,
Leytonstone, E11
Tel: 0181 534 2931

Stanley Gibbons Auctions
Ltd, 399 Strand, WC2
Tel: 0171 836 8444

Glendining's,
101 New Bond Street, W1
Tel: 0171 493 2445

G.W.R. Auctions
(Edmonton),
22 Bull Lane,
Edmonton, N18
Tel: 0181 8870525

Hamptons Fine Art
Auctioneers and Valuers,
6 Arlington Street, SW1
Tel: 0171 493 8222

Harmers of London Stamp
Auctioneers Ltd,
91 New Bond Street, W1
Tel: 0171 629 0218

Hornsey Auctions Ltd,
54/56 High Street,
Hornsey, N8
Tel: 0181 340 5334

Lots Road Chelsea Auction
Galleries,
71 Lots Road,
Worlds End,
Chelsea, SW10
Tel: 0171 351 7771

MacGregor Nash & Co,
Lodge House,
9-17 Lodge Lane,
North Finchley, N12
Tel: 081 445 9000

Thomas Moore,
217-219 Greenwich High
Road, SE10
Tel: 0181 858 7848

John Nicholson,
20 The Ridgway,
Wimbledon Village, SW19
Tel: 0181 944 5575

Onslow's,
Metrostore,
Townmead Road, SW6
Tel: 0171 793 0240

Phillips,
Blenstock House,
7 Blenheim Street,
New Bond Street, W1
Tel: 0171 629 6602 and
10 Salem Road, W2
Tel: 0171 229 9090

Rippon Boswell & Co,
The Arcade, South
Kensington Station, SW7
Tel: 0171 589 4242

Rosebery's Fine Art Ltd,
Old Railway Booking Hall,
Crystal Palace Station
Road, SE19
Tel: 0171 778 4024

Sotheby's,
34-35 New Bond Street, W1
Tel: 0171 493 8080

Southgate Auction Rooms,
55 High Street,
Southgate N14
Tel: 0181 886 7888

Town & Country House
Auctions,
42A Nightingale Grove, SE13
Tel: 0181 852 3145

Avon

Gardiner Houlgate
The Old Malthouse,
Comfortable Place,
Upper Bristol Road,
Bath
Tel: 01225 447933

Aldridges, Bath,
The Auction Galleries,
130-132 Walcot Street,
Bath
Tel: 01225 462830 & 462839

Bristol Auction Rooms,
St Johns Place, Apsley
Road, Clifton, Bristol
Tel: 0117 973 7201

Clevedon Salerooms,
Herbert Road,
Clevedon
Tel: 01275 876699

Phillips Auction Rooms
of Bath,
1 Old King Street, Bath.
Tel: 01225 310609

Phillips Fine Art Auctioneers,
71 Oakfield Road,
Clifton, Bristol
Tel: 0117 9734052

Taviner's Ltd,
Prewett Street, Redcliffe,
Bristol
Tel: 0117 9265996

Woodspring Auction Rooms,
Churchill Road,
Weston-super-Mare
Tel: 01934 628419

Bedfordshire

Wilson Peacock,
The Auction Centre,
26 Newnham Street,
Bedford
Tel: 01234 266366

Berkshire

Dreweatt Neate,
Donnington Priory,
Donnington, Newbury
Tel: 01635 31234

R. Elliott,
Chancellors, 32 High Street,
Ascot. Tel: 01344 872588

Holloway's,
12 High Street, Streatley,
Reading
Tel: 01491 872318

Martin & Pole,
12 Milton Road
Wokingham
Tel: 01734 790460

Thimbleby & Shorland,
31 Great Knollys Street,
Reading
Tel: 01734 508611

Duncan Vincent Fine Art &
Chattel Auctioneers,
92 London Street, Reading
Tel: 01734 512100

Buckinghamshire

Amersham Auction Rooms,
Station Road, Amersham
Tel: 01494 729292

Bourne End Auctions
Rooms, Station Approach,
Bourne End
Tel: 01628 531500

Hamptons,
10 Burkes Parade,
Beaconsfield
Tel: 01494 672969

Wigley's,
Winslow Sale Room,
Market Square, Winslow
Tel: 01296 713011

Cambridgeshire

Cheffins Grain & Comins,
2 Clifton Road, Cambridge
Tel: 01223 358721/213343

Goldsmiths,
15 Market Place, Oundle.
Tel: 01832 272349

Grounds & Co,
2 Nene Quay,
Wisbech
Tel: 01945 585041

Maxey & Son,
1-3 South Brink,
Wisbech
Tel: 01945 584609

Phillips Auctioneers,
Station Road, St. Ives
Tel: 01480 68144

Cheshire

F.W. Allen & Sons,
Central Buildings
15/15A Station Road,
Cheadle Hulme,
Tel: 0161 486 6069

Andrew Hilditch & Son,
Hanover House,
1A The Square,
Sandbach
Tel: 01270 762048/767246

Birchalls,
Cotebrook,
Tarporley
Tel: 01829 760754

Birchalls,
Hatton Buildings,
Lightfoot Street,
Hoole,
Chester
Tel: 01244 328941

Dockree's,
224 Moss Lane,
Bramhall,
Stockport
Tel: 0161 485 1258

Highams Auctions, Waterloo
House, Waterloo Road,
Stalybridge
Tel: 0161 338 8698 also at:
Southgate House,
Southgate Street,
Rhodes Bank,
Oldham
Tel: 0161 626 1021

Highams Inc.Rothwell & Co
(Auctioneers),
Waterloo House
Waterloo Road
Stalybridge
Tel: 061 303 2924

Frank R Marshall & Co,
Marshall House,
Church Hill,
Knutsford
Tel: 01565 653284

John Maxwell of Wilmslow,
133A Woodford Road,
Woodford
Tel: 0161 439 5182

Phillips North West,
New House,
150 Christleton Road,
Chester
Tel: 01244 313936

Phillips Fine Art
Auctioneers,
Trinity House,
114 Northenden Road,
Sale,
Manchester
Tel: 0161 962 9237

Henry Spencer Inc.
Peter Wilson,
Victoria Gallery,
Market Street,
Nantwich
Tel: 01270 623878

Wright Manley,
Beeston Sales Centre,
63 High Street,
Tarporley
Tel: 01829 260318

Cleveland

Lithgow Sons & Partners,
The Antique House,
Station Road,
Stokesley,
Middlesbrough
Tel: 01642 710158 &
710326

Cornwall

Jamaica Inn Gallery &
Auction Room,
The Old School,
Bolventor, Launceston
Tel: 01566 86020

Jeffery's,
5 Fore Street,
Lostwithiel
Tel: 01208 872245

Lambrays, incorporating
R J Hamm ASVA
Polmorla Walk,
The Platt, Wadebridge
Tel: 0120 881 3593

W H Lane & Son,
St Mary's Auction Rooms,
65 Morrab Road, Penzance
Tel: 01736 61447

David Lay,
Penzance Auction House,
Alverton, Penzance
Tel: 01736 61414

Phillips Cornwall,
Cornubia Hall, Par
Tel: 0172 681 4047

Pooley and Rogers,
Regent Auction Rooms,
Abbey Street,
Penzance
Tel: 01736 68814

Truro Auction Centre,
Calenick Street, Truro
Tel: 01872 260020

Cumbria

Cumbria Auction Rooms,
12 Lowther Street,
Carlisle
Tel: 01228 25259

Hockney & Leigh,
The Auction Centre,
Grange-Over-Sands
Tel: 015395 33316/33466

Mitchells,
The Furniture Hall,
47 Station Road,
Cockermouth
Tel: 01900 827800

Alfred Mossops & Co,
Loughrigg Villa, Kelsick
Road, Ambleside
Tel: 015394 33015

James Thompson,
64 Main Street,
Kirkby Lonsdale
Tel: 015242 71555

Thomson, Roddick &
Laurie, 24 Lowther Street,
Carlisle
Tel: 01228 28939/39636

Derbyshire

Richardson & Linnell Ltd,
The Auction Office,
Cattle Market,
Chequers Road,
Derby
Tel: 01332 296369

Neales,
The Derby Saleroom,
Becket Street,
Derby
Tel: 01332 343286

Noel Wheatcroft,
The Matlock Auction
Gallery, 39 Dale Road,
Matlock
Tel: 01629 584591

Devon

Bearnes,
Avenue Road,
Torquay
Tel: 01803 296277

Bonhams West Country,
Devon Fine Art Auction
House, Dowell Street,
Honiton
Tel: 01404 41872

Michael J Bowman,
6 Haccombe House,
Nr Netherton,
Newton Abbot
Tel: 01626 872890

Eric Distin Chartered
Surveyors,
2 Bretonside, Plymouth
Tel: 01752 663046 or
664841

Robin A Fenner & Co,
Fine Art & Antique
Auctioneers,
The Stannary Gallery,
Drake Road,
Tavistock
Tel: 01822 617799/
617800

Kings Auctioneers,
Pinnbrook Units,
Venny Bridge,
Pinhoe, Exeter
Tel: 01392 460644

Kingsbridge Auction Sales,
85 Fore Street,
Kingsbridge
Tel: 01548 856829

Phillips,
Alphin Brook Road,
Alphington, Exeter
Tel: 01392 439025 and
Armada Street, North Hill,
Plymouth
Tel: 01752 673504

Potbury's,
High Street,
Sidmouth
Tel: 01395 515555

Rendells,
Stone Park,
Ashburton
Tel: 01364 653017

G S Shobrook & Co,
20 Western Approach,
Plymouth
Tel: 01752 663341

John Smale & Co,
11 High Street,
Barnstaple
Tel: 01271 42000/42916

Sou'west Auctions,
Newport, Barnstaple
Tel: 01271 788581/850337

Martin Spencer-Thomas,
Bicton Street Auction
Rooms, Exmouth
Tel: 01395 267403

Taylors,
Honiton Galleries,
205 High Street, Honiton
Tel: 01404 42404

Ward & Chowen,
1 Church Lane, Tavistock
Tel: 01822 612458

Whitton & Laing,
32 Okehampton Street,
Exeter
Tel: 01392 52621

Dorset

Cottees of Wareham
The Market,
East Street,
Wareham
Tel: 01929 554915/552826

Dalkeith Auctions,
Dalkeith Hall,
Dalkeith Steps,
Rear of 81 Old
Christchurch Road,
Bournemouth
Tel: 01202 292905

HY Duke & Son,
The Dorchester Fine Art
Salerooms,
Dorchester
Tel: 01305 265080
also at:
The Weymouth Saleroom,
St Nicholas Street,
Weymouth
Tel: 01305 761499

House & Son,
Lansdowne House,
Christchurch Road,
Bournemouth
Tel: 01202 556232

William Morey & Sons,
The Saleroom,
St Michaels Lane,
Bridport
Tel: 01308 422078

Riddetts of Bournemouth,
26 Richmond Hill,
The Square,
Bournemouth
Tel: 01202 555686

Southern Counties
Auctioneers,
Shaftesbury Livestock
Market, Christy's Lane,
Shaftesbury
Tel: 01747 851735

Michael Stainer Ltd,
St Andrew Hall,
Wolverton Road,
Boscombe,
Bournemouth
Tel: 01202 309999

County Durham

Denis Edkins,
Auckland Auction Room,
58 Kingsway,
Bishop Auckland
Tel: 01388 603095

Thomas Watson & Son,
Northumberland Street,
Darlington
Tel: 01325 462559/463485

Wingate Auction Co,
Station Lane,
Station Town,
Wingate
Tel: 01429 837245

Essex

Abridge Auction Rooms,
Market Place, Abridge
Tel: 01992 812107/813113

Baytree Auctions.
23 Broomhills Industrial
Estate, Braintree
Tel: 01376 328228

Black Horse Agencies,
Ambrose, 149 High Road,
Loughton
Tel: 0181 502 3951

William H Brown,
Paskell's Rooms,
11-14 East Hill,
Colchester
Tel: 01206 868070

Cooper Hirst,
The Granary Saleroom,
Victoria Road,
Chelmsford
Tel: 01245 260535

Grays Auction Rooms,
Ye Old Bake House,
Alfred Street,
Grays
Tel: 01375 381181

Leigh Auction Rooms.
88-90 Pall Mall,
Leigh-on-Sea,
Tel: 01702 77051

Saffron Walden Saleroom,
1 Market Street,
Saffron Walden
Tel: 01799 513281

Trembath Welch
The Old Town Hall,
Great Dunmow
Tel: 01371 873014

Gloucestershire

Bruton, Knowles & Co,
111 Eastgate Street,
Gloucester
Tel: 01452 521267

Fraser Glennie & Partners,
The Old Rectory,
Siddington,
Nr Cirencester
Tel: 01285 659677

Hobbs & Chambers,
Market Place,
Cirencester
Tel: 01285 654736 also at:
15 Royal Crescent,
Cheltenham
Tel: 01242 513722

Ken Lawson t/as
Specialised Postcard
Auctions,
25 Gloucester Street,
Cirencester
Tel: 01285 659057

Mallams,
26 Grosvenor Street,
Cheltenham
Tel: 01242 235712

Moore, Allen,
33 Castle Street,
Cirencester
Tel: 01285 65183

Wotton Auction Rooms,
Tabernacle Road,
Wotton-under-Edge
Tel: 01453 844733

Hampshire

Andover Saleroom,
41A London Street,
Andover
Tel: 01264 364820

Fox & Sons,
5 & 7 Salisbury Street,
Fordingbridge
Tel: 01425 652121

Hants & Berks Auctions,
82, 84 Sarum Hill,
Basingstoke
Tel: 01256 840707
also at:
Heckfield Village Hall,
Heckfield

Jacobs & Hunt,
Lavant Street, Petersfield
Tel: 01730 62744/5

George Kidner,
The Old School,
The Square, Pennington,
Lymington
Tel: 01590 670070

May & Son,
18 Bridge Street, Andover
Tel: 01264 323417

D M Nesbit & Co,
7 Clarendon Road,
Southsea
Tel: 01705 864321

Odiham Auction Sales,
The Eagle Works,
Rear of Hartley Wintney
Garages, High Street,
Hartley Wintney
Tel: 01252 844410

Phillips Fine Art
Auctioneers,
54 Southampton Road,
Ringwood
Tel: 01254 473333 also at:

The Red House, Hyde
Street, Winchester
Tel: 01962 862515

The Romsey Auction
Rooms, 86 The Hundred,
Romsey
Tel. 01794 513331

Hereford & Worcs

Broadway Auctions,
41-43 High Street,
Broadway
Tel: 01386 852456

Carless & Co,
58 Lowesmoor,
Worcester
Tel: 01905 612449

Andrew Grant,
St Mark's House,
St Mark's Close,
Worcester
Tel: 01905 357547

Griffiths & Co,
57 Foregate Street,
Worcester
Tel: 01905 26464

Hamptons,
69 Church Street,
Malvern
Tel: 01684 892314

Morris Bricknell,
Stuart House,
18 Gloucester Road,
Ross-on-Wye
Tel: 01989 768320

Philip Laney
Malvern Auction Centre
Portland Road, Malvern
Tel: 01684 893933

Phipps & Pritchard,
Bank Buildings,
Kidderminster
Tel: 01562 822244/6

Russell, Baldwin & Bright,
Fine Art Saleroom,
Ryelands Road, Leominster
Tel: 01568 611166

Village Auctions,
Sychampton Community
Centre, Ombersley
Tel: 01905 421007

Richard Williams,
2 High Street,
Pershore
Tel: 01386 554031

Hertfordshire

Bayles,
Childs Farm, Cottered,
Buntingford
Tel: 0176 381256

Brown & Merry,
Tring Market Auctions
41 High Street,
Tring
Tel: 01442 826446

Hitchin Auctions Ltd,
The Corn Exchange,
Market Place, Hitchin
Tel: 01462 442151

Andrew Pickford,
42 St Andrew Street,
Hertford
Tel: 01992 583508

Sworders,
Northgate End Salerooms,
Bishops Stortford
Tel: 01279 651388

Vincent Auctions,
The Cranborne Rooms,
The Red Lion Public House,
The Great North Road,
Hatfield
Tel: 01920 460417 or
01707 323908

Humberside - North

Gilbert Baitson, FSVA,
The Edwardian Auction
Galleries, Wiltshire Road,
Hull
Tel: 01482 500500

H Evans & Sons,
1 Parliament Street,
Hull
Tel: 01482 23033

Humberside - South

Dickinson, Davy &
Markham,
10 Wrawby Street, Brigg
Tel: 01652 653666

Isle of Man

Chrystals Auctions,
Majestic Hotel, Onchan
Tel: 01624 673986

Isle of Wight

Phillips Fine Art
Auctioneers,
Cross Street Salerooms,
Newport
Tel: 01983 822031

Watson Bull & Porter,
Isle of Wight Auction
Rooms, 79 Regent Street,
Shanklin
Tel: 01983 863441

Ways Auction House,
Garfield Road, Ryde
Tel: 01983 562255

Kent

Albert Andrews Auctions &
Sales, Maiden Lane,
Crayford
Tel: 01322 528868

Bracketts,
27-29 High Street,
Tunbridge Wells
Tel: 01892 533733

Canterbury Auction
Galleries,
40 Station Road West,
Canterbury
Tel: 01227 763337

Mervyn Carey,
Twysden Cottage,
Benenden, Cranbrook
Tel: 01580 240283

Halifax Property Services,
Fine Art Department,
53 High Street,
Tenterden
Tel: 01580 763200
also at:
15 Cattle Market,
Sandwich
Tel: 01304 614369

Edwin Hall,
Valley Antiques,
Lyminge,
Folkestone
Tel: 01303 862134

Hobbs Parker,
Romney House,
Ashford Market,
Elwick Road, Ashford
Tel: 01233 622222

Hythe Auction Rooms,
35 Dymchurch Road, Hythe
Tel: 01303 267162

Ibbett Mosely,
125 High Street,
Sevenoaks
Tel: 01732 452246

Kent Sales,
Giffords, Holmesdale Road,
South Darenth
Tel: 01322 864919

Lambert & Foster,
102 High Street,
Tenterden
Tel: 01580 762083/763233

B J Norris,
The Quest,
West Street,
Harrietsham,
Nr Maidstone
Tel: 01622 859515

Phillips,
11 Bayle Parade,
Folkestone
Tel: 01303 45555

Phillips Fine Art
Auctioneers,
49 London Road,
Sevenoaks
Tel: 01732 740310

Michael Shortall,
Auction Centres,
Highgate,
Hawkhurst
Tel: 01580 753463

Town & Country House
Auctions, North House,
Oakley Road,
Bromley Common
Tel: 0181 462 1735

Walter & Randall,
7-13 New Road,
Chatham
Tel: 01634 841233

Peter S Williams, FSVA,
Orchard End,
Sutton Valence,
Maidstone
Tel: 01622 842350

Lancashire

Capes Dunn & Co,
The Auction Galleries,
38 Charles Street,
Manchester
Tel: 0161 273 6060/1911

Charles Edwards & Co,
4/8 Lynwood Road,
Blackburn
Tel: 01254 691748

Entwistle Green,
The Galleries, Kingsway,
Ansdell, Lytham St Annes
Tel: 01253 735442

Robt. Fairhurst & Son,
39 Mawdsley Street,
Bolton
Tel: 01204 28452/28453

Highams Auctions,
Southgate House,
Southgate Street,
Rhodes Bank,
Oldham
Tel: 0161 626 1021

Mills & Radcliffe Inc
D Murgatroyd & Son,
101 Union Street,
Oldham
Tel: 0161 624 1072

David Palamountain,
1-3 Osborne Grove,
Morecambe
Tel: 01524 423941

J R Parkinson Son &
Hamer Auctions,
The Auction Rooms,
Rochdale Road,
Bury
Tel: 0161 761 1612/7372

Phillips,
Trinity House,
114 Northenden Road,
Sale, Manchester
Tel: 0161 962 9237

Smythe's,
174 Victoria Road West,
Cleveleys
Tel: 01253 852184 &
854084

Warren & Wignall Ltd,
The Mill, Earnshaw Bridge,
Leyland Lane, Leyland
Tel: 01772 453252/451430

Leicestershire

Churchgate Auctions,
The Churchgate Saleroom,
66 Churchgate, Leicester
Tel: 0116 2621416

Gildings,
64 Roman Way,
Market Harborough
Tel: 01858 410414

Noton Salerooms,
76 South Street,
Oakham
Tel: 01572 722681

David Stanley Auctions,
Stordon Grange,
Osgathorpe,
Loughborough
Tel: 01530 222320

William H Brown,
The Warner Auction
Rooms, 16/18 Halford
Street, Leicester
Tel: 0116 2519777

Lincolnshire

Bourne Auction Rooms,
Spalding Road, Bourne
Tel: 01778 422686

A E Dowse & Son,
89 Mary Street,
Scunthorpe
Tel: 01724 842569/842039

Goldings,
The Saleroom,
Old Wharf Road,
Grantham
Tel: 01476 65118

Thomas Mawer & Son,
63 Monks Road,
Lincoln
Tel: 01522 524984

Henry Spencer & Sons,
42 Silver Street,
Lincoln
Tel: 01522 536666

Marilyn Swain Auctions,
The Old Barracks,
Sandon Road,
Grantham
Tel: 01476 68861

John H Walter,
1 Mint Lane,
Lincoln
Tel: 01522 525454

Merseyside

Cato Crane & Co,
Liverpool Auction Rooms,
6 Stanhope Street,
Liverpool
Tel: 0151 709 5559

Hartley & Co,
12 & 14 Moss Street,
Liverpool
Tel: 0151 263 6472/1865

Kingsley & Co,
3-5 The Quadrant,
Hoylake,
Wirral
Tel: 0151 632 5821

Outhwaite & Litherland,
Kingsway Galleries,
Fontenoy Street,
Liverpool
Tel: 0151 236 6561

Worralls,
13-15 Seel Street,
Liverpool
Tel: 0151 709 2950

Norfolk

Ewings,
Market Place,
Reepham,
Norwich
Tel: 01603 870473

Thos Wm Gaze & Son,
10 Market Hill, Diss
Tel: 01379 651931

Nigel F Hedge,
28B Market Place,
North Walsham
Tel: 01692 402881

G A Key,
8 Market Place,
Aylsham
Tel: 01263 733195

Northants

Corby & Co,
30-32 Brook Street,
Raunds
Tel: 01933 623722

Heathcote Ball & Co,
Albion Auction Rooms,
Old Albion Brewery,
Commercial Street,
Northampton
Tel: 01604 37263

Lowery's,
24 Bridge Street,
Northampton
Tel: 01604 21561

Merry's Auctioneers,
The Old Corn Exchange,
Cattle Market,
14 Bridge Street,
Northampton
Tel: 01604 32266

Nationwide Surveyors,
28 High Street,
Daventry
Tel: 01327 312022

Southam & Sons,
Corn Exchange,
Thrapston,
Kettering
Tel: 01832 734486

H Wilford Ltd,
Midland Road,
Wellingborough
01933 222760

Northumberland

Louis Johnson Auctioneers,
Morpeth
Tel: 01670 513025

Nottinghamshire

Arthur Johnson & Sons
Ltd, The Nottingham
Auction Rooms,
The Cattle Market,
Meadow Lane,
Nottingham
Tel: 0115 9869128

Neales of Nottingham,
192 Mansfield Road,
Nottingham
Tel: 0115 9624141

John Pye & Sons,
Corn Exchange,
Cattle Market,
London Road,
Nottingham
Tel: 0115 9866261

C B Sheppard & Son,
The Auction Galleries,
Chatsworth Street,
Sutton-in-Ashfield
Tel: 01773 872419

Henry Spencer & Sons Ltd,
20 The Square,
Retford
Tel: 01777 708633

T Vennett-Smith,
11 Nottingham Road,
Gotham
Tel: 0115 9830541

Oxfordshire

Green & Co,
33 Market Place,
Wantage
Tel: 01235 763561/2

Holloways,
49 Parsons Street,
Banbury
Tel: 01295 253197/8

Mallams,
24 St Michael's Street,
Oxford
Tel: 01865 241358

Messengers,
27 Sheep Street,
Bicester
Tel: 01869 252901

Phillips Inc Brooks,
39 Park End Street,
Oxford
Tel: 01865 723524

Simmons & Sons,
32 Bell Street,
Henley-on-Thames
Tel: 01491 571111

Shropshire

Ludlow Antique Auctions
Ltd, 29 Corve Street,
Ludlow
Tel: 01584 875157

McCartneys,
25 Corve Street, Ludlow
Tel: 01584 872636

Timothy Mear & Co
Temeside Salerooms,
Ludford Bridge, Ludlow
Tel: 01584 876081

Perry & Phillips,
Newmarket Salerooms,
Newmarket Buildings,
Listley Street,
Bridgnorth
Tel: 01746 762248

Somerset

Dores & Rees,
The Auction Mart,
Vicarage Street, Frome
Tel: 01373 462257

John Fleming,
4 & 8 Fore Street,
Dulverton
Tel: 01398 23597

Greenslades,
13 Hamet Street, Taunton
Tel: 01823 277121also at:
Priory Saleroom
Winchester Street, Taunton

Gribble Booth & Taylor,
13 The Parade, Minehead
Tel: 01643 702281

Black Horse Agencies,
Alder King, 25 Market Place,
Wells. Tel: 01749 73002

Lawrences of Crewkerne,
South Street, Crewkerne
Tel: 01460 73041

The London Cigarette Card
Co Ltd, Sutton Road,
Somerton
Tel: 01458 73452

Cooper & Tanner,
Frome Auction Rooms,
Frome Market,
Standerwick, Nr Frome
Tel: 01373 831010

Richards,
The Town Hall,
The Square, Axbridge
Tel: 01934 732969

Wellington Salerooms,
Mantle Street, Wellington
Tel: 01823 664815

Wells Auction Rooms,
66/68 Southover, Wells
Tel: 01749 678094

Staffordshire

Bagshaws,
17 High Street, Uttoxeter
Tel: 01889 562811

Hall & Lloyd,
South Street Auction
Rooms, Stafford
Tel: 01785 58176

Louis Taylor,
Britannia House, 10 Town
Road, Hanley,
Stoke-on-Trent
Tel: 01782 214111

Wintertons,
Lichfield Auction Centre,
Woodend Lane, Fradley,
Lichfield
Tel: 01543 263256

Suffolk

Abbotts Auction Rooms,
Campsea Ashe, Woodbridge
Tel: 01728 746321

Boardman Fine Art,
Station Road Corner,
Haverhill
Tel: 01440 730414

Diamond, Mills & Co,
117 Hamilton Road,
Felixstowe
Tel: 01394 282281

William H Brown,
Ashford House,
Saxmundham
Tel: 01728 603232

Lacy Scott,
Fine Art Department,
The Auction Centre,
10 Risbygate Street,
Bury St Edmunds
Tel: 01284 763531

Neal Sons & Fletcher,
26 Church Street,
Woodbridge
Tel: 01394 382263

Olivers, Olivers Rooms,
Burkitts Lane, Sudbury
Tel: 01787 880305

Phillips,
Dover House, Wilsey Street,
Ipswich. Tel: 01473 255137

Surrey

ABC Auctions,
Central Avenue,
West Molesey,
Tel: 0181 941 5545

Chancellors,
74 London Road,
Kingston upon Thames,
Tel: 0181 541 4139

Clark Gammon,
The Guildford Auction
Rooms, Bedford Road,
Guildford. Tel: 01483 66458

Crows Auction Gallery,
Rear of Dorking Halls,
Reigate Road, Dorking
Tel: 01306 740382

Ewbank Fine Art,
Welbeck House,
High Street, Guildford
Tel: 01483 232134

Hamptons, Fine Art
Auctioneers & Valuers,
93 High Street, Godalming
Tel: 014834 23567

Lawrences,
Norfolk House, 80 High
Street, Bletchingley
Tel: 01883 743323

John Nicholson,
The Auction Rooms,
Longfield, Midhurst Road,
Fernhurst
Tel: 01428 653727

Parkins,
18 Malden Road, Cheam,
Tel: 0181 644 6633 & 6127

Phillips Fine Art
Auctioneers, Millmead,
Guildford.
Tel: 01483 504030

Richmond & Surrey
Auctions, Kew Road,
Rear of Richmond Station,
Richmond
Tel: 0181 948 6677

Wentworth Auction
Galleries, 21 Station
Approach, Virginia Water
Tel: 01344 843711

P F Windibank,
Dorking Halls, 18-20
Reigate Road, Dorking
Tel: 01306 884556

Sussex - East

Ascent Auction Galleries,
11-12 East Ascent,
St Leonards-on-Sea
Tel: 01424 420275

Burstow & Hewett,
Abbey Auction Galleries
and Granary Salerooms,
Battle
Tel: 01424 772374/772302

Clifford Dann Auction
Galleries, 20-21 High Street,
Lewes. Tel: 01273 480111

Gorringes Auction
Galleries, Terminus Road,
Bexhill-on-Sea
Tel: 01424 212994

Gorringes Auction
Galleries,
15 North Street, Lewes
Tel: 01273 472503

Graves, Son & Pilcher, Fine
Arts, 71 Church Road, Hove
Tel: 01273 735266

Edgar Horn's Fine Art
Auctioners,
46-50 South Street,
Eastbourne
Tel: 01323 410419

Hove Auction Galleries,
1 Weston Road, Hove
Tel: 01273 736207

Raymond P Inman,
Auction Galleries,
35 & 40 Temple Street,
Brighton
Tel: 01273 774777

Lewes Auction Rooms,
(Julian Dawson),
56 High Street, Lewes
Tel: 01273 478221

Rye Auction Galleries,
Rock Channel, Rye
Tel: 01797 222124

Wallis & Wallis,
West Street Auction
Galleries, Lewes
Tel: 01273 480208

Watsons,
Heathfield Furniture
Salerooms, The Market,
Burwash Road,
Heathfield
Tel: 01435 862132

Sussex - West

John Bellman,
New Pound,
Wisborough Green,
Billingshurst
Tel: 01403 700858

Peter Cheney,
Western Road
Auction Rooms,
Western Road,
Littlehampton
Tel: 01903 722264/713418

Denham's,
Horsham Auction Galleries,
Warnham,
Horsham
Tel: 01403 255699/253837

R H Ellis & Sons,
44-46 High Street,
Worthing
Tel: 01903 238999

Nationwide
Midhurst Auction Rooms,
Bepton Road,
Midhurst
Tel: 01730 812456

Phillips Fine Art
Auctioneers,
Baffins Hall,
Baffins Lane,
Chichester
Tel: 01243 787548

Sotheby's in Sussex,
Summers Place,
Billingshurst
Tel: 01403 783933

Stride & Son,
Southdown House,
St John's Street,
Chichester
Tel: 01243 780207

Sussex Auction Galleries,
59 Perrymount Road,
Haywards Heath
Tel: 01444 414935

Worthing Auction
Galleries,
31 Chatsworth Road,
Worthing
Tel: 01903 205565

Tyne & Wear

Anderson & Garland,
The Fine Art Sale Rooms,
Marlborough House,
Marlborough Crescent,
Newcastle-upon-Tyne
Tel: 0191 232 6278

Boldon Auction Galleries,
24a Front Street,
East Boldon
Tel: 0191 537 2630

Thomas N Miller,
18-22 Gallowgate,
Newcastle-upon-Tyne
Tel: 0191 232 5617

Sneddons,
Sunderland Auction Rooms,
30 Villiers Street,
Sunderland
Tel: 0191 514 5931

Warwickshire

Bigwood Auctioneers Ltd,
The Old School, Tiddington,
Stratford-upon-Avon
Tel: 01789 269415

Locke & England,
18 Guy Street,
Leamington Spa
Tel: 01926 889100

West Midlands

Biddle & Webb,
Icknield Square, Ladywood
Middleway, Birmingham
Tel: 0121 455 8042

Cariss Residential,
20 High Street,
Kings Heath, Birmingham
Tel: 0121 444 0088

Ronald E Clare,
Clare's Auction Rooms,
70 Park Street, Birmingham
Tel: 0121 643 0226

Frank H Fellows & Sons,
Augusta House, 19 Augusta
Street, Hockley, Birmingham
Tel: 0121 212 2131

Giles Haywood,
The Auction House,
St Johns Road,
Stourbridge
Tel: 01384 370891

James & Lister Lea,
42 Bull Street,
Birmingham
Tel: 0121 200 1100

Phillips,
The Old House,
Station Road, Knowle,
Solihull
Tel: 01564 776151

K Stuart Swash, FSVA,
Stamford House,
2 Waterloo Road,
Wolverhampton
Tel: 01902 710626

Walker Barnett & Hill,
3 Waterloo Road,
Wolverhampton
Tel: 01902 773531

Weller & Dufty Ltd,
141 Bromsgrove Street,
Birmingham
Tel: 0121 692 1414

Wiltshire

Henry Aldridge & Son
Auctions, Devizes Auction
Rooms, 1 Wine Street,
(The Old Town Hall),
Devizes
Tel: 01380 729199

Hamptons,
20 High Street,
Marlborough
Tel: 01672 513471

Kidson Trigg.
The Estate Office,
Friars Farm, Sevenhampton,
Highworth, Swindon
Tel: 01793 861072/861000

Swindon Auction Rooms,
The Planks (off The Square),
Old Town, Swindon
Tel: 01793 615915

Dominic Winter,
The Old School,
Maxwell Street,
Swindon
Tel: 01793 611340

Woolley & Wallis,
The Castle Auction Mart,
Castle Street, Salisbury
Tel: 01722 411422

Yorkshire - East

Dee & Atkinson,
The Exchange, Driffield
Tel: 01377 253151

Yorkshire - North

Boulton & Cooper (Fine
Arts), St Michael's House,
Market Place, Malton
Tel: 01653 696151

H C Chapman & Son,
The Auction Mart,
North Street,
Scarborough
Tel: 01723 372424

Cundalls,
The Cattle Market,
17 Market Place,
Malton
Tel: 01653 697820

M W Darwin & Sons,
The Dales Furniture Hall,
Bedale
Tel: 01677 422846

GA Fine Art & Chattels,
Royal Auction Rooms,
Queen Street,
Scarborough
Tel: 01723 353581

Hutchinson Scott,
The Grange,
Marton-Le-Moor, Ripon
Tel: 01423 324264

Christopher Matthews,
23 Mount Street,
Harrogate
Tel: 01423 871756

Morphets,
4-6 Albert Street, Harrogate
Tel: 01423 530030

Nationwide Fine Arts &
Furniture, 27 Flowergate,
Whitby.
Tel: 01947 603433

Stephenson & Son,
Livestock Centre,
Murton, York.
Tel: 01904 489731

Geoffrey Summersgill,
ASVA, 8 Front Street,
Acomb, York
Tel: 01904 791131

Tennants,
Harmby Road, Leyburn
Tel: 01969 23780

Thompson's Auctioneers,
Dales Saleroom,
The Dale Hall,
Hampsthwaite,
Harrogate
Tel: 01423 770741

Yorkshire - South

Eadon Lockwood & Riddle,
The Sheffield Saleroom
411 Petre Street, Sheffield
Tel: 0114 2618000

William H Brown,
10 Regent Street, Barnsley
Tel: 01226 299221

William H Brown,
Stanilands Auction Room,
28 Nether Hall Road,
Doncaster
Tel: 01302 367766

Henry Spencer & Sons Ltd,
1 St James Row, Sheffield
Tel: 0114 2728728

Wilkinson & Beighton,
Woodhouse Green,
Thurcroft, Nr Rotherham
Tel: 01709 700005

Yorkshire - West

Audsley's Auctions,
(C R Kemp BSc), 11 Morris
Lane, Kirkstall, Leeds 5
Tel: 0113 2758787

de Rome,
12 New John Street,
Westgate, Bradford
Tel: 01274 734116

Eddisons,
Auction Rooms, 4-6 High
Street, Huddersfield
Tel: 01484 533151

Andrew Hartley,
Victoria Hall Salerooms,
Little Lane, Ilkley
Tel: 01943 816363

Malcolms No. 1 Auctioneers
& Valuers,7 Finkle Hill,
Sherburn-in-Elmet,
Nr Leeds. Tel: 01977 684971/
685334. (24 hours)

Phillips,
17a East Parade, Leeds
Tel: 0113 2448011

John H Raby & Son,
The Sale Rooms,
21 St Mary's Road,
Manningham, Bradford 8
Tel: 01274 491121

Scarthingwell Auction
Centre, Scarthingwell,
Nr. Tadcaster
Tel: 01937 557955

Whitby Auction Rooms,
West End Saleroom,
The Paddock, Whitby
Tel: 01947 603433

Windle & Co,
The Four Ashes,
535 Great Horton Road,
Bradford
Tel: 01274 57299

Channel Islands

Langlois Auctioneers &
Valuers, Westway
Chambers, 39 Don Street,
St Helier, Jersey
Tel: 01534 22441

Hamptons,Martel, Maides
Ltd,The Old Bank, 29 High
Street, St Peter Port,
Guernsey
Tel: 01481 713463

Ireland

James Adam & Sons,
26 St Stephens Green,
Dublin 2
Tel: 00 3531 760261

Mealys,
Chatsworth Street,
Castle Comer
Co. Kilkenny
Tel: 010 353 564 1229

Northern Ireland

Morgans Auctions Ltd,
Duncrue Crescent,
Duncrue Road, Belfast
Tel: 01232 771552

Temple Auctions Limited,
133 Carryduff Road,
Temple, Lisburn,
Co. Antrim
Tel: 01846 638777

Scotland

Christie's Scotland,
164-166 Bath Street,
Glasgow
Tel: 0141 332 8134

B L Fenton & Sons,
Forebank Auction Halls,
84 Victoria Road, Dundee
Tel: 01382 26227

Frasers Auctioneers,
8A Harbour Road,
Inverness
Tel: 01463 232395

William Hardie Ltd,
141 West Regent Street,
Glasgow
Tel: 041 221 6780/248 6237

J & J Howe,
24 Commercial Street,
Alyth, Perthshire
Tel: 018283 2594

Loves Auction Rooms,
The Auction Galleries,
52-54 Canal Street, Perth
Tel: 01738 633337

Robert McTear & Co
(Auctioneers & Valuers)
Ltd, Royal Exchange
Salerooms, 6 North Court,
St. Vincent Place, Glasgow
Tel: 0141 221 4456

Mainstreet Trading,
Mainstreet, St Boswells,
Melrose, Roxburghshire
Tel: 01835 823978

John Milne,
9 North Silver Street,
Aberdeen
Tel: 01224 639336

Robert Paterson & Son,
8 Orchard Street,
Paisley, Renfrewshire
Tel: 0141 889 2435

Phillips in Scotland,
207 Bath Street, Glasgow
Tel: 0141 221 8377 also at:

65 George Street,
Edinburgh
Tel: 0131 225 2266

L S Smellie & Sons Ltd,
Within the Furniture
Market, Lower
Auchingramont Road,
Hamilton
Tel: 01698 282007

Thomson, Roddick &
Laurie,
20 Murray Street,
Annan
Tel: 01461 202575

West Perthshire Auctions,
Dundas Street,
Cowie,
Perthshire

Wales

Dodds Property World,
Victoria Auction Galleries,
9 Chester Street,
Mold,
Clwyd
Tel: 01352 752552

G.H. Evans & Co
Auction Sales Centre,
The Market Place,
Kilgetty,
Dyfed
Tel: 01834 812793 & 811151

Peter Francis,
Curiosity Salerooms,
19 King Street,
Carmarthen
Tel: 01267 233456

Rogers Jones & Co,
33 Abergele Road,
Colwyn Bay,
Clwyd
Tel: 01492 532176

Morgan Evans & Co. Ltd,
30 Church Street,
Llangefni,
Anglesey,
Gwynedd
Tel: 01248 723303/77582

Morris Marshall & Poole,
10 Broad Street,
Newtown,
Powys
Tel: 01686 625900

Phillips in Wales Fine Art
Auctioneers,
9-10 Westgate Street,
Cardiff
Tel: 01222 396453

Players Auction Mart,
Players Industrial Estate,
Clydach,
Swansea
Tel: 01792 8466241

Rennies,
1 Agincourt Street,
Monmouth
Tel: 01600 712916

Wingett's,
29 Holt Street,
Wrexham,
Clwyd
Tel: 01978 353553

U.S.A.

Christie's East,
219 East 67th Street,
New York, NY10021
Tel: 0101 212 606 0470

Eldred's,
Robert C Eldred Co. Inc.,
1475 Route 6A,
East Dennis,
Massachusetts 02641-0796
Tel:0101 508 385 3116

Hindmans,
215 West Ohio Street,
Chicago, Illinois 60610
Tel: 0101 312 670 0010

Skinner Inc.,
357 Main Street,
Bolton, MA 01740
Tel: 0101 508 779 6241

Sloan's,
C.G. Sloan & Co.,
4920 Wyaconda Road,
North Bethdesda,
MD 20852
Tel: 0101 301 468 4911

INDEX TO ADVERTISERS

INDEX

Italic page numbers denote information and pointer boxes.

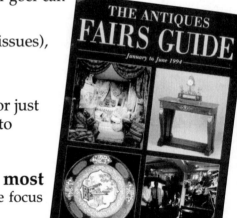

MILLER'S

Every two minutes someone, somewhere buys a Miller's guide

THE DEFINITIVE GUIDES TO ANTIQUES AND COLLECTABLES

M03 £10.99 — MILLER'S Classic Motorcycles PRICE GUIDE

M04 £19.99 — MILLER'S Collectors Cars PRICE GUIDE

M01 £19.99 — MILLER'S Antiques PRICE GUIDE

M05 £25.00 — MILLER'S Picture PRICE GUIDE

M02 £15.99 — MILLER'S Collectables PRICE GUIDE

M10 £9.99 — FURNITURE Antiques Checklist

M11 £9.99 — GLASS Antiques Checklist / SILVER & PLATE Antiques Checklist

M13 £6.99 — SILVER & SHEFFIELD PLATE MARKS

M06 £14.99 — Royal MEMORABILIA

M08 £14.99 — UNDERSTANDING ANTIQUES

M12 £9.99

M14 £6.99 — POCKET ANTIQUES FACT FILE

M07 £14.99 av. Oct.'94 — Rock & Pop Stephen Maycock

M09 £7.99 — ANTIQUES & COLLECTABLES The Facts At Your Fingertips

IF YOU WOULD LIKE TO PURCHASE ANY OF THE MILLER'S TITLES LISTED HERE, OR WOULD LIKE MORE INFORMATION ON MILLER'S BOOKS, fill in the order form attached and post to: **Reed Book Services Ltd, PO Box 5, Rushden, Northants, NN10 6YX** **or** phone through your order on our special **credit card hotline 0933 410511** quoting your credit card details and reference MIL6

ORDER CODE	TITLE	QTY	PRICE	TOTAL
	POSTAGE AND PACKING			FREE
	GRAND TOTAL			

I enclose a cheque for £ _____ made payable to Reed Book Services **or**

Please debit my Access ☐ Visa ☐ Amex ☐ Diners ☐ by £ _____

Card number: ☐☐☐☐ ☐☐☐☐ ☐☐☐☐ ☐☐☐☐

Expiry date: ☐☐☐☐

Signature: _____

MIL6

All available titles will normally be despatched within 5 working days of receipt of order, but please allow up to 28 days for delivery. Registered office: Michelin House, 81 Fulham Road, London SW3 6RB. Registered in England no. 1974080

If you do not wish your name to be used by other carefully selected organisations who may wish to send you information about other products and services, please indicate by ticking this box ☐

Title: _____ Initials: _____ Surname: _____

Address: _____

Postcode: _____

POST TO: Reed Book Services Ltd, PO Box 5, Rushden, Northants, NN10 6YX

THIS FORM MAY BE PHOTOCOPIED

LAKESIDE
limited

Old Cement Works, South Heighton,
Newhaven, East Sussex BN9 0HS
Telephone 0273 513326 Facsimile 0273 515528

LAKESIDE FURNITURE FEATURES STRONG,
CLASSIC DESIGNS WHETHER FOR THE AMERICAN OR
EUROPEAN MARKET. USING ONLY OLD OR WELL
SEASONED MATERIALS, THE HIGHEST
QUALITY IS ASSURED.

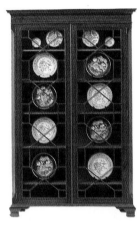

OUR SKILLED CRAFTSMAN MAKE
EACH PIECE INDIVIDUALLY TO EXACT STANDARDS
THERFORE WE CAN TAILOR TO SPECIFIC NEEDS.
WE CAN ALSO MANUFACTURE
CUSTOMISED DESIGNS IN A VARIETY
OF MATERIALS.

WE OFFER A FULLY COMPREHENSIVE
SERVICE FROM CONSTRUCTION AND POLISHING
TO UPHOLSTERY AND LEATHERING, CARRIED OUT
BY OUR OWN CRAFTSMAN.

WHOLESALE · IMPORTED · CHAIRS & DESKS

For further fine examples of our furniture see our display ad on pages 14 & 15